LONGHORN HOOPS

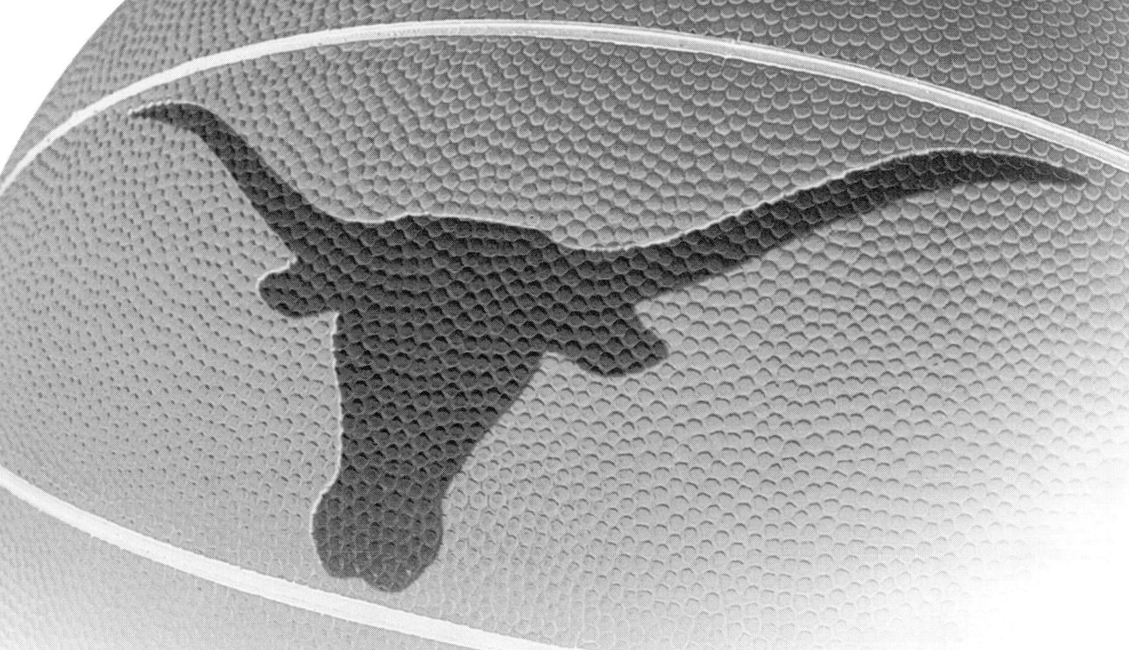

THE HISTORY OF TEXAS BASKETBALL

RICHARD PENNINGTON

FOREWORD BY DR. DENTON COOLEY

LONGHORN HOOPS
The History of Texas Basketball

University of Texas Press
P.O. Box 7819
Austin, Texas 78713-7819

Publisher's Cataloging-in-Publication
Pennington, Richard
Longhorn Hoops: The History of Texas Basketball / by Richard Pennington
Foreword by Dr. Denton Cooley. 1st edition.
p. cm.
Illus., charts, graphs, photos, index.
ISBN 0-292-76585-1
1. Basketball—Texas—History. I. Title
DDN 796.323'09764 LC GV 885.72 98-60912

Photos reprinted with permission from Texas Student Publications (*Cactus*), Ex-Students' Association (*Alcalde*), Austin History Center, UT men's and women's sports information departments, Jim Sigmon, Emma Lou Linn, Rodney Page, Dr. Denton Cooley, Mary Neikirk, Bill Sansing and Michael Sugrue.

Cover illustration by Steve Willgren
Book design by Terry Sherrell

Printed in the United States of America
at Morgan Printing in Austin, Texas

Foreword

While many sports can challenge the human body, mind and heart, none exceed basketball for developing physical and mental strength and imparting spiritual values. Surely, Dr. James Naismith never imagined the influence of his creation in 1891 when he sought a game that students could play inside during the long Massachusetts winters. Basketball soon spread throughout the United States and is today a global phenomenon that continues to inspire the athlete in each of us. Since only a hoop and a ball are needed to play, girls and boys on remote farms, in the suburbs and in the crowded inner cities can all learn the sport's basic skills rather easily.

As a child, I had a basket in my own backyard, which provided me with countless hours of challenge, fun and practice. As I grew older, I played in church and YMCA leagues, but my goal was to play first on my high school team and then at the University of Texas. I played center on the San Jacinto High School basketball team and in 1937 was honored by election to Houston's all-city team.

Subsequently, I enrolled at UT and with the confidence from high school behind me, I decided to try out for the freshman basketball team. If I made the team, I would satisfy my boyhood dream of playing in Gregory Gymnasium, the largest in the Southwest Conference. My first look inside Gregory Gym was somewhat overwhelming. The gym seemed massive to a 16-year-old college student! Because I did not have an athletic scholarship, I was a "walk-on" player. Competition to make the starting team was fierce. At the time, I was 6'4" and weighed 140 pounds, which made scrimmaging against the older and heavier boys a real challenge.

After playing freshman basketball, I hoped to make the varsity in 1939. In the late minutes of a preseason game with St. Edward's University, I got an unexpected chance to play. Somehow I made 12 points, and from that time on, I was a member of the team. I was even given a scholarship, which paid the handsome sum of $40 per month. Coach Jack Gray became a splendid lifetime role model for me and all of my teammates. One of my most inspiring and vivid memories remains the thrill of winning the conference championship in 1939 and participating in the NCAA regional tournament in San Francisco.

Not every season, however, can be a winning one. Often, victory must be balanced by the disappointment of defeat. Whether they win or lose, young women and men learn skills from team sports such as basketball that will help them prepare for the successes and failures that will inevitably confront them in life. They gain the spirit of competition, the companionship of teammates on and off the court and the ability to accept support from others. I believe that good sportsmanship and good citizenship have much in common.

Not all students at the University of Texas will have the privilege I enjoyed as a member of the varsity basketball squad, but there are many other opportunities during the college years to learn the lessons basketball teaches. Intramural basketball or even informal one-on-one games can provide a valuable balance to academic pressures. I firmly believe that students should participate in extracurricular activities like basketball to maintain their physical and mental health and to have a college experience that will give them a special kind of competitive edge.

To provide a lasting tribute, Richard Pennington has written *Longhorn Hoops: The History of Texas Basketball.* Pennington's superb research into the history of basketball at the University of Texas has allowed him to give his readers a fascinating account of the sport—from its beginnings outdoors at Clark Field to its present triumphs at the fabulous Erwin Center. This comprehensive book should be read by students, alumni, basketball fans and, especially, those of us fortunate enough to have worn the UT orange proudly on our basketball uniforms.

Certainly all alumni can anticipate exciting years ahead for competition in the Big 12 Conference, but we should not forget the excitement of the past and memories of those players and coaches who gave their best for their alma mater. An excerpt from Theodore Roosevelt's timeless prose summarizes my feelings about the sport: "It is not the critic who counts, not the man who points out how the strong man stumbles, or where the doer of deeds could have done them better. The credit belongs to the man who is actually in the arena...who at best knows in the end the triumph of high achievement and who at the worst, if he fails, at least fails while daring greatly, so that his place shall never be with those cold and timid souls who know neither victory nor defeat."

Hook 'em!

Denton Cooley, M.D.

Surgeon-in-Chief and President
Texas Heart Institute
Houston, Texas

UT letterman—1939, 1940, 1941

Preface

I was a high school student at a basketball game, of all things, at the moment I decided where to pursue higher education. Southern Methodist University and the University of Texas were playing at Moody Coliseum in 1970 when I—a Dallas native and fan of the Mustangs—noticed all the visitors in orange and white, displaying their Hook 'em, Horns sign and singing "The Eyes of Texas" and "Texas Fight." Before the game was over, my allegiance to SMU had faded. I was going to the big school, down in Austin.

Some of the sweetest memories of my UT years are of attending Longhorn basketball games at Gregory Gymnasium. My friends and I often went early, in order to sit at midcourt on the front-row bleachers. We were so close to the game, we could almost reach out and touch the players. By then, the old gym may have been long past its prime as a setting for college basketball, but we did not know that.

Several books, including one of my own, have recounted the history of Texas football. Longhorn baseball and track have been covered, too. It is high time that almost a century of UT hoops be studied and written about. While no one will claim that Texas has quite the blue-chip heritage of UCLA, Kansas, Indiana, Kentucky or North Carolina (and Tennessee and Louisiana Tech among the women), this is a fascinating tale with vivid personalities, some controversies, lots of victories and a few defeats.

Take a look at the banners hanging from the Erwin Center ceiling: You see one national championship for the men (1978 NIT) and one for the women (1986 NCAA) and a number of near misses. This book aims to show the depth and strength of basketball's tradition on the Forty Acres. Who remembers such old-time players as Clyde Littlefield, Holly Brock, Jack Gray, Bobby Moers or even Slater Martin or Raymond Downs or Jay Arnette or Larry Robinson? Who knows that female students began playing basketball at least five years before their male counterparts? And who is aware of the rise, fall and eventual rebirth of women's basketball at UT? In the following pages, you will see not just the athletes, but Texas coaches and fans and the various home facilities (primarily Clark Field, the Men's Gym, Gregory Gym, the Women's Gym [now Anna Hiss Gym] and the Erwin Center) in which the games have been played.

Basketball is the American game, conceived and nurtured entirely in the United States. Just 40 years after Dr. James Naismith procured two peach baskets and a soccer ball and originated basketball at the YMCA Training School in Springfield, Massachusetts, it had become the top participant/spectator sport in the country, best exemplified in intercollegiate play. It still answers the original need that gave rise to its birth: a competitive team game played indoors during the winter months. Even the uninformed observer finds basketball an easy sport to understand and appreciate. A well-played basketball game integrates many elements of athletic appeal, with running, jumping and throwing to a target, all in a way that utilizes speed, size and strength with coordination, cleverness and timing. Basketball, the most beautiful and exhilarating sport of all, has spread to the far-flung corners of the earth.

I thank men's athletic director DeLoss Dodds, who recognized the need for a history of UT basketball and commissioned me to put it together. Michael Ambrose did a fine job of editing the manuscript and offered other valuable advice. The support and encouragement of Bill Pierce, a fellow denizen of press row, was most helpful. Thanks also to George Breazeale, longtime writer for the *Austin American-Statesman;* I called on his sports history acumen several times over the three-year span of this project. My friend Travis Klein did some early design work and came to the rescue when computer problems arose. I'm in debt to Dr. Margaret Berry, the court of final appeal on all matters regarding University of Texas history. Terry Sherrell and Nancy Meredith of Morgan Printing not only dealt with a demanding author, they went above and beyond the call of duty to ensure a first-class book, which is dedicated to the love of my life, Eileen.

A few editorial notes are necessary. In its early decades, basketball at the University of Texas and elsewhere lacked competitive structure as YMCAs, high schools, colleges, semipros and barnstorming teams all played each other. Certain games made it into the historical record and others did not. Reporting of those games was quite spotty, too, a maddening state of affairs for any researcher. Cross-referencing of contemporary media guides shows some variation in final scores, order of games and sometimes even the winners of those games. I seek to provide an accurate account, given the often-haphazard archival resources we have inherited. Basketball season, which now lasts from November to March, was originally in January and February; due to this fact but mostly for the sake of convenience, I note each season by the year in which it ends. Dollar figures, scoring and rebounding averages are rounded off. I have attempted to keep separate the men's and women's sections of the book, except where unavoidable. Some secondary mascot names, such as the Texas "Steers," the Texas A&M "Farmers," and the Texas Tech "Matadors" have gradually fallen into disuse, as will be evident. Likewise, the "Lady" antecedent for women's teams is not employed herein. I recognize that some people will read only certain chapters or only the men's or women's sections, but in so doing, they will miss key information and the sense of a greater, evolving story. And because detailing basketball's myriad rule changes could get tiresome, I mention only the major ones or those that directly pertain.

Now, on to our topic, the history of Longhorn basketball!

R.A.P.
Austin, Texas

UT MEN

1906

Although 1906 was the first season in which the University of Texas fielded a representative men's basketball team, the game was being played informally at least a year earlier in gym classes and in students' spare time. Coeds had played basketball since 1900, and there may have been some early disparagement of the ostensibly noncontact "feminine" game. The beginning would have been further delayed if not for the arrival on campus of Magnus Mainland. He was a native of Scotland's Orkney Isles who already had experienced a successful football and basketball career at Wheaton College in Illinois. His team was runner-up in the first national basketball tournament, held in conjunction with the 1904 Olympics in St. Louis. A lineman on the UT football team in 1905 and 1906, Mainland (with some help from head football coach Ralph Hutchinson) had the initiative to organize, coach, manage and play on the first basketball team in school history. He convinced the Athletic Council to spend $125 to prepare an outdoor court on the southwest corner of Clark Field, located at the intersection of Speedway and West 24th Street.

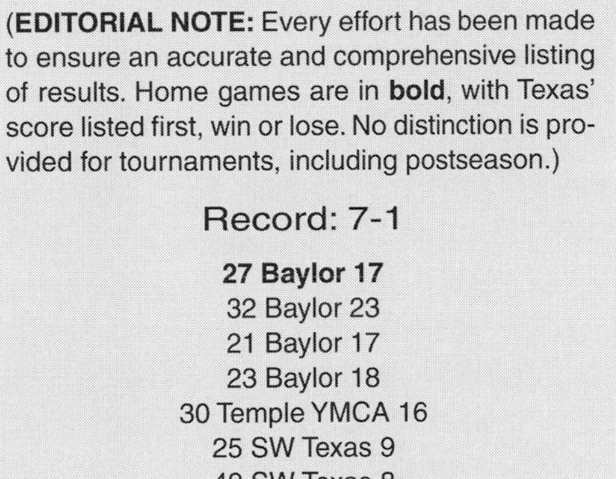
(**EDITORIAL NOTE:** Every effort has been made to ensure an accurate and comprehensive listing of results. Home games are in **bold**, with Texas' score listed first, win or lose. No distinction is provided for tournaments, including postseason.)

Record: 7-1

27 Baylor 17
32 Baylor 23
21 Baylor 17
23 Baylor 18
30 Temple YMCA 16
25 SW Texas 9
42 SW Texas 8
15 San Antonio HS 18

Of the 30 students who tried out for the team, 20 were retained. They supplied their own equipment, elected C.F. von Blucher as captain and staged an intrasquad exhibition on February 22 before a fair number of spectators. Another boost came when the Athletic Council bestowed official recognition on the sport; those who played in at least five games would receive the coveted "T."

Dr. James Naismith's 13 original rules underwent revision almost as soon as he committed them to paper. In 1906 (nine years after Yale and Penn played the first five-man college game), when basketball was just getting off the ground at UT, the center jump was held after every made basket; the legality of the dribble was under constant debate; the bottom of the basket was not yet left open; active coaching from the sidelines was discouraged; and player substitution was restricted. By choice, most free throws were shot underhanded. To the modern eye, basketball as it was played then and for years to come would seem excruciatingly slow, dull and unskilled.

After six weeks of practicing in all kinds of winter weather, the team played its first game when Baylor's six-man squad came to Austin on March 10. The Bears, who were taking a one-year hiatus from football, had these starters: center McDonald, forwards Wofford and Allison and guards Rohrer and Messingill. Their only substitute was Willis, the team manager. For Texas, it was Lawrence "Fuzzy" Feldhake at center, Mainland and Fred Ramsdell (a renowned

The first basketball team in University of Texas history. Founder-player-manager-coach Magnus Mainland, wearing his "T" sweater, is on the third row, far left. Captain C.F. von Blucher holds the ball.

football player and track star) at forward, and von Blucher and Leslie Gardner at guard.

Fewer than 100 people were in attendance on that historic day, which saw UT prevail by a score of 27-17. A strong south wind affected play, which was dominated by Mainland. After a single game, the team's 1906 home schedule was finished. A nine-man traveling squad went to Baylor two weeks later and won a three-game series in which the home team protested the play of Mainland (then in his sixth year of college competition) and the visitors protested nonregulation baskets. Both protests were waived. Baylor students attended the indoor games and cheered their team, also in its first year of existence. According to the *Austin Statesman*, "all three games were fast and hotly contested."

On the way back from Waco, Mainland and his compatriots stopped in Temple and beat the local YMCA club, 30-16. A second road trip was to the south. The team won two games from Southwest Texas Normal College but lost by three points to San Antonio High School (where basketball had been played for four years) amid squabbling about officials' calls.

Intercollegiate basketball at UT was off to a promising start, with seven wins and one defeat. But the financially strapped Athletic Council looked at the bottom line and saw expenditures of $146, receipts of $91 and a net loss of $55. Baseball and track were perennial money-losers, too, but those were well-established sports. It remained to be seen whether basketball had a future at Texas.

1907

Record: 5-4

35 Palestine YMCA 10
23 Decatur Baptist 24
38 Baylor 27
21 Baylor 23
23 Fort Worth YMCA 27
24 Baylor 28
40 Cleburne YMCA 36
36 San Antonio HS 16
Lakeside Institute—UT victory, but score unrecorded

Magnus Mainland was back as player-coach (and occasional referee) in 1907, along with three other T-men, Fred Ramsdell, Lawrence Feldhake and Leslie Gardner. The team played a nine-game schedule, of which little is recorded. On January 24, Palestine YMCA came to Austin for the season opener and lost, 35-10, before a sparse crowd at Clark Field. The first home loss in UT history was by one point to Decatur Baptist Academy in a game played in near-freezing weather. Baylor suffered a 38-27 defeat, with Ramsdell scoring over half of UT's points and freshmen Max Thomas and Walter Schafer showing promise as basketball players.

But the season's lone road trip was not too successful, as Texas lost two to Baylor and one to Fort Worth YMCA and beat Cleburne YMCA, 40-36. The final games were at home, two wins over San Antonio High School and one over Lakeside Institute, for a 5-4 record.

Their season over, the UT basketball team rested and took note of two things, one encouraging and the other much less so. Thomas W. Gregory, an alumnus and former regent, saw the need for a modern and spacious gymnasium in contrast to what the *Texan* called "that dark, dirty, unhealthy hole which we have so long called the gym."

The nameless gym, located in the basement of the Main Building, was not even adequate for basketball practice, not to mention intercollegiate games. And if the sport were to thrive at UT, a decent indoor arena would be necessary. Gregory, never mistaken for a crass athletic booster, was interested in providing a wholesome setting for Texas students, and if that included a basketball team representing the school, fine. In 1907, Gregory began a one-man campaign for a gymnasium expected to cost $75,000. He made a donation himself and urged faculty and alumni to contribute, hoping the money might be raised and the building erected within three years. Gregory's dream would come to fruition, but on a much larger scale than originally planned and many years later.

What the basketball team found distressing was a lack of support from the University. Despite Mainland's best efforts, the 1907 season had lost $189, and the Athletic Council planned to take another close look at basketball. Although the *Texan* indicated sufficient student interest, this statement appeared in the *University Record:* "Outside of the students who play basketball, very little attention is taken in this game at the University."

Mainland, an energetic older student who had influence with the student body and the Athletic Council, was gone. Fortunately, W.E. Metzenthin, a multisport athlete at Columbia and then head football coach, stepped forward. He agreed to coach the team and argued for the sustenance of basketball at UT. Player-manager Leon Goodman, assuming things would work out, began to arrange an ambitious schedule for 1908 that included the usual series with Baylor and San Antonio High School and a long road trip to either (a) Pine Bluff, Shreveport and Baton Rouge or (b) New Orleans, Mobile and Pensacola. At that time, most travel expenses were borne by the home team, so it actually cost less to play out of town.

In December 1907, Metzenthin ran the team through a number of lively practices at Clark Field. A *Texan* writer asked rhetorically, "May it not be that under such able coaching and stimulated by the awakening of college spirit, basketball at the University has entered upon a new and very successful era?"

But a meeting of the Athletic Council did not bode well for UT basketball. It would either be reduced to "minor-sport" status or dropped. Ramsdell, the team's star, refused to continue playing unless full support were given. The situation grew gloomier in January 1908, when the Baylor series was canceled, practice ceased and even interclass games were lethargic. Just as with football, baseball and track, interclass (and later, intramural) competition was fueled by male students' desire to join Varsity and possibly earn a letter.

Despite Metzenthin's support and the pleas of players and other students, the Athletic Council voted to do away with basketball as an intercollegiate sport. The council members regarded it as a two-year experiment that had failed, and their decision had a tone of finality. The 1908 schedule was canceled. Of course, the players were disappointed at this turn of events, but one of them, Morgan Vining, refused to let Texas basketball die.

1909

Record: 6-3

56 Austin HS 4
39 Deaf and Dumb Institute 9
21 Allen Academy 42
21 Allen Academy 38
21 San Antonio HS 19
34 Baylor 47
29 Baylor 21
42 Deaf and Dumb Institute 3
21 Austin HS 8

The exact nature of Morgan Vining's efforts to revive basketball is unclear, but he was widely acknowledged as the man most responsible. "It was through his constant application that student interest was aroused and a squad brought out to practice," claimed the *Cactus* yearbook. "We must give credit to Vining and his men for preserving a game that will mean much to Texas athletics in the future." W.E. Metzenthin agreed to continue his work as coach, the students wanted the game back and a number of challenges came from other institutions. Finally, the Athletic Council agreed to reinstate basketball as a major sport, including the giving of T's.

"Much interest is being centered in basketball, which was abolished last year and has been considered about dead ever since," said the *Austin Statesman*. "But on the contrary, it is very much alive due to several

W.E. Metzinthin, UT basketball coach from 1909 to 1911.

challenges Varsity has received from other teams in the state. A large number of men were out for practice the first day, including some from the football team.... Basketball is growing in esteem, and Texas should be represented in this form of athletics."

The *Texan* consistently urged the game's reinstatement partly because it was good training for football: "Several Easterners, coming from a section of the country where a recent basketball game was witnessed by more people than ever saw the Longhorns rout the Farmers [in football] on Clark Field, evidenced surprise that we had no Varsity five."

Manager J.D. Willis set up a nine-game schedule that included just two games on campus. Clark Field, which served as home to UT football, baseball, track and a wide array of student activities, was far from ideal as a basketball venue. Despite attempts to flatten the court, odd bounces of the ball happened often, reducing the quality of play. Basketball would become more popular and more secure as a major sport in the next few years, but playing outside at Clark Field was an increasing detriment.

The starting lineup for most of 1909 was comprised of Willis and W.H. Campbell at guard, Vining and Thornton Hardie at forward and Joe Estill at center. They blasted Austin High School, 56-4, and the Deaf and Dumb Institute (indelicately referred to as the "Dummies"), 39-9. That was followed by two losses to Allen Academy in Bryan and a two-point win over San Antonio High School. Baylor, laying claim to the mythical "state championship," came to Austin on February 27. A few days before the game, however, the UT team was thrown for a loop when Vining and Max Thomas announced that they were leaving to prepare for track season. But they were quickly persuaded to rejoin the team, which lost to the Bears, 47-34. The *Texan* reported that Vining and Baylor's E.A. "Happy" Ingram were the stars of the game.

A week later, when the two teams met in Waco, it was a different story. The Longhorns, strengthened by the addition of veteran M.F. Berry, upset Baylor, 39-21. The season ended with easy victories over the Deaf and Dumb Institute and Austin High School for a record of 6-3. In the 25th year of UT's existence, basketball was back for good at what the *Texan* called "the greatest state school in the South."

1910

Basketball was back, acknowledged as one of the four major sports at the University of Texas. But in fact there was just one major sport—football. It drew much larger crowds than baseball, track and basketball, it paid the freight for those and truly "minor" sports (tennis, cross-country, boxing, wrestling and others to come), and it stirred the passions of students, alumni and the press like nothing else. As the basketball team prepared for the 1910 season, they needed only to observe the hoopla surrounding the UT-Texas A&M football game, in which a week of campus rallies led 1,000 students to ride trains to Houston for the game. There is no indication that students had begun to follow the basketball team to out-of-town games then. According to the *Texan*, "basketball has not been a successful sport here in the past, but there is growing sentiment for it."

Record: 6-7

92 Deaf and Dumb Institute 14
35 Southwestern 13
70 St. Edward's 14
28 Baylor 31
31 San Antonio YMCA 19
21 Allen Academy 35
23 Allen Academy 24
40 Baylor 37
19 Decatur Baptist 28
26 Oklahoma 59
23 Oklahoma 63
35 Fort Worth Polytechnic 29
28 Waco YMCA 29

In W.E. Metzenthin's second year as basketball coach (he quit coaching football after the 1908 season), he had 35 candidates, of whom the key players were guards Max Thomas, Johnnie James and Lawrence Eastland, forwards Tom Moore, M.L. "Happy" Massingill and Thornton Hardie and center Emil Stieler. W.H. Campbell served as team manager. After a 78-point win over the Deaf and Dumb Institute, the team met Southwestern and won, 35-13, in a rough game that demonstrated both teams' lack of practice.

St. Edward's played basketball and had an indoor court, so the Longhorns paid a visit to south Austin and took a 70-14 victory. The *Texan* speculated that the team, with a 3-0 record, was the best in the five-year history of basketball at the University. But the orange and white would get a much stiffer test when Baylor came to town on February 5. Metzenthin installed a new offensive system that the *Austin Statesman* claimed "never fails to work.... The result will be seen in the game this afternoon." The result was a 31-28 loss to the experienced Bears before the largest home crowd yet, including the Longhorn Band. Unfortunately, Stieler, the UT center, missed the game because he was acting in a campus German play. Metzenthin understood; in addition to teaching and coaching, he led the Glee Club.

After a 12-point home win over San Antonio YMCA, the team embarked on a long road trip that encompassed the rest of the schedule. Even as the Longhorns climbed aboard the International and Great Northern train on February 22, Campbell was scrambling to arrange games. Some were played, and others (against Texas Christian and Austin College, for example) were not. Campbell expected a clean sweep and then, perhaps, a final game with Tulane to decide the "championship of the South."

Precious little information was recorded, or has survived, about the trip. It is known that Texas' victories over Baylor and Fort Worth Polytechnic Institute were interspersed with losses to Allen Academy (2), Decatur Baptist, Oklahoma (2) and Waco YMCA. "In the games with Allen Academy and Decatur, their coaches and other ineligibles were played, hence those games are not considered," sniffed the *Cactus*. "Oklahoma insisted on playing under intercollegiate rules, while our men were accustomed to those of the AAU."

Despite a 6-7 record, the *Cactus* awarded the state championship to UT. Basketball, growing in popularity all over the country, had taken root on the Forty Acres and was described by the *Texan* as "the ideal college game."

1911

Record: 1-4

61 St. Edward's 19
33 Baylor 34
19 Tulane 27
45 Alabama Polytechnic 27
15 LSU 40

Ex-player Thornton Hardie, then serving as manager, determined that the 1911 Longhorns would not face any team below the college level. No more YMCAs, high schools, academies or service teams. His was an idea ahead of its time, but as a result, the team ended up playing an abbreviated five-game schedule.

The key additions to the squad were center Joe McVeigh and forward Grady Ross, one of the first athletes to win four letters in basketball. The *Cactus*, using the florid prose of that time, said of Ross: "The little fellow...was a wonder in his way. Quick to grasp the elusive sphere and loath to turn it loose, except at the psychological moment, he was recognized by all as a man of inestimable worth to the team."

The season began on January 28 with a 61-19 defeat of St. Edward's, in which Morgan Vining scored 26 points and McVeigh 12. Bad blood lingered from the Texas-Baylor football game more than two months earlier involving, among others, Vining and M.L. Massingill. There was even some talk of halting athletic relations between the two schools (as had happened with UT and Texas A&M), but things cooled off. The Bears won, 34-33, in what the *Austin Statesman* called one of the best games ever played at Clark Field. A large crowd saw the Longhorns go up by nine points, but Baylor came back and won it on a last-second shot. The BU players felt pretty good about themselves, carrying Texas' scalp, as they beat St. Edward's later that night.

Coach W.E. Metzenthin was not discouraged by the loss, which exposed the team's weaknesses. He had a few days to rectify them before leading the Longhorns on the second out-of-state trip in school basketball history; the first occurred a year earlier when they crossed the Red River and played two games with Oklahoma. That was the Southern excursion Texas teams had dreamed of since 1907. While no wins were posted, the long journey through Louisiana, Mississippi and Alabama proved valuable. "The 1911 team was fortunate in having a splendid trip, which attested to Hardie's energy," the *Cactus* said. "They took a Southern tour, which was disastrous from the standpoint of victory but glorious for spreading the Texas spirit of good sportsmanship. Every report made mention of this fact."

First was a 27-19 loss to Tulane on an oblong (90' x 20') court at the YMCA gym on St. Charles Street in New Orleans. "There were no out of bounds lines," according to the *Austin Statesman*, "which arrangement tended further to confuse the Texas boys." It did not seem to bother Massingill, who scored 15 points. Alabama Polytechnic Institute (now Auburn) won, 45-27, also on an indoor court crowded with spectators. Metzenthin's players were unable to cope with the Tigers' speed. Worse yet was a 40-15 loss to Louisiana State in Baton Rouge. Tulane, Auburn and LSU were, like Texas, in the infant stage of their basketball history.

The team returned to Austin, weary and muttering as they trudged back to campus. Hardie tried but failed to arrange another game with Baylor, and UT students expressed some dissatisfaction that there had been just a single home game. While one win and four losses were nothing to be overly proud of, the Longhorns would not suffer another losing record until 1931.

1912

The *Texan* was rather optimistic in running an article headlined "New gymnasium now in sight." True, $65,000 had been subscribed in T.W. Gregory's campaign for a gym, but only a fraction was yet paid. To make matters worse, Gregory was involved in national politics and would soon move to Washington, D.C. to serve as attorney general in the Woodrow Wilson administration. The University's new gym remained a need and a wish but not a reality. Longhorn basketball players and supporters could only wonder how the sport might flourish with a decent facility in which to practice and hold games.

Record: 5-1

24 St. Edward's 7
39 22nd Infantry 33
32 San Antonio YMCA 31
37 San Antonio Turnverein 35
26 Baylor 38
41 San Antonio YMCA 22

Basketball was still on shaky ground at UT. When the Athletic Council appropriated just $50, the disheartened team feared that elimination might happen again. That was unlikely if only because W.E. Metzenthin, basketball coach the past three years, had begun serving as athletic director. His replacement for 1912, again without financial compensation, was J. Burton Rix, a Dartmouth grad who had coached the track team previously. "Rix took hold of the squad when it found itself without a leader and quickly demonstrated his ability to transform it into a quintet that was as good as any in the state," said the *Cactus*.

Rix, assisted by Carl Taylor, had some strong material in that 5-1 season, especially Joe McVeigh, Grady Ross, Morgan Vining, captain Johnnie James and Tex Schramm (father of the future Dallas Cowboy executive of the same name). Schramm, also the team manager, concocted "tag day," an attempt to get students in the Clark Field stands for the January 15 season opener. The opponent was a team of former college players hastily gathered by Mr. Matthews of St. Edward's. McVeigh was the leading scorer in a 24-7 victory.

The college-opponents-only philosophy had proven too costly, so UT was back to scheduling whoever was available and cheap (or generous with their own guarantees). The 22nd Infantry, unbeaten in the last two seasons, came to Austin on a warm day. According to the *Austin Statesman*, "the infantry team is famous for its great teamwork, and every member of the aggregation is an artist when it comes to 'shooting baskets.'" But the Longhorns were in shape and ready to put up a fight. For the first time, a 25-cent admission fee was charged, which deterred just a few fans. Texas won, 39-33, as Ross scored 12, James played a good defensive game and Schramm injured an ankle. The soldiers were not thrilled about playing on an outdoor court, something that was becoming rare. Schramm, who would serve as team manager again in 1913, took their views under advisement.

The team won a couple of close games in the Alamo City in early February. James, UT's husky guard, was ejected for rough play against San Antonio YMCA. His teammates urged the officials to reconsider, insisting that James always played like a perfect gentleman, but to no avail. Trailing by one point with time about to expire, Schramm scored the winning basket. Although the San Antonio Turnverein club refused to let Texas practice on its court before

Outdoor hoops on Clark Field.

the game the following day, the Longhorns managed a two-point win.

The Baylor Bears, said to have "put the kibosh" on several strong teams, were laying claim to the state title, but Rix and his players would not readily concede. Texas led by five points when the skies opened and turned Clark Field into a quagmire, sending players and fans running for cover. When the grounds had dried a few days later, Baylor was back, winning by a score of 38-26. The Bears' fine forward, McConnell, had 22 points. McVeigh scored 12 for UT before suffering a knee injury.

With Schramm and McVeigh out, James, Vining and Ross took up the slack in a 19-point win over San Antonio YMCA. The *Texan* noted that James seemed to be the chosen favorite of the 500 coeds present, and that colorful football star Arnold Kirkpatrick led impromptu cheers. The Longhorn-Bear rematch in Waco was canceled when Baylor officials imposed a quarantine on the campus due to a meningitis outbreak. While the players wanted another crack at the unbeaten green and gold, it was just as well because the money was gone, and they could not afford the trip. The 1912 season, which began amid such uncertainty, had gone rather well. Changes were afoot, as UT basketball prepared to enter its first golden era.

1913

"Basketball is no longer a minor sport at the University of Texas," said the *Cactus*. "It always has been so considered until this year Prof. Carl Taylor took charge of the work and infused new life into it. Coach Taylor hails from Drake, where he gained an enviable reputation in many college activities, not the least of which was basketball. Realizing the true merit of the game and seeking to put it on the same high footing as it is in the Eastern colleges, he devoted his time and energy to the molding of a quintet that would do credit to the University."

Taylor, also the UT track coach, inherited some good veterans and two frosh who would contribute substantially to the team's success over the next four years—guard Pete Edmond and center/forward Clyde Littlefield. Taylor arranged for the design of new uniforms featuring gray jerseys with an orange star. He had manager F.V. Lowry sell season tickets for the first time. And most significant, he found a makeshift gym that the Longhorns could call home. The Ben Hur Temple, at the intersection of Lavaca and West 18th Streets, was constructed in 1872 as an opera house for Turnverein, a German social society. Also used for dancing and gymnastics, the hall was far from ideal for basketball, but it served that purpose in 1913. Goals were erected on the balcony and in front of the stage, lines were drawn on the floor, bleachers were placed on each side of the pint-sized court, and it was ready to go. An estimated 350 people could squeeze in on both sides of the court, the balcony and the stage.

Record: 8-4

46 San Marcos Baptist 2
43 Southwestern 11
41 Baylor 15
36 San Antonio YMCA 14
24 Fort Worth YMCA 31
17 Decatur Baptist 20
18 Fort Worth Polytechnic 23
44 Waco YMCA 23
25 Baylor 33
70 Southwestern 7
57 Decatur Baptist 18
47 Waco YMCA 12

The first indoor home game in UT history took place there on January 13, 1913, a 46-2 drubbing of San Marcos Baptist Academy. A week later, Southwestern came to Austin for a night game (yet another novelty) and got crushed, 43-11. Tex Schramm scored 15 points, and Joe McVeigh played well, but the knee injury he had suffered the previous year continued to bother him. Former Texas coach J. Burton Rix served as the lone official. Twenty-point victories over Baylor and San Antonio

YMCA preceded a road trip that packed five games into four days. Taylor had hoped to take the team on a Southern tour, as in 1911, but it did not work out. In fact, the Longhorns would not leave the state again until 1923.

Fourth-year man Jack Garrett, who got sick and had to quit, was replaced in the lineup by the 6'2" Littlefield. He had not yet made an impact, but the *Daily Texan* (by then published five times a week) expected him to: "Littlefield, the freshman wonder in football, is out for a place on the team. His dexterity in handling forward passes on the gridiron gives promise of the skill he is showing on the courts."

In the first game of the trip, the Longhorns lost, 31-24, to Fort Worth YMCA. They played a doubleheader of sorts on February 6, falling to Decatur Baptist outdoors in freezing weather and dropping another game that night to Fort Worth Poly. UT salvaged some pride with a 44-23 win over Waco YMCA but lost to Baylor the next day. According to the *Austin Statesman*, the team returned, "telling a tale of woe, complaining of sore feet, charley horses, cold weather in north Texas and hard luck in general."

After a week of recuperation, Texas beat Southwestern, 70-7, with McVeigh the leading scorer. Decatur Baptist, a small school where basketball was played year-round, had defeated the Longhorns earlier in the season. Taylor's team was ready for the rematch at Ben Hur, beating the visitors by 39 points. McVeigh, Schramm, Ed Buddy and Lawrence Shea all scored in double figures.

The season closed on February 26 with a 47-12 defeat of Waco YMCA. That proved to be the final game played in Ben Hur Temple. The court was too small for basketball and for the number of spectators wanting in, it was off campus, and it cost money to rent for practice and games. While it had been a nice experiment, the Longhorns would be back at Clark Field the next three years. Pete Edmond, the dashing freshman guard who started every game, was chosen captain for the upcoming season. He was, said the *Daily Texan*, "a true representative of the 'Texas spirit,' which has come to stand for sportsmanship and manly playing." Little did anyone suspect at the time, but those last three victories over Southwestern, Decatur Baptist and Waco YMCA were the start of a 44-game winning streak, a Longhorn record that has endured for 80 years.

1914

The Texas basketball team welcomed its fourth coach in four years in 1914. L. Theo Bellmont, hired as the University's athletic director, had as his main task putting athletics on a sane and sound basis, pedagogically as well as financially. A graduate of the University of Tennessee, he coached nonvarsity basketball there and at YMCAs in St. Louis and Houston. Whether he really wanted this added responsibility at UT is unclear, but he would serve a pair of two-year stints at the helm, and his winning percentage of .886 (58 wins and nine losses) remains a school record. He was assisted by H.T. Ettlinger, a math professor and part of the athletic scene on the Forty Acres for two decades.

Record: 11-0

41 San Marcos Baptist 11
34 St. Edward's 18
25 Decatur Baptist 17
46 Southwestern 20
51 Baylor 14
25 Faculty All-Stars 19
53 Baylor 19
34 Fort Worth Polytechnic 25
34 North Texas 25
49 Southwestern 7
53 North Texas 22

Bellmont must have been dismayed when he first saw the basketball "facility" in the corner of Clark Field. The old playground was a near madhouse as more students than ever before participated in or tried out for intramural and intercollegiate sports. More than 500 could be seen at one time, training in football, soccer, baseball, track and basketball. Needless to say, it was not conducive to instruction in the finer points of the game.

The starters at the beginning of 1914 were Clyde Littlefield and Ed Buddy at forward, Carey Leggett at center and Pete Edmond and Gus "Pig" Dittmar at guard. Grady Ross, who lost his starting job to Dittmar, was the main substitute until midseason, when Leggett went to the bench and Littlefield moved to center. After several practice games with the scrubs, the Longhorns opened with a 41-11 victory over San Marcos Baptist. Littlefield scored 20 points in an equally easy defeat of St. Edward's.

Perhaps the toughest game was against Decatur Baptist, played under threatening skies before a large crowd. Due primarily to the efforts of Littlefield, Dittmar and Edmond, Texas won by eight. "The Baptists played a fairly good game," said the *Austin Statesman*, "but were outclassed by the Longhorn players, who used better tactics in many departments."

Southwestern and Baylor suffered lopsided defeats at Clark Field. In preparation for a four-game road trip, the "All-Stars" or "All-Americans" challenged the Longhorns in a fundraiser that was the season's biggest drawing card. The team was composed of W.E. Metzenthin of Columbia, J. Burton Rix of Dartmouth, Carl Taylor of Drake, Ettlinger of Washington and Vining and McVeigh of Texas. Perhaps player-coach Metzenthin was jesting when he said, "We're going to make Varsity look like a prep squad," to which captain Edmond stated that he and his teammates were not exactly shaking in their boots. According to the *Cactus*, "It was fast and snappy from start to finish, and the fighting spirit was always evident. The second half was a veritable football scrimmage." Texas won, 25-19.

The team left for Waco on the morning of February 13 and played Baylor that afternoon. Victorious, the Longhorns moved on to Fort Worth and beat Polytechnic Institute in a hotly contested game. They received a cordial reception in Denton before pinning a 34-25 loss on North Texas Normal College (now the University of North Texas). An estimated 1,000 people were in attendance, including many students of the College of Industrial Arts (now Texas Woman's University), who graciously rooted for the visitors from Austin. There was also a sizable crowd on hand in Georgetown when Texas beat Southwestern, 49-7. Littlefield scored 25 points and Ross 18 in that game.

The Longhorns returned, 10-0, but amid rumors that Bellmont had taken an ineligible player on the trip. He denied and explained, and the issue was soon dropped. UT's season closed on February 21 with a 53-22 defeat of North Texas in which Littlefield and Ross again were the stars. Bellmont, who refereed the game, said afterward, "The success of the season was due to the splendid offensive work of the guards and forwards. We have tried to strengthen our offense even at the expense of the defense. This is the new game, and it is successful."

He had promised the players an elaborate turkey dinner if they won every game, and they were so feted, courtesy of Mrs. Bellmont. While it had been a great season, there was more to come.

1915

Record: 14-0

33 Austin HS 12
46 St. Edward's 3
41 San Marcos Baptist 11
27 Dallas University 9
28 Decatur Baptist 25
53 TCU 27
28 Rice 14
31 Southwestern 21
52 Baylor 16
64 North Texas 13
30 Dallas University 13
39 TCU 25
60 Baylor 29
57 Baylor 19

Assisted by H.T. Ettlinger and gym coach Roy Henderson, L. Theo Bellmont led the Longhorns to another undefeated season in 1915. Tryouts and practice began on December 1. The "old men" (Clyde Littlefield, Gus Dittmar, Grady Ross and Pete Edmond) were augmented by freshmen H.C. Blackburn, a 6'4" guard, and Robert Blaine, who learned the game from Bellmont at Houston YMCA. He grabbed a starting job from the outset.

A loose-knit confederation known as the Texas Intercollegiate Athletic Association began in 1901, primarily for football, but winning it or the mythical state championship had meant little. Finally, there was a conference for the region's institutions that might rival the Missouri Valley Conference, the Western Conference (now the Big 10) or the Eastern League (now the Ivy League). Bellmont and Athletic Council chairman W.T. Mather were the key figures in forming the Southwest Conference, which began play in 1915 with these members: Texas, Texas A&M, Baylor, Rice, Southwestern, Oklahoma A&M (now Oklahoma State), Oklahoma and Arkansas. While football was the engine driving the formation of the SWC, basketball (as well as baseball and track) was also recognized, but the latter three schools did not participate in league play. It would be several years before basketball scheduling among Southwest Conference brethren was standardized. Although the resumption of athletic relations with Texas A&M excited UT fans, the Longhorns and Aggies would not meet in basketball until 1917.

Early-season wins over Austin High School, St. Edward's and San Marcos Baptist hardly extended the team. Nor did a 27-9 defeat of Dallas University played amid a brisk north wind. Dittmar, one of Texas' mainstays, suffered an ankle injury that sidelined him the rest of the 1915 season. Their drive for the inaugural SWC title thrown into doubt, the Longhorns found an able replacement in Blackburn. "Coach Bellmont shoved him into the breach, and the machine recovered itself and swept on to the undefeated goal," stated the *Alcalde*, UT's alumni magazine.

The 1915 Texas Longhorns were the heart of a 44-game winning streak. Coach L. Theo Bellmont and his key men—Grady Ross, Clyde Littlefield, H.C. Blackburn, Bob Blaine and Pete Edmond.

The closest game of the year was a 28-25 defeat of that tiny rival, Decatur Baptist. The first meeting between UT and the Texas Christian Panthers (soon to be renamed the Horned Frogs), scheduled for the wild outdoors of Clark Field, appeared to be canceled due to rain. But Eunice Aden, director of the Women's Gym, agreed to avail her facility to the men. It had very little room for spectators, but the game was held, and the Longhorns won, 53-27.

The Rice and Texas basketball teams met for the first time, also in the Women's Gym. The 5-0 Owls were expected to put up a tough fight, but they lost as Littlefield scored 14. The *Austin Statesman* was impressed with Littlefield in UT's February 8 defeat of Southwestern: "Littlefield played his usual strong game for Texas, especially on goal tossings. He made several star plays that were applauded." The *Cactus* said, "A true leader in every sense of the word and an athlete of unusual versatility and skill, Clyde was probably more instrumental than any other player in giving to the game this season its unprecedented popularity at the University."

He scored a school-record 28 points in the final home game of the season, a 52-16 win over Baylor. The team then headed north on what was supposed to be a six-game road trip. By that time, there was increased awareness of, and pride in, the winning streak, which had reached 23 games. Littlefield and Edmond reminded their teammates about it and the first SWC race.

They were never tested in beating North Texas and Dallas University, although the Dallas game, played on a slippery dance floor, gave Bellmont some concern. After seeing Texas defeat TCU, 39-25, Fort Worth basketball fans proclaimed the Longhorns the best team ever to visit their city. In a rough game—Ross suffered a broken nose—played before a hostile crowd, UT defeated Baylor, 60-29, in Waco. The score was even more lopsided in the next day's rematch, when Blaine scored 25. The game against Southwestern, still without a gymnasium, was rained out, and the Longhorns returned to Austin undefeated, their streak intact.

Bellmont chose his own all-SWC team, and it had a bright orange tint: Littlefield at center, Ross and Blaine at forward and Edmond and Blackburn at guard. (The consensus all-SWC team had Littlefield [his average of 19 points per game would stand as a conference record until 1944], Ross and Edmond, joined by Max Gilfillian and George Everett of Texas A&M.) The coach went into a lengthy denial of bias toward his own players and added, "Basketball as a college sport is rapidly coming into its own in Texas. The increased popularity of the game has brought to the surface a large number of capable players."

After two straight undefeated seasons, Bellmont could have gone ahead and named himself SWC coach of the year. There would be yet another season without defeat, but Bellmont had so much more to do; he found another man to coach the basketball team.

1916

Record: 12-0
102 San Marcos Baptist 1
80 St. Edward's 7
39 Southwestern 5
39 North Texas 19
51 TCU 20
44 Baylor 22
22 Baylor 9
41 Simmons 14
52 Southwestern 34
40 TCU 11
32 Rice 27
17 Rice 16

The Texas basketball coaching merry-go-round would continue for several more years. An unpaid position that offered its holder little in return for his time and trouble, it was given to Roy Henderson in 1916. He was the first UT alumnus to coach the team, and he concurred with L. Theo Bellmont's emphasis on offense. His words to the Longhorns before each game were simple: "Fellows, the score counts." And yet Henderson valued defense enough to keep one player, usually Gus Dittmar, as the "stationary guard" at the opponent's basket (much like a hockey or soccer goalie) even when Texas had the ball.

Dittmar's ankle injury had healed, and of the 50 students who tried out for the team, two newcomers helped forge a third straight undefeated season. They were A.B. Duncan, a 6'5" utility man, and Joe Thompson, another product of Bellmont's Houston YMCA program. "With [Pete] Edmond and Dittmar the guards, [Bob] Blaine and Thompson the forwards and [Clyde] Littlefield and Duncan the centers, the 1916 team was perhaps the best all-around team that Varsity has ever turned out," stated the *Cactus*. "Without hitch or flaw, these veterans of the game stood forth in all their splendor.... The spirit of the team, the harmony between the pilot and the crew, the enthusiasm of the 'rooters' all helped to place Varsity basketball in its proper place."

It may be indicative that of these six key players, only one, Thompson, was not a member of the UT football team. The presence, if not predominance, of football players on the basketball team would persist well into the 1940s.

The 1916 season, the last one played outdoors, began with the infamous 102-1 destruction of San Marcos Baptist. This hopelessly overmatched prep school had taken serious beatings at the hands of the Longhorns before, but never so bad as what happened on January 10 at Clark Field. Blaine scored 30 points, Littlefield 26, and so many baskets were made, the scorekeeper occasionally lost track. The Baptists would have been skunked if not for a free throw late in the game. And how rare was it to bust 100 in those days? Texas did not do it again for 40 years, until 1956. Bellmont realized the absurdity of playing such games and tried to go with a strictly collegiate schedule from then on.

The next two games were just slightly closer, 80-7 over St. Edward's and 39-5 over Southwestern. Bellmont, on a tour of midwestern colleges to study their athletic departments, heard of these scores. After witnessing a game between Northwestern and the University of Chicago, he boldly stated that Texas would defeat either one handily.

Henderson and an eight-member traveling squad did the Denton-Fort Worth-Waco circuit, winning all three games. They beat the North Texas "Pedoggies" (so called because it was a pedagogical, or teachers, school) by 20 with Littlefield scoring 22, they beat TCU and they beat Baylor on an inadequate indoor court.

A rematch with the Bears was held in the Women's Gym, won by Texas, 22-9. Victories followed over Simmons College (now Hardin-Simmons), Southwestern and TCU in which the combination of Littlefield, Thompson and Blaine proved too much. Rice gave them a pair of tough battles at the end of the season. First was a 32-27 UT win witnessed by 600 fans at Clark Field. It featured a nice scoring duel between Thompson (14 points) and Owl star Tom Tomfohrde (13). Just to be sure, Rice brought its own official, Mr. Stock of Houston YMCA. The Owls and Longhorns played a few days later in Houston, an indoor night game that was hard fought and thrilling. Rice led until the final two minutes but lost by a point.

Littlefield, one of the giants of Texas sports history, the winner of 12 letters in football, basketball and track, went on to coach UT track for four decades and had a six-year run as head football coach. In the 1950s, the Helms Athletic Foundation retroactively named him to its 1916 all-America basketball team. Littlefield was probably the key figure in three undefeated seasons, 40 straight wins (and counting) and booming interest in the sport. As much as Bellmont could not resist bragging about the team in Chicago, UT fans surely wondered how it might have fared in a national tournament. But that was more than 20 years in the future.

Other things were happening that would affect Longhorn basketball. Texas high schools had begun turning out better players, some of whom gravitated to Austin. The University's intramural program had existed for a few years but was formally instituted in 1916 by Bellmont, alumnus D.A. Frank and longtime director Berry Whitaker. Basketball was one of the seven sports provided, and in time it became the undisputed king of intramurals. Long before recruiting of athletes was an accepted practice, UT intramural basketball served as a "farm system" of sorts for the varsity. In future years, many students competed for teams representing their fraternity, boardinghouse or academic department, dreaming of playing for the school and earning a "T." Some of those dreams came true because Longhorn coaches learned to keep an eye out for top intramural athletes. And perhaps most important, the University of Texas basketball team would begin playing indoors in the 1917 season.

1917

While Thomas W. Gregory's drive to raise money for a functional and permanent gymnasium was pushed vigorously, the halfhearted response from alumni and other friends of the University caused the project to be quietly shelved. But the need had grown so urgent that in mid-1916, the Athletic Council went ahead and appropriated $8,500 to erect a temporary building adjacent to Clark Field. Even by the standards of the time, the Men's Gym was scarcely sufficient. Standing 115' x 105' and 23' high, it was built of wood, lacked restrooms and was poorly heated and lighted. Locker room facilities were rudimentary, to put it kindly. Yet the edifice was so much better than playing outdoors at Clark Field. For basketball purposes, the Men's Gym had room for 2,500 fans, a pinewood floor and an electric scoreboard. Another of the ugly, unpainted shacks adorning Speedway, it was described as "immense" by the *Daily Texan*. Over the next 12 years, it would serve the University well—or at least well enough—for basketball, rallies, commencements, convocations, concerts, dances and intramural sports.

Record: 13-3

52 SW Texas 15
34 Southwestern 14
30 Decatur Baptist 26
30 Rice 18
18 Rice 24
27 Baylor 19
19 Baylor 11
26 Rice 24 (2 OT's)
14 Rice 27
32 Baylor 15
31 Baylor 25
24 Southwestern 18
38 Texas A&M 16
24 Texas A&M 19
15 Texas A&M 29
24 Texas A&M 16

But the Men's Gym was not quite ready for the opening game of the 1917 season, under the direction of Gene Van Gent. A graduate of Wisconsin, the handsome new football-basketball-track coach held two practices daily, one indoors at the Women's Gym and one outdoors at Clark Field. Of the men who put together the 40-game winning streak, only two were back (Gus Dittmar and Joe Thompson), and other Southwest Conference teams had closed the gap on Texas. "The Longhorns do not appear capable of dominating the game any longer," wrote Ed Angly of the *Daily Texan*. "Time was, and not so distant either, that nobody doubted Texas would crush all opposition before her invincible five. But times have changed."

Thompson scored more than half the team's points in a 52-15 defeat of Southwest Texas at the Women's Gym. On January 24, 1917, 600 fans gathered for UT's inaugural game in the Men's Gym versus the Southwestern Pirates. After a preliminary game between the Beta Theta Phi and Sigma Alpha Epsilon

Just before tipoff between the Longhorns and Aggies.

fraternities, Texas won, 34-14. Decatur Baptist paid a visit the next night and gave Van Gent a scare, grabbing a five-point lead with three minutes left. "Varsity rooters made noise like an army of charging Huns," said the *Austin Statesman*, when two freshmen, Al DeViney and Guy Rogers, took control and sealed the victory.

The pinewood Men's Gym, built at a cost of $8,500, where UT played basketball from 1917 to 1928.

The SWC opener featured a fight between Della Valle of Rice and Thompson of UT, both of whom were ejected. The Owls' three-point halftime lead did not hold up, and again Texas was victorious. All things must come to an end, though, and the Longhorns' magnificent 44-game streak—a collegiate record that stood until the mid-1950s—was halted by Rice the next night at the Men's Gym. Even before the series, bold predictions had come out of Houston that the streak was doomed. Dodge scored 14 points in a 24-18 victory for the blue and gray. Dittmar was UT's only bright spot.

Baylor came to Austin and lost two close ones, the second of which was notable in that it followed a contest between coed teams; the UT freshmen beat the seniors. The revenge-minded Texas team met Rice in Houston and came away with a double-overtime victory that the *Daily Texan* called "the most nerve-wracking game in Longhorn basketball history," but the Owls came back to win the next night, 27-14, behind the shooting of Vance. Two outdoor victories over Baylor in Waco reminded UT's players of how fortunate they were to finally have a gym, even a temporary one.

After a lackadaisical defeat of Southwestern in Georgetown came the series that basketball fans had been waiting for—the Longhorns and the Texas A&M Aggies (more often called the "Farmers" then) on February 27 and 28. Texas won the first game, 38-16, before 1,500 fans at the Men's Gym. The starting lineup for UT was Jimmie Thomas and Bill Brown at guard, Dittmar at center and Joe Secor and Thompson at forward. For Texas A&M, it was Max Gilfillian and H.J. Burkett at guard, Marion Settegast at center and A.J. Price and Carlos Griesenbeck at forward. "Texas went into the contest last night with all the accoutrements of athletic warfare," reported the *Austin Statesman*. "The Varsity band led the rooters. The yell leaders pranced and 'performed' in most approved football-season fashion. The overcrowded gymnasium reverberated with lusty cheering."

The next night was even wilder as 700 Cadets traveled from College Station to support their team. The gym was nearly full, and officials had trouble clearing the floor to begin play. Before the opening tip, however, someone let loose an opossum with a placard reading "21-0" (the score of UT's football victory over Texas A&M three months earlier). Many enraged Aggies pounced on the innocent marsupial, even more Longhorns went to its defense, and the ensuing melee lasted several minutes. Texas A&M suffered a major loss in the second half when Gilfillian injured a knee, and Settegast fouled out. He refused to leave the game until he was coaxed by his teammates and assistant coach W.H.H. Morris. When UT won, 24-19, Aggie fans, believing the referee was less than partial, threatened to inflict bodily injury.

Texas lost the first game of the return series in College Station but won the second, 24-16, with 12 points from Thompson, to wrap up the 1917 SWC crown. When telegraphed word of the victory arrived in Austin, students started a bonfire and held a celebratory nightshirt parade. It was the kind of enthusiasm that had previously been reserved for football.

"The basketball games with A&M attracted more interest in the student body than ever before," said the *Alcalde*. "Games in the new gymnasium are especially interesting on account of the proximity of the specators to the game. The crowd extends right to the court lines.... The excitement is increased by reason of the fact that the ball frequently goes into the crowd, at times followed by the players."

1918

The 1918 UT basketball team. Captain Al DeViney holds the ball, and coach Roy Henderson stands to the right.

When the United States entered World War I, more than 500 of UT's male students, faculty and staff departed for military duties. That exodus included several members of the basketball team, as well as their coach, Gene Van Gent. His place was taken by 1916 coach Roy Henderson. Railroad travel during the war was chaotic, but the Longhorns managed to play a 21-game schedule that included three trips. Due perhaps to the weaker quality of play or the sobering effect of having friends and relatives fighting in Europe, attendance at basketball games declined somewhat in 1918.

"There have been no recent seasons," said the *Cactus*, "when training period opened with the Longhorns facing such gloomy prospects.... The dearth of experienced material stood in saddening contrast against yesteryears, when three or four veterans were always present to lighten the burden on the mentor. Coach Henderson merely shrugged his shoulders, said, *'c'est la guerre,'* and started to work on the hardest task that ever faced a Longhorn coach." His assistant was ex-player Jimmie Thomas.

Al DeViney, a sophomore, was the sole returnee. Henderson spotted and developed the talent of James Greer (who would lead the team in scoring) in the intramural ranks and freshman center Louis Smyth. Johnnie Gray, H.M. Russell, Otis Miller and William Hill also helped out during the season.

San Marcos Baptist, Southwest Texas and Southwestern each scored two points against UT in maulings at the Men's Gym. After beating the Pirates, the players were called into Henderson's office, where DeViney was chosen captain to the cheers of his teammates. With 14 points from Greer, the Longhorns dispatched Decatur Baptist and then got on a northbound train. Nursing injuries and sickness, they prepared to play four games in three days. On a sandy outdoor court in Denton, they lost to North Texas. They beat TCU in a rough game in Fort Worth on the afternoon of January 25, then traveled to Dallas and played Southern Methodist (under former UT coach J. Burton Rix) that night, edging the Mustangs, 22-21. The weary Longhorns stopped in Waco on the way home and lost a close game to Baylor, one of just two wins for the Bears that season.

With three days to rest, Texas then took on Baylor in the Men's Gym. Henderson hinted that his team was eager to feast on Bear meat, and he was right. DeViney and Miller starred in a 31-15 victory, the first of eight straight wins. UT took two from a strong Rice team in Houston. SMU, Oklahoma A&M (twice) and TCU all lost in Austin, thanks largely to the energetic play of Greer.

Record: 16-5

San Marcos Baptist—UT victory, but score unrecorded
SW Texas—UT victory, but score unrecorded
43 Southwestern 2
36 Decatur Baptist 22
20 North Texas 24
38 TCU 23
22 SMU 21
32 Baylor 36
31 Baylor 15
28 Rice 16
32 Rice 25
35 SMU 14
33 Oklahoma A&M 9
30 Oklahoma A&M 19
48 TCU 21
27 Texas A&M 15
12 Texas A&M 21
7 Texas A&M 8—A&M victory later forfeited
17 Texas A&M 12
36 Rice 40
27 Rice 31

Optimistic Longhorn fans anticipated a new addition to the Men's Gym trophy room, even with four games versus Texas A&M and two versus Rice still on the schedule. The first game with the Farmers was nip and tuck until the second half when UT pulled away. "Time and again, furious encounters took place in the shadow of the enemy goal, with the result that the ball soon was sent flying through the air to the Texas forwards" said the *Austin Statesman*. A&M won the next day's game, 21-12, in which Smyth and DeViney suffered wrist and knee injuries, respectively. E.M. Longcope and E.E. McQuillen were the key players for the Aggies.

The teams split two games the next week in College Station, although Texas A&M's 8-7 victory on February 21 was later forfeited because a player, Pat Dwyer, had been found ineligible. The conference race came down to the UT-Rice series in the Men's Gym. They were well-played, exciting games that often had the crowd on its feet. On the first night, Lawrence Kingsland scored 18 points to pace the taller and healthier Owls, and they won again to secure the 1918 SWC championship.

1919

When Roy Henderson threw out the balls for the first practice session in 1919, he could not have been too hopeful. Only H.M. Russell was back. But in short order, Al DeViney and James Greer showed up with releases from the Navy, and Louis Smyth reentered the University. Henderson found an outstanding young guard in George McCullough, and two brothers, Charles "Big" and Lee "Little" Dittert, had improved from the previous year. Things then seemed positively rosy for Henderson (interim AD while L. Theo Bellmont was in the military), whose statement, "we are on the eve of a great era," referred to postwar UT athletics in general. But he could have been speaking of the 1919 Steer basketball team, a group that would go 17-3 and bring the Southwest Conference title back to the Forty Acres.

Due to an influenza outbreak that killed over 200 people in Austin alone, University officials banned all social gatherings on campus during the month of January. So the first five games of the season were played in eerie near-silence at the Men's Gym before empty bleachers. Only players, coaches, trainers, officials and a handful of reporters were allowed in. As extreme as that action appeared, it was better than cancelation of the season, as had been briefly considered.

Record: 17-3

22 School of Military Aeronautics 15
25 Southwestern 12
37 TCU 17
52 North Texas 24
18 North Texas 25
33 SMU 19
40 TCU 25
21 Baylor 13
23 Rice 22
38 Rice 22
29 SMU 7
23 SMU 15
89 SW Texas 6
28 Rice 25
36 Rice 11
40 Baylor 7
28 Texas A&M 19
15 Texas A&M 22
20 Texas A&M 28
22 Texas A&M 15

Texas beat the School of Military Aeronautics, 22-15, in the opener. Former Longhorn Jimmie Thomas, who had been learning to fly at Camp Mabry, could still play the game; he scored 13 points, including "several baskets at almost incredible distances," said the *Austin Statesman*. UT had no trouble with Southwestern and TCU and expected none in a two-game series with North Texas. DeViney and Greer looked great in a 52-24 win, but the tables were turned the next night as the visiting Eagles won by seven.

The Longhorns got a clean sweep of SMU, TCU and Baylor on the road. After defeating the Bears, they had just eight minutes to catch the train to Austin. Wearing their basketball uniforms and carrying their bags, they sprinted to the station only to see the southbound train rolling down the tracks. Henderson and his players spent an uncomfortable night in the Waco train station.

Two more wins came in Houston, at the expense of the Rice Owls. In the first, UT came back from nine points down to tie it at 22. Then Greer, fouled just before the buzzer, hit a free throw to win the game. The influenza scare had abated enough for fans to be allowed back in the Men's Gym for basketball games, but there was a slim crowd for the series with SMU on February 7 and 8. Greer and McCullough sparkled for the Longhorns in both victories.

Henderson had a dilemma when he received a telegram from the coach at Simmons, stating that the Cowboys could not come to Austin for a scheduled game. Henderson hurriedly arranged a game with Southwest Texas, which was brutalized by a score of 89-6. Although the Longhorns had won eight straight, they were nevertheless jubilant to hear that Baylor had upset Texas A&M. "This is the only defeat that has besmirched the escutcheon of the Farmers and leaves them in the rear of Texas on a percentage basis," said the *Austin Statesman.* While scouting was rare and informal in those days, Henderson heard that Texas A&M was building a powerful basketball program, and indeed, the Aggies would dominate the SWC in the early 1920s.

Rice lost two in Austin, and Baylor took it on the chin, 40-7, setting up a four-game series between league leaders Texas and Texas A&M. The first two were played in College Station, and a split resulted. The championship series in Austin took place on February 28 and March 1. As was often necessary when Aggie rooters came en masse, extra seating was arranged in the Men's Gym. E.M. Longcope's 16 points led A&M to victory in the first game. A shoulder injury forced Greer to the bench early in the second game, and the Longhorns trailed by three when Henderson put him back in. He came through in a big way, scoring 12 points in a 22-15 win. Greer, the former intramural player, had not even expected to compete in 1919, but he led his team to the title and made all-conference. And he saved his best for last, against UT's ancient rival.

It is interesting to note that for the decade 1910-19, Texas had the fourth-highest winning percentage (.813) in the country, trailing only Navy, Creighton and California.

1920

The University of Texas welcomed back many students, faculty and staffers who had taken part in World War I. L. Theo Bellmont, survivor of a plane crash while training, resumed his duties as athletic director, and Gene Van Gent (coach in 1917) was to head the basketball team. But when Van Gent took a business opportunity in California, Berry Whitaker agreed to coach the 1920 Longhorns, as well as run the burgeoning intramural program. Roy Henderson served as Whitaker's assistant and coached the Shorthorns, a team of scrubs and ineligibles.

The granting of athletic scholarships at Texas was at least 15 years off; only gradually would it become an accepted practice. While the ideal was to recruit basketball players—or athletes of any sport—from students on campus, boosters were often eager to help. *The Longhorn T,* a publication of the UT athletic department, made this pitch in 1920: "An honor greater than any victory is Varsity's reputation as an exponent of clean and sportsmanlike athletics. The authorities and all T-men are directly responsible for the upholding of this high standard. Now, to the task of energetically, openly and cleanly securing promising athletes for future teams. Varsity does not condone the buying of or bidding for 'prep' school stars, but Varsity does believe in bringing the traditions of Varsity before the athletes of the state as an inducement to make Texas their institution. With this issue, a campaign is begun to arouse every T-man, ancient or modern, to his responsibility to secure at least ONE promising athlete for Varsity every year."

Record: 10-6
31 SW Texas 11
27 Southwestern 24
29 TCU 18
26 Simmons 9
28 TCU 21
9 SMU 19
26 Phillips 23 (OT)
44 Baylor 11
15 Texas A&M 16
8 Texas A&M 15
20 Rice 12
13 Rice 24
23 SMU 5
23 Southwestern 12
9 Texas A&M 27
13 Texas A&M 17

Whitaker's 1920 team was expected to contend for another Southwest Conference championship. In addition to seven lettermen, he beheld war veterans Bob Blaine and Joe Thompson, who had last played in

1916 and 1917, respectively. But it was a season of injury and sickness for many team members. The first reverse was Thompson's withdrawal from school following an operation.

UT got off to a 5-0 start but stumbled to 10-6, the worst record in a decade. After a 31-11 victory over Southwest Texas, the Horns helped inaugurate Southwestern's new gymnasium, reputed to be the best basketball court in Texas. The Pirates, playing before a big crowd, desperately wanted to defeat the visitors from Austin, but they lost by three points. TCU and the Simmons Cowboys fell in succession at the Men's Gym. The following night, the gym was the scene of the 1920 Texas athletic banquet, notable because Bevo, the original Longhorn steer mascot who had been branded by Texas A&M students, got served as barbecue.

And then it was time for the team to go upstate, where the results were mixed. In a victory over TCU in Fort Worth, Al DeViney suffered a knee injury. As for the SMU game in Dallas, the *Austin Statesman* had said, "little doubt as to victory is entertained by the Longhorn coaches." But the Mustangs won, 19-9, in a game marred by Blaine crashing into a brick wall, ending his season. Then or shortly after, center Charles Dittert got the flu, and his replacement, C.W. Knebel, had a back injury. Team captain H.M. Russell got the flu, and Lee Dittert and promising freshman Warner Duckett went out with bone bruises.

The crippled Longhorns faced Phillips University (a Southwest Conference member that one year) on January 27. The Haymaker football team had defeated Texas the previous fall, so Whitaker was pleased with a 26-23 overtime win. The *Daily Texan* upbraided fans who hooted when a Phillips player shot a free throw: "Texas spirit stands for fight but also for consideration and courtesy." Fan sportsmanship at Longhorn home basketball games remained a subject of discussion for five decades.

Even with substitutes playing most of the way, UT beat Baylor, 44-11, in a Saturday night contest. Ed Barrett, a small, speedy freshman forward, scored 22 points, and Duckett had 14. The Texas A&M Aggies, barreling to the only undefeated season in school history, had outscored opponents by a two-to-one margin when they came to Austin. Whitaker had enough healthy players to make a game of it, falling by one point. Barrett and George McCullough played well for the Steers, while center A.L. Forbes led the Aggies. Halftime of that game featured a three-round boxing match between local middleweights "Preacher" Andrews and "Lick 'Em" Brown. The Men's Gym was packed again the following night when Texas A&M won, 15-8.

UT split a home-and-away series with Rice and defeated SMU in a lively game. According to the *Daily Texan*, "there was a constant roar of yells and whistles that sounded like old times on Clark Field with the Farmers in town." Knebel scored 13 points and blanked Mustang star Alva McKnight. After beating Southwestern, the Longhorns traveled to College Station for two season-ending games with Texas A&M, which had long since claimed the SWC crown. The Cadets gleefully predicted certain defeat for Texas, and while it would be a hard row to hoe, one UT victory might be achieved because Russell and some other players were healthy again. As the *Austin Statesman* said, "the hoodoo which has been doing its best to deprive the University of all her men has eased up a little." But the Aggies won by scores of 27-9 and 17-13.

Not long after the season, Whitaker became head football coach, and Bellmont consented to handle the basketball program again. McCullough, all-SWC in 1920 despite an injured knee, was chosen captain for the next season.

1921

When George McCullough dropped out of school, his captaincy was transferred to Charles Dittert. But a confusing situation occurred with the arrival of another George McCullough, nicknamed "Hook" because of his large and nimble hands. A native of Missouri, he was 6'2" and 185 pounds of pure athletic talent. McCullough is regarded as one of the finest football players in early UT history, and he could dominate a basketball game, especially on defense. He and forward Phillip "Pap" Peyton had led a 1920 Shorthorn team that dealt misery to their opponents and sometimes to the varsity during practice games.

Since freshmen were no longer allowed to play varsity sports, a new team was formed—the Yearlings (sometimes called the Fish), coached by Clyde Littlefield. His 1921 team won eight of nine games and had players who would do quite well in later years, such as Abb Curtis, George Pendergrass, future coach Howard "Bully" Gilstrap, Manny Ponsford, Alphonso Ragland, Ivan "Bobby" Robertson and Vernon Schuhardt.

While the quality of basketball in the Southwest was continually on the rise, the number of athletes playing it year-round was small. The dominance of football can hardly be overestimated, and many young men of the time played basketball or baseball or ran track as an amusement or to stay in shape for the gridiron game each fall. So when L. Theo Bellmont called his squad together, typically few were ready for basketball season. In addition, Charles Dittert injured a knee before the first game, causing a lineup shift. Warner Duckett replaced him at center early in the season before getting moved out by four-year letterman H.M. Russell. These players got most of the court time in 1921: Russell, Peyton, McCullough, Ed Barrett and George Hill. Peyton, the team's best shooter, took almost every free throw, 155 out of 166.

Record: 13-5

34 SW Texas 6
25 Simmons 8
21 SMU 18
36 Southwestern 11
32 Baylor 10
18 Baylor 25
32 Rice 9
35 Rice 13
5 Texas A&M 23
16 Texas A&M 15 (OT)
25 Baylor 28
37 Baylor 19
27 SMU 21
24 Southwestern 15
36 Rice 31
22 Rice 24
16 Texas A&M 13
13 Texas A&M 18

As the season began, Texas' championship prospects did not look too bright, considering that most of the Texas A&M juggernaut was back. "Those who saw the Farmers in action last year know the almost perfect variety of game they put up," said the *Austin Statesman*. "However, if hard work and coaching can do anything for the Longhorns, Bellmont promises to have a good team."

And if the first five games—all victories—were any indication, it would be a nice season for UT. Southwest Texas and Simmons were routed at the Men's Gym, but the SMU Mustangs, a virtual two-man team with Leon Cooper and Jimmy Kitts, almost pulled an upset in their small, poorly lit gym. Lee Dittert's basket with 30 seconds left sealed a 21-18 victory.

Barrett had 12 points in a home win over Southwestern, and then it was on to Waco. Baylor finally had a place for indoor basketball, the Cotton Palace Coliseum. Its slick floor did not seem to bother the Longhorns, who roared to a big halftime lead and coasted in. Smarting over the previous night's defeat, the Bears, with wily coach Frank Bridges, sprang a surprise and won the second game, 25-18.

Bellmont ran some tough workouts to get the team's attention, and all looked well in a couple of victories over Rice in Austin, 32-9 and 35-13. As the Longhorns boarded the Sunshine Special for College Station on February 4 for a series with Texas A&M, they learned that the Aggies had just lost three of four to LSU and Tulane. "Even the most pessimistic among Texas fans are hopeful that the team will be able to win from the speedy A&M aggregation," said the *Alcalde*. "George McCullough, the big end of the football eleven, is a bear cat on the court. And Peyton is a great floor man, big, strong and aggressive."

In the first game, a convincing 23-5 A&M win, the Longhorns got frustrated and resorted to throwing up long shots. But they came back the next night and took a 16-15 overtime victory. When the Aggies tied it with two minutes left, "the house was in an uproar," said the *Daily Texan*. A.L. Forbes' missed free throw sent the game into OT, where the only score was Peyton's free throw. Neither coach substituted, and the 10 players were all exhausted when the final whistle blew. "It was veritable warfare from beginning to end, with State University in the lead throughout most of the game and with the Aggies fighting to the limit of their endurance for a victory," said the *Austin Statesman*.

The Baylor Bears came to Austin the following week for two games in which Bellmont expected his players to have blood in their eyes. But with Peyton sick and McCullough and Hill hurting, they were not at full strength and had the short end of a 28-25 score. Room was made that night in the gym for 100 members of the Texas Legislature, who were being lobbied to prevent the University from moving to a site near the Colorado River. By what the *Daily Texan* called "teamwork and the unbeatable Texas spirit," the Longhorns won the next night, 37-19. Peyton scored 17 and McCullough defied trainer S.N. Ekdahl's recommendations, discarded his crutches and played.

The Longhorns beat SMU in a slow, listless game in Austin and clipped Southwestern by nine. The roof of the Pirates' new gym leaked, and play had to be stopped several times to allow a janitor to mop the floor. The team went to Houston and beat Rice at City Coliseum but lost to the Owls the next day on a YMCA court. Peyton and Tim Timmons of Rice were the leading scorers in both games. The hostile crowd in the latter contest provoked a *Daily Texan* editorial entitled "Give the Players a Square Deal."

The Longhorns still had an outside shot at the SWC crown when Texas A&M came to Austin. The Aggies, directed by future UT football coach and athletic director Dana X. Bible, were greeted by more than 2,500 spectators in the Men's Gym on March 1 and lost, 16-13. Peyton, as usual, led the Horns in scoring, but the rebounding, defense and ballhandling of McCullough won raves from Bible and reporters. Excitement was at a high pitch the following night, and an equally large throng gathered, but Forbes, Pat Dwyer and George Hartung paced the Aggies to a five-point victory. Texas finished the season with a 13-5 record.

Basketball was not yet over at the Men's Gym. Forty high school teams from all over the state were arriving by bus and train for the inaugural University Interscholastic League tournament. Many current and former Longhorn players and coaches helped run the tournament, key among them Roy Henderson, athletic director of the UIL. When the tournament was over, Governor Pat Neff awarded cups and medals to the winners and runners-up. This event, which would grow to much larger proportions in future UT facilities (Gregory Gym and the Erwin Center), was off to a good start in the Men's Gym.

1922

It was not just for basketball that the Men's Gym got an extra 600 seats in late 1921, because the growing student body needed more room for all big indoor events. But the expanded gym still could not hold everyone who wished to see key Longhorn home games. L. Theo Bellmont's final season as coach was an exciting one with a record 20 wins. The team, whose jerseys were emblazoned with "Texas" (player numbers were added in the 1930s), came close to ending Texas A&M's reign of terror in the Southwest Conference.

If UT had lacked depth the previous season, that was not the case in 1922. Bellmont had many fine players, led by the incomparable Hook McCullough and top scorer Phillip Peyton. Six sophomores made the varsity, including 6'4" center George Pendergrass. Before the first game, however, Bellmont got word that poor grades might sideline captain McCullough, whom the *Austin Statesman* called "head and shoulders above other players...one of the greatest exponents of the indoor game who has ever worn the orange and white." Questions about his eligibility dogged McCullough throughout the season, which began with two lopsided wins over Southwest Texas. And Southwestern (a recent conqueror of SMU) offered the Steers no more competition on January 10 and 11. It was obvious early on that Bellmont had the makings of an excellent basketball team. That year, he emphasized teamwork, passing and taking fewer long shots, the hallmarks of recent Texas A&M teams. He also criticized UT's fair-weather fans and urged better treatment of opponents and officials.

Record: 20-4

55 SW Texas 10
42 SW Texas 15
53 Southwestern 20
36 Southwestern 19
36 SMU 17
27 SMU 15
45 Baylor 10
33 Baylor 15
40 Phillips 26
33 Rice 13
29 Rice 12
31 SMU 18
32 SMU 12
17 Texas A&M 20
16 Texas A&M 25
63 Trinity 8
30 Baylor 25
26 Baylor 35
38 Oklahoma A&M 13
28 Oklahoma A&M 8
21 Rice 8
36 Rice 11
19 Texas A&M 11
8 Texas A&M 20

Conference play began with two games against SMU in Dallas. The starters were McCullough and Bobby Robertson at guard, Peyton and Manny Ponsford at forward and Pendergrass at center. Texas toyed with the Mustangs and won both games, 36-17 and 27-15. A tougher time was expected from Baylor, which had already played 20 games on a tour through Louisiana, Mississippi,

Philip "Pap" Peyton (above) and George "Hook" McCullough (right), stars of the 1922 Horns.

Alabama and Georgia. Pendergrass outplayed the Bears' Ted Lyons, all-SWC the previous year, in two victories in Austin. Was it the finest team since the days of the 44-game win streak, when Clyde Littlefield, Pete Edmond and Gus Dittmar roamed Clark Field? Bellmont and his players were not saying so, but writers and fans did some sabre-rattling in their behalf.

Phillips, no longer in the SWC and therefore not hindered by strict eligibility rules, put up a hard battle before a big crowd at the Men's Gym, losing, 40-26. Peyton had 20 points in what the *Austin Statesman* termed "one of the prettiest and fastest hoop and ball exhibitions ever staged on a Texas court." The Owls of Rice Institute got their feathers plucked twice in Houston as Peyton continued his high-scoring ways.

A knee injury forced Robertson to miss two home victories over SMU, but he would be ready for the crucial series with Texas A&M. The biggest crowd yet in the Men's Gym saw a mighty tussle between the Horns and Aggies. Dana X. Bible's proteges inflicted a bitter double defeat (20-17 and 25-16) on UT and took over the SWC lead. Although Peyton and Robertson were hobbled somewhat, no alibis were offered when the maroon-jerseyed crew walked off the floor following the second game. They and their fans attended an all-University dance later that night at the gym.

Peyton, McCullough and Robertson were rested in a game with Trinity, coached by Leon Goodman, a member of the original UT basketball team in 1906. His Tigers were shown no mercy in a 63-8 blitzing. McCullough, thought to be ineligible, stayed at home while his teammates went to Waco on February 10. Somehow cleared at the last minute, he got to the Cotton Palace just before tipoff and played a stellar game as Texas won by five. Baylor fans constantly disputed with the referee, who was told that he should be wearing an orange uniform and was instructed to leave town. The Longhorns were pelted with various objects from the stands during and after the game. The next night, the Bruins exacted revenge with a 35-26 win spearheaded by the fast and shifty Ted Lyons.

Oklahoma A&M, a member of the SWC from 1922 to 1925, came to Austin and lost a pair of games by large margins. Bellmont, disenchanted with the late-season play of Pendergrass in the pivot, brought football star and intramural basketballer Tom Dennis onto the team and the starting lineup. Texas fans cheered him lustily. The most interesting moment of that series came when the Aggies' Peck hit a shot from 10 feet behind the half-court line.

The final four games of the season were played without Peyton, who had been declared academically ineligible. Texas won two from the woeful Rice Owls (1-11 in the SWC in 1922), marred by a foot injury to Ponsford, who crashed into the stands going after a ball. That set up a season-ending showdown with the Farmers in College Station. It would be a herculean task to win both, as was needed to take the crown; but one unidentified UT player told the *Austin Statesman*, "they beat us two games here, so why not return the compliment?"

Whether due to grades or injury, five Longhorns were out, and yet they won the first game by a score of 19-11. Texas A&M, led by center L.S. "Tiny" Keen, won the second game, 20-8, and the SWC title. The returning squad was met at the Austin train station by the Longhorn Band and numerous rooters. "This closed one of the most exciting and interesting chapters in University of Texas basketball history," said *The Longhorn T*. "But the Longhorns have failed to achieve the goal that the present age demands—to win the championship."

1923

Athletic director L. Theo Bellmont had the difficult and sometimes disagreeable tasks of making ends meet, building support among students, alumni and faculty, and upgrading facilities. Coaching UT basketball was something for which he had twice volunteered, but it was time to give that job to someone else. Bellmont, who would serve on the NCAA basketball advisory committee for a number of years, brought in young Milton Romney, a four-sport star at the University of Chicago. His primary duty was to assist Berry Whitaker with the football team. Romney headed the basketball program in 1923 (the first year in which home games were broadcast via radio), but because of circumstances beyond his control, he did not last long in Austin.

Record: 11-7
(does not include 6-game barnstorming tour in Iowa, Kansas and Missouri)

29 Southwestern 13
31 Southwestern 16
27 Oklahoma A&M 28
34 Oklahoma A&M 19
35 Baylor 18
23 Baylor 7
21 Texas A&M 27
25 Texas A&M 42
36 Rice 17
24 Rice 17
29 SMU 16
23 Baylor 18
19 Baylor 21
21 Rice 29
26 Rice 33
25 SMU 15
13 Texas A&M 16
18 Texas A&M 12

Missing from the previous squad were Hook McCullough, George Pendergrass and left-handed forward Manny Ponsford, whose chronic knee problems forced him to sit out the 1923 season. But that still left Phillip Peyton (who was to lead the SWC in scoring for the third straight year), Bobby Robertson, Vernon Schuhardt, Abb Curtis, Ed Barrett and Bully Gilstrap. The key newcomers were guard Alphonso Ragland and centers A.M.G "Swede" Swenson and Lester Settegast. Beginning on Christmas Day, 1922, Romney took eight players on a midwestern tour that involved six games with five teams: Des Moines University, Simpson College, Southwestern University (of Kansas), Hillyard (an AAU team from St. Joseph, Missouri) and the University of Missouri. They came back winless but much more experienced, having played some formidable opponents down to the wire. "The Longhorns absorbed six defeats on our midwestern trip, but they learned a lot of basketball in the absorbing," Romney said. "Every place we played, the fans and the teams were enthusiastic in their praise of the Texas University five. I am now more optimistic with respect to the Southwest Conference season. My squad did not play against these crack fives for nothing. It should serve us in good stead when we play the Texas A&M Aggies and the Baylor Bears."

Perhaps because they were all defeats, these games never made it into the UT historical record, although similar games in later seasons did. The Longhorns officially began their season on January 8 at the Men's Gym, playing host to Southwestern. Camp of the Pirates showed off his newfangled hook shot, sometimes from quite far out, but Texas took the opener, 29-13, and won again the next night. Barrett, who had received some criticism the last two years for excessive dribbling and shooting, made an effort to blend in with his teammates.

Another victory appeared certain when the Horns led Oklahoma A&M by 14 with nine minutes to go. Romney welcomed Peyton and Swenson to the bench, but the Aggies suddenly got hot and ended up winning the game, 28-27. Clifford Dean (20) hit two free throws in the final 30 seconds for Oklahoma A&M. A large crowd witnessed the defeat, which provoked some critics of the coach and his team, already trailing in the SWC race. The *Daily Texan* told its readers, "Texas students would do well to recall an ancient motto, 'Win or Lose, Texas Always.'"

At that time, the UT Board of Regents and the Athletic Council discussed and tentatively agreed to build a new gymnasium on what was called "Jordan Field" at the intersection of Speedway and West 21st Street. A proposed gym sufficient for physical education, intramurals and intercollegiate athletics, it aroused a lot of excitement, but it was just wishful thinking. The disappointment could be felt on campus when students realized that they were stuck with the Men's Gym, whose floor sometimes threatened to give way under the strain. Basketball, popular as it was, remained a financial liability and could not begin to pay for a quality gym. That dream was further delayed.

A return match with Oklahoma A&M in Stillwater produced a more agreeable result, 34-19, Longhorns, putting an end to all the grumbling. Next, Baylor came to Austin for a pair of games. Frank Bridges' players entered the Men's Gym wearing golden overcoats with a big green bear on the back. The cheerleaders, band and recently formed Texas Cowboys had the crowd in a continual uproar both nights for two victories. The brilliant play of Robertson and Peyton boosted UT to a 5-1 record, but a tough series with Texas A&M awaited them.

Before making the trek to College Station, the team went through some closed practices and got a pep talk from baseball coach Billy Disch. With Peyton, Settegast and Schuhardt sick, Romney could only hope for low-scoring games. If the Aggies' L.S. Keen and A.L. "Ox" Forbes were to run amuck, UT might get a couple of country cleanings, and that is just what happened. The Longhorns enjoyed a narrow halftime lead in the first game, but their shooting (a weakness all season long) went cold, and A&M won by six. The following night was even more decisive, 42-25. So early in the season, the Aggies already had a death grip on the SWC crown.

Rice lost two ragged games at the Men's Gym, 36-17 and 24-17. The *Austin Statesman* put the blame squarely on Phil Arbuckle's players: "No team which plays as roughly as the Owls do can hope to win.... The Longhorns play clean basketball. This system pays when the referee calls the fouls. Barry Holton, referee of last night's combat, became dizzy in the second half trying to keep account of the fouls."

The gym was packed again on February 20 for UT's best game of the season, a 29-16 lassoing and branding of the SMU Mustangs. Robertson and Ragland played well, and Peyton was at his best, scoring 20 points. In the following days, the team had to deal with two major distractions. First, Robertson and Settegast were injured when the motorcycle they were riding collided with a car. While Robertson's leg injury was bad enough, Settegast suffered a fractured skull that ended his season. Second, the long and drawn-out selection of E.J. "Doc" Stewart as the new Longhorn football coach was made. Newspaper stories mentioned, almost in passing, that Stewart would also be coaching the basketball team. Romney was a lame duck, and everyone knew it, but he tried to finish the season as best he could. After the accident to two of his key men, he found some intramural players to fill out the team.

In Waco for two games with Baylor, Romney and his squad dedicated the first to Robertson and Settegast, sending a get-well telegram to them in Seton Infirmary. Texas won that first game, 23-18, only after stopping a late Bear rally. The next night, however, the Longhorns lost a close one in which they trailed by seven points and came back to tie it, only to see Roy "Country" Williamson hit a long shot to win the game with 10 seconds left. Unlike the year before, there was high praise for Baylor's hospitality and sportsmanship.

Rice fans went slightly crazy when their team won two from UT. It was more of the heavy-handed tactics the Owls had used in Austin, drawing another vigorous response from the *Austin Statesman*: "Tonight's game was marred by inexcusable roughness on both sides. In fact, more than a third of the evening was spent in arguments with the referee as to whether or not various fouls were justifiable and in petty squabbles over minor points."

Carrying a three-game losing streak to Dallas, Romney fully expected a win because SMU's season was also in decline. The Ponies fell easy victims, 25-15, as Peyton and Swenson starred for Texas. All that remained was a home series with Texas A&M, SWC champion for the fourth straight season (but the last time for nearly 30 years). Robertson was sufficiently healed to play and give the Longhorn offense some much-needed punch. The first game was fast and furious, won by the Aggies, 16-13. But UT managed a six-point win to close the season. "That final series with Bible's quintet will always be remembered by the hundreds of Varsity rooters who packed the gym to capacity on both occasions," said the *Cactus*. "The brand of fight displayed by every man on the Texas five has never been surpassed."

1924

Doc Stewart was said to have begun playing basketball in 1893, two years after the game's invention. One of the first pros, the Ohio native became a coaching vagabond, piloting teams in basketball or football or both at Mt. Union, Purdue, Allegheny, Oregon A&M (now Oregon State), Nebraska, and most recently, Clemson, before he was enticed to Austin. He got off to a wonderful start, leading the Longhorn football team to an 8-0-1 record. His quarterback, Bobby Robertson, was captain of the 1924 basketball team that, to the surprise of nearly everyone, made history by going 22-0 and winning the Southwest Conference title, the first for UT since 1919.

Stewart implemented a new style of basketball, one that emphasized man-to-man defense, movement and crisp passing, and practically eliminated the dribble. The dribble, he insisted, should be used only in the most extreme emergency. His eight main players were guards Abb Curtis, Alphonso Ragland and Hubert "Birdie" Foster, forwards Robertson (an all-SWC guard in 1923), Manny Ponsford and Sandy Esquivel, and centers Lester Settegast and Carl "Carrie" Nation. Two, Esquivel and Nation, were sophomores and new to varsity competition. The others had previously run the gamut from mediocre to erratic to very good, so prognosticators had UT third or maybe fourth in the conference, behind TCU, Oklahoma A&M and Texas A&M. Because of a scheduling oddity, the Steers and Horned Frogs did not meet.

Athletic director L. Theo Bellmont arranged another preseason holiday trip, this time to Mexico. But political turbulence in Guadalajara and Mexico City caused it to be canceled. "We might get down to Mexico and not get back until time for the 1925 basketball season," Stewart quipped. That would have been mostly a sightseeing, goodwill tour, and the team needed work and competition. Since El Paso was somewhat of a basketball hotbed, he took the team there for eight games with local teams. The contests were played at night, before large crowds eager to see the men from the University of Texas. Stewart, who had some trouble teaching his system to the players, expected two or three wins, but he got seven against such teams as the Aztecs, the All-Stars, the Mormons, El Paso High School and Texas College of Mines (now UT-El Paso). The Longhorns toured the area with Esquivel and Ponsford, natives of El Paso, and were treated to a wild-game dinner across the border in Juarez.

Upon the team's return to Austin, grade reports from the registrar's office showed everyone eligible; there would be no flunkouts and no serious injuries in 1924. The season began in a strange way on January 9 against Southwestern. After six minutes, the Longhorns were leading, 3-2, when a transformer blew and the lights went out. While UT electrical engineering students combined their skill with the University's power house electricians in a vain effort to restore lighting, the Longhorn Band rendered noble service by playing for an hour. They finally quit, and 1,500 fans made their way from the darkened gym.

The two scheduled games against Southwestern were played, and Texas won both by four points. But in previous years, the Pirates had been just token opposition. If those two victories were indicative, UT was in for a long year. Such concerns found their way into the *Daily Texan* and *Austin Statesman*, but Stewart maintained his Sphinx-like attitude. "I don't know if we'll be good, bad or otherwise until I see the other Southwest Conference teams," he said.

Record: 22-0
(does not include 8-game barnstorming tour in El Paso)

20 Southwestern 16
21 Southwestern 17
16 Oklahoma A&M 14
22 Oklahoma A&M 15
32 Rice 14
40 Rice 22
19 Baylor 10
17 Baylor 10
33 Texas A&M 22
27 Texas A&M 16
38 Rice 10
32 Rice 9
22 Baylor 12
27 Baylor 24
19 SMU 13
15 SMU 11
30 Arkansas 26
32 Arkansas 21
17 SMU 9
29 SMU 13
24 Texas A&M 14
17 Texas A&M 11

Conference play began when highly touted Oklahoma A&M came to Austin. With the score tied at 14 in the final 10 seconds, Esquivel was fouled and missed both shots, but Nation grabbed the rebound and put it in to take a dramatic victory. Curtis' defense on Aggie star Sieler drew plaudits. And the interaction between referee Roy Henderson and the crowd was notable as fans booed, hissed and razzed him at every call they did not like. Henderson, coach of the Horns in 1916, 1918 and 1919, stopped the game and calmly informed the fans that a penalty to the home team might be imminent. Stewart then took the floor and asked the fans to tone it down, which they did. Chastened, they offered applause to Henderson and Stewart. UT president William Sutton, present in the Men's Gym crowd, apologized to Henderson for the offensive behavior, and all was forgiven. Texas won by seven the next night.

In a Friday afternoon game in Houston, the Longhorns led Rice by just two points at halftime, but a locker-room chiding by Stewart was effective, and they won, 32-14. Robertson had 14 points despite a stomach ailment. Ponsford (displaying a unique one-handed shot) and Esquivel scored 12 each in another easy win over the Owls. UT's stamina and conditioning paid off then and many other times in the 1924 season.

The Horns swept a low-scoring series with Baylor due to Ponsford's shooting, Robertson's floorwork and Foster's defense on the Bears' Bennie Strickland. Foster watched him with all the care and attention bestowed by an ardent wooer on his lady love. Although Texas A&M had not been doing so well, the Ags seemed rather confident of beating Texas in two games at the Men's Gym. But UT's gym, designed and built as a temporary measure, was showing its age after eight years. Lloyd Gregory of the *Austin Statesman* wrote, "The University of Texas is certainly in dire need of gymnasium facilities. The Varsity headquarters would not do credit to a second-rate college. If basketball continues to increase in popularity, a larger gym will have to be provided." Farsighted universities in Washington, Oregon, Iowa, Indiana, Minnesota and Pennsylvania had recently built modern fieldhouses to seat over 10,000 spectators.

The 1924 Longhorns, Southwest Conference champions, and the last undefeated team in school history. Coach Doc Stewart stands in the middle row, left.

Perhaps 3,000 fit into the Men's Gym on February 2 for the first of the UT-Texas A&M games, and Gregory estimated that twice that number wanted admission. He pointed out how much revenue was being wasted as a result. E.B. Darby, the Aggies' shining light, was kept in check by Foster, and Ponsford scored 16 in a 33-22 victory. The two teams played again the next night (something A&M coach Dana X. Bible did not like), and again the Steers won. The Aggies' early nine-point lead did not hold up largely because of the rebounding and shooting of Settegast.

Rice was blown out in two games, at which time people realized that the Longhorns, yet to feel the sting of defeat, were the class of the SWC. Premature though it was, some were talking about an undefeated season. And although Stewart had made a career out of sounding pessimistic, he did not discourage it: "If they finish unbeaten, the team will have proved themselves one of the strongest that has ever worn the orange and white."

The gym was full again on February 8 and 9 when Baylor and Texas met. While both were Longhorn victories, the second game required a frenzied comeback by the home team. Referee Red Brown had his hands full that night as Curtis was ejected for kicking the Bears' Warren Woodson. UT players contended that Woodson had engaged in overly rough play, and even more regrettable was the threat of a fight after the game.

Foster shut down flashy forward Gene Bedford in two close wins over SMU in Austin, earning at least a tie for the SWC title with six games left, all on the road. The Longhorns would prove their mettle in the final week, and not just because "Get Texas!" had become the rallying cry around the conference. On February 26, they embarked for Fayetteville, Arkansas, where the first Longhorn-Razorback games in history would be played. They had a close call the first night, a hard-fought four-point victory in which Robertson was the keystone. UT needed another second-half comeback to win the following game, 32-21. The players had dealt well enough with the 400-mile train ride, odd court and mad cheering of the Hog fans to win two games, but they were feeling the strain of a long season and playing not to lose. On the ride from Arkansas to Dallas, Stewart reminded them, "A team that won't be beaten, can't be beaten."

The weary Longhorns took two wins over SMU (17-9 and 29-13) and returned to Austin, rested a bit and then traveled to College Station for a two-game series to conclude the season. As much enthusiasm as they had aroused with 20 straight victories, they were still predicted to lose at least one to Texas A&M. Robertson scored 14 points in the first game, a 24-14 win before 2,000 yelling, swaying fans. The Aggies went down valiantly the next night, losing by six to the old foe they called "t.u."

"Magnificent fighting spirit on the part of the men, ably directed by the wizard of sportdom, 'Doc' Stewart, did the trick," said the *Cactus*. "The season was over before the amazed student body could rub its eyes and begin to realize that the team of '24 was a super-team.... Certainly, it made the greatest record, and did it in the face of the strongest opposition the Southwest has furnished since the cage game was introduced here."

More breathless praise from the *Alcalde:* "For once, one may deal in superlatives, without fear of being deemed either meaningless or inane—the Varsity basketball team of 1924 was the greatest, most formidable court machine that ever represented a Southwest Conference institution." Who is to say? After all, the 1920 Texas A&M team that went 19-0 might have quibbled with that assertion. Much has changed in UT basketball over the past 70-plus years. There have been better teams than Doc Stewart's 1924 Longhorns, but none can match their unblemished record.

1925

After a season-ending football victory over Texas A&M in brand-new Memorial Stadium, Doc Stewart "issued his clarion call for Longhorn basketeers," said the *Daily Texan.* Back from the great 1924 team were captain Lester Settegast, Hubert Foster, Sandy Esquivel and Carl Nation. Vernon Schuhardt, a veteran from 1922 and 1923, lent rebounding and defense. Stuart "Stud" Wright, Matt Newell and Maurice "Rosy" Stallter came over from the football team. Good material, but it soon became apparent that another SWC title was unlikely. While most pundits chose TCU, Stewart picked Oklahoma A&M.

Once again, the Longhorns took a preseason holiday tour. Stewart initially wanted to play Iowa, Chicago and other midwestern schools, but that plan fell through. Instead, they went to Dallas and played nine games in 10 days against local teams. They stayed in a dormitory at Dallas University and played their games in the State Fair livestock arena, which had been converted into a gym. These were clearly practice games, played before a smattering of fans, and yet they were recorded as the real thing. At any rate, UT split a pair with the Young Men's Hebrew Association, defeated the Boethians three times, beat Stowe's All-Stars, lost two to the Stickle Lumberjacks (AAU southern champions), and on New Year's night defeated Ragland's All-Stars. That team consisted of former Longhorns Alphonso Ragland, Bobby Robertson and Abb Curtis, plus frosh Joe King, Clen "Ox" Higgins, John Estes and Leo Baldwin.

Some SWC coaches had adopted or experimented with Stewart's no-dribble offensive system, but TCU's Matty Bell was not among them. He taught something called "dribble, pivot and pass," put on display before a capacity crowd at the Men's Gym on January 7. It proved to be a stirring game, won by the Longhorns, 14-13, in the final seconds on a shot by Esquivel. Victory was costly, however, because Schuhardt suffered a broken leg when he and Frog forward Jim Cantrell got tangled up out of bounds. The game really turned on an odd strategic move by Bell, who kept his ace, "Long" Tom George, on the bench the first 15 minutes of play.

Against a big team from Southwestern, with the score tied, Nation came off the bench to hit the winning basket. And the Horns beat the Buccaneers again the next night, 20-10, by jumping to an early lead. Esquivel was ejected for protesting the too-vigorous defensive play of an opponent. With a 3-0 record, they boarded the Katy train for Stillwater to take on John Maulbetsch's Oklahoma A&M Aggies. Players like E.M. Lookabaugh, George Conner, Clyde Hall and Gordon Perry could throw fear into most teams, and Stewart said he would be "tickled pink" to win one of two. It did not help that Settegast had an injured shoulder or that Nation and Foster were playing with chronic bad ankles or that the games would be held on the largest court in the

Record: 13-5
(does not include 9-game barnstorming tour in Dallas)

14 TCU 13
16 Southwestern 14
20 Southwestern 10
10 Oklahoma A&M 46
15 Oklahoma A&M 25
26 SMU 31
26 St. Mark's 13
21 St. Mark's 18
31 Baylor 21
16 SMU 15
12 TCU 31
19 Baylor 16 (OT)
20 Rice 16
14 Texas A&M 21
20 Arkansas 18
21 Arkansas 12
28 Rice 13
17 Texas A&M 13

conference. The first was a 46-10 disaster (then the worst defeat in UT history), and the second, although much closer, was another loss. To make matters worse, the crippled and travel-weary team stopped in Dallas and lost to SMU, 31-26.

"All I can say is that I'm glad to be back," Stewart stated, offering high praise for Oklahoma A&M and SMU. He vowed to give playing time to some heretofore substitutes, one being Newell. Inexperienced in basketball, he was still a fine athlete and an asset to the 1925 team. Another was Nesbit Cummings, a quick and smooth ballhandler but a defensive liability. Texas took two games from St. Marks, a San Antonio team headed by ex-Longhorn Ed Barrett. Somewhat reluctantly, Stewart began allowing Foster to dribble enough to open up the court, and it paid off in a 31-21 win over Baylor. Coach Frank Bridges used two complete teams, which he called the "greyhounds" and the "rabbits," to little avail. Esquivel was the leading scorer with 11 points.

Lester Settegast, Sandy Esquivel and Carl "Carrie" Nation.

SMU, flushed by a recent defeat of Arkansas, came to Austin on February 6. A capacity crowd saw the Mustangs miss three late free throws that would have tied or won the game as Texas escaped with a hectic 16-15 victory. Settegast displayed 1924 form, and Foster put the clamps on Pony star Gene Bedford. The Longhorns were trounced, 31-12, by TCU in Fort Worth, the first instance of a Frog victory over Texas in any sport. That game was refereed by Bridges, who was on the sideline the next day in Waco when his Bears took on UT. Nation sent the game into overtime, where the Horns took a three-point win.

In Houston, Rice was presented with a Valentine's Day gift in the form of a 20-16 defeat as a last-minute spurt allowed Texas to win its fifth conference game. The Longhorns stopped in College Station on the way home and helped dedicate Texas A&M's new 5,000-seat DeWare Memorial Field House. (It was quite a contrast to what they had in Austin. The state fire marshal had attended a recent game at the Men's Gym and issued a report declaring it a firetrap—jammed to the roof with spectators, the rickety wooden building had just two exits, smoking was permitted, and no fire extinguisher was present.) The Texas game was a homecoming event for Texas A&M alumni. Fans stood and applauded through most of the game, as the Aggies battled back from a four-point halftime deficit to win, 21-14.

With four games left in the season, UT was out of the SWC race, then tied between Arkansas and Oklahoma A&M. Then the highly favored, fast-breaking Razorbacks came to Austin for two games. Francis Schmidt's team, led by forward Rolla Adams and center Elbert Pickell, had recently scored 54 points against Texas A&M. But the Hogs' title hopes were dimmed with two losses to Texas, 20-18 and 21-12. Esquivel and Nation were the leading scorers, and the defensive work of Foster and Newell was excellent.

Thanks largely to Settegast's 14 points, Rice was beaten in a rough game featuring several uncalled intentional fouls. Stewart made an impassioned plea between halves for more fan support. "You men think you yell," he said. "Compared with the yelling of the Texas Aggies, your rooting is but a whisper. You'll have to give the team better support than you've been giving, if you expect us to win over the Farmers on Saturday night."

The good doctor got what he asked for, a large and loud house that helped the Longhorns win their season finale, 17-13, as both teams played like a championship was at stake. Texas A&M led the first 35 minutes, but late hoops by Esquivel, Settegast and Nation put Texas in front. Coach Dana X. Bible could only rub his bald head as the Aggies missed shot after shot.

While the Longhorns finished with a rush, winning eight of their last 10 games, it was a far cry from the glory of 1924. For the first time, no UT player made all-conference. Proud Texas schools were none too happy to see the SWC title leave the state (Oklahoma A&M won), but they had to get used to it because Arkansas would take the trophy each of the next five seasons.

1926

If the 1926 Longhorns were to prosper, much of the responsibility would rest on the lithe shoulders of captain Sandy Esquivel. Outstanding as a boxer, cross-country runner and basketball player, he welcomed a host of new team members. Football players Mack Saxon and Rufus King and track man C.B. Smith did not last, for various reasons. But Ed Olle (a transfer from Texas Military College) and sophs Joe King, John Estes, Ox Higgins, Charles "Red" Patrick and Leo Baldwin showed great promise.

The Southwest Conference had outlawed the increasingly popular holiday practice tours, which irked Stewart and some other coaches. The ruling was made because faculty representatives thought the game might be veering too far from the cherished amateur student-athlete ideal. They were right about one thing—basketball competition among SWC schools had never been more intense. The quality of play continued to rise, although so few intersectional contests were held that it was hard to gauge. And since there was as yet no tournament to determine a national collegiate champion, basketball cognoscenti gave undue attention to all-conference, all-regional and all-America teams. Throughout the season, they debated and speculated on who might be so honored, and when the final games were played, they weighed in with their considered opinions. Sportswriters, coaches, faculty members and even team trainers got newspaper space to present their all-SWC teams. Unfortunately, once again, no Longhorns made the consensus team, but Esquivel was chosen by several experts.

Before the season began, the pinewood floor of the Men's Gym got a thorough scrubbing and repainting. Esquivel, Estes, Baldwin, King and Maurice Stallter comprised the starting lineup in the opener with St. Edward's on December 18, which Texas won, 25-17. But the Saints came back three days later and took a one-point victory. Losing to a little school like St. Ed's was somewhat galling, but it got much worse as the Longhorns dropped two to Sul Ross on a YMCA court in San Antonio. Stewart got dubious results from using complete first and second teams.

UT's problems mounted in rapid succession. First, Matt Newell and Patrick were declared academically ineligible. Then Baldwin, a multisport star from Wichita Falls, suddenly quit the team, citing a lack of encouragement from Stewart. He was, however, sweet-talked into rejoining. Then came news that Stewart was resorting to an old-fashioned method of motivation, the paddle. When the coach detected a lazy or indifferent player, he stopped practice and applied a lick to the backside of the offending athlete. Subs and stars alike got spanked. "Those little taps sting terribly," King told the *Daily Texan*, "but they're just the thing to make a fellow think of what he's doing before he does it."

Stallter scored eight points in a 27-16 defeat of St. Edward's, but the Saints won the following night. Estes was out with an ankle injury, and Olle had a torn hand ligament and another problem with his leg. Although the season was off to a poor start (and against relatively weak competition), big crowds were coming to home games. The Horns picked up a little steam with two wins over Southwestern, and then it was time for SWC play to begin.

"TCU has the stuff," Stewart said before the Steers and Horned Frogs met on January 12. Their fine guard, Don Frazee, stayed in Fort Worth with a broken ankle, but Tom George, diminutive forward Frank Cantelmi and football star Raymond "Rags" Matthews were proven performers. The Men's Gym was full, the Longhorn Band was there and the players were ready for what the *Daily Texan* called "the attack of the vaunted amphibian horde." Texas led most of the way until Cantelmi got hot. He scored all of his nine points in the second half of a 20-16 victory. UT's center position was in good hands because Baldwin outplayed the lanky George.

Record: 12-10
25 St. Edward's 17
20 St. Edward's 21
18 Sul Ross 22
22 Sul Ross 25
27 St. Edward's 16
13 St. Edward's 25
24 Southwestern 20
21 Southwestern 14
16 TCU 20
17 Rice 22 (OT)
28 SMU 20
24 Centenary 18
23 Centenary 15
22 Baylor 29
12 Arkansas 35
7 Arkansas 27
19 SMU 26
35 Texas A&M 27
22 Baylor 19
23 TCU 21
27 Rice 9
32 Texas A&M 19

Several stiff scrimmages were held before the team entrained for Houston to take on Rice. When time ran out, the Longhorns were ahead by a score of 17-16, or at least so they thought. The official scorer said the teams were tied, sending the game into overtime. Ralph Nevinger scored all of the Owls' points, and UT was blanked, earning a dark corner of the SWC cellar. That turned out to be Rice's only conference win of the season.

SMU, with several big footballers on its team, came to Austin and played rough and tumble, but Texas won, 28-20, with a combined 16 points from Esquivel and Stallter. "The Mustangs are well-tamed and ready for the ladies' bridle path," joked the *Daily Texan*. Homer Norton's Centenary Gentlemen had a new gym in Shreveport, had beaten three SWC teams and were beginning a long and fruitless effort to win admission to the conference. Their left-handed captain, Red Lawrence, who spent his freshman year at UT, played well in two defeats at the Men's Gym, marred by hooting and jeering from spectators. Grandstand managers behind the Texas bench shouted comments and instructions, inspiring another *Daily Texan* editorial on student comportment at basketball games.

But that enthusiasm was counted on when Baylor played the Longhorns on January 30. With five sophomore starters (known alternately as the "Baby Bears" and the "Kid Kagers"), they might be susceptible to fan pressure customarily put on opponents in the Men's Gym. Lingering injuries to Olle, Estes and King, and Stallter's bout with tonsilitis, left Texas weakened. Center Louis Slade had 13 points in Baylor's first win over the Longhorns in three years. Jumping Joe King, despite a bad foot, scored 10 for UT.

Just before departing for the Ozarks to play the so-called "wonder team" of Arkansas, Stewart announced that nearly every player had come down with ptomaine poisoning. Emphasizing the David and Goliath theme, Stewart all but conceded defeat in the series, instructing his team to play defense and just hold the score down as much as possible. The Hogs' Elbert Pickell, Rolla Adams and 6'5" whiz Glen Rose ran rampant, winning, 35-12 and 27-7. Only Esquivel played well for Texas.

The team was further demoralized by a loss to the SMU Mustangs in Dallas. With a 1-6 SWC record and Texas A&M coming to town in a few days, they were stunned when athletic director L. Theo Bellmont unleashed a barrage of criticism at his coach. Sportswriters and others in the University community had grown somewhat disenchanted with Stewart for a number of reasons. Rumors of practicing on Sunday, questionable coaching moves and corporal punishment in practice were bad enough, but conceding defeat to the Razorbacks was too much. "Fans are tired of reading alibi after alibi and stories of the Longhorn team being incapacitated from ailments ranging from sore toes to ptomaine poisoning," the AD declared. "A waning spirit has been shown in the orange and white in the last two or three years. The University of Texas is fully strong enough to fight its battles without having excuses or alibis being offered for the showing of its teams. The University of Texas is not to be pitied...but the school is large enough to stand up before any of them, play games and take defeat as well as victory." Stewart, returning from Waco where he had witnessed the Baylor-TCU game, met with Bellmont, and they papered over their differences, but his time was not long on the Forty Acres.

The Longhorns and Aggies renewed their feud at the Men's Gym, which was packed to the rafters. One sportswriter claimed that 4,000 people were there that night to see Esquivel lead UT to a 35-27 win. Slim forward Hollis Tucker had 14 points for Texas A&M. "It was only by virtue of having a better-conditioned team, one that could stand 40 minutes of grueling basketball, that won the game for the Steers," said the *Austin Statesman*.

Journeying to Waco two days later, they beat Baylor by three and continued their successful march with a 23-21 win over TCU in Fort Worth. "Fighting like madmen from start to finish," said the *Daily Texan*, they won on King's basket with two minutes left. Intent on proving that the early loss to Rice was a fluke, they destroyed the Owls, 27-9, in Esquivel's final home game.

At DeWare Fieldhouse, the Longhorns beat Texas A&M for the seventh straight time, a decisive 32-19 victory that helped compensate for the agony they had endured most of the season. Stallter, one of two juniors on the 1926 team, was chosen captain for what would be Doc Stewart's last year at UT.

1927

The bloom was off the rose for Doc Stewart and the University of Texas. His football and basketball records had slipped, he paid too much attention to outside interests and he was tangled up in a power struggle that eventually brought down his boss, L. Theo Bellmont. While Stewart had some support, widespread speculation in the press about possible successors indicated that he would have a new address after the Longhorns' 1927 basketball season.

Practice began in early December, and it was soon apparent that some newcomers were making things hot for the veterans. Jake Looney, Charles Patrick and Steve Wray could play, but the real star was a polished and speedy forward named Holly Brock. He had led Beaumont High School to the 1925 state title and captained the 1926 Yearlings. The returnees for UT included Maurice Stallter, Ed Olle, Joe Estes and John King. And Stewart was delighted to learn that Carl Nation was back after a one-year absence. Probably the most talented Steer team since 1924, they lost five of their first eight games but finished second to Arkansas in the SWC.

The season opened with a 29-22 loss to St. Edward's, led by Harold Jansing and Sticks Reilly. But Brock (12) evened the count the next night in a 33-23 win. Hillyard, the 1925 and 1926 AAU champion based in St. Joseph, Missouri, came to Austin for a two-game series in late December. Regarded as a team of "giants" because they averaged 6'2", they had a number of former college all-Americans, including Forrest DeBernardi, Jimmy Loveless, George Starbuck and ex-Razorback Rolla Adams. Hillyard, which expected to put a knot on the collective head of the Longhorns, escaped with two close victories, one of them in overtime, when Starbuck took a pass from DeBernardi at a dead run and scored just as the timekeeper fired his gun. The *Austin Statesman*'s Frank White described the game as "one of those last-minute sporting finishes usually found only in novels and movies."

Record: 14-9

22 St. Edward's 29
33 St. Edward's 23
23 Hillyard 28
25 Hillyard 27 (OT)
26 SW Oklahoma 21
29 SW Oklahoma 27
17 SW Oklahoma 28
36 West Texas 41 (OT)
22 Baylor 16
24 TCU 28
33 Southwestern 27
28 Rice 19
31 Southwestern 14
35 Texas A&M 36
30 Rice 24
32 Arkansas 29
28 Arkansas 24
27 TCU 32 (OT)
23 SMU 25
41 St. Edward's 29
34 St. Edward's 20
25 SMU 23
39 Texas A&M 27

Texas won two and lost one in a series with Southwest Oklahoma. Brock, although rather weak defensively, led in scoring all three nights. Early in his sophomore season, he was being compared to the recently departed Sandy Esquivel. He might even fulfill Stewart's fond hopes of winning the 1927 Southwest Conference basketball championship.

In another "practice" game, so called because it was not against a conference team, the Horns lost to West Texas State, 41-36, in overtime. SWC play began on January 8 in Waco versus Ralph "Lone" Wolf's Baylor team. Billed as a clash between Brock and Keifer Strickland of the Bears, the game was won by UT, 22-16.

But the Horns suffered a four-point loss to TCU three days later as the all-around play of Rags Matthews, Frank Cantelmi and Clyde McDonnell kept the Frogs ahead most of the way. Olle, who played outstanding defense, fouled out late, and Stallter led Texas with 12 points. Cold permeated the old gym when Texas played Southwestern (followed by a game between Austin and Georgetown high schools), as fans' teeth chattered and the ball bounced off players' numb hands. UT trailed Kit Carson's Pirates at the half but came back to win, 33-27. Rice went down easily, and so did Southwestern again, leaving the Longhorns with a 6-7 record, 2-1 in all-important SWC games.

What happened on January 22 cast a pall over the 1927 season. The Baylor Bears were traveling to Austin when the team bus was struck by a train in Round Rock. Ten players died, and several other players, coaches and students were injured, causing the cancelation of BU's remaining games. Flags at the state capitol were set at half mast, 3,000 people gathered for a memorial service in Round Rock, and statements of condolence came from Stallter, Stewart, Bellmont and UT president Walter Splawn. (A survivor, John Kane, went on to become one of the most decorated American pilots in World War II.)

Because of that tragedy, UT's January 25 game with St. Edward's was postponed. The season continued as the Longhorns traveled to College Station to take on the Aggies. It had recently been announced that the 1927 UIL state tournament would be held there. Texas A&M's facility, everyone agreed, was large and comfortable for players and fans alike, while the Men's Gym in Austin was cold, with a bad floor and poor seating arrangements. The "temporary" wooden gym, then 11 years old and showing it, was simply inadequate to host the basketball tournament of the UIL, the largest organization of its kind in the nation. The Horns and Aggies engaged in a furious set-to, finally won by A&M, 36-35. The *Austin Statesman* called it "the most thrilling and exciting game played this season, before a rabid crowd that was fanatic in its enthusiasm." The leading scorers were Nation (13) and Brock (11) for UT and Stanley "Punk" Baker (12) and S.J. Clark (11) for the Ags. Proceeding to Houston, Texas beat Rice by six.

Then it was time for a visit from the fearsome Razorbacks, unbeaten and well on their way to another SWC title. Led by Tom Pickell, Glen Rose and Harold Steel and coached by Francis Schmidt, Arkansas was both big and fast. Even one UT victory seemed remote, but Stewart was not shy. "We'll give them both barrels," he told the *Daily Texan*. Using a quick, clever attack and a close man-to-man defense, the Steers scored a 32-29 victory that strained the vocal cords of 3,000 supporters. Stallter, Olle and subs like Looney and Patrick played well, but two late field goals by Brock made the difference. UT trod the heights of brilliance again the next night, winning by four. And again, it was Brock, that streak of human electricity, who vanquished the Hogs. Whitner Carry of the *Austin Statesman* wrote of "the drama, the frenzied excitement and the soul-stirring exhibition that took place within the walls of the old gym last night."

After twice pinning back the Razorbacks' ears and slowing but not stopping their triumphal march to the SWC throne, Stewart's team went on the road and lost close games to TCU and SMU. Texas led by one point with 10 seconds left when Frog forward Harry Taylor was fouled. He hit a free throw, sending it into overtime, where TCU outscored the Horns. Two days later in Dallas, SMU, with offensive stars Walter Allison and Alex Hooks, staved off a desperate UT rally to win, 25-23. Referee Ziggy Sears ruled that a long shot by Brock was released a split second after time elapsed; Stewart vigorously protested, but Sears was adamant.

Texas won two from St. Ed's and looked forward to the final games with SMU and Texas A&M, both at home. Rumor and speculation were rampant about Stewart, Bellmont and the UT athletic program. Stewart issued a statement that began, "Lest the uninformed give credence to rumors circulated by my adverse critics that I have unwarranted ambitions to wear the royal purple robes of the director of athletics..."

Still upset about Brock's disallowed game-tying shot a week earlier, the Horns were eager to beat SMU. So it was with a measure of glee that Texas took a stubbornly fought 25-23 win on February 19. Estes, the game's leading scorer, held Walter Allison to one field goal.

The team underwent a week of strenuous workouts before the season finale against Texas A&M. Whether he knew it or not, Doc Stewart was coaching his last game with the Longhorns, and he predicted a victory. But Dana X. Bible had his team keyed to a high pitch, too. "Chances are that the old gym will bulge to overflowing in its efforts to accommodate the crowd that will scramble for admission," said the *Austin Statesman*. The Longhorns jumped to a 14-point halftime lead and won, 39-27. S.J. Clark of A&M and Nation of Texas were the high scorers with 10 points each. In a few weeks, Clyde Littlefield was named as head UT football coach. Since he handled the track team as well, there was no consideration of Littlefield (former basketball star and coach of the frosh as late as 1927) taking on basketball duties. Stewart, who provided UT fans with many thrilling victories over the past four years, was gone. There was no hurry to find a replacement.

1928

Although he was not UT's first choice, Fred Walker agreed to coach the basketball team and assist with football and baseball for $4,000 a year. A graduate of the University of Chicago and an ex-major league baseball player, he had coached at eight different schools, most recently Loyola of New Orleans. Walker was a stern man, a disciplinarian who placed high demands on his athletes.

Aided by Marty Karow, another newcomer to Texas, he greeted 35 players at the Men's Gym in November 1927. They included captain John Estes, Joe King, Jake Looney, Ox Higgins, Steve Wray and the doughty Holly Brock. First-year men were W.H. "Sugar" Camp, Frank Cheatham, Alfred "Big Un" Rose and Nona Rees. Walker told them that he would emphasize speed and seldom use Doc Stewart's man-to-man defense. He reintroduced the dribble to Texas basketball, very good news indeed to Brock, Camp and Rees. Walker also began a curfew and closed the doors during practice to exclude overzealous followers and "coaches, sportswriters, managers, mascots and even the president of the University," according to the *Austin Statesman*.

Record: 14-5

33 St. Edward's 8
80 Academia Americana 10
37 Austin Athletic Club 20
45 San Antonio Elks 20
41 West Texas 33
23 SMU 39
26 Arkansas 42
29 Arkansas 59
71 St. Edward's 21
37 Rice 27
48 Southwestern 41
57 Baylor 36
36 Rice 34
51 Texas A&M 30
40 Baylor 25
25 SMU 44
39 TCU 32
25 TCU 29
30 Texas A&M 20

Walker's first team did not win the Southwest Conference, but it scored a lot of points. The Longhorns had broken 40 just twice in the previous five years; they did it eight times in 1928. The season began on a frigid night in the Men's Gym, as they outclassed St. Edward's, 33-8. Next was Academia Americana, a team from San Luis Potosi, Mexico, that had allegedly defeated several U.S. college teams. However, it was like some of the mismatches of 15 years earlier. When the smoke cleared, the Horns were ahead, 80-10, as Camp, Estes, Brock, Rose and King all scored in double figures.

Two more walkovers occurred in defeats of the Austin Athletic Club (composed largely of ex-UT players) and the San Antonio Elks. Despite the presence of big Adolph Dietzel, a future TCU star, the Elks had no chance and soon resorted to throwing up some outrageous long shots. Texas' first real competition came on January 3 in the form of West Texas, but Brock (18) and Camp (10) took care of the Buffaloes in a 41-33 victory. A 5-0 record and more than a two-to-one point ratio caused *Daily Texan* writers to ask if it might be a repeat of Stewart's great team of 1924.

They got their answer soon enough. SMU came to Austin and played a cool and deliberate game, winning by 16. Walter Allison scored 20 points for the Mustangs, who had an answer for everything Walker tried. UT's ill-arranged schedule followed with two games against the Razorbacks in Fayetteville. The fans went wild as the taller and superior Arkansans took the first one, 42-26, with Ralph Haizlip (16) and Tom Pickell (14) leading the way. Brock, Wray and Estes fouled out. It was even worse, 59-29, the next night, except that Wear Schoonover (14) joined in the Hogs' fun.

Having bitten the dust three straight times, the Horns arrived back in Austin undaunted. While it was of no immediate benefit to them, they got some good news. Thomas W. Gregory, who never completely stopped his campaign to erect a big new gym for the University, announced the beginning of the Union Project. It would combine the beneficence of alumni and the state legislature to build three much-needed facilities—a gym for men, a gym for women and a student union. This project had its roots in the 1924 campaign to build Memorial Stadium and was part of a far-reaching effort to create a greater University of Texas. An artist's rendering of the unnamed gymnasium-auditorium (bearing little resemblance to the final product) excited everyone's imagination, but no member of the 1928 Longhorns would ever play a game there. They had to make do with the Men's Gym, by then in a semi-delapidated condition. It seemed even more forlorn because adjacent Clark Field, the site of 30 years of UT sports history, was being razed as the basketball season went on. The *Austin Statesman*, noting that Texas A&M, SMU and Oklahoma had recently opened new field houses, made a couple of valid points: "No longer will other schools gather in the athletes merely because they have the facilities to accommodate them. [The gym] will have a basketball court that will enable all the students who have bought blanket taxes to gain admittance. At last, a person will be able to enjoy a basketball game in comfort."

Walker worked his players hard, hollering for "more fight and more fire and more punch." He had to be pleased with a 71-21 dismantling of St. Edward's. Brock (27) put on a fancy dribbling display that Stewart never would have permitted, while Rose scored 19 and Estes 13. It was the start of a seven-game winning streak. Rice, an SWC weakling in recent years, had an improved team with coach Pug Daugherty and players like Hank Grant and David Zuber, but the Owls lost to UT, 37-27. Because of final exams and an injury to Estes, the Longhorns barely beat Southwestern.

The 1928 team, which posted a 14-5 record, was led by captain John Estes (front row, center).

Razorbacks, in just their fifth year of intercollegiate basketball, had developed a monster program. From 1926 to 1929, they won 73 games and lost just six, three of them to Texas. The other teams in the conference were getting frustrated, and there was serious discussion about voting Arkansas out of the SWC, at least for basketball. Time, cost and bother of Texas schools traveling to the Ozarks were the reasons usually given, although these same factors affected the Razorbacks and made their accomplishment all the more impressive. But Francis Schmidt, the man most responsible for the Hogs' success, thought another, more cowardly, explanation might be involved. In agreement was Duby DuBose, *Austin Statesman* sports editor, who said that they were to Southwest Conference basketball what the New York Yankees were to baseball. In the end, of course, nothing happened except that Arkansas continued to win.

One year after the horrific accident that decimated its team, Baylor was back. Ralph Wolf was still coaching, and it so happened that his two best players, Keifer Strickland and Louis Slade, had survived. The Bears, who had the sympathy of opposing fans and players, won two SWC games and had a 7-2 overall record when they met Texas. But they lost by 21 at the Men's Gym. There was never a doubt, as Brock and Rose outscored Baylor by themselves and Walker experimented with different combinations. Sophs Cheatham and Rees showed promise for later in the season and for 1929 and 1930.

A big crowd in Houston turned out to see Rice and Texas. The Owls took an early lead, but UT came back and won, 36-34. Brock and Hank Grant of Rice both scored 15 points. Back in Austin, the Longhorns gave Texas A&M a lesson in basketball, ripping the Aggies, 51-30. It would have been worse, but Walker substituted liberally. Brock and Wray (despite an injured foot) were the headliners.

Baylor had held Arkansas to a low score and entertained hopes of beating UT at the Bears' Chapel Court. Big Un Rose of Texas played big, scoring 19 and grabbing most of the rebounds on the way to a 40-25 win. While Walker claimed that his team had played poorly and was dead on its feet, those comments may have been intended for readers of the Dallas newspapers, since the SMU game was next. Most observers thought the Longhorns looked excellent, with speed to burn.

Quite a few UT students traveled to Dallas to see the Horns and Mustangs. Their team got crushed, 44-25, as Walter Allison and Edwin Lindsey led the way. SMU was clearly the second-best team in the SWC in 1928. The best, needless to say, was Arkansas. The

Texas, not quite an also-ran, beat TCU in Fort Worth, 39-32. The result was uncertain until the final minutes, but Brock (15) played one of his greatest games, "the likes of which was never before seen in Fort Worth," said the *Daily Texan*. But the Horned Frogs turned the tables a week later in Austin, winning, 29-25. Center LeRoy "Slim" Eury and Rags Matthews scored from every angle and managed to shut Brock down. No one knew it at the time, but that was the last UT game ever played in the Men's Gym.

Finis was written on the 1928 season when the Steers beat Texas A&M, 30-20, in College Station before 3,000 agonized Cadets. Brock, Rose and Rees all played well and ensured the Aggies' ninth straight defeat. A 7-5 SWC record, 14-5 overall, was not bad for a team adapting to a new coach and a new system of play. Walker and his wife hosted the team dinner a week later, at which time the redoubtable Brock was chosen captain for 1929. They all got a shock in the early morning hours of March 25 when the flimsy, pinewood Men's Gym caught fire and burned to the ground. Early in the blaze, three-year letterman Joe King tried to go in and shoot one last basket, but he was forced out by the heat and flames. As a result of the fire, the Longhorn basketball team would be without a home for the next two years, and plans to build a new gym were thrown into fast-forward.

The *Alcalde* was somewhat wistful in recalling the Men's Gym: "The barren half acre of ashes left from the fire was a monument to a romantic Texas institution, for the gym, with all its total lack of beauty and its lack of accord with any conceivable architectural scheme for the campus, had held stirring events—rallies before the big football games, the college night ceremonies where freshmen were introduced to University group life in a most inadequate fashion, basketball games deciding championships and cultural performances where spectators sat on bleachers and collapsible chairs and heard the greatest artists of the world. The old shack had been condemned by state and city fire marshals.... University officials plead that the stark monstrosity was the only meeting place available, and fire marshals were benevolent in not enforcing the condemnation."

1929

Everyone was happy. Clyde Littlefield's Longhorn football team, which won the SWC crown, was being feted right and left. And the basketball players, many of whom played football, showed enough promise to rate as preseason cofavorites with Arkansas. It was a veteran squad with just two sophomores, Earl Taylor and Jim Fomby. Returnees included Big Un Rose, Nona Rees, Jake Looney, Steve Wray, Sugar Camp, Frank Cheatham and captain Holly Brock. The secret to Brock's success—apart from innate ability—was practice. He did not play football, baseball or run track, but he practiced and played basketball almost constantly, something rare in that era. Brock was a gym rat.

Record: 18-2

50 St. Mary's 30
45 SW Texas 16
27 SW Texas 18
73 San Antonio Elks 36
60 Daniel Baker 28
39 Daniel Baker 35
42 SW Oklahoma 28
22 Baylor 19
41 St. Edward's 27
29 SMU 19
56 Rice 25
33 TCU 27
32 SMU 33 (OT)
32 Arkansas 48
36 Arkansas 25
32 Texas A&M 29
57 Baylor 23
42 TCU 28
33 Rice 32
42 Texas A&M 31

Unfortunately, UT no longer had a gym. Memories of the much-lamented Men's Gym would grow fonder over the next two years as the team had to leave campus and play "home" games in very small facilities. The State School for the Deaf (insisting that it no longer be called the "Deaf and Dumb Institute") had recently erected a nice little field house on its south Austin campus. A basketball opponent for Texas two decades earlier, the school agreed to make the Silents' Gym available. Of the 20 games on the Longhorns' 1929 schedule, 15 were played there. With one-sixth the seating capacity of the Men's Gym, it precluded many people from seeing one of the best teams in school history. No tickets were sold to the general public, and blanket-tax and season-ticket holders were chosen by lottery.

The curtains went up on December 14 with a 50-30 thumping of the St. Mary's Rattlers. Brock's running mate, Camp, was the star in a 45-16 defeat of Southwest Texas. UT's passing and fast break were too much for the Bobcats, but a rematch the following night was considerably closer, a nine-point victory.

While Fred Walker attended a coaching convention in New Orleans over the holidays, Brock ran the team's practices and did it well. Somewhat aloof from his teammates in previous years, he had matured and was intent on making the 1929 season a good one. Walker was back in Austin for UT's 73-36 win over the San Antonio Elks. More resistance was expected from the Daniel Baker Hillbillies and their high-scoring star, Mac Miller. Texas won easily, and although Miller (18) was good, Brock (31) was great, "looking like a million bucks," said the *Austin Statesman.*

Walker believed that another romp over the Hillbillies was certain, so he started and played his subs most of the next night. It almost backfired as Daniel Baker led until the final two minutes, when Brock and Wray pulled out a four-point win. Another potential upset occurred at the Silents' Gym on January 9. Southwest Oklahoma, which had beaten the socks off several teams from Texas, led by four at the half. But Brock (17) and Camp (14) led a late rally to win. Holt had 16 for the Teachers.

As SWC play began, Walker went to Fort Worth to observe the Arkansas-TCU game. He got an eyeful. Since three-time all-conference forward Glen Rose was

Holly Brock was UT's most prolific scorer for three straight seasons.

gone, there was no way, it was thought, that the Razorbacks could be as good as the previous year. But they looked even better, defeating the Frogs with ease. In Waco, 1,200 people packed Baylor's gym and kept up a constant roar as the UT offense sputtered and the Bears hung in. Brock, Rees and Camp played a steady game, though, enabling the Horns to win, 22-19. After a rough and ragged victory over St. Edward's, Texas faced SMU in Austin. Although they had already lost two SWC games, the cocky Ponies, led by scoring aces Albert Brown and Elmo Johnson, expected to win. But Walker's team was ready to take them down a notch, and that is what happened, 29-19.

On the same night, Arkansas set a conference record by scoring 71 points against Baylor. Was Texas content to be runner-up in 1929? No other team was thought to have any chance of stopping the point-a-minute Hog juggernaut, and the series, on February 8 and 9, was widely anticipated. In the meantime, however, the Steers showed some offensive muscle in beating Rice, 56-25. Brock scored 17, and Looney, replacing the fouled-out Rees, had nine. Fans grumbled that referees Ziggy Sears and Dusty Boggess allowed too much roughness, accusing them of being asleep or perhaps stone dead.

The unbeaten Horns roared into Fort Worth and got more than they bargained for, edging TCU by six points. Brock scored 17 and the Frogs' Clyde McDonnell had 14 in a hot game from start to finish. In the stands that night were SMU coach Jim St. Clair and his team, who would make a desperate bid to beat Texas. Hostilities commenced in Dallas with an 8:15 p.m. tipoff. The lead seesawed back and forth, the game went into overtime and was finally won on a free throw by SMU center Al Brooks with 15 seconds left. "The day of miracles has not passed," the *Daily Texan* stated regrettably.

The Longhorns returned home disappointed, offering no excuses but swearing to wreak ruin and disaster on the Razorbacks. More than 1,000 students braved a snowstorm in Fayetteville to give Francis Schmidt and his team a rousing sendoff to Austin. Several out-of-town sportswriters would cover the series, and most of them anticipated a double defeat for the Longhorns. But UT fans recalled 1927, when Brock paced the team to two upsets over the red and white. There was quite a buildup for a series witnessed by no more than 600 fans in each game. Arkansas won the first game convincingly, 48-32. The Ozark twins, Wear Schoonover (18) and Tom Pickell (10) were most responsible for the Hogs' 31st straight win, while Rose led UT with 12. Don Legg of the *Austin Statesman* wrote: "One thing that impressed us was the speed of the Porkers when they broke for the Texas basket. Three of the young giants would come tearing down the floor with uncanny speed, and then the scorer would have to mark up two points for them.... This Schoonover is the best basketball player that we have ever seen."

The next night, Walker started Fomby and Cheatham, and they put the brakes on Schoonover and Pickell. Rose scored 14 as Texas took a big lead at the half and stalled much of the rest of the game. Brock, with nine points and skillful ballhandling, did his part, too. The Longhorns threw a bombshell into SWC camps with their 36-25 victory, ending the Arkansas win streak.

A fast finish was needed a few days later to beat Texas A&M before 3,000 leather-lunged Aggie fans. Brock scored half of UT's 32 points, while H.H. "Buster" Keeton had 10 for the home team. The Baylor Bears came to Austin for a midweek game, intent on proving that they could play with UT, and they did—for the first half. The Longhorns led, 24-17, at the break, but dominated the rest of the way and won by 34 points. Brock was a whirling dervish, scoring 24 and putting on a nice show of dribbling and passing.

Walker reminded his players of the near-loss to TCU earlier in the season, but the Horns had no trouble with Matty Bell's team, winning, 42-28. Brock had 17 points in that game and another 17 in a defeat of Rice in Houston. A big and enthusiastic crowd saw the Owls ahead by one with just a few seconds remaining. Brock dribbled, looked for the basket and passed the ball through a maze of arms to Looney, who hit a difficult shot to win it.

The SWC crown again belonged to Arkansas when the Aggies and Horns met in Austin for the season finale on Texas Independence Day. Brock, who was chasing Tom Pickell for league scoring honors, had shown his greatness again and again. But the setting left much to be desired. "Captain Holly Brock, for three years one of the best forwards to honor the school's court," said the *Austin Statesman*, "will see his last game with the Aggies and will be compelled to play before a small audience. What a difference from the grid game, in which 40,000 people gazed on a great Texas team.... Now the Texas cager, equally as great as Texas' pigskin artists, must finish a brilliant career before a crowd of 600 people."

UT got its 18th victory, 42-31. Brock, double-teamed the entire game, had 16 to win the SWC scoring title. When it was over, Sam Hart of the Athletic Council presented him with a gold watch as a token of his fine play over the past three years. The small crowd gave Brock a long and warm ovation.

1930

Record: 12-8

34 SW Texas 22
24 SW Texas 27
36 Daniel Baker 18
42 Daniel Baker 35
28 Oklahoma 46
30 Oklahoma 33
29 SW Oklahoma 36
49 San Antonio Elks 26
39 Rice 24
35 Baylor 32 (2 OT's)
19 Arkansas 22
29 Arkansas 27
42 Baylor 25
22 SMU 25
35 TCU 21
33 Texas A&M 25
31 Rice 23
21 TCU 26
50 SMU 14
20 Texas A&M 42

UT's long-awaited $500,000 auditorium-gymnasium was to be located on Jordan Field, northeast of the intersection of Speedway and 21st Street. Groundbreaking ceremonies were held on May 10, 1929. About 200 people (including UT President Harry Benedict, John McCurdy of the Ex-Students' Association and Governor Dan Moody) watched as Thomas W. Gregory turned the first spade of dirt. Designed by Greene, LaRoche and Dahl, the building would be erected by the Morgan Construction Company. Everyone thought, or at least hoped, that it would be ready for the last games of the 1930 Longhorn basketball season, but bad weather slowed the gym's progress.

Tow-headed Nona Rees, quarterback of the Texas football team, served as captain. Sugar Camp, Big Un Rose, Frank Cheatham and Jim Fomby were back, augmented by Wilson "Bull" Elkins. Although they would not be a strong offensive team, the Horns were a slight favorite to win the Southwest Conference. Coach Fred Walker, determined to end the four-year reign of Arkansas, knew that Francis Schmidt (the "miracle man" who led the Hogs to national prominence) had moved to TCU, and when they lost five early-season games, the Longhorns, Mustangs, Aggies, Bears, Owls and Horned Frogs had reason to hope. But new coach Chuck Bassett got Arkansas back on track for a fifth straight title. The SWC would never again see such a stretch of dominance.

The season began with a 34-22 defeat of Southwest Texas at the Silents' Gym. But the Bobcats returned the favor four days later on a slick court in San Marcos. Many of their long shots went in, and UT's comeback was not enough. Earl Taylor and Rose were the stars in two wins over Daniel Baker, but the team looked uninspired.

Walker knew he would need something better on a three-game road trip across the Red River. Big 6 champion Oklahoma had won 31 straight games, and the Sooners were eager to avenge a football defeat in Dallas the previous October. Hugh McDermott's team whipped Texas, 46-28, in the first game. Tom Churchill scored 16 and Gordan Graalman 13, while Rose (12) did most of the damage for the Horns. They made the Sooners sweat the next night, erasing most of a 10-point lead but still falling short. Over in Weatherford, Southwest Oklahoma was tough, too, beating Texas by seven points.

A 49-26 defeat of the San Antonio Elks in Austin concluded UT's nonconference schedule, leaving a 4-4 record. It was time to get serious, but with only Rose scoring, the Steers had an anemic offense. Fans yearned to see Holly Brock whiz downcourt and score baskets. Walker, irritated with press criticism of his team, felt vindicated by a 39-24 defeat of Rice in Houston. With a fast-break offense and stubborn defense, Rose led the way. Ray Hart had nine points for the Owls. A most interesting game took place on January 10 in Waco. Baylor had a small but athletic team with players like Raymond Strickland, Jake Wilson and Raymond "Mighty" Alford. The Bruins led at halftime, but Walker's tongue-lashing was effective, and UT tied it at 24 in the final seconds, sending the game into overtime. Baylor appeared to have it won when Taylor slipped through the defense and connected on a short shot. In the second OT, Rose scored the decisive hoop with 40 seconds left to win, 35-32.

Early in the season, the SWC standings had a familiar look with Arkansas and Texas on top. After a train ride from Austin to Muskogee, Oklahoma, and a bus ride to Fayetteville, the determined band of Longhorn cagers found themselves in the frigid wilds of the Ozarks. Some 2,000 fans braved subzero temperatures and a snowstorm to see the ballyhooed series. Arkansas had five key players (Wear Schoonover, Jim Pickren, Ken Holt, Roy Prewitt and Milan Creighton) but almost no reserve strength. As Walker's team invaded the Razorbacks' lair, they believed they might win one of two games. If so, it would be the first time in four years Arkansas had lost at home. The Hogs won, 22-19, as Schoonover had nine points. Taylor, better known for tennis than basketball, led UT with six. Camp was the star the next night, coming off the bench in a tight game and scoring 10 points to pace a 29-27 Longhorn victory.

With great pleasure, students observed construction of the big new gymnasium topped by skylights. But they soon realized it would not be ready in time for the SWC home opener against Baylor on January 25. The steel frame, roof and walls were up, and the Athletic Council considered holding games with the building in such a half-finished condition, but what an inauspicious debut that would have been for the finest gym in the entire Southwest. The council members wisely chose to get the building done and then open the 1931 season there. "Saturday's occasion [Texas versus Baylor] was supposed to be one of ceremony and pomp for the Steers," said the *Austin Statesman*. "Austin was supposed to witness the grand opening of the new gym. Old Man Weather smiled a wee bit and played a joke on the planners." The *Daily Texan* asked, in exasperation, "When, oh when, will our new gymnasium be finished and ready for basketball games?"

The Longhorns had a new home away from home. Austin High School's recently completed gym, costing $70,000 and with 1,500 seats, would be the site of UT's five remaining home games in 1930. So the Horns and Bears met there. Baylor's self-styled heroes, Raymond Alford and Raymond Strickland, planned to even matters, but Texas took a 42-25 win with Fomby scoring 14 and Rose nine. Although BU coach Ralph Wolf rode the referees, it did little good.

UT was confident of winning both games in the annual north Texas trip, but SMU pulled a shocker and won, 25-22. During that contest, Frank Cheatham and the Ponies' Bruce Kattman jawed and exchanged pleasantries throughout. The hot-headed Cheatham was not cooled down by a postgame shower because he went looking for Kattman, found him, and the two engaged in a fistfight. The incident made its way into the Dallas and Austin newspapers, and Walker belatedly kicked Cheatham off the team but not before a near-rebellion by the other players.

Seeking recompense for their loss to SMU, the Longhorns went to Fort Worth and beat the Frogs by 14. Roy Eury had 13 for TCU, while the fast-improving Fomby scored 12 for Texas. Francis Schmidt, whose TCU football team had won the SWC title, was getting a taste of losing in basketball. After a 33-25 defeat of Texas A&M at the AHS Gym, Walker crowed, "We're not out of it by any means."

And things looked even brighter with another home victory over Rice. The referees had their hands full with a crowd that booed often, once incurring a penalty shot. No fewer than four double fouls were called, Harry Norman of Rice and Rose had a fight, and the Owls' George McCarble challenged some fans to put up or shut up.

The Longhorns saw their title hopes go a-glimmering when TCU took a 26-21 victory in Austin. It was a miserable performance ("a tragic affair," according to the *Austin Statesman*), but they came back two days later and ripped SMU, 50-14. Rose scored 22, and Fomby had 14 in UT's biggest offensive display of the year. Rees' playmaking was superb. As well as the Steers did against the Mustangs, they were awful against Texas A&M in a bruising 42-20 loss. Ag center Shiro Hoke scored 16 in a game that delighted the fans in College Station.

While the season was over, Texas basketball remained in the news for several weeks. Fierce crosscurrents swept the athletic department as football and track coach Clyde Littlefield, baseball coach Billy Disch and acting athletic director H.T. Ettlinger sought to boot Walker. Some of his players felt the same way. Walker surely did not have a warm and lovable personality, but he could coach basketball. Furthermore, he had borne playing the last two seasons in the gyms at the State School for the Deaf and Austin High School and deserved to open the new UT facility in 1931. Don Legg of the *Austin Statesman*, Lloyd Gregory of the *Houston Post-Dispatch*, Jinx Tucker of the *Waco Tribune*, W.R. Beaumier of the *San Antonio Express* and other sportswriters weighed in on the subject. But Walker kept his job mainly because William Miller, editor in chief of the *Daily Texan*, disclosed the ouster plan and waged a vigorous editorial campaign against it. The skies cleared in late March when Walker was retained with a slight salary increase.

1931

"The massive structure of steel and bricks, padded with wood, rears its majestic head high into the heavens," wrote Don Legg of the *Austin Statesman*. "It stands as a silent tribute to the minds of dreamers who have fostered the idea for years and years, having their dream belittled and finally seeing it come to life. This new auditorium-gymnasium is a monument to Texas athletics and the high plane on which they stand."

Record: 9-15

69 San Antonio Triangles 47
25 St. Edward's 13
34 North Texas 33
26 North Texas 29
29 Centenary 31
22 Centenary 54
27 Oklahoma 28
33 Oklahoma 34
56 San Antonio Triangles 35
43 SW Oklahoma 32
50 Houston Triangles 38
75 Galveston All-Stars 29
21 Arkansas 29
27 Arkansas 25
19 TCU 40
32 SMU 51
43 Baylor 45
10 Texas A&M 34
41 SMU 33 (OT)
42 Rice 50
36 TCU 41
21 Baylor 34
16 Rice 23
29 Texas A&M 28

Named Gregory Gymnasium in honor of the man who carried its banner for 23 years, the building was opened in April 1930 for Round-Up, a gathering of students and alumni. With a Spanish renaissance exterior that reminded some people of a church, Gregory Gym would be much more than a place to hold basketball games. It had a tile pool (swimming became a varsity sport in 1931) and was the bustling hub of intramurals and physical education for UT's male students. A multipurpose facility from the start, it was the scene of commencements, cultural performances, inaugural balls, course registration and a bewildering array of other events. Well-designed, well-built and well-used, Gregory Gym would have a profound influence on student culture at the University of Texas over the next several decades.

And as a basketball arena, it was state-of-the-art for the 1930s, a palace that made other Southwest Conference facilities look like crackerboxes. The maplewood floor, built by meticulous Depression-era artisans, was ideal for the starting, stopping and jumping of athletes. The orange-and-white scoreboard at the gym's west end, operated by the University Co-Op, had an analog clock that wound backward. Gregory Gym's seating capacity, 7,500 with bleachers on the floor, would be exceeded many times in the 47 years it served as the home of UT basketball. The gym was often a crush of humanity during the UIL tournament, as well.

Jim Fomby captained the Horns in what turned out to be a doleful season, the last under Fred Walker's tutelage. Informal scrimmaging began in early October, and 500 people watched a practice game between Texas (starting with Wyatt Taylor and Ed Price in the backcourt, Fomby at center and Earl Taylor and Bull Elkins at forward) and Laurel Heights of San Antonio on November 22. The San Antonio YMCA Triangles lost, 69-47, as did St. Edward's, 25-13. The competition would get tougher very soon. Fomby scored 20 points in a close win over North Texas, but the Eagles won the rematch, 29-26. While there was a long way to go, it was soon apparent that the 1931 Steers were slow, poor shooters and ballhandlers and weak defensively.

Centenary came to Austin in mid-December and won two games. The first required a flurry of Gent baskets at the end, but the second was a 54-22 blowout that had some people consigning Texas' season to the junkheap even before SWC play began. "The

Gregory Gymnasium (below), home of Texas Longhorn basketball for 47 years. Thomas W. Gregory (right), the gym's namesake and the man most responsible for its construction.

team looked ill against North Texas and bedridden against Centenary," opined the *Daily Texan*. "The less said about it, the better."

Walker reconfigured his lineup and got much better results in two games with Oklahoma at Gregory Gym. Both were one-point losses. After that surprisingly strong showing against the Sooners, the picture brightened with four victories over the holidays. Elkins scored 18 in a 56-35 defeat of the San Antonio YMCA Triangles, and Earl Taylor had 11 as UT beat Southwest Oklahoma in Austin. In a foray to the coast, Texas defeated the Houston YMCA Triangles (with ex-Longhorns Holly Brock and Jake Looney), 50-38. Elkins (19) and Fomby (18) were the high-point men. The Galveston All-Stars went down easily, and the Steers felt almost bouyant as SWC competition began.

Gregory Gym had been in use for eight months before its formal dedication on Thursday, January 8, 1931 against five-time champion Arkansas. Wear Schoonover was gone, but the Hogs' reputation still gave everyone the knee shakes. What better way to inaugurate the building than with a victory over the champs? During pregame ceremonies, a high-minded, if somewhat naive 10-point code of conduct was announced by student leaders: (1) Treat opponents as guests; (2) never hiss or boo; (3) cheer to the end, whatever the odds; (4) accept decisions without protest; (5) do not abuse or make irritating remarks; (6) do not cheer when opponents are penalized; (7) applaud opponents' good plays; (8) never attempt to confuse opponents; (9) play fairly within the rules, for sport's sake rather than victory; and (10) win without boasting and lose without excuse. The sportsmanship code, which would have made basketball games at Gregory Gym exceedingly genteel, was impossible to enforce and would be widely disregarded in years to come.

Several former Texas players from the Clark Field and Men's Gym eras were in attendance that night, and they saw the team lose to the towering Razorbacks, 29-21, as Kenny Holt and J.R. Jelks led the way. Unlike in previous years, they used a slow and methodical attack to win. It was an uphill battle in the second game, but a sterling defense and Elkins' 11 points enabled the Horns to win by two. The *Alcalde* attributed UT's victory to "fighting spirit" rather than to basketball ability. "Retribution was dealt the Arkansas Porkers," said the *Austin Statesman*. "This victory took away part of the sting of Thursday night's defeat at the dedication ceremonies of Gregory Gym."

The Longhorns would find out if they were contenders or pretenders in a trip to Fort Worth and Dallas. TCU (with Adolph "Too Tall" Dietzel, Doc Sumner and Byron "Buster" Brannon) and SMU (with its equally impressive trio of Rhea Williams, Ray Johnson and Jake Reynolds) were not taking Texas lightly. It was the biggest crowd yet for a Frog basketball game, and the bad news came over the telegraph wires—TCU 40, Texas 19, a terrific blow to the team's SWC title hopes. Although he was occasionally triple-teamed, the lanky Dietzel scored 18 as the Frogs were never threatened.

The orange-clad warriors lost again the next night, 51-32, to SMU's fast-breaking team. They returned to Austin amid persistent rumors of Walker's firing. The coach, claiming to know nothing about it, worked furiously to get a winning lineup in time to meet the improving Baylor Bears. Earl Taylor scored 14, Elkins 12 and Fomby 11, but it was not enough as the Horns lost a heartbreaker to the Baptists, 45-43. Elkins put UT ahead with 20 seconds to go, but Raymond Strickland (23) hit a shot just before the gun sounded, plus a free throw, to win. The team was subdued but not disheartened because Fomby, whom Walker called "the greatest captain I've ever seen," sought to keep their spirits up by talking about winning the final seven games.

They went to College Station as underdogs for the first time in eight years. Texas A&M coach John Reid was confident, and Walker, for once, was not. In contrast to his predecessor, Doc Stewart, Walker usually had sunny things to say about his team's chances. Perhaps he foresaw his firing at season's end because Walker's attitude had grown bleak. A vocal crowd witnessed the Aggies' 34-10 victory, led by Shiro Hoke and J.C. Moody.

SMU brought its formidable hardcourt talent to Austin on February 10, but the Longhorns were out to repay evil for evil and upset the prancing Ponies. "Gregory Gym probably never again will be the scene of such a battle," the *Austin Statesman* dubiously predicted. Texas came from behind twice to tie the game and send it into overtime. Rhea Williams used his one-handed shot to score six points in the extra period, giving SMU a 41-33 win. Fomby scored 11, and Milton "Pap" Perkins rebounded in fine style for the luckless Horns.

Rice, which had not defeated UT since 1926, did it in Houston by rallying in the final 10 minutes. Blake Sellers scored 19 for the Owls and Virgil Dixon had 15, as did Taylor for the Steers. A woeful defense and no points from Fomby killed their chances to win. If that were not enough, TCU came to Austin and sent the Horns even further down a dismal road. Dietzel scored an SWC-record 26 points while his teammates mostly stood and watched. Sub forward Bill Kubricht scored five late points and nearly pulled out a victory for Texas, but the Frogs won, 41-36.

The oft-beaten Longhorns went to Waco and lost to Baylor, 34-21, as Raymond Alford, in perfect trim, scored 21. The Rice Owls got their first look at Gregory Gym in a 23-16 victory. "As a basketball contest, it was the poorest exhibition seen here this season, possibly in years," said the *Austin Statesman*. "...The game was an exceedingly dull affair, and a small-sized crowd was on hand to witness it."

With a 1-10 conference record, UT welcomed Texas A&M to Austin. The largest crowd of the season gathered, although no estimate was recorded. Due partly to the Depression and to having a poor team, attendance in Gregory Gym's first year was not at all good. Indeed, many people—not foreseeing the growth of the University and better times ahead—asked why such a large facility had been erected. More than one person was heard to say, "They'll never fill it up." Texas trailed the Farmers by one point in the final minute when Earl Taylor rebounded Elkins' missed shot and put it back in for a much-needed, much-desired 29-28 victory. The season was over, as was the losing streak. TCU won the Southwest Conference for the first time, and the Longhorns had the cellar to themselves.

1932

Fred Walker was out. The trouble pot had brewed for 18 months as a personality conflict with other Texas coaches, Walker's domineering tactics and the players' discovery that he regularly took and sold their complimentary game tickets brought things to a climax. The team signed a petition urging his dismissal, and captain Bull Elkins refused to play if Walker was retained.

The Athletic Council did not travel far to find a replacement. Ed Olle won six letters (two apiece in football, basketball and baseball) from 1925 to 1927, graduated and later earned a master's degree in business. He played semipro baseball and coached at El Paso High School before returning as business manager of the Longhorn athletic department. It was an important post since the department was in disarray and losing money hand over fist. In those economically tough times, attendance and revenue were down in football (the big daddy of college sports) and basketball. Before the 1932 season, Olle cut the price of tickets to games at Gregory Gym from $1 for adults and 50 cents for children to 50 cents and 25 cents. Less than 30 years old, he was on trial as the Longhorn hoop coach. But after the losing and dissension-torn season just past, great things were not expected. The Athletic Council was thankful Olle agreed to coach along with his duties in the business office. The Ex-Students' Association was happy to have another alumnus coaching an orange-and-white team. "It is a trend toward amateurism when the University is ready to depend upon its own," said the *Alcalde*. And most of all, the players were relieved to have Olle as their new coach. Possessed of a placid and likable manner, in stark contrast to Walker, he knew the players and they knew him. He realized the 1931 team, although not overly talented, had lacked spirit and cooperation. There was guarded optimism on the Forty Acres that the Longhorns would rise from the SWC cellar in 1932.

A dozen men who had been busy (in a losing effort) at Kyle Field on Thanksgiving day trotted onto the hardwoods of Gregory Gym a week later, joining those who just played basketball. Three footballers, Elkins, Ed Price and sophomore guard Bennie Rundell, were in the starting lineup most of the season. Bill Kubricht and John Tullis were the others. While the varsity practiced on the main court, the Yearlings, coached by Marty Karow, toiled on the small court erected on the gym's stage. It was hard for Olle not to notice the 1932 frosh, led by forward Jack Gray, who assembled a 12-1 record and provided his upperclassmen with some strong competition.

Olle took 25 players to San Marcos for the first game of the season. Southwest Texas, with its own new gym, opened with a 24-23 victory made possible by several UT blunders. In two home wins over Daniel Baker, lightfooted sophomore Glenn Thompson (12) and Kubricht (10) were the top scorers.

Texas' erstwhile conquerors, the SWT Bobcats, lost in Austin by a score of 25-13. The Steers then went to San Antonio and met Texas Chiropractic College, champion of the Texas Amateur Athletic Federation. The Hawks put up a fight, losing by six points. Elkins (16) and Tullis (10) led UT in scoring. Two city league teams, Nu-Icy and Dr Pepper, provided little competition at the Speedway basketball emporium.

Olle knew that was no way to get ready for fast-approaching Southwest Conference play. Texas split a pair of close games with Southwest Oklahoma and beat the 23rd Infantry, 41-16. The 18th SWC basketball campaign began in Fayetteville on January 8. The players were not expecting a bed of roses from the Hogs and their high-scoring captain, Ray "Hoot" Gibson. The Longhorns were up by a point with five minutes left, but UA center James "Doc" Sexton's free throws won it, 24-21. The next night, however, Texas overcame an eight-point deficit to grab an exciting 27-25 victory. Kubricht had 11 points and Price eight in a game that made the long trip back to Austin much more pleasant.

While Olle did not have any firsthand information, he was wary of SMU. But the visiting Ponies had lost some key personnel from their 1931 runner-up team and were destined to finish at the bottom of the conference in 1932. Displaying a strong defense and scoring regularly, the Steers beat SMU, 35-29, with 15 points from Kubricht and 11 from Tullis. Olle's scrapping and hustling team stalled in the final minutes to preserve the lead as 4,000 fans looked on.

Texas had served notice that it was no longer the SWC doormat. Olle worked wonders and produced a much-improved team, using a slow, deliberate attack unlike the fast break employed with former stars like Holly Brock, Big Un Rose and Sugar Camp. TCU, coming off a 25-point destruction of Rice, had more of the same planned for UT. "It is unlikely that the Longhorns will get anything but a banging at Gregory Gym Wednesday when they engage Francis Schmidt's Christians," said the *Austin Statesman.* They got banged, all right, 52-22, as the Frogs displayed an unbeatable brand of basketball. Adolph Dietzel, Buster Brannon and Doc Sumner were all in double figures, while Kubricht had eight for Texas.

In Houston, Rice got off to a big lead, but the Horns came back to tie it. Elkins, Tullis and Kubricht, the big guns of the UT offense, were strangely silent as Jake Hess led the Owls to a 25-22 victory. Olle was determined that the rematch with the Terrible Toads would be closer, but a packed field house in Fort Worth saw another easy TCU win. Adolph Dietzel (18) outscored the Longhorns by himself. The most encouraging thing for Texas was Rundell's defensive work on Doc Sumner.

Elkins was the star in Dallas, scoring 13 and hustling the whole game in a 29-17 lacing of SMU. Rhea Williams had 10 for the Mustangs. Texas A&M, languishing at the bottom of the SWC standings, had a natural yen for victory, and the Longhorns wanted to prevent that. There were plenty of fireworks at Gregory Gym on February 13 as Texas beat the Aggies by a point. The Horns led by nine at the half, but field goals began to fall fast and thick for A&M. After Charley Beard put the Ags ahead in the final minute, Price, with an assist from Rundell, used a nice two-handed set shot to win the game before 3,500 fans.

Record: 14-10

23 SW Texas 24
31 Daniel Baker 17
31 Daniel Baker 19
25 SW Texas 13
37 Texas Chiropractic 31
47 Nu-Icy 19
51 Dr Pepper 14
31 SW Oklahoma 29
24 SW Oklahoma 27
41 23rd Infantry 16
21 Arkansas 24
27 Arkansas 25
35 SMU 29
22 TCU 52
22 Rice 25
14 TCU 36
29 SMU 17
32 Texas A&M 31
28 Centenary 24
31 Centenary 32 (OT)
28 Baylor 35
26 Rice 19
30 Baylor 35
9 Texas A&M 14

Olle declined an offer to fly the team to Shreveport for a series with Centenary, so they rode the train. Thompson and Rundell rescued a game that was nearly lost because Olle chose to start his second-stringers. And the Longhorns did lose the second game to the Gentlemen, a 32-31 overtime affair.

Baylor and TCU were tied for the SWC lead when the Horns and Bears met in Waco. Texas had won 20 of the last 25 games against BU but not that night. In a hard-fought melee, with the lead going back and forth, Raymond Alford's 16 points enabled the Bruins to win, 35-28. As he did for much of the season, Olle went with his starting five (Kubricht, Price, Rundell, Elkins and Tullis) most of the way against Rice in Austin. Owl forward Jake Hess played well, but UT never trailed in what the *Daily Texan* called "a slow and laborious game."

The final home game of the season, against Baylor, was called "Ed Olle Night" in appreciation for what he had done. Taking a squad of fair ability in the wake of a bad season and building a strong foundation, Olle had the Longhorns at the .500 mark in SWC play, far better than early predictions. Player morale was high, and attendance had improved, albeit with reduced ticket prices. Be that as it may, Baylor was in the hunt for its first conference crown. Raymond Alford and Frank James had 10 points each in a 35-30 victory over UT. A nine-minute scoreless streak ended the Steers' upset hopes.

The season closed with what the *Cactus* called "a weird defensive battle," won by Texas A&M. Stalling, good defense and poor shooting by both teams led to a 14-9 Aggie victory in College Station. Texas finished the year with a 5-7 SWC record, 14-10 overall. It was hard to begrudge Baylor's championship. Five years after the Bear squad was decimated in a bus-train accident, the green and gold had slowly worked its way from the bottom to the middle to the top of the SWC. If the Gregory Gym sportsmanship code meant anything, UT fans did not mind seeing the conference pennant flying in Waco.

1933

As the Longhorns began preparations for 1933, their main loss was Bull Elkins, soon to be a Rhodes Scholar and eventually the president of two major universities. Coach Ed Olle predicted his team would pick up the loose crumbs of the Southwest Conference race, but captain Ed Price was a bit bolder: "We're going to surprise some of you crystal-gazers this year."

There was a sense of renewed vigor for Texas basketball due to the surprise showing of 1932, the return of good although not great players like Price, Bill Kubricht, Bennie Rundell and Glenn Thompson and the debut of sophomores Jack Gray and Jean Francis. Starters almost from the first scrimmage, Gray and Francis strengthened the team, but how would they respond to the varsity spotlight, not to mention the rawboned vets of Arkansas, TCU and other SWC teams? It had been nine years since UT won the league title, and no one—not even the lionhearted Price—claimed that it would happen in 1933. The Longhorns received scant mention as a dark horse, but that was all.

A home-and-home series with Southwest Texas produced two Steer victories as Kubricht and Francis were the leading scorers. The Javelinas of Texas A&I paid a visit to Gregory Gym in mid-December and lost two, 40-15 and 39-30. Texas missed Francis, who had the flu, but Gray was superb, scoring a total of 34 points.

Randolph Field, with several ex-West Pointers, was supposed to be tough, but UT brought the Aviators down to earth, 33-18. The Texas Chiropractic College Hawks, aided by TCU dropout Adolph Dietzel, presented no test in San Antonio. The Simmons Cowboys, winners of 46 of their last 48 contests, were swept in three games at Gregory Gym before a handful of spectators. And by a score of 68-28, the bearded players of the House of David bowed meekly to the power and speed of Texas as Gray (25), Kubricht (16) and Price (10) led in scoring.

The Longhorns' 10-0 record, earned against a bunch of "palookas" in the opinion of the *Austin Statesman*, was nonetheless impressive. With sophomore forward deluxe Jack Gray, they might surprise other teams of the SWC. The *Daily Texan* ran a front-page editorial entitled "A chance at a title" and urged students to load Gregory Gym's balconies when Texas met the defending champion Baylor Bears. Following the installation of loudspeakers, a public-address announcer, Weldon Hart, began working home games. About 4,000 fans showed up on a rainy night to witness a 48-26 UT victory. Baylor's 25-year-old captain, Abe Barnett, held Gray to six points, but Kubricht had 19, and Price was a whirlwind at guard.

A two-game series with Arkansas would be the acid test for Olle's Horns. Only then, halfway into the 1933 season, was it considered necessary to erect bleachers on the floor. For the first time in too long, the eyes of the SWC were on Austin in a game won by free throws. Unused to strict surveillance by officials, the Razorbacks came upon an exacting pair in Ziggy Sears and Bill Bushman, and three key players—Bruce Kendall, Hoot Gibson and Doc Sexton—fouled out. Gray scored 15 in a 36-28 Texas victory. The next night belonged to the Hogs, it appeared. They led most of the way, but UT caught and passed them at the end with some pressure free throw shooting by Francis. Gray, although closely guarded, scored 15 points as Arkansas coach Chuck Bassett fidgeted and cursed on the sideline. "It was one of the most sensational and thrilling contests ever staged at Gregory Gym," said the *Austin Statesman.* "When the Steers took the lead in the last three minutes of play, it seemed as though the great assemblage had gone wild.... Besides being a grand floor man with an eye that never loses sight of the ball, Gray is amazingly accurate with his one-handed shots at the basket."

Record: 22-1

42 SW Texas 12
49 SW Texas 13
40 Texas A&I 15
39 Texas A&I 30
33 Randolph Field 18
40 Texas Chiropractic 25
64 Simmons 20
52 Simmons 34
47 Simmons 25
68 House of David 28
48 Baylor 26
36 Arkansas 28
31 Arkansas 28
39 SMU 33
38 Texas A&M 31
59 Austin All-Stars 12
33 Baylor 28
31 TCU 29
33 Rice 24
28 SMU 27
26 TCU 42
59 Rice 31
51 Texas A&M 20

Gray was not the first player to use the one-handed shot, something long considered unnecessarily flashy and dangerous, rather like the behind-the-back dribble. Manny Ponsford used it a decade earlier, and SMU's Rhea Williams had done so, too. And Gray's teammate, Jean Francis, occasionally tried a one-hander. But none were as adept as Gray, who had perfected it while playing backyard games with his brother in Wills Point. When Olle saw the offensive advantage it promised, he and Gray began teaching the one-handed shot to varsity and freshman players. Made popular nationally three years later by Stanford's Hank Luisetti—who made it even more effective by jumping and shooting—and a staple of the game ever since, its origins were in the basketball backwater of Texas.

The fast-traveling Steers cleared another hurdle with a 39-33 defeat of SMU. Gray (16) and Kubricht (12) led UT scoring, while Clifton Wilhite had 11 for the Ponies in a game that hung in the balance until the final minutes. A large crowd, given to sporadic booing, filled the gallery and floor. With a record of 14-0 and four of the top seven scorers in the conference, it looked like the finest Texas team since the days of Doleful Doc Stewart. But Olle, noting that just two games had been played outside of Gregory Gym, cautioned his team against overconfidence before traveling to College Station. "We've been very fortunate so far, but the worst is yet to come," he said.

The Longhorns built a 14-point lead, but Joe Moody led the Aggies to within one. Fierce resistance enabled UT to escape DeWare Field House with a 38-31 victory. Mostly idle for two weeks for exams, the team kept its edge with a 59-12 defeat of the Austin All-Stars, the best of the city league players. Back in action on February 8 against winless Baylor, Texas needed a second-half rally to beat the Bears by five. Gray (13), with his dazzling one-handed shots, was irrepressible and cool under fire. The team returned to Austin and prepared for the season's biggest game, against TCU. Herschel "Slim" Kinzy was helping Frog fans forget about Adolph Dietzel. Other stars included Buster Brannon, Elbert "Flash" Walker, Doc Sumner, all-America football player Johnny Vaught and Richard "Speedy" Allison. Olle called them "a smart, experienced, fast bunch that makes few mistakes." Texas won, 31-29, in a wild game played before a record-breaking crowd. Actually, the Horns were coasting along with a 10-point lead when Price fouled out. TCU closed it to two before time expired.

Gray was quiet against Rice, but Francis (13) and Kubricht (11) picked up the slack in a 33-24 victory. The legality and fairness of using picks to free an offensive player was still under debate, but Olle's team mastered that technique in an increasingly favorable season. Just before the Steers' annual upstate trip, SMU coach Jim St. Clair foresaw a Texas defeat, and Olle said he might be right. UT got a scare from the Mustangs, winning by a single point. More than 2,000 fans in the SMU gym yelled themselves hoarse and thought their team had won when Smokey Zachary hit a fast-break layup with 10 seconds left. But umpire Frank Bridges (the former Baylor coach) called him for traveling and waved off the basket, so the fans unloosed their wrath. "For a time, the disturbance seemed serious, but athletic director Ray Morrison of SMU rushed to the scene and helped pull Bridges from the enraged Mustang partisans, and no damage was done," said the *Austin Statesman*.

Leading the SWC by two games, the Longhorns traveled west to Fort Worth and tasted the bitter dregs of defeat for the first time. Richard Allison scored 15 in a 42-26 Frog victory. Olle had a premonition that things would not be a breeze on that latterly northern cruise because both the Ponies and Frogs were loaded for Texas. With four games in 10 days, three of them on the road, his players were a bit tired, and it did not help that Gray was in a scoring slump. Despite the loss to TCU, the team still controlled its destiny. The last two games, against Rice and Texas A&M, were at home.

There was a complete reversal of form against the Owls. Kubricht scored 21, Gray 15 and Francis 10 in a 59-31 victory. And when the news arrived that Texas A&M had defeated second-place TCU, the title belonged to the Longhorns. Olle the coach had taken previously undistinguished material and molded it into a winner, while Olle the business manager saw attendance go up and UT basketball become more profitable. Even before the last game, all-SWC teams were announced, and the consensus had Gray, Kubricht and Price (head football coach 20 years later) joining Doc Sumner of TCU and Joe Moody of Texas A&M. The buzz was about Gray, called by some the greatest basketball player yet at Texas. Iconoclastic Waco sportswriter Jinx Tucker said he was overrated, and anyway, what about Clyde Littlefield? Or Hook McCullough, Bobby Robertson or Holly Brock? As if to answer Tucker, Gray put on a phenomenal shooting performance against the Aggies, tallying 32 points in a 51-20 victory. He broke the SWC record of 26, rendering Jocko Roberts' defense null and void. Roberts' instructions from A&M coach John Reid were simple: "Stop Mr. Gray."

UT's alumni magazine noted the startling 22-1 season. "The *Alcalde* would feel ungrateful if it did not take off its sombrero in the general direction of the 1933 basketball team which romped off with the conference championship and barely missed going through the season undefeated," it stated. "This year's showing is a demonstration of the efficiency of the present director, as well as the skill of the players. Hail and salute."

Basketball action inside Gregory Gym during the Steers' 1933 SWC championship season.

1934

In early December, Gregory Gym once again resounded with the thud of basketballs. Ed Olle's crackerjack team brought home the olive wreath in 1933, but he could hardly hope for a repeat because the Longhorns would be short and have scarcely any reserve strength. Three-fifths of the starting lineup—captain Ronald Fagan, Bennie Rundell and Jack Gray—needed time to recover from the bumps and bruises of football. Jean Francis and Glenn Thompson were back, as was 6'4" substitute center DeMoy Paulk. Jack Taylor and Richard Prigmore, up from the Yearlings, would make little impact in 1934.

What Austin sportswriters dubbed "the faithful five" was Fagan and Rundell (they had battled, sometimes bitterly, for the spot opposite Price in 1933) at guard, Gray and Thompson at forward and the 6'2" Francis at center. Preseason clairvoyants called it a passable team, but the Steers were devoted to their coach, and they had what no other team in the SWC had: Jack Gray.

The season began with two routs of Southwest Texas, 40-22 and 66-22. The Longhorns traveled by car to Monroe, Louisiana and engaged a team representing the Brown Paper Mills, winning by scores of 53-48 and 41-28. Francis was the leading scorer and defensive star of both games. But in the hamlet of Tullos, the Hunt Oilers introduced UT to a rough brand of basketball, a six-point victory aided, some thought, by an LSU referee.

After Christmas, a three-game series with Texas A&I was held at Gregory Gym. The first was a laugher for the Horns, the second was won by a late Gray-led rally, and the third went to the Javelinas. The teams were battling furiously at the end when a long shot by A&I forward McNabb dropped through the net for a one-point win to be savored in Kingsville. After a final tuneup victory against the local Magnolia Oilers, it was strictly business for Olle's team from then on.

They jumped right into the fire by playing their main contender, TCU, on the road. With a front line averaging 6'5", the Frogs swamped Texas, 59-31. Richard Allison scored 23, and Wallace "Hog Caller" Myers limited Gray to six points. It was such a thorough defeat, some UT players even showed displeasure with each other on the court. And no glad tidings were expected to emanate from Dallas when they met SMU. The Mustangs, led by Whitey Baccus and Smokey Zachery, were not exactly broken-down nags. It was not the first or last time Francis benefitted from an opposing defense focused on Gray. The lanky center scored 10 in a 27-22 victory in which no Steer subs were used.

On January 13, a colorful crowd of 4,000 saw Texas defeat Baylor with a combined 32 points from Francis and Gray. Much of the game, Fagan dribbled around and through Bear defenders. New UT football coach Jack Chevigny was introduced at halftime to applause and the blare of the Longhorn Band. Because Texas A&M had not won a game in Austin since 1923, the *Daily Texan* predicted John Reid's Farmers would leave town sadder but wiser. Olle put his players through the mill to ensure it. Although he gave no public indication, Gray was irked to read he was falling short of his 1933 performance. His point production was down, but a football knee injury had healed slowly. He was back in form against the Aggies, scoring 19 in a 34-29 loss. But Francis and Thompson were as cold as yesterday's flapjacks. "The lads from down the country deserved to win," conceded the *Austin Statesman*. "They won in the ancient, simple and infallible style—by taking the ball on the tipoff and keeping it, usually until they had made a basket."

Facing early elimination from the SWC race, Texas prepared for Rice. The Owls were perched atop the conference standings and had a good team with players like Floyd "Tree-Top" Kelly, Harry Journeay and R.T. Eaton. UT won a 40-38 heart-stopper as 4,500 fans roared their vociferous approval. Gray, in one of the best games of his career, slithered and twisted his way through the tight Rice defense for 24 points. And Olle's strategic move of inserting Paulk at center and moving Francis to forward paid dividends. Kelly had 16 for the Owls.

A fortnight off for exams was broken by one game with Olsen's Terrible Swedes, a Missouri-based semipro team that fancied itself "world champions." They used trickery, unorthodox play and a wide array of comical passes and shots. A sound team that won 120 of 128 games the previous year, the Swedes were nevertheless basketball burlesque. It appeared to be a typical winning exhibition by the renowned visitors who led by nine at intermission. But Francis and Gray started hitting, the gap was closed, and UT pulled ahead. The Swedes, no longer concerned about entertainment, tried frantically to get back in the game, but they lost by nine.

There was little time to ponder that pleasing victory. The team packed its uniforms and boarded a train for the Ozarks, expecting to win two and keep their slim title hopes alive. The first game went according to plan as Texas won, 28-26. Gray was outstanding, scoring 14 and turning back two Hog

Record: 14-8

40 SW Texas 22
66 SW Texas 22
53 Brown Paper Mills 48
41 Brown Paper Mills 28
22 Hunt Oilers 28
57 Texas A&I 46
31 Texas A&I 27
32 Texas A&I 33
49 Magnolia Oilers 28
31 TCU 59
27 SMU 22
44 Baylor 35
29 Texas A&M 34
40 Rice 38
40 Olsen's Terrible Swedes 31
28 Arkansas 26
29 Arkansas 32
31 Baylor 39
34 Rice 45
25 TCU 29
40 SMU 32
27 Texas A&M 25

rallies. UT seemed to have the second game in hand, but Taft Moody led a spirited comeback in the final two minutes to win by three. The real news out of Arkansas was that Ed Olle had resigned, effective at season's end. Popular with players, fans and the UT Athletic Council, Olle had done quite a service for three years. He was the busiest of Longhorn employees, working two jobs for the price of one. Rather amazingly, he had not gotten a raise in pay for the addition of basketball duties in 1932. In his office job, Olle served as executive, bookkeeper, financier, policeman and diplomat, and it was all done without fear or favor. He knew business managers were seldom criticized or fired—unlike basketball coaches—and had a growing family. "It was too heavy a burden," said Olle, who recommended that freshman and assistant varsity coach Marty Karow take his place. "I hated to quit. I'm a Texas man, and I wanted our team to win."

Weldon Hart of the *Austin Statesman* bemoaned his decision: "So Ed Olle will fade quietly out of the Longhorn court picture.... His brief spell at the helm will not be forgotten. We'll remember the coach who suited out each afternoon and was just one of the boys on the floor, who kept discipline but didn't 'ride.' He had some immortals—the cunning Price, the giant Kubricht, the incomparable Gray. Well, here's to the coach who was smart enough to lead his team to a championship and too smart to remain a coach too long."

Perhaps it was coincidental, but Olle's announcement, made before the second contest against Arkansas, preceded a four-game losing streak. The cellar-dwelling Baylor Bears, with 16 points from Benny Clark, won in Waco. And the Horns dropped a 45-34 decision to Rice in Houston. Gray had a great game, scoring 21 points as Houston alums cheered his every move and declared him the finest Longhorn of all time.

The players dedicated the February 22 game against TCU to their coach. Although the Horned Frogs were running away with the SWC crown, the *Daily Texan* anticipated a cage classic. Richard Allison, who was built like a double garage, and Gray, who scored baskets like he was eating peanuts, were tied for season scoring honors. The largest crowd yet at Gregory Gym, estimated at 7,000, saw the Horns lose a valiant and exceedingly rough game, 29-25. Wallace Myers' defense on Gray was again effective, and Herschel Kinzy had 11 for the Frogs. Something so prosaic as missed free throws may have kept UT from winning the game.

The home season ended three days later with a 40-32 defeat of SMU. Gray and Paulk had 10 points each for Texas, but the leading scorer was the Ponies' Smokey Zachery (18). Olle's last game as coach was a 27-25 win over Texas A&M in College Station, fought according to the best traditions of rivalry between the two schools. Playing days were over for Fagan, Rundell and Thompson.

Olle was stepping away from the game, and so was Francis Schmidt, longtime Arkansas and TCU football and basketball coach, then heading to Ohio State. During Schmidt's tenure in Fort Worth, the formerly hapless Frogs had won two SWC titles in each sport. His success, at least in part, may be attributed to open athletic recruiting. Other conference schools were doing it, or beginning to do it, if only to remain competitive.

1935

Marty Karow, an all-America fullback at Ohio State in 1926, came to Texas the following year as an assistant football coach. He helped Billy Disch with the baseball team and ran freshman basketball while Ed Olle tutored the varsity. Well acquainted with the players and eager for a head coaching job, Karow served notice that the 1935 Longhorns were ready to compete. Injuries and ineligibility, however, derailed an excellent year. It began with football injuries to two of his top players, Jack Gray (shoulder) and Jack Collins (ankle). Collins would not round into shape until February. Karow's early lineup consisted of Gray and Jean Francis at forward, DeMoy Paulk at center and Jerry Clifton and Paul Wittman at guard. The key subs were forward Jack Taylor and guards Marshall Pennington and Claude Harris. They first paraded before the home folks at Gregory Gym on December 13 in a 47-34 defeat of Southwest Texas. Gray and Francis, the gold-dust twins, displayed their marksmanship with 14 and 11 points, respectively. A nervous Karow paced along the bench, although his team had the game in hand. As part of what Karow called the "new deal" for fans, music was played over the public-address system before tipoff, and dances followed Friday night games. At halftime, various kinds of entertainment were offered: boxing matches, gymnastics, singing by the UT men's glee club and even an adagio dance by Margaret Russell and former Steer Bennie Rundell.

Southwest Oklahoma, a good team with lots of AAU experience, came to Austin for two games. The Teachers' Francy Young, a four-sport star, averaged 14 points per game in 1934, so the press conjured up a rivalry between him and Gray. He was outscored by Gray, 18 to nine, but it was Francis who won the game with a pretty side-court shot in the final minute. Texas triumphed again the next night, 50-33. Gray had the hot hand with 21.

After a 12-point defeat of Southwest Texas in San Marcos, UT fans grew optimistic. Karow used and improved the picks and screens Olle had taught, creating open shots. And the team was wont to work in sharp bursts, taking more chances and using a more varied attack. Gray, the captain, showed every indication of making his senior year a good one. In games against two San Antonio industrial teams before the Christmas break, the starters defeated the Magnolia Oilers, and the reserves beat the Finck Cigarmen. Texas got plenty of shooting practice in three defeats of newly renamed Hardin-Simmons in Abilene; only the last one was at all close.

Record: 16-8

47 SW Texas 34
35 SW Oklahoma 33
50 SW Oklahoma 33
38 SW Texas 26
42 Magnolia Oilers 28
38 Finck Cigarmen 32
54 Hardin-Simmons 25
45 Hardin-Simmons 27
36 Hardin-Simmons 30
47 Texas A&I 20
33 Texas A&I 23
38 SMU 36
24 TCU 21
44 Baylor 23
40 Texas A&M 41
28 SMU 32
27 Magnolia Oilers 37
35 Rice 49
30 Arkansas 47
33 Arkansas 23
23 Baylor 45
24 TCU 27
28 Rice 34
35 Texas A&M 25

The Longhorns were in fine fettle after beating Texas A&I twice in Austin. In the second contest, Javelina defender John Mark Dixon held Gray to four field goals. The *Austin Statesman* related this amusing anecdote: "Featuring a rather listless game was the unexpected appearance of a brindle bulldog who trotted onto the court while somebody was trying a free throw and visited the players at length while referee Dusty Boggess pursued him in vain. Shorty Alderson came to the rescue and dragged Bowser ignobly away by the collar."

Texas had a real dogfight in the Southwest Conference opener against SMU in Dallas. The Mustangs led by three at halftime, but UT, with 13 points from Francis, surged to a big lead with four minutes left. A frenzied Mustang rally was capped by Curly Haren's long shot in the final seconds. When referee Ziggy Sears blew his whistle for a violation away from the ball, disallowing the basket, 1,800 SMU fans went into an orgy of ref-baiting. Texas won, 38-36. After a three-point trimming of TCU (the Horned Frogs' first home loss since 1931), the hard-edged Karow could no longer suppress a smile. His team was unbeaten, Collins would be back soon, and seven of the 10 remaining conference games were at Gregory Gym.

Karow anticipated a battle royal against Baylor, calling that Bear team the best in three years. The Baptists, equipped with long-distance shooter Walter "Bunk" Bradley and a big man like Theo Alford, were fresh off an upset of SMU. Baylor coach Ralph Wolf jokingly offered to trade Alford for Gray, but Karow declined. It was a good thing he did because Gray (17) was largely responsible for a 44-23 defeat of the Bears in front of 3,000 fans. Paulk scored 12 and Alford nine for Baylor. Bradley was held scoreless by Wittman and Pennington.

The rampaging Horns finally lost on January 16. Texas A&M, with abundant size and experience, won a thrilling 41-40 game that saw the lead change hands 10 times. Gray, tightly guarded by Monte Carmichael, scored just seven points, while Aggie forward Tommy Hutto had 14. Karow seemed undaunted by the loss, but he knew that SMU, coming to Austin three days later, was not only playing well but still hopping mad about the controversial loss in Dallas. Weldon Hart of the *Austin Statesman* predicted Whitey Baccus would wear the Horns out. SMU's platinum-blond shooter had been doing it all year long. Baccus (10) had some help from Paul Briggs (13) in beating Texas, 32-28, in a rough game before 4,000 howling fans. Ref Dusty Boggess was razzed unmercifully throughout by Longhorn supporters because of his prolific foul-calling. For Gray, it was more of the same as opposing defenses continued to play him and practically ignore his teammates. He managed to score 10 against the Mustangs. Coach Jim St. Clair sent his team home while he stayed in Austin another day to marvel at the huge intramural basketball program operating in Gregory Gym.

The long exam period was broken only by a 37-27 loss to the Magnolia Oilers. But that was the least of Karow's worries. Rumors flew fast and thick that two Steers would soon be found ineligible, and they proved true. Clifton and Paulk were off the team. Francis first had the flu and then hurt an ankle in practice. Weakened, out of shape and carrying a losing streak, the Horns prepared for league-leading Rice in Houston. "We'll give them a scrap," Karow promised. Floyd Kelly and Harry Journeay had 10 points apiece in the Owls' 49-35 victory. Not even the genius of Jack Gray could prevail against Rice that night. He hustled on defense, rebounded, handled the ball and scored 21 points from inside and out. "Veteran followers of basketball agreed Gray gave the most masterful exhibition ever put on here by a basketeer," said an Associated Press report.

Since a big crowd was expected for both games with Arkansas at Gregory Gym, many fans showed up early. The Razorbacks, then tied with Rice for the SWC lead, had great players like Taft Moody and Ike Poole. The starting team averaged 6'3", prompting Frank Tolbert of the *Daily Texan* to remark, "They surely must have eaten their spinach in their young days." Only the court magic of Gray stood between the brawny Hogs and a sweep. Glen Rose's team fell behind early but finished with a rush, winning, 47-30. Moody and Poole combined for 36 points. But it was a complete reversal the next night as the Horns inflicted the first conference loss on Arkansas, 33-23. Four different Razorbacks were assigned to stop Gray (17), who played one of the finest games yet on the maples of Gregory Gym. A happy crowd of 4,000 cheered to the echo because the Longhorns would not be denied.

All-American Jack Gray. In the mid-1930s, he was widely regarded as the greatest Longhorn yet.

With that big victory under their belts, the team headed to Waco as top-heavy favorites over Baylor. But they were humbled, 45-23, when Ken Clark held Gray to six points, four coming at the free throw line. For the only time in his UT career, Gray fouled out. Theo Alford (15) and Mark O'Heeron (13) led the Bears in scoring. Yet another upset happened in Austin. TCU's Horned Frogs, winners of just one league game, eked out a 27-24 victory while the Gregory Gym choir sung its disapproval. *Austin Statesman* writer Weldon Hart, claiming TCU center Darrell Lester got away with murder on the court, blamed umpire Ziggy Sears in a long and sarcastic article.

UT, still groggy from the losses to Baylor and TCU, welcomed Rice to town. Karow and Owl coach Jimmy Kitts tossed verbal bouquets at each other's team. Fifteen points from Gray were not enough to prevent Rice's seventh straight win. A promising season that had turned sour ended on a positive note on March 6 when Texas beat Texas A&M, 35-25. Gray, with 11 points, won his third straight SWC scoring title. After the game, he was given the University Co-op's MVP trophy. Smiling broadly, the UT immortal stood in the center of mammoth Gregory Gym while the band played "The Eyes of Texas."

He was the first Longhorn athlete, of any sport, to receive consensus all-America honors, joining Lee Guttero of Southern California, Claire Cribbs of Pittsburgh, Bud Browning of Oklahoma and Leroy Edwards of Kentucky on the 1935 mythical team. Scribes in Texas took a while to assess the meteoric career of Jack Gray, the barrel-chested one-hand artist who topped the 1,000-point mark. They tried to remember any fanfare that had accompanied his arrival on campus in the fall of 1931, but there had been none, or at least nothing to suggest future stardom. Where had he come from? How had he done it? Though not especially quick or nimble, he was a man of iron, starting every football game his last two years and every single game of his three-year basketball career at Texas. All-SWC in football in 1934, he surely could have conserved his energy and been an even greater basketball player. Gray, who had imperfect support from his teammates the last two seasons, dealt with the pressure admirably. Furthermore, Olle and Karow never had to worry about his academics. "Throughout the Southwest, they are spinning the saga of this singular basketeer," said the *Austin Statesman*. "He was an athlete of surprising merit, and we may not see his like again."

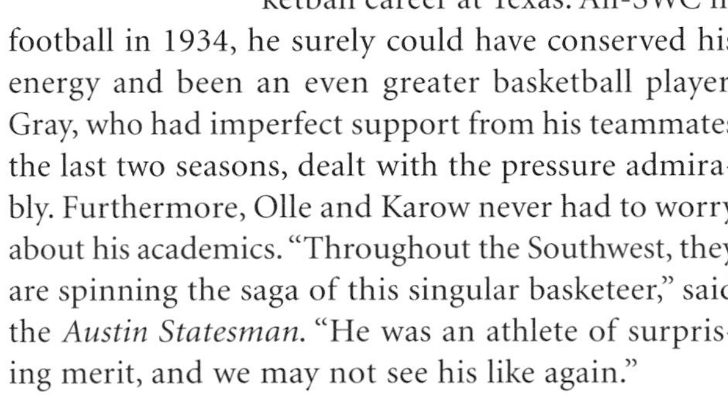

1936

It was an interesting situation. His playing days behind him, Jack Gray was named as an assistant coach for freshman football and head coach of the basketball Yearlings. Marty Karow retained his varsity basketball position but was demoted by Jack Chevigny from the varsity football staff to helping Gray with the frosh. Friction between Karow and Chevigny (himself under fire for declining Longhorn football fortunes) was complicated by the near-universal admiration of Gray. Athletes, students, coaches and alumni all wanted to keep him in Austin, perhaps one day as head basketball coach. That could not have made Karow overly secure.

The days of mass tryouts for varsity basketball were pretty much over by the mid-1930s, although coaches still kept an eye out for intramural stars. Gray had 64 aspirants for the Yearlings, while things were more settled on the varsity. Jack Taylor and Jack Collins (whose son by the same name would be a Longhorn football star 25 years later) were the main returnees. Promising sophomores included guards Don White and Warren Osborne, forwards Bill Baxter and Jerry Sparkman and center Henry Chovanec. Two more quality players, guard Jerry Clifton and center Joe Roach, were due to become eligible on February 1. Some railbirds speculated Taylor, the team captain, would soon be nudged from the starting lineup.

Karow's players needed time to adjust to the new three-second rule, designed to reduce congestion near the basket. That and elimination of the tipoff after a successful free throw drew the ire of traditionalists who sought to preserve the honorable Dr. Naismith's pastime. It would be further streamlined in 1938 when the tipoff after a made basket was junked. The new rules were the subject of a 20-minute demonstration for a small crowd attending the season opener against Southwest Texas in Gregory Gym on December 13. Texas lost to the Bobcats, 35-33, as Gid Campbell scored nine for the visitors. For those who chose to remain, the reserve squads then played an abbreviated game won by the Steers.

Record: 15-9

33 SW Texas 35
25 SW Texas 21
33 Sam Houston 29
23 Sam Houston 20
24 SW Oklahoma 25
29 SW Oklahoma 27
22 SW Oklahoma 19
23 Hunt Oilers 34
41 Rice 32
24 Baylor 23
31 SMU 33 (2 OT's)
30 Baylor 24
29 Olsen's Terrible Swedes 31
39 Olsen's Terrible Swedes 35
50 Hunt Oilers 46
38 TCU 25
37 Rice 33
30 SMU 44
35 TCU 27
43 Texas A&M 29
37 Arkansas 38
31 Arkansas 43
32 Texas A&M 27
16 Arkansas 27

In the return match in San Marcos, however, Texas won a close one with late shots by White and Baxter. Karow's young team was having problems with nerves, but there were plenty more "practice" games before the Southwest Conference race began. UT and Sam Houston State met in Missouri City to dedicate a new high school gym. Despite poor shooting and passing by most of the team, Taylor and Collins pulled out a narrow victory. And they beat the Bearkats in Huntsville the next evening, 23-20, rallying from six points down with five minutes left. During halftime of that game, Karow gave Collins a stern talking-to, claiming he had to find an extra measure of effort and aggressiveness. And although no one accused him of being another Jack Gray, who practiced with the team on occasion, Collins was on his way to a fine junior year.

Rankin Williams brought his Southwest Oklahoma Teachers to Austin for a three-game series in late December. Texas won two of them as Collins and his counterpart, Carl Nikkel, matched basket for basket. Olle and Karow hastily arranged a home game with the Hunt Oilers, a 34-23 loss that caused *Daily Texan* writer Joe Belden to label the Longhorns "weak." One game that was negotiated but fell through was with the New York Celtics, widely regarded as the best pro basketball team in the world with such players as Dutch Dehnert, Joe Lapchick and Nat Hickey. The finances were agreed upon, but the touring Celtics could not make it to Austin and missed a chance to put a bruising defeat on the young Longhorns.

Little chance for victory was seen against Rice. Jimmy Kitts' team, which shared the 1935 SWC title with Arkansas and SMU, was largely intact. R.T. Eaton and his teammates expected a night of relative peace and quiet after a wild victory over Baylor. With the

Horns up by eight at the half, many UT partisans adjourned to the Gregory Gym foyer and started smoking furiously and wishing the game was over. They had no need to worry because Taylor (15) and Collins (13) led a 41-32 upset that greatly chagrined the Owls. "Remember," Karow warned his players in the jubilant locker room, "we haven't won the championship, nor are we off to an undefeated season. Take it easy, will you?"

Karow remained doubtful on the way to Chapel Court in Waco. But the Horns overtook Baylor in the final minutes and won, 24-23. Baxter scored 10, and Texas was tied for the SWC lead. Just to show the precarious nature of a coach's life, rumors then began wafting that Karow's days at UT were numbered. He did not address them publicly, however, because there were games to be played and won. A big one approached in the form of SMU. For the past three years, Gray and Jean Francis had battled with the wearers of SMU's gaudy red and blue, and passions usually ran high. A return showing of the Longhorn-Mustang drama drew a large crowd that saw an unforgettable double-overtime 33-31 SMU win. Sparkman and Taylor brought Texas back from a 10-point deficit to tie the game "amid the wildest cheering the rafters of Gregory Gym have withstood in many seasons," said the *Daily Texan*. But the Ponies' Bill Blanton (14) and Curly Haren (10) were the big stars of the night.

Jack Taylor, Jack Collins and Bill Baxter, the top three players on the 1936 Texas team.

Gray's frosh, led by Willie Tate, defeated Schreiner in a game that preceded Texas and Baylor on January 18. Over 4,000 fans braved freezing weather to witness a rough game won by the Horns, 30-24. The Bruins, who indulged in strong-arm tactics most of the game, fell behind in the late minutes and began throwing up hope shots.

The torpor of the exam period was broken by a split with Olsen's Terrible Swedes and a surprising 50-46 defeat of the Hunt Oilers. Karow felt good as SWC play resumed; his team was 3-1, and Roach and Clifton were finally eligible. The husky Roach would be much needed against Arkansas, and Clifton was equally important. The most polished player on the team, the best passer and very fast, his main problem was the books. Regularly going on and off the ineligible list, Clifton was with the team for the rest of the 1936 season.

TCU came to Austin on February 8 and lost, 38-25, in a drab game in which the fans were too bored to boo. SWC champs in 1934, the Frogs had begun a long streak of mediocrity, finishing last in the conference seven consecutive years. Not until 1942 would they get out of the SWC dungeon. The Longhorns, facing six of their remaining seven games away from Austin, met Rice in Houston. Playing without Taylor (sidelined for the rest of the season with a leg injury), Texas proved that the earlier victory over the Owls was no upset. A packed house saw a hustling, cutthroat contest that featured some splendid dribbling and passing by Houstonian Warren Osborne, 14 points by Collins and two last-minute baskets by Baxter. Karow and his players were mobbed by scores of happy UT fans in what Houston sportswriter Lloyd Gregory called "the hardest-fought and most exciting cage contest played here in years."

To make it even sweeter, the Steers then shared first place with Arkansas. Their joy was short-lived, however, because SMU took a 44-30 win in Dallas. Bill Blanton and Lester Tipton teamed up to score 28 for the Ponies, but no Texas player reached double figures. Over in Fort Worth, UT beat the lowly Frogs, 35-27, behind 11 points by Collins.

The final home game of the 1936 season was against Texas A&M. Just as UT missed Taylor, the Ags missed sharpshooting forward Virgil Harris. Texas won comfortably, 43-29, thanks in large part to the visitors' zero-for-nine performance at the free throw line.

Trailing the Hogs by one game, UT went up to Arkansas where the hammer was poised to nail another SWC pennant to the mast. Glen Rose's defense was allowing just 24 points per game, and fine players like Jim Lee Howell, Ike Poole (consensus all-American in 1936), Elwin Gilliland and Don Lockard gave Razorback fans confidence. Their undersized court drew criticism from *Daily Texan* sports editor Stanley Gunn, who called upon the SWC to standardize courts around the league. UT's hopes flickered and died that night in the Ozarks but not before 1,500 fans were left limp in their seats. Collins and Roach had fouled out by the final minute when Osborne scored to put Texas ahead by one. But Lockard came right back, looping in the winning shot in the final seconds. And the Razorbacks won again the next night, 43-31.

Collins' 18 points in the season-ending victory over Texas A&M boosted him to the SWC scoring title. A Longhorn would not win it again until 1950. Actually, the season was not quite over. The 1936 Olympics in Berlin would be the first to include basketball, and three SWC teams (Arkansas, Texas and Rice) were invited to participate in the Olympic trials southwest district tournament in Houston on March 11. The cold-shooting Longhorns lost to Arkansas, 27-16.

1937

Although he enjoyed coaching basketball at the University of Texas and had done a fairly good job of it the past two seasons, Marty Karow validated the rumors by quitting in the summer of 1936. If AD and football coach Jack Chevigny did not fire Karow, he surely nudged him toward the door. Karow soon found employment at the U.S. Naval Academy, where he coached baseball and assisted with football and basketball.

While it was anchors aweigh for Karow, the Texas basketball job remained unfilled for several weeks. Problems with the football program outweighed such a matter. It was not a foregone conclusion that Jack Gray would move up to the varsity, but little effort was expended in searching for another man. Although Gray was unquestionably the key figure on the Longhorn team from 1933 to 1935, the captain his senior year and an unofficial coach, his only real experience was one season with the Yearlings. Just 25 when he accepted the job, Gray believed he was ready. And if the golden boy took a while to grow into it, no one at the University would mind too much.

Gray's football duties changed, too. Instead of heading the frosh team, he was varsity end coach. Because of a late-closing football season, he and two players (Jack Collins and Joe Roach) got a slow start on basketball practice. Bill Baxter, Don White, Jerry Clifton, Henry Chovanec, Warren Osborne, sophomore Willie Tate and others had worked out on their own since November 1, but not on the main floor of Gregory Gym. The Texas Centennial Exposition, featuring all sorts of flora, fauna and historical artifacts, had taken over. The debris was not cleared away and a new coat of varnish applied to the floor until the second week of December. The Steers squeezed in a few practice sessions on the tiny stage court and at Austin High School, but lack of work led to a terrible performance in the season opener against Southwest Texas in San Marcos. Out of 47 shots, only seven were made, and UT lost to the Bobcats, 24-20. In addition, poor passing and overall awkwardness were worse than typical for an early-season game. It was not the coaching debut Gray dreamed of. The rematch in Austin was much better, a 30-12 Longhorn victory keyed by 11 points from Collins and some classy play by Roach, a burly southpaw forward.

Gray and frosh coach Ed Price were quite pleased in mid-December when three fine athletes dropped in unannounced. Jimmy Britt, Elmer Finley and Oran Spears had played on the undefeated 1935 and 1936 teams of John Tarleton College. The trio spent a month at Rice, decided they did not like it there and transferred to Texas, where two former Plowboys, Baxter and Tate, were playing. As junior college graduates, they had to spend a year with the freshmen before getting three seasons with the varsity.

They arrived just in time to see a big game. Southern California was making a tour of the region and had already whipsawed Texas A&M, Rice and SMU. Sam Barry's Trojans brought basketball with a west-coast flavor, a conservative yet brilliant ball-control offense. Stars like Eddie Oram, Wayne Garrison and Carl "Buttercup" Anderson would match wits with UT's man-to-man defense. Some 2,500 people came away impressed with the Trojans' mastery of ballhandling and other basketball fundamentals. "No Southwest team at this stage of the season, if any time, ever has acquired the polish, poise and sureness of foot and hand which made Sam Barry's Trojans superior to Jack Gray's Longhorns," said the *Austin Statesman*. With that instructive 28-20 loss to USC, Texas basketball began to break out of a provincial mentality that had long ruled. Apart from biennial visits to Fayetteville, an occasional foray into Oklahoma and once to Shreveport, only in 1911 (the Tulane-Auburn-LSU trip) and 1923 (the seven-game barnstorming tour of Iowa, Kansas and Missouri) had the Horns left

Texas. College basketball was growing in popularity—a crowd of 18,000 had recently witnessed a game in New York—and Gray wanted UT to be part of it.

He took the team to south Texas for three games just before Christmas. Baxter, Tate and Clifton were largely responsible for victories over Texas A&I in Beeville and Kingsville. And Baxter had 12 points in a 36-26 defeat of the Sabinas Brewers in San Antonio. When Southwest Oklahoma came to Austin for a three-game series, Gray was dismayed to hear that his ace guard, Clifton, had gotten married and quit the team. The Longhorns won the first two of those games but missed Clifton's shooting and floorwork in a 34-22 loss. Clifton's replacement, Don White, was a defensive specialist. Just before SWC play began, the peripatetic Clifton showed up. Gray, later known as a coach who ran his teams with a firm hand, might not have forgiven any other player. But he and Clifton, teammates on the 1932 freshman team and then on the varsity, were friends.

Record: 13-10

20 SW Texas 24
30 SW Texas 12
20 Southern California 28
59 Texas A&I 36
37 Texas A&I 29
36 Sabinas Brewers 26
35 SW Oklahoma 30
35 SW Oklahoma 29
22 SW Oklahoma 34
21 TCU 23
16 SMU 27
23 Texas A&M 14
20 Rice 28
35 TCU 22
35 Olsen's Terrible Swedes 29
51 Austin All-Stars 10
39 Arkansas 28
43 Arkansas 31
31 Baylor 33
35 Rice 40
19 SMU 24
39 Baylor 40
37 Texas A&M 29

Heading north to play TCU and SMU, Gray quipped, "If we are successful this weekend, things will look mighty cheerful for the Longhorns." So far, though, they did not resemble SWC contenders. Some nights they did well, but just as often they looked like rookies playing on an indoor court for the first time. Collins was far below his all-conference form of 1936, Clifton was undependable, and Tate had yet to prove himself big-time varsity material. Baxter was doing better than expected, but he injured a leg against Southwest Oklahoma and aggravated it in practice.

All-America quarterback Sammy Baugh led TCU to its only Southwest Conference win of the year against Texas. Due to snow and ice, a scant crowd witnessed the two-point Frog victory. And in Dallas, UT was outclassed by the Ponies, 27-16. J.D. "Sniper" Norton, a fine sophomore forward, scored 18, while Collins had seven for the Horns. Gray offered no excuses, although the team bus stalled in the cold 30 minutes before game time, almost causing a late arrival. The gyms in Fort Worth and Dallas were frigid, a problem never experienced at Gregory Gym, where it sometimes got too warm. After lethargy befell the team upstate, Gray worked them hard in practice and preached rebounding. They would need it against Texas A&M, with 6'8" Dale Freiburger, who specialized in jumping and throwing the ball down through the basket, an emphatic shot later named the "dunk." Due to Collins' fine defensive work, Freiburger got no opportunity to display his unique shot in a 23-14 UT victory. Baxter (eight) was the game's leading scorer, while the Aggies' offense sputtered like the old family automobile.

A hotly waged game was expected between Texas and Rice in Austin on January 16, a few days after SWC president E.M. McDiarmid sent out a letter to "faculty representatives, coaches and officials, sportswriters, student leaders, cheerleaders and all concerned" regarding sportsmanship at conference basketball games. The customers were being asked to boo no more than absolutely necessary, and McDiarmid may have had Gregory Gym especially in mind. "Gregory rafterites have finesse and volume which their rivals cannot achieve," wrote Weldon Hart of the *Austin Statesman*. "There is a certain relaxed enthusiasm about their work which renders it all the more effective, and the accoustics are excellent. The architect must have been a basketball fan himself."

The spectators were slightly more cordial than usual in seeing the Owls take a 28-20 victory. Eighteen points came from Willis Orr, a rangy, acrobatic and tireless sophomore forward. Texas was relegated to also-ran status after just four games. While the ball seemed larger than the basket against Rice, that was no problem in a 35-22 defeat of TCU in Austin. Baxter (12) and Tate (11) were the top scorers. Two games filled the exam break, a 35-29 defeat of Olsen's Terrible Swedes and 51-10 over an all-star team from the Austin city league. Proceeds from the latter game went to relieve victims of flooding along the Mississippi River.

The Steers were idling along in sixth place when powerful Arkansas arrived in town, fully expecting two wins in the battle with SMU for Southwest Conference supremacy. Nearly 7,000 people packed Gregory Gym for some hoop-la, wondering if anyone might stop Hog star Don "Deadpan" Lockard. The 1936 champs received a sound beating from Gray's worthies, 39-28. Despite the best defensive effort of White, Lockard got 12. But Clifton was equally outstanding for the Longhorns, scoring 11 and displaying some clever footwork, pivoting and dribbling. Roach (13) and Tate (10) led another big UT victory the following night. Governor James Allred was at the press table at halftime when Dana X. Bible was introduced as the new UT football coach and athletic director. "Hired as the climax of a six-act play," according to the *Daily Texan*, Bible (who had coached Texas A&M in games at the Men's Gym) gave a brief speech.

Delighted about the two wins over Arkansas, the Longhorns cast baleful glances northward, fearing an upset in Waco. Gray said, "The Bears always put up a different type of game on their home court, and it's hard to beat them." Those fears were justified as BU won a spine-tingler, 33-31, on a last-minute shot by Ken Clark. Boyd "Jelly" SoRelle had nine for the Bears, and Clifton (11) reminded some Waco fans of the departed Theo Alford. That game could have gone differently except that Roach and Baxter had the flu, and Collins had an abscessed foot. The crippled Steers then went to Houston for a tiff with Rice. Holding the lead until the final minutes, they dropped a close one to the Owls as Chovanec scored 11 before fouling out.

Longhorn Band director George Hurt led a lively 30-minute program prior to the Texas-SMU game on February 20. The Mustangs (with the "Three Basketeers," J.D. Norton, Bill Blanton and Bill Dewell) won a rough and ragged game that displeased the Gregory Gym fans. Nevertheless, SMU had earned its first undisputed Southwest Conference trophy. That preceded a heartbreaking loss to Baylor. Baxter looked like the hero of a late and successful Texas rally, but Bubba Gernand made a wild and, some thought, lucky shot in the last five seconds to win, 40-39. Gernand, who alternately quarreled and laughed with Longhorn players and 4,000 fans, scored 17 points. Another very demonstrative player came to Austin for the season finale. Texas A&M's Johnny Morrow, on loan from the Aggie football team, howled at referee Dusty Boggess when called for his fourth and last foul. The crowd booed Morrow lustily, and he then invited any and all down for a session of fisticuffs. The game was a 37-29 Texas victory as Collins went out in style, scoring 13 points. And Clifton wrapped up an improbable career by being selected to the all-SWC team.

1938

Well before the first game was played, experts had written off the 1938 Texas Longhorns. "Expected to get nowhere," said the *Austin Statesman*. "Poor prospects," said the *Daily Texan*. "Discouraging prospects," said the *Alcalde*. Captain Don White disputed the notion that the team could not win, but there were reasons for all the gloomy predictions. Joe Roach had broken a leg in football and would not be back. Bill Baxter graduated early and chose not to play his senior season. Willie Tate had fallen short of expectations in 1937, and Henry Chovanec was a hard-working plugger but not the kind of athlete who won championships. Although Jack Gray's coaching skills would surely be challenged that year, things were not so bleak. He had two good little sophomores, Bobby Moers and Tommy Nelms. And those ex-John Tarleton players—Oran Spears, Jimmy Britt and Elmer Finley—were expected to make a big splash after gaining eligibility on February 1.

After many years of debate and experimentation, the abolition of the center jump after field goals was fully enacted, making basketball a faster and more strenuous game. That suited some of Gray's 1938 players more than others. Early in that season, some basketball fans were genuinely concerned about the health of players and predicted a bonanza for heart specialists a decade hence.

Gregory Gym first witnessed the new game on December 7 when Texas and Southwest Texas met. Two missed free throws by Nelms in the last minute allowed the Bobcats to escape with a narrow victory. But the Longhorns won, 22-16, in San Marcos. It was a defensive masterpiece ignited by the stocky, aggressive Moers, who raged up and down the court, intercepted passes and guarded his man tenaciously. Moers had chosen to play intramural ball in 1937 rather than work with Ed Price's frosh team. If that hindered him, it did not show. Moers was well on his way to becoming one of the best and most colorful Longhorn basketball players ever. Just 5'11" and 170 pounds, he asked no odds of any opponent, and the fans loved him. "He has basketball sense and that uncanny knack any great cager must have—the knack of being where the ball is," wrote Weldon Hart of the *Austin Statesman*. "Some have it, and some don't. It made Jack Gray himself the great player he was."

Two sure defeats were expected against the Dr Pepper team of Dallas and the Liberty Pipeliners of Overton. But behind the scoring of Warren Osborne and Tate, the Longhorns managed to win both, quieting their critics and heartening their coach. Early-comers to the Liberty game at Gregory Gym witnessed the Yearlings' defeat of Texas Lutheran; UT once again had a superb freshman team with future varsity contributors like Udell Moore, Chester Granville, Thurman "Slue" Hull, W.D. "Speedy" Houpt and Denton Cooley.

The Longhorns took a trip to east Texas to play two Lone Star Conference teams. Sam Houston won, 36-26, but Texas beat the Stephen F. Austin Lumberjacks, 31-23. Gray praised White's defense, Moers' floor work and Tate's shooting.

Hugh McDermott brought a sophomore-laden Oklahoma team to Austin for two games on December 30 and 31. He and Gray must have had an unusually congenial relationship because the Longhorns and Sooners scrimmaged three times before the first contest. Rebounding from a nine-point deficit created by the fast breaks and flashy dribbling of Sooners Jim McNatt and Marvin Mesch, UT got back in the game. The last two minutes were wild and full of thrills. Osborne, Tate and Moers were mostly responsible for a three-point win. But OU was in command the next night, winning by a score of 47-32.

A sprained wrist kept Moers out of the next game as Texas hosted the Colorado Springs Antlers. It was the fourth uniform Adolph Dietzel had worn in playing against the Steers. Gray was overgenerous, or perhaps trying to entice more fans to the gym, in calling Dietzel the best SWC player of modern times. He was tall and scored prolifically (his 12 points led the Antlers' victory), but in defense, passing, dribbling, hustle and other elements of winning basketball, he was not Gray's match.

The Longhorns had proven they were not the hopeless misfits they had been called a month earlier and were ready to begin conference play. If they were not of the caliber of Arkansas, they could still make things interesting. They hoped to get first blood against TCU, visiting on January 8. Some 4,500 fans saw an easy Texas victory paced by Osborne (13) and Chovanec (10). Even a stranger to Gregory Gym would have guessed league play was getting underway for all the boos and hisses raining down on the officials as of old.

In Dallas, UT took the court against the SWC champion Mustangs, then coached by Whitey Baccus. But the Horns were without Osborne. The senior guard stayed in Austin to focus on his law studies and never returned to the team. Gray and the other players were not greatly pleased with Osborne's sudden decision, but they moved forward. The game with SMU was an exciting one. Texas surged to the lead three times in the final minutes, but J.D. Norton (16) led a winning rally for the Ponies. Nelms scored 13 in a 39-18 defeat of TCU in Fort Worth, prompting Horned Frog coach Mike Brumbelow to lament, "Our big boys are too slow, and our little boys are too little."

Willie Tate (4) contends with a Texas A&M player for a rebound in the Longhorns' victory at Gregory Gym.

Gray missed the steady play of Don White (out with a knee injury) against Baylor. Tate was practically a one-man team, scoring 19, but Hubert Kirkpatrick and Bubba Gernand combined for 36 points in a 51-

45 victory for the green and gold cagers before 5,000 fans in Austin. During the exam period, Olsen's Terrible Swedes paid their final visit to Austin. As more than one pundit noted, they had begun to live down to their name—terrible. They had aged and brought an incomplete squad, having to recruit two local athletes to play the Longhorns. That was the first game in which Finley, Britt and Spears could play, and expectations were high. "Southwest Conference rivals, beware," Texas said with a 59-36 victory. Finley scored 17, and Moers, a dynamic, catlike player, was everywhere as the fans roared their approval.

SWC play resumed for Texas on February 4 in Waco. Hubert Kirkpatrick had recently eclipsed Gray's record by scoring 35 against TCU. And the new-model Steers were ready to avenge the earlier loss to Baylor. Fans were turned away from the game at Chapel Court, the last year it hosted Bear basketball. "They like their basketball rough in Waco, and old Chapel Court often resounds to the cracking of elbows against opposing ribs and skulls," wrote Weldon Hart of the *Austin Statesman*. "It is an ideal spot for Waco basketball games as the court can be readily returned to its original purpose and last rites said for maimed players and officials without the confusion of moving the bodies." The little gym was full of whooping fans who saw a thrill-packed game won, 46-45, by the Bears. Gray fashioned his defense to stop the wheeling, leaping Kirkpatrick, who still got 17 points. Tate and Moers combined for 26. Bubba Gernand, Baylor's court general, was so exhausted after playing the full 40 minutes that he passed out, lending credence to those who believed the game had become too stressful.

Rice guard Mike Seale scored 15 to lead his team out of a tie with TCU for the conference cellar. It was another one-point loss for Texas, and just before the long trip to Fayetteville. Arkansas finally had a regulation-sized court in its new $165,000 gym. UT's first experience there was rather unpleasant, a 74-38 drubbing. James Benton scored 20, Jack Robbins 18 and Don Lockard 12 in the record-setting performance. They did it with better athletes and by playing "fire department" basketball in which a Razorback would often grab the ball and all five would charge downcourt like firehorses on their way to a three-alarm blaze and then shoot with dispatch. Only Spears (14) played well for the Horns.

Texas rebounded from that bitter humiliation by throwing a scare into the Hogs the following night before falling, 42-37. Employing a slow passing game that knocked the Arkansas machine offstride, the Longhorns led only in the early minutes. Finley (14) and Tate (12) were the top scorers for UT.

Record: 11-11

31 SW Texas 33
22 SW Texas 16
33 Dr Pepper 30
27 Liberty Pipeliners 23
26 Sam Houston 36
31 Stephen F. Austin 23
31 Oklahoma 28
32 Oklahoma 47
30 Colorado Springs Antlers 34
33 TCU 21
26 SMU 29
39 TCU 18
45 Baylor 51
59 Olsen's Terrible Swedes 36
45 Baylor 46
41 Rice 42
38 Arkansas 74
37 Arkansas 42
35 Texas A&M 27
25 SMU 23
53 Rice 35
26 Texas A&M 31

The four-game losing streak ended on February 19 with a 35-27 defeat of Texas A&M in Austin. Spears held the Ags' leading scorer, Virgil Harris, to a single field goal, directed the Texas offense and slipped in nine points. SMU brought a 6-1 conference record to Gregory Gym but tumbled, 25-23, before 4,500 fans. Spears gave the high-scoring J.D. Norton trouble, but the game was won by the Longhorns' effervescent sophomore, Bobby Moers. Scoring 12 and playing the entire game, his speed, shiftiness and tantalizing feints kept the Mustangs in a dither. The home season ended with a 53-35 defeat of Rice in which Moers had 19 and Tate 17. UT football players, as was their custom, sat together on the north-side bleachers and gave an assortment of yells, mixing in jibes for the Owls' Frank Steen, the key figure in a disputed touchdown in a gridiron game the previous fall.

The Longhorns' final game was at DeWare Field House. Texas A&M charged into the lead in the last 10 minutes and held on for a 31-26 victory. Jimmy Clark scored 11 of his 15 points at the free throw line. A .500 season record and second-division status in the SWC were no worse than expected back in December, but the tide was turning. In Texas basketball history, 1939 would be a year to remember.

1939

It had been six years since the University of Texas won a fall-winter (football or basketball) championship. The 1939 Longhorn team, captained by Willie Tate, would have experience, speed and some fine sophomores but only average height. Defense might be a problem, too. Some fans, underwhelmed by Jack Gray's two-year record, thought it was time for him to produce a winner.

The season began on December 3 with a game versus the Liberty Pipeliners of Kilgore. That team, with Hubert Kirkpatrick (formerly of Baylor), Bill Blanton (SMU) and Don White and Bill Baxter (Texas), was expected to give the Steers all the competition they wanted and more. Tate scored 10, and Bobby Moers showed the same dash and fire that made him a fan favorite in 1938 in a 37-27 victory. UT looked potent in winning two from Southwest Texas, and then came the much-anticipated visit from Dr. Forrest "Phog" Allen's mighty Kansas Jayhawks.

Bobby Moers, UT's ballhandler and competitor extraordinaire.

Allen, who learned the game from its original source, Dr. James Naismith, had been coaching since 1908. He compiled a brilliant record (eventually winning 771 games over five decades), wrote books and gave lectures on all facets of basketball, often expressing his idiosyncratic ideas with a foghorn voice. Allen's Jayhawks played a smooth, intricate and deliberate game while Texas used the sort of go-go offense that made Allen hold his nose. It was the biggest intersectional game yet in Austin, bigger than the Southern Cal game of 1937. Gray's starting lineup was Moers and Oran Spears at guard, Chester Granville and Slue Hull at forward and Tate at center. Allen's crew appeared to be winning in the second half when the Horns came to life and put together a rally that had the gym in bedlam. Last-minute free throws by Spears and Tate won the game, 36-34. When the timer's gun went off, the football cheering section rushed the floor, pounded their basketball brethren and lifted them onto their brawny shoulders in an enthusiastic demonstration of school spirit.

A larger crowd the following night witnessed a 49-35 Kansas victory. George Golay (16) and Robert Allen (11) paced the Jayhawk attack. Even in defeat, Moers stole the show. Despite some errors and missed shots, he played tough defense, made several reckless offensive thrusts and outhustled everyone else. The referees, Dusty Boggess and young Doc Hayes (the future SMU coach), got a good going-over from the fans. *Daily Texan* sports editor Clarence LaRoche ripped Boggess and Hayes, although Kansas had to adjust to the SWC officials.

The All-College Tournament in Oklahoma City, which began in 1937, welcomed Texas into its 32-team field. Schools from Arizona to Texas to Missouri tussled in one of the country's strongest holiday meets, won the first two years by Oklahoma A&M. Not sure what to expect, the Longhorns blasted through their bracket, defeating Southeast Oklahoma, Westminster (of Missouri), Emporia State (Kansas), and tourney favorite Baylor before losing in the finals, 33-25, to Warrensburg (Missouri). The Mules' Al Shrik scored 16, while Moers led Texas with 14. Tate, who came down with the flu just before the tournament, played all five games and lost 18 pounds in the process.

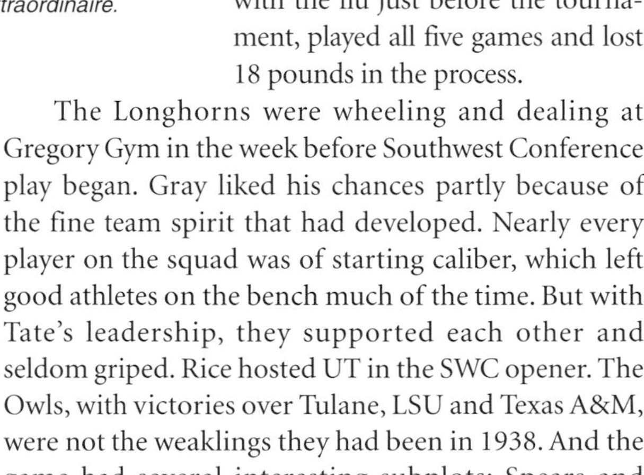

The Longhorns were wheeling and dealing at Gregory Gym in the week before Southwest Conference play began. Gray liked his chances partly because of the fine team spirit that had developed. Nearly every player on the squad was of starting caliber, which left good athletes on the bench much of the time. But with Tate's leadership, they supported each other and seldom griped. Rice hosted UT in the SWC opener. The Owls, with victories over Tulane, LSU and Texas A&M, were not the weaklings they had been in 1938. And the game had several interesting subplots: Spears and

Elmer Finley had been at Rice briefly; the Owls grabbed San Antonio star Bob Kinney when it looked like he would be wearing orange and white; and Rice's Frank Carswell, a boy-wonder shooter and ballhandler, was being touted in Houston as the equivalent of Bobby Moers. Buster Brannon's Owls hustled every minute and scored a startling 45-41 upset. Placido Gomez scored 12, and Levi Craddock and Ike Steakley got most of the rebounds that night in City Auditorium.

Record: 19-6
37 Liberty Pipeliners 27
57 SW Texas 31
45 SW Texas 31
36 Kansas 34
35 Kansas 49
41 SE Oklahoma 28
36 Westminster 24
34 Emporia 28
46 Baylor 38
25 Warrensburg 33
41 Rice 45
41 Arkansas 37
41 Arkansas 65
36 Baylor 31
47 St. Edward's 32
33 SMU 27
32 TCU 28
41 Texas A&M 37
38 SMU 21
41 Baylor 39
53 TCU 26
50 Rice 41
66 Texas A&M 32
41 Oregon 56
49 Utah State 51

Apart from Spears and Moers (who sustained a bruised hip), UT displayed an entirely inadequate defense against Rice. The bus trip back to Austin was shrouded in gloom, and the Horns licked their wounds in preparation for Arkansas. The Razorbacks, with John Adams and John Freiburger, were tall, talented and grim in their resolve to win the SWC again. Texas blew hot and cold during that series, winning the first, 41-37, and losing the second, 65-41. It was the last home conference game for a month, and everyone was asking, "What is wrong with the Longhorns?"

Smiling Jack Gray had a melancholy countenance and called the approaching game with Baylor a tossup, in spite of his team's earlier defeat of the Bears. There was a new gym on the Waco campus with a seating capacity of 3,700, and the fans that night saw a fast and rough game won by Texas, 36-31. Moers (13), with expert ballhandling and defense, showed Baylor sophomore Grady Vaughn (also being trumpeted as "the next Moers") a thing or two. During the exam period, UT defeated St. Edward's in a benefit game to fight infantile paralysis. Things were not going too well when Gray inserted a relative unknown, Denton Cooley. The skinny 6'4" sophomore announced his presence with authority, scoring 13 points. Although he would not start regularly until his senior year, Cooley contributed from then on.

As SMU coasted along with a 5-0 SWC record, Dallas sportswriters were beating the drum for the Mustangs, predicting an undefeated season. Gray complimented them, saying, "They're probably the most powerful team in the history of the school." And Whitey Baccus defied the time-honored coaches' custom of wailing to the four winds by announcing his Ponies would beat Texas on February 6. It was the eleventh meeting of Gray and Baccus, whether as players or coaches. Cooley entered a low-scoring game and lifted his team to a 33-27 victory before a capacity crowd in Dallas. Moers held J.D. Norton to a single field goal and directed an effective stall in the final minutes. A four-point defeat of TCU meant UT had won both games of its north Texas swing for just the second time in 15 years.

Before embarking for a game in College Station, Tate boasted, "We'll take those tin soldiers like Sherman took Georgia." It was not that easy. The Longhorns overcame 12 points by Bill "Big Dog" Dawson and a continual din by 3,000 Cadets to win, 41-37. Hull scored 14. Texas and SMU were tied for first place when the Mustangs came to Austin in an ugly mood, eager to vindicate themselves. Fan interest was unprecedented as business manager Ed Olle scrambled for ways to get more people into Gregory Gym. Thirty minutes before tipoff, the place was packed with 7,000 basketball fans. Wally Lawson, football player and president of the T Association, made a plea for good sportsmanship, and the crowd cooperated with a minimum of taunts at officials and the visitors in red and blue. They saw a smashing 38-21 Texas victory led by the inimitable Moers with 14 points. It was one of the best games of his flashy career. "Moers staged a one-man dribbling show probably never surpassed in the Southwest Conference, and his teammates furnished brilliant support," wrote Weldon Hart of the *Austin Statesman*.

With four games left on the schedule, all at home, the Steers were in good spirits. But there was no time to muse over that splendid defeat of SMU because second-place Baylor was next. Championship fever gripped the Forty Acres in February 1939. Huge crowds thronged Gregory Gym, and each successive victory got big headlines and adoring treatment from the *Daily Texan*. Bleachers on the gym's stage provided room for

500 more people to see the Horns and Bears. It was a dramatic game with the fans roaring and screaming, left in nervous exhaustion after UT's 41-39 victory. Moers and Granville combined for 22 points, and Grady Vaughn had 15 for Baylor in the bitter contest for SWC supremacy. Waco sportswriter Jinx Tucker vaguely intimated the officials were responsible for the Bears' defeat in Austin.

TCU, struggling through a miserable 2-17 season, would have loved nothing more than to bump off the high-flying Longhorns. A mere 5,500 people (considered a capacity crowd a year or two earlier) were in attendance for a 53-26 whipping of the Horned Frogs. Moers and Hull had 10 points apiece, and Cooley was the top rebounder. Demand continued to outstrip the supply of seats, but Olle and his student assistants found more room inside Gregory Gym when second-place Rice came to town. Somehow, 8,000 people squeezed in to see the Steers win, 50-41, and clinch a tie for the crown. Levi Craddock scored 15 for the plucked Owls, and Granville, Hull and Tate were in double figures for UT.

Just one more victory, against the Texas A&M Aggies (2-9 in the SWC), and another pennant could be hoisted at Gregory Gym. The Horns left no doubt, destroying their perennial antagonists, 66-32. Tate scored 20, and Moers played with customary abandon, thrilling the crowd of 7,000. Title-hungry fans crowded the court from all sides and gave the team a series of tremendous ovations. Even before the game, the Longhorns had been informed by SWC executive secretary Jim St. Clair of their selection to participate in the first NCAA Tournament. Tate and several teammates, unknown to Gray, had set an early-season goal of winning the SWC and getting into the tournament, and there they were. While it was nice to be in demand, they politely declined a spot in the two-year-old National Invitational Tournament in New York. Since they would be playing in San Francisco, the *Daily Texan* featured a front-page photo of Gray and the team, with this caption: "California, here we come."

Not so fast. There was an almost three-week delay between the SWC finale and their game against Oregon on March 21. Gray rested the team and tried to keep them fresh before the long westward train ride. The extra time allowed sportswriters and fans to assess the whirlwind 1939 season, in which more than 58,000 fans had crowded Gregory Gym for home games. The leadership of Tate, the dazzling play of Moers and the contributions of Spears, Hull, Granville, W.D. Houpt, Cooley and Finley were all noted, and any doubt about Gray's coaching was gone.

Thirteen players, Gray, trainer Milton Kelley and manager Albert Schwartz paraded out of a downtown store with 10-gallon hats and cowboy boots for the trip to San Francisco. A small crowd of well-wishers sang "The Eyes of Texas" at the train station as they departed. With stops in El Paso and Los Angeles, the trip took three days. The NCAA Tournament began in response to the artistic and financial success of the NIT. A small-college tournament in Kansas City had also begun in 1938. And the AAU had held a season-ending tournament in Denver for over a decade, but it was primarily for semipro teams. College basketball was still a regional affair with different styles of play—and sometimes different rules—in different parts of the country. Teams with the most intersectional experience were at a clear advantage, and Texas, with two games against Kansas and five at the All-College Tournament, was better off than some. Just eight teams were involved in a tournament that drew a total of 15,025 fans and lost $2,531. Oregon, Texas, Oklahoma and Utah State would play in San Francisco, and Ohio State, Wake Forest, Brown and Villanova met in Philadelphia. The two winners were to play for the first NCAA title in Evanston, Illinois.

The western regional games were played on a hastily arranged court at the Golden Gate International Exposition pavilion, most recently used as a bicycle track. UT had the bad luck to draw Oregon for a first-round opponent. Howard Hobson's Ducks (also known as the Webfoots) were tall and athletic, with a front line of 6'8" all-American Urgel Wintermute and two 6'4" forwards, John Dick and Laddie Gale. They had undergone trial by fire in an early-season barnstorming tour that included games in New York, Philadelphia, Buffalo, Cleveland, Detroit, Chicago and points west. The big Oregonians did not have much trouble with Texas. Moers tried to spark the team, but they were stale from the long delay and were simply overmatched. Wintermute scored 14 and Dick 13 in a 56-41 victory that saw Hull, Moers and Spears foul out. The Longhorns lost a close consolation game to Utah State and headed home. Salvaging their pride somewhat was the fact that the Ducks defeated Oklahoma and Ohio State on the way to the 1939 national championship.

1940

Most of the speed, cleverness and teamwork that carried UT to the 1939 Southwest Conference title was back. Except for Willie Tate, coach Jack Gray retained his key players: captain Oran Spears, Bobby Moers, Chester Granville, Slue Hull, W.D. Houpt, Elmer Finley and Denton Cooley. Sophomore Malcolm Kutner was one of a vanishing breed, an athlete who played both football and basketball. The enthusiasm of the Longhorns' championship season continued into 1940. While the opening game against a no-name school in earlier years drew little more than hard-core basketball fans and players' girlfriends, 4,000 people were at Gregory Gym to see Texas defeat Sam Houston, 57-37. Hull had the eagle eye that night, scoring 18 against the tall Bearkats.

The reserves got most of the playing time in an easy win over Southwest Texas in San Marcos, and even manager Bill Sansing was ready to go in when the gun sounded. Other than Finley (14), no Steer played very well. Professor Gray gave his students some hard work and a lecture or two about incautious long shots. While Tate was missed in the pivot position, Houpt and Cooley were capable. Houpt was bigger and more aggressive, but Cooley was a more polished player. Both were involved in a very successful season.

After two breathers, things were apt to be more difficult in a home series with Texas Tech. It was the first basketball meeting ever between the two schools. The Red Raiders, often called the Matadors, had been making gentle and persistent requests to join the SWC and would not gain admission for another two decades. Then playing in the Border Conference, coach Berl Huffman's team had eight lettermen back, including Marshall Brown. The Tech sports publicity office modestly referred to Brown as one of the greatest forwards in college basketball. But Spears stuck closer to Brown than an undersized collar in 20- and 11-point victories witnessed by a total of 10,000 fans.

Record: 18-5

57 Sam Houston 37
52 SW Texas 28
48 Texas Tech 28
41 Texas Tech 30
56 SW Texas 43
50 North Texas 29
57 North Texas 40
54 Manhattan 32
37 Temple 47
50 Rice 46
31 SMU 24
52 Arkansas 33
44 Arkansas 54
69 TCU 28
55 Liberty Pipeliners 33
60 Liberty Pipeliners 38
51 Baylor 47
42 SMU 45 (OT)
59 TCU 30
42 Texas A&M 31
60 Baylor 49
41 Rice 42
52 Texas A&M 53

Southwest Texas put up a bold front in Austin, losing by a score of 56-43. Houpt scored 19 and Hull 13, while Carter Lomax had 16 for the Cats. UT won a pair of home games against North Texas, running the early-season record to 7-0, but Gray knew his players had something besides the Eagles on their minds.

The 1939 All-College Tournament in Oklahoma City and the NCAA playoff games in San Francisco had whetted the Longhorns' appetite for travel and intersectional competition. Basketball impresario Ned Irish was having great success in staging doubleheaders at Madison Square Garden, New York's mecca of college hoops. The UT Athletic Council agreed to send the team there to meet Manhattan in the first part of a double bill that included Southern California and Long Island. While in the east, the Longhorns would stop in Philadelphia to play Temple.

Taking just one break for a workout at Butler University in Indianapolis, they rode the train northward. Gray's agile young men pulled into Grand Central Station, settled at the Hotel Picadilly, toured Gotham, saw a Broadway show and utterly destroyed the Manhattan Jaspers, 54-32, before 18,425 fans. That game, simultaneous with SMU's defeat of Loyola in Chicago, raised national esteem for Southwest Conference basketball nearly as much as UT beating Notre Dame and Rice beating Purdue on the same day in 1934 had done for SWC football. Houpt scored 17 and Moers 11 against the green-shirted Manhattan players. The sophisticated New York basketball fans were quite impressed with Texas' fast-break offense, and they were downright amazed by the ease and accuracy of the Longhorns' one-handed shooting. Popularized and taught by Gray since the early 1930s, this presented clear offensive advantages. While a few old-school coaches tried to resist, the evolving one-handed shot was gaining wide favor, as Texas' demonstration on the big stage made clear. The two-

Oran Spears displays the one-handed shot that so impressed the crowd of 18,000-plus at Madison Square Garden in Texas' 54-32 defeat of Manhattan.

handed set shot was far from dead, but its epitaph was being prepared.

The Horns' experience in Philadelphia was not so enjoyable. Temple, a better team than Manhattan (the Owls had won the NIT in 1938), took a 47-37 victory before 3,000 fans at Convention Hall. Center Don Henderson led Temple with 14 points, while Hull had 11 for Texas.

Upon arriving home after the long journey, UT had another bunch of Owls to prepare for. Rice, with Frank Carswell, Placido Gomez and soph star Bob Kinney, was on its way to a 25-4 season in which the Owls averaged nearly 60 points per game. Preseason prognosticators thought they would remove Texas from the SWC throne in 1940. The Owls played downtown at Sam Houston Coliseum, where 7,000 people (the biggest basketball crowd yet in Houston) gathered on January 6 to see the two conference big boys go toe-to-toe. Texas had not won in the Bayou City since 1934, but Spears rallied his forces and beat back a late Rice bid in a 50-46 victory.

The Longhorns returned to Austin justifiably happy and proud, in a good position to win their second straight conference championship and perhaps go further in the postseason. But Gray also needed to look to the future. The freshman teams of 1939 and 1940 would not provide much varsity material. When Gray lost Moers and Spears after the current season and Hull, Houpt, Granville and Cooley the next year, where would he be? This fearful near future could be traced primarily to a measly basketball budget. Kinney and other top young SWC players might have come to Austin if jobs were provided. Out-and-out athletic scholarships were still considered taboo at most schools, so in lieu of that, athletes worked on or off campus to cover their expenses. Some boosters took a humanitarian or philanthropic interest in star athletes, although this was more common in football than basketball. Much of it was sub rosa and the topic of contentious discussion by faculty, students and alumni. At any rate, UT was missing out on some fine basketball talent, and the cupboard might soon grow bare.

Gray's more immediate concern was a midweek game with SMU at Gregory Gym. He and Mustang coach Whitey Baccus were old friends (as was almost everyone with the genial Gray), but Baccus was ready to win. "It's been Texas upsetting SMU all along," he said. "Now the shoe is on the other foot, and I'd like to see how it fits." It did not fit well, at least not then. Before 7,500 fans, UT won a 31-24 defensive battle. Spears (nine) and Virgil "Country" Wilkerson (eight) were the leading scorers.

The Longhorns packed their bags and boarded an Arkansas-bound train. Granville rebounded, played good defense and scored 11 points in a 52-33 defeat of the rangy Razorbacks. A Texas sweep in Fayetteville had not occurred since 1924, and Glen Rose was not having any of it. His team, playing in a manner characteristic of the best that ever came out of the Ozarks, ended UT's 12-game conference win streak. John Adams and John Freiburger combined for 33 points in a 54-44 Arkansas victory as a capacity crowd of 1,500 gathered in the Hogs' two-year-old gym to see the tables turned. The *Daily Texan* reported 800 calls that night, asking for game results.

Frog filets were definitely on the Longhorns' menu on a snowy night in January. TCU, said to be much improved, with some good junior-college players, was buried, 69-28, before 6,500 fans. Moers (14) put on a great display of hustle, flash and marksmanship, well-nigh setting the Gregory Gym boards a-smoking. Gray liked to emphasize that his was a balanced team, and Moers never scored as many as 20 points, but he proved yet again his unique ability to win games and capture a crowd. Halftime of that contest featured Clyde Littlefield (recently recovered from a near-fatal bout with bronchial pneumonia) shooting a number of free throws to the delight of the crowd and football player Buddy Jungmichel doing an impromptu spin as a drum major.

Texas took two from the Liberty Pipeliners over the exam period. It was one of the last times the Steers would face a semipro team. The exam break gave sportswriters a chance to observe and pontificate on related issues. They commended the recent installation of new lights at Gregory Gym but bemoaned other things. A large "no smoking" sign was widely ignored, causing a sullen haze to float from the gallery down to the court. That situation was further complicated by the fact that Gray had recently turned to tobacco for consolation. Nevertheless, his father-in-law, former coach and athletic director L. Theo Bellmont, urged that the smoking ban be enforced. Second, the writers deplored the lack of glass backboards in Southwest Conference arenas. Fans who sat at each end of the court missed too much action behind a solid backboard, unnecessarily so. And finally, each of the gyms needed an electric clock operated by the timer. Some had no clock at all while Gregory Gym's old analog clock gave only an approximation of the remaining time. Gray, cool and calm as a player, was a nervous coach during a close game, repeatedly walking to the timer and inquiring how much time was left. Gray did, however, have the student manager keep detailed offensive and defensive charts for the Longhorns. The 28-year old maestro was one of the few coaches then to keep such a close statistical watch for each game and over the course of a season.

A huge crowd was expected when the Baylor Bears lumbered into town, and UT's field house was overflowing for the resumption of conference play. With Pete Creasey (all-SWC in 1939), slick guard Grady Vaughn and two fine new players, Frank Bryski and Joe Frivaldsky, the Bears were not to be trifled with. Moers, Texas' little big man, had a foot injury, and Houpt was battling ptomaine poisoning, but both played. UT won a 51-47 seesaw game that had 11 lead changes and was decided in the end by the Horns' conditioning. Moers (19) committed grand larceny on Baylor's ballhandlers and conjured tricks like Houdini. Houpt and Spears helped him turn the game in the late minutes.

Gray warned his SWC-leading team against overconfidence before the annual Dallas-Fort Worth trip. "We better snap out of it, or we'll get beat and beat bad," he said. While it was not bad, the Steers did lose a 45-42 overtime game in the frigid SMU gym. Five Mustangs went all the way. Forward Billy Sebeck's layup was the difference in a game that ended as fast and furious as the wildest-eyed fan could conceive. Sebeck was carried off the floor by members of the Mustang Band. The Longhorns took out their frustrations on TCU. Moers (15), Hull (13) and Granville (10) led a 59-30 vivisection of the poor Frogs, their 21st straight conference loss. "The small TCU gym was a little more than half filled for the game," said the *Austin Statesman*. "Local fans accustomed to seeing TCU beaten seemed to enjoy the Longhorns' splendid exhibition of passing, ballhandling and shooting. When Gray removed his regulars, a number of customers yelped in protest."

The loss to the Ponies stuck in UT's craw. On the bus ride home from Fort Worth, Granville stood up, glared at his teammates and asked, "What happened?" They expected to hear such pointed questions in Austin, but in the Hill Hall dining room, the Longhorn football team gave them 15 lusty cheers. The two-team (Rice and Texas) SWC race was speeding to a close. Both Gray's varsity and Ed Price's frosh beat Texas A&M in Austin, and the Horns won a bitter, grueling game against Baylor, 60-49. Some 4,000 fans filled McLean Gymnasium as Granville, Hull, Houpt and Moers kept Texas hot on the trail of another title. More than sheer talent, the will to win had driven them in 1939, and they still had it.

The Owl-Longhorn matchup in Gregory Gym on February 28 had everything: two outstanding teams, two fine young coaches in Gray and Buster Brannon, star players and a vocal crowd estimated to exceed 8,000. It was also the final home game for Moers, one of the most colorful and remarkable athletes in UT history. Supremely confident, no one loved the roar of the fans more than he. Twice all-conference in basketball and baseball, Moers also caught a touchdown pass during the 1938 football season. There was so much pressure and excitement inside the brick walls of Gregory Gym that night, even Moers was nervous and conservative at first. Rice, profiting from a wide disparity in free throws, won, 42-41, and the great gray Owl roosted high atop his SWC perch. The leading scorers were Moers (16) and Bob Kinney (15).

It seemed that the entire UT campus was heartsick about it, and that feeling was just exacerbated by a 53-52 loss to the Aggies in College Station. Substitute center Charlie Stevenson hit a long running shot with two seconds left to give Texas an inglorious exit amid questions of what might have been. Rice represented the Southwest Conference in the NCAA tourney, but for the Horns, an expected bid from the NIT or AAU never came.

1941

Once Bounding Bobby Moers departed, Texas basketball fans may have thought it would never be the same. The pulsating excitement of the past two seasons in which 37 games were won and just 11 lost, the overflow crowds at Gregory Gym and the Southwest Conference title runs—all these combined factors subsided a bit in 1941, basketball's jubilee season. Jack Gray's fifth Longhorn team (with captain Chester Granville, W.D. Houpt, Slue Hull and Denton Cooley) had enough T sweaters to make a good-sized tent. Malcolm Kutner and Udell Moore were back, and three strong players (6'5" Les "Pie" Sander, longshot artist Les Croucher and Tommy Nelms, a letterman in 1938 and 1939) would become eligible on February 1.

Other than Houpt, who had an injured ankle, the team looked good in early workouts. Cooley, bigger and more aggressive than before, showed an ability and willingness to mix it up underneath. The East Texas Lions, champions of the Lone Star Conference, were supposed to be double-tough. If so, they did not show it in the Gregory Gym curtain-raiser on December 6. Cooley (16) led the scoring parade in a 55-34 victory that was quite sharp for so early in the season. With just one game under their collective belt, the Longhorns entrained for Lawrence, Kansas. Phog Allen's Jayhawks had finished second in the 1940 NCAA Tournament and planned to keep their 21-game home win streak intact. Texas led by four at the half, but Kansas shifted to a more offensive strategy and surged ahead with the expert shooting of Howard Engleman (18) and Robert Allen (13) to win, 35-27. The Jayhawks won again the next night, but it was not easy. With 21 points from Granville, UT tied the game with two minutes left. Allen's free throw and Engleman's field goal gave Kansas a 48-45 victory.

Three games in three nights with two midwest powers, that was what Gray had scheduled. Oklahoma A&M, coached by Hank Iba, had won its last 46 games in Stillwater. UT put up a terrific battle before succumbing, 48-42. L.J. Eggleston scored 16 for

Record: 15-10

55 East Texas 34
27 Kansas 35
45 Kansas 48
42 Oklahoma A&M 48
52 SW Texas 36
30 Texas Tech 28
40 Texas Tech 44
49 SW Texas 39
43 Springfield 42
34 East Central Oklahoma 30
43 West Texas 40
38 Pittsburg State 39
48 Rice 37
38 Arkansas 50
34 Arkansas 44
35 SMU 39
43 TCU 39
60 Carr-Sweeney 41
58 TCU 39
45 Baylor 44
48 Baylor 52
42 SMU 36
42 Texas A&M 22
64 Rice 73
53 Texas A&M 36

the Aggies, and Houpt had 14 for the orange-clad visitors. Gray hated to lose, but he was pleased with his team's performance against Kansas and Oklahoma A&M. Even so, he took the players from the Austin train station directly to the gym for a two-hour workout.

The Longhorns were somewhat ragged in beating Southwest Texas, 52-36, before a small gathering. Texas Tech, a well-drilled, dangerous and unbeaten team, split a series in Austin. In the first game, left-handed J.B. "Whizzer" White scored 11 for the Raiders, but some fine shooting by Moore and two late free throws by Cooley pulled out a 30-28 victory. Tech won the next night behind 11 points from Byron Gilbreath.

Denton Cooley, Longhorn forward and center, 1939 to 1941.

Granville, known variously as "Trapper" and "One-Man Gang," played unevenly in the early part of 1941. He scored just two field goals in two games with Texas Tech and followed that with 23 points in a defeat of Southwest Texas in San Marcos. Before returning to Oklahoma for the All-College Tournament, Gray looked over his team and realized it would survive without Moers. Since no one picked the Steers to win the tournament (which included TCU, Baylor and Texas A&M) or the SWC, the pressure was off. They drew Springfield (Missouri) in the first round and appeared to have the game in hand, but the Teachers started a booming rally and took a three-point lead. While Hull (14) was the leading scorer, it was Granville and Cooley who won the game, 43-42, for Texas. East Central Oklahoma and West Texas were defeated by close margins, putting the Longhorns in the tournament finals against Pittsburg State of Kansas. UT built a 30-17 halftime lead but scored just eight points from then on to lose a shocker, 39-38, when Harvey King stole the ball and raced downcourt for a layup. Texas would play in the All-College Tournament many times in future years, but the trophy was never brought to Austin. There would not be a better opportunity than in 1941.

The loquacious Kutner started in place of Cooley in the SWC opener against Rice. Cooley, recovering from a cold and a bruised heel, later fought off Kutner's challenge for the starting job. Although Placido Gomez was out with an injury, the SWC-champ Owls looked formidable. Frank Carswell was back, and Bob Kinney had a new 6'6" teammate, Bill Tom Closs. The biggest crowd of the year, 7,200, congregated at Gregory Gym to see if Texas could avenge the bitter one-point defeat of a year earlier. The star of the game was Kutner, who scored 12 (as did his teammate Granville and Kinney of Rice) in a 48-37 upset. Not known as a finesse player, Kutner was all over the floor that night. In another novelty instituted by Gray, a small camera high in the rafters of Gregory Gym filmed the game.

The Horns went from one tough SWC contest to another. Arkansas came to Austin a few days later and swept Texas, 50-38 and 44-34, before crowds of about 7,000. As *Daily Texan* sports editor (and former student manager) Bill Sansing stated, "If John Adams is hot, it's Katy-bar-the-door because you haven't got a chance in 10." Adams was sizzling, but he had help from John Freiburger, Gordon Carpenter, Howard "Red" Hickey and Clayton Wynne. Averaging 6'5", they all wore numbers in the 70s. Glen Rose would later call the 1941 Razorbacks his greatest team; they went undefeated in the SWC, had a 20-3 season record and advanced to the second round of the NCAA Tournament. UT fans, upset over seeing their team get taken to the woodshed twice, received no merit badges from Emily Post, hissing, booing and throwing coins. But Adams and his teammates were utterly unaffected.

In Dallas, SMU got 19 of its 39 points on free throws in edging Texas as Virgil Wilkerson (15) led all scorers. Already spectators in the SWC race, the Longhorns found relief in Fort Worth. Just barely, though. Robert "Ghost" Groseclose and Leonard Cannady pulled TCU to within spitting distance of victory. Six players fouled out in UT's 43-39 victory paced by Hull (11).

With Sander, Croucher and Nelms finally available, Texas met a noncollegiate team, Carr-Sweeney, in

Gregory Gym for the annual polio fundraiser. It was a triple-header, beginning with a women's game (between Taylor's Green Devils and Sammie's), a high school game (Austin versus Waco) and the main event. Nearly 3,000 fans showed up because Bobby Moers was on the Carr-Sweeney squad, and they wanted to relive the great memories he had given them. Cooley scored 14 and Nelms 12 in UT's 60-41 victory. Moers had 13.

Hull, who had started almost every game since 1939, had an ankle injury and was not in the lineup against TCU. The team went out with a burst of speed and ran the Horned Frogs into submission, 58-39. Nelms, Hull's replacement, scored 11. The prelim game featured the Yearlings, led by John Hargis, and Tyler Junior College, led by V.C. "Buck" Overall; both Hargis and Overall had a future with the UT varsity.

The Longhorns went into Waco carrying hopes for second place in the SWC, but the Bears had similar notions. It was a typical slam-bang Texas-Baylor game with a garrison finish played as if the title were on the line. Cooley, a renowned pressure player, scored 14 in the 45-44 win, UT's sixth in a row over the Bruins. That streak came to an end a week later when Baylor took a wild and wooly 52-48 game in Austin. Grady Vaughn and poker-faced Frank Bryski boosted their team to victory, and Moore had 13 for the losing Steers. "Those very, very nasty Methodists are back in town," Sansing wrote in anticipation of the UT-SMU brouhaha. Basketball relations had been heated between the two schools for four years, and that game did nothing to cool them down. Texas won a rough game, 42-36, punctuated by a near riot when Moore and SMU's Grover Keeton piled into a backstop at the end of a fast break. Houpt played his best game of the year, scoring nine straight points early in the second half.

Texas A&M was gunning for the Longhorns. The February 27 game at Aggieland had been sold out for a week, perhaps because of the big football game in Memorial Stadium the previous fall. Kutner, one of the "Immortal 13" who beat the Ags, helped beat them in basketball, too. The khaki-shorted fans had scarcely begun to taunt and heckle before the Longhorns jumped to a 17-1 lead. Cooley defended and rebounded in fine fashion, Granville held high-scoring Bill "Jitterbug" Henderson to four points, Hull had 19, and Gray got his team out of College Station with a 42-22 win. They went straight to Houston and engaged the Owls for second place in the conference. Before 4,500 loud fans, the two teams singed the nets in a scoring duel won by Rice, 73-64. Seven players reached double figures, led by Frank Carswell with 19.

The weary Longhorns came home for the finale against Texas A&M. Granville scored 19 and Hull 13, trailing the Aggies' Bill Henderson (20) in what the *Austin Statesman* called "a loosely played, sometimes weird game." With that 53-36 victory, the Steers closed the season at 15-10. Not an all-SWC player among them, they came in behind Arkansas and Rice. Denton Cooley, who began as a skinny 16-year old freshman walk-on in 1938, earned three varsity letters and was Gray's workhorse in 1941. After completing medical school at Johns Hopkins University, he went on to become one of the premier cardiovascular surgeons in the world and helped found the Texas Heart Institute in Houston.

1942

Three days before UT's season began, the Japanese bombed Pearl Harbor, leading to full American involvement in World War II. A number of Longhorn players and even their coach would soon be called away to duties more pressing than the Southwest Conference basketball campaign. In the meantime, Jack Gray's brave lads were expected to fight a losing battle with the Fayetteville-Houston axis.

It was a woefully inexperienced team. Les Sander, Les Croucher and Malcolm Kutner were the only lettermen, and none had been a regular in 1941. And then there were the newcomers. Guard Lavoice Scudday, while short and slow, was a poised ballplayer. John Hargis (a talented leaper but indifferent on defense) and Otis Ritchey were 6'3" forwards. Squadman Frank "Big Chief" Brahaney and soph Dudley Wright brought hustle and polish, respectively, to the team. Kutner, an all-America football player, did not join the basketball squad until the fifth conference game. From this group, Gray pieced together a lineup to meet Southwest Texas in a home-and-home series beginning

Record: 14-9
55 SW Texas 30
50 SW Texas 36
36 SE Oklahoma 30
28 SE Oklahoma 25
61 Texas Tech 34
47 Texas Tech 36
49 Oklahoma City 32
55 Texas Tech 45
38 Oklahoma A&M 46
41 Pittsburg State 46
38 Rice 62
46 Texas A&M 32
32 SMU 31
31 TCU 33
58 Baylor 38
63 Sam Houston 48
46 TCU 57
60 SMU 43
34 Baylor 55
34 Arkansas 42
58 Arkansas 37
41 Rice 61
42 Texas A&M 46

on December 10. It looked like a hard winter for the Longhorns, but they got off to a good start, beating the Bobcats twice. Southeast Oklahoma, fresh off a split with Arkansas, lost two in Austin, 36-30 and 28-25. Scudday (11) and Sander (nine) led the Steers in those games. The second, played before 1,500 fans, was a rowdy event with tempers flaring constantly. "The Teachers used the primitive defensive strategy of pouncing upon the ballhandler and shoving him off the court," said the *Austin Statesman*. "The Longhorns, for self-preservation, had to join in this dizzy game of give and take."

Gray was happy. His 4-0 team, while wanting in the fundamentals of height, speed and shooting, had applied the lessons he prescribed. That little winning streak looked ripe for breaking as Texas Tech invaded Gregory Gym for two games. The Red Raiders' high-scoring trio of Elvis Erwin, Byron Gilbreath and Gabe Gilley were veterans of a 19-6 season in 1941. But Gray confounded Tech with a zone defense that stymied their clever block-out plays. Hargis (18) and Sander (16) played well, and the Horns triumphed, 61-34. It was closer the next night, but UT won again.

Weldon Hart of the *Austin Statesman* and Bill Whitmore of the *Daily Texan* finally called attention to a matter that did not begin with the 1942 Steer-Matador series: the wild boys of Gregory Gym, uninvited and unauthorized guests who regularly performed minor mischief. When disgruntled fans threw coins on the court, a horde of youths would pounce on them. The resultant mixups were amusing to some and appalling to others, especially because of the dirt and grime brought on the court. Hart and Whitmore implored the authorities to stop it, but these goings-on continued for years. There were no such problems at the All-College Tournament. Sander scored 16 in a 49-32 defeat of Oklahoma City. In the next round, the Longhorns met Texas Tech for the third time in eight days and won again, 55-45, with Scudday, Sander and Brahaney in double figures. Red Raider coach Berl Huffman, whose sideline antics always drew interest, was in fine form that day. Irked once by an official's call, he jumped to his feet, knocking over one of his players and then falling on a photographer. Lonnie Eggleston scored 20 in a 46-38 Oklahoma A&M victory, and Pittsburg State won by five, sending the Longhorns home. Another team competing in Oklahoma City was West Texas, with all-America forward Price Brookfield. Gray wistfully remembered how, four years earlier, that same Brookfield had ridden a freight car to Austin to meet Gray, asking for a job and a chance to play college basketball. The UT coach, perhaps unconvinced of the young man's potential, said he could not help, a decision he came to rue.

SWC play got underway on January 7 when Texas took on the high and haughty Rice Owls. Unbeaten in nine games, they had crushed Fordham at Madison Square Garden and LaSalle in Philadelphia. A crowd of 4,300 at Sam Houston Coliseum saw Rice blitz the Steers, 62-38, in an amazing display of speed, shooting and teamwork. Bob Kinney, a member of that year's all-America team with Brookfield, scored 23 for the Owls, and Sander held his own with 15.

Little note was taken of the return of Marty Karow to Gregory Gym. The former Longhorn coach, after two years at the Naval Academy, had been hired to run the Texas A&M baseball program in 1938, and he added the basketball job in 1942. Apart from Bill Henderson, the Ags did not have much of a team, and the Horns put the wood to them, 46-32.

After a three-hour workout, Gray and Ed Price left for Dallas a day before the team, to scout the SMU-Baylor game. On the way up, the two coaches discussed impending changes because Scudday, Ritchey and Croucher would soon turn in their orange-and-white uniforms for olive drab. Of course, virtually every other school was contending with the same thing. Texas defeated SMU, 32-31, in a seesaw tilt before 1,000 partisan Pony fans. The Longhorns, trailing by five at the half, were happy to see good-luck waterboy Billy "Rooster" Andrews (who had hitchhiked from Austin to Dallas) stroll into the locker room.

In Fort Worth, they learned that TCU's long stint as SWC doormat was over. Coach Hub McQuillan had recruited some junior-college hotshots from the midwest, ruffling feathers among certain of his fellow conference coaches who thought it was somehow unfair to seek players from outside of Texas. Bob McHenry and Max Humphries led the Horned Frogs to a two-point win in TCU's crackerbox gym that had the fans roaring to the very last. Although five players fouled out, some observers believed rough play common to other regions was being allowed and by abandoning rule-book strictness, the prestige and quality of SWC play might rise. But that was wishful thinking because tight officiating would remain a hallmark of conference basketball for decades to come.

Baylor, with its classy little guard, Dwight Parks, came to Austin with a 3-0 SWC record. The Bears left with a 3-1 record. It was a convincing 58-38 victory for UT, with Hargis (21) showing star potential. Croucher had 12 points, Scudday eight and Ritchey two in their swan-song game. Gray used the two-week exam period to remodel his team. To compound matters, Dudley Wright, expected to move into the starting lineup, had become academically ineligible. But it was not so hopeless; Sander, Hargis and Brahaney were playing well, and Kutner was finally available. Gray found another player in slender Curtis Popham, the former drum major of the Longhorn Band. The 1942 season was played out with a fair team very short on reserves. Gray tested them on February 6 against Sam Houston, beating the Bearkats, 63-48. Hargis (29) and Sander (17) were at their offensive best. That game, part of an annual benefit, raised $135, split between funds for infantile paralysis and Red Cross war relief.

Jack Gray and his starting five in early 1942: Les Croucher, Otis Ritchey, Frank Brahaney, Les Sander and John Hargis.

Reopening league play in Austin, TCU proved itself for real with a 57-46 victory. Brahaney (13) carried the load for Texas, but Bob McHenry, Max Humphries and Floppy Blackmon scored and controlled the backboards throughout the game. Hargis, who played poorly against the Frogs, made up for it in a 60-43 defeat of SMU, scoring 19. He had help from Kutner (14) and Brahaney (12). About 3,000 fans were there, slightly below average for a 1942 SWC game at Gregory Gym. Memories of the Bobby Moers era, with the gym packed for nearly every game, lingered. People realized what a rare entity Moers had been, and anyway, the team was not as good, and a war was going on.

In Waco, 2,500 fans razzed Kutner about Baylor's surprising 7-7 tie with the football Longhorns. The Bears unleashed some offensive power, jumping to a 12-point halftime lead and cruising to victory. Dwight Parks and Mark Belew combined for 31 points in a roughhouse game in which Sander fouled out early. Kutner got more attention from the fans in Fayetteville, but they ended up singing his praises because he was UT's leading scorer both nights. The Hogs won the first game, 42-34, behind 15 points from O'Neal Adams (the third of five brothers who played for Arkansas from the mid-1920s through the early 1950s). Evidently on their way to another undisputed SWC title, the Razorbacks were stunned by a 58-37 Texas victory. Kutner got most of his 14 points on fast breaks, using his speed to leave Arkansas players flat-footed.

SWC coleader Rice showed little appreciation for that upset, rolling over the Horns, 61-41. Bob Kinney, whom Gray called one of the conference's best ever, scored 18, and guard Chet Palmer had 17. The season ended in College Station, where Ag captain Bill Henderson predicted victory and got it. He scored 22 points, to the great pleasure of 4,000 leather-lunged Cadets. The final minutes were hectic, but Texas A&M held on for a 46-42 win.

The University of Texas got a lot of mileage out of Malcolm Kutner, who earned six letters in football and basketball. After World War II military service, he played five years with the Chicago Cardinals of the National Football League, twice making all-pro. His coach, Jack Gray, received notification of his acceptance in the Navy in mid-April. Initially serving as a physical training instructor in Corpus Christi, Gray was later shifted to more dangerous duty aboard an aircraft carrier in the Pacific Ocean.

1943

The nation was certainly on a wartime footing by 1943. Many schools considered suspending their athletic programs, and a few did. Texas AD Dana X. Bible insisted that would not happen in Austin, but several players and coaches were already participating in a life-and-death struggle overseas. Just as with football, many college basketball teams experienced sharp declines during World War II. And some, because of military personnel on campus, had a bonanza. The 1943 Longhorn basketball season was fraught with embarrassing possibilities. Jack Gray was in the Navy, as was his assistant, Ed Price. For the duration of the war (a term used often then), Howard "Bully" Gilstrap would coach the team. That was in addition to helping with football and track, his duties since returning to UT in 1937. A member of the basketball team in 1922 and 1923, he had coached the sport at Schreiner College. Gilstrap, hearty, loud-spoken and self-effacing, was not prepared for a three-year stint as Texas' basketball coach. To compound matters, the Longhorn football team would be playing Georgia Tech in the Cotton Bowl, and his attention there was required.

Three 1942 starters (Les Sander, Otis Ritchey and Lavoice Scudday) were in the service, and two players who were expected to contribute (6'7" John Langdon and Dudley Wright) did not make the academic grade but would gain eligibility on February 1. While Gray and Price offered encouragement and advice from afar, Gilstrap's eight-man team was on its own. Of the starters, four had played in 1942—guards Frank Brahaney and Curtis Popham, center John Hargis and forward Jack Fitzgerald. The main newcomer was Buck Overall, an all-American from Tyler Junior College who had worn out the Yearlings the past two seasons.

The opener, against Southwest Texas on December 4, would be the last home game for a month. A lackadaisical crowd of less than 1,000 saw a 47-27 UT victory. Gilstrap stayed behind while the team embarked on a six-game tour of south Texas. In his place, as substitute-substitute coach, was Clyde Littlefield, who began his great basketball career on the wild outdoors of Clark Field three decades earlier and most recently coached frosh hoops in the mid-1920s. He won five of those six games: 56-47 over Southwest Texas (Hargis scored 24), 45-33 over the Kelly Field Flyers, 41-27 over the San Antonio Aviation Cadet Center and 58-36 and 46-42 over the Randolph Field Flyers. The lone defeat was by five points to Corpus Christi Naval Air Station, coached by Lt. (J.G.) Jack Gray. That team, with former collegians like Bob Kinney of Rice and Bill Dewell of SMU and future Texas star Al Madsen, would go 23-0 in 1943 and be called the finest service team in the country.

UT's participation in the seventh annual All-College Tournament was in doubt for a while due to travel restrictions. Sixteen teams, rather than the usual 32, were playing, and the Horns were among them. Gilstrap, helping with Cotton Bowl preparations, rejoined the team when the train came through Dallas on the way to Oklahoma City. Hargis, Fitzgerald and Overall were in double figures in a 55-51 defeat of East Central Oklahoma. The Steers upset Oklahoma A&M but lost to Arkansas by 22 and concluded with a 38-32 win over Maryville (of Missouri) for third place.

TCU, which beat Arkansas in the tourney finals, had the role of SWC favorite, and Frog coach Hub McQuillan all but guaranteed a championship. The surprising Longhorns lacked height, at least until Langdon could play, and were seen as dark horses in early January. Rice, with 6'6" star Bill Tom Closs averaging 17 points per game, got a shock before 5,000 fans at Gregory Gym. Hargis scored 19 and Overall 16 in a 55-36 defeat of the Owls. Hargis proved he could play defense when the mood struck, holding Closs without a basket. If not for the long-range bombing of Willie Croucher (brother of former Longhorn Les Croucher) and Harold Lambert, it would have been worse for Rice.

In practice the day before the team left for Waco to play Baylor, Hargis collided head-on with substitute Lloyd Gregory, Jr. Both had severe gashes on their heads but made the trip anyway. Hargis seemed fine, scoring 21 in a 41-34 defeat of the Bears. Quite a few fans and even sportswriters were premature in saying the 1943 SWC race had a deep orange hue. But the Longhorns encouraged that sort of talk with a wild, scrambling 41-37 defeat of SMU. The Mustangs' big Tommy Tomlinson led all scorers with 15, but UT caught and passed them in the final minutes.

"I love the Aggies," Gilstrap declared on the way to College Station. "They treat you fine. We can stand plenty of noise." The Longhorns risked their 3-0 SWC record against Texas A&M, with 6'8" Jamie Dawson and stocky fireball Mike Cokinos. It was a rough game with 35 fouls called. The Ags closed a large gap at the end but fell nine points short. Overall, half of UT's double-barreled offense along with Hargis, scored 14, while Popham, who combined music and basketball, had 11.

The Longhorn Band gave Popham a big cheer before the game with TCU on January 19. It was an interesting contrast in style; the Steers played rather hastily and shot when they liked, but the Frogs were determined to run set plays. More than 6,000 fans showed up on a frozen evening in Austin, and they saw some nice man-to-man defense and a combined 25 points from Overall and Fitzgerald that easily beat TCU. Gilstrap commended the crowd for its support, and the old Bully-boy's coaching was finally earning praise as his team had won 13 games and lost just three. How was it happening?

"Cooperation," he said. "The finest all-around cooperation I ever saw. Jack [Gray] and Ed [Price] have helped me all they could. There were a lot of things I didn't know about the system, and the boys realized that. They came to the rescue. They've been assistant coaches as well as players. We've just been trying to work it out together."

It was a homecoming of sorts for Gray, who brought his Corpus Christi Comets to Austin for the annual charity game. He looked around Gregory Gym and remarked on its immensity and the number of nonbasketball lines painted on the floor. A big crowd turned out to see his servicemen thoroughly outclass the Longhorns in a game that degenerated into a rooster fight. Langdon and Wright were finally available, plus 5'9" freshman guard Roy Cox. The next fortnight in the compressed 1943 season would determine whether Texas was for real or not. In a high school gym in Houston, the Rice Owls made up for that earlier defeat, putting it on the Horns, 50-39. Skinny freshman forward David Cook scored 14 and Bill Tom Closs had 11 for the victory-hungry Owls. UT's comeback never got started as many long shots refused to fall.

Despite the loss, business manager Ed Olle and his assistant, Alice Archer, had to find and dust off the standing-room-only signs that got so much use during the Moers era. Arkansas and Texas were tied for the Southwest Conference lead, and the Gregory Gym boo-birds were always ready for the Hogs' Clayton Wynne, raucously hooting his every move. UT assumed undisputed possession of the lead with a 45-31 win as Overall took charge with 17 second-half points. The second game, dedicated to the hundreds of male students, including Popham, then being called up by the Army Air Force, was a 48-35 Texas victory in which Hargis (22) was superb. With 10 minutes left, Popham smashed into the Razorbacks' Jesse Wilson, who remained on the floor. While coaches and team doctors rushed to his side, several of Wilson's teammates seized Popham, which brought some Hill Hall residents—the Longhorn football team—onto the floor. The referees and police officers needed three minutes to clear it up before the game could continue.

Gilstrap took his players to north Texas, undoubtedly telling stories about the many times favored UT teams had been ambushed in Fort Worth or Dallas or both. It was rumored that TCU's recent poor showing derived from a squabble between Bob McHenry and Max Humphreys when the former won the MVP trophy in Oklahoma City. But the Horned Frogs seemed to get along well enough in a 49-44 overtime win. McHenry (15) tied the game with 15 seconds left in regulation, and his team scored five points and blanked the overeager Steers in the extra period. Hargis scored 17 and Overall 11, but they missed Popham's steady hand at the end. The next night in Dallas, forward Ben Harris

Record: 19-7

47 SW Texas 27
56 SW Texas 47
45 Kelly Field 33
41 San Antonio Cadet Center 27
58 Randolph Field 36
46 Randolph Field 42
50 Corpus Christi Air Station 55
55 East Central Oklahoma 51
45 Oklahoma A&M 36
44 Arkansas 66
38 Maryville 32
55 Rice 36
41 Baylor 34
41 SMU 37
54 Texas A&M 45
47 TCU 30
35 Corpus Christi Air Station 45
39 Rice 50
45 Arkansas 31
48 Arkansas 35
44 TCU 49 (OT)
56 SMU 65
51 Baylor 38
57 Texas A&M 55
59 Washington 55
54 Wyoming 58

had 20 points in a 65-56 defeat of Texas, sending the Horns back into a first-place tie with Rice. It was another rough game with 44 fouls called and two players (Brahaney of Texas and Rusty Baccus of SMU) ejected for fighting.

Where it once appeared the Steers had a firm grip on the SWC flag, they had to win the last two games just to share it with Rice. Back at home, bruised and disappointed, they met Baylor on February 27. The Bears, as slick as a wartime tire, took an early lead, but Overall (19), Hargis (12) and Brahaney (11) were hot, playing some of the prettiest Texas basketball since 1939 in a 51-38 victory. Weldon Hart of the *Austin Statesman* was convinced Overall was the best player in the SWC. The junior-college ex put on a show against Baylor with several sensational shots and impressive dribbling, passing and defense. He had stepped onto the UT varsity without an indoctrination period and took half a season to hit his stride, but he gathered momentum quickly. "Bucko is an all-court performer without equal," Hart wrote. "He does it all in a manner to justify Jack Gray's enthusiasm for him at Tyler Junior College. One of Gray's last official acts, before departing for the Navy, was to commit Overall to the Longhorn cause."

Frank "Big Chief" Brahaney puts up a shot during the Horns' surprising 1943 season.

The last home game of the season was against Texas A&M, coached in Marty Karow's absence by Manning Smith. It was a hectic, furious 57-55 UT win that earned an SWC cochampionship. Hargis scored 22 and Overall 17, while the Aggies were led by Jamie Dawson and Les Peden with 17 each. Gregory Gym fans contested officials' calls all night and tossed pennies when Brahaney and Mike Cokinos jousted too vigorously and got the boot. The game caused Dave Tipton, *Daily Texan* writer, to wax poetic: "There was blood on the moon, dear brother/There was hate in the hearts of men/Those Aggies from A&M/Visited Gregory Gym last night again."

A three-game playoff between Texas and Rice was rendered moot by the Owls' decision to play in the NIT; they lost the first game in overtime to St. John's. The Longhorns, after a three-week hiatus, would play in the NCAA western regionals in Kansas City. Although his team drew Washington, a tournament cofavorite (with Wyoming), Gilstrap was optimistic. "We'll have a chance," he said as the team departed. "We're not just going for the trip. We'll do everything we can to win." Before 8,000 fans at Municipal Auditorium, the Huskies jumped to a 13-point lead, but Texas came back. Hargis (30) was magnificent, and Overall (15) just slightly less so, but the real hero was little-used guard Roy Cox. Gilstrap put him in when a fourth Longhorn fouled out, and he coolly hit three baskets in the final minutes. Bill Morris scored 22 for Washington, which lost, 59-55.

Unlikely as it seemed, Texas was two victories away from the 1943 national title. If mighty Washington could be beaten, why not Wyoming? Since the western regional was considered much tougher than the east, that was the game. Beat the Cowboys (with player of the year Kenny Sailors and star center Milo Komenich), and the Georgetown Hoyas would be easy pickings at Madison Square Garden. It looked like that might happen early on. Hargis was again unstoppable, scoring 17 of the Horns' first 26 points as they took a 13-point lead. But Everett Shelton's bigger and stronger Cowboys had too much power for Texas, winning by a score of 58-54. Hargis (29) set a two-game tournament scoring record, and Overall had 14. Gilstrap made a serious error by not giving enough playing time to Cox, the slight freshman who could really play the game. Komenich scored 17, Jim Weir 13 and Sailors 12 for Wyoming, which went on to win the national championship.

1944

Bully Gilstrap lost nearly all of his team to graduation or the service. A collapsed lung ended the short and bright UT career of Buck Overall, who served as Gilstrap's assistant during the 1944 season. The only returnee, and thus captain, was sophomore guard Roy Cox, who had not played enough the previous year to earn a letter. College athletics, which provided desirable benefits to the civilian and military population, nevertheless suffered a further decline in quality. While American-led forces had gained the upper hand in World War II, there were another 18 months of horrific bloodshed to go. Page after page of the *Cactus* listed UT students and alumni fighting in the war and the inevitable casualties. In 1944, Gilstrap learned of seven former players—Bob Butler, Lavoice Scudday, Chester Granville, Henry Chovanec, Ned Sweeney, Warren Wiggins and Curtis Popham—who made the supreme sacrifice.

Because of the war, however, Cox got some fine new teammates. The Navy's V-12 program brought three Californians to Austin, Jeff Kemp, Joe Crowley and Al Martin. The 1944 Longhorns would be short. Kemp and freshmen Doug Stewart and Bob Summers barely topped 6'. There was one more addition, Slater "Dugan" Martin, who would come to eclipse all the others combined. Twice all-state at Jeff Davis High School in Houston, the 5'9" Martin was a basketball buzzsaw, a tireless hustler and ballhawk with quickness unlike anything seen at Gregory Gym. Even Bobby Moers would have been run ragged by Martin. It was another Houstonian, of an earlier vintage, who got Martin to the Forty Acres. Holly Brock, the star of the late 1920s, remained an enthusiastic booster of Texas athletics, and he urged Martin to become a Longhorn.

The season began at home on November 30 against Childress Army Air Field, coached by Lt. Lewis "Bullet" Gray of UT football fame. His team, with athletes from Ohio State, Princeton, SMU and Alabama, was bigger and older than the Steers. In contrast, wrote Morris Williams of the *Austin Statesman*, "Bully Gilstrap surrounded himself with a starting lineup that looked somewhat like a scrawny little prep outfit from deep in the heart of Texas." Yet Cox (19), Kemp (12) and Martin (10) led UT to a fast-paced 57-31 victory.

Kelly Army Air Field, 7-0 before visiting Gregory Gym, lost a double-overtime thriller that almost ended prematurely due to a free-for-all involving players and fans. Lt. Chris Hansen, a husky ex-Bradley star, scored 22 points despite razzing from the fans, which he seemed to encourage. But something caused him to snap, and suddenly he and UT football player Harlan Wetz were exchanging punches as a small mob surrounded them. Ten minutes were required to restore order, and the game was completed. Following that incident, *Daily Texan* sports editor Paul Tracy made yet another call to cut out the monkey business of football players as strongmen and fans throwing pennies and watching urchins scramble after them.

A two-day invasion of San Antonio Army camps produced victories over the Aviation Cadet Center and Randolph Field. The Chase Army Air Field Flyers came to Austin, coached by an old UT nemesis, Bubba Gernand, reputed to have once beaten the Horns with a late basket from the Colorado River bridge. He talked it and backed it up, a quality shared by one of his players, Al Madsen, soon to wear orange and white. Before a small, howling bunch of cage addicts, the Flyers won by two points. Although Cox scored 21, Martin may have been the dominant player on the floor. That was the first of five straight defeats attributable, in part, to the absence of the three Californians, gone home for the holidays. Southwestern, Kelly Army Air Field, Chase (again) and Corpus Christi Naval Air Station beat Texas at their respective gyms.

Record: 14-11

57 Childress Field 31
45 Kelly Field 42 (2 OT's)
44 San Antonio Cadet Center 38
45 Randolph Field 37
48 Chase Field 50
41 Southwestern 50
36 Kelly Field 45
50 Chase Field 64
42 Corpus Christi Air Station 55
47 Bergstrom Field 33
49 Southwestern 48
55 Baylor 37
50 Bergstrom Field 49
77 Texas A&M 40
54 Baylor 29
64 TCU 44
61 SMU 48
37 TCU 44
34 Rice 56
46 SMU 49
48 Arkansas 59
46 Arkansas 54
43 Rice 62
78 Bergstrom Field 65 (2 OT's)
81 Texas A&M 36

But the last two preconference games, against Bergstrom Army Air Field (47-33) and Southwestern (49-48) were victories. The latter was especially satisfying. Some of the 3,000 Gregory Gym fans had begun to depart since the Pirates, well-fortified by military men, had a two-point lead and the ball out of bounds with just 10 seconds to play. But Kemp stole it, scored a tying basket and calmly dropped in the winning free throw. Martin (14) turned in a colossal performance, one of his best yet. "Folks who haven't seen Slater Martin play basketball have missed the best personification of determination that ever hit Gregory Gym," wrote Weldon Hart of the *Austin Statesman*. "There have been smoother, fancier and better basketeers than the ex-Jeff Davis all-stater, but none who battled so wholeheartedly from whistle to gun." Hart lamented that Martin would soon get greetings from his Uncle Samuel in the form of an induction notice.

Bully Gilstrap (top row, right) and the second of his three wartime squads.

The 1944 Southwest Conference campaign began kindly for Gilstrap's young crew. Baylor and Texas A&M, hardest hit by military demands, could have combined their manpower and still had a weak team. Of the 24 conference games they played, just two—the Bears over the Aggies—were victories. Still, Overall (in charge while Gilstrap was in the hospital with the flu) took nothing for granted in preparing for Baylor, coached full-time by Van Sweet, a varsity player just one year earlier. In a 55-37 skinning of the Bears, Martin played his usual commando-style game for 40 minutes. His 15 points tied Cox, and Baylor center Marlin Hicks had 12.

While Martin was in Houston taking a physical exam, his teammates won an exciting victory in the annual charity game. The Bergstrom Flyers led by nine with four minutes to go, but Cox and Stewart began to close the gap. A Cox jump shot with 15 seconds left gave the Steers a 50-49 win. With four straight football losses and two in basketball, the Texas A&M Aggies thirsted for a defeat of the Longhorns. But January 15, 1944 was not the night. It was Martin's last game before joining the Navy, and Cox dedicated it to him. The Steers made his farewell party one to remember, scoring an SWC-record 77 points (the most in any UT game since 1928) to the Ags' 40. Martin, entering into the spirit of the thing, led with 18 points. Some 4,000 fans saw the stouthearted frosh close what looked like a truncated Texas career with a nice exhibition of court finesse. Martin meant more than points and defense, being so aggressive that he grabbed almost half of all loose balls; his speed and perpetual motion baffled the Aggies. It was quite an emotional goodbye to a freshman who had played just half a season, but Slater Martin was unique. Although he would be back, no one knew it at the time.

His replacement, Al Martin, did quite well (13 points) in his starting debut against Baylor in Waco. Kelly Avery had 12 for the Bruins, who lost, 54-29. The high-scoring Longhorns romped on to their fourth straight SWC victory, 64-44 over TCU in Austin. Two classy Californians, Kemp (23) and Crowley (16) sparked the UT offense to the pleasure of 2,500 patrons. Joe Wick (17) and Zeke Chronister (13) led the Horned Frogs. Their coach, Hub McQuillan, sweating profusely on the sidelines, beefed constantly to referees Jack Sears and Mike Williamson. Believing the Steers played too rough, he yelled several times to Gilstrap, "You've got a good football team!"

The Longhorns started their two-game north Texas jaunt with a 61-48 decision over SMU, paced by Kemp's 20 points and Cox's 14. But the Ponies' Dennis Haden led all scorers with 26. Gilstrap knew the schedule would soon get tougher, and it happened in Fort Worth. A capacity crowd at TCU's ramshackle field house found something to cheer about in the Frogs' 44-37 upset. Hub McQuillan, working the refs as he had in Austin, got a closely called game that saw three Steers foul out. Guard Stuart Allen rang the bell for 14 points, most of them from a distance.

Texas next met Rice in Houston. The Owls' 6'8" center, Bill Henry, was on his way to setting a new SWC scoring record. He, George Mikan of DePaul, Bob Kurland of Oklahoma A&M and other big players were causing a storm of controversy in the college basketball world. Tall enough and athletic enough to stand near the basket and deflect opponents' oncoming shots, they were called "mezzanine goons" by Kansas coach Phog Allen, their most faithful hater. Instead of raising the basket to 11 or 12 feet, as was discussed, goaltending would be ruled illegal after the 1945 season. Henry was a dangerous character against the Horns, scoring 19 in a 56-34 victory. He was ably assisted by Rusty Darling (15) and J.D. Thomas (12).

Once the conference leader, UT was in third place and sinking fast. The Longhorns shot poorly and got some bad breaks in a three-point loss to SMU in Austin. About 2,000 sorrowful fans sat in stunned silence after a rough-and-tumble game that was close all the way. The Ponies' Dennis Haden scored 16 and dominated the backboards. Cox had 12 points for UT, and nine came from Bob Fannin, a new player to the team, recruited by Gilstrap from intramurals.

All title hopes gone, the Longhorns traveled to Fayetteville to air their cage differences with the Razorbacks. Alarmed at a seven-point halftime deficit, Arkansas came out firing and hitting to take a 59-48 victory. Cox (17) and Deno Nichols (15) led their teams in scoring. The Hogs were in front most of the way the next night, stalling the final four minutes to win, 54-46.

Texas prepared for a midweek visit from Rice, the wrecking crew of the SWC. While their team lost (62-43), 3,500 Longhorn fans saw Bill Henry score 17 points with some sensational bank shots and tip-ins. Henry won high praise when people compared him to former Owl Bob Kinney. Perhaps to rekindle the winning spirit, Gilstrap agreed to play Bergstrom Army Air Field's team for the third time that season. A boisterous crowd of 1,200 soldiers and perhaps two dozen civilians gathered at the Bergstrom gym to witness a 78-65 double-overtime victory for the Steers. Former Purdue star Dan Waid scored 23 for the Flyers, and Kemp had 22 for Texas.

The season came to an end on February 21 in College Station against the downtrodden Aggies. It was actually close in the first half, with UT up by just 10. But a wild scoring spree ran to 81 points (to 36 for Texas A&M) before the game mercifully ended. Cox, fourth in SWC scoring, had 28, Summers 19, Fannin 15 and Kemp 11. It was a nice way to close a season that had grown dismal.

1945

"I wish Gray was back." Those words were spoken by Bully Gilstrap on the eve of his third and final season as coach of the Longhorns. But Jack Gray's military duties were not finished, so Gilstrap carried on. The 1945 team would be pieced together with Naval trainees, football players, transfers and other warm bodies. Only two players were back, captain Joe Crowley and Bob Summers, but Summers was ruled academically ineligible prior to the season opener. At 6'3", Jimmie Watson was the tallest player on the squad, followed by Bob Cleary and Bob Horneyer, both 6'2". Stan Graner had played at SMU and Guy Buccola at UCLA. Guard Don Wooten, with the Yearlings in 1942, served a hitch in the Army and was back in Austin, ready to play ball. Bobby Layne, better known for his football and baseball exploits, needed to lose some excess poundage, but Gilstrap was glad to have him. No one expected the Steers to contend for the Southwest Conference championship; the only question was whether they would beat anyone besides guaranteed cellar-dwellers Texas A&M and Baylor.

Those callow youngsters began the season at home on December 7 with a 41-39 defeat of Childress Army Air Field. Cleary (15) was the leading scorer, but Crowley won the game with a basket in the last 15 seconds. Against Southwestern the following night, Texas scored just seven points in the first half and yet managed to win by 10. Former (and future) Longhorn Roy Cox led South Plains Army Air Field into Gregory Gym. He scored only two points, and his Flyers lost, 51-50, as Texas came from behind again. Buccola scored 16 and played a smooth floor game, and Wooten's long shot in the last half-minute won it. "We're going to have to schedule some teams a whole lot better or a whole lot worse than us," said Gilstrap. "I can't stand any more of these."

In Georgetown, UT beat Southwestern again, but by a much higher score, 75-64. Horneyer scored 17, while former Aggie Nick Salibo had 21 on a variety of shots. The dauntless Steers finally tasted defeat, courtesy of Blackland Army Air Field. Shoddy ballhandling and free throw shooting may have lost the game, although 19 points by the Eagles' Billie Carruth had something to do with it. Gilstrap then took his players to Temple for a goodwill game with McCloskey Hospital. A 46-44 double-OT loss refereed by ex-Stanford star Hank Luisetti, it was witnessed by a crowd of wounded soldiers, some of them hobbling on crutches and others missing legs or arms. The experience brought the war home, and Gilstrap, almost at a loss for words, thanked them after the game. He called it "my happiest Christmas."

Record: 10-10

41 Childress Field 39
34 Southwestern 24
51 South Plains Field 50
75 Southwestern 64
32 Blackland Field 37
44 McCloskey Hospital 46 (2 OT's)
40 San Marcos Field 52
38 TCU 39
41 SMU 58
54 Baylor 36
49 Arkansas 40
38 Arkansas 74
47 Bergstrom Field 35
35 TCU 36
48 Rice 59
38 SMU 44
87 Texas A&M 59
54 Baylor 22
45 Rice 74
70 Texas A&M 35

He would have had an awful Christmas if UT had played in the All-College Tournament. As in 1944, his Naval trainees (mostly from California) went home, and the Oklahoma City meet had some teams ready and willing to whup the depleted Longhorns, so discretion was the better part of valor. They played one more home game, a 52-40 loss to San Marcos Army Air Field, and girded up their loins for the SWC schedule. Buck Overall, Gilstrap's student assistant and ad hoc trainer, was called up to the Army, and Buccola quit to focus on his studies. Hoping for the best but fearing the worst, the team went to north Texas. TCU center Gene Schmidt (12) led his team to a one-point victory, while Crowley had 10 for the Steers. It was not so close the next night at Perkins Gym in Dallas as SMU won, 58-41. Kelly Avery (a Baylor player in 1944) scored 24, and his more celebrated teammate, Dennis Haden, had 11.

Victory was all but certain against Baylor in a Saturday afternoon game in Waco. The Bears, on their way to a 0-17 season, were coming off a pair of 60-point losses to Arkansas. Wooten (14) and Cleary (11) helped build a commanding lead, so Gilstrap emptied the bench. When Layne, a second-, if not third-string hoopster, scored a layup, he got cheers from Rooster Andrews and the football players who had come up from Austin.

Gilstrap had 6'10" freshman George Kok in mind when he said, "They better move the Gregory Gym rafters up a few feet so that the giants from Arkansas can move around without bumping their heads." Shorter and less talented than the Razorbacks, UT oiled its racehorse offense as the best chance of staying close in two games on January 19 and 20. The bleachers and gallery were mostly full of fans who watched, disbelieving, as the Longhorns beat the towering Hogs, 49-40. Refusing to be awed by the mighty reputation of Arkansas, the band of undersized players forged an 11-point halftime lead, repulsed a late Razorback drive and coasted to victory. Kok scored 15, but he was given a run for his money by Cleary with 12 points and Horneyer with 10. Graner's dribbling in the final minutes gave people another reason to recall Bobby Moers. *Daily Texan* writer George Raborn called it "one of the most inspired performances ever seen at Gregory Gym." But the Porkers got a full measure of revenge the next night, winning, 74-38.

Wooten scored 10 and Layne eight in defeating Bergstrom Army Air Field in the annual charity game. And then it was back to business when TCU came to town. The big, rugged Horned Frogs put another one-point defeat on Gilstrap's team, 36-35. Their best player, Gene Schmidt, had been taken by the Navy, but Hoosier hotshot Leroy Pasco came through with 14 points. Despite the yells of Texas fans, Pasco was as serene as a monk when he made two free throws with just a few seconds left. Crowley had 10 for the Steers.

After seeing his team play rather passively in the TCU game, Gilstrap benched three starters, Wooten, Horneyer and Graner, against Rice. Nearly 5,000 fans showed up to see the Owls (on their way to a 20-1 season) and the great Bill Henry, a first-team all-American with a 23-point scoring average. The

Longhorns played hard against a taller and superior team, losing, 59-48. Henry scored 20, Bob Foley 15 and Murray Mendenhall 11 for Rice. Wooten, upset about not starting, scored a season-high 20. It was Bobby Layne's last game as a basketball player because the merchant marine was his address for the next several months. He would have excelled had he played the game more, but Layne lent vigorous ballhawking and considerable enthusiasm to the team in early 1945.

The audience at Gregory Gym on February 3 resigned itself to seeing SMU and Texas play a low-scoring, defensive game. The Longhorns lost, 44-38, because they could not score or rebound effectively. It was a miserable performance, although the fans seemed to enjoy the halftime entertainment provided by four singing and dancing UT coeds. Gilstrap was driving the delapidated yellow-and-black team bus to College Station when it broke down outside of Bastrop. The bus was hurriedly repaired, and they made it in time to beat the Aggies, 87-59. Wooten scored 25 and Cleary 14, while Charles Weinbaum had 19 for Texas A&M. That impressive showing preceded another one—albeit against another weak team—as Texas smashed Baylor, 54-22, in Austin. Wooten, Graner and Jack Wallace reached double figures, as did the Bears' Marlin Hicks. Referee Ziggy Sears was in a genial, expansive mood, ignoring many flailing arms and elbows and telling the coaches, "We don't have time to call all these violations."

The Longhorns' 20-game season, in which they never got more than 200 miles from Austin, was winding down. Bill Henry had a merry time of it in Houston, scoring 25 points in Rice's 74-45 rout. At 6'9" and 215 pounds of lithe muscle, he had become an SWC basketball legend. Every team in the conference threw its best men at Henry but to little avail. Gilstrap faced a much easier task in the season finale. A victory over the loud, brash corps from Texas A&M would soothe the pride of his team quite a bit. The game was remarkably free of rough stuff, given the "traditional enemy" angle. About 3,000 people saw a sweet 70-35 Texas victory, paced by Graner (22) and Cleary and Wooten (16 each). When Gilstrap and the players returned to their Gregory Gym locker room, a large orange-and-white cake awaited them.

1946

Along with assistant coach Ed Price, ex-sailor Jack Gray was just getting his land legs under him when practice started for the first postwar Longhorn basketball team. Five lettermen were back, none of whom had ever played for him. But Al Madsen, a 5'10" Wisconsin native, had been part of Gray's unbeaten 1943 Corpus Christi Naval Air Station team. Alert, agile, determined and daring, Madsen would be a key player for UT over the next four years. Roy Cox (in the military in 1945) was back, along with Don Wooten. Hopes went up with the arrival on campus of John Hargis, the high-jumping forward who had made all-SWC in 1943. But he registered too late and had to sit out a third season, so Hargis occupied himself by playing in the city league and averaging 30 points per game. The other big man, Robert Summers, sustained a rib injury that ended his season. Besides Ralph "Peppy" Blount (a football player and raconteur who served in the Texas Legislature as a UT undergraduate), Gray had no size in 1946. The Longhorns were not expected to be walking in tall cotton.

But they won their first seven games. It began with a 58-23 defeat of San Antonio YMCA and 40-33 over Kelly Air Force Base. Madsen and Cox combined for 26 points in beating Southwestern on December 12. Madsen, called "Cheesehead" by some teammates, had already put his stamp on the program. Picking up two technical fouls against the Pirates, he strutted about the court with the same cocky demeanor Bobby Moers had almost patented, but he did it with a sneer. Loved at Gregory Gym and loathed everywhere else, bellicose Al Madsen thrived on basketball pressure.

Little was known about the Southeast Oklahoma Teachers before they came to Austin for two games. Texas won the first in a slow waltz, 34-27, and the second in a 23-point rout. The first out-of-town game was against Southwestern, anxious to atone for that earlier defeat. Bob Hamric scored 15 for the Pirates, but forward Guy Buccola (18) led another UT victory. The war-born rivalry between the Steers and nearby Bergstrom Flyers flamed anew just before Christmas. Texas took a 53-45 decision in which Cox scored 17 and freshman Vilbry White 12. Former Kansas star Walt Quiring had 21 for the Flyers.

College athletic departments all over the country then were expected to go on a spending and building spree. Attendance was up for football and basketball, and many facilities that had been adequate in the 1930s were no longer so. Texas A&M announced plans to erect a new gymnasium, although G. Rollie White Coliseum would not become a reality until the 1955 season. While sellouts at Gregory Gym had been rare during the war, the student body was growing, and a problem was expected. So UT got into the act. A *Daily Texan* editorial urged that a 12,000-, 15,000- or even 18,000-seat field house be erected at the south end of Memorial Stadium. Because the student journalists did not consider costs and other priorities, athletic director Dana X. Bible suggested an alternative: Perhaps the military would donate an airplane hangar that could be brought to campus and converted into a gym. The field house issue got statewide press. Flem Hall of the *Fort Worth Star-Telegram* wrote, "The University's Gregory Gym, which seats 7,500 and has everything most coaches dream of, has been the standard by which all other such buildings in the Southwest have been measured for years. Now, just when TCU is talking about getting a modern gym about half as big as Gregory, Bible comes out with the statement that it isn't half big enough."

Record: 16-7

58 San Antonio YMCA 23
40 Kelly Air Force Base 33
42 Southwestern 28
34 SE Oklahoma 27
54 SE Oklahoma 31
54 Southwestern 47
53 Bergstrom Air Force Base 45
34 Oklahoma A&M 69
52 Rice 55
43 TCU 41
47 Arkansas 55
63 Arkansas 90
46 Texas A&M 42
54 Bergstrom Air Force Base 39
57 TCU 42
70 SMU 69
48 TCU 46
36 Baylor 51
71 Rice 46
44 Texas A&M 50
42 Baylor 43 (2 OT's)
50 Rice 48
41 SMU 35

Of course, nothing happened. Not a shovel of dirt was turned, and no airplane hangars found their way to the Forty Acres, but getting another, bigger gymnasium would be a well-discussed matter in the next three years.

Gray knew his bantam-sized team would be in fast company in the All-College Tournament. In the opening round, they met defending national champion Oklahoma A&M, with its 7' all-American, Bob "Foothills" Kurland. It was a slaughter from the beginning, 69-34. Kurland scored 24 and set up many other baskets for his Aggie teammates. They won the tournament and after the season a second national title for coach Hank Iba. The Longhorns lost again at Oklahoma City, 55-52 to Rice, but beat TCU by two. Cox had 42 points against UT's two conference rivals.

Faced with the bleak prospect of doing battle with the tree-toppers from Arkansas, Gray and the team departed for Fayetteville. *Austin Statesman* writer Morris Williams contended it would be a moral victory if the Longhorns could walk out of the Arkansas gym after the second game—presumably another defeat—under their own power. The Razorbacks did win both, but the first was no rout, 55-47. Big George Kok scored 17 playing part-time, and Bill Flynt had 12. All those fears were justified the next night as Gene Lambert's team went Hog-wild, 90-63. Kok got 26 points, while Cox led Texas with 19.

Losing four out of five, Gray tried a new lineup dictated, in part, by injuries to Cox (hip) and Madsen (ankle). Texas A&M's 6'8" Jamie Dawson, back from two years in the military, was having a fine season. The largest crowd in the Speedway structure since 1943 saw UT win a thriller, 46-42. Madsen's ankle did not hurt too much since he played a sparkling game, scoring 25. A collision between Dawson (18) and Blount resulted in five stitches for the former and three lost teeth for the latter.

More than 5,000 fans attended the annual charity game at Gregory Gym. Texas beat Bergstrom Air Force Base, 54-39, the last time the Longhorns ever played a military team. Max Cohen proved himself a capable center against the Flyers and earned more playing time the rest of the season. TCU's slick guard, Leroy Pasco, all-SWC in 1945, was fourth in the nation in scoring when the favored Horned Frogs came to Austin. But he was overshadowed by Madsen and Cox in a 57-42 Texas victory. Madsen did a lot of damage in the 25 minutes he played before fouling out; the Southwest Conference was learning that his bite was even worse than his bark.

The Longhorns went to Dallas in search of their first conference victory away from home. Whitey Baccus' Mustangs had some good basketball players (such as Brian Lloyd and Johnny Zatopek) and a football player dabbling in the sport (Doak Walker), but SMU remained winless within the loop. The Ponies put up fierce resistance, jumping to a 14-point halftime lead and staying ahead until the final minutes when Madsen (26) and Cox (12) won it. Zatopek had 22 and Walker 12 for SMU. Buccola, in California because of his mother's death, happened to have his flight grounded in Dallas just before the game started. He hustled out to Perkins Gym, borrowed a pair of shoes and scored nine valuable points for Texas.

Much as he had done the night before against SMU, redheaded Roy Cox limped into the game at Fort Worth and hit the winning shot, beating TCU, 48-46. It was Texas' third defeat of the Frogs in 1946. Howard Overbeek (15) and Leroy Pasco (13) were TCU's top scorers, while Madsen, Ronald Pearson and White had 10 each for the Steers, winners of the north Texas series for the first time in seven years.

The surprising Golden Bears of Baylor hosted Texas on January 31. Winless the year before, they got some players back from the military and some fine frosh and were on their way to a conference title and NCAA Tournament appearance. Never before or since has the SWC seen such a dramatic worst-to-first change. The primary reason was a pious young man named Jackie Robinson. An ordained minister who also played flawless basketball, the 6'1" Robinson had led Fort Worth Paschal High School to the state championship in 1945, gaining the praises of coaches and officials who called him the greatest player yet to perform in the UIL tournament. Jack Gray was one of Robinson's admirers, but he would like to have seen him in a Texas uniform. Baylor's top scorer and primary ballhandler, he was the focus of the Longhorn defense. It was estimated that 95 percent of Baylor students attended games at 3,000-seat McLean Gym, and they raised the roof whenever the Bears scored. Texas led by one at the half, but Madsen soon fouled out, and Robinson took things in his own hands as Baylor won, 51-36.

Thanks largely to the ministrations of new UT trainer Frank Medina, Cox was healthy again. In a 71-46 spanking of Rice (minus Bill Henry, who did not play his senior year) before 6,500 fans at Gregory Gym, he scored 28 points, the most in an SWC game that season. An unheralded freshman, Don Scharlach, led the Owls with 14. Texas did not look good in workouts prior to meeting Texas A&M in College Station, and with seven straight wins over the Ags, an upset was quite possible. Marty Karow got a sweet victory as his team took an early lead, held it and fought off several UT rallies. Jamie Dawson scored 21 and got a lot of help from Oscar White (13) and a little from Bill Yeoman, future University of Houston football coach. Wooten scored 15 for the Longhorns.

The team came home amid criticism that they played poor defense. Not only was that true, but they could not rebound to save their lives. Anticipating another win over Texas and an SWC crown, Baylor alumni planned a big postgame celebration at the Driskill Hotel. For a while, it appeared that the Baptists would be holding a pity-party downtown. The Longhorns and Bears played a tremendous game, one of the most exciting ever at Gregory Gym. The teams were tied at the half, they were tied at the end of regulation, and they were tied at the end of the first overtime. Pandemonium reigned among the 7,500 fans as a White long shot and a Madsen layup put the Horns ahead by three, but Mark Belew scored for Baylor and made it one. Madsen grabbed a rebound with 30 seconds left and tried to stall, but three Bears converged and sent him sprawling. No foul was called, and center Bill Johnson took off to score the winning basket until he was fouled by Wooten. Johnson made both free throws, and suddenly the game was over. The fans screamed bloody murder, and a group of UT football players charged referee Johnny Morrow in a menacing way, but Gray intervened and escorted him to safety. To compound matters, the timekeeper, former Texas star Sandy Esquivel, made a blunder that cost several precious seconds. *Daily Texan* writer Jack Gallagher stated, "Jack Gray's team was the victim of some of the rawest decisions ever handed out on a basketball court."

Such a disappointing loss did not hurt the Steers in their final two games. In Houston, they trailed Rice by three with five minutes to go, but Cox and Blount hit three late field goals to win, 50-48. The Owls' Bill Tom led all scorers with 14. The lowly SMU Mustangs did not submit without a fight before a crowd of 6,000 in Austin, but UT administered their twelfth SWC defeat, 41-35. Cox scored 16 and Madsen 12, including the last five.

Jack Gray considered himself a better coach the second time around, smarter and more patient. He had done an outstanding job in 1946. Just out of the Navy, he took a bunch of short players without much college experience and developed them into a strong team that finished third in the SWC. Except for Wooten, his top men would be back in 1947, joined by some good freshman and military veterans. University of Texas basketball was entering another golden era.

1947

Along with Arkansas, SMU and defending champion Baylor, Texas was thought to have a good shot at winning the Southwest Conference title. But the 1947 Longhorns did that and much more, forging a reputation as one of the greatest teams in school history. It was a veteran squad, in more ways than one. Of the eight players who earned letters that year, seven had served in the war effort: Roy Cox (Army Air Force), Al Madsen (Navy), Slater Martin (Navy), John Hargis (Marines), John Langdon (Army), Dan Wagner (Navy) and Tom Hamilton (Army). Only sophomore Vilbry White had been a civilian. Coach Jack Gray, too, was a World War II vet. Those were not striplings Gray tutored in 1947; several were in their mid-20s and had seen combat. Happy to have survived (Langdon experienced frostbite in the Battle of the Bulge) and be back on campus, they loved basketball and played to win.

If that were not enough, Bill Sansing, student manager of the 1939 team and later an Air Force intelligence officer, had been hired to start the UT sports information office. He produced the first basketball media guide, boomed players for all-conference and all-America honors and dubbed Cox, Madsen and Martin the "Mighty Mice." Due to the burgeoning student body, which had recently surpassed 15,000, business manager Ed Olle regretfully concluded that Gregory Gym tickets would be sold to the public only if room was left after the students got in. The first four games of the season were nowhere near sellouts. But when it became apparent that Texas was having an extraordinary season, the gym was packed regularly. Tickets were rationed, so students attended alternating games. Quite a few even traveled to Waco, College Station, Houston, Dallas or Fort Worth to see the Longhorns play—and win—in their "away" orange uniforms.

The season began at home on December 2 with a decisive win over North Texas, 63-41. Martin, who used his spare time during the war shooting baskets in the hold of a ship, had lost none of his speed and dash, leading UT with 14 points. People who wondered if the frail-looking Cox might get shoved aside by more gifted teammates saw him score 12 and prove his continuing value. Pete Shands' Eagles lost again the next night, 66-40.

Stiffer competition was expected from the Houston YMCA Triangles, a team led by former Rice all-American Bill Henry. But when Texas jumped to a 27-9 halftime lead, it was all over. The Continental Air Liners, an AAU club based in Denver and coached by Chuck Hyatt, boasted a number of seasoned ex-collegians from the midwest. One of them, Howard Shannon, had an unusual running jump shot, a further evolution of the one-hander Jack Gray made popular in the 1930s. The Air Liners held a small lead for 13 minutes, but Cox (11) led UT to a 46-34 victory. It was the last time for 10 years that the Longhorns would face a semipro team, once a regular part of the nonconference schedule.

While some people doubted the wisdom of the eastern and midwestern trip that followed, Gray wanted to harden his team for the All-College Tournament and the SWC title chase. The Longhorns embarked on a 10-day, 4,000-mile train trip that included games with Canisius in Buffalo, Long Island in New York and DePaul in Chicago. If they did well, it would help boost the prestige of the SWC and the University of Texas. A crowd of 7,796 in Buffalo's Memorial Auditorium saw Niagara beat Montana State and Texas come from behind four times to down Canisius, 52-46. The Griffins' Hank O'Keefe led all scorers with 14, followed by Cox (13) and Martin (12) of UT. The highlight of the trip was playing in Madison Square Garden against Clair Bee's Blackbirds, then averaging 90 points per game and recent victors over Oklahoma A&M. The LIU attack was built around diminutive shotmaker Jackie Goldsmith and 6'5" center Dick Holub. As in Buffalo, the Horns had to adjust to tight officiating. Wilbur Evans of the *Austin Statesman* wrote, "The big town was pop-eyed here as the strains of 'The Eyes of Texas' filled the air in this Valhalla of basketball, for Jack Gray's Texas Longhorns gave little old New York the surprise of its life in upsetting Long Island University, 47-46, before 18,453 fans." This time it was the big men, Hargis (15) and Langdon (13), who led the scoring parade with several assists from Madsen. In the second game, Arkansas lost to New York University.

The Steers boarded a train at midnight and headed for Chicago. Ray Meyer's DePaul team had won the NIT two years before and had some top players back, including 6'8" Ed Mikan, younger brother of the recently graduated all-American, George Mikan. Gray, pleased with the team's showing against Canisius and LIU, was convinced his gamble of sacrificing height for speed had paid off. After the curtain-raiser at Chicago Stadium (North Carolina versus Northwestern), UT got a brusque display of midwestern ball from the Blue Demons, especially when it became clear that the Longhorns were in command. The DePaul players used roughness flagrant enough to evoke boos from local fans. Sharp-eyed Roy Cox, the hottest thing Chicago had seen since the great fire, scored 19 while Hargis and Martin had 10 apiece in a 61-43 win. The Demons learned crime did not pay when Texas made 26 of 31 free throws.

It was a victorious tour, a clean sweep. And yet there was little time for celebration before the Oklahoma City tournament began. The 7-0 Longhorns were given a good chance to win there and had become favorites in the conference. Hargis (16), Madsen (13) and hook-shot artist Tom Hamilton helped tame the Missouri Tigers, 65-46. Texas again showed an ability to identify and adapt to an opponent's weakness. Oklahoma A&M, the defending national champion, held on for dear life in the final minutes of a 40-39 semifinal victory before a standing-room-only crowd of more than 5,000. Oklahoma City sportswriters called it one of the best and most exciting games in the history of the 11-year-old tournament. Freshman forward Bob Harris, after a hairline foul by Hargis (17), made one of two free throws in the last half-minute to win. Oklahoma A&M annexed the title the following night after Texas defeated Oklahoma, 62-50, for third place. Hargis, the tournament MVP, rebounded well and poured in 22 points. Martin had 16 and Cox 10. The Horns led the star-filled Sooners by 15 at the half and interspersed a fancy stalling game with occasional drives to the basket. Gray emptied the bench in the last four minutes. Phog Allen, whose Kansas Jayhawks did not play in Oklahoma City, was impressed with Texas' shooting, defense and team spirit.

UT had not played a home game in nearly three weeks, and demand for tickets was sky-high. *Daily Texan* sportswriter Josef Weinberger, noting that, practically demanded construction begin immediately on a new facility. "The only answer to the complex seating problem is a new field house, and it should be started as soon as feasible," he wrote. "It has become apparent that Gregory Gym no longer satisfies the needs of a large student body." At the same time, a group of businessmen announced plans for a 10,000-seat arena (with 30-lane bowling alley and ice hockey rink) to be located at 23rd Street and East Avenue, adjacent to the new highway soon to be built. While Interstate 35 became a reality, Austin's putative sports arena did not.

Record: 26-2

63 North Texas 41
66 North Texas 40
53 Houston YMCA 23
46 Continental Air Liners 34
52 Canisius 46
47 Long Island 46
61 DePaul 43
65 Missouri 46
39 Oklahoma A&M 40
62 Oklahoma 50
68 SW Texas 37
62 TCU 46
45 Baylor 38
56 SMU 36
67 Rice 53
63 Southwestern 39
61 Texas A&M 41
72 TCU 44
58 SMU 51
69 Texas A&M 40
70 Baylor 52
67 Rice 60
49 Arkansas 44
66 Arkansas 46
64 SWC All-Stars 52
42 Wyoming 40
54 Oklahoma 55
54 City College of New York 50

The general public was afforded its last glimpse of the Longhorns on January 3 when they faced Milton Jowers' Southwest Texas Bobcats. An inexperienced team facing the rampaging Texas quintet that had won nine of 10, the Cats got destroyed, 68-37. Halftime entertainment by a couple of lightweight boxers was more interesting than the game.

Gray made no predictions about the SWC race, saying simply, "Anything can happen." He realized every other team in the league had its guns centered on Texas. TCU, just 1-22 overall in 1947, put up a good fight before bowing to the Longhorns' speed and skill, 62-46. The pesky Frogs hit what was considered an amazing 42 percent of field-goal attempts. But Hargis scored 20 points in 30 minutes and Langdon 16. Slow, rather awkward and considered the team's weak link, Langdon was getting better. The Longhorns were out to avenge the previous year's controversial loss to Baylor. Bill Henderson, coach of the Bears, was alternately brash and deferent to UT. Initially promising no overtime game "because we'll be too far ahead," he later changed his tune and declared Gray's team the best in Texas history, on a par with top teams like Oklahoma A&M, Kentucky and Kansas. A packed house of 4,000 in Waco saw Hamilton hit four late hook shots and carry the Horns to a stirring 45-38 win. The Bruins, with 11 points each from Jackie Robinson and freshman Jamie Owens, attempted to counter Texas' swift attack with a slow, deliberate style, but that did not last long. Martin (18) played a whale of a game, holding Bill Johnson to a pair of free throws.

SMU, winner of the Big 6 holiday tournament, came to Austin for a mid-week game and was soundly defeated, 56-36. More than 7,000 fans jammed Gregory Gym to see Hargis sizzle, scoring 23 points in the first half, 30 for the game. Bombarding the hoop from all angles with his flat one-handed jumpers, he came within two points of tying his coach's scoring record. A great leaper and tough as barbed wire, Hargis was an unlikely basketball star. He had come to UT way back in September 1940, hoping to play baseball for Billy Disch, but he gave that up when he outscored better-known ex-high school basketball stars. Brilliant in the 1943 NCAA Tournament, his three years away from college basketball had not hurt Hargis a bit. When 1947 was over and done, he would be a second-team all-American. The first Longhorn to play in the National Basketball Association, Hargis spent four years with the Anderson Packers, Fort Wayne Pistons and Tri-Cities Blackhawks.

The biggest crowd yet to attend a basketball game in Houston gathered at Sam Houston Coliseum to see the Owls and Horns go at it. Harmon Walters scored 14 points and Bill Tom 12 for Rice in a game that was tied at the half. Texas had a big rebounding edge with Langdon, Hargis and Hamilton, and four players were in double figures in a 14-point win preceded by the Shorthorns' victory over the Owlets. During the two-week exam break (interrupted by a 24-point defeat of Southwestern), UT fans had time to ponder their team. It was almost certainly better than the wartime club that reached the NCAA semifinals, but what about Bobby Moers and the 1939 team? What about that 22-1 team in Gray's sophomore year? Or the undefeated 1924 Longhorns? The quality of SWC basketball had grown so much since then, and seeing was believing. While the 1947 team appeared to be the best yet, the season was far from over.

Victory! Pictured inside their Gregory Gym locker room after defeating Arkansas for the 1947 SWC title are Tom Hamilton, John Hargis, Jack Gray, Al Madsen, Slater Martin, Roy Cox, Dan Wagner and John Langdon.

Conference play resumed on February 3 against Texas A&M. Although the Ags had absorbed an 84-18 loss to Kentucky earlier in the year, they were coming on with high-scoring freshman Bill Batey. A collision with Madsen five minutes into the game cost Batey three teeth. His absence was felt by the Aggies, who went down, 61-41. Hargis and Cox scored 19 and 14, respectively, fed nicely by Madsen as UT got a fifth conference win.

The north Texas journey often ended in gloom, but not that year. In the beginning of the TCU game at Will Rogers Coliseum, the Steers were as cold as the ice rink the court sat on, but they warmed up as the night progressed. Leroy Pasco, twice all-conference, played poorly, and his teammates were no match for Texas. Hargis scored 21 and Martin ran the ball at his usual breakneck pace in a 72-44 victory. The Longhorns had considerably more trouble in Dallas before a sellout crowd of 2,800. Tommy Tomlinson (17) and Burt Rollings (12) kept the Mustangs in front until Madsen took command late in the second half, pulling away to win by seven. The scoring was well distributed among Gray's seven key players.

SMU helped the cause, however, by sweeping two games with Arkansas, leaving UT alone in the conference lead. Texas A&M coach Marty Karow was staying awake nights vainly planning a defense to stop the Longhorns. They taught the Aggies a lesson in basketball, winning, 69-40 in College Station. During the riotous last eight minutes, a fistfight, the constant roar of the Aggie Band and aggressive tactics on the court led to a masterpiece of chaos. One brazen Texas fan who refused to stop ringing a cowbell was seized by a dozen Cadets and unceremoniously tossed over a ten-foot balcony rail. It was for good reason that Aggies warned visiting teams and fans, "Beware DeWare."

Baylor, the dethroned champion, came to Austin but never really had a chance. Hargis scored 17, Langdon 12 and Hamilton 11 as 7,000 fans cheered a 70-52 win. Bill Johnson, hero of the Bears' triumph a year earlier, tallied 13. The game was marred by considerable rough play and a feud between Madsen and Jackie Robinson that almost resulted in a double ejection. It was thought that Rice was doomed to a disastrous evening in Gregory Gym, and although the Owls lost (67-60), the issue was in doubt for some time. The Steers made up a five-point deficit as a partisan crowd—all students—screamed wildly throughout the game. Bill Tom scored 29 for Rice, while Hargis (18), Madsen (17) and Martin (11) led UT. Wilbur Evans of the *Austin Statesman* wrote: "Jack Gray seems to be blessed with basketeers who hit their peak under pressure, boys like Slater Martin, who shine brightest when the hour is darkest...and Al Madsen, who was omnipresent on offense and defense against Rice."

Gene Lambert's rangy Razorbacks were in second place entering the season-ending series with Texas. Tales of sickness and injury came out of the Ozarks, but Gray told his players not to believe a word of it. A very full house (8,000) at Gregory Gym waited an extra half hour because the train carrying Arkansas had been delayed. Although Texas won, 49-44, the Hogs led most of the game. George Kok had 17 points and SWC scoring leader Al Williams 11. It was the only season the 6'10" Kok did not make all-SWC, but the fans loved him. Displaying the kind of sportsmanship SMU's Doak Walker had in football, he got an ovation from the UT crowd. A late surge, led by Martin, won it for the Horns. The pressure off and the title theirs, they had a much easier time the following night, winning by 20. An equally big crowd, including Governor Beauford Jester, saw Texas finish with a 12-0 SWC record.

Kok and Williams stayed in Austin a few days longer, joined by Jackie Robinson and Bill Johnson of Baylor, Leroy Pasco of TCU, Mike Garcia of Texas A&M, Tommy Tomlinson and Bob Prewitt of SMU, Bill Tom and Harmon Walters of Rice and Baylor coach Bill Henderson. The Southwest Conference All-Stars met the champion Longhorns at Gregory Gym in a charity game originated by sports information director Bill Sansing and sponsored by the *Austin Statesman*. The all-stars practiced together just once and lost by 12. While there was some talk of making it an annual event in Austin, held in conjunction with the UIL tournament, the game was never repeated.

What Gray really needed was some competition during the 2 1/2 weeks before the NCAA Tournament. Perhaps it was the aura his team had built, but not even a hard scrimmage could be arranged. As a result, the Horns were somewhat stale when they got to Kansas City to play Wyoming on March 21. With the best record (24-1) in the country, however, they had a real chance to win the eight-team tournament and bring the trophy to Austin. A round-trip train ticket to Kansas City cost just $37.50, and quite a few Texas fans were there to show support. Four Cowboys remained from the 1943 national champions, and four Longhorns (Hargis, Langdon, Cox and Jack Fitzgerald) had been on the team that lost to them in the regional finals. Wyoming's 22-4 record in 1947 was due largely to guard Jimmie Reese and center Mike Todorovich. The famed Texas fast break was slowed to an uncertain shuffle by the Cowboys' clever defense and too many missed shots. Trailing most of the way and staying close only with unflinching grit, the Steers' money players, Madsen and Martin, scored eight points in the final seven minutes when Wyoming tried to stall. A long shot by Martin with 35 seconds left provided the winning margin in a tense 42-40 game. Eleven points and lots of rebounds by Langdon had kept them in it.

Some 9,500 people fit in 8,000-seat Municipal Auditorium the next night for the regional finals between Texas and Oklahoma. Despite a 12-point victory over the Sooners early in the season, UT had plenty of respect for them. There was even more high drama to come. Trailing by four in the final minute, the Horns made a spirited comeback with field goals by Wagner and Martin, and then a free throw by Madsen made it 54-53, Texas. But OU's Ken Pryor dribbled the ball across midcourt and sank a 40-foot shot, dealing a heartbreaking loss to the finest team that had yet come out of the Southwest Conference. Several players stared, dumbfounded, at the scoreboard as time expired and another beat his fists on the floor. Martin scored 18 and Sooner all-American Gerald Tucker 15 in a game that would be recounted many times in the future. A few tears were shed in the locker room, but the team had to hurry because there was a train to catch and another game to play.

Gray tried to keep his players' spirits up on the way to New York. There was little consolation in playing for third place against City College of New York at Madison Square Garden before OU and Holy Cross contested the national championship (won by the Crusaders). Texas took its final victory, 54-50, as Martin and Madsen used their speed in spurts, and Hargis (17) outhustled the Beavers' forwards, Sonny Jameson and Joe Galiberz. And so it was over. Twenty-six wins and two last-second defeats, both by a single point. Fans who saw the 1947 Longhorns at Gregory Gym or elsewhere never forgot them. Such a team passed but seldom.

1948

Jack Gray, the dean of Southwest Conference basketball coaches, was still helping out with UT football, scouting opponents for Blair Cherry. That cut into his availability to the team somewhat during the first month of practice, but he anticipated another fine season. Four starters were certain: Captain John Langdon, Slater Martin, Al Madsen and Tom Hamilton. The fifth spot was contested by Vilbry White and Sidney "Chick" Zomlefer, twice an all-SWC baseball player. His high school team in Chicago had won 98 straight games, and he missed being one of what athletic director Dana X. Bible called "the thump-thump boys." Austinite Philip George, mascot of the team during his childhood, was expected to help off the bench. For the first time in six years, freshmen were not allowed to play on the varsity.

The season opened with two home games against Sam Houston, which had a couple of big, athletic players in Murray Mitchell and Don Walker. Over 6,000 people were present both nights to see near upsets, averted primarily by Martin, Hamilton and Madsen. Although the speed and timing of the 1947 juggernaut were not there yet, the season was young. Based on his performance against the Bearkats, Zomlefer had won the starting job over White.

Bobby Moers, by then a practicing physician, was in the audience at Sam Houston Coliseum on December 8 to see the Steers defeat Texas Tech, 51-42. Red Raider center Don Grove scored 20, but most of his points came after the game was decided. The next night, it was Texas and LSU while Rice, which beat the Tigers, met Texas Tech. Martin, who had but one point against the Raiders, scored 19 in a 50-31 romp. Bob Meador had nine for the Bayou Bengals, who were too slow to keep up with Gray's whippet-like team.

North Texas, too, provided little competition for the Horns, losing two in Austin. That 6-0 record would get tested in another trip to the northland to play City College of New York in Gotham and St. Joseph's in Philadelphia. Spirits were high, but there was no big sendoff rally. While it was UT's fourth trip to New York and the third in two years, a country-boys-go-to-town air still prevailed. A capacity crowd in the historic, triple-tiered, smoke-filled Madison Square Garden got its money's worth, seeing Washington State defeat Manhattan and the Longhorns edge Nat Holman's CCNY Beavers, 61-59. It was a bad night for the home teams. Hamilton, 6'3" and 210 pounds, may have resembled a football player, but he did quite well (22 points) as Texas withstood a late CCNY rally. It was an exciting game won on sheer nerve since the Horns blew an 18-point first-half lead. Irwin Dambrot (15) and Sonny Jameson (13) led in scoring for the Beavers, who recalled the narrow loss to Texas in the NCAA tourney eight months earlier.

Down in Philly, it was another doubleheader, UT versus St. Joseph's and Kentucky versus Temple. The shortage of reserve power that had shown up earlier was even more evident, but the Longhorns pulled out a 61-57 victory. Madsen's 19 points and terrific floor work put them in front, but he, Zomlefer and Hamilton fouled out, leaving Martin, Hargis and the subs to gallantly hang on in the final minutes. Al Goukas led the Hawks with 13. Weldon Hart of the *Austin Statesman* accompanied the team on the New York-Philadelphia swing and drew five conclusions: (1) Eastern fans, coaches and writers had a healthy respect for Gray and the Longhorns; (2) they knew more about basketball, by and large, than people in the Southwest; (3) Texas had another sharp team;

(4) Martin and Madsen deserved to be mentioned in the same breath as Bobby Moers; and (5) UT would have trouble repeating as champion of the SWC because of a lack of depth.

After saying hello to their families on Christmas day, the Longhorns left for Oklahoma City with a good chance of becoming the first SWC team since TCU in 1942 to win the All-College Tournament. Texas put the quietus on Georgia Tech, 54-45, as Martin scored 20 and Hamilton 15. Martin Keener paced the Yellowjackets with 15. While the Texas and Alabama football teams were preparing to clash in the Sugar Bowl, the basketball teams met in a game that was nearly as rough. Forty-eight fouls were called, and Vilbry White had to receive medical treatment after getting upended by a Crimson Tide player. The Horns won, 40-31, leading to the title game with another heavyweight, Oklahoma A&M. Eerily reminiscent of the previous season, the Aggies won by a single point. Bob Harris, who beat UT with a free throw in 1947, did it again in 1948 with a field goal in the last five seconds. Madsen injured an ankle early in the game, but White (recovered from that nasty spill against Bama) did well in his place.

Record: 20-5

55 Sam Houston 47
56 Sam Houston 40
51 Texas Tech 42
50 LSU 31
51 North Texas 39
60 North Texas 49
61 City College of New York 59
61 St. Joseph's 57
54 Georgia Tech 45
40 Alabama 31
31 Oklahoma A&M 32
59 Rice 44
45 TCU 39
69 Texas A&M 48
57 SMU 51
49 TCU 41
62 SW Texas 32
39 Baylor 48
47 Rice 54
40 Arkansas 54
54 Arkansas 43
32 Baylor 29
47 SMU 45
54 Texas A&M 34
43 New York University 45

Texas returned to Sam Houston Coliseum to open its defense of the SWC title against Rice. Trailing by two at halftime, the Horns staged a dazzling comeback to win, 59-44. Madsen, despite a sore ankle, scored 15 points. The Owls' sterling Bill Tom (21) looked like he could win the game by himself, but the smooth UT ballhandlers got a well-earned victory. Insisting the age of miracles had not yet passed, Gray worked his players as if TCU (4-42 in 1947 and 1948) had a chance. The Horned Frogs proved him right, losing by just six in a loosely played game that ended with Zomlefer and Brock Jerrell exchanging blows. Gray, initially thankful the game was held at Will Rogers Coliseum and not TCU's old campus gym, had second thoughts because the floor, lying atop an ice rink, was wet and slippery.

The Steers were not expected to spare the rod when Texas A&M, another weak team, came to Austin on January 17. Hamilton scored 20 and Martin 17 in a 69-48 stampede that had 7,600 fans screaming. "There have been better games played in Gregory Gym," wrote Jack Gallagher of the *Austin Statesman*, "but the spacious arena has seen few teams that handled the ball as flawlessly, guarded as well and hit its shots as unerringly as Gray's whirling dervishes did in the second half.... Martin is on his way to becoming one of the greatest all-around basketball players in Longhorn history."

As part of the ongoing saga, a committee of the UT Development Board met with 50 prominent alumni to discuss plans for a 20,000-seat coliseum, costing an estimated $2 million and to be located south of Memorial Stadium. University architects had already begun to design such an edifice. *Daily Texan* writer George Christian, in an article about people criticizing Gregory Gym, asked them to consider the truly awful facilities serving some Southwest Conference schools. At any rate, no new gym was built.

During the two-week break for final exams, basketball practice was rare. Finally, activities resumed against SMU in Dallas. Martin (22) was as hot as a witch's cauldron against the Mustangs in a 57-51 victory. Texas had not lost a game at the gym on Speedway in two years when TCU came to town. Nearly 8,000 fans saw the Horns extend that streak, winning by eight points. Julius Dolnics and Bob Young had 11 each for the artless Frogs, while Martin scored 15 and Hamilton 14. Substitute Philip George scored 10 and grabbed more than his share of rebounds.

After outscoring Southwest Texas by an almost two-to-one ratio in the annual charity game, it was time for the showdown in Waco, the Mighty Mice against those masters of maple mischief, the Baylor Bears. Both teams were undefeated in conference play. Minister Jackie Robinson and his brethren had just sent the big Hogs reeling back to Fayetteville with two losses. While the Bears had their claws sharpened, Gray was not afraid, not with Slater Martin on his team. "Slater's one of the great college players in the country," he said.

Martin held Robinson to two points, but soph Don Heathington rang up 24 in Baylor's 48-39 win before an overflow crowd.

The Gregory Gym locker room was full of gloom after a 54-47 loss to Rice. Warren Switzer and Bill Tom combined for 35 points, and the Owls overcame a 17-point deficit to win. It was a stunning upset in which Joe Davis' team was given an inch and took a mile, humbling the Horns. Undefeated just eight days earlier, they found themselves on the brink of elimination from the SWC race, heading to Arkansas. A throng of 4,000 filled Razorback Field House to see Gene Lambert's team take a 54-40 win. George Kok (26) was dominant, especially in the second half. As Gray pointed out, the play of both teams was hindered by a dusty and slippery floor. Lambert and Arkansas AD John Barnhill promised to have it in better shape the next night. Gray devised a brilliant offensive plan that had Martin, 5'10", in the pivot and Langdon outside, drawing Kok with him. It was surprisingly successful, and the Steers won, 54-43, to earn a split. Martin scored 20 and the cagey Madsen 11 as tempers flared after the game. Razorback fans tried to attack officials Johnny Morrow and Bill Keeling, but Arkansas coaches escorted them away.

Vilbry White played a smart, steady game in that victory and won the starting job that had belonged to Zomlefer through most of the season. He was in the lineup on February 25 when the newly crowned Bears came to Austin. Not a player from either team reached double figures, but it was a heck of a game, conducted before 8,000 fans. With the score tied and 20 seconds left, Al Madsen, always at his best when the going was toughest, hurtled down the lane, scored a layup and added a free throw. UT won it, 32-29. Nine points do not describe the superb play of the Wisconsin Wizard who ran the offense, played great defense and caused all sorts of trouble for Baylor. When the game was over, there was joyous delirium as every Longhorn rode to the locker room on the shoulders of Texas fans. "Jack Gray's the greatest coach in the world," shouted Madsen. "The greatest in the world!"

That win over Baylor brought a bid from the NIT, so perhaps there would be a Garden party in 1948. Two more SWC games remained to be played, though. SMU came within two points of an upset in Austin, but the freezing tactics of Martin (21) and Madsen in the last three minutes were successful. And the Mighty Mice were on the run in College Station, whipping Texas A&M, 54-34, before a crowd of 3,300.

There was no time to waste, as the Horns boarded a New York-bound train the following morning to meet New York University, led by future NBA star Dolph Schayes. They checked into the Paramount Hotel, attended the Marcel Cerdan-Lavern Roach boxing match and worked out at the 69th Regiment Armory. They were in fine shape but underdogs to the Violets. Trailing by seven midway through the second half, Martin and Madsen engineered a spirited drive that put Texas ahead, 43-39, with 3 1/2 minutes to play. Negating UT's effort to stall, NYU tied it up and then, with just six seconds on the clock, Dick Kor fired a long shot that went in, winning the game and sending the Longhorns home. Schayes (14) and Madsen (12) were the top scorers.

Baylor enhanced Southwest Conference prestige by winning twice in the NCAA Tournament, only to lose to Kentucky in the championship game.

1949

"The Longhorn five carried their supporters from the heights of glory to the depths of despair during the hectic season of 1948-49," summarized the *Cactus.* "Their success ranged from mediocre to sensational, and their losses varied from heartbreakers to humiliation." Shorter in stature than in the previous season and relying on even fewer players, Texas still managed a 17-7 record. The incomparable guard duo, Slater Martin and Al Madsen, was back, along with Vilbry White, Philip George and Tom Hamilton. Sophs Frank "Pancho" Womack and 6'4" (a size that would have been described as "giant" or "elongated" 20 years earlier) Wilson Taylor were the only reliable subs.

Jack Gray, in his 10th season at the UT helm, had a reputation as one of the best young coaches in the nation. With a 62-14 record the past three years, he had not done it by scheduling preconference patsies, and there was more of the same in 1949. A capacity crowd

Slater Martin, probably the finest Longhorn of the pre-integration era.

at the Parker Agricultural Center (a.k.a. the "Cowbarn") in Baton Rouge saw the Steers open with a 60-45 defeat of LSU. Martin, who had 19 points, held Tiger ace Bob Meador scoreless. The next night, however, they got bounced, 56-39, by Tulane in New Orleans as 5,400 partisan fans bellowed encouragement. The Green Wave's fast break and dominance of the backboards made the difference in the second half.

The dramatic one-point loss to Oklahoma in the 1947 NCAA playoffs was still on the Horns' minds as they prepared to play the Sooners in Norman. Ken Pryor, who had hit the winning shot that night, was still on Bruce Drake's team. A newcomer was 6'11" soph Marcus Freiburger, a Texan who chose to matriculate north of the Red River. He was the focus of one of the first all-out basketball recruiting battles, something Gray found distasteful. Freiburger was neutralized in Texas' 49-40 victory, accomplished with Martin on the bench most of the second half due to fouls. Madsen (17) and OU's Bill Waters (14) led their teams in scoring.

The home opener was on December 10 against North Texas. Gregory Gym had been equipped with improved lighting and a long-sought feature—glass backboards. In two victories over the Eagles, Hamilton scored 43 points. Gray's team headed back to the east coast for games with NYU and St. Joseph's. Such trips (by train but soon to be by airplane) were beneficial in several ways. They were enjoyable to the players and thus a carrot in recruiting. They gave UT basketball national media attention inconceivable had the team played only regionally. And they were financially helpful to the basketball program. Students who purchased blanket taxes essentially got in free, and Gregory Gym could not hold all of them, not during the slap-happy Martin-Madsen years. So Texas' visits to Madison Square Garden were necessary. But Longhorn players, coaches and the few local sportswriters who traveled with them had begun to notice a disturbing trend. Too many fans were betting and had more interest in point spreads than quality of play or who won the game. It was the very intersectional doubleheaders Texas participated in that led to the point-shaving scandals culminating in 1951. In a related matter, it had become apparent to New York fans that their schools (primarily NYU, Long Island, CCNY, Manhattan and St. John's), which had once beaten the tar out of the imports, could no longer do it. "Something terrible has happened lately," wrote Gayle Talbot, a transplanted Texan then writing for the Associated Press in New York. "The outlanders aren't scared any more, especially such hardened visitors as those from the states of Kentucky, Missouri, Oklahoma, Texas, Utah and California. What they have been doing to members of the subway circuit is sinful."

A rematch of the two-point loss to NYU in the previous season's NIT turned out differently, a 58-57 Longhorn victory in which the Violets came back from 18 points down to nearly win the game. Gray, upset over a series of late calls against his team, got a technical foul from referee John Nucatola when the Texas coach took the basketball and bounced it 20, 40 or perhaps 100 feet in the air (the ball went higher with every retelling of the story). He sat down and put his head in his hands, waiting for the ball to descend.

At Philadelphia's Convention Hall, recently the site of the Democratic and Republican national conventions,

UT met St. Joe's, a giant-killer that had recently beaten Oklahoma A&M. Led by Paul Senesky, Jack Ramsay (a future NBA coach) and Hank Dudek (father of a future Longhorn by the same name), the Hawks were ahead by eight with 10 minutes left. But Martin, Hamilton and White led a 13-5 run and effectively froze the game for an exciting one-point victory.

Thriving on big-time basketball, the Longhorns got more of it in the Oklahoma City dribble-derby. Slater Martin carved another notch in his brilliant cage career by scoring 25 points in a 56-47 defeat of Colorado A&M. The next game was against Baylor, minus Jackie Robinson, three times all-SWC and a member of the 1948 U.S. Olympic team, who had a calcium deposit on his knee. The Bears did not miss him much; their superior height played the biggest role in a 49-36 victory, a dogfight most of the way. UT beat Alabama, 60-39, for third place in the tournament. The Tide had nothing to match the sparkling play of Martin, Hamilton and White. Taylor looked good in a reserve role.

After defeating the yellow-clad Sam Houston Bearkats in Austin by 29 points, UT traveled to Dallas to start SWC competition. The 9-2 Longhorns were healthy and had a good chance at the title. They did not, however, make the AP's first top-ten poll, announced in January 1949. Doc Hayes' Ponies had early jitters, allowing Texas to build a 12-point halftime lead and roll on to victory. Martin (15) shut down SMU star Jack Brown, but his counterpart, Bob Prewitt, scored 22. Gray's request that the TCU game be held on campus and not in icy Will Rogers Coliseum was summarily denied. The Horned Frog band played "Back Home in Indiana" for the five Hoosiers who made up the starting team. One of them, 29-year old Julius "Daddy" Dolnics, scored 17, as did Madsen, Martin and Hamilton in a 59-46 UT win.

Rice brought a 4-8 season record into Gregory Gym, but the Longhorns were cautious. Gray had a hunch the Owls would offer serious competition, and they did. An overflow crowd, with fans in aisles, doorways, the stage and the floor could not believe what they saw. Texas shot two of 27 in the second half and lost, 45-37. Rice's 12-rebound edge contributed to the upset in which 6'9" Bill Tom scored 16 points.

The gym was again packed when Baylor came to town for a 3:30 p.m. midweek game. It was moved up because Governor Beauford Jester's inaugural ball would be held there that evening. The Steer-Bear encounters in Austin the past two years had produced unforgettable, scintillating games. The 1949 contest fell just short of that as Texas won, 40-37, thundering back into the SWC race. Hamilton (16) had his hook shot working beautifully, and Madsen came off the bench, despite four fouls, and repelled every Baylor threat. He and Martin put on a dazzling exhibition of dribbling in the final minutes. That was the last game in the career of the Bears' Bill Johnson, who was badly hurt in a car accident a few days later.

After the two-week exam layoff, Oklahoma came to Gregory Gym for the first time since 1938. Nearly 7,000 fans saw a game with superb shooting and ballhandling, rallies and counter-rallies. Martin suffered a bloody nose in a collision with Marcus Freiburger and had to leave the game, but he was back two minutes later. He scored 23 in a 59-53 victory in which Texas matched the Sooners in rebounds despite a serious height disadvantage. Prairie Lea's gift to the Longhorns, Vilbry White, scored 21 in a 50-41 defeat of Texas A&M at DeWare Field House. Martin had a red-hot duel with the Ags' soph guard, Jewell McDowell, said to have been "stolen" away from UT in the recruiting process. The burr-headed Amarillo product was a fierce competitor who did not rattle easily. When Madsen and Martin taunted McDowell at the free throw line, he laughed and converted.

Arkansas began playing home-and-home series with its SWC rivals in 1949. The Hogs, fresh off a defeat of Baylor, came to Austin with a typically big team but one more mobile than in the past. The biggest of them, 6'8" Bob Ambler, scored 21 and got a bunch of rebounds in a 60-54 Arkansas win. Madsen scored six points in the last 90 seconds as the Steers tried to come back, but a pressure defense allowed two easy Razorback baskets. The two teams met four days later

Record: 17-7

60 LSU 45
39 Tulane 56
49 Oklahoma 40
49 North Texas 41
68 North Texas 47
58 New York University 57
55 St. Joseph's 54
56 Colorado A&M 47
36 Baylor 49
60 Alabama 39
69 Sam Houston 40
50 SMU 44
59 TCU 46
37 Rice 45
40 Baylor 37
59 Oklahoma 53
50 Texas A&M 41
54 Arkansas 60
50 Arkansas 54
56 Texas A&M 43
36 Baylor 31
49 Rice 65
81 TCU 60
40 SMU 54

in Fayetteville, and Texas was eager to return the compliment. Although Ambler was out with an ankle injury, the aggressive Hogs won by four. Hamilton and three Arkansas players scored 13 each, but the game's top performer was Martin, who had 16 of UT's last 20 points and nearly won the game himself.

The troubled Steers, beaten in their last two starts, met Marty Karow's Aggies in Austin on February 16. Texas A&M had not won at Gregory Gym since 1934, and Jewell McDowell and his teammates were making noise about ending that streak. But the Ags, those respecters of tradition, went down, 56-43, as Hamilton scored 17 and White (fourth nationally in shooting percentage) 14. Martin bottled up McDowell.

In a stormy contest in Waco, Texas climbed back into second place with a 36-31 defeat of Baylor. Madsen rallied his team to erase a five-point deficit with 11 minutes remaining. The game had everything—ball thievery, shots from all angles and excitement at a fever pitch. After the buzzer, angry fans rushed referee Ziggy Sears. Two policemen, coach Bill Henderson and AD Ralph Wolf could not ward off the pushing swirl of roused Baptists (some yelling, "kill him!"), and even the strains of the Baylor alma mater did not work. Sears' hair was pulled and his shirt torn before he reached safety. SWC executive secretary James St. Clair commended Baylor authorities for trying to control it, but he blasted the fans responsible, calling the matter "an indictment against the supporters of intercollegiate athletics." Ironically, most observers agreed the game had been well officiated.

After that little soiree, the Longhorns went to Houston to engage Rice. The spectacular career of Slater Martin had been thoroughly chronicled in his home town, and in the days preceding the game, the Houston newspapers were filled with stories and photos of the ex-Jeff Davis star. A huge delegation of friends and family turned out to welcome their hero back home for the last time as a collegian. Overheated City Auditorium was packed to the ceiling with 3,500 fans who witnessed a 65-49 mauling of UT. It was the worst defeat since Gray's return from the service four years earlier. Texas' lack of height and quality reserves was becoming evident as the season drew to a close. Madsen and the Owls' Bill Tom both scored 21 points.

The TCU game in Austin was special for two reasons. Eight members of the 1924 Longhorns held a reunion, were feted at Hill Hall and recognized at halftime. Only coach Doc Stewart (killed in a 1929 hunting accident) and Carl Nation were not there. They marveled at the changes in the game and recounted tales of the Men's Gym and the hardscrabble life of a college basketball player then. As for the game (an 81-60 Texas victory), a slim crowd of 4,500 got to see history when Martin reenacted the gold rush and scored 49 points. With encouragement from the fans, his teammates passed him the ball again and again, and he scored UT's last 18. In the bedlam-filled locker room, Gray raved about "the greatest exhibition of shooting I ever saw." It was an SWC record, a Gregory Gym record and the second-highest total in the nation that year. Although Gray, Hank Iba of Oklahoma A&M and Buster Brannon of TCU all called Martin the finest basketball player in the country, he was not a consensus all-American.

An NIT invitation looked possible before the Texas-SMU game on March 1. The careers of two Longhorn greats, Martin and Madsen, ended in a dismal 54-40 loss to the sophomore-laden Mustangs. Before 7,000 spectators at Gregory Gym, Bob Prewitt and George Owen combined for 35 points. Martin was prolific if not accurate, hitting six of 23 shots.

Daily Texan writer Lou Maysel assayed the players leaving the team and those soon to join and prophesied the age of speed at UT was over. Jack Gray would face a major rebuilding job as the new decade dawned.

1950

Many people viewed the departed Slater Martin as the greatest Longhorn basketball player ever, and what he did in the pros verified that perception. In 11 years with the Minneapolis Lakers and St. Louis Hawks, he made all-NBA seven times, was on five championship teams and later gained admission to the Basketball Hall of Fame in Springfield, Massachusetts. Martin had been the premier player during an era of brilliant Southwest Conference basketball. He, teammates John Hargis and Al Madsen, Jackie Robinson of Baylor, George Kok of

Arkansas, Bill Henry of Rice, Leroy Pasco of TCU and others had elevated the quality of competition in the conference. But the 1950 season was not yet over before people began speculating about its future. The SWC's woeful 12-39 intersectional record and declining attendance begged for explanation. Possible reasons were the continued dominance of football on the high school and college level; a revulsion toward betting and point-shaving scandals that caused the conference to impose stringent rules upon itself; too many Texas universities pursuing too few high school stars; a belief among athletic directors that basketball was a financial loser; small, ancient gyms that failed to wow out-of-state recruits; and a delay in racial integration.

Record: 13-11
48 Oklahoma 65
35 Texas Wesleyan 38
54 North Texas 51
64 North Texas 47
42 West Texas 46
58 Arizona 50
84 Trinity 37
46 Houston 44
35 Wyoming 44
48 Alabama 41
49 Baylor 41
51 Arkansas 60
43 Baylor 49
55 Rice 52
48 Texas A&M 46
45 Oklahoma 55
37 Arkansas 51
69 TCU 57
34 SMU 51
38 TCU 51
47 SMU 46 (OT)
41 Baylor 43
55 Rice 41
53 Texas A&M 52

"SWC basketball has come upon evil days," wrote Morris Williams of the *Austin Statesman*. "Gone are the recent years of glory when Texas, Baylor, Arkansas and Rice were busily building up prestige in the post-war roundball world. What's happened? Is this the leveling off, the end, maybe, of a brief but crazily splendid era—an era which dangled its magic wand of greatness over a few favored coaches and players and turned thoughts of fans toward national championships?"

The NBA virtually ignored players from the Southwest Conference. Two other crude measuring sticks—consensus all-Americans and NCAA performances—are indicative. Since 1935, five SWC players (Jack Gray of Texas, Ike Poole of Arkansas, John Adams of Arkansas, Bob Kinney of Rice and Bill Henry of Rice) had won first-team consensus all-America honors. But in the next quarter-century, the conference would produce just one such player, Jim Krebs of SMU in 1957. The SWC had a representative in the NCAA Tournament each of those 25 years, but in 17 instances, the team lost its first game. Six times (Texas Tech in 1962, Texas in 1963, SMU in 1967, TCU in 1968, Texas A&M in 1969 and Texas in 1972), the SWC team won its first game and was then ousted. Twice (Baylor in 1950 and SMU in 1956), the league's standard-bearer reached the Final Four and lost in the semifinals. Of course, that is not to say the Southwest Conference underwent a drastic weakening, no quality athletes performed, there were no exciting games or title chases or interesting controversies. There were plenty of the above in the following years, but the fact remains, SWC basketball failed to keep pace with the rest of the country.

As for the 1950 Longhorns, prospects were not encouraging. "It looks like a long, hard winter," Gray said. "I've had enough trials and tribulations to fill a library." Tom Hamilton and Frank Womack (key players on Bibb Falk's national champion baseball team) were back, but the other vet, Wilson Taylor, soon quit to focus on his studies. For the season opener at Oklahoma, Gray had a starting lineup of Hamilton and Notre Dame transfer Bill McGee at forward, 6'5" Don Klein at center and Womack and Luther Scarborough at guard. The green Longhorns got ripped, 65-48, before 4,500 fans. Hamilton, who would carry the load all season, was the top scorer with 22. There was no shame in losing to a classy team like OU, but when they got beat by three at home by little Texas Wesleyan, some fans actually booed. The Rams, with UT transfer Louis Zastoupil, celebrated as if they had won the national title. In that game, Scarborough suffered a broken rib and collapsed lung that sidelined him for the season.

Just when it looked like the *Alcalde*'s fearful prediction of the most disastrous season since 1931 would be a reality, things improved as the Steers won two from North Texas, 54-51 and 64-47. The leading scorer in both games was Bill Huffman, a 6'1" senior who had seen scant playing time the past three years. Not a great defender, Huffman nevertheless became one of Gray's more dependable players in 1950.

After losing to West Texas by four, the Longhorns went to San Antonio for two games at the new Alamo Stadium Gym. Undefeated Arizona took a tumble, 58-50, as Hamilton scored 25 and Womack clung like a leech to Wildcat star Leon Blevins. The Longhorns no longer seemed so impotent, and an 84-37 defeat of Trinity, the biggest score since the war years, was proof.

The University of Houston, in its fifth year of college basketball, brought a team to Austin on December 20 and appeared to have the game in hand, but Huffman tied it and Hamilton won it with eight seconds left for a 46-44 victory that caused a small yet vocal crowd to mob the Longhorns. Dick Berg led the Cougars with 15 points.

Texas entered the All-College Tournament with a 5-3 record, and fans realized that with just one star, the old warhorse Tom Hamilton, Gray had done another fine job of molding a team that would win some games. A zone defense harassed Wyoming in the first round at Oklahoma City, but guard John Pilch (12) helped the Cowboys to a 44-35 victory. UT led all the way in a seven-point defeat of Alabama and beat Baylor, 49-41. Perhaps because it was a consolation game and he did not want to tip his pre-SWC hand, Bear coach Bill Henderson chose to rest Don Heathington and his other starters in the second half. That had something to do with the Horns scoring the game's last 19 points.

Tom Hamilton unleashes a hook shot against the Arkansas Razorbacks.

Conference play began in Fayetteville. The Razorbacks were good despite a losing record attributable to playing tough teams like Oklahoma A&M, Illinois, Indiana and Kentucky. Jim Cathcart and Hamilton both scored 17, but Cathcart had more help in a 60-51 Arkansas win. Bob Ambler did yeoman work under the backboards for the Hogs. Unlike in the holiday tournament, Baylor used its top players the whole game against Texas in Waco. Heathington, all-SWC for the third straight year, headed a lineup with five seniors. Unable to fathom the Steers' tight zone defense, Baylor still managed to win, 49-43. It was 40 minutes of spine-tingling basketball with 12 lead changes. Hamilton's hook was not dropping, but he still got 13 points, four less than Heathington.

When UT hosted Rice on January 12, the doors of Gregory Gym were open to the public for an SWC game for the first time since 1946. Because demand for seating by the student body had declined, business manager Ed Olle announced that plenty of tickets were available. To the business office, a big crowd with lots of paying (i.e., nonstudent) patrons was preferable to an equal number of students. Six thousand fans saw the Longhorns rally after a stumbling start to beat the Owls, 55-52. Substitute guards Bobby Joe Clark and George Cobb played well, and Joe Ed Falk threw in 15 points. Hamilton's driving hook with 40 seconds left clinched the game. Joe McDermott (15) of Rice missed two free throws and made two turnovers in the final minute.

The gym was packed when upstart Texas A&M came to Austin two days later. Hamilton, scoreless from the field, hit a free throw to tie it up in the last minute, but Falk was the hero with a twisting shot at the buzzer that drew a deafening roar of approval from the crowd as Texas won, 48-46. Refs Whitey Baccus and Adolph Dietzel ruled it good despite vigorous protests from Marty Karow and the Aggies. Walter Davis of Texas A&M (16) and McGee (11) had high-point honors.

For the second time in 1950, the Longhorns lost to Oklahoma. The annual March of Dimes benefit raised $4,500 as Wayne Glasgow (21) led the Sooners to a 55-45 win. It was the last game for McGee, UT's second-leading scorer, who was ruled academically ineligible. Conference play resumed when Arkansas, then coached by Presley Askew, invaded Gregory Gym. Thanks in part to a seven-minute Texas drought, the Hogs built a 22-point lead and took an easy victory. Hamilton was the game's top scorer with 17.

He followed that with a career-high 31 in a 69-57 defeat of TCU, snapping the Horns' two-game losing streak. Womack played a good defensive game, and Huffman had 11 points against the young Horned Frogs, who were led by Harvey Fromme (12). After five straight home games, Gray's Steers went to Dallas and got walloped by SMU, 51-34. Paul "Cotton" Mitchell scored 14 for the Ponies, seeking their first SWC title since 1937. UT's nine-game win streak over TCU came to an end at Will Rogers Coliseum, still bearing faint olfactory memories of a recent stock show. Hamilton scored 24 and Frog guard Tommy Taylor 17 in a 51-38 decision. The Longhorns were within four when Womack fouled out, leaving a much weaker defense.

The tables were abruptly turned when SMU came to Austin and lost a stirring one-point overtime game. An unheralded sub, James Dowies, and Huffman closed the Mustang lead at the end of regulation. Eight of Texas' nine points in OT came on Hamilton's hook shots. "The gun fired, leaving the Texans out in front, 47-46, and Hamilton with a tired victory grin adorning his face as he was literally ganged by victory-drunk Texas supporters," wrote Bill Lee of the *Austin Statesman*. Jack Brown, Charlie Lutz and Paul Mitchell had 13 each for the Ponies.

The 100th meeting of Texas and Baylor (the oldest basketball rivalry in the state, beginning in 1906) was a crashing, heartbreaking 43-41 defeat by the Bruins. The leading scorers were Hamilton (16) and Don Heathington (13), seniors who had gone head-to-head many times in the past four years. Baylor guard Gerald Cobb came off the bench, and as the Gregory Gym capacity crowd roared, made a jump shot, a lightning dash to the basket and a free throw in the final 90 seconds to win it.

Last-place Rice, then holding its games in the Houston Public School Field House, fought UT on even terms in the first half but wilted and lost, 55-41. Dowies, in the starting lineup for the first time, scored 16 to tie the Owls' gangling Joe McDermott for high-point honors. Huffman had 15. Texas A&M, still steamed about that last-second loss in Austin, led most of the way in the season finale, but a Huffman layup and a Womack free throw brought the Steers a 53-52 victory. Jewell McDowell had 19 for the Ags and Hamilton 18 for Texas. The Dallas senior was the first UT player to lead the SWC in scoring since Jack Collins in 1936. Equally outstanding in basketball and baseball—he earned four letters in each sport—Hamilton had a heck of a career wearing orange and white.

1951

Missing almost half of his offense in the person of Tom Hamilton, UT coach Jack Gray still viewed 1951 with optimism. But surviving the early season might be tough, he warned. Captain Frank Womack was back along with Joe Ed Falk, Jim Dowies and Don Klein. They were joined by three sophs—high school teammates George Scaling and Cecil Morgan and an intense little jumping jack named Leon Black. Transfers Ted Price (Kentucky) and Jimmy Viramontes (New Mexico A&M) were the long and short of it at 6'8" and 5'7". The 1951 Longhorns would not be the most talented team, surpassing 60 points just three times, but they compensated with an abundance of character, discipline and desire.

The curtain went up in early December with two home games against Sam Houston. Viramontes drew howls of delight from 3,000 fans with his passing and ballhandling, evoking memories of the Mighty Mice of the late 1940s. Falk scored 18 as the Steers opened on a victorious note, 51-44. They were outlasted by the stubborn Bearkats the next night in a one-point overtime loss that might have been avoided, but Texas missed three free throws in the last 10 seconds of regulation. Dowies and Sam Houston's Tom Sewell both scored 16.

UT shot just 17 percent in the first half, losing to Oklahoma, 49-35, in Norman. The speedy Sooners were in command all the way, causing the *Daily Texan* to describe Gray's team as "more courageous than talented." It was too early to make such judgments. Scaling replaced the ill Womack when Texas Wesleyan came to Gregory Gym, and he scored 16 in a 63-41 victory. Dowies, a hard-charging, aggressive player, had 20, quite a few of those points the result of nifty assists from Viramontes.

The SWC was again getting beaten to a fare-thee-well in intersectional games when Texas made another northeast trip. No one could stop Canisius' big men, Randy Sharp (20) and Don Hartnett (15) in the Griffins' 59-45 win. Buffalo sportswriters were most impressed with the play of Scaling (13) and Viramontes. St. John's and Holy Cross played first in a Madison Square Garden doubleheader with Texas and Manhattan following. A crowd of 14,000 saw an exciting game as the inexperienced and outmanned Longhorns rallied to tie it at 46 in the final minute. Victory was within reach when Scaling stole the ball and passed to Luther Scarborough, but the referee called him for an offensive foul, leading to Jim Garvey's game-winning free throw. Scaling had 18 and Junius Kellogg 14 for the Jaspers. Later in the season, Kellogg blew the whistle on the point-shaving scandal that shook college basketball. More than 30 players (widely considered just a fraction of those involved) from Manhattan, City College of New York, Long Island, New York University, Kentucky, Bradley and Toledo had conspired to fix games, usually winning by less than the point spread. Basketball was threatened, but it survived and thrived.

The Longhorns returned home from New York with a 2-4 record. For the first time, they played in a midseason tournament other than the one in Oklahoma City. The *San Antonio Express-News* brought Texas, SMU, LSU and Alabama together, and the SWC regained some prestige when its members defeated the Southeastern Conference teams. Dowies scored 14 and Black (in his first start) 13 as UT beat LSU, 68-53. So it was the Longhorns and the Ponies in the tournament finals. Texas blew a nice first-half lead and watched Derrell Murphy tie the game and then win it with a hoop in the last 15 seconds.

Playing again in the All-College Tournament, UT met Vanderbilt, a team packed with Indiana schoolboy stars and averaging 66 points per game. But with 17 each from Dowies and Scaling, the Horns scrapped their way to a 55-49 triumph. They next played Oklahoma A&M, Hank Iba's Missouri Valley Conference powerhouse. No Texas player reached double figures in that nine-point loss, but there were many chances to win. Guard Gail McArthur scored 13 for the Aggies. In the last game in Oklahoma City, Alabama got 30 points from Paul Sullivan and Bob Schneider to beat Texas, 54-41. Scaling scored 15, and Black exhibited a stellar floor game.

Record: 13-14

51 Sam Houston 44
54 Sam Houston 55 (OT)
35 Oklahoma 49
63 Texas Wesleyan 41
45 Canisius 59
46 Manhattan 47
68 LSU 53
50 SMU 52
55 Vanderbilt 49
38 Oklahoma A&M 47
41 Alabama 54
59 Baylor 58 (2 OT's)
56 Rice 54
42 SMU 39
50 Arkansas 42
29 Texas A&M 32
53 TCU 43
47 Oklahoma 49
77 Rice 51
34 TCU 49
41 SMU 54
38 Arkansas 40
51 Baylor 43
42 Texas A&M 40
33 Texas A&M 45
35 Texas A&M 34
32 Texas A&M 33

Conference play began on January 3 against Baylor, a team even younger than UT. About 4,000 people at Gregory Gym saw the Horns and Bears fight tooth and nail through regulation and two overtimes before Falk made a winning free throw with two seconds left. Dowies, who scored all five Texas points in the first OT, had 17 and Klein 16. Gordon Carrington, one of four Bruins to foul out, scored 11. Gray did not let the celebration last long. The Steers got their first look at Rice's new $1.1-million, 6,200-seat facility (named Autry Court a decade later), complementing its new 70,000-seat football stadium. Texas was cruising toward victory in the last minute when field goals by Jim Gerhardt, Charlie Tighe and Maurice Teague brought the Owls to within one point. But Black dropped in a free throw, and time ran out. UT won, 56-54, in a game that started slowly and ended in an uproar.

Before the SMU game in Austin, a storm broke with Gray at its epicenter. He told *Houston Post* writer Jack Gallagher that the slowdown, ball-control style of offense was hurting the game and with it, fan interest. He called the Oklahoma City tourney "one of the dullest you ever saw." A member of the NCAA rules committee, Gray favored a shot clock or some other way to speed up play. The Associated Press sent Gallagher's story across the nation, and in response, various coaches agreed or disagreed. For example, Nat Holman backed Gray. But Hank Iba and Phog Allen got their noses bent out of shape, as did Presley Askew of Arkansas.

Gray put his men through some stiff workouts and installed a couple of new plays in preparation for the red-hot SMU Mustangs, winners of eight of their last nine. If experience was a teacher, the Horns were likely to be taking lessons, but they won, 42-39, before 7,000 wildly cheering fans. Scaling and the Ponies' Paul Mitchell both scored 12. Womack and Scaling held high-scoring Fred Freeman to three. In Fayetteville, Dowies and Scaling combined for 25 points in pacing UT to its fourth straight SWC win, 50-42. Seven-foot center Billy "Toar" Hester scored 10 early points but none after getting double-teamed. Gray froze the ball much of the second half, proving he could play the slow-down game when he saw fit. Those were not the Razorbacks who had ruled the conference for much of the past 25 years. Whatever their secret had been, they were fading; Arkansas would win just one title in the 1950s and none in the 1960s.

Texas A&M's Mutt-and-Jeff combination of Walter Davis and Jewell McDowell beat the Longhorns in College Station, 32-29. That game epitomized ball control, for which Aggie coach John Floyd made no apologies. The maroon and white took solace in ending a run of eight consecutive lickings dished out by Gray's teams. The Steers waded back into the thick of the fight with a 53-43 defeat of TCU before a packed house in Austin. The frontline of Dowies, Falk and Klein got most of the rebounds, and Scaling, performing ably in every facet of the game, scored 20. A stouthearted defense was thrown at Buster Brannon's fast-breaking Frogs, whose scoring leaders were Harvey Fromme (13) and George McLeod (11). Although it had previously been reserved for football victories, the lights of the UT Tower were turned orange in celebration.

Much as Texas perennially led the Southwest Conference in football attendance, so it was in basketball, and 1951 was no exception. The conference average of 2,300 was boosted by a number of 5,000-plus crowds at Gregory Gym. More surprising was the Longhorns' undisputed possession of first place at the halfway mark, due in large part to the coaching genius of Gray, who could make a fair team good and a good team great.

In the annual benefit game on February 5, the OU Sooners took a two-point victory in which Marcus Freiberger (21) rattled the rims with old-time fervor. Texas closed the gap in the final minute and appeared to have sent the game into overtime when Dowies hit a shot, but the ref disallowed it because of a foul on Womack. Rice, which had lost its last 16 games away from Houston, visited four days later and was dealt more misery, 77-51. UT shot 56 percent from the field to leave the Owls groggy. Scaling (20), Falk (16) and Dowies (13) led the Horns, while Rice's Joe McDermott got most of his 17 points when the game was effectively lost.

Just when things looked rosy, the Longhorns dropped three in a row. First was a 49-34 defeat by TCU in Fort Worth before 5,100 fans. George McLeod scored 19 and dominated both backboards in a thorough spanking of Texas. Next was SMU in Dallas. Doc Hayes' fourth-place Ponies scored a stunning 54-41 upset with 32 points from Jack Brown and Derrell Murphy. Ahead all the way, they began freezing the ball with 10 minutes left. The weary Steers braced for a home game with Arkansas, and the third straight defeat was administered, 40-38. Firebrand guard Jimmy Viramontes led a late rally that fell just short. As the team sank in the SWC standings, Gray and his players showed the strain by carping after the game and into the next day about a first-half mistake by referee Whitey Baccus that cost two points, the Razorbacks' margin of victory.

Down but not out, the Longhorns turned back Baylor, 51-43, in a bitterly fought game in Waco. Ralph Johnson, the Bears' SWC-leading scorer, got 16 points, while Scaling and Dowies combined for 38. Womack, never a big scorer, played his usual fine floor game and defense. In the regular-season finale, UT nipped Texas A&M, 42-40, before 8,000 enthusiastic fans. Gray employed a full-court press the entire game in which Dowies (12) was the top scorer. The result was a tie for the championship among Texas, A&M and TCU. Glory had been a long time coming for the Ags, who last won the title in 1923, and the Frogs (1934).

To determine the NCAA tourney representative, a three-way playoff was set up by a series of coin flips, all advantageous to Texas. The Aggies defeated TCU in Waco and then met the Horns in a best-of-three series. The first game, in College Station, was a 45-33 A&M victory. Jewell McDowell, shut out by the Horns just a week earlier, was splendid with 14 points. UT, facing elimination, rose to the occasion at home in a 35-34 win. The final minute was fast and rough, capped with a stolen pass by Viramontes, a Falk miss and then a rebound by Black, who was fouled by Walter Davis. His free throw with seven seconds left was the margin of victory. In a carbon copy of that game, the Ags won the next night, 33-32, with Leroy Miksch canning a late free throw. Thus ended a 17-year A&M jinx at Gregory Gym.

It was also the end of the magnificent coaching career of Jack Gray. He announced in late March that he was resigning, a development that shocked the UT athletic department. Enormously popular with his players, colleagues and alumni, Gray also had a growing family to support. His meager salary was not enough, and he and AD Dana X. Bible failed to see eye-to-eye. Although Bible had coached basketball at Texas A&M in the 1920s, he was first and foremost a football man. That was problematic for Gray as was his dislike for the increasingly crucial matter of recruiting. No one had asked Gray to come to Austin in 1931, but he came and made a lasting impact as a two-sport athlete and hoop coach. In 1951, he entered the oil pipeline business. No less successful in that endeavor than in athletics, Gray went on to become a wealthy man. He continued to live in Austin, stayed involved with the University of Texas and was one of the first inductees to the Longhorn Hall of Honor.

1952

Record: 16-8

48 Oklahoma 44
61 North Texas 56
55 North Texas 50
57 East Texas 49
68 Sam Houston 41
55 LSU 59
64 Tulane 78
63 Murray State 64 (OT)
58 SMU 42
51 Texas A&M 52 (OT)
65 Vanderbilt 49
43 TCU 52
41 SMU 31
62 Arkansas 51
60 Rice 53
43 Oklahoma 39
51 Texas A&M 40
58 Baylor 46
57 SMU 49
59 Baylor 71
47 TCU 54
38 Texas A&M 34
54 Rice 48
44 Arkansas 45

Except for the two seasons in which Marty Karow ran things, only Texas alumni had coached Longhorn basketball since 1932—Ed Olle, Jack Gray, Bully Gilstrap and Gray again. The big job at UT, head football coach, had recently been awarded to Ed Price, and seven of eight "major" sports were under Texas men. With the departure of Gray, athletic director Dana X. Bible and the Athletic Council sought a new basketball coach, preferably one with an orange-and-white pedigree. Although they took four months, there is little indication a widespread search was done. In July 1951, Thurman "Slue" Hull was appointed to fill the pontoon-sized shoes of Gray, who probably gave his blessing.

Hull first played in Gregory Gym in 1935, leading his Hughes Springs High School team to third place in the UIL state tournament. Part of the great Tarleton College teams that won 86 consecutive games, he arrived in Austin in 1939 and played for Gray with Bobby Moers, Chester Granville and Denton Cooley. After serving in the Army during World War II, Hull coached at Temple High School and Lamar Junior College (he had a 46-31 record with the Cardinals) and then returned to Austin. He could not have been more different from his ex-coach. Gray was a disciplinarian, a hard-driver who instilled a strong work ethic in his players. He commanded respect. Hull, on the other hand, was more likely to pat an athlete on the back and ask him to do his best. Hull's assistant was Marshall Hughes, a Tarleton teammate in the late 1930s. The 1952 Texas basketball media guide described Hughes as "a scholar as well as a coach and an athlete," and that was the truth. In addition to coaching in high school and junior college, he earned a master's degree and enrolled at UT in 1950 to start work on a doctorate in physical education. Hughes volunteered to help Gray and soon became the freshman coach and varsity assistant, jobs he held throughout Hull's five-year tenure. A nice man, he was even less assertive than Hull. The *Alcalde* was wildly flattering in opining that the combination of Hull and Hughes was like having Hank Iba and Adolph Rupp on the same staff.

Returning from the 1951 tri-champs were captain Don Klein (also a javelin chucker on Clyde Littlefield's track team), Jim Dowies, George Scaling (third in SWC scoring in 1951), Jimmy Viramontes, Leon Black, Ted Price and Cecil Morgan. Two fine players, Gib Ford and Billy Powell, were up from a 10-2 Yearling team. With the Korean War going on, nearly every man on the squad was in Army, Navy or Air Force ROTC. While not favored to win the Southwest Conference—TCU was—the team had experience, size, speed, ballhandling and depth. Only the defense was suspect. Hull had stepped into a nice situation with the 1952 Longhorns.

He won his first game, a 48-44 trimming of Oklahoma in Norman. Price, who had improved considerably in the off-season, scored 13 points. Both teams substituted freely as UT broke a four-game losing streak to the Sooners. North Texas, with a victory over Texas

A&M, came to Austin for two games and lost both by five points. Dowies and the Eagles' Pat Kelley were the top scorers the first night and Price and Dick Woodward the next night.

Scaling, a 5'11" package of hustle, conditioning and shooting skill, scored 17 in a 57-49 defeat of the East Texas Lions before 1,500 fans. "He waded through the East Texas floormen Tuesday night like a revenuer eluding hillbillies," wrote Charley Eskew of the *Austin Statesman*. Yet another teachers college, Sam Houston, took a 27-point beating at Gregory Gym, and then it was time for some serious competition.

Coach Thurman "Slue" Hull (right) and his assistant and eventual successor, Marshall Hughes.

The undefeated Longhorns boarded a Louisiana-bound train on December 16. They had heard about LSU, with all-Southeastern Conference guard Joe Dean and 6'9" soph Bob Pettit, and both were poison. Dean (eventually the Bengal athletic director) scored 13 and Pettit 30, including a field goal that broke a late tie and let LSU win, 59-55. Price (19), Dowies (15) and the ballhawking Viramontes kept Texas in the game, but Pettit was simply too much. Klein fouled out trying to guard him, and no one else had much luck. Bob Pettit went on to all-America honors and a long, distinguished career with the St. Louis Hawks. Tulane put the most decisive loss (78-64) of the season on the Horns the following night. Cliff Wells' Green Wave shot 46 percent and rolled over the visitors from Austin before 2,700 fans. Husky center Don Holt had 23 points and a plethora of rebounds, while Scaling (20), Dowies (16) and Viramontes (13) led the Steers.

Hull bemoaned his team's defensive work and vowed to improve in time for Murray State at Gregory Gym. The unbeaten Thoroughbreds, averaging 72 points per game, brought Bluegrass-style basketball to Texas. A small crowd saw an exciting game that went into overtime and culminated with Charley Lampley's winning free throw after time had expired to give the Thoroughbreds a 64-63 victory. Price and Murray State's Ben Purcell both scored 20.

Texas, a fixture of the All-College Tournament for more than a decade, chose to forgo it in 1952 and did not return to Oklahoma City until 1967. A new feature was the preseason SWC Tournament held in Dallas in conjunction with the Cotton Bowl, rather like the well-established Sugar Bowl cage meet in New Orleans. Inviting one outside school (Vanderbilt that year), all seven SWC members played games in the Automobile-Aviation-Recreation Building on the grounds of the State Fair. With 33 points from Dowies and Powell, Texas beat SMU, 58-42. The same two were the top scorers against Texas A&M, but Jewell McDowell, often a tormentor of the Horns, tied the game in regulation and won it in OT. In the third-place game of the tourney, which was won by TCU, UT and Vandy met. Ford made his starting debut against the Commodores and played well, as did Powell (16) and Dowies (13) in a 65-49 victory. A total of 10,000 people attended the tournament, a marginal financial success.

For just the second time in six years, the Longhorns did not take a trip to Madison Square Garden in 1952. Although TCU and Texas A&M were not deterred from playing there, a lot of schools refused, not even for a big payday. It was the hour of trial for college basketball after a full year that brought discredit to the game. Arraignments, court dates and ex-players and mobsters going to jail had dented its glory and spectator appeal. And fairly or not, Madison Square Garden was perceived as the prime den of iniquity. Except for a trip in 1954, Texas was through with early-season games at the fabled Garden.

As they had demonstrated in Dallas, the TCU Horned Frogs were the class of the league. With every starter back from the 1951 tri-champs, they were the first SWC team to break into the AP's top 20. In Fort

Worth, George McLeod and Harvey Fromme combined for 40 points in a 52-43 win. Scaling and Dowies had 11 each on a night when little went well for the Steers.

Back in the friendly confines of Gregory Gym, stalwarts Scaling (15) and Dowies (13) led the way in a 41-31 defeat of SMU. Ford and Powell scored just two points each, but they controlled the backboards against the smaller Mustangs. Both teams shot poorly from the field (Price was one for 11) in a sloppy game decided by free throws. Arkansas came to town four days later. The Hogs, in the first losing season in school history, were deprived of their star center, Billy Hester. Rumored to have been part of a fixed game between Arkansas and Kentucky two years earlier, he quit and said he was "going back to the farm." Texas stemmed three Razorback rallies and finished with a scoring spree in a 62-51 victory. Powell, the San Antonio springboard, grabbed 11 rebounds and joined Dowies (16) as the game's top scorer. Walter Hearns replaced Hester and led the Hogs with 15.

UT journeyed to Houston to meet the young Rice Owls, with 6'6" soph Gene Schwinger. He scored 26 points and showed why he would become the finest SWC player of the early 1950s. In a 60-53 Longhorn victory, Scaling and Price got 16 each. Hull's team overcame its own futility and a nine-point deficit, putting the ball on ice with eight minutes left. Another early freeze almost cost Texas the game against Oklahoma. A Gregory Gym crowd of 3,000 saw the stall begin with seven minutes remaining and the Horns up by just three. OU's Bob Waller tied it at 39, but Klein came up big in the final 30 seconds by scoring a basket, causing a Sooner turnover and getting a key rebound. Price, with 15 points, pulled out of a scoring slump. As Black, Ford and Powell got better by the game, Hull hoped to stay within striking range of TCU.

To do that, the Horns had to defeat visiting Texas A&M, then minus flashy two-time all-SWC guard Jewell McDowell. He graduated early, much to the relief of the Longhorns. A capacity crowd screamed its appreciation of a 51-40 Texas victory as Dowies (19) halted a late rally and smart floorwork by Viramontes and Ford led to some easy baskets. Walter Davis—who would win a gold medal in the high jump at that summer's Helsinki Olympics—had 20 for the boys from the Brazos Valley. To make it even sweeter, news came that the Frogs had lost to Arkansas, pulling UT into a first-place tie.

Beaten just once at home, the Horns met Baylor (with a 3-16 season record) on February 5. If they could stop the scoring antics of Ralph Johnson, little trouble was expected. Johnson, a 6'3" lefthander with a deadly hook shot, had led the conference in scoring in 1951. And there was the matter of attendance. Following the postwar enrollment boom, the UT student body declined from 17,000 to 12,500, still far more than could fit into Gregory Gym, but the demand was not the same as in the frantic Slater Martin years. While some sellouts continued to occur, it was only by urging the general public (virtually warned not to bother in previous years) to come and join the students. Just 3,500 people were there to witness the Longhorns' 58-46 victory over the Bruins. Dowies had 22 points and Klein and Ford slapped some tight defense on Johnson, who scored a season low of nine.

SMU had won three straight before hosting Texas in crowded Perkins Gym, but the Mustangs missed star forward Derrell Murphy, out after midterm exams. While Jack Kastman (15) and Henry Holm (13) stepped up to replace him, the Ponies fell victim to a sparkling display of backboard control and Price's tip-in mastery. UT's six-game win streak came to a halt at McLean Gym in Waco as Baylor rocked the Longhorn dream boat with a 71-59 thumping. Ralph Johnson (22), the night's brightest star, had help from Howard Hovde (13) and Bill Harris (12). Bill Henderson's Bears tore the Texas defense asunder as Klein, Dowies, Black and Powell all fouled out.

The conference race was still a two-team affair when the Horns and Frogs tangled in Austin. The *Daily Texan* called it the game of the year, and attendance (7,500) reflected that. TCU had not won at Gregory Gym since Bully Gilstrap was coaching Texas, and the Frogs needed all their basketball savvy to pull out a 54-47 victory. Due to foul problems, George McLeod played just 16 minutes, but he scored 14 points. The SWC crown as good as theirs, the Frogs' locker room had cheerful smiles and backslapping while a funereal air prevailed across the way. "The boys played hard," Hull said, "but the shots didn't fall when they should have."

At College Station, the score was tied at 34 with two minutes left when Price tipped in Dowies' miss, and Scaling blew through the Texas A&M defense for a layup in a four-point Texas victory. Walter Davis kept the Ags in the game with 15 points. The Longhorns overcame the A&M ball-control methods and loud, taunting fans and got a taste of Aggie hospitality when the air was let out of a tire on the team bus.

Texas fans had their first chance to see Gene Schwinger when Rice came to Gregory Gym. He scored 16 points in a 54-48 loss to the Steers. While Dowies (25) was the only other player to reach double figures, Ford, the sure-handed Amarillo soph, played his usual fine defensive and rebounding game. Although Black did not score, he got some of the loudest cheers from the 3,000 fans present. At 5'8", he often outjumped much taller players and was Hull's iceman when it was time to stall.

The season ended in Fayetteville. Coach Presley Askew had been harassed into leaving, and a nice crowd gathered to pay tribute to him and, perchance, witness a Razorback upset. Dowies (15) and Klein (13) had the Horns up by one, but sophomore guard Tyron Lewis threw in a 55-foot shot at the buzzer, giving Askew an unforgettable going-away present.

1953

Slue Hull's second Texas team lost some height and scoring punch from 1952, and the Yearlings offered no real help. The key newcomers were a pair of 6'7" transfers—Fred "Goose" Saunders (from Schreiner College) and Bob Waggener (Western Kentucky). They joined lettermen George Scaling, Leon Black, Cecil Morgan, Gib Ford and Billy Powell. Although he was not named captain until the end of the season, Black held the team together from the first scrimmage through the last, title-deciding game. The Longhorns were not expected to be there since preseason forecasting had them fifth or sixth in the Southwest Conference.

One day after Waggener broke a hand in practice, the season got underway with a narrow 48-47 defeat of Oklahoma at Gregory Gym. Powell scored 12 points, and three Sooners had 10. As had been done many times before, the *Daily Texan* sought to improve fan conduct at home games with a stern editorial about jeering, howling and stomping while opponents shot free throws, asserting that such conduct "dishonors the University of Texas." The Colorado A&M Rams had already played and won three games when they came to Austin and lost a rough, lopsided contest, 63-46. In the prelim, Marshall Hughes' frosh defeated national champion Wharton Junior College, with Wayman "Jiggs" Buchanan leading the way. His 21 points per game in 1953 was the highest average yet for a Yearling.

Record: 12-9
48 Oklahoma 47
63 Colorado A&M 46
59 Tennessee 66
66 Vanderbilt 84
51 Oklahoma 72
43 Baylor 57
52 TCU 64
58 Texas A&M 54
55 TCU 48
64 SMU 53
62 Arkansas 57
42 Texas A&M 51
59 Baylor 60
58 Rice 46
68 Texas A&M 49
70 Arkansas 65
79 Houston 65
80 SMU 52
56 Rice 61
77 Baylor 65
50 TCU 68

The Horns hit the road and played Tennessee in Knoxville on December 18, the first basketball meeting between the two schools. Scaling and the Vols' Carl Widseth both scored 16 as Tennessee came from behind to win, 66-59. Texas was fading even before Powell, Ford and Saunders fouled out. Two days later in Nashville, UT dropped another one, 84-66, to Vanderbilt. It was the most points given up by a Longhorn team since 1946. Dan Finch, the Commodores' junior forward, scored 21 to lead both teams.

Gib Ford, perhaps UT's best all-around player, broke his hand in practice and was sidelined for several weeks. The first game without him was against OU in Norman, where the Sooners dominated the backboards and the scoreboard to win by 21 points. Texas, flagging when the SWC Tournament began in Dallas, finished in a dismal seventh place. It began when Baylor took a 57-43 victory with Scaling and the Bears' John Starkey scoring 21 apiece. Texas and TCU were close during most of the second-round game, but the Frogs pulled away to win by 12; gangling center Henry Ohlen had 18 points. The Horns did manage a 58-54 defeat of Texas A&M to avoid last place. SMU pulled a shocker by winning the tourney with victories over A&M, Arkansas and Rice. It was the last year for the financially shaky meet in Dallas because Rice AD Jess Neely reissued an invitation to hold it at Rice Gym. His offer was

Gib Ford (31) shoots in the Longhorns' 58-46 win over Rice. Fred Saunders and Leon Black follow.

accepted, and the erstwhile Cotton Bowl Tournament moved to Houston the next year.

Perhaps because UT had lost five of its last six games, Gregory Gym was only half full when defending champ TCU came to town. Buster Brannon's Frogs had treated the Horns terribly in Dallas. Hull went with just six players (Scaling, Powell, Black, Morgan, Saunders and sub forward Jim Richardson) in a spasmodic 55-48 upset. Although Henry Ohlen was the game's top rebounder, he made just three of 15 shots. The victory was sealed by Hull's application of a semistall in the final minutes as the Frogs were forced to foul. Powell scored 18 and Saunders 11.

In what the *Austin Statesman* described as "one of the most spirited exhibitions by a Texas team in several years," the Horns beat SMU, 64-53, on the Ponies' home court. Grabbing an early lead and fighting off repeated challenges, Texas had just two starters playing toward the end because Saunders fouled out, Powell was injured, and Morgan crashed headlong into a brick wall while chasing a loose ball. Scaling (22) and SMU's Jack Kastman (11) were the game's leading scorers.

Glen Rose was back as coach at Arkansas, and one of his stars was the son of a former Hog player and coach, Gene Lambert. The Longhorns, with Powell and Morgan healthy, were at full strength when Arkansas visited. The much bigger Razorbacks were in command until a second-half full-court press proved effective. A tense crowd of 6,500 witnessed UT's 62-57 victory, led by Saunders (20). The difference was made at the free throw line as the Steers connected on 30 of 51 and the Hogs just 11 of 23.

To everyone's amazement, UT was winning without Ford, the talented forward. But it ended when the Aggies took a 51-42 victory behind 17 points from Rodney Pirtle and 13 from Leroy Miksch. Texas' shooting was as cold as the weather outside DeWare Field House. Morgan got in trouble with some Cadets in the game's closing minutes. He put a hard foul on guard Don Binford after a fast break and was nearly mobbed by fans in the gym's north end. Texas players and coaches came to his rescue, as did the referees and Aggie coaches. After the game, a maroon partisan took an errant swing at Leon Black.

Despite that loss, other SWC teams were still looking at the Longhorn posterior. Ford and Waggener had recovered, so the team was at full strength upon meeting the Bears in Waco. Over 3,000 fans packed into the little sweatbox known as McLean Gym to see Baylor earn a 60-59 squeaker. Even with Ford's close-to-the-vest defense, John Starkey scored 25 points. The Bears led by two when Scaling was fouled at the buzzer. As the hushed crowd looked on, he made the first free throw but missed the second. Black (20) played one of his best games in defeat. Then in the 13th year of a basketball career that began in a tiny east Texas town, Black was a remarkable athlete. With excellent coordination and explosive reflexes, he could dunk a ball or rocket up between two bigger players for a rebound. It was only in his senior year that Black was called upon to score, and he proved himself capable. United Press International named him to its "Small America" team (players 5'10" and under) in 1953.

Gregory Gym was again full when the Horns hosted Rice and the celebrated Gene Schwinger. Ford hustled, scored 17 points and grabbed 15 rebounds while holding the Owls' star to 12 points in a 58-46 victory. SWC officials, known for their quick whistles, sent six players to the bench with excessive fouls. Out to avenge the earlier loss to what the *Daily Texan* called "Ol' Army," Texas did so with an impressive 68-49 victory keyed by Powell's 16 points. Leroy Miksch, often a thorn in the Longhorns' side, scored 16 for Texas A&M, but the Ags were surprisingly inept. If there was ever a need for a shot clock, that game proved it because Morgan held the ball near midcourt for the last three minutes, and the Aggies refused to come out after him.

Coupled with a Baylor loss, Texas was riding high in the saddle, leading the SWC before the Arkansas game. While the Hogs would have loved nothing more than to tag the Horns with their third loss, Hull's sharpshooters were too much. Texas led by 12 when Raymond Shaw and Orval Elkins brought Arkansas to within two in the final two minutes. But timely free throws by Morgan, Black and Waggener kept UT in front, 70-65. If Hull was not Jack Gray, his team had nevertheless come a long way on hustle and determination, and there was more winning yet to come.

The March of Dimes game, a Gregory Gym institution since 1939, featured the University of Houston, coached by Alden Pasche. His 6'8" center, Gary Shivers, tied Powell for scoring honors with 21 in Texas' methodical 79-65 win before 1,700 fans. In a game with little real significance, the Horns lost Black, their spunky little guard, with an ankle injury. He was scarcely needed against last-place SMU, which got clobbered, 80-52, UT's highest point total in nearly four years.

With all the security of a boy passing a graveyard at night, the Steers ventured to Houston and got a rude welcome from the second-place Owls. Texas had won seven straight over Rice, but Gene Schwinger scored 22 and Maurice Teague 11 as a throng of 6,200 saw the Owls grab the SWC lead with a 61-56 win. Black, taped all the way from his toes to his knee by trainer Frank Medina, tried unsuccessfully to play.

In the final home game, Scaling got a career-high 25 points as the Horns beat Baylor, 77-65, to pull into a tie with Rice and TCU for first place. John Starkey also had a fine game with 21 for the Bears. It was not a great surprise for the Frogs and Owls to be at the top as the season neared a close, but Texas? That was most unlikely. Rice was upset by SMU, leaving all eyes on Will Rogers Coliseum where TCU and Texas met. The Horned Frogs led by one at halftime, scored a quick eight points and turned a close game into a 68-50 rout to win their second straight SWC championship. Scoring honors went to Henry Ohlen (18) of TCU and Scaling (15). Connecting on just four of 24 shots in the second half, the Longhorns were miserably off form.

Hull put the uniforms in mothballs, but he had reason to feel upbeat. His 1953 team, seen as an also-ran at the start of the year, had surpassed all expectations. And an SWC title, or at least a portion of it, was on the horizon.

1954

Perhaps because SWC championships had been coming at four-year intervals (1939, 1943, 1947 and 1951), the Longhorns were not quite expected to gain admission to the throne room in 1954. There was a marked lack of speed, defense and outside shooting, but the core of Billy Powell, Gib Ford and Fred Saunders guaranteed a fairly good team. Coach Slue Hull moved Ford to guard and installed Bob Waggener at forward, while sophs Philip Kidd and John Schmid alternated at the fifth spot throughout the season. Wayman Buchanan, the big scorer of the 1953 frosh, had a negligible impact.

UT did not start with a weak opponent at Gregory Gym. Instead, the Horns traveled to Stillwater and met Oklahoma A&M, with 6'11" Bob Mattick and Mack Carter, the "Borger Bomber" who had left Texas to play college hoops. Stage fright struck all of the Longhorns except Saunders (12) as they shot 10 of 45 from the field in a 54-37 defeat. Carter had 13 for the Aggies.

Lamar Junior College had become four-year Lamar Tech since Hull's departure from Beaumont, and he brought the Cardinals in for a game. They had already defeated Texas A&M by 20 and lost to Baylor when UT took an 81-61 victory on December 5. The Goose (Saunders) flew high with 19 points, while Gene Carpenter led Lamar with 17. That was Texas' 11th straight win at home, stretching back to the 1952 season, a streak that ended with a visit from Oklahoma A&M, rated No. 5 in the nation. The Ags escaped defeat by the skin of their teeth, 62-60, before 6,000 fans. There was action aplenty with five lead changes in the last two minutes, and the Steers were ahead by one with just 20 seconds left. But forward Tom Fuller made a 20-foot shot, and a free throw by Dale Roark ended the rousing game. The big men, Bob Mattick (21) and Saunders (18), led their teams in scoring.

Bouncing back into the win column with a four-point home victory over Houston, the Longhorns got good performances from Saunders (26 points and strong defense on the Cougars' 6'8" Gary Shivers) and substitute guard Charles Warren (13 points and many assists). That game was but a tuneup for UT's eastern invasion—Duquesne in Pittsburgh and Manhattan in New York, evoking memories of Jack Gray, whose teams won eight of 12 in the east and five of seven at Madison Square Garden. The Dukes had two towering stars, Jim Tucker and Dick Ricketts, and a super-soph in Si Green. The game was televised in Pittsburgh's Golden Triangle, where optimism was as abundant as pig iron. Ranked No. 3 and destined to finish second in the 1954 NIT, Duquesne had a big, fast and superb basketball team. Temperatures were near zero, about like Texas' shooting in a 71-58 loss to the doughty Dukes. Hardly resembling the team that had played Oklahoma A&M to a standstill 10 days earlier, the Horns fell behind early and were never in it. Waggener and Ford both scored 16, three less than Fletcher Johnson, Duquesne's rubber-legged reserve center. Hull made no excuses: "They were just too much for us. Too much speed and too much height."

Record: 16-9

37 Oklahoma A&M 54
81 Lamar Tech 61
60 Oklahoma A&M 62
68 Houston 64
58 Duquesne 71
62 Manhattan 56
72 Alabama 52
66 Arkansas 65 (OT)
58 Rice 65
54 TCU 47
64 Arkansas 61
49 Texas A&M 46
74 Rice 66
80 Houston 79
75 SMU 69
63 Baylor 67
64 Texas Tech 56
51 Rice 61
66 Texas A&M 49
78 Baylor 63
63 SMU 90
67 Arkansas 57
68 TCU 59
62 Rice 70
71 Rice 72

The Longhorns traveled on to New York, where Ned Irish said everything was hunky in big-time college basketball. Attendance at Madison Square Garden, which he operated, was up, and fixed-game scandals were in the past. The Jaspers were not the toughest of opponents for the visitors in orange. UT shot to a 19-point halftime lead but grew cold as Manhattan narrowed it to one with six minutes left. Schmid had a steal and three free throws to put the Horns ahead at the end, 62-56. Saunders, in early foul trouble, scored 18 points in just 27 minutes of playing time. On their way home, the Longhorns stopped in Syracuse to catch an NBA game between the Nationals and the Minneapolis Lakers with UT-ex Slater Martin.

Back in Austin, neither flushed with victory nor crestfallen, the Horns prepared for the SWC tourney. Hull and his aide-de-camp, Marshall Hughes, knew their team could score and rebound, but they had trouble stopping opponents. No. 17 Rice, fresh off a Madison Square Garden victory of its own (over St. John's), was the strong favorite to win the three-day event at Rice Gym. Joining the seven SWC teams was Alabama, with a gang of sophomores who recently had won the Birmingham Classic. The Crimson Tide and the Horns were even at halftime, but Powell, UT's fiery redhead, scored 16 points in a 72-52 win. Jerry Harper had 19 for Bama. In the semifinals, Texas and Arkansas went into overtime in a spine-tingler. Orval Elkins put the Razorbacks up by two, but with 15 seconds left, Powell drew a two-shot foul. He made the first, missed the second but grabbed the rebound and hit a game-winning jumper. Rice also needed an OT victory (over SMU) to reach the finals. Gene Schwinger scored 24, and the Owls capitalized on numerous UT errors in a 65-58 win. The tournament was a prelude to the SWC race in which Rice and Texas were clearly the top teams.

It began five days into the new year in Fort Worth. TCU's 30-year-old campus field house, used for practice and nonconference games, had recently burned to the ground. Will Rogers Coliseum was not ideal for basketball, so the Fort Worth school system offered the use of its new 3,500-seat gymnasium. The Horned Frogs, SWC champs or cochamps the last three seasons, were off to a poor start. But against Texas, Buster Brannon's forces threatened to make it a runaway in the first half, only to see the Horns come back for a 54-47 victory. Saunders, with a hook shot that reminded people of Tom Hamilton, scored 16 and Powell and Ford 11 each. Waggener's defense on Henry Ohlen helped the cause, too. One of the loudest-cheering fans that night was former Longhorn Leon Black, then a soldier at nearby Fort Bliss.

Norman Smith scored 24 for Arkansas, but he got little help from his teammates in a 64-61 UT victory in

Austin before 6,500 fans. Glen Rose substituted often and urged his players to be aggressive, and as a result, the game sometimes resembled a back-alley tussle. Saunders (17) fouled out with five minutes left but was capably replaced by Jim Richardson as the Horns held on to a narrow lead. Powell (19) clinched it with three free throws.

It was the last year for DeWare Field House, a place where chicken wire once separated the court from the leather-lunged Aggies who made a game there seem, in the words of SMU's Doc Hayes, "like 40 minutes in Korea." G. Rollie White Coliseum was under construction when the Longhorns visited. But there was trouble in Aggieland. Two starters, Don Moon and Rodney Pirtle, had quit in disgust over coach John Floyd's slow-paced offense. Floyd denied reports that the team, then 1-10, had threatened to quit en masse and was only talked out of it by an assistant coach. The decimated Aggies fought UT to the hilt, losing by three points. Powell led the Longhorns with 14, and Saunders and Waggener scored 12 each and held 6'8" Roy Martin to three. Pat McCrory, a diminutive jump-shot artist, scored 12 for A&M.

Rice, paced by the velvet touch of Gene Schwinger, came to Gregory Gym for a big game that drew a big crowd—7,500. The Owls' nine-point halftime lead looked safe, but Saunders' hooks kept dropping, and Hull moved Powell, who was playing with a bad ankle, into the post, drawing Schwinger outside. The strategy worked as Texas tied it up and went on to finish brilliantly with a 74-66 victory. Owl guards panicked under the defensive pressure of Ford, who scored 14. Much as he had since his sophomore year, Ford did it all—scoring, rebounding, playmaking, defense and whatever else the team needed to win. In a year when Frank Selvy of Furman and Bevo Francis of Rio Grande were scoring obscenely, Ford played well and never even made all-SWC. (As a member of the Philips 66 Oilers, however, he would earn a spot on the U.S. Olympic team in 1956 and later become CEO of Converse.)

Fifteen days after beating Rice, the Longhorns started playing basketball again. The exam-period delay made Hull grumble, but there was nothing he could do about it. Even practicing was difficult because Gregory Gym was given over to course registration. To get ready for the resumption of SWC hostilities, the Horns went to Houston and played Alden Pasche's Cougars and came away with an 80-79 win. Saunders scored a career-high 28, including two free throws in the final half-minute. It was a team victory against an inspired UH club led by Gary Shivers (17) and Jackie Bell (15).

Notorious morning glories in the SWC garden, the Horns were determined not to fade. They faced a crucial battle with point-happy SMU, winless in Austin since 1949. Texas' 75-69 victory retained first place. The capacity crowd never took an easy breath, and the issue remained in doubt until the end. The Mustangs fell before UT's balanced attack as Saunders, Kidd, Schmid and Powell all reached double figures. Stylish guard Art Barnes had 16 for SMU.

The taciturn Hull reminded his team of the previous season when they got upset by Baylor in Waco. Once again, that old black magic the Bears weaved so well in their little abode spelled defeat for Texas, 67-63. Murray Bailey (21) and Tommy Strasburger (18) did most of the damage. Despite the loss, UT still had a tenuous grip on first place. Recently turned down for SWC admission for the 23rd time, Texas Tech came to Austin for the annual charity game. The Longhorns, looking forward to their showdown with Rice, were erratic in a 64-56 win paced by Richardson (18). Gene Carpenter had 14 for the Red Raiders. The prelim game was between Austin and McCallum high schools, the latter coached by a former UT star (Jimmy Viramontes) and featuring a future UT star (Jay Arnette).

The Steers could only wonder if the familiar February skid-row jinx had begun when Rice beat them, 61-51, in Houston. Gene Schwinger was splendid, scoring 24 and getting 23 rebounds to help the Owls wrest the SWC lead from Texas. Monte Robicheaux's defense thwarted the UT guards. Saunders had 18 points, but he and Ford were weakened by a virus. Just when expectations were lessening, lowly Texas A&M came to town and lost a 66-49 game that was as lackluster as an old wedding ring. Saunders and Ford were not even needed because Richardson again proved himself a quality player with 23 points. And for the Ags, James Addison scored 23 and was no slacker on defense. The Longhorns outrebounded them by an almost two-to-one margin. Many of the 6,000 fans who had begun the game with a derisive chorus of "The Farmer in the Dell," ended it by applauding the visitors' efforts.

There was another rout at Gregory Gym four days later, and this time Baylor got the worst of it, 78-63. The game marked the return to form of aces like Powell, Ford, Saunders and Waggener. When the lead reached 25, Hull cleared his bench. Albert White (15) was the Bears' lone bright spot. The grinding SWC race was into its last mile when the Horns went to Dallas to meet the Mustangs. They suffered a humiliation of biblical proportions, getting walloped by SMU, 90-63. The hot-shooting Ponies could do little wrong, especially in the first half when they built a 53-31 lead. Ford had an uncharacteristically poor game, going scoreless and committing three fouls. Derrell Murphy (24) was one of five SMU players in double figures. The pain was assuaged by news that Baylor had pulled an upset on Rice, so the Horns and Owls remained tied for the lead.

Although treading on slippery ground of late, the team returned home for one workout and then left for Fayetteville, heads up, jaws set, shirttails in. A victory would tie the all-time Texas-Arkansas record, then favoring the Hogs at 32-31. Three regulars fouled out, leaving Ford, Richardson, Kidd, Schmid and Warren to stall and hold onto a narrow lead before an overflow crowd of Razorback fans. They not only held on, they extended it a bit, winning, 67-57.

The Rice Owls defeated SMU on the same night Texas beat TCU on the hallowed hardwoods of Gregory Gym, 68-59, to earn a share of the 1954 SWC championship. Saunders (23) and Powell (16) paced the Horns, and Ford's floor play was impeccable. Whenever he went to the bench for a rest, the team seemed to sag. Center Charles Brown scored 26 for the dethroned Frogs.

While the NIT had indicated a willingness to take the SWC runner-up, no one anticipated a best-of-three playoff to determine the representative to the NCAA tourney, by then the clear winner of that 15-year-old popularity contest. So the pressure was turned up; the winner would go to Kansas City, and the loser would go home. The NIT got underway while the Owls and Longhorns were playing. Rice rapped the Steers, 70-62, in Houston and made a down payment on a date with Oklahoma A&M. A full house of 6,500 saw the Owls use a full-court press and Gene Schwinger score 25 points. The season's fifth meeting of the two teams was in Austin on Monday, March 8. (If necessary, a final playoff game would be held in Waco.) The gym was as full as the fire marshal would allow. A basket by Ford put the Horns up, 71-70, with 10 seconds left, and the Owls hurried downcourt. Schwinger would have taken the decisive shot, but he had fouled out for the first time in his illustrious career. Buzzy Brian missed a shot, and the rebound went to James Beavers, who coolly lofted a left-handed hook that dropped through the net just before the buzzer, leaving Gregory Gym silent except for the whoops of the Owls and a small cadre of their fans.

1955

The 1954 SWC cochampionship, surely the high-water mark of Slue Hull's tenure, was followed immediately by the worst season in Texas basketball history. "It could be a long, cold winter of pointless nights," bemoaned Mike Quinn of the *Daily Texan*, and he was far from wrong. The situation might have been truly horrendous if not for the arrival of Raymond Downs, destined to become one of the greatest Longhorn point-makers ever. His high school coach in San Antonio was Ed Kelley, a former UT football and basketball player who taught Downs several tricks of the trade. Misidentified at first by the *Austin Statesman* as Raymond "Brown" and by the *Alcalde* as "Terry" Downs, he was lightly recruited and spent a year at Del Mar Junior College. When Kelley advised Hull of Downs' potential (he scored 40 points several times at Del Mar), a scholarship was offered, so he came to Austin and sat out the 1954 season. During that time, Downs grew an inch to 6'4", added 15 pounds of muscle and honed his game. Downs made an impression on the coaches and players with his ambidextrous shooting and overall hoop savvy.

But the focus was on fellow sophomore Ellis Olmstead, who had what no coach can impart—size. At 6'10", he was the tallest player yet to wear orange and white, but he was slow, inexperienced and lacked the killer instinct that came naturally to Downs. Hull looked around at his prospects and indicated that he was counting on Olmstead to develop. Two more sophomores, guard Norman Hooton and forward Bill Groogan, contributed substantially over the next three seasons. Lettermen Philip Kidd, John Schmid and Wayman Buchanan were back, too.

Due partially to an injured ankle, Downs got off to a slow start, hardly scoring a point and giving little hint of future stardom. Twenty years had passed after the last meeting of the Steers and Hardin-Simmons. On the first day of December, 5,000 fans at Gregory Gym saw Bob Tremaine and Delnor Poss combine to score 33 points and give the Cowboys a seemingly safe five-point lead with two minutes left. But Texas put on a nice comeback, capped by Hooton's two baskets, to tie and win an exciting 59-57 contest. Olmstead scored 15 and looked surprisingly adept at the post position, rendering the mournful wails of preseason observers wrong. Or so it was hoped. No one knew that the next 15 games would be losses.

The first was one of the closest, a 70-63 defeat by No. 11 Oklahoma A&M in Austin. Hank Iba, lacking a big man like Bob Kurland or Bob Mattick, set aside his famed ball control for a faster-paced game. It was a Texan, Mack Carter (17), who put on as smooth a display of basketball finesse as Gregory Gym had seen in some time. Olmstead scored 16 and rebounded well, drawing praise from Iba. The return game, at Gallagher Gym in Stillwater, featured a barrage of second-half shooting by Carter (21) as the Cowboys (a name gradually gaining favor over "Aggies") won, 77-49. Carl Shafer handcuffed Olmstead, and Downs did not play because his foot was in a cast. Schmid led the Longhorns with 13 points.

The Houston Cougars, with 7' center Don Boldebuck, came to Austin and beat UT for the first time, 79-58, before a sparse gallery. Boldebuck scored 32 and former Longhorn Joe Palafox 15, while Hooton (16) was the lone bright spot for Texas. "An uninteresting game," claimed the *Austin Statesman*, and the loudest cheers of the night were reserved for a group of young tumblers who performed at halftime.

Texas was in fast company at the Birmingham Classic, as Alabama, Wake Forest and West Virginia boasted their own star players in Jerry Harper, Dick Hemric and "Hot Rod" Hundley, respectively. The Horns lost two games and finished last in the tournament. Bama won, 89-54, as Harper (23) was one of four Crimson Tide players in double figures. Buchanan had 15 for Texas. And Hemric scored 40 in a 95-71 defeat by the Deacons. An even bigger surprise than Buchanan's showing against Alabama was substitute forward Charles Howard, who rebounded expertly and scored 23 points in the loss to Wake Forest. On the same trip, UT met Vanderbilt in Nashville. The Commodores had recently beaten TCU by 22 and may have expected another blowout, but the game was tied at 43 with 15 minutes left and remained close until four Longhorn regulars fouled out. Then Vandy pulled away to a 27-point win. Forward Bobby Thym tallied 30 points and Buchanan 22 for Texas. Downs (11) had his best game yet.

Just as in Birmingham, last place in the SWC tourney belonged to Texas. Olmstead and John Fortenberry of Texas A&M both scored 21 in the Ags' 66-61 first-round victory. Buchanan, the object of high expectations and some criticism the previous year, scored 22 in the Horns' 77-63 loss to SMU. And following the script to the letter, UT lost to Baylor by 14. Hooton, out with a bruised shoulder, was missed, but Buchanan came on strong with 26 points, eight less than the Bruins' Murray Bailey.

While Gene Schwinger of Rice had gone on, the league welcomed four fine sophomores in 1955: Jim Krebs of SMU, Jerry Mallett of Baylor, Dick O'Neal of TCU and Raymond Downs of Texas, although the latter had not yet done anything to merit inclusion in the group. SWC play commenced when the Horns met and lost to Doc Hayes' Ponies before just 3,500 fans, the smallest home crowd for a conference game in several years. Speedy Joel Krog had 23 points for SMU and Buchanan 14 for the Steers. By that time, some UT fans had consigned the season to the junkheap and begun to gaze with adoring eyes at Marshall Hughes' Yearlings. Kenneth Cleveland, Barry Dowd, Kermit Decker, Bobby Puryear and John Shaffer were winning and promised to upgrade the Longhorns considerably in seasons to come.

Minus the senior leadership provided the year before by Billy Powell and Gib Ford, the team was also weak in rebounding, passing and defense. Hull was

Record: 4-20

59 Hardin-Simmons 57
63 Oklahoma A&M 70
49 Oklahoma A&M 77
58 Houston 79
54 Alabama 89
71 Wake Forest 95
67 Vanderbilt 94
61 Texas A&M 66
63 SMU 77
75 Baylor 89
51 SMU 74
67 Baylor 85
64 TCU 79
52 Rice 58
52 Houston 59
74 Texas Tech 79
75 Arkansas 74 (OT)
70 Rice 79
80 Texas A&M 76
56 TCU 75
74 Arkansas 79
74 Texas A&M 64
61 Baylor 89
80 SMU 93

Raymond Downs, the great scorer of the 1955, 1956 and 1957 Texas Longhorn teams.

desperate, so he retooled the offense and tried an all-sophomore lineup against Baylor. UT lost to the Bears, 85-67, but the game was notable for the belated emergence of Downs. Recovered from an ankle injury, Downs scored 38 points, the second-highest total in Texas history. "It was a typically partisan Baylor crowd," reported the *Austin Statesman*. "The game, as always, was rough, and boos—over anything—from the crowd were the rule rather than the exception."

On the verge of a disastrous season, the Horns journeyed to Fort Worth and lost to TCU, 79-64. Dick O'Neal, the Frogs' 6'7" soph sensation, scored 42 points, and he would have had more but UT stalled the last four minutes in an effort to preserve Slater Martin's SWC record of 49. That strategy was roundly booed by the TCU crowd. Downs was held to 16 by Ray Warren.

In a meeting of cochamps fallen on hard times, 1-12 Texas and 5-8 Rice met in Austin. Don Suman's Owls were carried from the door of defeat by big Joe Durrenberger and guards Bobby Brashear and Monte Robicheaux. Downs scored 16 for the Longhorns, who led early in the second half but ended up losing, 58-52. Buchanan, not known for his rebounding, pulled down 11.

After the long exam break, the Horns sought a victory against two nonconference foes. In Houston, they lost to the Cougars by just seven in the team's best performance since early on, as Downs kept it close with 19 points on an assortment of drives, hooks and fadeaway jumpers. He had an uncanny knack of using his hips to draw fouls and then converting free throws. The red-shirted Raiders of Texas Tech rode into Gregory Gym on February 3 and nipped the Steers, 79-74. Jim Reed, DuWayne Blackshear and Gene Carpenter scored most of Tech's points and formed a sagging defense around Downs (20).

With the dubious distinction of holding a 15-game losing streak, easily the longest in a half-century of UT basketball, the Horns prepared to tip off with Arkansas, 3-2 in the SWC. Given the dire situation, the team was not in low spirits. "With a few breaks here and there, we can still win some games," Downs said. Sure enough, Texas managed a 75-74 overtime defeat of the Razorbacks. Downs (41) was nothing short of magnificent, but he got help from Olmstead, who had 12 points, 17 rebounds and a key blocked shot. The long drought ended on a rainy night when the Gregory Gym roof leaked, interrupting play several times. Norman Smith had 20 for the Hogs, whose coach, Glen Rose, said, "It was a good game, OK, the kind the spectators like. A tough one to lose, though. This boy Downs looked great."

Buchanan injured an ankle against Arkansas and was out the rest of the season. His teammates lost to Rice, 79-70, in Houston. The epitome of balanced scoring, the Owls had six players in double figures. Downs (30) continued his scoring spree, and Hooton tossed in 14. It was cold down in the cellar, but UT had company in Texas A&M, en route to the same 4-20 season record. A crowd of 6,000 gathered in spacious new G. Rollie White Coliseum to watch a nerve-shattering 80-76 Texas win keyed by a basket and free throw by Olmstead in the final half-minute. Double- and triple-teamed, Downs still scored 39, including 23 from the line. Center George Mehaffey led the Ags with 22 in what Hull called "a sweet victory."

The TCU Horned Frogs, in the thick of the SWC race, paid a visit in mid-February and won easily, 75-56. The press played up the O'Neal-Downs scoring duel, won by the Frogs' flat-topped star, 36 to 22. In attendance that night was Tom Hamilton, then playing pro baseball. "Downs is a great player," he said. "He has the finesse I wish I could have had when I was at Texas."

With six straight wins over Arkansas, Hull's Horns entered Fayetteville with some hope of victory. But Hog center Pete Butler scored a career-high 31 points as his team snuffed a late Steer rally to win, 79-74. Downs had 22, and Hooton and the Hogs' Terry Day (both ejected when they tussled in Austin) scored 16 and 17, respectively.

Downs got his fourth foul with 10 minutes left but still scored 31 against Texas A&M in a ragged, foul-infested 74-64 victory at Gregory Gym. Many of the 3,500 partisans recognized Downs' special talent and chanted his name whenever he went to the bench. Olmstead scored 15 and Howard 10, while Groogan led the team with 12 rebounds. John Fortenberry scored 18 for the Ags. Baylor was the last home game of UT's long season. Waco sportswriters, with encouragement from the Bear sports information department, were hailing Jerry Mallett as "another Tom Gola" (LaSalle's 1954 all-American). Mallett was quite ordinary that night, scoring just eight points, but the Bruins won, 89-61, in their most lopsided victory yet over the Horns. Downs scored 31, yet none of his teammates had more than seven.

As the season reached its merciful end, Hull seemed absent-minded and depressed, as though shadows were lurking. The Longhorns lost to conference champion SMU in Dallas, 93-80. Lumbering Jim Krebs led the Ponies with 22, while Hooton (29) took advantage of their defensive obsession with Downs (26). Although he got going when the season was almost half over, Downs scored 400 points in 1955, just one shy of John Hargis' Longhorn record. But Downs would obliterate that mark and several others in the next two years.

1956

The so-called fabulous freshmen who moved up to the varsity helped make Texas basketball respectable again. But really, the survivors of the Bataan Death March that was the 1955 season were responsible—Raymond Downs, Norman Hooton, Ellis Olmstead, Wayman Buchanan and Bill Groogan. While the *Alcalde, Daily Texan* and *Austin Statesman* spoke of the "new-look" Longhorns, only one sophomore, guard Kenneth Cleveland, made the starting lineup for the opening game against West Texas, champion of the Border Conference. Downs, who had been unstoppable in preseason scrimmages, scored 31 points as UT won, 85-73, before a crowd of 4,500 at Gregory Gym. Ray Burrus had 24 for the Buffaloes.

A stronger test was expected when the Longhorns met Oklahoma A&M in Stillwater. Hank Iba's Cowboys held the upper hand most of the game, but UT stayed close. Trailing by one in the last minute, Downs sank a jump shot, Olmstead created a turnover, and Downs scored again for a 59-56 upset win. It was the first home opening loss in Oklahoma A&M history, and Texas fans had a tangible reason to believe the awful experience of 1955 would not be repeated. In Bartlesville two days later, the Horns took the court against the Phillips 66 Oilers, AAU and National Industrial Basketball League champions, a team stocked with former all-Americans. Sent to do a job few college teams would undertake, the Longhorns got crushed, 92-66. Burdette Haldorson (21) led the big hardwood veterans, while only Downs (19) and Olmstead (17) had success for Texas. Their frustrated teammates resorted to throwing up long shots, and Cleveland suffered a leg injury that kept him out for several games.

Record: 12-12

85 West Texas 73
59 Oklahoma A&M 56
66 Phillips 66 Oilers 92
58 Oklahoma A&M 61
91 Phillips 66 Oilers 108
83 Auburn 76
86 Mississippi 72
66 TCU 60
72 Rice 80
71 Southern California 63
67 TCU 73
63 SMU 66
67 Arkansas 70
74 Texas A&M 75
58 Rice 83
86 West Texas 79
80 Baylor 73
96 SMU 109
74 TCU 67
72 Texas Tech 84
69 Arkansas 79
94 Rice 82
101 Baylor 95
98 Texas A&M 70

The same two Oklahoma aggregations came to Austin the following week. The Cowboys corralled the Steers, 61-58, before 5,500 customers. Iba raged on the sideline as his team lost much of a big lead, even though Downs (28) had fouled out. Two late free throws by guard V.R. Barnhouse brought a smile back to Iba's face. And Downs (26), Buchanan (18), Hooton (16) and Olmstead (12) were no match for the high-octane Oilers who roared past UT, 108-91. Their coach, ex-OU Sooner Gerald Tucker, was impressed with Downs. "He's got a lot of moxie, and he's clever at drawing fouls," Tucker said. "I think he could play in our league."

With a 2-3 record compiled against strong competition, the Horns traveled to Montgomery, Alabama for the Blue-Gray Tournament and did something Jack Gray's greatest teams never accomplished, coming home with a big trophy. It was a pleasant occurrence, considering *Sports Illustrated* had recently proclaimed the SWC the weakest major conference in basketball. There were admittedly some dogs (Baylor, TCU and Texas A&M went a combined 16-55 that year), but UT had defeated Oklahoma A&M, Rice had wins over Oklahoma, Tulane, LSU and Kansas, and SMU counted Minnesota, Wisconsin and Kansas among its victims. The Longhorns beat two Southeastern Conference teams on the way to the tourney championship. First, they overcame a 14-point halftime deficit to edge Auburn, 83-76. Olmstead was a lion on the backboards, Downs scored 31, and Kermit Decker played a fine outside game. The next night, the Steers stepped into the limelight with an 86-72 win over Mississippi. Downs scored 29, and Decker, the pride of Hutto, Texas, had 17. They returned to Austin the next day secure in the knowledge that they had a much better team than in 1955. Mark Batterson of the *Austin Statesman* wrote, "A year ago, there were highly vocal critics aiming barbs at Texas basketball coach Slue Hull. But these days, he is being pointed out on public thoroughfares as a genius."

The fifth annual Southwest Conference Tournament got underway in Houston with a 66-60 victory over TCU. Dick O'Neal had 21 points in the first half but just eight in the second due to Olmstead's defensive work. Hooton and Downs combined for 41 points. Rice's 6'10" sophomore star, Temple Tucker, scored 31 in a lively 80-72 win. The ubiquitous Downs, ninth in scoring nationally, got 24. And in the last game of the tournament, Texas spotted Southern California a six-point halftime lead and came back to win by eight. Downs scored 24 points, half of them on free throws, while Jack Dunne and Danny Rogers had 17 each for the Trojans. The tournament drew 30,000 fans to Rice Gym and made a small profit, but coaches Doc Hayes (SMU), Ken Loeffler (Texas A&M) and Glen Rose (Arkansas) wanted to end it. Their views did not prevail, however, and the tourney continued for another four years.

The real thing, SWC competition, began with a 73-67 loss to TCU in Fort Worth. Early in the game, Dick O'Neal's errant elbow put a big gash over Downs' right eye, sending him to the bench for eight minutes. The Longhorns, who had trailed at halftime in 10 of their 11 games, were 15 behind at the break and never quite closed the gap. Many of the 2,800 in the gym came to see all-America running back Jim Swink, who—when he got in—scored one point and almost double-dribbled three times. The football-basketball tandem, once so common, had almost vanished by then, but Swink, King Hill of Rice and Del Shofner of Baylor were keeping it alive.

Hull drilled his players in preparation for SMU, then in a stretch of brilliance that included SWC titles in 1955, 1956, 1957 and half of one in 1958. With Jim Krebs, Rick Herrscher, Larry Showalter, Joel Krog and Bobby Mills, the No. 10 Mustangs were potent, balanced and experienced. They won, 66-63, but not before fighting off a late surge led by Hooton and Groogan in front of 7,500 Gregory Gym partisans. Downs scored 23 despite close attention from the Pony defense. Olmstead, although scoreless, had 12 rebounds and several blocks. Krog led SMU with 17 points.

It was root Hogs or die when Arkansas came to town. Decker scored the first eight points, but the Horns fell behind by 16, rallied to within one and lost, 70-67. Terry Day (17) was one of four Razorbacks in double figures, while Downs, UT's ambidextrous artisan, scored 24. The trend of narrow SWC losses continued in College Station, where the short Aggies took a 75-74 victory as Fritz Connally and George Mehaffey riddled Texas' man-to-man defense. Downs (24) and Hooton (18) led the Steers.

After four defeats by 13 points, the team may have felt snakebit. Against Rice, Downs was held scoreless for most of the first half, but Olmstead took up some of the slack. Still, Temple Tucker, Joe Durrenberger and Gerry Thomas ran away to an 83-58 win, Rice's seventh straight over the Horns. While they were in Houston, a press leak made public what had long been speculated—that Hull would retire from coaching at the end of the season. When asked, UT athletic director Dana X. Bible confirmed that Hull's resignation letter was in hand. Attention turned quickly to possible successors, primarily frosh coach and varsity assistant Marshall Hughes, Slater Martin and TCU's Buster Brannon, although the latter received scant consideration. The name of Slater Martin was revered by those who knew Texas basketball. Then having the finest season of his NBA career, Martin was unlikely to stop playing and come to the rescue of his alma mater for a much smaller salary. Furthermore, he had no coaching experience, but that did not stop some lobbying on his behalf by Houston alumni. Hughes was respected as a tactician, handler of young athletes and scout. He had coached Tarleton College in the late 1940s and the Yearlings from 1950 to 1956, but those positions were quite different from heading the varsity at a big school like UT. At any rate, Hughes wanted the job and he got it in early February, assuming extra duties before the 1956 season was out. While it was a sad situation for Hull, still the head coach, they worked together for the remaining games.

Perhaps it was coincidental, but the season changed when Hull's resignation became public, as the Horns won seven and lost two. Their five-game losing streak ended in Canyon where they beat West Texas, 86-79. Bill Henderson brought his Bears to Austin and appeared to have the game won, leading by 12 with eight minutes to play. Texas then put on a big surge that thrilled 5,000 fans and clipped Baylor, 80-73. Louis Estes (28) led the Bruins, and Downs, with 32 (12 of 16 from the field) eclipsed John Hargis' season scoring record. The real hero of the evening was Hooton, who scored the game's last seven points.

SMU had recently vanquished its main contender, Arkansas, when the Longhorns went to Dallas. Downs scored 32 of UT's 96 points, but it was not enough because the red and blue tallied 109, and 50 came from Krebs. The 6'8" Missouri native took advantage of a poor Texas defense with hooks, tip-ins and a few outside shots to hit the half-century mark, breaking the record held by Slater Martin and Dick O'Neal of TCU. The Mustangs were being acclaimed as the best SWC team since Baylor lost to Kentucky in the 1948 NCAA title game.

The Texas-TCU matchup at Gregory Gym on February 11 featured two mediocre teams with one great player on each. Dick O'Neal scored 29 for the Frogs and Downs 31 for the Longhorns in a 74-67 victory that handed TCU sole possession of the SWC cellar. Hooton scored 17, and Decker made a number of steals and handled the ball well.

Texas Tech, destined for an NCAA Tournament spot in 1956, had been asking and practically demanding admission to the conference in recent years. A large coliseum under construction in Lubbock would be the SWC's biggest and best, and finally the Red Raiders got the votes in what was primarily a football matter. They would begin conference play in the 1958 season. In the meantime, however, they came to Austin for the annual charity game and won by 12 in a comedy of errors with poor shooting and too many fouls. Downs (24) injured a knee, but trainer Frank Medina thought he would be ready for Arkansas.

It was Glen Rose Night in Fayetteville, as a host of Hog cage greats returned to honor the Arkansas coach. In UT's first visit to the Razorbacks' 4,000-seat Barnhill Fieldhouse, Downs was held to a season-low 12 points. The shooting accuracy of Jerald Barnett (26) and Manuel Whitley (21) enabled the red and white to win, 79-69.

Downs, described flatly by the *Daily Texan* as "the greatest basketball player in University of Texas history," scored 32 in a wild and rough 94-82 win over Rice. He had help from Hooton (29) and Olmstead (16), while Temple Tucker (26) did what Jim Krebs and Bill Russell of San Francisco had made popular—guiding teammates' missed shots into the basket, something soon labeled "offensive goaltending" and ruled illegal. Tempers flared all evening as 6,000 rabid Gregory Gym fans booed, threw pennies and unnerved referees Don Rossi and Bill Keeling. When Downs fouled out, he returned to the court for some not-so-friendly repartee with Tucker.

For the first time since 1951, Texas won in the Bears' den, 101-95. The phenomenal Downs went on a scoring rampage that included 18 of 30 field goal attempts and 13 of 17 free throws for 49 points. He might have gotten 60, but Baylor used a five-man defense toward the end, causing 3,000 of its fans to hoot disapproval. Downs tied Martin's school record and fell one short of Jim Krebs' new SWC mark. Hooton, Cleveland and Olmstead had 13 each, and Louis Estes 21 for the Bears.

A home victory against Texas A&M would give the Steers a 12-12 season record, a far cry from the 4-20 of a year before. Texas fans, notorious for their bad manners, heard from student body president Roland Dahlin before the game, and they were fairly cooperative. The Longhorns presented Hull with a 98-70 victory. Cleveland and Decker, sophomore guards who came on late in the year, scored 14 and 12, respectively. Downs had 33. He was again a member of what the UT sports information office called the "300 Club," consisting of players who had scored at least 300 points in a season. Those preceding Downs were Jack Gray (1933), John Hargis (1943 and 1947), Slater Martin (1948 and 1949), Tom Hamilton (1949 and 1950), Jim Dowies (1951 and 1952), George Scaling (1953), Fred Saunders (1954) and Billy Powell (1954). But Downs' whopping 625 points in 1956 was another matter entirely. He was in a club by himself.

1957

Marshall Hughes must have been pinching himself. His original purpose at the University of Texas was to earn a doctoral degree, but he became part of the Longhorn basketball program and after seven years almost by happenstance found himself the head coach. His academic work had ceased while he pursued the unexpected opportunity, and had he been successful, Hughes might have made coaching a career. But his three-year stint as ruler of the roost at Gregory Gym, while not without moments of triumph, can be summarized in one word: decline. His assistant was ex-Steer Jimmy Viramontes, who had won two district titles at McCallum High School in Austin and aided in the development of Jay Arnette, author of a 21-point-per-game average for the 1957 Yearlings and a future varsity star.

Every player from Slue Hull's last team (the highest-scoring in UT history) was back, plus two promising sophomore forwards, Brenton Hughes—no relation to the coach—and Richard "Bub" Farrell. Athletic victories of any kind were welcome on the Forty Acres after an awful 1-9 football season that led to the resignation of Ed Price and the hiring of Darrell Royal. No one, however, predicted an addition to the trophy cases in the Gregory Gym foyer because SMU was considered a shoo-in for the Southwest Conference championship.

A month before the season began, cocaptains Raymond Downs and Norman Hooton were part of an SWC all-star team that played the U.S. Olympic team at the new SMU Coliseum (later renamed Moody Coliseum). The Olympians, with Bill Russell, K.C. Jones and ex-Longhorn Gib Ford, won the game, 90-66.

Things got off to a fine start with a 103-68 smothering of North Texas at Gregory Gym. Downs scored 29 points in barely half the game, and the twin-guard menace of Kenneth Cleveland and Kermit Decker combined for 33. Unfortunately, Hooton took a bad spill and broke a bone in his wrist. The fans got a demonstration of entertaining fast-break basketball that harked back to the racehorse style of the 1947 team with Slater Martin, Al Madsen and John Hargis. Running, Hughes believed, would help offset a lack of size and prevent opponents from shackling Downs with zone defenses.

The team's first road games were in the Pacific northwest. No. 13 Oregon State held a four-point halftime lead, but fell, 64-63, to the fine shooting of Cleveland and John Shaffer. The Beavers' Dave Gambee scored 24 and did a good job of defense on Downs. In the prelim game, Oregon got a 33-point whipping from Portland. But the next night in Eugene, Texas lost to the Webfoots, 65-64. The Horns were lethargic early, going scoreless a long stretch of the first half, but Downs (31) and Decker led a last-minute rally that ended just short. Oregon was led by massive Howard Duffy (13).

Record: 11-13

103 North Texas 68
64 Oregon State 63
64 Oregon 65
68 Oklahoma 62
68 Tulane 65
67 Vanderbilt 94
93 Hardin-Simmons 64
76 Arkansas 89
101 Baylor 84
59 TCU 54
76 Baylor 87
85 TCU 76
66 Rice 76
66 Arkansas 67
77 SMU 68
59 Oklahoma 71
67 Texas A&M 69 (OT)
95 Baylor 68
56 SMU 79
63 Rice 79
77 East Texas 71
55 Texas A&M 61
54 Arkansas 70
60 TCU 74

In what later seemed a prescient action, the SWC office suggested that each school hold a meeting of athletic officials and student leaders in an effort to improve sportsmanship at league basketball games. Athletic director Dana X. Bible (soon to turn that job over to Ed Olle) called a confab with Hughes, Downs, Hooton, assistant dean of students W.D. Blunk and sports information director Wilbur Evans. They acknowledged that fan behavior at Gregory Gym was often nothing to boast of and that UT had never won the SWC sportsmanship trophy, which originated in 1948. By *Daily Texan* editorials and pleas from the public-address announcer, they hoped to rein in the most rambunctious of students, who comprised the large majority of home crowds. The gym was full when Big Red came to town and lost, 68-62. Don Schwall (20) and Joe King (18) led Oklahoma, and Downs scored 22 and Brenton Hughes 15 for the Longhorns. Texas track star Eddie Southern, owner of an Olympic silver medal, was honored at halftime.

Hughes then took his team on a brief tour of Dixie. Although Hooton was still out and Ellis Olmstead stayed home with a throat infection, the Horns grabbed a 68-65 victory over previously unbeaten Tulane in sweltering New Orleans. Downs wheeled and dealed for 24 points, breaking Slater Martin's career scoring record. Tom Murphy and Calvin Grosscup led the Greenies with 22 and 21, respectively. Vanderbilt took the measure of the Longhorns in Nashville, 94-67. In shooting, rebounding and defense, the Commodores left no doubt about their superiority.

Having traveled 3,000 miles and played five games in eight days, the shorthanded and roadweary Steers hosted Hardin-Simmons. Bob Tremaine, the Cowboys' all-time scoring champ, had 22 points, while Downs and Farrell got 23 each in a 93-64 Texas victory. A spirited Gregory Gym audience saw good showings from subs John Shaffer and Barry Dowd. Decker, whose explosive speed was hindered by a thigh injury, managed to score 12.

At the SWC tourney in Houston, a flu epidemic affected players on nearly every team. But a little virus could not stop the mighty SMU Mustangs, who won the crown. Texas lost to Arkansas, 89-76, in the opening round. The Hogs fashioned a deep sagging defense for Downs, but the muscular, gum-chewing San Antonian still scored 31. Although Hooton returned to the lineup, he showed signs of a long layoff, missing 10 of 11 shots. UT beat Baylor, 101-84, and TCU, 59-54, to finish in third place as Shaffer worked his way into a starting position. Sickness and injury had turned a deep team into a thin one, and only seven players got into the game against the Frogs.

Conference play began in Waco, where Jerry Mallett led a hot Baylor team to an 87-76 victory. Often criticized for not living up to his potential, Mallett scored 31 and was master of both backboards, limiting the number of Longhorn shots. Much was made of Downs' "feud" with Baylor, and he certainly had scored a lot of points against the Bears (including 33 in the SWC tourney), but it was mostly coincidental because what team had he *not* torched? At any rate, they solved the riddle of Raymond Downs, holding him to six shots from the field and 14 points. Decker (15) was the top Longhorn.

Hoping to make amends for a disappointing game, Texas welcomed Buster Brannon's Horned Frogs to

Austin. Dick O'Neal was back for his senior year, and he had extra help from 6'5" soph Ronnie Stevenson. O'Neal (25) and Stevenson (18) were good, but Downs was simply great in an 85-76 win. He rebounded, played stout defense against the taller TCU players and scored 34 points on 11 of 14 from the field and 12 of 13 from the charity stripe, adding more points to his UT career scoring record. Decker had 18 and Farrell 15, and Cleveland's ballhawking contributed to the victory.

Three days later, Texas lost a home contest to Rice, 76-66, as 7,500 fans roared and demonstrated their stern disapproval. Many tumultuous basketball games had been held at Gregory Gym since its opening in 1931, and many more remained in its future, but the night of January 11, 1957 was infamous. Boos rocked the building every time officials Larry Covin and Bo McAlister made a call against the Longhorns, and that was not all. Fans threw pennies, cups and various and sundry other debris onto the floor in protest, resulting in several stoppages of play. The refs, Hughes and cocaptains Downs and Hooton each took the microphone and asked for calm. A forfeit, to be registered as a 2-0 Owl victory, was a drastic but real possibility. The game was played out, and when it was over, the crowd poured onto the floor to further berate Covin and McAlister, who were escorted to safety by police. UT athletic officials, embarrassed and concerned about the incident, met the following morning to seek a solution.

Jack Gallagher of the *Houston Post* wrote, "Texas officials long ago gave up attempting to curb the tribal instincts of the student body.... With a new field house, they can move the spectators farther away from the court and mingle Austin townspeople with the students in the hope that the adult influence might be a settling factor." A new field house, of course, was a decade-long topic of discussion, as year after year of Longhorn recruits were told they would be playing in a modern and much bigger arena by their senior seasons. Bible retorted that money for such a facility was not available and that the immediate problem was crowd control at Gregory Gym.

Lou Maysel of the *Austin Statesman* echoed Gallagher's comments: "The University of Texas has a full-fledged crisis on its hands in the form of the howling rabble that turns out for basketball games at Gregory Gym.... It's a Roman holiday for that element of the UT enrollment that has not completely bridged the Darwinian evolution from primitive ape to civilized man." Maysel also called for a new field house and in the meantime, urged the dispersion of the Hill Hall athletes who congregated on the north bleachers and regularly gave unshirted hell to opponents and refs. He suggested that new football coach Darrell Royal impose some discipline on his troops and in fact use them to elevate student behavior.

The aftermath of that game extended all the way to Fayetteville the next week. Texas lost to the Razorbacks, 67-66, after blowing a nine-point lead with six minutes left. It was a different set of officials, but they called only eight fouls on the Hogs, who averaged 21 per game, and they seemed quick on the whistle for traveling and other floor violations by the Steers. Whether officials sworn to impartiality would consciously favor one team over another was doubtful, and anyway, Arkansas had a 72-41 rebound advantage.

"The eyes of Texas are upon you," and "Mob participation means dismissal." The *Daily Texan* ran these words above an open letter from Downs and Hooton and a stern, unyielding message from UT president Logan Wilson the day before the Longhorns met SMU at Gregory Gym. Howard Grubbs, executive secretary of the SWC, would be there, although he denied it was because of the rowdy actions of a week before. In the first home game ever televised, Texas was supposed to have little chance at victory against the No. 3 Mustangs, who had won 20 straight conference games, had an all-American and future NBA player in Jim Krebs and two more all-SWC players, Bobby Mills and Larry Showalter, and an excellent coach, Doc Hayes. SMU had built a fearsome reputation among its conference foes, but all of Hughes' players were healthy and ready to go.

Sportswriters dubbed UT's 77-68 win "the miracle on Speedway," and Bob Halford of the *Austin Statesman* claimed that the eight Longhorns responsible deserved to have their names etched alongside the "Immortal 13" who had upset Texas A&M in a titanic 1940 football game. Raymond Downs, Norman Hooton, Ellis Olmstead, Kermit Decker, Kenneth Cleveland, Bub Farrell, John Shaffer and Barry Dowd were the Ponies' masters that Friday night. An overcapacity crowd of 8,000 was loud but well-behaved after repeated scoldings in the press. Downs (28 points and 13 rebounds) was the tremendous performer Austin fans had grown accustomed to watching, and Shaffer came off the bench for 15. Hughes had done a good job of preparing his team for battle and was cool under fire once the game began. He cherished the victory and was effusive in his praise for the team and fans, transformed from an unruly mob into an appreciative audience.

Unfortunately, that game preceded the two-week exam layoff. There was no competition, and just a few practices were held at St. Edward's since Gregory Gym was used for registration. The first game after the break was a 71-59 loss to OU in Norman in which only Downs (26) played well. No one knew it then, but the season was turning sour. While Hughes had been to the mountaintop with the big win over SMU, most everything was downhill from there, not just in the 1957 season but for the remainder of his brief UT coaching career.

The young men representing Texas Agricultural and Mechanical College won their first SWC game, a 69-67 overtime defeat of UT at G. Rollie White Coliseum. George Mehaffey scored 23 points, including the winning field goal with three seconds left, but Decker was fouled at the buzzer. As he stepped to the free throw line, the referees huddled with the timekeeper and concluded, to the Longhorns' vehement protests, that the foul occurred after time had expired.

Remembering with anguish the Bear hug put on them in Waco, the Steers ripped Baylor, 95-68, before 7,500 fans. The biggest factor in the game was the ability of the UT guards, Cleveland, Decker and Hooton, to steal the ball and make successful fast breaks. There were more gray hairs for BU coach Bill Henderson, whose team could not hit the side of a barn.

The Ponies routed UT, 79-56, in another televised game at SMU Coliseum. Five players were in double figures for Doc Hayes' team, and their Texas counterparts ranged from cool to frigid. Downs, leading the nation in field goal accuracy with 57 percent, hit just four of 24. Brenton Hughes did yeoman rebounding work, however. After that game, Pat Truly of the *Daily Texan* wrote a column refuting one in the *Dallas Morning News* which called Krebs "the Southwest's greatest basketball player." Truly proceeded to document why Downs was superior to the big, if not agile, SMU center, and added: "We still contend that there are basketball players in this area who are the equals, if not the betters, of Krebs. In fact, Texas Southern, with the nation's best Negro team, is said to have a couple of boys who top anyone in the SWC."

The conference remained almost a decade away from racial integration of its basketball squads. While no visiting team had yet brought a black player into Gregory Gym, the Longhorns had been competing against integrated teams for years—in the NCAA Tournament, the All-College Tournament in Oklahoma City, and on trips to New York, Buffalo, Chicago, Philadelphia, Pittsburgh and Oregon. If there was no rush to integrate (black undergraduate students first enrolled at UT in 1954), nor were there any of the shameful episodes in which SEC or ACC teams refused to play against integrated squads.

Five weeks after getting their feathers ruffled at Gregory Gym (in a victory, nonetheless), the Rice Owls played host to Texas, and justice was both swift and brutal in a 79-63 defeat of Hughes' team. A crowd of 4,000 was rather rowdy itself, and Downs was subjected to a severe beating. He got cut over one eye in a three-on-one collision four minutes into the game and caught plenty of elbows from Temple Tucker and Tom Robitaille. Back home in Austin, Downs, a tough customer, scored 28 in a narrow defeat of East Texas.

The SWC's most bitter rivalry was renewed when Ken Loeffler brought his Aggies to Austin. By a score of 61-55, Texas A&M won there for the first time since 1934. George Mehaffey was injured and did not play, but sophomore center Jim McNichol stepped up and scored 24 to pace the maroon-clad visitors. Ever since January 11, a game highlighting the shady demeanor of local fandom, only angels had attended, and nary a penny was thrown. A capacity crowd that cheered the officials' entrance turned mean when the game was lost, as some fans took to their pockets and rained the court with pennies.

Downs brought a sensational three years of scoring at Gregory Gym to a close when the Longhorns played Arkansas. He had just 18 points, and no teammate even broke double figures in a 70-54 loss to the rough-and-ready Razorbacks. Although Texas held high-scoring Freddy Grim to six points, soph sub Harry Thompson took up the slack with 20. The Horns looked lead-footed and paralyzed in their last home game.

And they failed to escape the cellar (sharing it with Texas A&M) by losing to TCU, 74-60. Other than Groogan's 17 points, Downs had no help. He scored 25 and received a long ovation when the Fort Worth crowd expressed appreciation for the greatest Longhorn scorer of all time. It was also a finale for Dick O'Neal, who held the same lofty niche in Frog basketball history. Neither one ever played for a champion, but they had worn out the nets over the past three years, combining for more than 3,200 points.

1958

Dissension had something to do with the Longhorns losing seven of their last nine games in 1957. The reliance on Raymond Downs was heavy, and some of his peripheral teammates resented having to throw the ball into the post and watch him shoot; when he did not get it, UT's all-time scorer sometimes had screamed. Marshall Hughes and his players were going to see how they might do without Downs. The Horns would have more balanced scoring, obviously, and they would be short and fast, depending on hustle and outside shooting. Jay Arnette, a high-jumping 6'2" forward, was the key newcomer.

Hughes lined up some confidence-builders to start the season. Bub Farrell scored 15 points and grabbed 12 rebounds in a 62-45 defeat of Texas A&I before 2,500 fans at Gregory Gym. As he had promised, Hughes used a lot of players, 14 to be exact, and eight of them scored. The Javelinas were led by Jay Hawley (11), who had played freshman ball at UT three years earlier. The Horns were hot and cold in a 79-59 defeat of Trinity with Farrell again the top scorer and rebounder. And the McMurry Indians provided no competition whatsoever, losing, 73-41.

Another home game took place on December 14, against high-scoring Tulane. Cliff Wells' Green Wave was unbeaten, having played a similar set of lightweights, Tampa and Louisiana College. Texas trailed at the half but came alive behind the shooting of Farrell (19), Brenton Hughes (14) and Kenneth Cleveland (13) to win by a score of 75-64. Defensive action by Cleveland and Kermit Decker started one fast break after another. Guard Gary Stoll scored 18 for Tulane.

Although a 4-0 record looked nice, it was just shadow-boxing at that point. When the Steers traveled to the midwest, they took their lumps. At Brewer Fieldhouse in Columbia, the classy Missouri Tigers won with ease, 82-61. Sonny Siebert and Al Abram combined for 37 points as Mizzou outshot, outrebounded and played more aggressively than the visitors from the Lone Star State. Most of John Shaffer's 13 points came late and made the score look somewhat respectable. UT practiced in Kansas City before moving on to Wichita. While the tall and talented WSU Shockers won, 82-66, the three fastest Longhorns, Decker (22), Cleveland (11) and Arnette (11) played well.

That was the last game of the 1958 season against a non-SWC team. There would be three games with conference brethren in the Christmas tourney in Houston, followed by a 14-game championship race (rather than 12, as it had been since 1928) due to the addition of Texas Tech. Rice was favored to win the tournament and the conference title and then do something in the postseason, as SMU had done in reaching the 1956 NCAA Final Four. The Owls achieved none of those things. UT assistant coach Jimmy Viramontes was in charge of the team while Hughes remained in Austin awaiting his first-born child. The Horns lost to Arkansas, 83-67, a game in which Decker scored 21 points. They overcame a sizable first-half deficit to beat Baylor, 61-59, with Cleveland and Decker combining for 31. Gene McCarley led the Bruins with 14. Decker, the top scorer in the tournament, headed a gallant but losing effort against SMU, 83-75. Going over and around the Ponies, his shooting was excellent. Rick Herrscher scored 24 for Doc Hayes' crew.

Record: 10-13

62 Texas A&I 45
79 Trinity 59
73 McMurry 41
75 Tulane 64
61 Missouri 82
66 Wichita State 82
67 Arkansas 83
61 Baylor 59
75 SMU 83
55 Arkansas 57
50 Texas A&M 71
82 Baylor 61
68 SMU 82
73 TCU 69
68 Rice 102
71 Texas Tech 59
58 TCU 88
74 Texas A&M 68
66 Texas Tech 93
64 Baylor 65 (OT)
73 SMU 89
86 Rice 78
60 Arkansas 74

They began playing for keeps on January 4 when Arkansas came to town. Arnette got his first start because Shaffer was out with a thigh injury, and Farrell, whose production had dipped in Houston, quit the team. As cold as last week's turkey sandwich in the first half, the Horns picked it up in the second with Brenton Hughes, Bobby Puryear and Cleveland leading the attack. But Freddy Grim (17) and Larry Grisham (14) kept the Razorbacks ahead the whole way, and they won by two.

The Steers invaded Aggieland and got thumped, 71-50, before 3,000 khaki-clad fans. Wayne Lawrence, a big soph from Connecticut, was unstoppable inside with 22 points and 11 rebounds, and the Texas A&M defense kept Hughes' sharpshooters out of range all night. Arnette was UT's high-point man with 13. A much-needed boost in morale came when the Horns beat Baylor, 82-61, in front of the season's biggest home crowd yet, 5,000. Hughes surprised the Bears with a zone defense, and the team shot 46 percent and won the rebound battle. Shaffer, healthy again, scored 16, as did Cleveland. Tom Kelly and Rex Hughes had 12 each for Baylor, destined for a last-place finish.

There was another televised game in Dallas, something still rare enough to cause excitement. It was held at SMU Coliseum, known as "the house that Krebs built" in honor of the 6'8" Moses who led the Mustangs to three SWC titles and national prominence and was then playing for the Minneapolis Lakers. With senior Rick Herrscher and four sophomores starting, the Ponies kicked the Horns, 82-68. The SWC's No. 1 crowd-pleaser, guard Max Williams, scored 23 and harassed Texas' guards most of the game, and Bobby James scored 20 and collected that many rebounds. If he had not done so already, Arnette signaled his arrival with 22 points, hitting 11 of 19 from the field. Arnette was uncommonly cool for a soph, and when he fouled out, SMU pulled farther ahead.

TCU, winner of the SWC Tournament and just coming off a 24-point defeat of Rice, had tremendous firepower, a great rebounding reputation and Ronnie Stevenson, generally considered the league's best player. The Frogs did not expect to lose in Austin, but they did, 73-69. A crowd of 3,500 saw Brenton Hughes score 21 points and grab 13 rebounds, they saw Arnette score 18 and show more signs of greatness, and they saw sharp ballhawking from UT's guards, as deft a band of thieves as Ali Baba and his buddies. The Longhorns made 21 of their 25 free throws. Stevenson (15) was not such a world-beater, and 6'10" postman H.E. Kirchner went scoreless and had one rebound. If not on the order of the 1957 "miracle on Speedway," it was nonetheless an eye-opening triumph. "This was one of our finest efforts ever," Hughes said, and the Horns basked in praise over the two-week exam layoff.

Play resumed on February 4 in Houston. The Rice Owls, starved for the kind of victory demanded by their critics, delivered a 102-68 defeat of Texas. With Tommy Robitaille (24), Dale Ball (21) and Temple Tucker (17) showing the way, the blue and gray shot 60 percent and forged by far its biggest margin of victory in a series that began in 1915. Sophomore whiz Jay Arnette scored 21 for UT. The Owls were ahead by 45 with four minutes left and continued pouring it on until coach Don Suman, taking a hint from Hughes, finally put in his subs.

After that merciless beating by Rice, the Longhorns hosted Texas Tech, the baby of the conference. Polk Robison's Red Raiders were holding their own and more with an exciting brand of basketball keyed by guard Gerald Myers (the future Tech coach) and Leon "Podd" Hill, a graceful 6'5" hustler. They seemed to have an insatiable desire to win and prove themselves. Two UT student groups presented Robison with a hat and spurs before the game, and thus ended the night's hospitality. Over 6,000 enthusiastic fans saw the Horns give Tech a 71-59 initiation. Of the starters, only Arnette failed to reach double figures. Neither of the Raiders' two stars played well; Charley Lynch (17) was their top scorer.

Tigers at home and lambs on the road—that described UT ever since Raymond Downs' 49-point eruption against Baylor in 1956. Might the routine change in Fort Worth? No. Brenton Hughes hurt a knee against Texas Tech, Shaffer had a cold, and Arnette sprained an ankle in the first half of an imminently forgettable 88-58 loss to TCU. Ronnie Stevenson and H.E. Kirchner combined for 51 points and were most responsible for a 64-36 rebounding edge. The lone Texas player in double figures was Ed Russell, a 23-year-old Army veteran who never earned a letter.

Brenton Hughes, a doubtful participant against Texas A&M, had his leg bandaged tightly by trainer Frank Medina and went ahead and played. He scored just six points, but his 14 rebounds and defense characterized a hard-fought 74-68 win before 7,000 fans in Austin. Barry Dowd scored 12 off the bench. For the boys from the Brazos basin, Neal Swisher scored 20 and Archie Carroll 18.

On that same night in Lubbock, Texas Tech whipped Arkansas before a crowd of 10,275, then the largest ever to see a basketball game in the state. Hughes had been to Lubbock Municipal Coliseum a couple of times on scouting trips, unlike his players. In fact, of the 12 previous UT-Tech encounters beginning in 1940, 11 of them had been at Gregory Gym and one at a neutral site. By a score of 93-66, Leon Hill (27), Charley Lynch (23) and Gerald Myers (14) were afforded vengeance for what happened 10 days earlier. Only Decker and Brenton Hughes reached double figures for Texas.

It was the battle of the oft-beaten when the Bears and Longhorns met before an overflow crowd in Waco. The game went into overtime, and things looked good for UT when Shaffer hit two free throws to go ahead, 64-63, with nine seconds left. But guard Charley Pack made a long buzzer-beater to win by one. BU's Bob Turner was the game's leading scorer with 21.

As the Longhorns returned to Austin and prepared for two more home games, *Austin Statesman* sports editor Lou Maysel penned a column on a familiar topic—UT's need for a new gym. Noting SMU's and Texas Tech's impressive new structures, he asked why Texas, a school supposedly rolling in money, did not have one, too. Maysel proceeded to explain the various reasons why the financing for such a facility was more difficult than it appeared. He pointed out that alumni donations (which had built Memorial Stadium in 1924) could not do it, the UT athletic department could not do it, and the University itself could not do it because of higher priorities, as the baby-boom generation approached college age. But, he suggested, perhaps the three might combine resources and build a $4-million coliseum holding 15-18,000. "A patch of land has already been earmarked for the building," he wrote. "It's that parking lot just to the south of Memorial Stadium. However, it looks like it will be five or more years before ground will be broken there. But that wait can probably be shortened somewhat if the problem is tackled aggressively now." On the contrary, nothing substantial happened, and Gregory Gym continued to serve as the home of UT basketball for nearly 20 more years.

The Longhorns, fighting to stay out of the cellar, hosted SMU in late February, but there would be no upset that night. Rick Herrscher connected on nine of his first 10 shots and finished with 28 points in the Mustangs' 89-73 victory. Decker had 19, most of them on driving layups. An 86-78 defeat of Rice occurred when the players ignored Hughes' repeated instructions to go slow; he had lost control of the team. The bespectacled Cleveland, a crowd favorite since the first time he stepped on the court at Gregory Gym, scored 23 and handed out several assists. Brenton Hughes, still playing on a bad leg, had 22 points and 14 rebounds. Dowd was the apparent victim of an Owl body block with 45 seconds left, but no foul was called, provoking another shower of pennies, which in turn caused *Daily Texan* writer Carlos Conde to do a good-natured column on that age-old issue, sportsmanship at Gregory Gym. He urged fans not to go overboard, but he also made it clear that the crowd at a college basketball game ought not be held to the same standard as tennis or the opera.

The Horns girded their loins and headed to the Ozarks. Arkansas had a lot on the line in the final game of the season. Some 5,000 fans packed Barnhill Fieldhouse to see the Razorbacks beat UT, tying SMU for the conference title. With Freddy Grim (18) in charge, they methodically hammered the Texas defense. Shaffer (15) and Decker (12) led the Steers. Communication problems and the players' decaying respect for Hughes had been constant factors. At 5-9 in the Southwest Conference and 10-13 overall, it had not been a terrible season, but the next one would be.

1959

Entirely too much hope was placed on the sophomores joining the UT varsity in 1959, especially the big men, Wayne Clark and Albert Almanza. Clark, at 6'11", was the tallest player in school history, but like Ellis Olmstead before him, was slow, inexperienced and not at all aggressive. Almanza, the 6'8" Latin with a touch of satin, was a native of Chihuahua, Mexico who had played high school ball in El Paso. Twenty-two years old, Almanza was agile and had a nice variety of shots. Seven other sophs played roles of lesser importance on Marshall Hughes' third team. Since Brenton Hughes was academically ineligible, leadership fell to Bobby Puryear and Jay Arnette. Undoubtedly the best of the Longhorn players, Arnette suffered a broken nose before the season opener on December 2.

Texas overcame first-night jitters before a home crowd of 3,000, beating the McMurry Indians by 25. Clark, Arnette, Almanza and walk-on guard Donnie Wilson all scored in double figures. A big victory margin over a little school like McMurry was nice, but how would the team fare in rugged Southwest Conference competition? Only hard-core orangebloods anticipated the Steers having more than a .500 record. There were five more games before the SWC Tournament, time to gain experience and build a nucleus that could be adequate in 1959 and maybe contend in the following two years. An 83-74 loss to Trinity, however, was a harbinger of things to come. Arnette, who left the game early when his nose was reinjured, scored 18 points and Clark 16, while Bob Galkowski led the scrappy Tigers with 16.

Oklahoma State—no longer A&M—was still coached by Hank Iba, and he was still playing the slow game that infuriated Jack Gray in the 1930s. Holding the ball, passing and dribbling until a safe shot developed, the black-clad Cowboys conquered Texas, 66-39, behind 30 points from center Arlen Clark. The Longhorns shot just 19 percent, but at least Clark and Almanza rebounded well. Nevertheless, Charlie Smith of the *Daily Texan* lamented that the win over McMurry might have been the season's last. If Smith was somewhat pessimistic, he was not too far off the mark.

After three games in Austin, Hughes took the team on the road for two games in Louisiana that went quite similarly. UT led Tulane for the first 35 minutes, and then the Green Wave's poise and experience began to show. Vic Klinker scored 22 en route to a 61-51 victory. Almanza had 20 for Texas. Encouraged by their showing in New Orleans, the Horns then met LSU in Baton Rouge. They were up by three at the half, but Dick Davies (16) led a surge that gave Tiger fans something to cheer about. Both teams shot miserably—LSU 10 of 48, UT 17 of 59—but Davies and his teammates had many more trips to the foul line.

Wolves had already begun to howl for Marshall Hughes, but his two big sophomores, Clark and Almanza, were getting a crash course in varsity hoops, and the team appeared to be making strides. Hughes, who had played for Pete Shands at North Texas, welcomed his old coach to Gregory Gym. It was no time to be sentimental, however; the Longhorns beat the Eagles, 76-54. Arnette celebrated his 20th birthday by scoring 29 points, and Almanza and Clark held center Jim Mudd to seven, one-third of his season average. "This win gives us a much better outlook for the tournament," Hughes said.

Arnette did not play in the SWC tourney due to a serious foot infection. Without his scoring and reassuring influence on the court, the young Horns were in trouble. They suffered a 12-minute dearth of field goals and lost to Rice, 62-43. Texas Tech stole a victory with two free throws by Gene Arrington in the last six seconds. Clark scored 18, Almanza 16 and unknown Billy Davenport, starting in place of Arnette, 10. It was Texas and Baylor for last-place "honors." The score was tied at the half, but the Bears ran off eight straight points and proceeded to win, 75-54. Only Clark (17) and Almanza (10) reached double figures. BU was led by Gene McCarley with 18. Although his team was at the muddy bottom of the heap, Hughes remained calmly determined: "On the whole, I feel good...if you can ever feel good about losing."

The Longhorns were back in Houston for the SWC opener against Rice. With 30 points from Almanza, they shocked the Owls, 61-58. Texas trailed by 14 with 16 minutes left as Hughes rotated his bench and starters in search of outside shooting. Besides Puryear (10), he did not get much, but Almanza played splendidly, hooking, jumping and following up like a demon. Tom Robitaille had 13 for the Owls, whose 10-game win streak against UT came to an end.

Exhilarated over the momentous upset and temporarily tied for the lead with half of the conference, Texas hosted a shorter but faster, better-shooting and more experienced SMU team. The Longhorns turned in a fine first-half performance but wilted at the foul line and under the boards and fell, 73-55. Davenport had the tough task of guarding slick Max Williams, who scored 10 and set up many of SMU's points. Bobby James had 30 for the Ponies, and Almanza led Texas with 14. "You can't hit one of 11 free throws [in the second half] and expect to win," said assistant coach Jimmy Viramontes. SMU, in contrast, was 25 of 28 from the line.

Record: 4-20

73 McMurry 48
74 Trinity 83
39 Oklahoma State 66
51 Tulane 61
47 LSU 52
76 North Texas 54
43 Rice 62
57 Texas Tech 59
54 Baylor 75
61 Rice 58
55 SMU 73
78 TCU 86
47 Texas Tech 64
29 Texas A&M 73
51 Baylor 62
38 Oklahoma State 58
74 Arkansas 77 (OT)
54 Texas Tech 76
58 Baylor 60
61 SMU 78
59 TCU 72
61 Texas A&M 71
56 Arkansas 63
63 Rice 54

Arnette had practiced, and he made the trip to Cowtown, but just could not play against TCU. He was sorely needed to cope with Buster Brannon's all-senior lineup. Musclemen Ronnie Stevenson and H.E. Kirchner combined for 59 points and 36 rebounds to ease past the Horns, 86-78, before 3,700 fans at Fort Worth Public Schools Gym. Puryear, the No. 2 free throw shooter in the nation, paced Texas with 17. No UT player reached double figures in a 64-47 loss to Texas Tech in Austin. For the shorter Red Raiders, who had a two-to-one rebound margin, Leon Hill scored 26 and James Wiley 16. The enthusiasm of the crowd of 3,500 died a slow death as the Tech lead grew. "It was one of the poorest performances of the year for the troubled Longhorns," wrote Wick Temple of the *Austin Statesman*, "a stumbling, bloody, hairy monster of a basketball game."

A precursor of the high-flying leapers soon to rule the game, Jay Arnette dunks against Trinity.

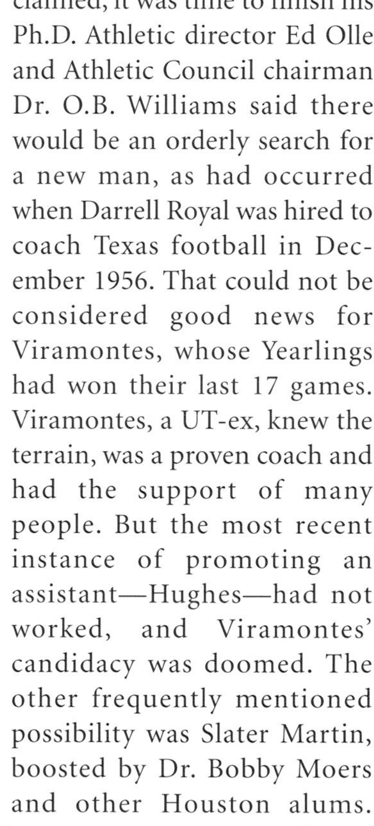

Hughes, for once, did not disagree. He promised changes, but he had few viable options. The loss to Texas Tech seemed to prove that Gregory Gym was no longer the basketball burial ground for visitors it had long been, its mystique past. Some UT fans manifested their unhappiness by hanging Hughes in effigy from the mustang statue in front of Texas Memorial Museum and again from one of the flagpoles on the south mall. Ed Price had been the object of many necktie parties when the 1956 football season went bad, and there it was again. The situation got worse, much worse, in College Station, where 6,200 roaring fans watched their team maul the Longhorns, 73-29. Although Aggie coach Bob Rogers put in his subs with 15 minutes left, UT scored just 12 points in the second half. Archie Carroll (22) and Wayne Lawrence (18) had enough points between them to defeat the Horns.

That was one of the lowest ebbs in UT basketball history, and Hughes and the players knew it. Yet they had a fine Saturday afternoon practice, went up to Waco and nearly beat Baylor, winner of three straight. The return of Arnette (15) helped considerably. Carroll Dawson (17) led the green-garbed Bears to a 62-51 victory at McLean Gym, the little crackerbox inferior to many high school gyms, then in its final year of service.

During the two-week exam period, Hughes announced his resignation, effective at season's end. He said he had considered the action for several months and that the team's 3-12 record and being hanged in effigy had not driven him from the game. Instead, he claimed, it was time to finish his Ph.D. Athletic director Ed Olle and Athletic Council chairman Dr. O.B. Williams said there would be an orderly search for a new man, as had occurred when Darrell Royal was hired to coach Texas football in December 1956. That could not be considered good news for Viramontes, whose Yearlings had won their last 17 games. Viramontes, a UT-ex, knew the terrain, was a proven coach and had the support of many people. But the most recent instance of promoting an assistant—Hughes—had not worked, and Viramontes' candidacy was doomed. The other frequently mentioned possibility was Slater Martin, boosted by Dr. Bobby Moers and other Houston alums. Martin, however, had a recent one-game experiment as player-coach of the St. Louis Hawks and did not enjoy it, claiming he was ill suited to coaching. Shortly before withdrawing his name from consideration, Martin made some ears perk up with this statement: "There's nothing wrong with the Southwest Conference coaches except they can't get material. People in the conference concentrate on football too much, and basketball has just become a girls' sport."

Hughes had nine more games to coach, and a successor would not be named until well after the season. In Stillwater, Arlen Clark found the UT defense to his liking and scored 24 to lead Oklahoma State to a 58-38 victory. The Longhorns made a gallant stand for 30 minutes but slumped and scored just two field goals the rest of the way. Arnette had 10 points.

The game between the Horns and Hogs was on regional TV, perhaps one reason Gregory Gym was just half-filled. The score was tied at the end of regulation when Clark missed a short jumper that would have won, and Clyde Rhoden (29) hit a layup with 20 seconds left in overtime to give Arkansas a 77-74 victory, breaking the hearts of UT fans. Puryear scored 22, Almanza 16 and reserve forward Jerry Don Smith 14. While it was another loss, the Longhorns played with poise and teamwork, even in the last tense minutes. "Texas and Arkansas treated the southwest's television basketball audience to an interesting exhibition Saturday," wrote Lou Maysel of the *Austin Statesman*, "much to the relief of a segment of UT exes who feared more embarrassment for their school."

Smith earned a starting job with his showing against the Razorbacks, and he scored 17 in a foul-filled 76-54 loss in Lubbock. Texas Tech was also led by a surprise starter, Wade Wolfe (15). Texas had another chance to halt the eight-game losing streak when the Baylor Bears came to Gregory Gym. The Horns' six-point lead vanished when they got the shakes early in the second half, and from then on, the two teams were never more than four points apart. Carroll Dawson (18) dropped in a field goal in the waning seconds to give BU a 60-58 win. Arnette, once again the dashing driver of earlier days, scored 24, and Clark and Smith had 11 each. With five games remaining on the schedule, chances for victory were dwindling. UT had not won in Dallas since 1953, and SMU continued that trend by a score of 78-61. Clark had another good showing with 14 points, Almanza had 13 points and 10 rebounds, and Arnette scored 12 despite injuring his nose once again. Kim Nash, Steve Strange and Bobby James were too much for the Longhorns. But for the first time in five years, the Mustangs did not win at least a share of the SWC championship.

While three of the last four games were at home, an upset of league-leading TCU was unlikely. The Frogs had an 18-rebound edge and won, 72-59, but Texas made it interesting, cutting a 19-point lead to five with four minutes left. That was when TCU went on a tear of its own to seal the victory. Puryear scored 22 for the Longhorns. The SWC basketball title won by the Frogs matched that earned by their football team in the fall.

The dust-smeared Horns sought their second conference victory, and fourth overall, against Texas A&M in Austin on February 24. Hughes hoped his players remembered the 73-29 disaster five weeks earlier in College Station. It was close, but with Wilmer Cox supplying the gas, the Aggies roared down the stretch to win, 71-61. Cox shared high-point honors with Neil Swisher (21), who became the most prolific scorer in A&M history that night. In a losing effort, Arnette (32) was fantastic, a combination sprinter and high-jumper who made shots from everywhere and dunked occasionally. Several Ags tried to cover him, but none were successful. The crowd of 5,500 booed lustily and littered the floor when referee Odell Preston called a technical foul. And fistfights after the game came within a hair of turning into the sort of riot that occurred at Clark Field in 1955 after a Longhorn-Aggie baseball game.

Glen Rose's Razorbacks, also trying to avoid their worst record ever, welcomed UT to Barnhill Fieldhouse, and the Longhorns went down again, 63-56. Texas shot just 23 percent and did not handle the Arkansas defensive pressure well. Puryear (22) was the leading scorer in that loosely handled game.

The only SWC team Texas had beaten all season, Rice, came to Austin for the last game of Hughes' coaching career. The Owls had been hot lately, winning their last three games, and Tom Robitaille had 42 against the Ags. The Longhorns held him to 14 on the way to an edifying 63-54 victory. Arnette scored 27, and free throw accuracy was another key factor as Texas made 29 of 32. Hughes, who received gifts from his players, students and even the officials before tipoff, got the game ball afterward. When the buzzer sounded, many in the crowd of 3,000 swarmed onto the floor to congratulate Hughes and the team. His voice a little husky, Hughes said, "I'm glad we could close it out like this. I thought the kids played a fine game, especially on defense."

Things never quite got off the ground for Marshall Hughes. Some problems were of his own making, and others were not. He had experienced a unique run in the UT basketball program, spanning the entire decade of the 1950s. Hughes wasted no time in completing the requirements for a doctoral degree, wrote a practical dissertation entitled "Standards for facilities in physical education in senior high schools" and joined the faculty of Southwest Texas State.

1960

The coach-seekers cast their net wide, all but snuffing Jimmy Viramontes' chances. Names discussed in the press included Oklahoma State assistant Sam Aubrey, Milton Jowers of Southwest Texas, Abe Lemons of Oklahoma City and Babe McCarthy of Mississippi State. The first three did not fit the profile of a coach who had made it on a big stage. Lemons, of course, was destined to work in Austin 17 years hence. And McCarthy, whose Bulldogs defeated No. 1 Kentucky in 1959, chose to stay in Starkville and joust with a state government terrified about interracial athletic competition.

Tobacco Road went into shock when Duke coach Harold "Hal" Bradley announced he was accepting an offer from the University of Texas. He had coached the Blue Devils for nine years, compiling a 168-77 record, producing an all-American (Dick Groat), reaching the NCAA playoffs in 1955 and twice being named Atlantic Coast Conference coach of the year. A native of Westford, New York, Bradley graduated from Hartwick College and coached at his alma mater for three years before moving to Duke. *Sports Illustrated* had recently named him one of the top 12 coaches in college basketball, in part because he won with half the scholarships of North Carolina and N.C. State, two foes in the fiercely competitive ACC. People in Durham could not believe Bradley was heading off to the football-mad Southwest Conference, but he welcomed the opportunity to rehabilitate Texas basketball. The 47-year-old father of two would get $11,000 per year, a figure some faculty and alumni considered excessive.

Lured away from Duke, coach Harold Bradley led UT to a conference title and a spot in the NCAAs for the first time since 1947.

After a two-hour meeting with sportswriters at the Driskill Hotel, Bradley was variously described as a Yankee scholar who became a Southern gentleman and someone with the poise and speaking manner of a General Motors executive. Bradley retained Viramontes as assistant coach, was diplomatic in assessing the quality of play in the SWC (although he had yet to see a game) and believed a scholarship was a fair exchange for both school and athlete. With his hiring and athletic director Ed Olle's assurances that a new field house was in the near if indeterminate future, Longhorn fans had reason to hope.

Bradley inherited an oddball mixture of seasoning and youth likely to produce erratic play, at least early in the 1960 season. Seven lettermen were back, plus Brenton Hughes after his one-year hiatus, junior college transfer Donnie Lasiter, and three sophomores, forward Jimmy Brown and guards Bill Brown and Taylor "Butch" Skeete. An advocate of the running game, Bradley worked his players hard on defense, conditioning and fundamentals. "You win your games during practice," he said. "By the time the game comes around, it's in the lap of the gods. The main thing is to get the boys to think 'winning.'"

In addition to the optimism always present with a new coach, there was an extra measure because of Bradley's blue-chip background. And UT fans blithely assumed that if Darrell Royal could take a 1-9 football team and metamorphose it into a Sugar Bowl participant in one year, Bradley might perform a similar miracle in basketball. He was introduced before a Gregory Gym crowd of 3,500 on December 1, 1959, when his Longhorns defeated McMurry, 95-54. Jay Arnette scored 22 and Hughes 17, while the Indians were led by Toby Burkhardt (18). Against Trinity, the Horns proved the "wait and see" offense of the past season was dead, running up a 21-point lead before relaxing for an 86-78 victory. Arnette, who could jump like a kangaroo, scored 31. Don Hrebec had 24 for the Tigers.

Untested so far, UT trampled Tulane, 94-71. Arnette was again the high-point man with 25, and Wayne Clark held all-SEC center Vic Klinker without a field goal. Guard Dick O'Brien scored 18, but most of the Greenies were as cold as a barefooted iceskater. The fourth game at Gregory Gym produced a fourth victory, equaling the number of wins in all of the 1959 season. Arnette scored 20, Lasiter 19 and Hughes 15 in an 84-67 defeat of LSU. After leading the first 10 minutes, the Bayou Bengals could not penetrate a tight zone defense, and Clark, Hughes and Albert Almanza commanded the backboards. Joe Clune scored 27 for LSU.

Abe Lemons' Oklahoma City Chiefs had gone 20-7 in 1959 and played in the NIT. The Longhorns ventured away from home for the first time and lost to OCU, 98-90, as Fred Moses and Rex Norton wiped out a 12-point Texas lead. The following night in Tulsa, however, Arnette scored 28 in a 67-57 defeat of the Golden Hurricane. Lasiter (11) did a good job as playmaker, and Bill Brown overcame a shaky start to score 10. No other Longhorn was in double figures.

Eight teams converged on Houston for the final SWC Tournament in late December. Although it was more popular with fans than ever and generated welcome revenue, the coaches had reasons to dislike the intraconference meet. The surprise of the young season was Harold Bradley's 5-1 Texas Longhorns, with Arnette scoring 26 points per game and Hughes making almost 70 percent of his shots. But Texas A&M and SMU were expected to carry the big sticks, both in the tourney and the conference race. If the Steers shot poorly against Rice, they compensated at the free throw line for a 79-53 win at packed Rice Gym. Clark (18) was the game's leading scorer. But Carroll Broussard and Wayne Lawrence combined for 50 points as A&M beat the Horns and went on to win the tournament. By the same 10-point margin, Arkansas defeated UT behind Clyde Rhoden's 21.

As the quality of competition toughened and scouting intensified, Bradley's team had been prevented from running so much and forced into the halfcourt game. But Arnette, Clark and the other Longhorns had won respect from their peers and among themselves. They approached the SWC race with something resembling confidence.

A Gregory Gym crowd of 6,500 hooted, hollered and stomped its feet in edgy anticipation throughout the Texas-SMU game on January 5. Hughes, a man of many moves under the basket, scored 19, and showboat Max Williams had 16 for the Ponies. Arnette, who bruised a knee in the opening minutes, was not up to his usual firebrand level and scored just 10 points, but he sank a driving layup with two seconds left, posting a dramatic 58-56 victory. A mob poured onto the court to celebrate as the disconsolate Mustangs just got out of the way. While Bradley was exceptionally cool on the bench, he received a nerve-wracking introduction to SWC basketball.

Record: 18-8

95 McMurry 54
86 Trinity 78
94 Tulane 71
84 LSU 67
90 Oklahoma City 98
67 Tulsa 57
79 Rice 53
74 Texas A&M 84
58 Arkansas 68
58 SMU 56
52 Rice 50
72 Arkansas 66
61 Texas A&M 72
62 Baylor 68
89 North Texas 78
98 TCU 77
75 Texas Tech 66
69 SMU 65
79 Texas A&M 62
74 Texas Tech 61
68 Baylor 62 (OT)
71 Arkansas 57
86 Rice 62
73 TCU 81
81 Kansas 90
61 DePaul 67

Still in the clouds after beating one of the conference's supposedly elite teams, UT headed to Houston. Reserve forward Jerry Graham hit three clutch free throws in the final 10 seconds to beat Rice, 52-50. Lasiter (18) and the Owls' James Davis (16, including a 45-foot shot at the buzzer) were the top scorers. Pushovers in the past, the Horns had become a team to approach with care, and they won another close one at home, 72-66, over Arkansas. The Razorbacks had vanquished Texas 12 straight times beginning in 1955 and erased a 13-point deficit in just six minutes, but Hughes' two free throws and an effective stall won the game. Clyde Rhoden and Ronnie Garner, high school teammates from Hot Springs, combined for 36 points, and Arnette and Lasiter had 20 each.

Texas A&M, 10-0 and No. 8 in the nation before losing a squeaker to SMU, hosted the league-leading Horns. The ancient rivalry was renewed before 8,500 fans, about one-fifth of them rooting for Texas. Arnette, with his leaping shots and defense-probing drives, had many admirers around the SWC, but he scored just 14 and fouled out with eight minutes to play. The star of the evening was Carroll Broussard (29), the smooth-as-silk sophomore forward who detested all things orange. Broussard, who would be a three-time all-conference player, led the Ags to a 72-61 victory.

Bill Brown quit the team just before a 68-62 loss to Baylor in Heart O' Texas Coliseum, the Bears' new off-campus facility resembling a barn. BU overcame a five-point UT lead behind the shooting of Richard Tinsley (16) and the rebounding of subs Johnny West and George Graves. Burly center Jimmy Brown led the Longhorns with 17 points. Bradley later identified the loss to Baylor as his team's wakeup call, and indeed it was, as they proceeded to win the next nine games. The Longhorns came out of the exam period with an 89-78 defeat of North Texas in Denton. Jim Mudd, ninth in the nation in scoring, tallied 36 but got little help from his Eagle teammates. Arnette and Almanza combined for 38 as UT shot 72 percent in the second half.

Defending champion TCU, hard-hit by graduation, came to Austin in the unfamiliar position of underdog. Lasiter, Arnette and Hughes stole the ball repeatedly in the early minutes of the game in which Texas blistered the Horned Frogs by 21 points. Two purple-clad players did well, however, Bobby Bernard (23) and Tommy Meacham (16 points and 13 rebounds). Another easy home win came against Texas Tech, 75-66. Hughes, an unusually good passer for a forward, handed out 13 assists and scored 11 points, Lasiter held the Red Raiders' stellar sophomore guard, Del Ray Mounts (who had scored 35 against Arkansas), to 16, and Almanza played strong defense and rebounded well. It had taken him a while to adjust to the intensity Bradley required. "He demands a lot of you, but that's the way it should be," Almanza said.

A highly partisan crowd of 9,000 in Dallas saw the Longhorns wipe away six years of failure and frustration in two hours with a 69-65 victory over SMU. They built a 17-point lead, big enough to trade Doc Hayes' crew field goals for free throws in the final minutes and still come out ahead. Arnette scored just seven, but Almanza and Brown combined for 36 points and 28 rebounds. Kim Nash and Mad Max Williams had 14 each for the Mustangs.

Brenton Hughes quipped that he would jump off the Tower if the Longhorns did not win their next game. It was the mighty (Texas A&M) versus the bold (Texas) in a basketball showdown at Gregory Gym, filled beyond capacity. An estimated 2,000 people were turned away, and not only for the game. There was a reunion of Longhorn basketball players, including Clyde Littlefield, Abb Curtis, Ed Olle, Jack Gray, Dr. Bobby Moers, John Hargis and others who had built the UT hoop tradition. The gym was full by halftime of the freshman game in which Shelby Metcalf's Fish beat Rodney Pirtle's Yearlings in overtime. In the main event, however, the Ags could not keep pace with the Longhorns. Arnette (25) and Almanza (18 points and 11 rebounds) keyed a 79-62 victory in which the chorus of "poor Aggies" rang down from the rafters. Gregory Gym rocked with tension and emotion as Bradley's players lifted him onto their shoulders and carried him from the court. A *Daily Texan* photo of the scoreboard was captioned, "sweetest sight in the world." Texas A&M coach Bob Rogers, a hard but gracious loser, paid high tribute to UT and Arnette in particular: "He's hell on wheels. I'll see Arnette for a week at nights jumping and sailing through the air. On that court, he's the greatest player in the conference."

There was some concern that Texas was walking into Polk Robison's trap in Lubbock, but the Longhorns stampeded to another victory, 74-61. Texas Tech could not handle the shooting accuracy, fast breaks and tough defense of the visitors in orange. Almanza scored 22, while James Wiley had 17 for the Red Raiders. Referee Odell Preston drew the ire of many of the 7,100 fans who rained paper and ice on the floor.

The 68-62 score by which Baylor beat UT in Waco was repeated in Austin, but it was the Bears' turn to lose despite some very aggressive defense. The Longhorns held onto their share of the SWC lead with 25 points from Almanza (including four of the team's eight in overtime), 18 from Arnette and 12 from Hughes. Forward David Pearce led the Bruins with 26. Treading warily into the land of opportunity in severe winter weather, the Horns belted Arkansas, 71-57, and took sole possession of first place. Sprinting downcourt every chance they got against the slower Hogs, they looked like the champions they were soon to be. Skyscraping Wayne Clark had one of his best scoring (16) and rebounding (12) games of the year.

An 86-62 defeat of Rice, coupled with an SMU loss, meant Texas was crowned the 1960 SWC cage champion with a berth in the NCAA playoffs. Almanza (22) and Arnette (20) were the Horns' top scorers, while Austinite Mike Maroney led the Owls with 13. From rags to riches, from chumps to champs, from the outhouse to the penthouse, the Longhorns had made a magnificent turnabout in just one season with the school's first undisputed SWC title since the glory days of 1947. Arnette, with 440 points and counting, had earned recognition as one of UT's all-time greats. Bradley stood in the victorious locker room eating an apple and saying in his Yankee brogue, "A coach always has hope. I knew we could do it if the boys would work hard. We had to get them to believe." A happy bunch of players showered and departed Gregory Gym that foggy night to gaze upon an orange Tower. The following afternoon in the Moore-Hill dining room, a rare thing happened when the basketball team got a standing ovation from coaches, athletes, cooks, waiters and everyone else present.

With the pressure off, the champions took a header in Fort Worth, losing to TCU, 81-73. The Frogs had five players in double figures, while Lasiter (22) led the Steers. Not ranked in the AP's top 20 at the end of the season, UT was nevertheless going to meet the Kansas Jayhawks at Ahearn Fieldhouse in Manhattan, Kansas. The NCAA Tournament had expanded to 24 teams since Texas last played, and Arnette dared to dream that the lean and hungry Horns could win the whole thing. But Clark and Brown fouled out with 10 minutes left, the game still hanging in the balance. Future pros Wayne Hightower (34) and Bill Bridges (17) took control and led the Jayhawks to a 90-81 victory. The crowd of 12,500 was enthralled with the play of Arnette, who scored a career-high 34. The season ended the next night with a consolation-game loss to DePaul. Arnette was again superb, scoring 29 points. Howie Carl had 19 for the Blue Demons.

A few days later, Arnette was playing left field for Bibb Falk's Longhorn baseball team, earning his sixth letter in two sports. He joined such luminaries as Jerry West, Jerry Lucas and Oscar Robertson on the 1960 U.S. Olympic team, was named Amateur Athlete of the Year by the Texas Sports Writers Association, played minor league baseball and had four years with the Cincinnati Royals of the NBA.

1961

He had waved a wand, transforming the downtrodden Longhorns into Cinderella winners, so Harold Bradley was expected to do more great things in 1961 and the seasons to follow. UT fans hoped the basketball program was on the sort of upward trajectory SMU had experienced in the mid- and late 1950s or better. Some dreamed of attaining the lofty status of Kentucky, North Carolina or Oklahoma State, three Southern schools that had won NCAA titles. While that might have happened, it did not for various reasons. The Texas athletic department was oriented to football, the key moneymaker and alumni-pleaser. Thirty-year-old Gregory Gym presented many limitations, and Bradley had some of his own, including public relations and recruiting. The Longhorns would win two Southwest Conference championships and share another during his eight-year reign, but they were just another face in the crowd, another earnest challenger far from the national spotlight.

Bradley, whose Sunday afternoon television show began in 1961, missed Jay Arnette and Brenton Hughes. "Those two equal three," he said. "In speed, toughness and experience, you have to figure that the loss of Arnette and Hughes is equal to the loss of three starters." But he still had Albert Almanza (a member of Mexico's 1960 Olympic team), Wayne Clark, Donnie Lasiter, Jimmy Brown and Butch Skeete. And five sophomores would earn letters in that season. The veterans and newcomers blended smoothly in the opener, a 77-54 defeat of Howard Payne before 4,500 fans. Soph guard Robert Ledbetter (14) led UT, while Dobie Craig scored 13 for the Yellow Jackets.

Trinity, with losses to Texas A&M and Rice, also fell to UT, 71-59, in the annual March of Dimes game. Bradley changed lineups throughout the season, with only Lasiter starting every game. Jack Dugan moved up before the Horns met Oklahoma City. A 6'7" forward, he did not play freshman basketball but starred in intramurals and pickup games, was spotted by assistant coach Jimmy Viramontes, made the varsity and lettered three years. By the 1960s, it was rare for a nonbenchwarmer to be drawn from the student body rather than recruited. Dugan and his teammates took the floor against Abe Lemons' Chiefs, who won by four. The speed and accuracy of Larry Jones (16) and Gary Hill (15) offset Texas' height advantage. Almanza and Lasiter had 10 each in Bradley's first home loss, one that did not sit well with the fans, who cluttered the court with paper, disregarding the coach's "be nice" letter published in the *Daily Texan*.

Two more rookies, Coyle Winborn and Jimmy Gilbert, started against Tulane in New Orleans, but they combined for just three points in a 63-49 loss characterized by poor second-half shooting. Ahead by six points with 10 minutes to go, the Longhorns went cold. Almanza had 16 points for UT, the Green Wave's Jim Kerwin scored 17 and center Jack Ardon had that many rebounds. A third straight loss came in Baton Rouge, courtesy of the LSU Tigers, 62-59. Texas trailed by 12 at the half, but Lasiter (19) led a rally that fell just short. LSU guard Ellis Cooper had 20 points, most of them from the free throw line. While Bradley did not publicly identify the culprits, he blamed a lack of effort, especially in rebounding, for the three defeats.

The Tulsa Golden Hurricane (coached by Clarence Iba of the famous hoop family) blew into Austin and got upset, 80-70, in overtime. Texas led all the way until a basket by John Jones of Tulsa tied it at 68 near the end of regulation. Three quick jumpers by Brown rendered the five-minute extra period free of suspense. Almanza (20) and Tulsa's David Voss (17) were the top scorers.

In place of the defunct SWC Tournament, Bradley put the team in a pair of doubleheaders. The first, called the Aluminum Bowl Classic, was held at Barton Coliseum in Little Rock. Tennessee took a 13-point lead in the first seven minutes, but Almanza (19 points and 13 rebounds), Lasiter (15) and John "Mutt" Heller (14) brought the Longhorns back to tie the game at 51 and then win it, 77-73. Bobby Carter scored 17 for the Volunteers. Alabama, defeated by Arkansas, had a 1-6 record, but the Tide played tough, losing to UT by a point. Almanza and Lasiter (21) shared scoring honors, while Larry Pennington had 27 for Bama. Bradley, although pleased with the victories, was still not overly impressed with his team, which tended to get flustered at critical times.

The final warmup before the SWC race was at Autry Court in Houston. Poor shooting plagued Texas in a 48-44 loss to Clemson, but the Horns made 53 percent the next night against Mississippi State, collaring the Bulldogs, 93-82. They made a fast trip from the ridiculous to the sublime, according to *Austin Statesman* writer Jerry Wizig. In a roughhouse affair with 57 fouls called, Skeete and Almanza combined for 44 points, while MSU's Jerry Graves scored 34.

With a 6-4 record, UT entered the legalized fratricide known as SWC competition, one of three favorites (along with Arkansas and Texas A&M) to win the title. Over 6,000 fans converged on Gregory Gym on January 4 to see the Horns and Razorbacks. Pregame entertainment featured the Longhorn Band and Irene Reeb twirling a flaming baton in the darkened gym. Texas' defense of the conference championship began with a 68-58 victory. Clyde Rhoden, a 6'3" stick of dynamite in 1960, had an injured ankle and was not quite so explosive, leaving Jerry Carlton as the only Hog with a trace of speed. He scored 18, one more than Almanza.

TCU had just three SWC victories in 1961, and one of them came at the Longhorns' expense in Fort Worth. A veritable monsoon raged outside while there were thrills galore inside in a 95-94 four-overtime Horned Frog victory. Skeete, a slightly overweight substitute the year before, played a heroic game, going 57 of 60 minutes, crashing into a wall once and scoring 34 points. Phil Reynolds had 27 for the Frogs. After a basketball game resembling an old-time marathon dance, the players staggered to their locker rooms. Bradley described it as a nightmare and pointed to the 34-10 disparity in fouls called by referees Bo McAlister and Odell Preston.

A Slater Martin from the west—that is how Texas Tech fans thought of Del Ray Mounts. Scarcely recruited, he flourished in Lubbock, becoming a tight little bundle of nerves and steel, a cold-eyed operator with a warm hand. At 21 points per game, Mounts was a better scorer than Martin had been, and in an era dominated by taller players. Most coaches and writers considered Martin (recently retired after 11 NBA seasons) a superior defender, but both played with fierce determination. Mounts scored most of his 17 points in the first half of a 63-55 loss in Austin. The Red Raiders, with a thin bench, used just six men and tired noticeably in the final minutes. Almanza, Brown, Skeete and Lasiter broke double figures for the winning Horns.

Frosty Heart O' Texas Coliseum was the scene of the Longhorns' only SWC road victory of the season. They won, but just Bear-ly, 59-58, over Baylor. Neither team scored in the final four minutes, as first Texas and then Baylor stalled and missed free throws. It came

Record: 14-10

77 Howard Payne 54
71 Trinity 59
49 Oklahoma City 53
49 Tulane 63
59 LSU 62
80 Tulsa 70 (OT)
77 Tennessee 73
79 Alabama 78
44 Clemson 48
93 Mississippi State 82
68 Arkansas 58
94 TCU 95 (4 OT's)
63 Texas Tech 55
59 Baylor 58
81 Texas A&M 76
59 Rice 63
63 SMU 70
68 Baylor 65
59 Arkansas 74
71 SMU 65
81 Rice 79
69 Texas A&M 86
79 TCU 77
60 Texas Tech 63

down to Bruin guard Jerry Spence's last-second shot, which did not fall. Almanza had 19 points, and Spence had 17 for BU.

More Aggies than usual were expected to make the trip to Austin, prompting business manager Al Lundstedt to warn UT's late-arrivers. As a result, 3,000 people were pounding on the doors of Gregory Gym when it opened, and the two frosh teams got the rare opportunity to play before a bustling throng. Further complicating matters was the recent hiring of sports information director Jones Ramsey away from Texas A&M. Carroll Broussard, the smoothest Frenchman since Maurice Chevalier, amassed 37 points, but his Aggies fell, 81-76. The UT bench strength was evident when Lasiter got in foul trouble and was replaced by Gilbert, who scored 16 and played a fine ballhawking game. Almanza carried the biggest load for Texas, scoring 23 and grabbing 10 rebounds. Fans displeased with the referees' calls responded with boos, paper and coins, causing Ag assistant coach Shelby Metcalf to quip, "Heck, on a good night here, a quick guard can pick up two dollars in change easily."

The 19-day exam layoff hurt the Longhorns, who dropped a 63-59 decision to Rice in Houston. Lasiter, with 20 points, was the game's leading scorer. Not afraid to take the big shots, the modest Longview native had always wanted to be a Longhorn, and he started every game of his two-year career in orange and white, making all-SWC in 1961. Almanza, however, had a miserable game against the Owls, with just three points and two rebounds, temporarily losing his starting job. Doc Hayes' Ponies dealt Texas a 70-63 defeat before 7,500 fans at SMU Coliseum. After a seven-minute second-half span in which they were outscored, 23-7, the Horns were never in contention. Almanza was back, however, scoring 21 and getting nine rebounds. Jon Larson had 16 for SMU, and stars Jan Loudermilk and Steve Strange scored 15 and 11, respectively.

Close observers of SWC basketball noted the trend toward winning at home and losing on the road, a bad sign for a weak league. Some thought it had developed into a game of fouls and free throw shooting and that officials were too easily influenced by crowds. Due to the recent incursion of pro sports into Texas, the colleges were going to have to compete or fans might find new allegiances. Bradley saw a need for better-trained officials and more coordination between them and coaches before and during the season. Without direction from the Dallas-based SWC office, however, the future of college basketball in the region could turn dim.

The hapless Baylor Bears came to Austin and led well into the second half before losing, 68-65. Richard Tinsley, Baylor's best player, scored 18 points before fouling out for the 11th time that season. Lasiter scored 21, and Almanza, Clark and Winborn were mostly responsible for UT's 52-27 rebound edge.

Arkansas coach Glen Rose, a plainspoken man whose SWC basketball roots went back more than 35 years, had recently advocated integration. He believed that long-armed black athletes would help his school and other conference schools compete on a national level. That was still a few years away. In the meantime, Rose's Hogs got off to a blazing 14-1 start and were never in trouble, winning by a score of 74-59 in Fayetteville. Freewheeling Ronnie Garner had 21 points for Arkansas, and Almanza led UT with 17.

SMU and Texas met at Gregory Gym in a rare Saturday afternoon game dictated by the television cameras of ABC. It was the first nationally broadcast SWC game ever, and the fans at home saw a good one. The Longhorns won, 71-65, behind Lasiter's 21 points and Almanza's 18 points and 18 rebounds. Jan Loudermilk (16) led the Mustangs, who converted 23 of 24 free throws. The man calling the game was Curt Gowdy, a member of the Wyoming team that had beaten Bully Gilstrap's Longhorns in the 1943 NCAA semifinals, and one of the officials, ex-Sooner Kenny Pryor, hit the long shot that beat Jack Gray's team in the 1947 Final Four.

The days of the SWC basketball calender were dwindling down to a precious few when UT played host to John Frankie's Rice Owls. The blue-clad visitors were hot and led until Dugan stole a pass and forged a three-point play with 1:25 left. Texas held on to win, 81-79, after which many of the 5,000 fans swarmed the floor. Lasiter (22) turned in his usual fine performance as the team's quarterback, and Clark and Skeete had 15 each. Mike Maroney and Olle Shipley led Rice with 26 and 19, respectively.

As he had done earlier in the season, catlike Carroll Broussard scored 37 against UT in Texas A&M's 86-69 win at packed G. Rollie White Coliseum. Played amid a background of noise from the Aggie corps, it was no game for the weak of ear, and both teams gave all-out efforts. Lasiter had 24 for the Horns, who left College Station defeated for the sixth straight time.

Due to injuries and other problems, Buster Brannon could only suit up seven players when TCU met Texas in Austin. The Horned Frogs nearly pulled off a big victory but fell two points short. A trio of seniors (Lasiter, Almanza and Clark) and soph Robert Ledbetter did nearly all of the scoring for UT, while TCU's Billy Simmons and Phil Reynolds had 19 each.

Texas Tech, the baby of the SWC, won its first title after beating UT, 63-60, in Lubbock before 10,380 delirious fans. The Longhorns threatened to spring an upset, twice leading by 11, but lost their shooting touch in the final minutes. Harold Hudgens and Del Ray Mounts (who played with an eight-inch scalp wound) combined for 37 points for Polk Robison's champions, and Lasiter led Texas with 20. Apart from the consistent play of Lasiter, the 1961 Longhorns were a team that never quite jelled. Bradley shrugged his shoulders, said, "I can't explain it," and looked to the next season.

1962

"We'll have more speed, but some of our new boys will have to come through for us," said coach Harold Bradley. "I think we'll have an interesting ball club to watch." Of the four "new boys" on the 1962 Longhorns—guard Jimmy Puryear (brother of Bobby Puryear, a UT player in the late 1950s), forwards Joe Fisher and Ron Weaks and center Mike Humphrey—none were in the starting lineup for the season opener against Howard Payne in Austin. The Yellow Jackets gave the 4,000 fans some uneasy moments before bowing, 81-68. Texas got 19 points from Jimmy Brown, who had suffered through an awful junior season, shed 15 pounds and was the star of fall practice. Texas Wesleyan was overmatched and lost, 92-66. Mutt Heller, possibly the first basketball player-swimmer in UT history, scored 18, while freshman center Irvin Rue had 16 for the Rams.

Tulane was expected to bring some big-time competition to Gregory Gym, but the Green Wave washed away after the first 10 minutes in a 90-65 Texas victory. Fisher and Butch Skeete (14 each) were two of the seven Longhorns in double figures, just the sort of balanced scoring Bradley liked. Tulane star Jim Kerwin scored 14, too, but he missed 13 of 18 shots from the field. Fun and frolic was over for Texas in a 77-75 loss to LSU before 3,000 jeering, stomping and sometimes vicious fans. Sam Chase, a deft guard from Indiana, scored 25 points, and Maury Drummond got 18 rebounds for the Tigers, who had recently lost to Rice. Brown and Skeete both scored 19, and the latter was hit by a flying piece of ice as fans littered the floor with debris throughout the fiercely contested second half.

Record: 16-8

81 Howard Payne 68
92 Texas Wesleyan 66
90 Tulane 65
75 LSU 77
60 Louisville 76
78 Western Kentucky 68
82 East Texas 67
88 Mississippi 71
84 William & Mary 71
66 Texas Tech 77
73 Arkansas 59
64 Rice 89
64 Texas A&M 57
95 Trinity 89
76 Baylor 71
82 SMU 84 (OT)
83 Rice 82
48 Texas A&M 54
81 Baylor 66
64 SMU 69
71 Texas Tech 84
61 Arkansas 60
71 TCU 68
73 TCU 61

As the Longhorns departed for Louisville and the Bluegrass Tournament, Bradley noted his team's 52 percent shooting, as well as its lax defense. Freedom Hall (capacity: 18,000) was just one-third full when Texas met Peck Hickman's Louisville Cardinals. Center Bud Olsen worked his way through the UT zone and man-to-man defenses for 28 points and 21 rebounds, and teammate Jadie Frazier had 20 points before fouling out in the Cards' 76-60 victory. Skeete led the Horns with 20, and Jack Dugan had 14 points and 15 rebounds. Bradley came down with the flu and was hospitalized, so Jimmy Viramontes ran the team the next night, defeating Western Kentucky, 78-68. The Hilltoppers shaved much of a big UT lead in the final minutes, mostly by the scoring of Bobby Rascoe (29). While poor free throw shooting had hurt the Longhorns against Louisville, they went to the line as eagerly as a daily-double winner at Churchill Downs against WKU, converting 24 of 28. Humphrey showed promise of basketball stardom with 15 points and 13 rebounds,

Fan participation was the norm at Gregory Gym basketball games in 1962.

and Jimmy Gilbert, playing again after a hand injury, was a vital part of the UT attack. Skeete, the only Longhorn on the all-tournament team, was no great athlete. He overcame slowness afoot by effort, smarts and clutch shooting.

Skeete's backcourt running mate, Gilbert, scored 21 points in an 82-67 defeat of East Texas State attended by fewer than 1,000 people because classes had been dismissed for the holidays. Bill Mayes had 27 points for the Lions in a game that inaugurated the $2,000, four-sided scoreboard hanging from the Gregory Gym ceiling. Players, coaches and fans had long complained about just having one high in the gym's west stands.

In the first game of a pair of doubleheaders hosted by Texas Tech, the Longhorns defeated Mississippi (much as their football counterparts would do three days later in the Cotton Bowl), 88-71. Five Texas players hit double figures, and guard Don Kessinger led the Rebels with 26. And the Horns beat William & Mary, 84-71, amid the almost constant tooting of referees' whistles. Balanced scoring again proved better than one individual star, as the Indians' Kirk Gooding had 24 points.

Back to the South Plains for the second time in a week, UT fell to the defending SWC champs. Del Ray Mounts, Harold Hudgens and their Red Raider supporting cast turned away the Horns, 77-66. Heller was the top Texas scorer, with 15, one more than Dugan and Gilbert.

Arkansas, with a 9-1 record against some good competition, came to Austin and got bopped, 73-59, before 6,000 fans. With nearly 40 turnovers, equally divided between the teams, it was not a pretty game. Jerry Carlton, the second-leading scorer in the conference, was held to nine, and Tommy Boyer, the Hogs' other star, made just three of 17 shots. Heller scored 17, and Dugan had 14 points and 11 rebounds.

Next on the schedule was TCU, with its plush new 7,166-seat Daniel-Meyer Coliseum. But the UT team bus had barely reached Round Rock before it was pulled over by a State Highway Patrol car and informed that 16-degree weather and icy roads in Fort Worth had caused the game to be postponed. The extra practice session at Gregory Gym availed little in light of an 89-64 trouncing by Rice in Houston. Behind Larry Phillips (23) and sophomore star Kendall Rhine (18 points and 12 rebounds), the Owls grabbed an early lead and sprinted to victory. Only Brown and Dugan (15 each) played well in a game that did nothing for UT's confidence.

The last team to hand Texas such a thorough paddling was Texas A&M in 1961, and the Ags were coming to town. Carroll Broussard was back, and he had more help from JC transfer Bennie Johnson and sophomore star Bennie Lenox. It was standing room only at Gregory Gym, and few could forget the 64-57 Longhorn victory. Skeete and Broussard led their teams in scoring, with 17 and 15, respectively, and the extracurricular activities were something else. Late in the first half, a free-for-all broke out involving players and about 300 fans. Broussard and Heller had been jostling each other before Heller scored a layup, got fouled hard by Broussard and landed on his head. The Texas forward was knocked unconscious, blood streaming from a gash over his eye, as tempers started to flare. Play briefly resumed when elbowing turned into fisticuffs. Players from both benches joined in, as did a nest of Aggie fans, quickly offset by Longhorn supporters. Fighting lasted about a minute before the officials (Shorty Lawson and Peyton Shelton), coaches and policemen could restore peace. The Longhorn Band played "The Star-Spangled Banner," and the game was finished without further incident.

"Strange it was that the biggest blowup Gregory Gym has ever seen should come at this time," wrote Lou Maysel of the *Austin Statesman*. "UT officials have been engaged in a campaign to improve crowd behavior.... The main problem is that Gregory Gym concentrates too many strong vocal chords and too many husky pitching arms into too small an area."

The two-week exam break ended with a 95-89 victory over Trinity at Alamo Stadium Gym in San Antonio. The scrappy Tigers, led by Gaylan Stroth (25) and Jim Potter (23) earned UT's respect. Dugan had 19 points and 12 rebounds, and four free throws by Gilbert halted a late Trinity rally. SWC play resumed with a 76-71 defeat of last-place Baylor, then coached by Bill Menefee. Both teams shot over 50 percent, but the Texas bench made the difference with Humphrey, Fisher and Puryear helping to turn the Bears back again and again. The top scorers were Roy Wolfe (21) of BU and Gilbert (20).

Losers of their last three games, the SMU Mustangs welcomed UT to Dallas. Skeete put on a great aerial gunnery show, hitting 11 of 12 from the field in an 84-82 overtime loss. His 24 points matched the Ponies' Jan Loudermilk. Seven players fouled out, five of them wearing orange. "We just ran out of players," Bradley said, while the Mustang Band played "Taps."

An equally close game took place in Austin four days later. Brown scored a career-high 27 to lead the Horns past Rice in an 83-82 game that ended in wild disorder. When Puryear missed a free throw with :03 left, Kendall Rhine grabbed the rebound and quickly called timeout, but the clock ran down to :01, not enough time to get a decent shot. A number of Owls charged the scorer's table, and fans came onto the floor and exchanged pleasantries with Rhine, Mike Maroney, Olle Shipley and others. Coach John Frankie had his hands full getting the Owls to their locker room without further escalation of violence.

Seven games remained, and it had already been a cage season to remember—not for the mediocre basketball played, but the incidents appertaining thereto. Gregory Gym had no monopoly on such things, and if Bradley and his players had any qualms about going to College Station, it did not show, except that UT had lost every game there since Raymond Downs' sophomore year. "G. Rollie White ought to have armed guards at the gate to check for clubs, hatchets, slingshots and other havoc-making devices," wrote Wes Hocker of the *Daily Texan*. The sellout crowd and Aggie Band were as loud and unnerving as usual, but nothing bad happened other than a 54-48 defensive struggle won by the men in maroon. Carroll Broussard was at his best, with 25 points and 10 rebounds. Ron Weaks, whose hustle in the Rice game earned him a starting position, led UT with 13.

Weaks went scoreless in Waco, but the Longhorns won by 15. The difference was free throws because both teams made 22 field goals. A remarkable 37 of 39 from the line carried Texas to its fifth SWC win before just 2,500 onlookers at Heart O' Texas Coliseum. Rebounding numbers also favored the Longhorns, 45-27. Baylor's Roy Wolfe scored 26 and Skeete 20.

Texas was 29-2 at home in the Bradley era when SMU came calling. The Ponies won it, 69-64, as Doc Hayes got 52 points from his front line of Jan Loudermilk, Dave Siegmund and Jim Hammond. In another game won with free throws, technical fouls on Gilbert and Viramontes hurt the Horns, led by Brown (13).

Bradley, courted by several schools after UT's big turnaround in 1960, gave every indication of being happy in Austin. His name was mentioned when the Syracuse job came open two years later. One of Bradley's predecessors, Jack Gray, was introduced (along with the 1951 SWC tri-champs) at halftime of the Longhorn-Red Raider game. When a reporter asked

Gray, an oil pipeline mogul, if he missed coaching, he responded pithily: "Hell, no." Texas Tech looked like the best team to visit Gregory Gym all season, winning, 84-71, behind Roger Hennig's 20 points. Del Ray Mounts, nearing the end of his colorful career, scored 19 and covered a lot of ground on defense. Gilbert and Fisher combined for 25 points in a losing effort.

UT ate high on the Hog in Fayetteville, taking a one-point victory. Skeete rang up 11 straight points, and then the Horns went scoreless the last four minutes, with just enough of a margin to hold off the Razorbacks when Tommy Boyer (20) missed a shot at the buzzer. Only 21 fouls were called, 11 on Texas and 10 on Arkansas. That was worth noting only because of the ensuing scandal. Gene Roswell of the *New York Post* claimed "shenanigans" in Southwest Conference basketball, with officials allegedly attempting to influence point spreads. Roswell's sources were bookies, among the most suspicious people in the world, and no proof was ever presented. But the FBI and Texas Department of Public Safety took the charge seriously, as did the SWC office. Each of the 22 officials voluntarily took lie-detector tests, and two were quietly stricken from the list. Their identity was not revealed, nor were the facts surrounding the case. Those who worked the remaining games did so under considerable pressure because the faint finger of suspicion pointed at all of them.

Texas and TCU, a pair of teams on the outside looking in, had two back-to-back games due to the postponement in early January. The first was in Austin, a 71-68 Longhorn victory before just 2,500 fans. Brown and Frog guard Phil Reynolds scored 17 each, although the latter made just eight of 22 shots. And the stone-cold Frogs nearly got run out of their new gym when UT piled up a 24-point lead and coasted to a 73-61 win, the first in Fort Worth since 1954. Gilbert led the Longhorns with 17, and Johnny Fowler (21 points and 16 rebounds) was TCU's bright spot. The season over, Bradley thanked the Texas fans and promised better times ahead. The 1962 Yearlings, recruited and coached primarily by Viramontes, won all 12 games and planned to shake things up when they joined the varsity.

1963

Seven lettermen were back from a team that went 16-8 the year before, coming in fourth in the Southwest Conference. The vaunted sophomores included 6'8" John Paul Fultz and 6'5" Larry Franks in the front court and Jimmy Clark and Tommy Nelms (whose father of the same name had played with Bobby Moers 25 years earlier) in the backcourt. Jim Bob Smith, coached by UT-ex Leon Black at Lon Morris Junior College, was another savvy guard. With speed, size and experience, it was the most promising Longhorn team since Jay Arnette and company won the title in 1960. Harold Bradley and SMU's Doc Hayes were on the spot as coaches of the SWC preseason favorites. In the wake of the point-shaving investigation—which produced a lot of smoke and little if any fire—some new officials had been hired, and all were urged to be extra conscientious. The coaches vowed to help under a "gentleman's agreement" whereby they would remain on the bench during conference games.

Fultz, Franks and Clark joined Jimmy Gilbert and Jack Dugan in the starting lineup for the season opener with Howard Payne. The Yellow Jackets brought a 13-game winning streak to Gregory Gym, but it came to an end on December 1 as the Horns ran at every opportunity and won, 77-53, before 4,500 fans. Clark, who hit his first five shots, led all scorers with 16. And nearly everyone contributed in a 71-38 defeat of East Texas State. Joe Fisher had 14 points and nine rebounds, and guard Ben Riley scored 11 for the Lions.

After those two breathers, UT went on a Louisiana hayride. Jim Kerwin, Tulane's all-America candidate, had missed two games with a torn thigh muscle. But he played against the Horns, firing away 30 times and scoring 26 points, followed by center Bob Davidson (17 points and 11 rebounds). The Green Wave lost, 81-72. Mike Humphrey led Texas with 14, and four teammates reached double figures. In Baton Rouge, however, clutch free throw shooting down the stretch enabled LSU to gain a 75-66 victory. Texas led most of the game but finally succumbed to the scoring and rebounding of Dick Maile and Maury Drummond. Jimmy Gilbert had 20 points before fouling out. Despite the loss, *Daily*

Texan sportswriter (and future UT sports information director) Bill Little said the Longhorns had the makings of a great team.

Arkansas, similarly flattered after a 9-1 start in 1962, had stumbled to 5-9 in the SWC race, so it was too early to tell. And the Longhorns were just beginning a four-game losing streak in which they looked anything but great. They fell to Oklahoma State, 69-65, in Austin. In an interesting contrast of UT's speed and the slow, methodical OSU offense, the Cowboys, who shot 65 percent from the field, prevailed in a tightly called game. If not for some damaging tactical errors in the closing minutes, Texas might have won. Soph center Gene Johnson (22) led Hank Iba's team, and Gilbert had 15 for the Horns.

The shakedown cruise before league play took Texas out to the west coast. The California Golden Bears, national champs in 1959 and runners-up the next year, were still tough. With a front line averaging 6'9", they were certainly tall. UT's basket was fogged in worse than the San Francisco airport in the first half, and that slow start proved fatal in a 70-62 loss. Just three of the Longhorns' first 17 shots went in. Dick Smith (21) was effective from the outside for Cal, and 13 points from Dugan was the best Texas could offer. Things hit rock bottom the next night against No. 8 Stanford. UT's shooting, rebounding and ball control (25 turnovers) were quite poor as the Indians won, 72-46. Tom Dose scored 19 points and dominated interior play. Heavy substituting by the Indians mattered little because the lead continued to mount, and nothing Bradley tried could pump life into the Longhorns.

Record: 20-7

77 Howard Payne 53
71 East Texas 38
81 Tulane 72
66 LSU 75
65 Oklahoma State 69
62 California 70
46 Stanford 72
63 Denver 52
40 Texas Western 45
54 Rice 49
69 Arkansas 63
76 Baylor 38
78 Texas Tech 58
88 Trinity 54
73 TCU 56
70 Texas A&M 59
77 SMU 62
90 Texas Tech 76
75 TCU 59
83 Texas A&M 73
92 SMU 76
77 Rice 59
99 Arkansas 86
48 Baylor 55
65 Texas Western 47
68 Cincinnati 73
90 Oklahoma City 83

In the Sun Bowl Tournament in El Paso, they snapped out of it with a 63-52 defeat of Denver. Bradley got fine work from Humphrey (19), Mutt Heller and Ron Weaks (12 each), while Tim Vezie (12) led the Pioneers. With the SWC race looming in less than a week, the victory provided a sharp improvement in team spirit. But Texas Western, which had other ideas about holiday cheer, won the championship game, 45-40, when the Longhorns had too many fouls and too few rebounds. Bradley was assessed a rare technical foul with 12 seconds left, to the delight of a hostile crowd of 4,500 at Memorial Gymnasium. Heller and the Miners' Jim "Bad News" Barnes were the top scorers (10 each) followed by Nolan Richardson (the future Arkansas coach) with nine.

That was an impressive showing against a fine Texas Western team, but UT's 4-5 record entering conference play gave no hint of what was to come. Kendall Rhine, a 6'9" junior, was being touted as the finest Rice player since Gene Schwinger or Bill Henry and possibly the conference's next all-American. But he scored just 13 points when the Owls lost in Austin, 54-49. Led by Fisher (16), UT's pressing, aggressive tactics took control with three minutes left. Gilbert's four free throws in the final 72 seconds wrapped up a game that had 18 lead changes.

When Texas' band of basketball troubadours arrived late in Fayetteville because of nasty weather, the afternoon game with the Razorbacks was rescheduled for 7 p.m. Height usually makes right, and Arkansas had four 6'6" players in the starting lineup, but the Longhorns made off with a 69-63 victory keyed by Franks' 19 points. Although the husky Nacogdoches soph made four of five from the field and 11 of 12 from the free throw line, he did not collect a single rebound. Larry Wofford and Tommy Boyer combined for 35 for the Hogs, harried by UT's man-to-man defense.

Humphrey (21 points and 15 rebounds) starred in a 76-38 mangling of Baylor at Gregory Gym. The Bears did not even get a taste of honey in a lopsided game witnessed by 4,000 patrons. Winston Moore, averaging 20 points per game, was held to 12. With their high-intensity defense and 58-percent shooting, the Steers were really coming around. "They just completely overpowered us," said BU coach Bill Menefee. "Texas is the best team we've played this year."

Nine thousand fans were expected to cram Texas Tech's hothouse when UT visited Lubbock, but zero-degree weather kept it to 7,600. The Red Raiders, participants in the NCAA tourney the past two years, missed Del Ray Mounts and his pals. Puryear, a fine defensive player and underrated on offense, threw in some long-range bombs early, and a 78-58 rout was on. Fultz (20 points and 11 rebounds) got a bloody lip in scrambling for a loose ball. It was a bitter defeat for the once-mighty Raiders, whose tempers flew toward the end, as did pennies and other projectiles from a rude crowd. Two Tech students took it upon themselves to apologize to Bradley after the game, however. With that win and a loss by Texas A&M, the Horns had first place to themselves, and yet none were among the SWC's top ten scorers.

All-SWC performers Jimmy Gilbert (above) and Mike Humphrey (right).

Lou Maysel of the *Austin Statesman* called Bradley "a cage magician...[who has] transformed a dozen bumpkins into impressive-looking chargers who look like they might run away with the SWC championship." A fine team was expected in 1964, not 1963, but Bradley was not wont to take credit. "If you start winning," he said, "a lot of your problems just disappear. This thing is like a snowball, and it started for us in El Paso." The snowball was getting bigger and moving faster with each game. After a 34-point drubbing of Trinity in San Antonio, Texas resumed SWC play against TCU in Austin. Frog-hunting was never so easy. Buster Brannon's team was in the midst of a dreadful 4-20 season, and the game's outcome (73-56, Longhorns) was never in doubt. Gilbert (10 of 11 from the field), Puryear, Humphrey and Heller were all in double figures, and Fisher had 14 rebounds. TCU center Archie Clayton played well, getting 19 points and 13 rebounds.

Head cheerleader Bill Melton urged UT students to attend the Tuesday night game in College Station and help serve as an "equalizer." From time immemorial, few Longhorn fans had traveled to remote College Station for sporting events, nowhere near the number of Ags who came to the relatively cosmopolitan state capital and a campus that was nearly half female. G. Rollie White Coliseum was full that night, and 8,500 fans saw the Aggies' 30-game SWC home winning streak come to an end, 70-59. Gilbert (23) and Puryear (19) dismissed the bedlam in Texas' first victory there in eight years. Only Bennie Lenox (26) gave the Horns any trouble.

Texas' share-the-wealth plan continued in the 100th meeting with SMU, a series that began in 1918. Five Longhorns were in double figures, led by Humphrey (15 points and 10 rebounds) in a 77-62 victory before 8,000 happy fans. The SMU scouting report said to limit the outside shooting of UT's Jim-dandy guards, Gilbert, Clark and Puryear, and the Ponies were successful but at the cost of opening things up inside. Dave Siegmund scored 22 for SMU and Gene Elmore 12. Texas Tech took a 14-point beating at Gregory Gym three days later as Franks (18) and Fisher (11 points and 11 rebounds) led the way.

Donning their traveling uniforms again, the Longhorns belted TCU in Fort Worth, 75-59, making believers of the Frogs for a second time. Ahead by just six at the half, UT rolled up 20 points in seven minutes to notch a 10th straight win. Humphrey (19) and TCU's Don Kosick (17) were the top scorers.

With a three-game lead, Texas was riding to the title on greased skids, and a victory over Bob Rogers' Aggies would clinch at least a tie. Paced by Franks' 24 points, the Longhorns won, 83-73. Lenox scored 43 points to break Carroll Broussard's school scoring record. It was a one-man show for the Ags, whose offense consisted mostly of Lenox dribbling downcourt, looking for his shot and taking it. He took 29 of them, more than the rest of his teammates combined.

That was the basketball side of it. An SWC official had declared four days earlier that crowds seemed to be on better behavior. He rued making that statement after the events of February 19, 1963, which made 1962 look tame. Gloating Longhorn fans sang the familiar chant "poor Aggies" ("poor Teasips" when the shoe was on the other foot) toward the end of the game. When the buzzer sounded, a well-organized phalanx of Aggies moved out of the bleachers and across the court. They made threatening signs, shouted crude challenges and asked for the very violence that occurred. "It was like the Red Sea crashing down on Pharoah and his boys," said the *Daily Texan* of the inevitable confrontation. An estimated 2,000 people crowded the court, perhaps a quarter of them engaged in hand-to-hand combat lasting fully 10 minutes. The Longhorn Band again played the national anthem, and public-address announcer Wally Pryor called first for order and then for doctors to treat the injured. Helping campus and city gendarmes, UT athletic director and football coach Darrell Royal and his Aggie counterpart, Hank Foldberg, used what moral authority they could to end the fighting, some of which spilled outside. Gregory Gym had witnessed some big-time melees, and there were a few remaining in its future, but nothing like what happened that night. Administration and student leaders at both schools gave it their own spin and then denounced the violence. A *Daily Texan* editorial castigated the Aggies for "acting like animals" and half-seriously suggested that Texas A&M be abolished. Lou Maysel repeated his theme about the inadequacy of Gregory Gym and wrote that if the situation did not improve, perhaps Longhorn-Aggie basketball games should be held at neutral sites such as Dallas, Houston or San Antonio. The SWC needed national exposure, but not the kind it got in a half-page spread in the *Chicago Daily News*.

SMU Coliseum was full when Doc Hayes' Mustangs and the high-rolling Longhorns met, but many of the red-and-blue faithful were gone with five minutes left when Bradley emptied his bench. Texas played an outstanding game, winning, 92-76, behind 21 points from Humphrey and 18 from Dallas native John Paul Fultz. Dave Siegmund (28) kept SMU close for a while, but not long. It was UT's most decisive win over the Ponies in 10 years. "Praise to the victors," Hayes said. "They keep the pressure on you constantly." When the team returned home, they got a nice welcome from students and other fans on the north side of Gregory Gym. "The SMU newspaper [the *Daily Campus*] had some stuff about us being overrated and a bunch of goons and things like that," Gilbert commented. "We were ready to play."

The *Thrasher*, Rice's student newspaper, carried the same "overrated" charge, but why? UT, after defeating the Owls by 18 in Houston, had a 13-game winning streak, was ahead of second-place Texas A&M by four games and had two players (Gilbert and Humphrey) who would earn all-SWC. The Horns were making plans for the NCAA Tournament, while their conference brethren were playing out the string. Texas beat Arkansas, 99-86, in the last home game of the season with Franks, Heller and Humphrey the top scorers. Tommy Boyer had 24 points for the Hogs.

With just lowly Baylor to dispose of, the Longhorns looked at the prospect of going through the SWC schedule undefeated and becoming the first team to do so since Jim Krebs and SMU in 1956. But the resentful Bears, nursing memories of the terrible beating they took in Austin, proceeded to upset UT, 55-48. Roy Wolfe's successful 80-foot heave at the end of the first half was part of an 18-point BU scoring spree. It was so dark inside Heart O' Texas Coliseum, a fan almost needed a flashlight to see the baskets, but Bradley would brook no excuses: "It never helps to lose, and with all due regard to Baylor's fine effort, some of our boys didn't have their heads in the game."

After the bubble was burst in Waco, there were just four days to prepare for a first-round game with Texas Western in Lubbock. Don Haskins' 19-6 Miners, who beat Texas in their home tourney nine weeks earlier, were again favored. The Longhorns were champions of a league that had lost its standing as a basketball power center over the last dozen or so years, measured by any criteria. And Texas Western coaches scouting the stinker of a game played in Waco may have taken

UT a bit lightly. It was a pro-Miner crowd at Lubbock Municipal Coliseum, with cheerleaders, band, drill team and west Texas fans always glad to heap scorn on a team representing the big school in Austin. But the days of wine and roses continued when the Horns used a second-half outburst to win, 65-47. They had a 34-26 rebounding advantage over the muscular Miners (primarily because Jim Barnes got some quick fouls and sat out nearly half the game), Humphrey scored 18 and Fultz 16.

On the jubilant flight home, Fultz and Nelms warbled the lyrics to "Kansas City," but that was 40 miles from Lawrence, the site of their next game. It was with fearsome Cincinnati, the two-time national champion, No. 1 team all season long, with two all-Americans, Ron Bonham and Tom Thacker. The Bearcats, coached by Ed Jucker, had lost just six games in the past three years. If the Horns could play good defense, hit from the outside, stay out of foul trouble and not get overawed by the glory surrounding Cincinnati, they might win and put the SWC back on the map. But most experts gave Texas less chance than an ice cube in the desert. While the Longhorns' 19-6 record was better than that of some teams in the final Associated Press top-ten poll, at least they were among 27 teams listed as "others receiving votes."

The game was close throughout, but the Bearcats won, 73-68. Two free throws by center George Wilson (25) with 18 seconds left put it out of reach. Bonham (24) and Thacker (14) showed the fastest hands since Houdini. Franks scored 18 before fouling out, and Gilbert and Fultz tallied 13 each. The Horns shot 55 percent against the famed Cincinnati defense, but 17 turnovers hurt the cause terribly.

In the consolation game, Gilbert and Humphrey were the top scorers in defeating Abe Lemons' Oklahoma City Chiefs, 90-83. It was the first 20-win season since 1948, and coaches and sportswriters in Lawrence seemed sincere in declaring Texas the finest Southwest Conference team they had seen in a decade.

1964

Austin felt an odd mixture of sorrow and elation as the 1964 season approached. President John F. Kennedy had been assassinated in Dallas just 10 days before the first game. Despite grief across the land, life did go on, and sports proved a helpful distraction. Just a Cotton Bowl win over Navy separated the UT football team from the national championship, and sweet memories of the 1963 basketball season lingered. They continued to linger for more than thirty years because Harold Bradley commemorated the 13 straight Southwest Conference victories by having the scores painted, in orange and white, on the steps leading from the home locker room down to the maplewood floor of Gregory Gym.

And the gym itself was different. A $1.75-million annex, 11 years in the planning, had been erected on its south side. Unlike the original, it was no architectural gem, just a windowless brick box. But function is beauty, and the annex took care of some crying needs for intramurals and physical education. Specifically built *not* for intercollegiate athletics, the annex nevertheless helped UT hoops. With four full-sized basketball courts, it enabled gym rats of all levels to play more, and when necessary, the varsity and frosh teams practiced there.

Jimmy Viramontes, an assistant coach, scout and recruiter the past eight years, had won the top job at West Texas State. Viramontes was replaced, of course, but his contributions would be missed in the seasons to come. The cognoscenti predicted another SWC title for Texas. No. 9 in the nation as the season began, the Longhorns got no impact players from a 3-9 Yearling team. Jimmy Puryear (hand), Jimmy Clark (knee) and Mike Humphrey (ankle) were injured before the opener with Howard Payne on December 2, but only Puryear was unable to play. UT got off to a fast start, winning four home games over a span of eight days. While Howard Payne had two players, Robert Springer and Ted Hobby, with more than 20 points, the Yellow Jackets lost, 89-58, before 3,000 fans at Gregory Gym. In the epitome of balanced scoring, five Longhorns had 14 points. One of them, Tommy Nelms, did a fine job of filling in for Puryear. And Texas Wesleyan went down without a whimper, 81-46, as Joe Fisher hit all nine of his field-goal attempts.

Tulane was having a tough time of it in early season games. The Green Wave had suffered two 30-point blowouts, and it happened again in Austin. John Paul Fultz (21), Larry Franks and Humphrey (18 each) led the way in a 95-63 victory in which the Longhorns shot 59 percent. Fisher had 10 rebounds, four more than Bob Davidson, the Southeastern Conference rebound leader in 1963. After jumping to a 10-1 lead against LSU, it appeared that Bradley's club was off to another easy win. But the Tigers climbed back in with 24 points from Dick Maile, mostly on long, soaring jumpers, and 21 from Sam Chase. UT did not seal the 70-65 victory until Clark hit six free throws in the final minute. Fisher, off to a good senior year, had 22 points and 15 rebounds.

The winning continued in the first part of a sashay into Oklahoma and Kansas. OU led by three with a minute left when the Texas press began paying dividends. Clark and Jim Bob Smith scored after steals, and Clark added two free throws in an 81-78 win that disappointed a crowd of 5,200 in Norman. Fisher had 14 points and 17 rebounds, while Bill Wilson scored 21 for the Sooners. "Texas sure is big and strong and was able to throw a lot of weight around the boards," said OU coach Bob Stevens. The razor-sharp Wichita State Shockers put a 76-57 defeat on the Longhorns. And it was a Texan, Dave Stallworth, who did the most damage with 16 points and six rebounds. Fultz came off the bench and scored 12 on a bad night for UT. "It's terrible to have to learn a lesson like that," said Fultz. "We were all lousy." One game remained on the road trip, against Oklahoma State, and the Horns could only hope that Stillwater did not run any deeper than the trouble they encountered against Wichita. But an agonizing 17-point first half gave them little chance of beating the Cowboys. Fultz and James King of OSU both scored 16 points as Hank Iba's team won, 69-53.

Record: 15-9

89 Howard Payne 58
81 Texas Wesleyan 46
95 Tulane 63
70 LSU 65
81 Oklahoma 78
57 Wichita State 76
53 Oklahoma State 69
71 Princeton 84
69 Pennsylvania 61
83 Baylor 59
53 Arkansas 58
60 Texas A&M 65
103 Trinity 59
90 Texas Tech 94
74 SMU 76 (OT)
79 TCU 62
98 Rice 80
78 Texas Tech 76
66 SMU 82
71 TCU 70
93 Rice 83
105 Baylor 77
80 Arkansas 67
63 Texas A&M 65

The Charlotte Invitational was a homecoming of sorts for Bradley, who had not been back to North Carolina in four years. One of his ex-players at Duke, Lefty Driesell, was coaching Davidson, the tourney's host team. Humphrey, Franks and Fultz kept UT close to Princeton but lost, 84-71, because of one player. All-American, future New York Knick and U.S. Senator Bill Bradley was phenomenal, scoring 46 points on a variety of shots, including a 25-foot hook and several jumpers that seemed to find the basket by radar. During one six-minute stretch in the first half, Bradley scored 17 points. Pennsylvania had only mortals on its team, and the Quakers lost to Texas, 69-61.

Puryear's hand had healed, and he was in the lineup when Baylor (a loser by 51 points to 1964 national champion UCLA) came to Austin to start conference play. Many students were still away for the holidays, and the game was on television, so the gym was just half-full; in the 50th season of SWC hoops, attendance would drop by 14 percent. The Longhorns remembered the previous year's upset and smashed BU, 83-59, behind Fultz (22) and Franks (15). Spencer Carlson, a 215-pound strongman, powered in 19 points, but Winston Moore, the closest thing to a star the Bears had, scored just four.

The next four conference games (wrapped around a 103-59 destruction of Trinity) were grandstand specials, close and exciting games. And Texas finished on the short end each time, halting talk about a championship redux. The Fayetteville crowds were smaller and less fanatical since the Hogs had sunk into mediocrity, but Glen Rose, nearing the end of a long coaching career, had his team ready to play. The flat-footed Longhorns shot 31 percent and watched a five-point lead wither in the game's late minutes. When the fans smelled victory, cries of "sooey pig" filled the air at Barnhill Fieldhouse. In a bitter 58-53 upset, Fisher and the Razorbacks' Warren Vogel both scored 17.

Memories of the 1963 rumble were fresh in people's minds as Texas A&M (which had just admitted its first female students) came to Austin. UT ticket manager Al Lundstedt tried to steer Aggie fans to balcony seats, away from the bleachers, and unprecedented security, including the Aggies' own military personnel, guaranteed relative calm. Close to 8,000 fans filled the gym for the Saturday afternoon game. Bennie Lenox had piled up 53 points against Wyoming in the All-College Tournament two weeks earlier, and his offensive moves and springy legs reminded some orangebloods of Jay Arnette. He scored just 17, but three quick jumpers in the second half choked off a UT rally, and the Ags took it, 65-60. "I'll tell you what's wrong with Texas," Lenox said. "They miss ole' [Jimmy] Gilbert, but they ought to be glad they had Nelms [16]. He kept them in the game."

Texas Tech athletic director Polk Robison estimated that if Lubbock Municipal Coliseum were big enough, 18,000 people might be in attendance at the Longhorn-Red Raider game on February 1. It was a dubious achievement, but Tech fans had gained a reputation as the SWC's meanest, and they chose Mike Humphrey as their target, riding him unmercifully. He felt it, going scoreless and getting just two rebounds in a 94-90 loss scarred by a total of 61 fouls. Soph stars Norman Reuther and Dub Malaise (who drew comparisons to Gerald Myers and Del Ray Mounts) combined for 42 points, and veteran Tom Patty had 19 for the Raiders. UT's Franks and Fultz scored 19 apiece as the defending champions were barely above winless Baylor and TCU in the standings. "Heavy hangs the head that wears the crown," said Fisher.

Longhorn center Joe Fisher muscles by a Texas Wesleyan player in the second game of the 1964 season.

Two free throws by Clark appeared to seal a narrow win over SMU in Austin, but Gene Elmore (28 points and 13 rebounds) scored with just five seconds left to send the game into OT. Pony guard Jim Brockman converted both ends of a one-and-one free throw situation, handing the Horns a 76-74 defeat. Fultz was not much of a defender, but he hit all eight of his shots from the field, and Clark (17) played every minute. Fickle Texas fans were beginning to ask, what was wrong with the Longhorns?

Nothing that a game against TCU would not cure. A sign at the entrance of Daniel-Meyer Coliseum said, "Kick 'em while they're down, Frogs," but the drought ended with a 79-62 UT victory. Bradley, who doubted some of his players' effort over the past few games, was pleased. Fultz, roving from corner to corner, scored 22, two more than Frog sophomore Gary Turner. In another out-of-town game, Texas beat Rice, 98-80. Kendall Rhine, the Owls' 6'10" star who led the conference in scoring and rebounding in 1964, had 23 points and fouled out with eight minutes left. Herb Steinkamp and Larry Phillips, Rhine's frontcourt sidekicks for three years, had 22 and 20, respectively. Fisher and Franks combined for 51 points, and Clark played a fine game. But Humphrey, still weak from a bout with measles, reinjured his ankle against the Owls. Relations between Bradley and his all-SWC center had deteriorated, and he soon quit the team.

Texas Tech, battling with the Aggies for first place, came to Austin and lost a pulsating 78-76 game. UT led most of the way, but Gene Gibson's team rallied sharply and went ahead with three minutes left. Then a Franks hook shot and a pretty tip-in by 5'9" Jimmy Clark put the Longhorns in front, and they were never caught again. It was like old times at Gregory Gym, with a victory and a big, enthusiastic crowd. Fisher collected 15 rebounds, and Franks had 16 points. Despite a hip injury, Norman Reuther scored 19 for the Red Raiders.

With wins over TCU, Rice and Texas Tech, the Steers were feeling much better and entertaining hopes of an NIT bid. But they got submarined by SMU in Dallas, 82-66. It was tied at intermission, and then the Mustangs warmed up, forcing UT into a pressing defense. The officials did not hesitate to call fouls, which the home team usually converted into points.

As he was for much of the season, Joe Fisher was the leading scorer (18) and rebounder (13) in a 71-70 defeat of TCU at Gregory Gym. The *Daily Texan* called it a battle of have-nots, and *Austin Statesman* writer Bob St. John called it a game between the sick and the dead, but Bradley called it a victory. Two free throws by Fultz with 41 seconds left gave UT a one-point lead, and Gary Turner's long hook shot at the buzzer missed. Ambidextrous guard Bobby McKinley scored 25 for Buster Brannon's Horned Frogs. Fisher was sharp (23 points and 13 rebounds) in a 93-83 defeat of Rice in Austin. He was ably assisted by Franks (17), Fultz (17) and Puryear (14). The Owls' Kendall Rhine (27) broke Gene Schwinger's career scoring record, although just 1,500 people were there to observe.

UT's 105-77 defeat of the Bears in Waco was a record of another sort, the 300th win of Harold Bradley's distinguished coaching career. Fultz, the soft-shooting Dallas junior, hit 13 of 16 from the field for a total of 29 points, and Baylor forward Spencer Carlson was also quite impressive with 34. The game was marred by a fight between Jim Bob Smith of Texas and Melvin Ellison of Baylor, both of whom were tossed.

The last home game of the year matched the Horns and Hogs, who had started UT on a four-game tailspin in January. There were bad passes, elbows thrown and whistles galore in Texas' 80-67 victory. Fisher scored 20 and collected 13 rebounds, and Jim Magness (21) showed no conscience in launching 20 shots from all over the court. The Longhorns had won, but it was a rather sad home closing, in front of just 2,000 fans.

While beating the new champion, Texas A&M, would have relieved some disappointment, it did not happen. Twice in the last 10 seconds, Smith had game-winning one-and-one free throw opportunities, but he came up empty, to the relish of more than 8,000 screaming fans at G. Rollie White Coliseum. Texas lost the game, 65-63. Fultz had 14 points and 14 rebounds, and Puryear held Bennie Lenox to 13 points. Their 13-1 conference record matched that of UT in 1963, but the Aggies were promptly bounced by Texas Western in the NCAA playoffs.

1965

Would the University of Texas really leave the Southwest Conference? In what was entirely a football matter, the SWC had imposed scholarship limitations and taken disciplinary action over some minor irregularities, and neither the UT athletic department nor the Board of Regents liked having someone try to put a ring through Bevo's nose. A philosophical cleavage had the big state schools (and Texas was the biggest) on one side and the smaller private schools on the other. But since UT's conference roots went back half a century, the issue was finally resolved—or at least papered over—and the institutions stayed together.

A handful of sophomores and junior college transfers joined the Longhorn basketball team before the 1965 season. Although none made the starting lineup for the first game, that could change; when he saw a team going nowhere, Harold Bradley was quick to put a senior or two on the bench and give the younger players a chance to develop. The main addition to the UT basketball program was assistant coach Leon Black, the little leaper who captained the 1953 team. Since then, he had served a hitch in the Army and coached in high school and two junior colleges, Schreiner and Lon Morris. The latter school had gone to the national JC tournament finals in 1963, when Black was named coach of the year. His duties in Austin were to help Bradley, scout, recruit and oversee the frosh, coached by two more ex-Horns, Jimmy Gilbert and Brenton Hughes.

Texas Tech was given the nod as the Southwest Conference favorite, with Texas A&M, SMU and Texas close behind. But basketball in the conference seemed to be weakening, which Bradley attributed to (1) high school coaches who regarded the sport as more of a duty than a pleasure, (2) gyms that were often locked by 4 p.m., and (3) UIL rules that prevented year-round organized practice. These factors were not conducive to turning out high school and future college basketball stars. The pipeline was at a trickle. "Basketball is almost impossible to predict from year to year and from game to game," wrote Lou Maysel of the *Austin American-Statesman*. "This might be a compliment if the level of play in the league were high. It's pathetically low, and except for rare peaks, the disparity between SWC basketball and the rest of the nation is alarming."

Record: 16-9
104 Texas Wesleyan 84
94 Mississippi 67
75 LSU 83
73 Oklahoma 86
69 Oklahoma State 73 (OT)
77 Nebraska 73
93 Howard Payne 74
66 Georgia 60
49 Florida 62
62 Texas Tech 66
64 TCU 77
95 Baylor 74
82 Trinity 68
89 SMU 79
76 Rice 63
65 Texas A&M 63
81 Arkansas 65
75 Rice 72
73 Texas Tech 87
70 SMU 73
74 Arkansas 72
86 Texas A&M 71
84 TCU 63
79 Baylor 75
78 SMU 80

At any rate, the 1965 UT season began with a game against the Texas Wesleyan Rams at Gregory Gym. Bradley's starting five was John Paul Fultz at center, Larry Franks and Paul Olivier at forward and Tommy Nelms and Jimmy Clark at guard. Despite the usual opening night jitters, they raced to an easy 104-84 victory, with six players in double figures. The high-point man was Ram guard Larry Phelps, who hit all 11 field-goal attempts and totaled 26.

The Longhorns took an early road trip, playing Ole Miss and LSU. Because of a Rebel football game in Oxford, the basketball game was held in Tupelo, at a high school gym capable of seating 2,000 souls, with a court at least 15 feet short of regulation size. Fultz and Franks combined for 32 points in a 94-67 win. Glenn Lusk scored 13 for Mississippi. Two days later in Baton Rouge, fans yelled "Tiger bait!" as the Longhorns took the floor. All-SEC forward Dick Maile got in early foul trouble but had plenty of help from Bill Wilson (21) and Harry Heroman (20) as LSU won, 83-75. A frantic rally led by Olivier (20) in the game's final minutes was not enough. Bradley chided his players in the locker room and said, "You can't give 50 percent effort and expect to win basketball games."

The Big 8 Conference invaded Gregory Gym in mid-December, and the first of three games caused Bradley's countenance to turn dark. Oklahoma, 7-18 in the previous season and winless in two games thus far, was superior to Texas in shooting, rebounding and defense, winning by 13. Except for Nelms, Olivier and Franks, the graying Longhorn coach had no kind words for his team. James Gatewood scored 21 for the Sooners, who dictated the game's slow pace. Hank Iba had just led the U.S. Olympic team to a gold medal in Tokyo, and his Oklahoma State Cowboys were winners, too. They took a 73-69 overtime victory before 2,000 fans in Austin. A basket by Fultz sent the game into OT, and he cut the Cowboys' lead to two with 36 seconds left and could have tied it again in the final seconds, but he missed two free throws. Gary Hassman (23) of OSU was the game's leading scorer, and Nelms had 15 for UT. It was a spirited showing against a quality opponent, and Bradley found reason for optimism. "A tough schedule like ours will either make men or children," he said. "And I believe they're beginning to look like men." Nebraska, the recent conqueror of No. 1 Michigan, also came to Austin. Cornhusker guard Fred Hare scored 33 and grabbed 13 rebounds, but UT offset that one-man performance in a 77-73 victory that ended with fans on the floor hugging the tired Longhorns and lots of smiling faces in the locker room. Soph Bo Rothchild (22 points per game as a Yearling, with a high of 43) came off the bench and hit two quick baskets as Texas took the lead for good.

Franks (20) and JC transfer Mickey White (19) helped turn back Howard Payne before the Longhorns headed to the Gator Bowl Tournament. About 6,500 fans at Jacksonville Coliseum saw Texas meet Georgia, led by guard Jimmy Pitts, the SEC's top scorer. Rothchild (18) helped pull out a hard-earned 66-60 win over the Bulldogs. Pitts was as good as advertised, scoring 27 and keeping his team close. By no means a beautiful basketball game, it was nevertheless UT's third straight victory. That streak ended the next night against a tall Florida team. Bradley shuffled the deck and used three new starters, Rothchild, White and guard Mike Gammon, but Texas fell behind by 15 at the half and lost, 62-49. No Longhorn was in double figures, and the Gators' 6'9" Gary Keller scored 21. As the team flew back to Austin, Bradley considered his players well-tested and ready for SWC competition.

The Longhorns and Red Raiders played a close, bruising game in Gregory Gym, but when it was over, Texas Tech was in front, 66-62. Olivier had 15 points for UT, and Dub Malaise 21 and Norman Reuther 18 for the visitors. A wild-eyed 6'6" junior southpaw, Reuther hustled more than any other player on the court. "He looks like a blacksmith, but he gets the job done," Bradley said in a compliment of sorts. After just one conference loss, *Daily Texan* sports editor Paul Burka wrote, "Scratch Texas from this year's likely title contenders."

Not since the four-overtime epic of 1961 had TCU bested the Longhorns, and the Frogs had not won any SWC game since 1963. They had a fine JC transfer, Gary Turner, and four sophs in the starting lineup when the teams met at Daniel-Meyer Coliseum. The Frogs led from start to finish and took a 77-64 upset victory with 17 points each from Stan Farr and spitfire guard Wayne Kreis. Turner scored just 10 but collected 16 rebounds. Fultz, who had lost 12 pounds from a recent bout with tonsillitis, managed to score 15.

Baylor, also eager to escape doormat status, had adopted a faster-paced offense, and forward Darrell Hardy was on his way to becoming the Bears' first all-SWC player in five years. Dissatisfied with his defense and guard play, Bradley kept trying new combinations. The one he tried on January 12 worked as Texas blitzed BU, 95-74, in Austin before 2,500 fans. Hardy was shut down by Fultz and White, who scored 16 each. On that happy note, the Longhorns stopped for the exam break, then resumed play with an 82-68 defeat of Trinity in San Antonio. The Tigers' Pete Rannuci bombed away, taking 25 shots (some from 30 feet out) and scoring 22, but Franks was two points better. Texas played a sloppy game, however, causing one courtside wag to note, "Bradley's passing game is even worse than [Darrell] Royal's."

Franks rang up 24 points when the Horns toppled SMU, 89-79, at renamed Moody Coliseum in front of a sellout crowd. With senior Bill Ward, junior Carroll Hooser and the sophomore troika of Charles Beasley, Denny Holman and Bob Begert, it was the strongest Pony team since Jim Krebs departed the Hilltop. But their visitors from Austin shot 64 percent. Clark (16) had one of his best games of the season, and Gammon (14) drew praise from Bradley. Ward had 20 for SMU.

Tied with four other teams for second place behind Texas Tech, the Horns returned home to play the Rice Owls, who were having a difficult season (2-22 overall). Bradley had considered benching Franks just a month earlier, but the senior forward came through with another excellent showing, 20 points and 19 rebounds, in UT's 76-63 victory. Tommy Nelms, back from an ankle injury, provided a steady influence for the Longhorns. Doug McKendrick of Rice scored 25 and fouled out with two minutes left.

Riding the crest of a four-game winning streak, the Horns traveled to College Station to engage the defending champion Ags. John Beasley (22 points per game) was proving himself a worthy successor to Carroll Broussard and Bennie Lenox. The 8,000 basketball maniacs who filled G. Rollie White Coliseum witnessed a 65-63 UT victory. Gammon, Olivier and Franks had 11 apiece, and Beasley was supplanted by Paul Timmins (21) as Texas A&M's top scorer. Longhorn reserve John Bush found the whole thing too intense and fainted in the locker room after the game.

Bradley was disappointed to see just 5,500 fans in Gregory Gym when the Horns and Hogs tipped off. Olivier scored a career-high 26 as Texas breezed to an 81-65 win. The slender Dallas junior would never be a defensive stalwart, but he sure had a pretty jump shot. Franks continued his rebound binge with 13. Ricky Sugg and Orval Cook scored 13 each for Arkansas.

UT's seventh straight victory came in Houston, but the Owls put up a fight before losing by three. Had they not missed some layups and free throws in the closing minutes, they could have won. Doug McKendrick and Larry Tiner combined for 42 points, while the big two for Texas were Franks (20) and White (18 points and 13 rebounds). Rice coach George Carlisle was dejected and kept saying "if only" after the game, and Bradley paid tribute to the effort of the losing team. That was followed by another away game, against league-leading Texas Tech, zooming along at 87 points per game. Lubbock Municipal Coliseum was full, and another 2,000 people paid to watch on closed-circuit television in the building's annex. With 30 points from Dub Malaise, the Red Raiders overpowered UT, 87-73. Norman Reuther scored 17 and held Franks to two. A 15-point Tech scoring spurt in the first half effectively ended the game. White had 16 for Texas.

If that did not end the Longhorns' title hopes, a 73-70 home loss to SMU did. The Mustangs led the entire game until White stole the ball and went in for a layup to put Texas ahead by one. But Bill Ward and Charles Beasley sank two free throws each to win a stemwinder. White and Nelms had 19 and 18, respectively, more than any of the balanced Ponies.

Presumably playing for second or third place, UT went to Little Rock and squeezed by Arkansas, 74-72. In a great seesaw battle with 19 lead changes, Fultz, playing with four fouls, scored the Longhorns' last seven points. Nelms had a superb game as Texas' floor general. Hog forward J.D. McConnell (15) led his team in scoring.

Two days later, a bombshell dropped in Lubbock when Texas Tech announced that Norman Reuther had not passed the required 20 hours in the previous two semesters. Rather like what had happened when

Arkansas won the 1933 SWC football race with an ineligible player and had to vacate the championship, the Red Raiders were out. To Reuther's credit, he was a dean's list student, taking premed courses, and no one accused him or the school of cheating. "The king is dead, long live the king" were the sentiments of SMU, Texas and Baylor, who became the new leaders with three games to play.

The Bears soon lost, bringing it down to the Ponies and Horns. Texas A&M was out of the race, but the Ags would have dearly loved to spoil things for their old rivals. John Beasley, who had scored at least 30 points in his last five games, was tremendous, getting 40 points and 15 rebounds in an 86-71 loss to Texas. None of the Longhorns' big men could stop him, and the Gregory Gym crowd of 7,800 showed its appreciation for Beasley with a standing ovation. Despite a 19-rebound deficit, UT played a strong game. Beasley's 38 points the following Tuesday night helped the Ags beat SMU in College Station, while Texas was downing TCU in Austin, 84-63. Franks scored 21, and Fultz (a much better defensive player than in his first two years) did not allow Frog star Gary Turner any field goals in the second half.

Again with an eye on each other, SMU and Texas won. The Mustangs beat Arkansas in Dallas, and the Horns edged Baylor in Waco, 79-75. UT's hopes looked dimmer than the lights in Heart O' Texas Coliseum when they fell three points behind with six minutes to go, but the Steers then scored 11 straight. White had 19 points, tying BU's Darrell Hardy and Ed Horne for scoring honors. It meant UT was the 1965 SWC cochampion, along with SMU, the third title in Bradley's six years in Austin.

The Longhorns returned to Waco four days later in a playoff with SMU to see who would represent the conference in the NCAAs. With the score tied at 78 in the final minute, Mustang guard Denny Holman drove on Clark, somehow avoiding an offensive foul. Holman's shot was blocked by Mickey White, and then the ball bounced to Bob Begert. After a wild scramble under the basket, Begert grabbed it, put it up and scored as time ran out. Bill Ward had 26 points for Doc Hayes' team, and Fultz, whose hook shot was working nicely, got 22. SMU held a 41-27 rebound edge. "We lost and they won," said a grim Bradley. "That makes the difference between a good game and a medium game."

1966

The long-delayed racial integration of SWC sports began when Oliver Patterson and James Means joined the UT track team in 1963, and it really became a fact when Jerry LeVias signed a football scholarship with SMU and James Cash a basketball scholarship with TCU. Cash, an A-student who led Fort Worth Terrell to the state title of the Prairie View Interscholastic League (flip side of the UIL during the segregation years), got offers from 96 schools, including TCU, Texas and Texas Tech. Cash finally decided to stay in his hometown and join Buster Brannon's Horned Frogs, playing freshman ball in 1966. SWC coaches held their own counsel on the subject, but they were looking to black athletes to upgrade basketball in the league. Instead of having them boost the Missouri Valley, Big 8 and other conferences, why not give black athletes a chance at the best schools in Texas? Harold Bradley made no secret of his desire to get Cash into a Longhorn uniform and was rather upset when his offer was declined. A black walk-on had tried and failed to win a spot on the 1965 team. Bradley and assistant coach Leon Black continued seeking young men to integrate UT basketball, but it did not happen quickly or easily. Of course, 1966 was a watershed year since Texas Western, with five black starters, defeated Adolph Rupp's all-white Kentucky Wildcats in the NCAA title game, something later known as the *Brown v. Board of Education* of college basketball.

Bradley's teams had won or shared the SWC championship three times in six years, a remarkable achievement considering the low level of Texas basketball before his arrival. While it would be another six seasons until the Horns won it again, they were able to avoid the 4-20 nadirs of 1955 and 1959. Mostly because the 1966 team lacked height and defensive prowess, UT was assigned a second-division preseason status, but Bradley felt otherwise. "This should be a very exciting team to watch," he said. "We plan to run on our opponents when

Gregory Gym, well past its prime by 1966, was still a great place to observe a college basketball game.

we can." Mickey White was the only returning starter, but there was plenty of new talent with JC players Dale Dotson, Noel Stout and Charlie Turnbough and two youngsters, Gary Overbeck and Billy Arnold, who had each scored 19 points per game for the Yearlings. For the first time in his tenure, Bradley chose a team captain, senior forward Bob Ittner, who had amassed 44 points and 34 rebounds in his varsity career. Ittner was not in the starting lineup when UT met Texas Wesleyan at Gregory Gym for the season opener. Dotson scored 18, and Turnbough had 12 rebounds in a 99-79 victory, Bradley's 100th at Texas. Little sharpshooter David Weber scored 36, nearly half of TWU's total.

In a Saturday afternoon home game, the Longhorns used speed and muscle to defeat Ole Miss, 80-71. Mickey White scored 15 and Arnold and Dotson 13 each. Mike Gammon, the guard who was expected to make the offense go, had a thigh injury that kept him out the first nine games, but Arnold and Dotson were filling in quite well. The Rebs' SEC brothers, the LSU Tigers, presented a much sterner test. Harry Heroman, who had caused Texas so much trouble in Baton Rouge the season before, did it again, scoring 27 and retrieving 12 rebounds en route to a 76-66 LSU win. Poor shooting and turnovers plagued the Longhorns, and a full-court press did not slow their Louisiana guests. *Daily Texan* columnist John Anders wrote of the 2,500 fans: "Some of the torrents of abuse leveled on referees last Monday night would have shocked Lenny Bruce, much less a starry-eyed freshman coed at her first UT basketball game."

In the week preceding the next game, Texas sports fans did not have their minds on basketball. Football coach and athletic director Darrell Royal was being wooed by his alma mater, the University of Oklahoma. One member of the OU Board of Regents even called Royal's departure "cut and dried," but DKR politely declined the Sooners' offer and stayed in Austin to win more SWC and national titles. By coincidence, Bradley's team was headed in that direction when the Royal-to-OU story was peaking, but it was to Stillwater, not Norman. Texas beat the Oklahoma State Cowboys at their own game, ball control and defense, pulling out a 56-51 victory. Soph forward Larry Lake made the most of his first start, scoring 12, playing good defense and securing some key rebounds. But Texas lost by 11 to Nebraska the following night in Lincoln. The game was close until the final three minutes, when a 12-point Cornhusker flurry decided things. Nate Branch, Grant Simmons and Stuart Lantz combined for 53 points and 32 rebounds, almost equal to UT's totals. Junior forward Minton White scored 12 for the Horns.

Before the team set off for two distant tourneys, Bradley's only gripe was about a lack of second effort on rebounds. That could be a problem against a tall team like Memphis State, host of a tournament at Mid-South Coliseum. Stout (19) and Dotson (18) packed the hottest pistols in an 80-72 upset of the Tigers. Staying close in the rebounding department, the Longhorns showed surprising poise when it got close. Guard Mike Butler led Memphis State with 15 points. In the finals against Northwestern, a late rally from 13 points down put Texas ahead by one with a minute left. But Jim Pitts tipped in a teammate's missed shot to win it for the Wildcats, 73-71. Paul Olivier, a big part of UT's drive at the end, scored 13.

Once again matched up with the host team, the Longhorns tangled with Seattle in the American Legion Tournament in 12,000-seat Seattle Coliseum. The Chieftains were big and strong, and Bradley tried another combination of players. Texas fell behind early but stayed within distance until the last five minutes when an Arnold field goal was all the Horns could manage. Olivier and Mickey White both scored 14, while Seattle, looking for all the world like the Boston Celtics of the west, got 45 from Tom Workman and Elzie Johnson. Guaranteeing UT an unsuccessful visit to the Puget Sound area, soph guard Russ Critchfield bombed in 36 points in an 82-77 California victory. "He was better than we thought," said a wistful Bradley about Critchfield, who made 13 of 20 from the field and 10 of 12 free throw attempts. Mickey White played another fine two-way game for Texas with 16 points and 13 rebounds.

The Steers' 4-5 record was nothing special, but they were coming off six straight tough road games. As Bradley pointed out, "We could have played a lot of easy teams at home during December and built up a winning record. I think we're ready to go." Gammon was back in time to meet the low-flying Rice Owls, losers of their first nine games. UT won, 94-85, as Gammon played a masterly floor game, aiding the point totals of Mickey White (19), Olivier (18) and Overbeck (13). Owl ace Doug McKendrick had 22 points.

The drama was not quite the same as the last time the two teams met, but the result was the same—SMU beat Texas. Because of TV coverage in the Dallas area, Moody Coliseum was less than half full as Doc Hayes' Ponies raced past the Longhorns, 99-78. When Carroll Hooser (20) fouled out with seven minutes to play, SMU was up by 12, but the lead did not shrink. The Mustangs shot 64 percent and halted the UT fast break. Mickey White (20) and Dotson (17) were the highest-scoring Longhorns. White was again outstanding (20 points and 19 rebounds) in an 89-74 loss to Baylor at Gregory Gym on January 11. Center Darrell Hardy scored 24 but yielded high-point honors to teammate Jimmy Turner (26). The versatile Hardy also had 14 rebounds and a number of assists. Lake, an unpolished player but not timid, scored a career-high 20. Although the team looked a bit ragged, Bradley found some bright spots.

The Horns and Hogs met in Fayetteville to battle for sixth place in the SWC. Glen Rose's last Arkansas team had an all-senior lineup that had started most games for three years, but junior guard Tommy Rowland was the chief instrument of Texas' torture. He scored 27 points before fouling out in a 93-82 victory, the most points a Razorback team had ever scored against UT. Olivier (23) played well for the Longhorns, and Mickey White had 19 points and 12 rebounds.

And things only got worse with Texas A&M (4-0 in the SWC) coming to Austin. Shelby Metcalf's team featured King Kong and Godzilla, a.k.a. John Beasley and Randy Matson. The 6'9" Beasley was having the greatest scoring season in conference history, 31 points per game, and Matson drew even more fan and media attention. Holder of the world record in the shot put and two years away from an Olympic gold medal, he had not played basketball since his senior season at Pampa High School. Matson shed a few pounds and claimed the center position for himself, scoring a little, rebounding well and intimidating some opponents. The Aggies trailed by 13 at the half and felt the collar getting tight, but they refused to choke before 7,000 howling fans at Gregory Gym. With just 15 second-half points, the Longhorns made A&M's comeback much easier, and the Ags rode off with a 64-57 victory. Of their two celluloid monsters, just Beasley (22 points and 12 rebounds) had a strong game, while Matson looked like he should have stayed with track and field. Mickey White and Turnbough combined for 34 points for the Horns, who seemed to be headed for a bad-to-terrible season.

Dark clouds were forming over Gregory Gym when exam time came around. After the two-week layoff, UT met Howard Payne in Brownwood. The game was no breather because the Longhorns had lost four straight and the Yellow Jackets had a nine-game win

Record: 12-12

99 Texas Wesleyan 79
80 Mississippi 71
66 LSU 76
56 Oklahoma State 51
64 Nebraska 75
80 Memphis State 72
71 Northwestern 73
80 Seattle 95
77 California 82
94 Rice 85
78 SMU 99
74 Baylor 89
82 Arkansas 93
57 Texas A&M 64
95 Howard Payne 83
87 Texas Tech 74
77 TCU 75
110 Texas A&M 82
85 TCU 77
86 Texas Tech 117
91 Rice 82
69 SMU 71
74 Arkansas 70
71 Baylor 88

streak. Texas took it, 95-83, as Dotson and Howard Payne's Eddie Nelson scored 21 each.

Many people viewed Harold Bradley as something of a curmudgeon, but he would surprise them at times with his statements. When Houston beat Texas A&M (twice), TCU (twice) and Baylor, he said SWC schools should not have played Guy Lewis' Cougars because the much lower academic standards of UH provided a major recruiting advantage. He lumped Oklahoma City and Texas Western in with what *Austin American-Statesman* writer Fred Sanner called "outlaw schools," all bound for the NCAA playoffs. And on a different subject, Bradley told Sanner, "I think Texas Tech has the worst crowd in the United States.... We enjoy a good, clean rivalry, but the attitude and feeling of the Texas Tech crowd takes all the fun out of the game for the visiting team." He did not like the way the fire marshal let in too many people, who crowded the floor, harassed opponents and sought to influence officials. And why, Bradley asked, make a hero out of Norman Reuther, whose academic ineligibility cost the Red Raiders the 1965 SWC title? Lubbock, naturally, was indignant, but the red carpet treatment was extended to the Longhorns. From the airport to the hotel to the coliseum, local citizens—some possibly sincere—clapped and cheered. The Texas Tech Saddle Tramps instructed the sellout crowd to cheer wildly when the Red Raiders had the ball but be silent when the Horns had it. The plan backfired because Texas was a much better team that night, roaring to an 87-74 win behind Dotson's 22 points and Stout's 20. Of the vaunted Raider attack, only guard Bobby Measells (32) played well. It was a very sweet win for the Longhorns, and a coaching coup for Bradley.

James Cash scored 27 points and grabbed 18 rebounds in a losing effort for the TCU Wogs in the prelim game at Gregory Gym. The varsity teams then played an exciting game before 3,700 fans. The Longhorns came back from 12 points down to tie it at 75 on a basket by Mickey White with 1:43 left. They regained possession and stalled until Dotson sank a 20-foot jumper just before the buzzer, pleading, "Baby, go through the hole!" Dotson and TCU's Rich Sauer (22) tied for scoring honors.

G. Rollie White Coliseum was swelled past its capacity as UT paid a visit. The Aggies remained unbeaten in SWC play and were preparing a spot in the trophy case with seven games to go. But the surging Steers did it again, routing Texas A&M, 110-82. Stout hit 13 of 17 shots and totaled 33 points. "When they keep going in, you have to keep throwing them up there," said a tired but happy Stout. His performance caused Bradley to recall some of Jay Arnette's best games in 1960. John Beasley's 38 points made him the all-time career scoring leader at A&M. The giant-killing Longhorns climbed the beanstalk one more time in Fort Worth when they beat TCU, 85-77. Mickey White, Dotson, Arnold and Olivier reached double figures. Mickey McCarty (18 points and 14 rebounds) helped prevent a UT runaway.

Dub Malaise, who had scored 83 points in Texas Tech's last two games, came to Austin and poured in a Gregory Gym-record 50 points in a 117-86 thrashing of the Longhorns. Like John Beasley of Texas A&M, Malaise was called an all-America candidate by his school's sports information department, and he was one that night. Tech also got 27 points from Norman Reuther and 19 from Bob Glover. Having recently snapped a 28-game losing streak, Rice hosted UT in Houston. Just 1,500 people were there to see the Horns turn back the Owls, 91-82. It was a close game with 14 lead changes, but Texas found the key to victory in the late minutes. Mickey White (26) and Doug McKendrick (24) led their teams in scoring.

Doc Hayes, the Norman Vincent Peale of SWC basketball, brought his hot SMU Mustangs to Gregory Gym for a Saturday afternoon game. He had been playing, officiating and coaching hoops for 45 years and claimed it was not a life-or-death matter. "We'll be happier if we win, but we'll live if we lose, and it's taken me a long time to come to that conclusion," he said. UT had the Ponies tied at 69 when guard Denny Holman split the defense for a driving layup with 15 seconds on the clock. Stout had 21 points, but 50 percent free throw shooting cost Texas the game.

Captain Bob Ittner moved into the starting lineup on the basis of his play against SMU, and he came through, scoring 14 and getting seven rebounds in a 74-70 home defeat of Arkansas. A sparse crowd of 2,200 saw the Horns ensure Bradley's 31st year without a losing record. The season ended in Waco, where Papa Bear Darrell Hardy scored 40 points, got 25 rebounds and proved himself one of the finest players in BU history. Mike Gammon scored 16 for the Longhorns. The 88-71 defeat left Texas with a 12-12 record, 7-7 in the Southwest Conference. Not great, but better than had been predicted.

1967

The Longhorns again lacked height inside, and the biggest player, 6'7" Gary Overbeck, had taken a lot of criticism for his not-so-splashy sophomore season. What Harold Bradley's eighth Texas team mostly had was a wealth of outside shooters like Mike Gammon, Dale Dotson, Billy Arnold and Noel Stout. A hand injury kept Arnold out of the first five games of the year, but he was not needed in a 106-63 defeat of Texas Wesleyan before 4,500 fans at Gregory Gym. Stout scored 18, and a couple of sophomores, guard Larry Smith and forward Scotty Brown, played well.

Record: 14-10

106 Texas Wesleyan 63
80 Mississippi 82
114 LSU 78
76 Oklahoma State 70
85 Howard Payne 82
93 Arizona State 81
87 Iowa State 101
87 Montana State 91
89 Arizona State 88
74 Massachusetts 85
71 Arkansas 62
82 TCU 96
82 SMU 73
70 Texas Tech 68
59 Texas A&M 68
86 Baylor 88
81 Rice 73
67 Arkansas 61
81 Rice 76
75 Baylor 101
78 Texas Tech 88
72 Texas A&M 58
88 TCU 79
83 SMU 92

UT went on the road, first facing Ole Miss in Oxford. Gammon and Larry Lake were the top scorers for the Horns, who came back from 17 points down only to fall mortally wounded before a final Rebel charge, 82-80. Jerry Brawner had 17 points and 18 rebounds in Mississippi's victory. The following night in Baton Rouge, UT took control early and blistered LSU, 114-78, with the reserves doing most of the second-half damage. The Tigers could in no way match the quickness and pinpoint gunnery of the Steers, who shot 66 percent from the field. The scoring aggregate was a school record that would last another five years. Brown (20) and Overbeck (18) led UT, while Brad Brian scored 21 for LSU, coached by Press Maravich. His son, Pete, was getting considerable attention on the Tiger frosh team.

Gammon's thigh injury was back, so he did not play against Oklahoma State. It was the 30th Longhorn-Cowboy meeting in a series that began in 1918, when then-Oklahoma A&M was a fellow SWC member. Hank Iba, the 62-year-old coaching legend, was trying to bounce back from a disastrous 4-21 record in 1966, but UT won by six. Stout scored 21, and Charlie Turnbough (with minor injuries to his hip, knee and back) had a seven-point second-half splurge just when the Horns needed it, leaving the Cowboys to do a dainty sidesaddle out of Austin. Twenty straight second-half free throws enabled Texas to beat a determined Howard Payne team, 85-82, in Austin. The Yellow Jackets led twice by seven points, thanks mostly to their post man, Dan Smith, who displayed a dandy fallaway shot. Six Longhorns reached double figures.

It was tournament time. Texas had not won a basketball meet since the 1956 Blue-Gray Tournament, and it did not happen in 1967. The Sun Devil Classic, played in Veterans Memorial Coliseum in Phoenix, started with UT and host Arizona State. Arnold scored 18 points in the first half, and Turnbough had 19 of his career-high 24 points in the second half as the Horns beat the Sun Devils, 93-81. To win the tournament, Texas would need to control Iowa State star Don "Kangaroo" Smith, who had scored 41 points and collected 18 rebounds in defeating Southern California. Smith was not quite so great (24 points and 11 rebounds) the next night, but the Cyclones led by 29 points in the first half and dealt UT a sound defeat, 101-87. Stout scored 17, and little Larry Smith caught the crowd's fancy with his quickness and hustle.

The Longhorns had played in the All-College Tournament 10 times but not since 1951, Jack Gray's last year at the helm. And their 1967 appearance would be the last for two more decades. They lost in the first round to Montana State, 91-87, as Bobcat sophomore Jack Gillespie rang up 36 points. The victory really came at the free throw line, where Montana State took 14 more shots than Texas. Overbeck had 20 points and 10 rebounds in a tense one-point defeat of Arizona State, the second victory over the Sun Devils in nine days. Guard Roger Detter (22) kept ASU close. The Massachusetts Redmen, representing the Yankee Conference, got 34 points from forward Bill Tindall, zipping past UT, 85-74, in the last game in Oklahoma City. He, Joe DiSarcina and John Lisack had too much quickness for the Longhorns. Stout and Dotson both scored 15.

It was a bad year for the Southwest Conference, the worst ever if measured by the record against outside opponents—just 38 percent of the games were victories. UT went to the post in SWC play with Arkansas at Gregory Gym. First-year coach Duddy Waller had been left with a pig in a poke, bereft of experienced talent other than Tommy Rowland. The Razorbacks played slowdown basketball as a means of survival, and it was effective, but they still lost to Texas, 71-62. Rowland equaled his 19-point average, one less than Longhorn forward Charley Turnbough. A steady performer who often appeared to stand flat-footed, Turnbough had inside fakes that frustrated opposing players.

Bradley prepared his team to meet TCU at Daniel-Meyer Coliseum. The Frogs' speed, backboard strength, shooting balance and depth showed they had improved from the doormat status of the early and mid-1960s. With 14 straight points late in the first half, school was out, and TCU took a 96-82 victory. Big men Mickey McCarty, James Cash and Stan Farr got second and third shots throughout the game. Frog guard Wayne Kreis scored 23, while Stout and Dotson combined for 41.

Billy Arnold eludes SMU's Bill Voight in an 82-73 upset of the defending SWC champion Mustangs.

The Longhorns returned to Austin, but they had to face SMU, the two-time defending champion with four starters back from the 1966 team. Two of them, Charles Beasley and Denny Holman, would make all-SWC, and center Lynn Phillips would be sophomore of the year. But UT climbed Mount Everest with a mighty defensive effort and 52 percent shooting. Arnold scored 23 in the 82-73 Texas win, while Bob Begert had 16 points and 11 rebounds for the Ponies. "Texas deserved to win," said SMU coach Doc Hayes. "They beat us in everything except effort. They just made fewer errors than we did." There was another home win four days later, 70-68 over Texas Tech. A 10-foot hook by Vernon Paul tied it up for the Red Raiders with just over a minute left. Texas, out of timeouts, coolly ran the clock down to the final seconds before Dotson passed to Overbeck. He whirled left and hit the winning shot, heading off to two-point Valhalla and leaving Gene Gibson's team with a 2-11 record. Stout had 22 points for the Longhorns.

Like two maddened bull elephants in a telephone booth, the Steers and Ags met in College Station. Texas A&M entered the game with the memory of a 28-point licking the last time the two teams played. But Ol' Army, using the walk-it-up offense, won by a score of 68-59. Sonny Benefield and Billy Bob Barnett had 14 points apiece for the victorious Aggies, whose happy fans swarmed the court after the buzzer.

The Longhorns were glad to resume play after the exam period but distressed over the departure of Dale Dotson due to grades. The JC transfer had started 38 of 39 games during his UT career and ran the offense. It was a major blow. Dotson was missed in an 88-86 loss to the Bears in Waco. Darrell Hardy scored 31 points, and his diminutive teammate, Randy Thompson, hit two late free throws to beat the Horns. Twenty turnovers, including several critical ones in the final minutes, doomed Texas' effort, although Arnold (20), Stout (19) and Overbeck (16) did well. The fracas was played before 4,800 restless natives at Heart O' Texas Coliseum, and when the refs called consecutive technicals on BU players, fans threw ice, cups and other debris on the court, stopping play for ten minutes.

Feathers flew when Rice came to Austin on February 7. Turnbough (17) and Arnold (16) led the scoring in UT's 400th Southwest Conference win, 81-73. Guard Mike Inselmann had 17 for Don Knodel's Owls, beginning a gradual climb out of poverty row.

Texas got off to an 11-point lead after six minutes against the Razorbacks in Fayetteville, and that padding made the difference in the wake of later trials and tribulations. Benton Cone (17) and Tommy Rowland (16) kept Arkansas in the game, and the action got heated in the final minutes. But speed and rebounding carried UT to a 67-61 win. Arnold scored 22 and Stout 15 despite early foul trouble.

A wild 81-76 Texas victory took place in Houston. Substitute center Mike Lochner's defensive work helped wipe out a 12-point Rice lead, and the Horns had it won in the final minute when Owl guard Greg Williams put a hard foul on Lake, who responded. Before anyone knew it, both benches and the entire lower stands of Autry Court emptied. The fighting went on for a minute before officials Joe Shoshid and Charlie Lutz and other cooler heads could break it up. In the confusion and mayhem of what the *Daily Texan* called "a near-Valentine's Day Massacre," the Longhorns' unattended gear next to the bench was pilfered. Bill Doty scored 29 for Rice and Arnold had 20 for Texas.

More inhospitable feelings between host and guest were on display when Baylor came to Austin and took a staggering 101-75 victory behind 22 points apiece from Darrell Hardy and Jimmy Turner. The Bears swept UT for the second straight year. First, Bradley threw in the towel, and then some of the 4,500 fans threw other objects. Warned by the officials to stop, they refused, and the Longhorns were assessed four technical fouls. Bradley said a crisp requiem over his team's performance, perhaps the worst of the season. Abb Curtis, a 1920s-era UT basketball player and long-time supervisor of SWC officials, was dismayed by the upsurge of bad behavior around the league. "We've tried everything we know to improve the situation, and we're just at wits' end," he said. "It's not confined to this conference. It's all over the United States, worse in a lot of places than it is here."

The Horns and Red Raiders played a tight game for 37 minutes until the home team ran away with an 88-78 win before 8,000 relatively calm onlookers at Lubbock Municipal Coliseum. Texas Tech hit 12 of 14 from the free throw line at the end, spelling defeat for Texas. Due to excessive turnovers against Rice and Baylor, Bradley set aside the running game for a more deliberate offensive approach. Turnbough (10 of 16 from the field) had 22 points and Stout 19. Tech's Vernon Paul strolled the lane for 21 points and 13 rebounds.

The two teams were going nowhere, but when UT and Texas A&M met, anything was possible. As a result, Gregory Gym had 75 policemen and several photographers on duty for the game. Bradley's team avenged the nine-point loss in College Station with a 72-58 win. The second-half defense was terrific, holding the Ags to seven of 24 field-goal attempts. One player, however, stood out, as Billy Bob Barnett (20) bulled his way underneath and flung slingshot strikes from outside. Stout scored 16 for the Horns. Dueling for second place (SMU won the title by four games) were Texas and TCU in Austin on the last day of February. It was a rough game, halted twice by rhubarbs, but the Horns won, 88-79. Overbeck was the dominant player on the court with 20 points and 18 rebounds. Wayne Kreis (19) led the Horned Frogs in scoring.

UT's season closed in Dallas and not on a happy note. The Longhorns led SMU, 60-48, with 14:43 left, causing some early celebrating by a group of their fans at Moody Coliseum. But the Mustangs outscored Texas by 21 points the rest of the way. Bob Begert and Denny Holman combined for 41 points, and Stout (21) came through with another fine effort for the Horns.

In a postseason interview with George Breazeale of the *Austin American-Statesman*, Bradley talked about the departing players, such as Stout, Gammon and Turnbough, those returning, like Arnold, Lake and Overbeck and the next year's rookies. He gave every indication of eagerness to continue coaching the Longhorns, perhaps into the 1970s. So fans were surprised to learn of his resignation in mid-May. A diabetic, Bradley was not in the best of health, and that was the main reason he gave. Although the basketball program appeared to be losing steam, he denied pressure to quit or any friction within the UT athletic fraternity. But Bradley's occasional public comments about the dominance of football in Texas had cost him some support. His Longhorn teams won 125 games and lost 73, winning or sharing the SWC crown three times. Although Bradley had been in Austin just eight years, his age and record made people view him as an elder statesman like two other retirees, Doc Hayes of SMU and Buster Brannon of TCU. Athletic director Darrell Royal praised Bradley, and Lou Maysel of the *Austin American-Statesman* wrote, "A good gambler is one who knows when it's time to get out of the game, whether he's winning or losing, and it would seem to apply to the very risky business of coaching, too. This might best explain the sudden resignation of University of Texas basketball coach Harold Bradley, who certainly goes out a winner."

1968

Speculation about Harold Bradley's replacement began almost immediately. Some sports writers floated the name of Don Haskins of UT-El Paso (formerly Texas Western), the 1966 national champion. And Slater Martin, boomed for the Longhorn job after Slue Hull and Marshall Hughes left, was again mentioned. But Martin, away from college basketball for 18 years, had recently become coach and general manager of the Houston Mavericks of the new American Basketball Association. (The Dallas Chaparrals were also original members of the ABA, which gave ex-SWC stars a chance at pro ball. Kendall Rhine of Rice, John Beasley of Texas A&M, Charles Beasley of SMU and Darrell Hardy of Baylor were among those who played in the league, which merged with the NBA nine years later.) But the media never hired a coach, and the man who received almost sole consideration from athletic director Darrell Royal and the Athletic Council was 35-year-old Leon Black.

Two days after Bradley quit, the job was given to Black. He was orange to the core, a former UT player and Bradley's assistant the past three seasons. But it started even before that. He grew up in a tiny east Texas town, reading about the exploits of Bobby Layne on the football field and Jack Gray's Mighty Mice on the basketball court. Intense as a player and coach, Black set a goal of "making the University of Texas in basketball what it is in football." He was not naive, however, realizing that UT's high academic standards made recruitment of top hoopsters difficult. Another problem was venerable Gregory Gym, which had been obsolete for at least a decade. It was by far the oldest facility in the Southwest Conference, and some high school stars took one look at it and crossed Texas off their lists.

Black's assistants in 1968 and for several seasons to follow were Jim O'Bannon, who played at TCU in the mid-1950s, and Bennie Lenox, one of the all-time greats of SWC basketball during his playing days at Texas A&M. Five lettermen were back, but Larry Lake was hobbling from a broken foot, and Larry Smith had undergone spinal surgery in the spring. While there was some doubt regarding Smith's availability, he played most of the season, albeit often in pain. The key newcomers were forwards Wayne Doyal, who had scored 17 points per game for the frosh, and junior college transfer Kurt Papp. After scrimmages with Southwest Texas and St. Mary's, the Longhorns began the toughest nonconference schedule yet.

Leon Black's UT head coaching debut was a success, a 95-82 defeat of Mississippi before a big crowd in Austin. Doyal had a nice introduction to varsity competition, scoring 27 points, eight more than Gary Overbeck. Thirty turnovers, however, were an indication of the poor ballhandling that would hurt the Horns all year long.

LSU had not had a good basketball team since the departure of Bob Pettit in 1954, but things appeared to be changing because of a gangly 6'5" soph guard with floppy hair and socks to match. "Pistol" Pete Maravich, a prolific scorer (45 points per game with the Tiger

LSU's Pete Maravich, a basketball immortal, paid a visit to Austin early in the 1968 season.

freshman team) and a wizard with the ball, was the focus of all 5,000 fans at Gregory Gym. His dazzling pregame routine drew some hoots and a lot of admiration. John Matzinger and Billy Arnold had the difficult job of trying to defend against Maravich, who scored 42 points on 15 of 39 from the field. Some of those shots came off his fingertips from exceedingly long range. Papp scored 20, and Overbeck had 17 points and 14 rebounds in Texas' 87-74 loss. Plans to play LSU again in 1969 and 1970 fell through, so that was the last time the Steers saw Maravich, destined to be the greatest scorer in the history of college basketball, long before the advent of the three-point shot.

Three tough games in five days, in New York, Provo and Boulder, began on December 7. Lou Rossini's New York Violets played in Madison Square Garden, a new version of the fabled arena, but it was not their facility that worried Black. "No one on our club comes close to being as quick as their guards [Jim Miller and Adolfo Porrata]," he said. "We may be like worn-out cats chasing freshly rested field mice." NYU took a 75-67 victory behind a combined 36 points from Miller and Porrata. Overbeck was easily the top Longhorn with 23 points and 13 rebounds. Brigham Young, the NIT champ two years earlier, had won 24 straight games at home. The Cougars, with advantages in size and experience, made it 25 with a 13-point defeat of UT. Despite close coverage by Ken McWilliams, BYU's Randy Schouten scored 24, the same as Overbeck. Black, who always preferred to carry the game to an opponent, was forced to use a slow, deliberate offense because of the turnover epidemic. The long junket ended with a 90-75 loss to Colorado. Buffalo guards Pat Frink (32) and Chuck Williams (25) were too much for the Horns. Arnold scored 20 and Overbeck 17. So Black and his hoop practitioners returned to Austin with a four-loss skein.

Their next game was on the road, too. Hank Iba, seeking career win number 734, felt confident as his Oklahoma State team held the ball with the score tied at 54 in the final seconds. But guard Kenny O'Neal was called for charging, and Doyal converted two free throws despite Cowboy fans' best efforts to disconcert him. Overbeck, who had a chronic knee ailment, played all 40 minutes. He suffered a shoulder separation in workouts the following week and was unable to go in a home game against California-Santa Barbara. With Overbeck on the bench, Gaucho center Leroy Jackson had his way, scoring 25 and grabbing 12 rebounds. But Doyal and Papp combined for 43 points in an 87-75 UT victory.

The Longhorns had won three and lost four, slightly better than the average for SWC teams, which continued to receive lessons in humility during the preconference schedule. Texas got three more such lessons in the Far West Classic in Portland. Oregon State used 19 points from 7' soph Vic Bartolome and a suffocating man-to-man defense in tripping UT, 54-42. It was the fewest points the Steers had scored in five seasons. When Doyal and Lake were hospitalized following attacks of intestinal flu, Texas was shorthanded in meeting Pete Carril's Princeton team. Papp fouled out early in the second half, leaving Overbeck and four guards on the floor. They could not hold the pace against the Tigers and lost, 95-77. But Arnold threw in 38 points, the fifth-best mark in UT history. A 70-57 loss to Oregon was not a great surprise after the Horns made just six first-half field goals. Arnold scored 20 and the Ducks' Ken Smith 26.

Record: 11-13

95 Mississippi 82
74 LSU 87
67 New York University 75
50 Brigham Young 63
75 Colorado 90
56 Oklahoma State 54
87 Cal-Santa Barbara 75
42 Oregon State 54
77 Princeton 95
57 Oregon 70
84 Texas Tech 72
84 SMU 80
66 TCU 65
80 Arkansas 85
87 Texas A&M 88
68 Rice 64
58 Baylor 74
105 Texas A&M 117
79 Baylor 65
94 Rice 83
79 Texas Tech 60
83 SMU 72
65 TCU 71
73 Arkansas 74

The same team that shot a miserable 38 percent in those three games in Portland connected 56 percent of the time in an 84-72 defeat of Texas Tech in Lubbock. Overbeck, suffering the effects of shoulder and knee problems, played superb defense on Red Raider star Vernon Paul and had 25 points and 19 rebounds to lead the way. Gene Gibson's team staged two stout rallies in the second half but fell short. The Longhorns' victory was achieved in spite of travel problems due to icy weather, as they went from vagabonds to kings in the course of one day.

The three-time defending champion SMU Mustangs came to Austin on January 6, but it was a different and weaker team with a 1-10 record. Bob

Prewitt was attempting to succeed Doc Hayes, the SWC's all-time winningest coach. Some 5,000 people witnessed a tight game that finally went to the Horns, 84-80. All five UT starters were in double figures, capped by Arnold (26), while Bill Voight scored 23 for SMU. Voight and Doyal scuffled in the final 15 seconds, something Roy Edwards of the *Dallas Morning News* sought to turn into a cause celebre by saying Doyal kicked Voight.

A four-game TCU winning streak ended at Gregory Gym, 66-65, but not without a battle. The Longhorns blew a nine-point halftime lead only to be rescued by Overbeck's offensive and defensive work at the end. He hit what turned out to be the game-winning hoop with 1:08 left and blocked a shot by the Frogs' Tom Swift. Overbeck and Arnold had 22 points apiece, while man-mountain Mickey McCarty tied Rick Wittenbraker (18) for TCU's high-point honors.

While the *Daily Texan* averred that Black wore a flattop to avoid tearing his hair out, his patience appeared to have paid off in the form of a 3-0 SWC record. Smith's development as a ballhandler had freed Arnold to be a pure shooter, and Arnold was less of a defensive liability than in earlier years. Overbeck was playing splendidly. Doyal and Papp were pleasant surprises. Black had no regrets about the murderous early-season schedule: "Playing good competition always helps. It makes us realize where we need to improve. And if you play poor teams, there's no incentive." Yes, the Longhorns felt pretty sassy on their way to Little Rock, but that did not last long. In the 1,000th game in Arkansas history, the opportunistic Hogs took advantage of UT fouls and Overbeck's ankle injury to win, 85-80. Soph center James Eldridge had 25 points and 13 rebounds, and Doyal scored 22 for Texas.

Mastermind Shelby Metcalf and his two junior strongmen, Ronnie Peret and Billy Bob Barnett, led the Texas A&M Aggies into Gregory Gym, where they were greeted by 8,000 fans. In a fiercely contested game, the Ags erased a 12-point deficit to win, 88-87, behind John Underwood's 27 points. Overbeck tried to play, but his ballooned right ankle prevented it. Arnold tallied 36 before fouling out, a fate afflicting Papp and Doyal, too. As UT players and other students hit the books during the exam break, the eyes of college basketball were on Houston—the Astrodome, specifically. The Houston Cougars (eight years away from SWC membership), led by Elvin Hayes, and national champion UCLA, with Lew Alcindor, did battle before 55,000 fans and a nationwide TV audience. UH won, 71-69. If the SWC needed evidence that basketball was truly a big-time game, it was provided on January 20, 1968.

The Longhorns and Owls tussled in Austin in front of 3,000 people. Overbeck scored 20, and the speed of Arnold and Smith beat the Rice press to take a four-point win. Smith held Owl star Greg Williams to two-of-11 shooting, but Black was again irked by the number of turnovers. "It was a long way from being a classic ballgame," said Rice coach Don Knodel.

Bill Menefee must have been doing it with smoke and mirrors. How else could his Baylor Bears be sitting easily atop the conference standings? He had two fine rookies in sweet-shooting Larry Gatewood and Tommy Bowman, a 6'4" leaper who was the SWC's second black player. Bear fans dared hope it was the finest team since Jackie Robinson and the 1948 NCAA runners-up. While BU won, 74-58, at Heart O' Texas Coliseum, a couple of lesser lights, Russell Kibbe (21) and David Sibley (17), paced the Bruins. Twenty-four turnovers just killed the Horns' chances at victory.

Although a whopping 222 points were scored at G. Rollie White Coliseum, more than half, 117, were by the Aggies. Billy Bob Barnett scored 32, and Overbeck, a premature candidate for Medicare playing on courage alone, had 41 points and 14 rebounds, a tremendous performance. Coach Shelby Metcalf insisted the defenses were not bad, but the offenses were just that good; Texas shot 62 percent and Texas A&M 58 percent.

Black publicly said all the right things about the visiting Baylor Bears, who possessed a two-game lead in the SWC. Privately, however, he convinced his players the Tuesday night game was the Alamo, Little Big Horn and Normandy wrapped into one. Arnold and Overbeck, on their way to all-SWC recognition (UT's first since Larry Franks in 1965) scored 20 points each in a rousing 79-65 victory. The Longhorns shot 67 percent and had a nine-rebound edge. Bowman displayed great agility under the basket and kept BU close most of the way.

Texas' 13th straight win over Rice came at Autry Court as the Horns rambled to a 20-point halftime lead and a 94-83 triumph. Overbeck waded through the Owl defense for 28 points, while Doyal and Arnold had 19 each. Greg Williams and Larry Miller combined for 48 for Rice.

Something was happening. UT caught Texas Tech napping at the starting line and made the Red Raiders pay dearly for it in a 79-60 win that had 5,500 Gregory Gym fans in hysterics. Black's hot Longhorns found themselves in a three-way tie for the conference lead. After Overbeck reinjured his ankle, the scoring burden fell on Arnold, and he came through with 32 points, nine of 14 from the field. Lee Tynes had 19 for Tech.

The winning continued with an 83-72 defeat of SMU in Dallas, the Longhorns' first victory there in three years. And because Baylor and Texas A&M had lost, first place belonged, improbably, to the Steers. The teams were tied at 70 with 5 1/2 minutes to go when Texas reeled off 11 straight points. Lynn Phillips of the Mustangs, capitalizing on Overbeck's injured ankle, wheeled and dealed for 31 points. By no coincidence, the big UT run began when Phillips fouled out.

The SWC was headed for a Keystone Kops finish. After four glittering wins, UT had a blowout on basketball's glory highway in Fort Worth. With a 71-65 victory, TCU pulled into a tie with Texas and Baylor for the lead. Bill Swanson scored 19 for the Horned Frogs, and Mickey McCarty and James Cash pulled down a combined 32 rebounds. Except for Arnold (28), the Horns looked strangely inert and had many sins of omission and commission.

On March 2, the last day of the regular season, TCU beat Baylor in Waco, and Texas lost a heartbreaker to Arkansas in Austin, 74-73. The Longhorns led by nine twice, but sweaty palms were evident in the late minutes, while Duddy Waller's Razorbacks felt no pressure. James Eldridge scored 23 for the red-clad visitors and Arnold 18 for UT. Overbeck gave it his best (13 points and eight rebounds), but he could scarcely move. The Horns had made their stretch run with just seven players and finally went on the ropes out of sheer exhaustion.

1969

Austin American-Statesman writer George Breazeale recalled the strenuous—if not brutal—training program to which Bear Bryant had subjected his Texas A&M football team 15 years earlier in Junction and compared that to what transpired at Gregory Gym for six weeks preceding the 1969 UT basketball season. Leon Black and his assistants, Bennie Lenox and Jim O'Bannon, worked the young men under their direction very hard, paring the team down to 10 players. Despite returning three starters (Larry Smith, Kurt Papp and Wayne Doyal), the Longhorns were expected to wind up in the lower precincts of the Southwest Conference.

Joining that threesome in the starting lineup on opening night were 6'3" soph guard Billy Black and 6'6" JC transfer Bruce Motley. UT encountered Ole Miss in Oxford on December 2. The tall and talented Rebs failed to take advantage of 22 Texas turnovers and lost to their SWC visitors, 67-63. Doyal was six of seven from the field for a total of 16 points, just one less than Ken Turner of Mississippi. All in all, Black's players made a passing grade on their first pop quiz. Two days later and a few miles eastward, they played an Alabama team that had lost to Duke by 38. But C.M. Newton's Crimson Tide forgot that and roared to an 88-62 victory, complete with a 49-26 rebound edge. Bama guard Gary Elliott camped on the edges of the UT zone defense and poured in 21 points. "There is absolutely no bright spot in the game that I can find," Black mused. "We just weren't ready."

Texas played only three pre-SWC home games, and the first was against Colorado. Although the Buffaloes won, 73-64, they met a Longhorn team that played with the alertness, effort and discipline Black preached constantly. Colorado forward Cliff Meely scored 24, while Papp led UT with 21.

Fresh off that performance, the Horns moved to New Orleans for a battle with Tulane in a series that had begun in 1911. Scouting reports about the Green Wave's scoring artistry and depth proved true as UT absorbed a 108-95 defeat. Both teams used racehorse tactics throughout, but Tulane had some real stallions, primarily forward Johnny Arthurs (36). Motley (25), Doyal (20) and Papp (19) led the Longhorns. The setting was not for those with sensitive ears due to the din of the Tulane band and students repeatedly banging a courtside gong.

In the Volunteer Classic in Knoxville, Dick Garrett and Chuck Benson scored 14 points each in Southern Illinois' 58-37 victory. It was the puniest offensive output for Texas in a decade, and not a single Horn reached double figures. Black's assessment of the team's fourth straight loss was blunt: "We were as bad as I've ever seen us...the worst we've looked in any game in the last two years." Perhaps it was the sight of Sooner red or just determination to erase the sting of that awful first-round defeat, but the Steers rose to the occasion and smashed Oklahoma, 65-46. It was an amazing reversal there in the foothills of the Smokies. Papp and Motley combined for 38 points, and UT won the rebound battle despite the presence of two big future NBA players, Garfield Heard and Clifford Ray. Smith, Billy Black and Marcus Whitson provided fine guard play for Texas.

A second straight cage triumph occurred when the Horns strapped Southern Mississippi, 89-72, at Gregory Gym before a sparse crowd. They did it with a good showing on the backboards, a defense that forced the Southerners to shoot off balance most of the night, and some help from the bench. Motley continued his strong early-season play with 19 points and 11 rebounds. Southern Miss was led by Wendell Ladner (soon to play alongside Julius Erving for the New York Nets of the ABA), with 22 points and 18 rebounds.

Twenty-six points by Papp was not enough in a 66-60 home loss to Oklahoma State. Sophomore phenom Amos Thomas (eight) was less than phenomenal, but his teammate, guard Sparky Grober, scored 20, mostly in the second half. "I thought we played pretty well in spots," conceded Cowboy coach Hank Iba. "Texas didn't do anything we weren't expecting, except to use the full-court press in the last few minutes."

The Horns again traveled to the southeast for a tourney, this time the Charlotte Invitational. They trailed Wichita State, 43-36, at the half, got a charge of inspiration and went on to edge the Shockers by three. The scoring pyrotechnics came from UT's Billy Black (24) and Ron Washington (22) of WSU. That victory, so heartening to Black, earned Texas the right to face No. 3 Davidson in the tournament finals. The Wildcats unleashed all the fury they could muster in a 98-76 victory highlighted by 28 points from Mike Maloy and 25 from Houston native Jerry Kroll. Motley's 23 points helped the Horns close the lead to 10 once in the second half.

Record: 9-15

67 Mississippi 63
62 Alabama 88
64 Colorado 73
95 Tulane 108
37 Southern Illinois 58
65 Oklahoma 46
89 Southern Mississippi 72
60 Oklahoma State 66
84 Wichita State 81
76 Davidson 98
63 TCU 59
62 SMU 68
67 Arkansas 59
82 Texas Tech 64
57 Texas A&M 65
70 Rice 76
57 Baylor 71
69 Texas A&M 70 (OT)
58 Baylor 63
81 Rice 80
64 TCU 54
69 SMU 71
69 Texas Tech 82
65 Arkansas 69

Because of a long layoff prior to SWC play, Black imposed two-a-day workouts. He wanted his team to maintain conditioning and be ready to play a good 40-minute game against the defending champ TCU Horned Frogs. Johnny Swaim's purple phalanx, smarting from a loss to SMU, fell for the 10th straight time at Gregory Gym, 63-59. Despite a short bench and foul trouble, the Longhorns stubbornly clung to their control game, coming from behind five times in the second half. Papp scored 17, and Doyal and Larry Smith 15 each for UT, while James Cash had 20 points and 12 rebounds for TCU. Black called it "by far the most intelligent game we've played this year."

SMU's super-soph forward, Gene Phillips, once scored 81 points in high school and averaged 35 per game with the 1968 frosh. The younger brother of Mustang center Lynn Phillips, he was destined to lead the SWC in scoring all three of his varsity seasons. Doyal held him to 15 when UT visited Moody Coliseum on January 11, but SMU won, 68-62. The Horns were ice cold in the second half, making just three field goals in the first 15 minutes. Papp had a nice game, however, with 22 points and 15 rebounds.

Black, Lenox and O'Bannon had worked hard on the recruiting trail, amassing a fine Yearling team with players like Joe "Scooter" Lenox (younger brother of UT's assistant coach), Eric Groscurth and Richard Langdon (son of 1940s player John Langdon). As yet undefeated, they drew a big crowd for the game with Tyler Junior College, led by star guard James "Poo" Welch. With 27 points from Lenox—Welch scored 30—the Texas freshmen won. That game preceded a 67-59 varsity win over Arkansas, one of the Longhorns' best showings of 1969. Doyal hit a long jumper 34 seconds into the game, and UT led from then on. Papp and the Hogs' James Eldridge both scored 21. Arkansas coach Duddy Waller could only lament his team's poor performance.

Fifteen days removed from the battle arena, the Longhorns looked like world-beaters in an 82-64 pasting of Texas Tech in Lubbock. They outrebounded the

Red Raiders by 13, played a fanatical zone defense and shot well. Papp scored 28, and reserve center Mike Smith drew special praise from Black. Pessimists had abounded after the crushing losses to Bama and Southern Illinois in December, but the Horns appeared to have left the gloom behind with a 7-7 record, 3-1 in the conference. That turnaround was followed by one of a different sort, as they lost five straight games and eight of the last 10.

First came a meeting with the neighborhood bully, Texas A&M. The Ags, who had already begun to show their heels to the rest of the SWC, had a big, strong team, led by Ronnie Peret and Billy Bob Barnett. Just 6,500 fans were in Gregory Gym that night for the game; sellouts had become rare in recent years and the crowds somewhat tamer. It was an even match until the final six minutes, and then the Aggies' size, experience and depth showed. The Horns could not control Peret (26) inside, and A&M won, 65-57. Doyal hit two-thirds of his shots for 25 points.

Rice fans were in a bit of a frenzy when the Owlets scored an upset of the Yearlings, and then the same thing happened with the big boys. The 76-70 win was Rice's first over Texas since 1962. Guard Tom Myer scored 23 and center Steve Wendel blocked half a dozen shots in the game at Autry Court. Doyal (15) and Whitson (14) led the Horns in scoring.

Larry Gatewood and Tommy Bowman combined for 39 points in Baylor's 71-57 thrashing of UT in Austin. The game was close until Papp (13 points and 12 rebounds) fouled out with 12 minutes left. The hard times continued in College Station, where Texas lost, 70-69, in overtime. G. Rollie White Coliseum was full and loud, as it usually was when the Horns visited, and they smelled an upset in the air. Fine second-half shooting, a disciplined offense and hustling defense rocked Texas A&M's boat, but the unsinkable Aggies, led by 23 points from Billy Bob Barnett, won it. Doyal finished with 26.

For the second time in eight days, Baylor walked down victory lane at UT's expense, this time in the Bears' den, Heart O' Texas Coliseum. They got a dandy performance from Tommy Bowman—26 points and 12 rebounds. Papp had a career-high 30 points. When Bill Menefee's Bruins pulled ahead with 11 minutes left, they went ultraconservative, taking just eight more shots the rest of the way.

Gregory Gym was half-full for Texas and Rice, two of five teams then sharing the SWC cellar. Papp, the 6'6" El Paso native, again had a hot hand, scoring 29 points, including both ends of a one-and-one free throw situation with nine second left. That enabled the Horns to win a cliffhanger, 81-80. Owl guard Greg Williams essayed some heroics of his own with 33 points.

The usually bleak confines of Daniel-Meyer Coliseum looked just lovely to UT basketball fans after a 64-54 defeat of the Frogs. Doyal played one of the best games of his career, scoring 28 and holding James Cash to five. Guard Larry Smith, who scored 10 and ran the Longhorn offense so well, came down with the mumps, ending a spirited but ill-fated varsity career.

He was missed in UT's final three games, all defeats. Doyal and Papp combined for 47 points in a 71-69 loss to SMU at Gregory Gym. For the Methodists, Bill Voight had 24 points, and the Phillips brothers combined for 31. It was the older one, Lynn, who won the game for SMU, hitting a 12-foot shot from the side of the lane with just seven seconds remaining. The last home game of the season was an 82-69 loss to Texas Tech. Gene Gibson, the Red Raiders' coach, had already been notified of his dismissal, and the players vowed to win the remaining games for him. (They lost the finale to Baylor.) Center Steve Hardin was all-universe that night, scoring 29 points, mostly on hooks and jumpers. Papp and Doyal both had 18. The game was not entirely devoid of excitement because some of the 3,000 fans, in disagreement with the work of refs Larry Covin and Shorty Lawson, threw "ice missiles" (ice inside a folded paper cup after a soft drink had been consumed) on the court.

It ended in Fayetteville on March 4. The last-place Razorbacks, with four starters out, fielded a seven-man team but still managed to beat UT, 69-65. The officials seemed eager to get the lackluster game over with, so they called few fouls, resulting in a lot of back-climbing for rebounds and karate-chopping on defense. Papp and Doyal both scored 18, one less than James Eldridge of Arkansas.

Leon Black refused to do a lengthy postmortem on his second season as coach of the Longhorns. It had not been easy or pleasant, and there was a long way to go in the rebuilding program. A new five-year contract indicated that his bosses had faith in him. "Last year is over, and as far as we're concerned, we're not going to bring it up again," he told Lou Maysel of the *Austin American-Statesman* in between rounds of visiting with coaches and inspecting the play of prospects in the UIL tournament at Gregory Gym. "We're going to work to get better for the future."

1970

Darrell Royal's Longhorn football team was going for the brass ring again—another undefeated national championship—so spirits were high on the Forty Acres. Things were happening on the basketball front, as well. With better personnel, Texas would junk the control offense of 1969 in favor of fast breaking and pressing, a style fans always preferred. What they really preferred, of course, was winning, and a poll of the eight Southwest Conference coaches pointed to UT as the slight favorite. Wayne Doyal was back for his senior year, joined by the ex-Yearlings once touted as among the best in the nation. Of that group, just two, forward Eric Groscurth and guard Scooter Lenox, went on to earn three varsity letters. Lynn Howden, a 6'7" sophomore, had averaged 25 points and 15 rebounds for the LSU freshman team but chafed at the notion of helping Pete Maravich set scoring records and got out of Baton Rouge as soon as he could. The most significant addition, from a sociological or historical standpoint, was a quick 6'1" guard named Sam Bradley, the first black basketball player in UT history. Recruited out of San Angelo as a track man, he scored 12 points per game for the 1968 frosh, sat out the 1969 season and came back to join the Longhorns. Bradley, a fine defensive player and floor man, started several games for the 1970 Horns, but his contributions decreased as the season went on.

Wayne Doyal launches a picture-perfect jumper.

Although his first two teams compiled losing records, Leon Black and the staff were working feverishly to improve the program. They brought in another strong recruiting class and put together a tough pre-SWC schedule. And they welcomed the formation of a booster club, the Longhorn Rebounders. This group actually began at the end of the 1969 season. Its president, Howard Chalmers, was a Texas graduate who occasionally substituted for Wally Pryor as the Gregory Gym public-address announcer and did some radio work. Other key members included Kentucky alumni and fans who had moved to Austin in 1967 when IBM opened its plant in the northwest part of the city. Those fans, who kept an eye on their beloved Wildcats, appreciated college basketball, winning basketball, big-time basketball. The club wanted more of the general public attending home games, a statewide radio and TV hookup and most of all, a new facility. "We hope that in time, city and University officials will see the need for a new place to play, possibly by the end of next year," Chalmers said with great optimism.

Black designed flashy new uniforms with two horizontal stripes and an interlocking "UT" on the hip, earning approval from *Daily Texan* fashion editor Frenchy Golding. She modeled them and concluded, "They're not flattering to those with wide hips, but the orange-and-white knee-socks are *tres chic....* The Longhorn look for the 70s is simply ravishing, a most delightful change from the dull, plain-Jane uniforms of past years."

The 64th Texas basketball season began with a rush, three home games in eight days. The "new look" Horns beat Ole Miss, 95-84, before 5,000 fans. Howden, familiar to some of the Rebs from his one season at LSU, scored 23 and collected 15 rebounds. The Tide was supposed to be rising at Alabama, but the Longhorns had no trouble with C.M. Newton's team, winning by a score of 90-63, atoning for the humiliation

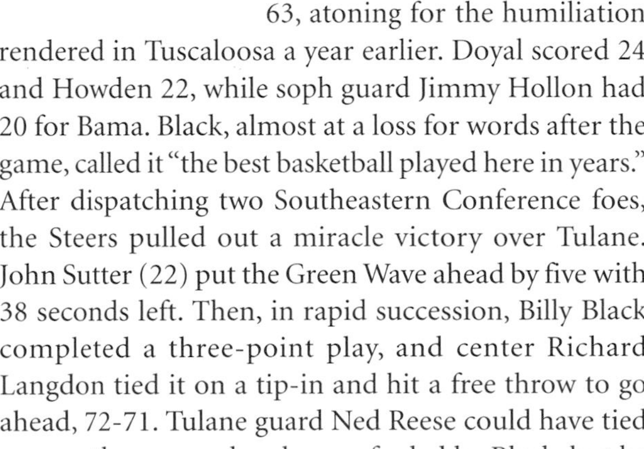

rendered in Tuscaloosa a year earlier. Doyal scored 24 and Howden 22, while soph guard Jimmy Hollon had 20 for Bama. Black, almost at a loss for words after the game, called it "the best basketball played here in years." After dispatching two Southeastern Conference foes, the Steers pulled out a miracle victory over Tulane. John Sutter (22) put the Green Wave ahead by five with 38 seconds left. Then, in rapid succession, Billy Black completed a three-point play, and center Richard Langdon tied it on a tip-in and hit a free throw to go ahead, 72-71. Tulane guard Ned Reese could have tied or won the game when he was fouled by Black, but he missed the front end of a one-and-one. Thus ended a hoop contest with three technicals, one fight (Groscurth was ejected) and fans filling the antiquated gym with boos, throwing paper cups and even a pair of shoes on the court.

That three-game winning streak comprised the best start for a Texas team since 1963, although it ended abruptly on a west coast road trip. Doyal sustained an ankle injury in practice and was unable to go against Cal-Santa Barbara in tiny Robertson Gym. The Gauchos roped the Longhorns, 100-85, with a fine all-around game from forward LeRoy Jackson. Black, who started four sophomores and a junior, was not surprised by such a denouement. He did, however, get a combined 40 points from Howden and Bruce Motley.

Record: 11-13

95 Mississippi 84
90 Alabama 63
72 Tulane 71
85 California-Santa Barbara 100
54 UCLA 99
51 Oklahoma State 54
76 Brigham Young 73 (2 OT's)
61 Florida State 82
73 Ohio 65
55 Seton Hall 56
59 Baylor 81
75 Arkansas 69
81 Texas A&M 87
96 SMU 83
75 Rice 67
55 TCU 80
69 Texas Tech 81
70 Texas A&M 79
71 Texas Tech 90
93 TCU 84
67 Rice 75
81 Baylor 70
61 Arkansas 78
85 SMU 74

UT then proceeded to the college basketball capital of the world, Pauley Pavilion. Lew Alcindor, largely responsible for UCLA's national titles in 1967, 1968 and 1969, had gone on to the pros, but the Bruins were still a mighty team. They dealt a lot of misery in a 99-54 rout, the worst loss in Texas history, coincidentally John Wooden's 500th career win. Groscurth, Doyal and Howden barely reached double figures, while UCLA, with a horde of lightning-fast athletes, was led by John Vallely (24), Sidney Wicks (20) and Henry Bibby (18). Black, who insisted his team was better than what it showed in California, called for a tougher road attitude.

Riding so high earlier, the Longhorns saw their record fall to 3-3 after a 54-51 loss to Oklahoma State in Stillwater. Hank Iba renewed the patent on his controlled-offense philosophy once again as the Cowboys fought off a late Texas rally. Iba, coaching in his 41st and last season, had an 18-5 record against UT. Doyal and OSU's Sparky Grober both scored 14. Bradley, recently recovered from a hamstring problem, had 13.

Back home on December 20, Texas rebounded with a double-overtime 76-73 defeat of a veteran Brigham Young team. The Cougars got a combined 48 points from post man Scott Warner and guard Doug Howard, while Doyal had 23 and Lenox 21. A lot of the Horns' baskets were set up by guard Terry Mullin, a New York native who played on San Jacinto's JC national champion team in 1968.

UT took off for the Sunshine State, first stopping in Tallahassee. Big, quick and strong, read the Florida State scouting report, and the Seminoles proved it with an 82-61 victory. The most impressive was 6'9" Dave Cowens (a future Boston Celtic great), who scored 19 and got 20 rebounds. Coach Hugh Durham waited until the lead approached 30 points before putting in his reserves. After that sobering loss, the Longhorns went to Miami for the Hurricane Classic. Their first-round opponent was No. 5 Ohio University, with wins over four teams from the Big 10. Regardless of the Bobcats' reputation and their own road shortcomings, the Steers sprang a 73-65 upset before 2,000 people at Miami-Dade North Fieldhouse. They battled Ohio on even terms for most of the first half until Doyal went on a scoring spree. After building a 12-point lead, UT's victory was secured due to the ball-control skills of Billy Black. The Horns were not as sharp in the finals against Seton Hall, but they were up by three with 1:09 left and Bradley at the free throw line. He missed, and soon after, the Pirates' Mel Knight scored. Bradley was fouled again, and again he missed. The final seconds under the Seton Hall basket were a wild melee, with Knight tipping in a shot to win, 56-55. UT got 39 points from Howden and Doyal and 16 rebounds from Groscurth.

Leon Black was not crazy about starting conference play against Baylor in Waco. The 7-3 Bears had knocked off two previously unbeaten teams (New Mexico State and Wyoming), and Tommy Bowman and Larry Gatewood had long been tough on the Horns. And there was a new man in green and gold, forward William Chatmon, who would make all-SWC twice. More than 7,000 fans crowded the cow palace on the Brazos to witness an 81-59 BU victory. Gatewood had 24 points and Chatmon 16 points and 12 rebounds. UT shot poorly and had more turnovers than Pepperidge Farm.

Groscurth scored 20 and Doyal 17 in a 75-69 defeat of Arkansas in Austin on January 10. A 19-point Longhorn lead was sliced to four by the last two minutes, and the Hogs frantically tried to break up Texas' delay game. Their fouls sent Groscurth to the free throw line, where he made six of six. Another key element was Bradley's tight defense on Arkansas guard Almer Lee, who hit just four of 22 from the field. Gregory Gym was full three days later when the Horns and Aggies tangled. The mere sight of each other was usually motivation enough, and both teams were medium desperate to stay alive in the SWC race. Shelby Metcalf's marauders came charging from behind to hang an 87-81 loss on UT. Ag forward Mike Heitmann scored 25 and 7' center Steve Niles 20, while Howden and Doyal had 17 each for the Longhorns.

Character and determination were called for when UT met SMU in Dallas, and those qualities were abundant in the Steers' 96-83 victory. Like princes of paradox, they practiced the good side of the hoop art with five players in double figures and a school-record 67 rebounds. "It was just a tremendous performance," said Black, and he was not referring to the 36 points by Mustang scoring machine Gene Phillips.

Less than 24 hours after 35,000 students registered for spring classes, Gregory Gym was ready for a basketball game, a high-noon face-off with Rice. The Cinderella team of the SWC so far, Don Knodel's Owls were coming off a glass-slipper upset of Texas A&M. Black had healthy respect for Rice guards Tom Myer and Gary Reist, but he went with a zone defense that proved successful in a 75-67 win. Howden provided most of the heroics with 25 points and 13 rebounds. The Rice bench rode the officials the entire game, leading to the ejection of one player.

After beating the Mustangs and Owls, Texas turned around and lost four straight, ending all title aspirations. First, it was an 80-55 drubbing by TCU in Fort Worth. Jeff Harp scored 19, and Doug Boyd collected 24 rebounds for Johnny Swaim's spirited Frogs. In the tomblike UT locker room, Black sought slivers of sunshine but found few.

The Texas Tech Red Raiders, averaging five rebounds less than their opponents, had an edge of 15 over the Longhorns, forced 18 turnovers and got some resulting easy baskets in an 81-69 win. Lithe forward Gene Knolle had 20 points and 18 rebounds, while Doyal and Howden scored 19 each. "It was an excellent game," said Tech coach Bob Bass, who had been hired away from the Denver Rockets of the ABA. "It's a little tougher to win in Austin than at some of the other places around the league."

It was the defending champs (Texas A&M) versus the preseason favorites (Texas) in a game for pride and fifth place at G. Rollie White Coliseum, a place lovingly known as a snake pit to visitors, especially those in orange. Black made some lineup changes with Lenox, Motley and Billy Black joining Doyal and Howden, but it did not help. The Ags won, 79-70, with a combined 61 points from Steve Niles, Mike Heitmann and Bill Cooksey. Doyal and Motley had 16 each in the sixth straight loss to A&M, breaking a record that was set when Dana X. Bible coached the Farmers a half-century earlier. It happened as the band played the war hymn and 5,000 fans locked arms and swayed back and forth in the best Aggie tradition.

Could UT cool off the red-hot Raiders? For a half, it appeared possible, but then Texas Tech's two imported gunners, Greg Lowery (from Florida) and Gene Knolle (New York) riddled the Horns' alternating defenses. They combined for 60 points in a 90-71 Red Raider victory before a full house in Lubbock. UT lost all semblance of a disciplined attack in the second half.

Their once-promising season in shambles, the Longhorns revived and beat TCU by nine at home. With Doyal scoring 26 and Groscurth getting 18 points and 12 rebounds, UT led all the way. Billy Black, who had replaced Bradley in the back court, played a steady game and scored 14. His coach of the same name (they were unrelated) was happy and relieved to end a four-game losing streak: "We wanted this one, and we went out to get it."

The Rice Owls, heading to their first undisputed SWC crown since World War II, scored a 75-67 triumph over UT at packed Autry Court. Their fans adopted Aggie-like cheers and chanted, "Beat the hell out of Texas." Tom Myer rained in 27 points and running mate Gary Reist had 20 for Rice. The spotty Horn offense was led by Lenox (17), and sub forward Sammy Hyde collected 10 rebounds.

It was double, double, Doyal and trouble for Baylor in Austin. The Longhorn senior forward scored 26 points and collected eight rebounds in an 81-70 victory before 5,300 spectators. He was matched on the other side by William Chatmon (28 points and 10 rebounds). Ten straight free throws in the final minute ensured victory over the Bears.

The Arkansas Razorbacks were a paltry 4-18, and their coach, Duddy Waller, had announced the end of his four-year hitch. The Hogs pounded the erratic Horns, 78-61, at Barnhill Fieldhouse, dominating every aspect of play. Robert McKenzie had 23 and Almer Lee 21 for the home team, while Doyal (19) was UT's best.

A disappointing season came to an end on March 3 in Austin when Texas hosted Bob Prewitt's SMU Mustangs. With a little help from his teammates, Doyal scored a career-high 35 points in an 85-74 win. The Texas defense clamped down on Gene Phillips (23) in the second half, and a 15-rebound edge helped the cause. Doyal went to the bench with 53 seconds left, to the sustained applause of 4,000 fans. A three-year starter, he totaled 1,062 points, second in UT history behind Raymond Downs. Mostly an outside shooter, Doyal had 51 percent accuracy, and had he not been so team-oriented, he could have put up more impressive numbers. Through no fault of his own, he never played on a championship team or made all-Southwest Conference.

1971

John Mark Wilson, most prominent of the sophomore "baby bulls," suffered a knee injury in October and was out for the season. "Not only will he put it in the hole, but he will go get it if it doesn't go in," is how Leon Black described the 6'7" Odessa native who scored 25 points per game for the Yearlings. Others from that group included 6'10" B.G. Brosterhous, 6'8" Ralph Elliott, 6'7" Jack Louis and guard Mike Dukes. The add-and-subtract game continued with the recruitment of Tyler JC guard Jimmy Blacklock (the Longhorns' second black player), but forward Eric Groscurth underwent a spinal operation and was sidelined for the season. Even without Wilson, Groscurth and Sam Bradley, a recent dropout, UT was expected to field a competitive team in 1971.

The hoop campaign began with an 80-78 loss to No. 14 Florida State at Gregory Gym before 5,000 onlookers. The Horns came back from 13 points down to almost tie it in the final seconds. Ron King scored 23 for the Seminoles, while Howden had 18 points and a school-record 24 rebounds for the home team. Billy Black, converted from guard to forward for his senior season, scored 17.

Texas' first road trip was to the Deep South. The H-men of Alabama, Wendell Hudson, Jimmy Hollon and Allan House, scored 20 points apiece in the Crimson Tide's 90-78 win. Billy Black and Howden combined for 38, and Blacklock (16) provided most of the outside scoring punch. Two days later, the Horns encountered Ole Miss in Oxford. The Rebels had just unveiled a Pete Maravich-clone named Johnny Neumann. A 6'6" sophomore forward with lots of offensive savvy, he averaged 40 points throughout the season before jumping to the pros. Billy Black (23) held Neumann to 29, but the Longhorns still lost by five. Poor shooting and 24 turnovers, some of them crucial, kept Texas from victory. And victory had been a precious commodity in Black's three-plus seasons at the helm, coming less frequently than defeat.

The Horns had a three-game homestand just before the exam period, which had been moved from January to December, coincidentally aiding basketball practice and scheduling. L.C. Brasfield scored 37 and Greg Starrick 23 for Southern Illinois, but the Salukis fell to hot-shooting Texas, 107-100. Billy Black (31) was superb. Supposedly a fast-break team, SIU could not stop the Longhorns' running game. Maximum effort and aggressiveness were there again when UT beat Southern Mississippi, 95-80, behind 27 points and 13 rebounds from Howden and the slick ballhandling of Blacklock. Ricky Ragland led the Southerners with 18. Billy Black scored the most important of his 24 points at the free throw line with 11 seconds left to give the Horns a rousing 72-71 victory over Oklahoma State. Tony Kraus (22) paced the lonesome Cowboys, coached by Hank Iba's successor, Sam Aubrey.

During the two-week break for exams and the Christmas holidays, the University of Houston got a tentative OK to join the Southwest Conference, something made official in the 1971 spring meeting. The Cougars did not begin conference play in football or basketball until 1976, however. Once contemptuously referred to as "Cougar High" because of its lower academic standards—a major recruiting advantage—UH was in. How and why? It was a way for the SWC to strengthen its slipping hold in Houston, which was becoming a pro town with the Oilers, Astros and Rockets. And there was no denying that UH had a good all-around athletic program. The Cougars had been ranked as high as No. 3 in football, and Elvin Hayes carried them to the 1968 Final Four in hoops. Their bid for admission was sponsored by UT, and once crosstown rival Rice consented, it was a done deal.

Leon Black's 3-3 Longhorns returned to the basketball wars in late December at the Milwaukee Classic. Dukes held Wisconsin star Clarence Sherrod to 13, but the Badgers' rebounding mastery put Texas in a big hole, a 25-point hole early in the second half. Despite 30 points from Blacklock (the most he ever scored in a UT uniform), Wisconsin won, 89-73. Brosterhous, a horrendous one-of-15 from the field in that game, made up for it with 23 points in an 85-76 defeat of Dartmouth. Scooter Lenox, back from a shoulder injury, added 13, mostly from downtown. The Indians were led by soph guard James Brown (15), who later made a name for himself broadcasting pro football and basketball.

Leon Black (top row, right) and the 1971 Horns.

There was one more tuneup before the SWC race commenced, against Tulane in New Orleans. Although they outscored the Green Wave, 35-8, over a 14-minute span, the Horns had to hold on at the end for a 74-70 conquest. Billy Black and Tulane soph Jim Kwiatowski shared scoring honors with 17.

The loop opener was with Arkansas. Despite memories of poor performances and galling defeats in the hills in recent years, Texas took control and charged to an 88-79 victory. Billy Black (24) had another solid night, and Blacklock (22) consistently broke through the Razorbacks' pressure defense. Center Bobby Vint scored 26 for Arkansas and its new coach, Lanny Van Eman. His tenure was just slightly more successful than that of his predecessor, Duddy Waller. Arkansas basketball was living on memories of the 1920s, 1930s and 1940s.

With six victories in the last seven games, Black believed the Horns had turned the corner. They missed Groscurth and Wilson but were getting better-than-expected play from Billy Black and Howden. The main difference, though, was Blacklock, providing 17 points and six assists per game. He gave his teammates the warm, secure feeling that the Texas offense was in skilled hands. Not at all demonstrative, Blacklock seemed unfazed by pressure. But he made just three of 15 shots in a 77-70 loss to Baylor before a full house in a Saturday afternoon game in Austin. Howden (25 points and 14 rebounds) and the Bears' William Chatmon (23 points and 11 rebounds) were the best players on the court. Black was subdued in the locker room after the game, mentioning bad shots and a late breakdown in discipline.

The shooting malady followed the Longhorns to Lubbock, where they lost to Texas Tech for the fourth straight time, 68-62. And although no Red Raider topped 6'6", UT was outrebounded, too. Guard Steve Williams, who always seemed to save his best for Texas, scored 16. As they were wont to do, the SWC refs called it close with 51 fouls. There was plenty of noise inside the coliseum as 9,648 people demanded blood, ragging UT players about their long hair and the recent Cotton Bowl loss to Notre Dame. The Tech band added to the festive atmosphere by playing the Notre Dame victory march.

Much had happened since the Longhorns' 107-100 trimming of Southern Illinois on December 10, and lately it had not been good. They carried a two-game losing streak to Carbondale to meet coach Paul Lambert's operatives and won again, 89-81. Dukes, scrambling to regain his starting job from Lenox, had a great night, scoring 24 (seven of 10 from the field and 10 of 10 free throws) and playing tough defense. Greg Starrick scored 26 in the Salukis' 14th home loss in the past seven seasons.

TCU visited Austin on January 30. The Yearlings and Wogs played a prelim game won by the former, 131-68. The man who really made the scoreboard groan was 6'6" forward Larry Robinson, who scored a freshman-, UT-, Gregory Gym- and Southwest Conference-record 55 points, pulled down 28 rebounds and blocked several shots. He, Lawrence "Spider" Johnson, Harry Larrabee and Dennis Shidler were the core of a third straight talented freshman class, the best evidence that Black's rebuilding program was working. As for the varsity, TCU had not won in Austin since 1959, but Johnny Swaim had a couple of JC transfers who planned to do something about that. Eugene "Goo" Kennedy and Simpson DeGrate combined for 46 points and 24 rebounds as the Frogs leaped over Texas, 76-70. Howden, Brosterhous and Blacklock fouled out, and a knee injury to Dukes ended his season and, as it turned out, his career.

Record: 12-12

78 Florida State 80
78 Alabama 90
84 Mississippi 89
107 Southern Illinois 100
95 Southern Mississippi 80
72 Oklahoma State 71
73 Wisconsin 89
85 Dartmouth 76
74 Tulane 70
88 Arkansas 79
70 Baylor 77
62 Texas Tech 68
89 Southern Illinois 81
70 TCU 76
84 Rice 68
84 SMU 83
78 Texas A&M 69
67 Baylor 88
55 Texas Tech 70
87 Arkansas 88 (OT)
64 Texas A&M 65
71 TCU 74
96 SMU 88
94 Rice 88

With one foot in the grave, the Horns prepared to play the SWC-champion Owls. Black remained cheerful despite the losses. "Our kids deserve to win, the way they've been trying so hard," he said. "We're not a great ballclub, but our players are giving a good effort every game. Sometimes, there's nothing you can say but 'keep on trying.'" They defeated Rice, 84-68, before 6,000 fans as six UT players reached double figures. Fireworks erupted just before tipoff when Owl coach Don Knodel protested the Longhorn Band's playing of "The Eyes of Texas." Whether or not it was music-appreciation night, Black had a 20-point lead with two minutes left, enabling him to play his subs.

Gene Phillips of SMU, two-time SWC player of the year and a shoo-in for a third such award, was averaging 28 points per game. Billy Black got the honor of trying to stop him when the Horns and Ponies met at Moody Coliseum. Phillips had 24 points and 11 rebounds and was a key figure in SMU's comeback from 11 down to tie the game at 83. The Mustangs possessed the ball and went into an agonizing two-minute stall before Phillips committed a turnover and then fouled Brosterhous, who hit the winning free throw with 17 seconds left. Howden led UT with 22 points and 10 rebounds.

A six-game, three-year losing streak to Texas A&M came to an end with a 78-69 defeat of the Ags at Gregory Gym. Inside muscle had been the main factor in that stretch, but it was not subtle enough for the refs because 7' Steve Niles, 6'8" Rick Duplantis, 6'7" Jeff Overhouse and 6'6" Chuck Smith were directed to the bench with five fouls apiece, and the Longhorns got 34 points on free throws. Blacklock and A&M's Jeff Howard scored 23 and 18, respectively.

It did not seem to matter to SWC opponents if the Longhorns were winning or losing—attendance always swelled when Texas came to town, claimed Craig Byrd of the *Daily Texan:* "'Beat the hell out of TU.' At A&M, that chant is a prayer. At Texas Tech, it's a threat. And at Arkansas, it's a religious duty. Everywhere else around the Southwest Conference, it's merely a burning compulsion. 'TU' stands for 'The University,' doesn't it?" William Chatmon led a Baptist revival in Waco, scoring 23 points and securing 24 rebounds in BU's 88-67 win over the Longhorns. The teams matched mistakes for most of the first half with missed shots, bad passes and defensive lapses, but Bill Menefee's Bears snapped out of it, while UT never did. That was the beginning of a five-game losing streak.

Texas pulled into a 49-49 tie with Texas Tech midway through the second half before freezing. Not a Longhorn point was scored for over eight minutes, and by then, the Red Raiders had a 70-55 win sewed up. Greg Lowery (20) and Gene Knolle (17) were double trouble, and Ron Douglas had 15 rebounds in Gerald Myers' first win at Gregory Gym as a coach. Blacklock scored 20 for the Longhorns, who played another home game four days later against Arkansas. Tight and cautious, UT got off to a bad start, but the 4-17 Hogs, who twice had 11-point margins, seemed intent on giving it away. When guard Almer Lee (27, including an odd five-point play) fouled out, the Horns caught Arkansas, pushed ahead and were caught, themselves. The game went into overtime and was won by the Razorbacks, 88-87, when Blacklock (21) missed a free throw with four seconds left.

UT and Texas A&M were suffering from the same strange poison, an inability to win at home. But that trend stopped in College Station, where three turnovers in the waning minutes and a short jumper by forward Jeff Howard gave the Aggies a 65-64 win. Lenox, who scored 18 like Howard, had a chance to win it and silence a loud, unnerving crowd, but his last-second shot did not drop.

They had led the SWC race almost from the beginning, and the TCU Horned Frogs needed just one more win to clinch the crown. Black's Longhorns followed their usual pattern of dropping behind early, courageously clawing back into the game and losing toward the end. Eugene Kennedy had 26 points and 19 rebounds, and Simpson DeGrate scored 21 in the 74-71 TCU win at Daniel-Meyer Coliseum. Lenox led Texas with 22. Billy Black and Coco Villareal were tossed for fighting with four minutes left.

Lenox and Blacklock hit for 26 each in the home finale, a 96-88 defeat of SMU. The 4,000 fans present got to see an unforgettable performance by Gene Phillips. The 6'4" Houston native made all of his 11 free throw attempts and 20 of 38 from the field for 51 points. With one game left, he had scored 1,917 points, far eclipsing the SWC career mark left by another red-and-blue player, Jim Krebs. Phillips was accorded a two-minute ovation by the Gregory Gym crowd.

Forty-five points from the Lenox-Blacklock backcourt tandem carried Texas to a 94-88 defeat of Rice in Houston. Gary Reist, who started every game for three years, led the Owls with 37. A sad postscript was added to UT's 12-12 season when reserve forward Ralph Elliott died in a traffic accident near his hometown of Denison during Easter vacation.

1972

It was a "must" year for Texas basketball. The Longhorns needed to win, if not the Southwest Conference title (for which they were favored), then over half of their games. Leon Black undoubtedly had the deepest and strongest team of his tenure, with lots of experienced players and two fine sophomores. Harry Larrabee, a 5'10" guard who was slow afoot but had quick hands, grew up in the crucible of Indiana high school basketball. The other newcomer, forward Larry Robinson, had been anointed the crown prince and future king of SWC hoops. A whiz as a freshman (34 points and 17 rebounds per game), Robinson could play inside or outside, and his coaches and teammates loved him. A bit of history was made when Jimmy Blacklock was elected captain, the first black athlete to hold that position on a UT team. No one could doubt that integration had occurred by 1972; each member of the all-SWC team was black, and Mississippi and Alabama, the first two opponents for the Longhorns, had begun the process themselves.

If Robinson made it on the varsity level and Texas won, perhaps Gregory Gym would fill up more frequently. The once-majestic building, while still structurally sound, had become antiquated, and yet a student body of 39,000—not to mention another 200,000 Austin residents—seldom occupied all 7,800 seats. Even so, Frank Erwin of the UT Board of Regents had made an auditorium/coliseum with twice the capacity of Gregory Gym a high priority. A committee had been appointed and was quietly studying how to fund, design and erect such a building.

After scrimmages with Stephen F. Austin and Southwest Texas, the Horns hosted Ole Miss for the season opener. Three late turnovers halted UT's momentum and allowed the Rebels to escape with a 79-78 victory. Scooter Lenox and Duaine Boucher of Mississippi both had 23 points. Another SEC team, Alabama, paid a visit to Gregory Gym, and again it was a tense game right down to the buzzer. The Crimson Tide, led by the magic of forward Wendell Hudson (31 points and 20 rebounds) came back from a 12-point deficit but lost, 85-83. Robinson, the blue-chipper from Hobbs, New Mexico, scored 24, grabbed 12 rebounds and made some key defensive plays.

Lenox and John Mark Wilson teamed up for 49 points in a 90-83 defeat of Oklahoma City, leaving Abe Lemons' Chiefs 0-3 with losses to TCU, Baylor and Texas. From there, Black and his basketball entourage went to Manhattan to engage Kansas State. The Longhorns needed good rebounding and error-free play to beat the hulking Wildcats, and they could manage neither in an 87-60 thrashing. Guard Dan Beard (23) and center Steve Mitchell (19) led an early scoring rampage, and the game was effectively over. Except for B.G. Brosterhous (16 points and 13 rebounds), Texas played meekly and gave little indication of becoming an outstanding team. The last game before exams and the holidays was a 28-point destruction of Stetson, a tiny Florida school just beginning to play major-college basketball. Sixteen days later, with most of the students out of town, UT held off Centenary, 81-77, before 3,000 fans at Gregory Gym. It was the first meeting of the Horns and the Gentlemen since 1931. Robinson scored 26, Larrabee (starting for Lenox, who had a foot injury) 20, and Brosterhous had a game-saving block at the end. Larry Davis and James "Skeeter" Horne scored almost two-thirds of Centenary's points.

UT took its 5-2 record to the Bruin Classic in Los Angeles, where the first-round opponent was a precocious and yet fearsome UCLA team. Averaging 112 points per game and on their way to an eighth national championship in nine years, the Bruins had marvelous 6'11" sophomore Bill Walton, Keith Wilkes, Henry Bibby, Larry Farmer, Greg Lee and a bench full of high school all-Americans. The beating (115-65) was slightly worse than the one administered two years earlier, as Walton scored 28 points, got 24 rebounds and dominated the game in ways statistics cannot tell. "Walton gave what seemed to be a masterful exhibition," wrote Lou Maysel of the *Austin American-Statesman*, "often soaring above his fellow citizens like a porpoise leaving the water to tip in an offensive rebound or spear a defensive chance, which he usually disposed of like a hot horseshoe." The Longhorns snapped back the next night with an 86-69 defeat of Arizona. As he had been against the Uclans, Robinson (26) was the leading scorer. Jim Huckestein tallied 28 for the Wildcats.

Lenox, Larrabee, Eric Groscurth and Lynn Howden had a variety of physical ailments, but they all participated in a 78-70 win over Georgetown. It was let-them-play night at Gregory Gym in one of the roughest home games in some time. Hoya ace Michael Laughna scored 25, while Groscurth continued his fine play, moving Wilson out of the starting lineup. Pre-SWC competition concluded with a 67-61 defeat of Oklahoma State in Stillwater. Mike Jeffries scored 18 for the Cowboys, and Robinson (14) led the Horns before going out with an ankle injury. Shortly before the SWC race began, the NCAA rescinded the rule against freshmen playing varsity football and basketball, effective in the summer. An item long debated, it was done primarily to reduce costs. Black responded by saying, "This will make it a whole new ball game." While Texas would field a junior varsity team (known as the Shorthorns) in both sports for the next few years, the best players went straight to the varsity. The Yearling hoop team then being coached by Bennie Lenox was the last, and it was not a strong one. Only Chris Voegele and Jay Lapeyre ever lettered, and they were bit players.

Robinson handled the ball like a guard, rebounded like a center and shot like a Marine marksman in UT's 87-63 defeat of Rice. He had 35 points and 11 rebounds, prompting this comment from Owl coach Don Knodel: "I don't think I've seen any big man in this league any better than Robinson. He's a great one, with all the tools." Texas Tech coach Gerald Myers, in Austin to scout the game, made similar remarks.

Baylor had compiled a 10-2 pre-SWC record, so Black and Bear coach Bill Menefee exchanged the usual flattery before their teams met at Heart O' Texas Coliseum, recently

Record: 19-9

78 Mississippi 79
85 Alabama 83
90 Oklahoma City 83
60 Kansas State 87
86 Stetson 58
81 Centenary 77
65 UCLA 115
86 Arizona 69
78 Georgetown 70
67 Oklahoma State 61
87 Rice 63
77 Baylor 75
68 Texas Tech 79
117 Arkansas 93
80 SMU 85
75 TCU 88
80 Texas A&M 71
83 Rice 67
90 Baylor 70
76 Texas Tech 81
92 Arkansas 86 (OT)
93 SMU 81
80 Texas A&M 73
72 TCU 65
91 SMU 89 (OT)
85 Houston 74
55 Kansas State 66
70 SW Louisiana 100

equipped with a rubberized court, sort of the basketball version of artificial turf for football. As people eventually learned, however, grass works better in football and maplewood is best for basketball. More than 9,000 fans watched Texas go Bear-hunting, winning in Waco for the first time in seven years. It was a thrilling game that recalled the barnburners of the late 1940s. There were 13 lead changes in the last eight minutes, culminating in Robinson taking a pass from Brosterhous and hitting a 15-foot jumper to win, 77-75. He finished with 22 points, three less than Baylor's Roy Thomas. The Longhorns made 13 of 15 free throws down the stretch.

The fire marshal closed the doors of Gregory Gym five minutes before tipoff between Texas and Texas Tech. An estimated 8,000 people (500 with reserved seating, a recent innovation) saw the Red Raiders win, 79-68, with 28 points from Greg Lowery. They shot 62 percent, played tenacious man-to-man defense and put on a fine exhibition of basketball. Fiery sophomore guard Richard Little, who encouraged the razzing of the crowd, surely got the last laugh. "I'm still so shell-shocked," Black mused, "I won't know until I watch the film whether Tech's offense was that good or our defense was that bad."

Larry Robinson, a prime mover in two Southwest Conference title runs.

The Arkansas-Texas A&M game a week earlier had ended in a brawl. Guard Martin Terry, a junior-college transfer, scored 46 points and proved handy with his fists. There was another fine newcomer for the Hogs, 6'8" Dean Tolson, who had averaged 30 points per game as a freshman. Tolson (33) and Terry (25) combined on some eye-popping alley-oop buckets, but it was not nearly enough. The Longhorns, with a 58-37 rebound edge, hung a 117-93 defeat on their visitors from the Ozarks. In a racehorse game, as the score indicates, Lenox (23) was one of six UT players in double figures.

A half step slow all night, the Horns fell to SMU by five in Dallas. The Mustangs got 42 points from their three guards, Zack Thiel, Bobby Rollings and Larry Delzell, but their main man was forward Ruben Triplett (24 points and 10 rebounds). Robinson had 33 points and 11 rebounds before fouling out. An 88-75 loss to TCU in Fort Worth was the lowest point of the 1972 season. Other than Robinson (31), there was little to cheer UT fans, as the team had numerous offensive and defensive breakdowns and some very clumsy miscues early. Johnny Swaim's defending champion Frogs took their 17th straight SWC win at Daniel-Meyer Coliseum.

Daily Texan writers Alan Truex and Joe Phillips all but called for Black's head, but things started to change with an 80-71 tumbling of Texas A&M in Austin. Robinson had a typically fine game (26 points and 10 rebounds), and Howden, Larrabee and Wilson did well off the bench. Aggie guard Mario Brown, who had been hitting almost 60 percent of his shots in SWC play, was just three of 17. In a reminder of rowdy times past, some A&M cadets were victims of attack outside Gregory Gym; in one instance, a gang of football players pummeled one measly Ag.

It was a touchy situation, but Black had to act. He put his captain, Jimmy Blacklock, on the bench and started Harry Larrabee along with Lenox in the backcourt. Blacklock, who scored 400 points in 1971, had played tentatively and made repeated turnovers. Larrabee, a better outside shot and ballhandler, was more adept at running the offense, and he was in for good. Although not thrilled with the development, Blacklock handled it fairly well, and he still had some contributions to make to the 1972 Texas season. Rice, winless in the SWC, remained that way after an 83-67 Longhorn victory at Autry Court. Robinson had 24 points and Howden 19 points and 11 rebounds. He was not the most graceful player (and a broken thumb did not help), but Howden's muscle was needed against the Owls. He had recently passed Gary Overbeck as the UT career rebound leader.

Lenox and Robinson combined for 45 points in a 90-70 defeat of ice-cold Baylor in Austin on February 15. The Bears hit just 25 of 70 shots and were never in it. Senior forward Pat Fees scored 20 and collected 11 rebounds. "Texas was obviously ready to play," said BU coach Bill Menefee.

Robinson had perhaps his worst game of the year in an 81-76 loss to Texas Tech in Lubbock—seven points, two rebounds and five fouls. When he took a seat, the Red Raiders extended their lead to 15 with just over two minutes left. But Robinson's teammates did not give up. They ripped off 12 straight points before Tech was able to stop the run. The Raiders soared on the wings of Greg Lowery (31) and Ralph Palomar (28). Wilson (22) led UT.

Texas remained one of five teams in the race by taking a 92-86 OT win over Arkansas at Barnhill Fieldhouse. Martin Terry and Dean Tolson were again superb (34 and 19 points, respectively), and Robinson had 23 for Texas. But it was the littlest Longhorn, Larrabee, who stood tall at the end. He stole a pass and made five free throws in the last 30 seconds. It was a costly victory because Wilson (19) sustained an ankle injury that sidelined him the rest of the way.

The title-hungry Longhorns had more trouble with Ruben Triplett (24), but they put together a 93-81 victory over SMU before a large and loud throng at Gregory Gym. Robinson scored 37, and Brosterhous, playing with an injured shoulder, had 15 points and 14 rebounds.

"The best player in the conference" is what Shelby Metcalf called Robinson after watching the Longhorn forward score 25 points in an 80-73 defeat of Texas A&M in College Station. The Ags strained every sinew in their bodies to stay close in the second half, and as often as not, Lenox' long jumpers kept them down. Randy Knowles scored 23 for the maroon and white, a week removed from a riot/basketball game with Baylor.

UT's fieldhouse was packed to the rafters for the TCU game, the regular-season finale. Whoever lost was through, while the winner shared the SWC crown with SMU. Blacklock came off the bench and helped break the Frogs' pressure defense, and Robinson (26 points and 15 rebounds) was Mr. Cool at the free throw line, canning five late ones in a 72-65 victory that was a long time coming for Leon Black. His postgame interviews, after getting tossed in the shower, were conducted with a smile as big as a rainbow. Simpson Degrate and Evans Royal combined for 35 points for the ex-champs.

A playoff game with SMU at a neutral site was imminent, and Black expressed a preference for Hofheinz Pavilion in Houston, but Heart O' Texas Coliseum was selected. Knowing the winner would move into the NCAA Tournament, Pony fans traveled 100 miles south and Longhorn fans 100 miles north, and enough Waco citizens were interested to fill the big barn. It took an extra period to decide, but Texas came out on top, 91-89. Robinson (30 points and 12 rebounds) and Brosterhous fouled out, leaving Black with a lineup of cripples and reserves. Seldom-used forward Jack Louis forced a turnover, blocked a shot and got a big rebound in the last frantic minute. "It was a gutty ball game," said the oft-maligned Black, who suddenly had the job security of a Supreme Court justice.

The team was hurting. Brosterhous (shoulder), Howden (ankle and thumb), Lenox (thigh and foot) and Larrabee (ankle and leg cramps) were bad off, but worst of all, Robinson broke his right foot in Waco. With 546 points, he had enjoyed the second-most productive season in Longhorn history, but he was on crutches, in a soft cast from calf to toe. Trainer Frank Medina worked feverishly with Robinson, who chose to play—or at least try—against Houston in Las Cruces, New Mexico. Guy Lewis' Cougars, four years away from full SWC membership, were 20-6 with big athletes like Dwight Davis, Dwight Jones and Steve Newsome. They were heavy favorites to win and proceed in the tournament. Black's optimistic comments were regarded as so much whistling past the cemetery, but he looked like Nostradamus after the Longhorns pulled a shocking 85-74 upset. Robinson (just announced by the SWC office in Dallas as player of the year) managed to get 23 points and 14 rebounds. His mobility and jumping were limited, but he went 35 minutes. Groscurth, Lenox, Larrabee and Brosterhous also reached double figures. Davis and Newsome combined for 51 of UH's 74 points. It was one of the biggest upsets in UT history, provoking several hours of wild celebration on the Drag, west of campus.

Black and the team received a tumultuous welcome at Austin Municipal Airport, and the loudest cheers were reserved for Robinson. They had five days to reflect on the victory (including a rare basketball pep rally in front of Gregory Gym), rest and get ready for a second-round game with Kansas State in Ames, Iowa. Jack Hartman's Wildcats had put a 27-point defeat on UT in December and won their last nine games. One proud Longhorn in attendance that night was Raymond

Downs, who predicted the sun would shine on Black's team: "Don't be surprised if they start to win and win big. This team has all kinds of talent." But the Horns ran out of band-aids and miracles, falling to KSU, 66-55. They came back from 11 points down to take a slim lead with 4:44 to go and then succumbed to the bigger and deeper Cats. Robinson, playing virtually on one leg, scored 22 points, two more than Dan Beard of the winning team. In the consolation game, Southwestern Louisiana showed no mercy to the beat-up Longhorns, winning, 100-70. Bo Lamar, the leading scorer in the nation, hit 36 points, his average exactly. Groscurth (21) led UT, and Robinson rested his aching foot.

A long and satisfying season was over. The seniors went out as winners, the younger players could look forward to more of the same, and coach Leon Black had vindication, if he ever needed it. Gregory Gym had been packed in the final home games, as full of noise and color as it was during the glory days of Jay Arnette, Slater Martin, Bobby Moers or Jack Gray.

1973

Leon Black's Southwest Conference cochamps returned six lettermen—Eric Groscurth, B.G. Brosterhous, John Mark Wilson, Jack Louis, Harry Larrabee and Larry Robinson. While no one disputed that Robinson was the central figure in the 1972 title drive, all had contributed. For the first time in 25 years, freshmen were eligible for varsity competition, and UT had found a good one, Dan Krueger, a 5'11" Wisconsin native. The Longhorns' upset of Houston in the NCAA Tournament had helped convince him to come to Austin. Krueger would forge a fine career over the next four years, twice making all-SWC.

The new facility was being planned, but those in charge insisted it would be more than a gymnasium. In fact, a name was chosen ("Special Events Center") even before B.W. Crain, Jr. was selected as the architect. Still far from a reality, it would be built in an area bound by 15th Street on the south, 18th Street on the north, Red River Street on the west and Interstate 35 on the east. Coinciding with the decision to erect a new UT baseball stadium, its impetus can be traced to Frank Erwin of the Board of Regents. A master power broker, he spearheaded the expansion of the UT System and oversaw numerous projects on the flagship campus in Austin. Erwin, Black, J. Neils Thompson (longtime SWC faculty representative and Athletic Council member) and Jack Gray took a number of trips around the country, inspecting new facilities and making plans for the one in Austin. In the meantime, however, Gregory Gym would suffice.

Brosterhous and Wilson suffered ankle injuries in preseason workouts and were on the convalescent list a fortnight before the opening game with South Alabama. But they, along with Robinson, supplied 55 points in an 81-67 home victory. Darius Segure had 16 points and 11 rebounds for the Jaguars.

UT toured the Magnolia State in early December and got two unexpected defeats. In Oxford, Mississippi's stifling zone defense and backboard strength, combined with poor shooting by the Horns, equaled a 78-58 loss to the Rebels. Seven-foot center Fred Cox scored 19 for Ole Miss, but the big shock for Texas was Robinson's anemic showing, zero points and two rebounds. The Longhorns moved downstate to Starkville and dropped an 80-69 decision to Mississippi State. Robinson spent more than half the game on the bench in foul trouble. His teammates battled on, however, reaping another solid scoring and defensive performance from Brosterhous. Larry Fry led the Bulldogs with 15 points and 11 rebounds.

The slumping Longhorns returned to Austin to face Oklahoma State. The Cowboys were not exactly shaking in their Converse All-Stars at UT's 33 percent shooting. Unable to hit a number-two washtub in both games in Mississippi, Black's forces made 39 of 70 shots in an 86-66 defeat of OSU before a crowd of 4,500. Robinson reassured Texas fans that his skills had not deserted him with 29 points and nine rebounds. Groscurth and Louis were zonebusters, scoring 16 and 15, respectively. Andy Hopson had 19 points and 10 rebounds for Oklahoma State.

Texas was expected to tread softly at Mid-South Coliseum against No. 19 Memphis State. The Tigers, coached by Gene Bartow, were loaded with talent, especially Ronnie Robinson, Larry Finch and Larry Kenon, all of whom had pro ball in their futures. But the Longhorns scored 14 straight points in a five-minute span in the second half and relied on Larrabee's late free throw shooting to win, 80-79. Robinson had 26 points for the Horns and Kenon 28 for the Tigers, who would end up losing the NCAA title game to Bill Walton and the UCLA Bruins.

Three thousand fans witnessed Oklahoma City's 79-77 victory at Gregory Gym. For the connoisseur of fine cage play, there was not much to recommend the game, but those who liked to watch tempers fraying at the seams may have enjoyed it. OCU forward Marvin Rich won the game with a last-second shot from the top of the key. Wilson (25) played well for Texas. But Robinson and the Chiefs' Ronald Brown got into a tussle and were ejected. Coach Abe Lemons was tagged with three technical fouls after just 6:40 of play and was also invited to leave by referee Harlan Voyle. He went up to the gallery but was spotted by Voyle and sent ignominiously to the visitors' locker room.

At the Poinsettia Classic in Greenville, South Carolina, 7'1" Fessor "Moose" Leonard shredded UT's inner defense for 33 points as Furman won, 101-95. The Purple Paladins led by as many as 20 before Robinson (26 points and 10 rebounds) launched a comeback that brought the Horns to within three in the final minute. They salted away Pepperdine, 97-81, for third place in the tournament. William "Bird" Averitt, key to the Wave's offense, was held to four of 18 from the field.

There were two more road games before SWC play commenced. Black expected a big challenge from Oklahoma and its 6'9" freshman, Alvan Adams. The future Phoenix Sun was excellent, scoring 23 and getting 19 rebounds in the Sooners' 81-78 win. Robinson scored 20 despite a knee injury, the severity of which was not at first realized. He limped through Texas' 81-79 overtime defeat of Centenary in Shreveport, scoring 14 points and collecting three rebounds. The team doctor examined him and determined the problem was not tendinitis, as previously believed, but a broken kneecap. A lot of Longhorn hearts were broken, too, when Robinson's junior year ended prematurely.

Black and assistant coaches Bennie Lenox and Dale Dotson had a week to retool the team before the SWC opener. Life without Larry Robinson began on January 13 in Baylor's tiny, ancient McLean Gym because Heart O' Texas Coliseum had suffered tornado damage. Some 3,300 fans squeezed into the old place and saw the Bears turn back UT, 85-79. Wilson poured in a career-high 34 points, but it was not enough, as Jerry Ahart scored 26 and Charlie McKinney 25 for the Bears.

John Mark Wilson rebounds. Looking on intently are Eric Groscurth, Harry Larrabee, Ira Terrell of SMU, B.G. Brosterhous and referee Shorty Lawson.

Groscurth (20) and Wilson (17) led the Horns to an easy 85-68 defeat of Tulane. The debris of UT registration was evident all over Gregory Gym, with mutilated computer cards everywhere and signs on the walls indicating "natural sciences," "business administration," "nursing" and other academic majors. There had not been enough time to set up bleachers on the floor, so all 2,500 fans observed the proceedings from the gallery. Gregory Gym was in better condition three days later when Lanny Van Eman's Razorbacks met the Longhorns. Martin Terry and Dean Tolson combined for 49 points in a 76-72 Arkansas victory. Black was irked after the game, wondering how his team could fail to convert the Hogs' 32 turnovers into more points. "It was bad," he said. "There's not a single phase of the game we played well in."

Pat McClellan, a 6'3" guard with good basic basketball skills, completed a meteoric rise when Texas played the Aggies in College Station. He was a walk-on, a member of the Shorthorns (averaging 15 points per game), moving up to the varsity and then a starting position. G. Rollie White Coliseum, with its usual frenzied crowd, was a tough place to debut, so Bennie Lenox, an ex-Aggie, tried to calm him down. The Longhorns dropped to 0-3 in the conference with a 69-64 loss. Brosterhous, Groscurth and Louis fouled out, leaving Larrabee, one soph and three frosh on the floor, and they nearly managed to win. In contrast to his morose comments following the Arkansas game, Black was pleased with the effort expended by the young team.

The object of a fierce recruiting battle after leading San Antonio Jefferson to the 1972 state championship, Rick Bullock had chosen to pursue higher education at Texas Tech. He was quite a load, standing 6'9" and weighing 235 pounds and was a major reason the Red Raiders were on their way to the SWC title. But Bullock was relatively quiet in Tech's 73-64 overtime win in Lubbock. Ron Richardson had 20 points and 16 rebounds, and Ed Wakefield scored 10 straight in the extra period. Louis (18) led the Longhorns. Buck Harvey of the *Daily Texan* insisted he did not mean to be critical, but things seemed to be going backward. He recalled 1971, when Texas had a plethora of freshman and varsity talent, and surveyed the current team, which he described as "one of the most amazing groups of 6'3" walk-ons and unheard-ofs ever amassed into the same gym." Knowledgeable as only a student journalist can be, Harvey tolled the bell for Black and predicted a bleak future for UT hoops.

Brosterhous' parents, who had come down from Oregon for the game with Rice, looked on approvingly as he got 26 points and 10 rebounds in an 88-73 victory. Krueger scored 10 in his first start, while Mark Wehrle (22) led the cellar-dwelling Owls. Everyone seemed to agree that SMU had the best players—if not the best team—in the SWC. Ruben Triplett had been joined in the frontcourt by Ira Terrell (like Texas Tech's Rick Bullock, destined to earn all-conference honors thrice) and Sammy Hervey, who had put up some outrageous offensive numbers in high school and junior college. The Pony Express delivered an 82-75 victory at Gregory Gym on Saturday, February 3. Bob Prewitt's big three scored all but 16 of SMU's points. The Longhorns shot 55 percent, made just eight turnovers and caused the Mustangs to sweat in the late minutes.

Record: 13-12

81 South Alabama 67
58 Mississippi 78
69 Mississippi State 80
86 Oklahoma State 66
80 Memphis State 79
77 Oklahoma City 79
95 Furman 101
97 Pepperdine 81
78 Oklahoma 81
81 Centenary 79 (OT)
79 Baylor 85
85 Tulane 68
72 Arkansas 76
64 Texas A&M 69
64 Texas Tech 73 (OT)
88 Rice 73
75 SMU 82
69 TCU 62
77 Baylor 64
74 Arkansas 86
71 Texas A&M 68
77 Texas Tech 80 (OT)
75 Rice 68
89 TCU 69
83 SMU 77

"Reluctant participants in the hard-times classic" was how George Breazeale of the *Austin American-Statesman* characterized the Texas-TCU game in Fort Worth. The Frogs, with their aesthetically challenged vertical-stripe uniforms, scored just 26 points in the first half but were competitive in the second in a 69-62 loss to the Horns. Wilson (23) and Brosterhous (22) led UT, while 6'11" Bill Bozeat had 16 for TCU, all in the second half.

Retiring coach Bill Menefee brought his Baylor Bears to Austin and lost, 77-64. Although the Forty Acres were covered with ice, it was warm inside Gregory Gym, at least for the Longhorns, who hit 58 percent of their shots. Wilson scored 27, Brosterhous busted Lynn Howden's career rebounding mark, and the pudgy Larrabee showed why, appearances notwithstanding, he was such a fine player. Going nearly 40 minutes, as he often did, he made his teammates better. Charlie McKinney had 20 points and 10 rebounds for the Bruins.

UT was outplayed, outrebounded and outscored in an 86-74 loss to Arkansas at Barnhill Fieldhouse. It would have been worse had Longhorn reserves not narrowed a 21-point gap in the last seven minutes. Martin Terry (31), Rickey Medlock (15) and Dean Tolson (14) made most of the noise.

Another full house gathered at Gregory Gym to see the Horns smite the burly Aggies, 71-68. A malfunctioning scoreboard necessitated some hasty cooperation among clock operator Gary Ball, public-address announcer Wally Pryor and refs Paul Galvan and Billy Cowan. Larrabee scored a career-high 27, including four late free throws, while Randy Knowles, who had piled up 70 points in Texas A&M's last two games, was held to nine. Gerald Myers' Red Raiders already had a hammerlock on the 1973 SWC crown when they came to Austin. Instead of a nine-point overtime loss for Texas, as had occurred in Lubbock, it was a three-point OT loss. Richard Little (25) and Ron Richardson (19) paced the Raiders, while Larrabee had 18 for UT. Texas Tech was equal to every salvo the Longhorns could fire. "This is the road we've been down all year," said a dejected Black. "'Almost' won't get you a nickel cup of coffee."

When Texas met Rice at Autry Court, barely 1,000 souls were in attendance. Most college basketball fans were across town, watching No. 7 Houston play Jacksonville. The Owls had a small lead with three minutes left, but McClellan, Brosterhous and Larrabee erased it and cruised to a seven-point win. Black, a fervent believer in the one-at-a-time philosophy, was happy to get it.

Lynn Royal, a fine-looking freshman, scored 21 points in TCU's 89-69 loss in Austin. Brosterhous and Larrabee had 18 apiece and Louis, who had improved considerably as the season went on, scored 16. Almost all of the Longhorns were sharpshooters that night with 63 percent from the field.

The season ended in Dallas, where people were mourning the deaths of former SMU coach Doc Hayes and his wife in a traffic accident. On top of that, several Mustang stars were squabbling and playing lackadaisical defense. The game between the two cochampions of 1972 ended with UT up, 83-77. It was less of a shootout than a popgun affair, but seniors Jack Louis (23), B.G. Brosterhous (17) and Eric Groscurth (10) went out in style. Sammy Hervey scored 26 for the Ponies. While Black was not inclined to make excuses or what-ifs, his team had not done badly. They lost seven conference games by an average of seven points, and a healthy Larry Robinson would have affected that considerably.

1974

"This is a year of excitement," claimed the Longhorn media guide. "...It marks the beginning of construction of one of the most long-awaited facilities in Texas sports. Twenty-five years ago, people talked of a basketball palace at the University of Texas which would be second to none in the nation. For 25 years, the dream has remained dormant. During 1974, construction is slated to begin on the new special events center." Described by the *Alcalde* as "UT's Astrodome," the 16,000-seat structure (originally pegged at $19 million) was expected to be ready for the 1977 season, but that was too optimistic. Gregory Gym, which was to serve as the home of Texas basketball for another four seasons, was making it hard for Leon Black and assistant coaches Dale Dotson and Skip Adams to recruit. Most of the young men they sought wanted an arena that was big, shiny and new, and the venerable gym on Speedway simply did not qualify.

The 1974 recruiting class, while far from a bust—four players earned three letters before they were through—was not a great one because there were no blue-chippers, no difference-makers. A lot was riding on the vets. John Mark Wilson, a tri-captain along with Harry Larrabee and Larry Robinson, had to quit playing because of his crippled knees. Robinson underwent a second knee operation in the summer, and no one knew if he would regain the spring and mobility that made him one of Texas' finest ever. Larrabee and Dan Krueger gave the Horns a set of short but talented guards.

The first three games of a challenging 12-game preconference schedule were at home. Mississippi floated into town on December 1 and dominated the Longhorns in a 75-59 win before 6,000 fans. Rebel guard Dave Shepherd scored 24, while Robinson looked rusty, hitting just three of 17 shots. UT was led by frosh guard Hank Bauerschlag (16). Robinson's performance against Mississippi State two days later was much better (25 points and 15 rebounds), but Texas still lost, 87-82. The Bulldogs had the poise to fight off a desperate Texas bid in the late minutes. Soph guard Rich Knarr beat Larrabee like a bass drum, scoring 32 points for the SEC visitors. No. 13 Kansas State had the horses, and their thoroughbred tendencies paid off in a 71-63 victory over UT. Jack Hartman's Big 8 champs won their third game, while Leon Black's Horns went 0-3. Lon Kruger (16) of the Wildcats and Larrabee (14) were the top scorers in the game, the first in which an experimental 30-second shot clock was used.

The Horns put on their traveling shoes and headed to Des Moines for a game with Drake. But they fell behind the taller and stronger Bulldogs by 17 at the half, and a nice comeback powered by JC transfer Tyrone Johnson (13 points and 10 rebounds) was not enough. Larry Haralson and Craig Davis rang up 38 of Drake's points. Black, who sought a reversal of fortune in Stillwater, did not get it. Oklahoma State used a pair of hot-shooting guards, K.C. Kincaide and freshman Ronnie Daniels, to turn back the Longhorns, 83-73. Larrabee and Tyrone Johnson both had 20 points in UT's fifth straight loss but one that gave Black encouragement. "I'm proud of these kids," he said. "I've never been 0-5 in my coaching career before, and I could have scheduled some wins.... We've got quality people with potential, and we're learning every time we go out there. Against this caliber of competition, you pay for every mistake you make."

With 19 points and 22 rebounds from Robinson, UT threatened to repeat the previous year's upset of Memphis State. The teams were tied at 78 with three minutes left when Gene Bartow's Tigers scored 10 consecutive points, attaining a 90-82 win at Gregory Gym. Billy Buford and Dexter Reed (23 each) were among five Memphis State players in double figures. It was the same song, seventh verse against Centenary on December 22. Robert Parish—getting ready for a 20-season NBA career—scored 29 points and got 14 rebounds as the Gents overcame a 13-point deficit to win, 97-94. Robinson (29 points and 14 rebounds) was outstanding, and he had help from freshman center Tommy Weilert (20), Tyrone Johnson (13) and Larrabee (12). Texas seemed ready to answer, once and for all, the question of how a team could be so consistently competitive and still not win.

Off to the worst start in school history, the young and hungry Longhorns traveled to Portland to play in the Far West Classic. Ron Lee scored 26 points in Oregon's 78-66 win over UT. Krueger and sub forward James Price came off the bench to keep it close. Duck coach Dick Harter flattered his SWC guests by calling them the best 0-8 team he had ever seen. And West Virginia coach Sonny Moran offered similar kudos when his Mountaineers edged Texas, 80-79. Robinson (25) and Jerome Anderson of WVU (22) were the top scorers in a game that hung in the balance until the very end. Nine straight losses recalled three of UT's worst seasons, 1931, 1955 and 1959, which led to the retirement of coaches Fred Walker, Slue Hull and Marshall Hughes, respectively. The streak ended with an inartistic 77-65 defeat of Army for seventh place in the tourney. Larrabee scored 15 and Greg Fountain 19 for the Black Knights.

Black repeatedly told his team to point toward conference play, they were getting better, they had met some tough competition, and to keep their heads up. But Texas had two more intersectional basketball rivers to cross, and both were defeats. Gary Link scored 22 and Al Eberhard 16 in Missouri's 86-76 win at Columbia. With Robinson and Krueger in foul trouble, young players like Ed Johnson, Phillip Davis, Bruce Baker and Rich Parson did well off the bench in the second half. In Austin, the Longhorns bowed to Oklahoma, 80-76, closing pre-SWC play with a 1-11 record. Barely a minute was left, the score was tied, and UT possessed the ball when the Sooners' Mike McCurdy picked off an errant pass and darted downcourt for the winning hoop.

He had remained cheery because his team was giving full effort, and Black may even have dreamed the impossible dream, that the Horns could sneak up on people and contend for or win the SWC. Regardless of Texas' awful record, it was not the year of the locust, and his players were with him. "We'll be there when it counts," Weilert said. "You've got to believe."

More than 6,000 fans had every reason to believe after witnessing UT's 104-53 annihilation of TCU at Gregory Gym. Dan Krueger, an emerging star, led the scoring parade of six Horns in double figures. It was the most thorough SWC victory since Arkansas ripped Baylor, 94-28, in 1945. Frog coach Johnny Swaim was beside himself after the game. He bolted the locker-room door and gave his players a tongue-lashing. Later, meeting with reporters, he smoked a cigarette and said, "They whipped us every way you can. I, as a coach, am ashamed."

SMU star Sammy Hervey was not only incorrigible, he was ineligible due to academics. The Mustangs, preseason cofavorites with Texas Tech, still had Ira Terrell, however. He played a fine game at Moody Coliseum, scoring 37 points and grabbing 14 rebounds despite being double-teamed throughout, but Texas won, 87-82. The Horns' bench depth paid off in the late going as more players were run at the tiring Terrell. Black, the recipient of two technical fouls, was praised by Dallas sportswriters for his handling of personnel during the game. After just two conference wins, the Longhorns were being taken seriously.

The college basketball world was buzzing about Notre Dame putting a halt to UCLA's 88-game winning streak when Texas and Rice met in Houston. The Horns were shaky and a bit undisciplined in the first half, but Robinson (32) and Price (15) carried them to an 82-71 win. Tim Moriarty, Danny Carroll and Scott Fisher had 12 apiece for Don Knodel's Owls.

Interest ran high when the two conference leaders, UT and Texas Tech, met at Gregory Gym for a Saturday afternoon game in late January. The Longhorns came from 15 points down to go ahead by one on a bucket by Robinson (38) in the final minute. Orangebloods in the throng of 7,000 believed it could only bring victory, but there was too much octane in the Red Raiders' tank to let that happen. While Rick Bullock, William Johnson and Richard Little combined for 67 points, it was the less-celebrated Phil Bailey and Steve Trncak who won the game at the end. Black, who had a shouting match with Tech coach Gerald Myers at the scorer's table, said it was decided by free throws, of which the red-clad visitors made 17 of 25 and Texas just five of 12.

Were the Horns back to their losing ways? No, they hit 13 of their first 18 shots against Texas A&M and cooled down only slightly the rest of the way, taking a 98-90 home victory. The Aggie zone defense was a step slow in covering Robinson (30), Krueger (24) and Larrabee (18), all of whom played 40 minutes. Randy Knowles scored 30 for A&M, whose coach, Shelby Metcalf, offered this quote: "Texas put on a fantastic shooting exhibition. Heck, I couldn't let our guys shoot from there without having a guilty conscience." A packed Gregory Gym could still intimidate opponents. With nearly 8,000 fervent fans sitting oh-so-close and the band and cheerleaders going at it, Metcalf took a look around and decided not to start his freshman guard.

Robinson, who had recently passed Wayne Doyal as the No. 2 career scorer at UT, led the Hog-killing brigade in a 96-81 defeat of Arkansas in Fayetteville. He poured in 38 points and grabbed 14 rebounds, prompting Dean Tolson (who had 29 points and 19 rebounds, himself) to say, "Robinson is a bad dude. But then again, he always has been." Some Arkansas boosters departed the premises when their team fell behind, 61-37, and missed a big comeback by Lanny Van Eman's forces to within nine before the Longhorns put a stop to it.

Baylor coach Carroll Dawson recalled how his last-second shot had given the Bears a big win at Gregory Gym in 1959. But that Longhorn team did not have Larry Robinson, and the 1974 team did, which is the main reason BU lost, 93-79. Robinson continued his string of superlative performances with 29 points and 15 rebounds. Baylor's frontcourt defense (Lee Griffin, Charlie McKinney and Gary McGuire) tried to stop Robinson with scant success, partly because Larrabee and Krueger were hitting from outside. Griffin scored 24 for the Bruins. Several hundred fans remained after the game and listened to public-address announcer Wally Pryor relay a radio broadcast of SMU's defeat of Texas Tech, putting the Longhorns in a tie for the lead.

That was very nice, but the same Ponies came to Austin four days later and beat Texas, 74-72, before 8,000 screaming fans. SMU coach Bob Prewitt, rumored to be on the way out and soon replaced by Pan American coach Abe Lemons, had Ira Terrell (25) and Oscar Roan, a tight end on the SMU football team, muscling Robinson all game long. The star Longhorn forward got 32 points, anyway. Larrabee's two free throws tied the game with 14 seconds left, but Zack Thiel did the same thing on the other end of the court seven seconds later to win it.

Black tried to warn his players. The 51-point defeat of TCU did not mean they should let up; in fact, the last-place Frogs were liable to have blood in their eyes. And the coach was right, as the Longhorns suffered a 72-71 OT loss in Fort Worth. SWC officials had long been criticized for their eagerness to blow the whistle, but Denny Bishop and LaVon Boyette called so few fouls that Texas took just 14 free throws and TCU just four, none of them in regulation. Robinson scored 29 points in a defeat that left Texas 7-14 overall and behind the eight ball in the conference race.

Record: 12-15

59 Mississippi 75
82 Mississippi State 87
63 Kansas State 71
72 Drake 80
73 Oklahoma State 83
82 Memphis State 90
94 Centenary 97
66 Oregon 78
79 West Virginia 80
77 Army 65
76 Missouri 86
76 Oklahoma 80
104 TCU 53
87 SMU 82
82 Rice 71
81 Texas Tech 85
98 Texas A&M 90
96 Arkansas 81
93 Baylor 79
72 SMU 74
71 TCU 72 (OT)
85 Rice 76
75 Texas Tech 74
88 Texas A&M 81
99 Arkansas 82
95 Baylor 84
61 Creighton 77

The surging Rice Owls, winners of three of their last four games, came to Austin looking for another victory. The last time they had won at Gregory Gym (1957), most of their players were in kneepants. It was a sloppily played game, won by the Longhorns, 85-76. Krueger rendered a 24-point performance and was at the center of an explosive sequence of events with three minutes left. Texas led by three when he hit a driving layup and was fouled by Tim Moriarty, who protested enough to merit a technical. Krueger converted both free throws and threw in a 25-foot bomb on the inbound play for six quick points. He overshadowed a fine game by the Owls' Danny Carroll (22 points and 16 rebounds). Black said gleefully, "We'll take it. We'll take anything we can get at this point."

Black's teams had lost 10 straight to Texas Tech, dating back to 1969. And in the last two seasons, the Red Raiders had made a fetish of winning close games, but they came out on the short end of a 75-74 verdict in Lubbock before 9,567 customers, some of whom threw ice and insults when things did not go their way. The fans may have taken their cue from Tech coach Gerald Myers, who ragged the officials all night long. Rick Bullock, the big player with the soft hands and light feet, was in early foul trouble and scored just nine points. Teammates Grady Newton and William Johnson combined for 41 points and 33 rebounds, more than half of Tech's totals. For the Longhorns, the great Robinson came through with 30 points and 14 rebounds. Extra motivation may have derived from comments by Shelby Metcalf of Texas A&M and Johnny Swaim of TCU that the Red Raiders would probably win the game and the SWC crown.

Although the Ags were out of the race, a record crowd of 8,241 gathered at G. Rollie White Coliseum to see them play the visiting "teasips." The place was so loud, it was shaking, but UT stayed cool. The senior leadership of Robinson (34) and Larrabee (26) was invaluable, and Krueger managed to secure 11 rebounds in the Horns' 88-81 win. Ed Johnson, always clever around the hoop, had 18 points and 12 rebounds. Randy Knowles (21 points and 13 rebounds) was the Aggies' best. The game ended unpleasantly when Texas A&M freshman guard Mike Johnson took a poke at Larrabee, causing both benches to empty.

The Larry and Harry show made its final Gregory Gym appearance on February 26 against Arkansas. Prime movers in the 1972 cochampionship run, they had the Longhorns on the verge of another title in 1974. Texas was tight early, but the Hogs got roasted, 99-82, before a packed house. Rickey Medlock and Dean Tolson combined for 47 points, while the two men of the hour, Robinson and Larrabee, totaled 48. Both received sustained ovations from the crowd and their teammates when Black pulled them toward the end of the game.

On March 2, Texas Independence Day, the Longhorns achieved freedom of another sort with the first undisputed SWC title since 1963. They got it with some help from the SMU Mustangs, conquerors of Texas Tech in Lubbock earlier in the day. Heart O' Texas Coliseum was full, the Baylor defense was designed to stop Robinson, and Charlie McKinney (24 points and 22 rebounds) was too quick for UT centers Tommy Weilert and Rich Parson. Nevertheless, Texas won, 95-84, with 26 points from Krueger, 22 from Larrabee and 20 from Robinson, named SWC player of the year for the second time. Robinson, who led the conference in scoring (22 points per game in the full season and 28 in SWC play) was the first Longhorn to do that since Billy Arnold in 1968, and 15 years would pass until it happened again.

And Black, the object of alumni grousing two months earlier, was chosen coach of the year. He had performed a remarkable feat with the 1974 Horns. "They could have died of a broken heart during the preconference losing streak," wrote Lou Maysel of the *Austin American-Statesman*. "But they pulled off a tremendous coup.... What has changed mainly for Black is an unbelievably long run of bad luck with injuries, although a partial turnover in manpower and a lesson or two in public relations may have helped."

The Longhorns had grown accustomed to the SWC's 30-second experiment, but there would be no shot clock in the playoffs. The Super Pit on the North Texas State campus in Denton was the scene of the Longhorns' first-round NCAA date with No. 19 Creighton, coached by Eddie Sutton. Every player in the Blue Jays' starting lineup was between 6'4" and 6'8", and they were led by forward Gene Harmon, an 18-point-per-game scorer. Giant-killers against Houston in 1972, it looked like the Horns would do it again, holding a 57-51 lead with 9:30 left. But then Creighton put on a full-court press and scored 17 straight points, leaving a partisan Texas crowd subdued as the game was lost, 77-61. Harmon scored 22 for the Blue Jays, and Robinson 20 for the Longhorns. Although Creighton was a taller, more poised and experienced team, Black could only puzzle over UT's late self-destruction.

1975

Leon Black knew it was rebuilding time. His student assistant in 1975 was Harry Larrabee, largely responsible (along with Larry Robinson) for two SWC trophies adorning the foyer of Gregory Gym. Dan Krueger and Ed Johnson led a group of seven lettermen and two frontcourt newcomers, Mike Murphy and Gary Goodner. The age-old recruiting promise, "You'll be playing in a new arena by your senior season" would come true for Murphy and Goodner three years hence. Some players had to step up, and after a scrimmage with Southwest Texas and the Orange-White game, Black did not know who that would be.

The young Longhorns, with just one senior and two juniors, faced another difficult pre-SWC schedule, beginning with Brigham Young in Provo. It did not help that several Texas players were suffering from the flu when they took the court against the big Western Athletic Conference team. Gifford Nielsen, better known as quarterback of the Cougar football team, scored 19 points in an 80-72 defeat of UT. Murphy, honored with Robinson's number, 41, had a nice debut—16 points and 11 rebounds. But the Horns shot just 35 percent and were badly outrebounded, chilling indicators of things to come.

The first home game of the season was a 10-point loss to Murray State. Racer guards Jesse Williams and Zack Blasingame picked apart the Texas zone defense for a combined 39 points. Ed Johnson (16) and Tyrone Johnson (15) led the weakened and flat-footed Longhorns. Only a late surge against the Murray State subs made the score respectable.

Krueger, the team captain, was hospitalized with infectious mononucleosis, missed the next four games and really did not hit his stride until SWC play began. Taking his place in the backcourt, or trying to, were Hank Bauerschlag, Pat McClellan, junior college transfer Jeff Boothe and Tommy Delatour, who had spent the past two years on the Texas junior varsity. They took a brief tour of the southland, stopping first in Shreveport. Leon "Black Magic" Johnson had 25 points and Robert Parish 17 in Centenary's 96-71 throttling of the Horns. The Gentlemen shot 64 percent and had a 16-rebound edge. Tyrone Johnson (14), UT's top scorer, said of Parish: "He should be a pro now. He's wasting his time playing college ball." About 3,000 fans gathered in Tad Smith Coliseum to see Ole Miss and Texas tangle. Bob Mahoney (21) had the Rebels up by 16 at intermission, and things looked hopeless, but Bauerschlag scored 25 second-half points to forge a tie with eight minutes left. Still, the Horns lost, 82-74.

Back in the friendly confines of Gregory Gym, the Longhorns played a strong game against Drake but fell in overtime, 103-98. A jump shot by Ed Johnson (24) put Texas ahead by 11 with 6:34 to play. However, the Bulldogs took command gradually and then with a rush. The extra period was close for the first two minutes, after which it was all Drake. Larry Haralson led the Missouri Valley Conference team with 30 points. Reminiscent of 1974 when the Longhorns dropped their first nine games, they went 0-6 when Oklahoma State won, 73-63. Ronnie Daniel and Olus Holder scored 18 each, and Andy Hopson collected 19 rebounds for Guy Strong's Cowboys. UT held a one-point halftime lead but grew cold in the last 20 minutes. For the fifth straight game, no Longhorn player had as many as 10 rebounds. And to compound matters, one of the key big men, Tyrone Johnson, suffered an ankle injury that kept him out for the next five weeks.

Krueger was back, or maybe halfway back, and he made a lot of difference in a 63-59 victory over Northwestern before 2,000 fans at Gregory Gym. His 11 points, five assists and steadying influence were needed in a hotly contested game with 13 lead changes. That December 23 victory made Christmas a little merrier in Austin. Wildcat coach Tex Winter paid tribute to the Longhorns' energetic performance, and Black said, "Having Dan out there was worth a great deal to us. He's one of the best guards in the country."

The next game was at the 14,000-seat LSU Assembly Center, later named in honor of Pete Maravich. Dale Brown's Tigers could have used an extra 40-odd points, Maravich's usual output, in a 78-63 loss to UT. Superb defense and a newly discovered ability to cope with late-game pressure helped the Horns win. Murphy scored 26, and Rich Parson got 10 rebounds for Texas, while Glenn Hansen (16 points and 13 rebounds) led the Bayou Bengals. The excitable Brown was tagged with two technical fouls.

Missouri soph Scott Sims picked Krueger's pocket twice in the final 70 seconds, enabling the Tigers to take a rough and exciting 64-60 victory at Gregory Gym.

Jim Kennedy scored 19 for the Big 8 visitors, and Bruce Baker had a season-high 18 for UT. At the half, the all-time Longhorn team was announced, consisting of Jack Gray, Bobby Moers, Slater Martin, Jay Arnette and Larry Robinson, the first four of whom were present and got an appropriate cheer from 3,000 fans. A panel of 73 coaches, officials, writers and players were doing the same thing at each of the SWC schools to commemorate 60 years of conference basketball. And the man who got the most votes of all was Martin, followed closely by his late-1940s contemporary, Jackie Robinson of Baylor.

UT traveled to Mobile for the Senior Bowl Tournament, first beating Louisiana Tech, 81-68, before a paltry 600 fans. Murphy (16) led four Longhorns in double figures, while Mike McConathy scored 14 for the Bulldogs. South Alabama, host of the tournament, still had some players who had helped engineer a 14-point defeat of Texas in the 1973 opener. The Jaguars, averaging 98 points and 60 rebounds per game, appeared in control of affairs early. But Ed Johnson (18), Delatour (16) and Krueger (13) came alive and put the Horns up by five at the half, and that was the final margin in an 80-75 victory. Johnson was chosen most valuable player in UT's first tournament championship since 1956.

The recent turnaround, with four wins in the last five games, had come against teams with losing records, but so what? The Longhorns were happy to be winning again, and the memory of 1974 was fresh. They were defending SWC champs, after all. Because of a scheduling quirk, however, they did not begin conference play for two more weeks and lost their competitive edge. The 30-second shot clock used the previous season was gone, largely due to Eddie Sutton, the aggressive new coach at Arkansas. He successfully politicked against it. A graduate of Oklahoma State and a devotee of Hank Iba, Sutton liked to play slow and wait for a good shot, if not a perfect one. As the season developed, some teams began reverting to the stall, a ploy never popular with fans. Texas and SMU kicked off conference play in Dallas, where the Ponies got 17 points from John Sagehorn to win going away, 74-59. Black evinced keen disappointment in his team's showing: "We just didn't play well and got what we deserved." That was against a Mustang team without star center Ira Terrell, suspended for one year for associating with an agent.

In three days of practice before meeting Texas Tech at Gregory Gym, Black called for more intensity, rebounding and defense. The old gym was packed for the Saturday night game, one that concluded in dramatic fashion. With the score tied, Krueger drove along the key for a layup, but 6'6" William Johnson blocked it, provoking screams of goaltending from the UT bench. After a timeout, Johnson launched a fallaway jumper over Parson to win it, 59-57. Johnson and Phil Bailey had 20 each for the Red Raiders, and Krueger managed 15 for Texas.

The Heartbreak Horns lost again, 74-72, to TCU at Daniel-Meyer Coliseum. They made a courageous comeback from 16 points down, and Krueger's 15-foot jumper sent it into overtime. But two turnovers and half a dozen missed shots, some from close range, killed their chances. Lynn Royal had 16 points and Bill Bozeat 11 for the Horned Frogs, while Krueger and Ed Johnson scored 15 and 14, respectively.

Record: 10-15

72 Brigham Young 80
69 Murray State 79
71 Centenary 96
74 Mississippi 82
98 Drake 103 (OT)
63 Oklahoma State 73
63 Northwestern 59
78 LSU 63
60 Missouri 64
81 Louisiana Tech 68
80 South Alabama 75
59 SMU 74
57 Texas Tech 59
72 TCU 74 (OT)
74 Texas A&M 80
52 Arkansas 56
63 Baylor 62
60 Rice 59
70 Baylor 69
68 Rice 62
70 SMU 62
63 TCU 62
51 Texas Tech 78
56 Arkansas 68
63 Texas A&M 74

Texas A&M coach Shelby Metcalf, the sage of the Brazos, had written his doctoral dissertation on crowd behavior at SWC basketball games. And what he saw on February 1 at Gregory Gym was typical for the ancient rivalry—7,000 fans all but participating in a game played with unflagging fury. Krueger (30) put Texas ahead by two with 7:18 left, but the Ags were in charge from then on, winning by a score of 80-74. Metcalf got 17 points from John Thornton, 16 from Sonny Parker and 13 from Ray Roberts. Officials Tommy Taylor and Shorty Lawson did a whistle duet, calling 57 fouls.

The UT cagers were going after Pork skins at Fayetteville and appeared on the way to victory when Arkansas scored 10 straight points and won, 56-52. Weilert and Kent Allison (16 each) led their teams in scoring. It was a game featuring physical contact, two technical fouls and several outbursts of temper, all of which pleased a crowd of 5,906. The television screen did not convey all that happened at Barnhill Fieldhouse. A recently formed group of fans known as the "Mad Hatters" dressed in garish garb, stationed themselves behind the visitors' bench and hurled a steady stream of insults. Ice and coins were thrown, too.

Black looked over the wreckage of a 0-5 SWC record and said, "We're gaining experience but losing basketball games." They were about to start winning because the soft part of the schedule had arrived. Dan Krueger was the key to most of the victories that followed. He made two free throws with 10 seconds left to take a 63-62 lead over Baylor in Waco. The Bears' Billy Carlisle was fouled soon after that but missed the front end of a one-and-one, and the game was over. Ed Johnson and James Weaver of BU were the top scorers with 19.

Krueger's two free throws with 35 seconds left gave UT a three-point lead against Rice in a game that ended with the Longhorns ahead, 60-59. Owl coach Bob Polk was content to play at a snail's pace, once having his players pass the ball for two minutes to force a change in Texas' defense. A slim Gregory Gym crowd booed incessantly. Krueger had 17 points and 11 assists, while Tim Moriarty scored 20 for last-place Rice.

The Bears and Horns met for the second time in eight days, and the result was startlingly similar. Billy Carlisle of Baylor made just one of six potential free throws in the last three minutes, while Krueger was a cool six of six down the stretch in Texas' 70-69 home win. He finished with 19 points, six assists and just two turnovers in 40 minutes. "Dan's a winner," Black said. "We knew that when we recruited him. He could average 25 points per game if we needed him to."

Twenty-five is exactly what Krueger scored in a 68-62 defeat of Rice in Houston, but no last-second heroics were necessary. The Owls made just 22 of 63 field-goal attempts, and only guard Charles Daniels (27) could hit. Danny Carroll pulled down an impressive 21 rebounds.

Bob Prewitt's SMU Mustangs had lost four of their last five outings, and they fell again in Austin, 70-62. The game was tied at 58 with five minutes left when the Longhorns reeled off 12 straight points. Delatour scored 20, and Tyrone Johnson, back from a mid-December ankle injury, had 12. Joe Swedlund led the Ponies with 14 points. Krueger worked his magic one more time in a pulse-pounding 63-62 win over TCU at Gregory Gym. Four of his teammates (Johnson, Johnson, Weilert and Delatour) outscored him, but he was surely the one to take the big shot. Gary Landers had given the Frogs a one-point lead with 27 seconds left, so Krueger surveyed the defense and drilled a 20-foot basket. Lynn Royal scored 19 for TCU, and Bill Bozeat had 13 points and 13 rebounds.

The Longhorns, winners of six straight games, left town for the first time in two weeks to play the Texas Tech Red Raiders, who had an even longer winning streak of eight. Rick Bullock, leading the SWC in scoring and rebounding, had been quiet in the earlier game in Austin, but he scored 27 points in Tech's impressive 78-51 win. Tyrone Johnson had 14 points and 12 rebounds, while Krueger played a miserable game, making just one of seven shots. The Raiders, Aggies and Razorbacks, clearly the top echelon of the SWC in 1975, were engaged in a furious fight to the finish. Black took no pride in the spoiler role because he wanted to win, but there were no more victories for Texas that season.

Eddie Sutton brought perhaps the best Arkansas team in 30 years to Austin on March 4. Since his hiring a year earlier, Sutton had complained about officials, competition, budgets, facilities (he had no kind words for Gregory Gym) and almost everything pertaining to the SWC. Although he stepped on a lot of toes, some people regarded him as a much-needed breath of fresh air. The Razorbacks made just 10 of 29 shots in the first half and trailed by five, but Sutton straightened them out in the locker room with some strong words. Charles Terry, brother of ex-Hog great Martin Terry, scored 18 points in the visitors' 68-56 win. Krueger (16) and Tyrone Johnson (15) comprised most of UT's offensive output. The *Daily Texan* speculated about "dark days" for Black, who seemed haggard and drained after the loss to Arkansas.

Tyrone Johnson, who had considered quitting a few weeks earlier due to injury, scored a team-high 21 (his best as a Longhorn) in a season-ending 74-63 loss to Texas A&M in College Station. All-SWC performers Barry Davis and Sonny Parker combined for 31 points and 20 rebounds. The Aggies had won the title, their 20 victories were a school record, and they were headed for the NCAA playoffs. Shelby Metcalf celebrated by swigging champagne in the locker room at G. Rollie White Coliseum.

1976

Construction of the Special Events Center had gone slower than expected, pushing its completion date back a year. But the striking, circular building dubbed the "Super Drum" by the media was gradually taking shape across the street from Brackenridge Hospital, and anticipation of the approaching new era in Texas basketball was felt by everyone. Other things were happening in the bicentennial year, as well. The University of Houston became a full-fledged member of the Southwest Conference, causing fears of Cougar domination that proved unjustified. The number of conference games on television doubled, with several weeknight games being aired. And the SWC instituted a postseason tournament, a staple of the Atlantic Coast Conference for years and an idea whose popularity was growing. Texas coach Leon Black questioned the desirability of making the regular-season champion prove all over again its right to an NCAA playoff berth. As George Breazeale of the *Austin American-Statesman* wrote, "The SWC's new brain child represents the ultimate implementation of the theory that sports turnstile-keepers learned long ago: eternal hopes mean extra gate receipts."

Black was still talking about building a national contender in Austin. He had used a lot of players in 1975, sometimes at the expense of winning games, to prepare for a better 1976 (the last year for a junior varsity program), but the annual sportswriters poll conducted by the *Lubbock Avalanche-Journal* put the Longhorns seventh out of nine teams. Dan Krueger was back for his senior year, serving again as captain, and there were three frosh—6'5" Ovie Dotson from San Antonio, 6'8" Carl Belcher from Houston and a slim 17-year-old guard from Pennsylvania named Johnny Moore. He had been located by UT assistant coach Skip Adams while playing in an all-star game in Pittsburgh and was undaunted by the prospect of going to school so far from home. Sports information director Jones Ramsey said, "Moore's got charisma.... With his ability and moves, and the way he owns the crowd, he'll fill up this place and the new one, too."

The Longhorns helped Oklahoma inaugurate its new 12,000-seat Lloyd Noble Arena but were ungracious visitors in a 60-55 victory. Krueger scored 22 points, mostly on long-range jumpers, drives and a couple of off-balance shots in the lane. Gary Goodner scored 16 and Ed Johnson had 12 rebounds. Rick McNeil tallied 14 for the chilly (36 percent) Sooners. From Norman, UT trekked north to Stillwater to engage Oklahoma State. The Cowboys rallied to win, 88-73, with 34 points from Ronnie Daniel. Krueger, who fouled out for only the third time in his four-year career, combined with Moore to score 22 of the Horns' first 28 points.

Mississippi had beaten Texas five straight times, and the Longhorns repaid that southern hospitality with a 67-65 victory at Gregory Gym. Rebel coach Cob Jarvis complimented Moore, who led a second-half comeback and scored 22, the same as Walter Actwood of Ole Miss. Black won his 100th game as UT head coach when the Horns downed California-Poly Pomona, 77-66, in Austin before 2,000 fans. Krueger scored 26 and Moore 19, while the Broncos, playing their first year of major-college basketball, were led by Jack Gamulin (21) and Joe Sills (20). After starting the previous two seasons with nine and six losses, respectively, the Longhorns' early 3-1 record looked quite nice.

Record: 9-17

60 Oklahoma 55
73 Oklahoma State 88
67 Mississippi 65
77 California-Poly Pomona 66
79 Centenary 87
63 Fairleigh-Dickinson 59
86 Brigham Young 91 (OT)
86 Cornell 60
70 Centenary 75
70 Baylor 72
84 SMU 96
77 Baylor 82
61 Texas Tech 67
58 Houston 63
59 Arkansas 57
74 Rice 56
70 TCU 73
60 Texas A&M 72
69 Texas A&M 85
76 SMU 79
60 Texas Tech 71
95 Houston 86
68 Arkansas 75
90 Rice 70
81 TCU 89
90 SMU 103

The first part of a home-and-home series with Centenary began in Shreveport on December 13. Robert Parish, playing with a sprained foot, scored 29 in the Gentlemen's 87-79 win. UT stayed close for the first 35 minutes, but 17 turnovers and a 13-rebound deficit took their toll.

Krueger (22) and Mike Murphy (20) scored more than half of the Longhorns' points.

They got back on the winning track with a ragged 63-59 defeat of Fairleigh-Dickinson before 2,000 fans in Austin. Al LoBalbo, basketball coach at the small New Jersey school, went ballistic on the bench, watching SWC refs Tony Stigliano and Jim Harvey call 12 offensive fouls. "We've played all over the country, and I've never seen officiating like this," he muttered after the game. "It's hard to make any comment on our offense because the officials never gave us a chance to get it started." FDU forward George Lighty led both teams in scoring with 24.

Krueger registered a career-high 35 points in Texas' 91-86 overtime loss to Brigham Young in the first round of the Kiwanis Invitational in Norfolk. Given up for dead after trailing by 14 at the half, the Longhorns clawed back and nearly won. The Cougars were led by Jay Cheesman (26) and Verne Thompson (21). UT shot 61 percent the next night and had a 14-rebound edge over a tall Cornell team, taking an 86-60 win. Murphy (20) was one of five UT players in double figures, while their Ivy League opponents got 20 points from center Stan Brown. It was a poorly attended tournament, as only 1,100 people witnessed the Longhorns' two games.

The cover of the Longhorn basketball media guide featured Dan Krueger and Leon Black in front of the partially finished Special Events Center.

The final nonconference game of the season was a 75-70 loss to Centenary in Austin. Robert Parish, the least-publicized great player in the nation (he did not even make second-team all-America), had 32 points and 14 rebounds before fouling out with three minutes left and the Gents clinging to a fragile three-point lead. But the Horns could not capitalize on that golden opportunity and got beat. Krueger scored 28, keeping his field-goal percentage at 59 percent by hitting 12 of 20 and staying among the NCAA free throw leaders by sinking four of four. Murphy had another fine game with 21 points and 14 rebounds.

SWC play began at Gregory Gym when the Longhorns entertained Baylor. The Bears had a nine-point lead at the half, extended it to 15 and saw it shrink to two in the game's frantic last seconds, which featured a tussle between Goodner and Arthur Edwards. BU's Memphis recruits, Larry Spicer and Tony Rufus, combined for 44 points in the 72-70 victory. Texas got 21 points from Moore and some overdue contributions from the bench, especially Belcher and Dotson. "We were going through the motions defensively for 25 minutes and just waited too long," Black said.

The Longhorns had two road games in three days, beginning with Sonny Allen's SMU Mustangs. He had brought a reputation for racehorse offense to Dallas, but pressure defense was just as responsible for a 96-84 defeat of Texas. The Saturday afternoon game was practically over with 10 minutes left because the Ponies had a 31-point lead, although a combination of SMU second-stringers and a good UT rally affected the final count. Moore (22) and SMU's Ira Terrell (21) led their teams in scoring. At Heart O' Texas Coliseum, Baylor guards Billy Carlisle, Danny McDaniel and Tom Callahan penetrated the UT defense repeatedly, building a nine-point lead with nine minutes to go. Bear coach Jim Haller then called for the delay game, evincing boos from many of the 6,300 fans present. The Longhorns got to within one, but Larry Spicer and Tony Rufus made some key shots in an 82-77 win for the green and gold. Moore (18) and Belcher (17) were two poised freshmen.

Tempers were by no means tepid when the Horns and Red Raiders met in Austin, as officials LaVon Boyette and Alex Louis called four technical fouls in trying to keep order. Rick Bullock had 32 points and 17 rebounds in Texas Tech's 67-61 win, the eighth straight at Gregory Gym. The three UT frosh, Moore, Belcher and Dotson, were all in double figures. For the first time all season, Black went with a straight man-to-man defense, but the Longhorns could not seem to get any breaks.

Houston and Texas had last met in a regular-season basketball game in 1955, and much had happened since then. Guy Lewis' Cougars had been to the mountaintop, or at least close, with Elvin Hayes in the late 1960s and did a lot to hasten integration of the SWC, of which they were finally a member. At seven-year-old, 10,000-seat Hofheinz Pavilion, the Cougars jumped to a 20-2 lead after five minutes, dooming the Longhorns to a fifth straight conference loss. To their credit, Black's players did not give up and brought the final score to 63-58. UH's star guard, Otis Birdsong, had a quiet 17 points.

The Longhorns were winless in the SWC but not hopeless, as Eddie Sutton brought his Arkansas Razorbacks into Gregory Gym. While they had yet to gain national fame as the "triplets," Marvin Delph, Ron Brewer and Sidney Moncrief adorned the Hogs' roster. UT threw a smothering zone defense on them and got some clutch shooting and rebounding on the way to a 59-57 win before 5,000 screaming fans. Krueger, Moore, Goodner and Murphy reached double figures, and Dotson, Rich Parson and Tommy Weilert all helped end the victory drought. Delph scored 16 for Arkansas but made just eight of 23 from the field. Sutton continued to flout the SWC coaches' "gag rule," bellyaching about two late traveling calls and making accusations of home cooking, officiating influenced by the crowd.

Things were really bad in Houston, where six players who had been kicked off the 2-14 Owl squad formed the Rice Alternate Team, a.k.a. RAT, and challenged the remaining players to a public game to see who would finish the season. Rice coach Bob Polk did his best to ignore the controversy, and the fans were ignoring the team as a whole; just 1,000 showed up at Autry Court to see an easy 74-56 UT win, keyed by 17 points from Krueger.

Just when they were getting used to winning again, the Longhorns dropped a 73-70 game to TCU at Gregory Gym. Texas took 24 more shots and outrebounded the Horned Frogs by 21, but 26 percent shooting from Moore and Krueger did not help, nor did some crucial late turnovers. Only Murphy (16 points and 11 rebounds) played well for UT, while coach Johnny Swaim got 20 points from Randy Boyts and 18 each from Rick Hensley and Gary Landers. "I saw something in Fort Worth that had us 25-point underdogs to Texas," said Landers, a senior who had lost five times to the Horns. "But I had a feeling we had a chance."

The Longhorns and league-leading Aggies had two straight games together, first in Austin and then in College Station. A pair of fine frosh, Karl Godine and Jarvis Williams, had helped Houston Kashmere win two state championships, and both were in the starting lineup for Texas A&M when the old rivals tipped off before a packed house on January 28. Partisan fans were hopeful when a Goodner hoop with 11 minutes left put the Horns up by one, but that was, rather amazingly, the last UT field goal of the evening as the Aggies ran to a 72-60 victory. Veterans Barry Davis and Sonny Parker combined for 42 points and 24 rebounds. The rematch at Aggieland was a fight-infested 85-69 A&M victory. Krueger led the Longhorns with 26, while Godine had 24 and Parker 21 for the Ags.

Leading SMU by three and in possession of the ball with 2:30 left, Texas was in fairly good shape, but a series of turnovers led to six points for the Mustangs, and they stole a maddening 79-76 game in Austin. Guard Mike Jaccar scored 20 and Ira Terrell (who never lost at Gregory Gym, in high school or college) had 19 points and 13 rebounds. Krueger scored 28 for the snakebitten Horns.

Mired in eighth place with a 2-9 SWC record, UT went to the South Plains to meet 9-2 Texas Tech. The Longhorns shot 34 percent and played a lifeless game that distressed Black greatly, losing by a score of 71-60. Rick Bullock's 23 points made him the Red Raiders' all-time leading scorer.

In desperate need of a confidence-boost, Texas hosted Houston at Gregory Gym before 4,300 spectators. The Cougars were having trouble winning on the road, a trend that continued in a 95-86 Longhorn victory. UH got 34 points from Otis Birdsong and 20 from forward David Marrs but could not stay with the Texas fast break. Krueger and Moore, the coldest of the Longhorns in Lubbock, poured in a combined 50 points, and Ed Johnson (who had just returned from a foot injury) scored 14 points, got 15 rebounds and forced several Houston turnovers.

For the first time since 1968, Black took the team to Little Rock to face the Razorbacks. Barton Coliseum, recently damaged in a storm, held 7,200 fans who witnessed a 75-68 Arkansas victory. Daryll Saulsberry and Charles Terry, two of five Hogs in double figures, took control of the game in the second half. The Longhorns shot poorly, committed 18 turnovers and missed many opportunities.

They were in Arkansas when the long-rumored news broke that SWC faculty representatives had declared Karl Godine and Jarvis Williams of Texas A&M ineligible. It all began in September when Black sent a letter to conference commissioner Cliff Speegle, suggesting an investigation of the circumstances of their recruitment. The SWC hired an agency, which determined that "athletic interests" of A&M had provided the two young men with new cars, jobs paying unusually high salaries and washer-dryers for each of their mothers. Godine and Williams appealed, were reinstated briefly by a federal judge and finally ruled ineligible by the SWC for the rest of the 1976 season and all of 1977. A&M was reprimanded and lost two scholarships, but no games were forfeited by the new champs. However, Aggie supporters vociferously denounced Black, and with the exception of Sonny Allen of SMU, none of his fellow conference coaches came to his defense. Black acknowledged writing the letter but refused to provide extra information to an increasingly aggressive media. For the remainder of the season, basically the last 10 days of February, his life was made miserable.

The final home game was a 90-70 defeat of the hapless Rice Owls, "a game as exciting as watching a sailing regatta without wind," according to the *Daily Texan*. Elbert Darden scored 24 for Rice, and Goodner had 23 points and 18 rebounds for UT. Krueger, a staple of Longhorn basketball since 1973, scored 16 in his last game at Gregory Gym.

Krueger tickled the twine for 25 points in an 89-81 loss to injury-hampered TCU before a meager crowd in Fort Worth. The Horned Frogs, recent victims of Rice, got all but one point from Gary Landers, Randy Boyts, Robert Hollie and Thomas Bledsoe. It was the first time in 17 years that TCU had swept Texas.

The regular season ended with the Longhorns 9-16 overall and 4-12 in the conference, not a record that would ordinarily warrant postseason play, but the SWC's tournament was soon to begin. Theoretically, Rice or Texas (the bottom) could beat Texas A&M or Texas Tech (the top) and go on to the NCAA playoffs, although that did not happen in 1976. The Longhorns dropped a 103-90 decision to SMU at Moody Coliseum. Ira Terrell and Pete Lodwick of the Ponies scored a combined 52 points, while Krueger ended a fine career with 27 points (492 for the season, fifth highest in UT history). Weilert, Moore and Johnson all had 15.

But the real news was Leon Black's announcement of his resignation after the game. While the Godine/Williams matter had wounded him, he insisted that was not the reason for quitting. Rather, his own assessment of the Texas basketball program, coupled with the approaching completion of the Special Events Center, convinced him that another man should coach the Longhorns. He stoutly denied any pressure from athletic director Darrell Royal and professed his love for the University of Texas, staying in the UT athletic department in several less-visible jobs for the next 20-plus years. By consensus, Black had been the "cleanest" coach in the Southwest Conference, and he never took his frustrations out on the wrong people, as some coaches tended to do. Leon Black, who oversaw integration of Longhorn basketball, left with two SWC titles and a record of 106-121 in nine seasons.

1977

On the heels of a season-ending loss to SMU, the team bus had barely rolled into Austin before athletic director Darrell Royal began receiving applications and recommendations for a successor to ex-coach Leon Black. It was a job coveted by many people, if only because the Special Events Center was inching toward completion. Whoever was hired would have the honor of playing the last season at Gregory Gym and the first at the big new facility, which was expected to be the best in Texas and adjoining states. Bill Blakeley of North Texas and Wayne Yates of Memphis State were two candidates mentioned in the media, but Royal seemed to have his eye on AE "Abe" Lemons of Pan American, a small school in the Rio Grande valley. Sixteen days after Black's resignation, Lemons was introduced by Royal as the 20th coach in seven decades of University of Texas basketball. He was unlike all the others.

Lemons served in the merchant marine during World War II, played basketball at Oklahoma City University and coached there from 1956 to 1973. His Chiefs won 309 games and lost 179, reached postseason play nine times and led the nation in scoring three times. Lemons had an even higher winning percentage in three years at Pan Am, where he was also athletic director. Although Lemons claimed to be happy there, he yearned to perform on a bigger stage, and when Royal, his fellow Oklahoman (they had known each other since the 1940s) called, Lemons was ready to bargain. They agreed on a five-year contract at about $30,000 per year.

Far from an unknown figure in Austin, Lemons and his OCU teams had played the Longhorns numerous times, and other Southwest Conference teams, too. Bobby Knight of Indiana, Eddie Sutton of Arkansas and Guy Lewis of Houston were among coaches who hailed the move. But it was hard to say if Lemons' fame derived more from hoop acumen or comedy. The cigar-smoking, 53-year-old part-Cherokee Indian had a droll, spur-of-the-moment wit and was one of the greatest quote-makers in all of college athletics. A backporch philosopher, he was capable of delivering a stream of hilarious stories and one-liners and yet spewing venom, showing kindness to strangers and yet putting players deep in his doghouse. He spoke forthrightly, an admirable trait but one that would cause him trouble at UT. A walking, talking, wisecracking bundle of contradictions, Lemons was, above all, a fine basketball coach.

It was unclear, however, just what kind of team he would field in 1977. Leon Black and his assistants were responsible for two additions to the team, men who would play major roles in the success of the next few years—Jim Krivacs and Ron Baxter. A 6'1" guard from Indianapolis, Krivacs had been waiting in the wings during the previous season, giving Dan Krueger and Johnny Moore plenty of competition in practice. He had spent his freshman year at Auburn, saw little playing time and transferred to UT. An outstanding long-range shooter, Krivacs was somewhat of a defensive liability. Baxter, a brawny 6'4" forward who could operate at guard in a pinch, was coplayer of the year in the tough Los Angeles high school system. Assisting Lemons was Barry Dowd, a Longhorn player in the late 1950s who had coached at UT-Arlington for the past 10 years. Practices under Lemons consisted of lots of full-court scrimmaging, usually refereed by Krueger, a student assistant.

Lemons expressed disappointment with the team's status on the eve of the season opener with Oklahoma State. "We're not where I wanted to be at this stage," he said. "We're still looking for someone who likes to play defense and has that rare talent of running to the other end and throwing the ball in the basket. It'll be a miracle if they play good. Seems like whatever I say, they do the opposite." Nevertheless, Lemons' debut was a success, a 74-73 overtime defeat of the Cowboys at Gregory Gym. Long a believer in giving the crowd a ton of thrills, the new UT boss had just about all the excitement he could stand as his team blew several leads. The winning points came on a goaltending call against Oklahoma State's Andrew Jones on a shot by Krivacs. Gary Goodner of the Longhorns and Olus Holder of the visiting team were the top scorers with 19 apiece. The so-called "Alcindor rule" (passed in 1968 because of the dominance of Lew Alcindor, who had since taken the name Kareem Abdul-Jabbar) outlawing the dunk shot had finally been rescinded by the NCAA, and Austin fans got a look at it when Goodner busted one on the Cowboys' 7'3" center, Lonnie Boeckman.

Dave Bliss brought his OU Sooners to Austin and hung a 60-56 defeat on Texas, thanks largely to a combined 38 points from guard Cary Carrabine and forward John McCullough. Turnovers and poor shooting from the field and the free throw line cost UT the game. Krivacs (13) led the team in scoring, as he did two days later in a sloppy 78-63 win over Wisconsin-Stout. He hit 11 of 14 shots, including the kind of rainbow jumpers Longhorn fans soon came to associate with him. Baxter (20) had a two-fisted slammer-jammer that rocked the old gym, while center Brian Kennedy scored 22 for the Blue Devils. A third home victory came when UT stood off Southern California, 66-61. The lightning-quick Moore, perhaps the first player in Longhorn history to wear double-zero on his jersey, scored 22 points, and Greg White had 17 for Bob Boyd's Trojans. Mike Murphy went scoreless but grabbed 13 rebounds in a game that elicited a few compliments from Lemons, although he was concerned about a weak bench.

Darrell Royal's retirement after a great 20-year run as football coach had the attention of most UT sports fans when the Longhorn basketball team took to the road for the first time. Gary White scored 28 and Rickey Brown 21 in Mississippi State's whirlwind 91-89 overtime victory. Krivacs was hot again, scoring 27 points. His coach was hot, too, but in a different way. Lemons blasted the Southeastern Conference officials and Bulldog coach Kermit Davis for his team's roughhouse tactics. "I'll say one thing for sure," he fumed. "Mississippi State played its way right off our schedule tonight."

In contrast to the methods employed by his predecessor, Leon Black (or most coaches, for that matter), Lemons ran a loose ship for out-of-town games. No curfews, no blackboard sessions and no restrictions on when or where or what to eat. He expected his players to be ready and focused for every game, but he was not their guardian. "You think they can't get into sin before 10 o'clock?" he rhetorically asked Lou Maysel of the *Austin American-Statesman.* "If I find somebody goofing off, I'll do something, but otherwise I don't care what they do." He also preferred to schedule games in big cities likely to contain some UT alumni, places that might have a broadening influence on his players. During Lemons' years in the merchant marine and as coach of two little independent schools, he had done a lot of traveling. And whether it was an opponent he had faced many times before or one utterly unknown to him, Lemons put little faith in scouting reports.

December 23 was homecoming of a sort when Lemons took his Longhorns to Oklahoma City after a two-week exam layoff. He had played for the Chiefs and coached them for nearly two decades, and some of his former players were on hand to say hello. Guard Allen Leavell (18) led an early second-half drive that put OCU in front for good, although Texas made it close at the end before losing, 66-65.

Record: 13-13

74 Oklahoma State 73 (OT)
56 Oklahoma 60
78 Wisconsin-Stout 63
66 Southern California 61
89 Mississippi State 91 (OT)
65 Oklahoma City 66
67 Providence 81
76 Rhode Island 66
59 Texas A&M 68
73 Baylor 75
87 Texas A&M 73
73 SMU 74
73 Texas Tech 72
81 Houston 95
58 Arkansas 86
74 Rice 68
89 TCU 80
105 Centenary 81
75 Baylor 72 (2 OT's)
79 SMU 69
81 TCU 69
69 Texas Tech 87
84 Houston 95
61 Arkansas 73
90 Rice 51
70 Baylor 72

Basketball-hungry citizens stood on snow-stacked street corners in Providence, trying to get tickets to the Friar Invitational, but the Civic Center had a capacity of just 12,150. The tournament, underwritten by a large local bank, was very well run and a financial plum to the four teams involved—Providence, Rhode Island, Michigan (1976 NCAA runner-up and then No. 1 in the nation) and Texas. Lemons, not painfully shy about publicity, took the town by storm, as people were fascinated by the crusty southwesterner who had been compared more than once to Will Rogers. Dave Gavitt's Friars, who had lost just six of their last 73 games at home, strummed the Longhorns, 81-67, behind 26 points from guard Joe Hassett. Krivacs had 22 for Texas. The loss looked a little better after Providence beat Michigan in the championship game. Moore and Baxter combined for 41 points in UT's 76-66 defeat of Rhode Island in the consolation game. Sly Williams scored 27 for the Rams, who had entered the tourney with a 7-0 record. Senior post man Rich Parson, a clunky, wide-bodied player, had been booed by Gregory Gym fans early in the season but refused to be discouraged. He played aggressively, rebounded and made himself one of Lemons' reliables for the rest of the 1977 season. "I'm going to play him whether they like it or not," Lemons said after Parson's strong showing in Providence, and the boos stopped.

While there would seem to be nothing new under the basketball-coaching sun for Abe Lemons, his teams had never competed for a conference championship. The media practically awarded the SWC crown to Arkansas before the race began, assigning Texas and Texas A&M spots somewhere in the middle of the nine member schools. Not all of the tension over the events late in the 1976 season had dissolved when the two teams met in College Station, but orange and maroon were never compatible colors, anyway. Steve Jones scored 24 points in the Aggies' 68-59 win, "a classic display of bad basketball," according to George Breazeale of the *Austin American-Statesman*. Nowhere were the Longhorns worse than at the free throw line, making just five of 19. "This wasn't the worst performance of the year," Lemons said. "It was the worst performance of my life.... I guess the long trip over here did it." Shelby Metcalf, not a bad quipster himself, was just glad to get a victory.

Gregory Gym was a sweltering battle pit when the Horns hosted Carroll Dawson's Baylor Bears, who emerged as victors, 75-73. BU shot 74 percent from the field in the first half but had to withstand a late comeback led by Moore (22), Goodner (20) and Baxter (19). John Danks, an energetic freshman forward from Kentucky, displayed the kind of defense Lemons liked. The Bears got 22 points from Arthur Edwards.

The sophomore guard duo of Moore and Krivacs combined for 43 points in an 87-73 defeat of Texas A&M in Austin before a near-capacity audience. And Parson, the 6'8" Oregonian, had possibly his best game as a Longhorn with 17 points and 12 rebounds. The Ags, looking nothing like the team that went 26-4 in the SWC the previous two years, were led by freshman Steve Sylvestine (17).

A notoriously bad free throw shooter, Gary Goodner deserved better. He had played a fine game (14 points, 12 rebounds and enough picks to free Krivacs to score 22), but there he stood at the line while 8,446 SMU fans urged him to miss. The Longhorns trailed by one, and the clock showed six seconds when he launched an air ball. And yet the game was not over because Krivacs stole the inbounds pass and flipped the ball to Moore, whose 24-foot shot was too strong. With 20 points apiece from Pete Lodwick and Joe Swedlund, the Ponies won a rhubarb-filled contest, 74-73. The seventh loss of the young season equaled the number Lemons had endured in his last two years at Pan American. The UT coach, who liked to wear bright floral shirts during games, sometimes just put his head in his hands and moaned. He could not get used to losing and did not want his players to, either. Yet attendance at home games was up, and there was a sense that Texas basketball was finally turning into something more than an interlude between football and spring football. If the 1977 Longhorns had not thrown fear into the hearts of other teams, no one could doubt that the quality of play was much improved over the past decade.

Texas Tech paid a final visit to Gregory Gym and appeared to be on the way to a rout, leading by 14 points after 11 minutes of play. But Krivacs, Moore, Goodner, Baxter and Parson resurrected the Horns, and they came up with a 73-72 win before 5,500 fans. Krivacs hit two free throws to tie and go ahead with 17 seconds left, and then Goodner blocked Mike Russell's shot at the other end of the court. "We hustled and deserved to win," said Danks, who played 25 minutes in relief of the foul-plagued Moore. When the game was over, a mob of fans, one carrying a "we love Abe" sign, surrounded Lemons and television interviewer Frank Fallon. Red Raider coach Gerald Myers could only lament his team's 19 turnovers.

Krivacs' injured ankle did not prevent him from playing against Houston, but there was bad news on the academic front. Center Gary Goodner, a catalyst for some of UT's basketball success, had not passed enough courses and was out. For the game with the Cougars, Lemons chose to start 6'10" junior Tom Nichols in place of Goodner. Texas was no match for UH, led by incomparable guard Otis Birdsong, who scored 43 points in a 95-81 win at Hofheinz Pavilion. The second-leading scorer in the nation (and the SWC's first consensus all-American in 20 years), he was en route to the greatest offensive showing in the history of the conference—30 points per game and over 1,000 points for the season. Asked what he thought of Birdsong, Lemons replied mirthfully: "He's terrible, a poor shooter, not smart, shoots off the wrong foot, a real dog."

If Birdsong was a canine, Gregory Gym looked like a kennel when Arkansas came to town. Sidney Moncrief (leading the nation in shooting percentage), Ron Brewer, Marvin Delph and a roster of fine players were then 13-1 and on their way to the SWC crown but a first-round exit from the NCAA Tournament. The Razorbacks' 30-year drought was clearly over because they would finish first or second in the SWC from 1977 to 1985. Coach Eddie Sutton had a good thing going in Fayetteville. A crowd of 7,800 saw the Hogs inflict a brutal 86-58 defeat on Texas. The triplets were responsible for 56 of those points, including enough dunks to intimidate the referees, in the view of the *Daily Texan*. Among UT's players, only Baxter (16 points and 11 rebounds) held his own. The loss was so thorough that Lemons made no humorous comments afterward—postgame interviews were usually a roaring comedy hour—but he wielded a verbal machete at the quality of SWC officiating. The sneaker-clad Solomons who oversaw the Texas-Arkansas game assessed him yet another technical foul. Lemons, who had coached independents for 21 years, was still an independent, and when he learned that SWC commissioner Cliff Speegle desired a meeting, he claimed to await "ten lashes with a wet noodle."

Jim Krivacs (left) and Johnny Moore (below), UT's backcourt tandem of the late 1970s.

His team's 74-68 defeat of Rice in Houston was of less than epic proportions. "I ain't knocking winning," Lemons said. "But it's not often you can play that bad and win." Baxter scored 17 and Parson 13, and Ovie Dotson, in his first start of the year, got 10 rebounds. Elbert Darden scored 28 for the Owls, whose coach, Bob Polk, announced his resignation before the game. It had not been a successful run for Polk, since his teams won just 17 games in three years and just one on the road.

The TCU Horned Frogs, in the midst of an atrocious season (0-16 in the SWC, 3-23 overall), got squashed, 89-80, in Austin. Krivacs threw in arching jumpers from all over the court for 34 points, while Moore had 17 assists, seven steals and some dipsy-doo passing that the fans loved. Tim Marion and Daryl Braden had 22 points each for the Frogs. Coach Johnny Swaim summarized the game thus: "We told our kids Krivacs could hit those moon shots from 25 or 30 feet, but they stood there and watched him shoot."

The Longhorns were back in action at Gregory Gym the following Tuesday against Centenary, just coming off a defeat of Pan American, Lemons' old team. Forward Bobby White, averaging 22 points per game, was held to 10 by Dotson as the Gents suffered a 105-81 defeat. Their coach, Riley Wallace, was socked with three technicals and sent to the locker room early in the second half. Krivacs scored 28 and Baxter had another excellent game with 25 points and 13 rebounds. Lemons inserted substitute guard Hank Bauerschlag, and he responded by scoring 15 points and handing out four assists.

Carroll Dawson had suddenly resigned halfway through the Baylor season (succeeded by Jim Haller), and star forward Tony Rufus quit, but the Bears played UT tough at Heart O' Texas Coliseum before losing, 75-72, in double overtime. The hero of the game was Parson, who rebounded Baxter's missed shot with five seconds left and put up a five-foot shot that touched nothing but net. Moore scored 20, including a crucial three-point play at the end of regulation, and Larry Spicer had 22 for BU.

Time was running down on Gregory Gym. SMU's last visit there was not a pleasant one for followers of the Mustangs. Moore, recalling the one-point loss in Dallas, said, "I just wanted to kill them" after UT's 79-69 win. He and his backcourt buddy, Jim Krivacs, had 22 points each, and Dotson collected 13 rebounds, while T.J. Robinson scored 19 for the Ponies. Despite a late 17-point SMU spree, Lemons was happy for the win. Having once described his team as "a bunch of leftovers," he had changed his tune somewhat. "These guys are really making me proud," he said. "It kinda makes me wish I hadn't said all those ugly things about them at the beginning of the year."

The winning streak became six after an 81-69 defeat of TCU at Daniel-Meyer Coliseum. Johnny Swaim had recently made some Lemons-like comments about his own players, saying they were not inclined to play defense and were wild shooters. The Longhorns went 25 for 27 at the free throw line, but they lost the rebound battle, 35-29. Moore scored 27 points for Texas and Tim Marion 18 for TCU.

Mike Russell scored 32 points and got 12 rebounds in Texas Tech's 87-69 defeat of UT on a Saturday afternoon in Lubbock. He took full advantage of Parson, who was suffering stomach pains late in the season. Moore scored 23 for the Longhorns in a game enlivened by technicals on Lemons and Dowd. Lemons was furious afterward, chomping on a cigar and issuing stern denunciations of Denny Bishop, who imposed the two T's, and other "rabbit-eared refs." And the players, Baxter in particular, were not fond of the Red Raider fans, many of whom threw lemons and other citrus fruits. But Gerald Myers defended his fans and said, "It's no picnic down in Austin. They weren't giving pats on the back and saying 'nice shot.'"

Guy Lewis of UH agreed, calling Gregory Gym "an equalizer." His Cougars had been winning lately, and they won again, 95-84. Otis Birdsong bombarded UT's zone defense for 35 points, and Cecile Rose had 20. Baxter (17) led five Longhorns in double figures, but the team was tired, having played five games in 11 days. Seven thousand fans got the most excitement when Dotson blocked Birdsong's attempted dunk at the end of a fast break.

Because of injuries, sickness and dropouts, Dan Krueger was needed to hold a five-on-five scrimmage. It had been a long, hard winter for the Horns, who had a date with the soaring, scoring Razorbacks at newly enlarged Barnhill Arena. Eddie Sutton's team was the first from the SWC to warrant a top-ten ranking since the Jim Krebs-led SMU Mustangs in 1957. Arkansas rode the heroics of Marvin Delph (28) and Sidney Moncrief (19) to a 73-61 victory featuring lots of ferocious close-in combat. Krivacs scored 20 for Texas.

For the 20th straight time, Rice lost at Gregory Gym, and it was not even close: 90-51. Krivacs scored 31 points and earned a technical foul, just as he had against Arkansas, prompting him to say, "The refs are on a power trip or something." The Owls, meanwhile, were basketball mediocrity personified.

One of the first-round games in the SWC's postseason tourney was played in Austin, where Texas met Baylor, neither of whom had a snowball's chance in hell of getting by Arkansas or even Houston and moving into the NCAA playoffs. Sherman Patton's 25-foot shot just before the buzzer gave BU a 72-70 victory. Krivacs (24) and the Bears' Arthur Edwards (21) were the leading scorers.

The season was over. Abe Lemons had captivated the fans with his exuberance, turning UT hoops inside out. But he was glum, calling 1977 his longest season ever. He said ominously, "I'm not long for this league. I won't be in this league more than two years, I'll guarantee you that. I gotta find something else to do or I'm going to ruin the Texas program. They're not going to let me stay."

It was just a postgame, postseason depression for a man used to winning most of the time. Many exciting and satisfying events loomed in the near future, and Lemons was usually at the center of them. From a historical perspective, though, the key fact is that college basketball had bid adieu to Gregory Gym after 47 years. There was an annex on the south side, trees had sprouted and matured on the west and north, and wooden benches in the gallery had been worn smooth by the posteriors and feet of countless thousands of fans, but the gym still looked about the same as when it was unveiled in 1931. Easily the best facility in the Southwest Conference in the early years, Gregory Gym was far from that in the 1960s and 1970s. Intramurals and recreational sports continued to put it to good use, and Longhorn volleyball teams would play there until 1990. It got a $26-million renovation in 1996 and 1997 in order to serve future generations of UT students. If buildings could talk, Gregory Gym might have more stories to tell than any other on the Forty Acres.

1978

The 1978 Texas Longhorns were not expected to do anything special, even with four starters (Gary Goodner, Jim Krivacs, Johnny Moore and Ron Baxter) back. Of the seven newcomers, only one turned into a major contributor, and he was among the least touted: Tyrone Branyan, a California JC transfer located by Abe Lemons' chief recruiter, Steve Moeller. Branyan was a slow, low-altitude 6'7" forward, but he could play the game, especially on the offensive end. By the time Southwest Conference competition began, he was a fixture in the lineup.

The season started on November 26 in Baxter's hometown, Los Angeles, against Southern California. A 10-point halftime lead vanished because of too many turnovers and a scoring surge by the Trojans' Cliff Robinson (19) and Paul Henderson (18). Baxter, who had a large cheering section in the crowd of 3,900, got 20 of his 24 points in the second half, but it was not quite enough as USC took a 65-64 victory.

Three days later came the big event, the opening of the $37-million, 16,231-seat Special Events Center. University officials had hoped to inaugurate it with something other than a basketball game, but delays in construction prevented that. They also gnashed their teeth at the media's almost constant use of the term "Super Drum" well into the early 1980s. Five hundred feet in diameter and 97 feet tall, it was a flat-roofed, steel-framed edifice of reinforced concrete, precast panels and glass. On the inside and outside, the building still had a rough, unfinished look when 12,650 hoop fans and curiosity-seekers attended the Texas-Oklahoma game. UT business manager Al Lundstedt reported more than 2,000 season tickets had been sold, costing $52 for 13 games. The contrast between the Super Drum and old Gregory Gym could not have been more stark. It was away from the center of campus, with parking on-site and in several nearby state-owned garages. Restrooms, concessions and other amenities were no longer difficult to find, and the 21-inch theater-type seats found favor with everyone. A large scoreboard/message board hung from the ceiling, and acoustical materials and speakers allowed for precise, high-quality sound control. Games would be played on a portable court (225 pieces of 4' X 8' maple, each weighing 175 pounds) with orange trim and "Texas" in lariat script at both ends. Because it was a multipurpose building, also to be used for concerts, speeches, trade shows and other events, compromises were made in its design. From a basketball standpoint, some of the home-court advantage was lost; fans were no longer within arms' reach of the players. But only the most sentimental alumni could have yearned for Gregory Gym after the move. It had taken a long time and a lot of Frank Erwin's political will, but UT finally owned a big-league, showplace facility.

On a cold, drizzly evening, the first game ever held there was a prelim, a three-point victory for Jody Conradt's Texas women's team over Temple Junior College. That was followed by some pomp and circumstance as the entire Longhorn Band played "The Eyes of Texas" and an oversized Texas flag was unfurled. Finally, the Longhorns and Sooners tied one on. OU had the top scorer, John McCullough (30), but UT had the speed and reflexes to win, 83-76. Krivacs (22) led five Horns in double figures. Texas players gave the building's floor and lighting good marks, although it did not quite feel like home yet. Baxter called the Super Drum "outta sight," while Krivacs said, "It's a thrill playing here. This is a first-class place, and we expect Texas to have a first-class program." Lemons, who had the last word on most subjects, offered this comment: "Seems like we're on the road, getting ready to catch a bus. But wasn't that a lovely crowd?"

The Longhorns had further opportunity to get used to their new arena when they hosted two Southeastern Conference teams in quick succession. They dropped Mississippi State, 81-69, despite a 17-rebound deficit. Krivacs (19) and Rickey Brown (15) were the leading scorers. Brown's coach, Ron Greene, harassed the officials constantly and drew three technical fouls before getting tossed. Ten years after Pete Maravich lit up Gregory Gym, LSU was back, a team with potential but terribly young—11 frosh on the 15-man squad. Texas jumped to a 16-2 lead, and Dale Brown's Bayou Bengals were never able to catch up in an 82-66 loss. Krivacs threw in 30 points, and "Junior" Moore, who Lemons persuaded to be a passer before a shooter, had 10 assists. UT's guard combo worked well together, as the 1978 and 1979 seasons would attest. Senior forward Mike Murphy, all but immortalized the previous year by Lemons' classic put-down, "You scored one more point than a dead man," got a rare start against LSU.

Krivacs' quick release was on display for everyone to see at old Gallagher Hall when he scored 42 in a 108-87 defeat of Oklahoma State. From the start, the Horns ran with telling effect, and their defense held Cowboy guard Mark Tucker to seven points, 13 below his average. Lemons, pleased with the smell of success, declared it his team's best game yet.

Except for 6'8" Bo Jackson (18 points and 24 rebounds), UT had no trouble at all with Alaska-Anchorage, forcing 30 turnovers and beating the Sea Wolves, 87-65, before 10,500 fans in Austin. Krivacs and Baxter combined for 46 points in the last game before final exams, which gave Texas a 5-1 record.

The Longhorns were back in action on December 17, taking the measure of Centenary, 105-73, in Shreveport. Riley Wallace, coach of the Gentlemen, got 20 points from Chris Cummings and 16 points and 16 rebounds from Bobby White, but he freely conceded the SWC visitors had more talent and intensity than his team. Lemons did frequent subbing, trying to find a fifth starter, and Branyan (12 points and five rebounds) appeared to be moving out of the pack of contenders.

Paul Hansen, Lemons' assistant at Oklahoma City for 18 years, brought his Chiefs to the Super Drum to meet Texas. Baxter had a career-high 32 points, 11 rebounds, two assists and two blocked shots as the Longhorns breezed, 88-71. But the burly Texas forward had help because Krivacs scored 25 and Branyan 14, and reserve Phillip Stroud got eight points and 11 rebounds. "It was a hard win, a lot harder than the score indicated," Lemons said, referring to OCU's vigorous three-quarter-court press.

The Milwaukee Classic, a tournament the Longhorns had played in seven seasons earlier, was next on the schedule. The games were played as outside temperatures hovered between two below zero and ten above. Army, coached by a young Mike Krzyzewski, operated at two speeds, slow and slower, but it seemed to work. The Black Knights brought a 7-3 record into the tourney and played UT down to the wire before losing, 74-73, in front of a crowd of 10,938. They had the game's top two scorers, Gary Winton (24) and Matt Brown (20). "If anybody could spell his name, the Army guy [Krzyzewski] would be coach of the year," Lemons said of the man who later led Duke to two national titles. The victory set up a game against Marquette, the defending NCAA champion. Although Al McGuire was no longer coaching the Warriors, they retained some familiar names like Butch Lee (1978 national player of the year), Jerome Whitehead, Jim Boylan and Bernard Toone. They won it, 65-56. Lemons thought Marquette was somewhat brutal under the basket and so informed the men in striped shirts. Whitehead (21) and Baxter (18) led their teams in scoring.

Was it an aberration, or was the SWC improving? A 65-percent winning clip seemed to suggest the latter, and again Arkansas led the way. The Hogs had steamrolled the conference (16-0) in 1977, and appeared to be just as strong, but Texas, Houston and one or two others had ideas about bringing the mighty Razorbacks down. If the results of the SWC opener were indicative, it could be the Horns, who met TCU in Fort Worth on January 5. The Frogs had been shocked at the beginning of the season when coach Johnny Swaim suddenly quit, saying he was "tired of smelling sweaty jock straps and hearing basketballs bounce." His 32-year-old assistant, Tim Somerville, moved up, but he had little with which to work. Texas gave Somerville's Frogs a terrible beating, 90-41. Understandably frustrated and embarrassed, TCU players Aurdie Evans and Mike Dreyspring threw too many elbows at the end for Lemons to ignore. "Sure looks like TCU's going to have a long year," he said. "Those two guys are bad enough players, but we still don't know what kind of fighters they are." Krivacs scored 20 for Texas, and freshman guard Dave Shepherd had 16.

More serious competition was expected from Texas Tech with star center Mike Russell, but the Red Raiders lost, 101-86, before a near sellout, 14,900 fans at the Super Drum. Only Kent Williams (24) scored consistently for the red and black, while Baxter, Branyan, Krivacs, Moore and Goodner ranged from 25 down to 12 points. The game ended with a steal by Baxter and a dunk, followed by a two-minute ovation from the big crowd, twice what would have fit into Gregory Gym. "We had Texas Tech for breakfast," Baxter said brashly, "we get Houston for lunch and Arkansas for dinner. If we're hungry enough, we'll win."

Lunch was served the following Tuesday night at Hofheinz Pavilion, where the Horns devoured Houston, 100-89. Rendering a third straight superb performance, Texas broke the Cougars' 11-game home winning streak. Mike Schultz scored 19 and collected 12 rebounds for UH, while Krivacs scored 29, Baxter 23 and Branyan (shooting 69 percent in the SWC so far) 22. Not the most imposing of athletes, Branyan had a knack for getting to the right spot on the court, making layups and set shots. Lemons, a man of few compliments, said of Branyan, "He's a heck of a player. He's like the white buffalo, the rarest of them all."

Dinner in Baxter's grand scheme was a rather unforgettable sold-out evening in the Super Drum, a 75-69 upset of No. 3 Arkansas, with its fabled triplets, Sidney Moncrief, Ron Brewer and Marvin Delph. Most of the Hogs looked a bit fatigued, playing their fourth game in eight days, but not Moncrief. The 6'4" jumping jack made nine of 11 shots, all six free throws and got seven rebounds. Moore was no less sensational, hitting 10 of 14 from the field, grabbing six rebounds, making seven steals and handing out eight assists. It was a big win before a big crowd, and although Lemons denied it, he had a tear in his eye when the school song was played after the game, which catapulted the Longhorns to No. 15 in the Associated Press poll.

Just as there were traffic snarls and other problems inevitable with the opening of such a large new facility, a snafu arose when 1,200 late-arriving people bearing general admission tickets were denied entry because the Super Drum was full half an hour before tipoff. Some public and private disagreements ensued between the building management and the UT athletic department over just what had occurred and how to prevent such things in the future. But most of the news was good, extremely good. Just over halfway through the home season, it appeared that the new arena and a winning team were producing a financial windfall. Thirteen games at Gregory Gym in 1977 had netted about $55,000, while just eight games thus far in 1978 brought nearly five times that amount. Besides the number of fans, the nature of those fans was changed. In the Gregory Gym days, students who had paid the blanket tax comprised the large majority of every crowd, and they brought in very little revenue. But the Super Drum crowds were comprised more of townspeople, families and alumni, with some students sprinkled in. It was, without a doubt, a more mature and sedate crowd, and security was much improved. The era of fans rumbling on the court during and after games (such as the infamous 1963 Longhorn-Aggie game) was over. And Gregory Gym never had anything like the Burnt Orange Room, where season ticket holders gathered before and after each home game to socialize and discuss hoops. When Lemons made an appearance following a big Longhorn victory, there was no better place to be.

Rice, destined to share the SWC cellar with TCU, came to Austin and lost, 78-64. Branyan and Moore combined for 41 points, and the Owls' Elbert Darden had 16. The game was notable for the "Schuler Shuttle," named after Rice coach Mike Schuler, who substituted players 99 times before the game ended. He had learned the strategy as an assistant in the Atlantic Coast Conference, watching Dean Smith of North Carolina, but Lemons was irked: "There's no point in it, no rhyme or reason. It just delays the game. All they need is a few clowns to make it a circus."

Record: 26-5

64 Southern California 65
83 Oklahoma 76
81 Mississippi State 69
82 LSU 66
108 Oklahoma State 87
87 Alaska-Anchorage 65
105 Centenary 73
88 Oklahoma City 71
74 Army 73
56 Marquette 65
90 TCU 41
101 Texas Tech 86
100 Houston 89
75 Arkansas 69
78 Rice 64
79 Texas A&M 77 (OT)
78 Baylor 76
85 SMU 80
73 Houston 72
71 Arkansas 75
87 TCU 60
102 Rice 86
90 Texas A&M 66
77 Baylor 79
78 Texas Tech 63
82 SMU 74
90 Houston 92
72 Temple 58
67 Nebraska 48
96 Rutgers 76
101 North Carolina State 93

New members of basketball royalty, Lemons' Longhorns expected and got a tough game in College Station, finally winning in overtime, 79-77. They wiped out three eight-point Aggie leads in the second half and had what it took at the end. Krivacs scored 26 and Baxter 22, while Branyan had perhaps his worst (five of 17) shooting game as a Longhorn. Texas A&M's celebrated pair, Karl Godine and Jarvis Williams, rode the bench, as Joey Robinson (23), Willie Foreman and Wally Swanson (15 each) did the heavy lifting. In the hot, packed and jubilant visitors' locker room, Lemons hollered, "We were resurrected. I believe in life after death. I surely do."

Another cardiac caper loomed when Baylor paid its initial visit to the Super Drum. The Bears, coming off an overtime loss to Arkansas, had the league's most dynamic player, Vinnie Johnson, a 6'2", 200-pound package of muscle and basketball know-how picked up on the playgrounds of Brooklyn. Moore held him to 21 (just five in the second half) in UT's 78-76 victory witnessed by 13,225 patrons. Despite a 24-point, 16-rebound game by the Bruins' Russell Oliver, Baxter

(29 points and 11 rebounds) was the money player in the late going with drives, jumpers and defensive work that won raves from BU coach Jim Haller.

Lemons predicted his team would lose a conference game eventually, but he just did not know when or against whom. Texas won at Moody Coliseum for the first time in four years, edging SMU, 85-80. Krivacs (30) found gaping seams in the Mustangs' zone defense and had target practice. The victory was aided by a series of late SMU turnovers. Reggie Franklin and Joe Swedlund combined for 45 points for the Ponies, who outrebounded Texas by a 48-31 margin. Although the Horns were winning, they were not a strong team on the boards.

"It's hell to lead a whole ball game until the last few seconds and then get beat," said Guy Lewis after his Houston Cougars lost, 73-72, in Austin. Branyan went from goat to hero; he committed five turnovers but hit two free throws to tie and go ahead with 18 seconds left. Defensive pressure from Ovie Dotson and John Danks helped on a night when the flu-weakened Longhorns played poorly. Cecile Rose (23) bombed away from the outside, and Charles Thompson and Mike Schultz had their way inside, but Texas won for the 17th time in 19 starts, moving up to No. 12 in the nation.

The hills were alive with basketball when Arkansas and Texas clashed at Barnhill Arena on February 1. Eddie Sutton, whose Razorbacks were 19-1 and trailed only Kentucky in the national rankings, deserved much credit for the SWC's resurgence. He welcomed the challenge from the Longhorns, claiming UT was a newly awakened giant. Perhaps, although four wins by eight points suggested they were less than overpowering. With 6,485 fans loudly calling the Hogs, Arkansas came back from 11 points down to win, 75-71. Thirty points by Marvin Delph and aggressive defense (including some illegal hand-checking, in Lemons' view) put them on top at the end, evening the series. The starting five for Texas were all in double figures, led by Moore (17). Despite the loss, the Longhorns found solace in their showing against a great Arkansas team in a hostile environment.

Partly because of the Super Drum's inadequate lighting—a problem soon resolved—UT had just one home game on television, against the lowly TCU Horned Frogs. The commentator was former UCLA coach John Wooden, who praised the ascendant Longhorn program but was too candid to put it in the highest echelon. The game, an 87-60 Texas win, was basically a replay of what happened in Fort Worth a month earlier. Steve Scales scored 27 for the Frogs and Krivacs 23 for UT, and Dotson had a couple of crowd-pleasing dunks.

Lemons' earlier "clowns" comment drew a response when Texas and Rice met at Autry Court. Of the 4,500 fans present, several hundred with painted faces, stick-on noses and other Bozo-type accoutrements waved balloons and were not shy with their taunts, but the UT coach was unfazed. "I was in the war with the Germans and Japanese," he said. "I've seen bigger wharf rats than these clowns." He was more concerned about what happened on the court, where the Owls erased Texas' 17-point halftime lead only to fall, 102-86. Krivacs (36) and Allen Reynolds of Rice (29) were the top scorers. Mike Schuler's frenetic substituting had eased a bit.

After six days' rest, the Horns welcomed Texas A&M to their beautiful new home. Despite collecting 22 fewer rebounds than the Ags, Texas won a laugher, 90-66, in front of a crowd of 15,200. Krivacs scored 34, and Moore passed out 16 assists. Willie Foreman of A&M (19) showed no qualms about shooting 27 times, although just eight went in. UT's victory was the 20th of the season, the first time that mark had been reached since 1963. Lemons, not one to be impressed with dry statistics, had done it eight times before, but not at a big school like Texas. His ability to motivate players (or more accurately, get them to motivate themselves), simplify the game and capitalize on strengths had never been so fully recognized. The Longhorns had one of the best coaches in the nation.

He blamed himself for UT's 79-77 loss to Baylor at Heart O' Texas Coliseum, saying the team was not ready to play. Vinnie Johnson scored 29 and was the main candidate for the role of hero, but it went instead to seldom-used guard Jim Vaszauskas, whose two free throws with nine seconds left won it for BU. Baxter, guarded tightly by Russell Oliver, had 17 points and 13 rebounds for the Horns. "Too bad the Baptists don't drink," Lemons told Jim Trotter of the *Austin American-Statesman*. "This would be a good night for them to celebrate."

The always-demure fans in Lubbock questioned Lemons' attire, heritage and coaching ability, but it made no difference in Texas' 78-63 win over Texas Tech. That result was made even more pleasant by Houston's upset of No. 1 Arkansas, leaving the Horns and Hogs tied for first in the SWC. Baxter led UT with 23 points, and the chilly Red Raiders got 17 from Mike Russell.

The following week, the Abe Lemons Show (produced by former player Hank Bauerschlag) featured what appeared to be the viewing window of a drive-in funeral parlor. The coach, dressed in black with a lonely posey in his hands, played the part of a corpse as an organ hummed sadly in the background. He then popped up and said, "We're not dead yet!" They were alive enough to beat SMU, 82-74, and earn a cochampionship with Arkansas. Nearly 15,000 people looked on in the Super Drum as the Mustangs refused to go down easily. The backcourt leadership of Phil Hale and 32 points from Jeff Swanson kept them close until midway through the second half. With 30 points and 12 rebounds, Baxter led the Horns in a victory that ensured a bye to the SWC tourney finals, to be held 11 days hence. The players cut down the nets, and athletic director Darrell Royal went to the locker room to offer congratulations. Lemons claimed he was going off for a rest at some undetermined place. "I'm not exactly happy," he said. "I'm glad, kind of like when you've gone to the dentist."

After the first round (played at four sites), the SWC Tournament was a sold-out, three-day affair held at the Summit in Houston. Although it was an upset, not everyone was surprised when UH beat Arkansas, earning a place in the finals against Texas. The Cougars, losers of two to UT in the regular season, had a longer bench and more on-court muscle. They established control early and held off the tenacious Longhorns for a 92-90 victory. Charles Thompson scored 23 and Ken "Juice" Williams 18, and tourney MVP Mike Schultz got 16 rebounds. Krivacs and Baxter combined for 49 points, but Goodner's showing hurt. In 14 minutes, the UT center had two points, five fouls and no rebounds. Lemons screamed about some calls that did not go his way as Texas lost the game and a chance to play in the NCAAs. Houston was in, and Arkansas got an at-large bid, but the Horns were out.

The 41st annual National Invitational Tournament, an event whose luster had dimmed considerably since the last time Texas participated in it (1948), made a bid that was accepted, somewhat glumly, by the head coach. Assistants Barry Dowd and Steve Moeller and the players were eager to compete, but Lemons said, "It's been a long damn year, and I need to be out finding a post man." At any rate, Lemons had a team in the NIT for the third time. The March 10 first-round game at the Super Drum required some schedule-shuffling with the boys' and girls' UIL state tournaments (they were thrilled with the new setting), and the Longhorns tipped off against Temple on time. Shooting just 31 percent and trailing by seven at the half, UT's season appeared to be almost over. Lemons had some choice words for his players, and what a difference it made in the last 20 minutes as Texas KO'ed the Owls, 72-58. Krivacs, surpassing Larry Robinson's season scoring record, had 23 points and Baxter 16, while Tim Claxton led Temple with 15 points and 13 rebounds. It was Lemons' 400th career victory.

The second-round game was with Nebraska. A mixup by NIT officials led to some tension between the two schools, both of whom were under the impression the game would be held on their respective home courts. Lemons was adamant, telling anyone who would listen that the game would not be played in Lincoln and even threatening to put his lawyer friend, Richard "Racehorse" Haynes, on the case. With profuse apologies from NIT president Peter Carlesimo, Nebraska relented. The Cornhuskers were determined to slow the game's tempo, and though they were successful, UT was always in control. For one of the few times all season, the Horns won the rebound battle, and they won the game, 67-48. Krivacs scored 18 and Carl McPipe 16 for Joe Cipriano's Nebraska team as 13,000 people watched.

Lemons feigned indifference about going to the NIT semifinals, asking, "Is it still in New York?" Admittedly, most attention was focused on St. Louis, scene of the NCAA Final Four, of which Arkansas was a participant. The Razorbacks lost their semifinal game, and such a result was expected when UT met Rutgers in sold-out Madison Square Garden. It was the first time a Longhorn team had played there since 1968, while the Scarlet Knights, their campus 45 miles away in New Jersey, had played 17 games at the Garden in the previous four seasons. They had two players, James "Dunkmeister" Bailey and Hollis Copeland, who had started on a 31-2 Final Four team in 1976. But their array of defenses had no answer for the marksmanship of Krivacs (25), Branyan (24) and Baxter (19) as UT romped to a 96-76 win. While Goodner neutralized Bailey, Copeland scored 25 for Rutgers. Lemons, who dazzled the New York media with all sorts of tales and jokes, was finally enjoying himself and offered kudos to his players.

Texas was the second straight SWC team to reach the NIT finals, following Otis Birdsong and the

Abe Lemons and his NIT champions celebrate at Madison Square Garden.

Houston Cougars in 1977. The opponent would be North Carolina State, a one-point victor over Georgetown. The Wolfpack, four years removed from an NCAA winner, averaged 84 points per game and was bigger at every position. But October's question marks had become March's exclamation points as the Longhorns dominated, roaring ahead by 24 points and taking a 101-93 conquest for the NIT title, the greatest prize in UT basketball history. Krivacs (33) and Baxter (26 points and 12 rebounds) were voted co-MVPs of the tournament, although Moore was no less deserving. The Wolfpack (led by Hawkeye Whitney with 22) pressed but never got a steal, and Baxter's full-court passes set up one easy hoop after another. "Texas beat us badly," said N.C. State coach Norm Sloan. "They were a lot quicker than we thought. There are some great athletes on that team."

It was a shining moment for the University of Texas, the Southwest Conference and Abe Lemons, who received a kiss on the cheek from UT president Lorene Rogers. Gary Goodner, Tyrone Branyan, Jim Krivacs, Johnny Moore, Ron Baxter and their teammates, unlikely champions, brought a big trophy home to Austin. The 1978 season, which began with a loss on the west coast and ended with a win on the east coast, had been a glorious one.

1979

For a basketball program coming off such a successful, high-profile season, Texas recruited miserably; none of the freshmen or junior college players brought in ever made an impact, and the Longhorns would be needing help soon because Johnny Moore, Jim Krivacs and Tyrone Branyan were seniors. Coach Abe Lemons acknowledged the vital importance of recruiting. "You've got to get the best there is, no matter where they're from," he said. "A doctor can bury his mistakes, but mine are still on scholarship."

The Special Events Center, more popularly known as the Super Drum, no longer had the look of a construction site. The rough edges long since smoothed out, it was almost universally admired as an arena for basketball and other events. The Longhorns had averaged 12,400 in attendance there in 1978 and had a 15-0 home record. Fans could note two new features as the 1979 season began. A large orange-and-white banner, commemorating the NIT championship, hung from the rafters at the south end. It was followed by another 20-plus banners to acknowledge the long and proud history of UT basketball, beginning with the first Southwest Conference title in 1915. The other change pertained to the Super Drum's court. The immediate out-of-bounds areas had gotten bold markings identifying just who played there—"THE UNIVERSITY OF TEXAS" lengthwise, "LONGHORNS" along the baselines and "SWC" at each free throw line. And the familiar Longhorn logo appeared on each side of the half-court stripe.

UT had a No. 6 preseason ranking and the pressure of being the near-unanimous favorite to win the conference. Not only that, but Moore, Krivacs and the other vets had Salt Lake City (site of the NCAA Final Four) on their minds. The 1979 season commenced with another first, an exhibition game against a non-U.S. college opponent. The Longhorns blew out a Canadian team, the University of Windsor, but Baxter suffered a bruised knee, which, added to an earlier ankle injury and some excess pounds, led to a subpar year for the all-SWC forward. He was able to play in the real season opener, a 76-71 loss to Long Beach State. The 49ers' Ricky Williams, every bit as quick as Moore, had 26 points and some late free throws to ice the game.

If the Horns got more competition than expected in California, they got mighty little in the first home game, against an NAIA team, Northern Montana. Texas blistered the Northern Lights, 148-71, setting school and conference records for points scored. Moore had 19 assists and Krivacs 43 points against a terribly outmanned club, but the former showed no sympathy: "If they didn't want to play us, they shouldn't have scheduled us." Two days later, a second-half surge was needed to subdue Arkansas State by a score of 68-54. Led by Anthony Myles and Marvin Jarrett, the Indians had a 37-25 rebounding edge and were not bothered by UT's matchup zone defense. Baxter and Branyan (19 points each) pulled the Horns through. Lemons, upset with his players' lack of enthusiasm in practice, called them "a bunch of zombies," but they finished a three-win week at the Super Drum by demolishing a highly regarded Brigham Young team, 96-57. Texas outrebounded the Cougars, who averaged 6'9" in the frontcourt, and held soph star Danny Ainge to 18 points. Branyan scored 35, and Phillip Stroud had 11 points and 13 rebounds and played some tough interior defense.

The Longhorns, who looked so good against Brigham Young, shot poorly, committed needless fouls and displayed little teamwork when they fell to Oklahoma, 71-65, in Norman. Cary Carrabine hit three late baskets to hold off a UT charge at the end. Branyan did his part on offense, getting 27 points. "Tyrone is a smart player. He's coming on," Lemons said of his unflappable forward who played for championship teams on the high school, junior college and collegiate levels.

Moore expressed the opinion that Texas' rather poor start could be traced to overconfidence, and Krivacs, in a deep shooting slump, did not spare himself any blame. He made just five of 18 from the floor in the Longhorns' 85-70 defeat of Oklahoma State in Austin. Branyan kept them afloat again with 28 points and 13 rebounds, while Mark Tucker scored 16 for the Cowboys. Both teams seemed to have trouble adjusting to the new (and long called-for) three-man officiating crew. Another uninspired win came at the expense of Hardin-Simmons, 68-58. Krivacs scored 24, and Dave Shepherd came off the bench and added 15, but Baxter was, by his own admission, terrible. The season was young, they had won five of seven games, and yet everyone was asking, "What is wrong with the Longhorns?" Nothing that a big, talented center would not cure, in the view of *Austin American-Statesman* writer Carter Cromwell. Such an individual was not a member of the 1979 Texas team, though.

For the first time in 18 years, UT did not play in a midseason tournament. There was, however, another trip to the west coast. Baxter snapped out of his lethargy long enough to score 17 and grab nine rebounds in a 70-53 defeat of Pacific, ending the Tigers' 13-game home winning streak. Better defense and shot selection helped considerably. Terence Carney scored 16 for Pacific. The Longhorns got a look at an all-American and future pro when they met Bill Cartwright and the San Francisco Dons. The 7'1" center with lethal elbows had 24 points and 12 rebounds in his team's 69-48 victory. Texas was in the game with four minutes left and then went stone cold. Only Branyan (22) had any success.

There was more hand-wringing as the Horns prepared to start conference play. Their first foe was TCU. Coach Tim Somerville, waging a long, steep fight to bring the Horned Frogs out of the basketball doldrums, had fashioned a 5-5 pre-SWC record by playing a lightweight schedule. The game was never close after Texas jumped to a 20-8 lead, finally winning, 92-63, before

7,500 fans at the Super Drum. Krivacs totaled 29 points, while Mark Nickens had 20 for the Frogs, whose main goal in the second half was keeping the score down. Lemons was not happy with the play of his bench, other than forward John Danks.

Due to a scheduling quirk, the next four games were on the road, beginning on a frozen, overcast day against Texas Tech. The Red Raiders had beaten No. 8 Michigan and were eager to regain a position in the SWC elite. They shot 62 percent (as compared to UT's 37 percent) in an impressive 92-74 victory. "Tech looks like we did last year," Lemons said. "They played with a lot of enthusiasm." Kent Williams and Ralph Brewster combined for 35 points for Gerald Myers' crew, while Baxter (29) led the Longhorns. In a reminder of bygone days, Houston had a football player in its lineup. Leonard Mitchell, a 6'7", 260-pound defensive tackle, started at center for the Cougars, who were coming off a game with Arkansas in which they led by 23 and then lost because of an 11-minute scoreless stretch. They showed the effects of that defeat in a 75-57 loss to Texas. It was one of the Longhorns' best games yet, as they shot well, played good defense and ran the offense crisply and with purpose. Branyan (18) led four UT players in double figures, but George Walker of UH was the game's top scorer with 20.

The third of the four straight road games was against 10-0 Arkansas, the nation's tenth-ranked team. The Razorbacks were riding the exploits of Sidney Moncrief, one of the all-time greats of SWC basketball. Leading his team in scoring (25 points per game), rebounding (12) and intangibles, Moncrief knew how to win. He had 22 points and U.S. Reed 17, but the Hogs fell to UT, 66-63, ending their 35-game home winning streak. And it happened under some harrowing conditions, as many of the 9,312 fans threw ice, cups and coins. Baxter was hit twice while attempting a free throw, causing Lemons to rage at the referees. Krivacs scored 21 and Moore (blanked in the Houston game) 17. Those clever students at Rice had not yet tired of the clown motif and were out in full force again, chanting "We want Abe" long before the game started. Krivacs (30) took the Owls' frosh guards, Bobby Tudor and Willis Wilson, to school in a 94-81 Texas win. Elbert Darden scored 30 for Rice, whom Lemons complimented afterward.

The Longhorns played their first home game in sixteen days, against Southern California. San Francisco's Bill Cartwright had demonstrated that UT had trouble with big men, and Cliff Robinson was a fine one, having led the Pacific 8 Conference in scoring as a freshman. But Stroud and the rest of the Texas interior defense sagged on Robinson, holding him to 13 points and 10 rebounds in an 87-68 whipping of the No. 20 Trojans. A crowd of 15,500 (including several pro scouts) and a nationwide television audience saw the Horns play a solid 40 minutes. Al McGuire, working the game for NBC, repeatedly expressed amazement at Branyan's unorthodox play, but after the Longhorn forward compiled 25 points and nine rebounds, McGuire was glad to name him as the game's MVP. The ex-Marquette coach also offered this opinion: "Basketball has really come a long way here. A few years ago, they played in a small gym, and now they play in one of the best facilities in the nation. I tell you, I've never seen so much orange in my life."

Shelby Metcalf was slowly building a powerful team at Texas A&M. His Aggies could boast wins over Indiana, Kentucky, San Francisco and Nevada-Las Vegas, were ranked No. 15 and shared the SWC lead with Texas. They had more size and, by most accounts, more pure talent, and their pregame comments did nothing to hurt the Longhorns' motivation. It was a big 89-66 UT victory, with 14,503 fans raising the roof at the Super Drum. Branyan and Krivacs teamed up for 57 points, Moore had 14 assists, and there was plenty of time near the end for showboating. David Britton, A&M's loudest talker before the game, went zero-for-six from the field, but like most of his teammates,

Record: 21-8

71 Long Beach State 76
148 Northern Montana 71
68 Arkansas State 54
96 Brigham Young 57
65 Oklahoma 71
85 Oklahoma State 70
68 Hardin-Simmons 58
70 Pacific 53
48 San Francisco 69
92 TCU 63
74 Texas Tech 92
75 Houston 57
66 Arkansas 63
94 Rice 81
87 Southern California 68
89 Texas A&M 66
77 Baylor 76
98 SMU 62
79 Houston 53
58 Arkansas 68
73 TCU 60
95 Rice 52
65 Texas A&M 57
102 Baylor 83
63 Texas Tech 56 (OT)
66 SMU 81
70 Houston 65
38 Arkansas 39
76 Oklahoma 90

could hardly believe the thoroughness of their defeat. He predicted a different outcome when the two teams met in College Station.

Heart O' Texas Coliseum, a building best suited to livestock shows with manure and hay inside and out, was the scene of the Texas-Baylor game, and the Longhorns got the blue ribbon in a 77-76 victory. Six clutch free throws in the final 40 seconds, four by Stroud and two by Krivacs, preserved the victory, witnessed by 9,200 fans. Branyan and Krivacs continued their high-scoring ways with 26 and 23 points, respectively, while Vinnie Johnson (27) led the Bears. Lemons complained about the officials' reluctance to call offensive fouls on Johnson for backing in and muscling defenders before taking his shot, talents he would use to good effect in the NBA.

The No. 17 Longhorns were rolling with six straight wins, and the schedule looked good—six of the remaining nine games were in Austin. It would help, however, if Baxter could get in gear because his total of 28 points and 13 rebounds in the last four games had not helped much. SMU was not the team to beat UT. The Mustangs had lost three straight games, and injuries and sickness slowed two of their best players, Brad Branson and Billy Allen. Texas jumped to a 23-point halftime lead and stretched it to 47 before relenting in a 98-62 win at the Super Drum. Krivacs scored 24 and Moore had 13 assists, frequently making the impossible pass look routine. "Well, we're still alive," said a wistful Sonny Allen, SMU coach. "This is not a great place to start a winning streak."

A 79-53 crunching of Houston at the Super Drum was entirely without suspense. Baxter (11 of 14 from the field and eight rebounds) played well, as did Stroud (10 points and 14 rebounds). Krivacs' second basket broke Raymond Downs' UT career scoring record of 1,513, although he claimed not to care about the achievement. Guy Lewis' Cougars were awful, shooting just 31 percent.

The Longhorns had yet to lose at the Super Drum in 25 games, which would seem to indicate the home-court advantage was not completely lost when they departed Gregory Gym after the 1977 season. That magnificent stretch was halted on the first day of February when Arkansas imposed its slowdown offense and won, 68-58, before a crowd of 15,300. Sidney Moncrief (23) and Branyan (19) led their teams in scoring, but it was the extracurricular activities that made the game distinct. Moore, who often tried to draw offensive fouls with a theatrical touch, jumped in front of U.S. Reed at midcourt near the end of the first half, but no call was made. Razorback coach Eddie Sutton came off the bench and began lecturing Moore on the impropriety of his move, which brought Lemons storming onto the scene. The two grappled, yelled at each other and did not stop until assistant coaches Barry Dowd and Pat Foster and UT police pulled them apart. Just 10 years earlier at Gregory Gym, such a scene probably would have flown out of control. Sutton, the victorious coach, was somewhat apologetic after the game, but Lemons insisted he had a right to defend Moore and blasted Sutton, threatening to "liquidate his ass" and "tear his Sunday clothes" in the event of a recurrence. While both men had behaved indiscretely, it was no great surprise because Southwest Conference basketball had improved so much (at least at the top) and coaches were under fierce pressure.

The 1979 Texas-Arkansas game at the Special Events Center included a gentlemanly halftime discussion between Abe Lemons and Eddie Sutton.

The Longhorns did not let the loss to Arkansas slow their momentum, winning the next five games. They went to Cowtown and had a tougher time than expected before beating TCU, 73-60. Krivacs scored 20 and Baxter 19. Steve Scales had 14 points and 10 rebounds for the dissension-riddled Horned Frogs.

Stroud had a career-high 23 points and 14 rebounds as UT breezed by Rice, 95-52. Brian Burns, one of four freshmen starting for the Owls, scored 15. Many of the 8,689 fans left the game early when

Lemons began substituting, but they missed a splashy ending when Moore stole the ball, flipped it underhand against the backboard and did a one-hand stuff at the buzzer. The dunk, in its third year back in college basketball, was an art form, and its foremost practitioner on the Texas team was senior Ovie Dotson. When a home game was in the bag, the crowd would chant his name and go nuts when he threw one down.

After a six-day rest, the Horns went to Aggieland, determined to avoid the defeat promised them in Austin. Flawless in the first half with 68 percent shooting and a 15-point lead, they survived some furious pressure from Texas A&M in the second half and won, 65-57. It was no game for end-of-the-benchers or Dotson's meaningless dunks; all five starters played 40 minutes. Moore scored 23 and David Britton 18 for the Ags, absorbing their third straight loss. Lemons, the object of some criticism after his wild-eyed act in the Arkansas game, said sarcastically, "I'm going to charm school and listening to chamber music. Gee whiz, golly yes, Moore played a great game. He played lovely. See how my language has changed?"

Each of the last 10 Texas-Baylor games had been decided by five points or less, but that ended with a 102-83 Longhorn win in Austin to remain a game ahead of Arkansas in the SWC race. Branyan connected on 16 of 20 shots for 41 points, despite everything BU could do to stop him. "We fronted him, we backed him, we double-teamed him, but nothing worked," said Bear coach Jim Haller. Vinnie Johnson shaked and baked for 21 points, Pat Nunley scored 20, and Terry Teagle, a freshman and future star, had 13.

When Texas lost to Texas Tech on January 6, the team was playing poorly and doubting itself, but 12 victories in the last 13 games seemed to indicate the 1979 Horns were as tough as the 1978 version. Lemons downplayed the revenge angle when the Red Raiders came to Austin. UT blew a 14-point lead and nearly lost when David Little's shot went in and out, sending the game into overtime. Baxter took charge, scoring eight of the Horns' 11 points in a 63-56 win, clinching a tie for the SWC crown.

Lemons was unwilling to share it with Arkansas, but that is exactly what happened after UT lost to SMU in Dallas. It was a shocking 81-66 loss to a Mustang team that had fallen to Texas by 36 points earlier and was on a five-game losing streak. Brad Branson scored 20 points, Richard Harris had 15 rebounds, and Reggie Franklin blocked five shots against the 11th-ranked Longhorns. "We just stood around and got beat," Lemons said. "I don't know why SMU played so well. If I knew, I'd be in the investment business."

As the top two seeds, Texas and Arkansas had byes into the semifinals of the SWC Tournament, a Summit conference attended by more than 15,000 people in Houston. The Longhorns had yet to win a single game in the four-year-old tourney, losing to SMU in 1976, Baylor in 1977 and Houston in 1978. They met the Cougars and prevailed, 70-65, with some clutch free throws by Moore and Baxter, necessary because of frigid (29 percent) field goal shooting in the second half. Ken Williams led UH with 25 points. That put Texas and Arkansas, two teams that loved each other like a cobra and a mongoose, in the finals. Except for the last two minutes, the game was "about as exciting as a bowl of cold soup," according to Jim Trotter of the *Austin American-Statesman*. The style of play was set when the Razorbacks held the ball for more than two minutes before taking a shot. Arkansas won, 39-38, when all-American Sidney Moncrief hit a free throw and layup with 16 seconds left. Branyan (21) was the leading scorer in a game in which only 71 shots were attempted. "We need a shot clock," Baxter said, as the Hogs and their fans celebrated. "A 39-38 game, and we're supposed to be college ball players. That's high school!"

Despite the loss, UT received an at-large berth in the 40-team NCAA Tournament, and the opponent was Oklahoma, an early-season conqueror of Texas. The 20-9 Sooners and the 21-7 Longhorns met in Dallas, drawing many football analogies in the media, although Barry Switzer and Fred Akers stayed home to watch the game. OU, with its first Big 8 championship in 30 years, shot 62 percent in a 90-76 win that ended Texas' campaign. Sophomore guard Raymond Whitley was most responsible, scoring a game-high 25 points, five more than Branyan. It was a sad ending for some fine Longhorn players, losers of three of their last four games. But they had accomplished so much in 1978 and 1979, winning 47 games, a share of two SWC championships and an NIT title, and making an NCAA appearance. Krivacs was UT's all-time leading scorer, and Moore had started every game, 113 of them, of his college career. He went on to play nine years with the San Antonio Spurs, twice leading the NBA in assists.

1980

"We're hoping to win some ball games," UT coach Abe Lemons told a crowd of 3,000 after a preseason intrasquad contest. "We're hoping to win them all. But if we don't, don't gripe at me. Gripe at the players." Lemons, entering his 25th year in the profession, and assistants Barry Dowd and Steve Moeller had put together a fine recruiting class. The two most promising rookies were guard George Turner and 6'10" center LaSalle Thompson. They could have pursued higher education at any number of schools but were persuaded to come to Austin. The spotlight was really on forward Ron Baxter, the only returning starter and the undisputed leader of the team. Lemons was pushing, if not riding, Baxter to return to the level of play he exhibited during that glorious 1978 season. If he was a proven performer, his fellow forward was not. John Danks had started just once in three years, averaging three points and one rebound per game. But Danks, who always played with intensity, would prove to be one of the Longhorns' pillars.

Danks made 11 of 14 shots and grabbed nine rebounds in the season-opening 83-76 defeat of Northwestern Louisiana. The Demons had some quick inside players, such as Earnest Reliford (21) and Frederick Piper (18), who gave Thompson some trouble.

At venerable Boston Garden, the Horns met Harvard, an also-ran in the Ivy League but a team that threatened to score an upset by shooting 71 percent in the first half. Superior depth and the hot hand of Turner (25) staved off embarrassment as UT won, 85-73. Lemons moaned about freshman mistakes—three first-year men (Turner, Thompson and guard Fred Carson) started—and Baxter said, "These guys need to realize they're not in high school any more." He referred primarily to Thompson, who managed to secure just four rebounds and got a seat on the bench much of the second half.

Back home, the Longhorns stung Vermont, 90-71, before a crowd of 8,078. It was not a thing of beauty with 55 fouls, 50 turnovers and countless other mistakes by the two teams. Baxter and Danks combined for 43 points and 17 rebounds, and Ken Montgomery (a transfer from North Carolina State) played well in reserve against the Catamounts.

After three mediocre victories over weak opponents, it was put up or shut up time in Chicago. DePaul, experiencing a hoop rebirth with longtime coach Ray Meyer, had been in the 1979 NCAA Final Four. The Blue Demons were led by a couple of all-Americans and future pros, Mark Aguirre and Terry Cummings. While Lemons feigned fear before the game, Danks did not. "We're going there with the intention of winning," he said. "They only put five men on the court, too." UT played with poise all the way and had a chance to win, but DePaul took it, 66-60. Baxter (21) scored one more point than the celebrated Aguirre. "They gave us everything we wanted and more," Meyer said. "Baxter's a fine player."

David King of the *Daily Texan* wrote, "'Oh, come all ye faithful' should be the theme song over the Christmas holidays because only the truly faithful will come to see Biscayne, Hardin-Simmons and Murray State." Thompson, Montgomery and Danks were the leading scorers in Texas' victories over those teams. Biscayne and Hardin-Simmons went down easily enough, but the Murray State Racers came within two points of winning. Turner, who was best known for his long-range jumpers and sharp drives to the basket, turned in the defensive play of the game with 10 seconds left to secure UT's sixth win, 65-63.

San Francisco, 9-0 with three starters back from the team that stomped the Horns the previous season, visited on December 27. Dan Belluomini's Dons had plenty of depth and a frontcourt averaging 6'9". Texas was somewhat successful in controlling the tempo, trailed by six at the half, made some defensive adjustments and gained a 65-61 victory before 11,081 delighted fans. Turner and USF's Quintin Dailey shared scoring honors with 16 points. "How sweet it is," Lemons said in the locker room while smoking a big Cuban cigar.

That surprising win hardly compared to what happened in Las Cruces two days later. New Mexico State halted UT's momentum with a 77-61 upset, not the kind of showing likely to inspire confidence for the approaching Southwest Conference race. Turner and the Aggies' Greg Webb both had 19 points in a physical game. Lemons, who claimed the Missouri Valley Conference referees "raped" his team, vowed never to play another MVC team.

Texas Tech tripped the Horns, 57-54, in the conference opener at the Super Drum, just the second UT loss in the big arena in 39 games. Texas got 17 more rebounds and 10 more shots than the Red Raiders but still managed to lose because Kent Williams hit five late free throws. Turner had a miserable game, making just one of seven shots and committing a crucial turnover at the end.

Turner claimed some teammates blamed him for the defeat and chose not to go to Dallas for the SMU game two days later. The response from the coaches and players was a combination of anger and molly-coddling. Turner was a very talented athlete but also a moody and immature one, destined to have a short career at UT. The "other" freshman guard, Carson, more than compensated for Turner's absence in an 85-75 defeat of the Mustangs at Moody Coliseum. Baxter moved to the backcourt, and freshman Bill Wendlandt got his first start at forward. The star of the evening was Thompson (25 points and 17 rebounds). "When LaSalle comes to play, the man can be awesome," Carson said.

Turner was back with the team but not starting when Texas and Houston met at Hofheinz Pavilion. He helped turn a close game into a rout in the final minutes. "Everything's cool now, no problems," said the temperamental guard who had 12 points and five assists in UT's 99-73 win. He got a warm reception from teammates Ron Baxter, John Danks (the game's top scorer with 24) and Henry Johnson. The Williams cousins, Rob and Ken, combined for 36 points, but Cougar coach Guy Lewis called his team's performance "awful." Some fickle fans agreed, chanting "Guy must go" without realizing the greatest era of UH basketball was just around the corner.

The Longhorns were loose and ready for a Saturday afternoon home game with Arkansas. Bad blood between Lemons and Razorback coach Eddie Sutton seemed to have subsided as they buttered up each other's team. In a battle of wits and strategies, zone defenses and careful play, Arkansas came out on top, 55-50, before 12,148 fans. Baxter scored 17 for UT, while Alan Zahn had 16 for the victorious Hogs.

Record: 19-11

83 NW Louisiana 76
85 Harvard 73
90 Vermont 71
60 DePaul 66
88 Biscayne 63
86 Hardin-Simmons 64
65 Murray State 63
65 San Francisco 61
61 New Mexico State 77
54 Texas Tech 57
85 SMU 75
99 Houston 73
50 Arkansas 55
95 TCU 65
77 North Texas 79 (OT)
48 Baylor 62
53 Texas A&M 56
87 Rice 76
113 SMU 80
59 Arkansas 60
84 Houston 82
90 TCU 62
99 Baylor 61
61 Texas A&M 84
76 Texas Tech 63
76 Rice 56
67 Houston 47
62 Arkansas 64
70 St. Joseph's 61
76 SW Louisiana 77

TCU, a horrendous 13-66 over the past three seasons, had a new coach, Jim Killingsworth, who sought to make the Horned Frogs as competitive as they had been under Johnny Swaim in the late 1960s and early 1970s. The Killer had a long way to go, as seen by his team's 95-65 loss to the Longhorns in Austin. Although Danks and Baxter had 24 points apiece and Montgomery added 21 off the bench, Texas did not play especially well. Tom Douglass, a walk-on guard, outscored the prize frosh, Turner and Thompson, which puzzled Lemons. "We just put them out there and hope they hustle," he said. "It's nothing personal. I'm not playing favorites. All my favorites have graduated."

Taking a break from the conference wars, UT met North Texas at the Super Pit in Denton. Just a filler game and a chance to smooth out some rough edges for the Horns, it was serious business for Bill Blakeley's Eagles because a win over the two-time cochamps of the SWC would enhance their reputation considerably. A crowd of 8,100 was thrilled to see North Texas overcome a nine-point deficit in the last minute; freshman guard Pat Hicks' 35-foot prayer at the buzzer sent it into OT. And then they won, 79-77, starting a three-game losing streak for the Longhorns.

Not only was Texas' psyche bruised, but several players had minor injuries. Baxter, who had a sprained ankle, should have sat out the Baylor game, but the team needed him. At Heart O' Texas Coliseum, the Longhorns scored just 10 points in the final 10 minutes of a 62-48 loss. Terry Teagle, the Bears' soph star, scored 18 points. Lemons delivered a bitter commentary on his team after the game but made an exception of Baxter, who wept in an otherwise deathly quiet locker room.

Lemons searched for a way to pull the Horns out of a slump resulting in five losses in the last eight games. It hardly helped that the best Texas A&M team in decades was up next. Shelby Metcalf's Aggies had a frontcourt of Vernon Smith, Rynn Wright, Rudy Woods and freshman Claude Riley, touted as "the

lights had been installed around its sloping walls, and after each Longhorn basketball victory—the men or the women—it was bathed in a lovely orange glow. More distressing was the ticket situation. Bob Rochs, Al Lundstedt and others in the UT athletic department were shaping a new ticket policy. Except for the premiere games, students were not attending in big numbers, leaving too many seats unfilled. "We've been criticized for having empty seats because we've been holding tickets for the students," Rochs said. Various alternatives were tried, but largely due to student apathy, the Texas athletic department began focusing on ticket sales to the general public. That led to predictable complaints from students who felt they were being marginalized. One *Daily Texan* editorial was entitled "Something's rotten in Bellmont." The Erwin Center, more than twice the size of old Gregory Gym, was not so fearsome to visiting teams, just by its design. In addition, there were fewer students, far removed from the court, giving it even more of a sedate feel. With increased security on hand, the Erwin Center was light years from the wild and woolly times at Gregory Gym. The era of student-dominated crowds at UT basketball games was over.

The season got off to a rocky start when coach Abe Lemons and assistants Barry Dowd and Steve Moeller were subpoenaed to testify before a federal grand jury investigation of gambling. Lemons evidently did not like Moeller's testimony and summarily fired him, leading to a bitter, backstabbing feud. Each pointed an accusing finger at the other for weak recruiting. Of the four recruits brought in before the 1981 season, only one, 6'9" forward Mike Wacker, could be called a blue-chip prospect. Furthermore, Moeller claimed Lemons' tendency to criticize his players, publicly and privately, was hurting the program.

"So this was going to be the year Texas basketball hit the skids, the year a lot of people were going to have the last laugh on the wisecracking Okie," wrote Bill Sullivan of the *Austin American-Statesman*. Lemons himself did little to dispel the idea that, even with LaSalle Thompson in the middle, the seniorless Horns were likely to have some hard times. The starting lineup for the opener against Pacific included Thompson, Wacker, Henry Johnson, Ken Montgomery and JC transfer Virdell Howland. It was not a good day for Longhorn fans; the football team lost to Texas A&M at Memorial Stadium in the afternoon, and the basketball team fell to the Tigers, 78-77, at the Erwin Center a few hours later. The battle of the big men was not even close as Ron Cornelius got 34 points and held Thompson to six. But Texas' gentle giant came back and scored a career-high 30 in a 91-76 thumping of Biscayne in Miami. Ray Harper, a 5'11" freshman guard, went 40 minutes and got 16 points and some praise from Lemons.

George Turner, who had caused equal amounts of happiness and dismay during his one year with the Horns, was kicking around at a couple of junior colleges in California. There were more Turner-like problems, however. Fred Carson got his feelings hurt over one of Lemons' critiques and missed two practices. And reserve forward Daryl Bushrod walked out of the Erwin Center at halftime of a 101-82 defeat of New Mexico State. Montgomery bombed the Aggies for 34 points, and Thompson (24 points and 13 rebounds) was again outstanding. It was Johnson's turn to star two days later against Long Beach State as the 6'6" forward rang up 30 points in a 92-67 victory over the 49ers in Austin. "Texas is a powerful team," said Long Beach coach Tex Winter, an old friend of Lemons. "They're not very fast, but they have quick hands. They just dominated us on the boards."

The Horns' game with Southern California on December 9 was a dream come true for Johnson, who had grown up a mile from the Los Angeles Sports Arena. He did well there against the Trojans, but his 24 points were not enough in an 89-81 loss. Purvis Miller, USC's big center, led an early second-half spurt that ended the suspense.

Four days later, Texas hosted Ray Meyer's De Paul Blue Demons. The Longhorns had not faced a No. 1-ranked team since 1972, when UCLA mauled them by 50 points. Moody but talented forward Mark Aguirre was having another all-American season, and he poured in 25 points in an 83-65 defeat of UT before a near-sellout crowd. Johnson was the only Texas player with the quickness to match the Blue Demons in a game that resembled quarterhorses versus Clydesdales. Thompson, who was big and strong but a half-step slow, had 22 points and 13 rebounds. Lemons needed better play from his second forward spot, where Wacker, Bill Wendlandt, Bushrod and Howland accomplished mighty little during their time on the floor. UT had problems, as Honest Abe would attest.

Hoping to snap a two-game losing streak and build some momentum for the SWC race, Texas entertained North Texas. While the Eagles focused their attention on Thompson, Johnson hit for 36 points and Wacker 18 in a 103-82 victory. The momentum did not last long because the Longhorns fell to South Carolina, 74-70, before 5,629 boisterous Gamecock fans. Freshman center Jimmy Foster had 24 points and 12 rebounds for USC. Lemons was less than kindly toward his two young guards, Carson and Harper: "Damn, they were terrible. We didn't get anything out of either one of them. Not a thing."

The final tuneup for the SWC season was a 91-68 runaway defeat of Harvard. Montgomery led all scorers with 22 in a foul-infested game that saw Thompson exchanging shoves, elbows, menacing glares and heated words with several Crimson players.

Lubbock Municipal Coliseum was the site of the first conference game. The Texas Tech Red Raiders were short (no starter was taller than 6'6") and quick. Tech got 27 points from Jeff "Skywalker" Taylor and just two turnovers in beating UT, 89-79. Thompson and Johnson scored 18 apiece for the Longhorns, who had three days to regroup from the defeat before playing SMU in the Erwin Center. The Ponies were coming off a 42-point loss to Arkansas and had a weak inside game, but Texas had its own troubles; five players had minor injuries or sickness. With four seconds left in overtime, Thompson blocked Dave Gadis' shot, then Gordon Welch grabbed the ball and banked it in to give SMU a 53-51 win. Howland and the Mustangs' Dave Piehler both scored 18.

If a semblance of offensive continuity were to develop, that was an opportune time with high-rolling Houston and Arkansas coming up next. A pair of local teams, St. Edward's and Huston-Tillotson, played a prelim game before the Longhorns and Cougars tipped off. Guy Lewis had some fine young talent, especially sophomore guard Rob Williams and frosh forwards Clyde Drexler and Michael Young, both of whom liked to get out and go and make the spectacular play. Williams, who would lead the SWC in scoring in 1981, handled the ball well and possessed an uncanny shooting touch. His showing in a 91-71 rout of Texas was breathtaking—16 of 22 from the field and eight of 10 from the line for 40 points, plus a few fancy passes to set up teammates for scores. It was UH's first win in the Erwin Center.

Eddie Sutton's Razorbacks had achieved the hat trick (three victories) against UT in 1980 and were favored to win again at Barnhill Arena on national television. Amid deafening noise, the Horns amassed a 10-point lead with 11 minutes to play, when Arkansas began chipping away. U.S. Reed's open shot from the lane in the final seconds was off the mark, and Texas escaped with a 62-60 win. Lemons, who hid his eyes when Reed took the last shot, praised his young guard tandem: "Fred and Harper are awesome. I'm sorry I said all those things about them before. Neither one of them choked."

It was one of the most satisfying victories in Lemons' long career, and he hoped it might turn the Longhorns' season around, but it did not. Bad news was coming. Henry Johnson, whose poise and leadership were keys to the win in Fayetteville, was on shaky academic ground. His final game before being declared ineligible was a lackluster 66-64 loss to TCU in Fort Worth. Just a few miles up the road in Denton two days later, the Horns dropped a one-point game to North Texas when Thompson (26 points and 21 rebounds) missed one of two free throws at the end. He completely dominated inside play, prompting Eagle coach Bill Blakeley to say, "Thompson was ungodly." Carson was equally complimentary, calling Thompson superior to Ralph Sampson of Virginia and Sam Bowie of Kentucky.

Baylor fans who had seen their team compile a 5-0 SWC record were beginning to think 1981 might be

Record: 15-15

77 Pacific 78
91 Biscayne 76
101 New Mexico State 82
92 Long Beach State 67
81 Southern California 89
65 DePaul 83
103 North Texas 82
70 South Carolina 74
91 Harvard 68
79 Texas Tech 89
51 SMU 53 (OT)
71 Houston 91
62 Arkansas 60
64 TCU 66
74 North Texas 75
75 Baylor 70
67 Texas A&M 63 (OT)
40 Rice 46 (OT)
83 SMU 63
48 Arkansas 54
59 Houston 75
88 TCU 84
82 Baylor 84
79 Texas A&M 108
65 Texas Tech 54
90 Rice 80
58 Rice 44
66 Texas Tech 58
76 Arkansas 73
59 Houston 84

the year of the Bear, ending a three-decade drought in titles. With Lemons juggling his lineup and looking for someone to replace Johnson, Texas seemed unlikely to halt BU. But the Horns jumped to a 20-point lead and held on for a 75-70 win before 11,141 spectators in Austin. Thompson had 26 points and 15 rebounds, and Wacker held Terry Teagle to 16 points.

Lemons took a liking to all-American football player Kenneth Sims and brought him to College Station as his "bodyguard and advisor," but the big man could not prevent Reveille IV, Texas A&M's canine mascot, from attacking Wendlandt and Howland in pregame warm-ups. The Aggies, defending champs of the SWC, were having a hard time, and a 67-63 OT loss to their ancient rivals only made things worse. Thompson came through with 32 points, almost half of Texas' total. Lemons was pleased to win but incensed over some calls and noncalls at the end.

Playing with newfound confidence, the Longhorns expected to boil Rice, although forward Ricky Pierce was scoring 20 points per game. The Owls had not beaten UT in Austin since 1957 when Raymond Downs bestrode the Gregory Gym hardcourts like a colossus. That long streak came to an end when Mike Schuler's team took an excruciatingly slow 46-40 overtime win. Lemons and his players were quite critical of themselves, while Bill Sullivan of the *Austin American-Statesman* wrote, "SWC basketball, 1981, is a great, big bore, an attraction with all the raw spectator appeal of watching paint dry on a summer afternoon.... It has also become a case for the 30-second clock." The Owl-Longhorn game was so boring, fans were leaving when the overtime session began.

Howland and Harper teamed up for 49 points in Texas' 83-63 romp of SMU at Moody Coliseum, avenging an earlier loss to the Mustangs. In a game that was never in doubt, the entire Longhorn team played well, recording 26 assists. Dave Piehler had 25 points for the cellar-dwelling Ponies.

Not always the best of friends, the Horns and Hogs met in Austin on February 3. The last four games between the teams had been decided by 10 points. Although standout guard Darrell Walker had been benched for disciplinary reasons, Arkansas waltzed across Texas, 54-48. There were some critical turnovers, but the game was really lost by poor Longhorn shooting—19 of 52 from the field and 10 of 19 on free throws. Thompson (17) and U.S. Reed (16) led their teams in scoring.

Abe Lemons (top row, far left) and the 1981 Horns.

For Lemons, whose frustration boiled over in the loss to the Razorbacks, it was more of the same in Houston. He refused to talk to the media after UH took a 75-59 victory. Rob Williams scored 32, topping the 1,000-point mark in his young career. The only Longhorn who showed any sign of life was Montgomery (22), while Harper had an awful game and Wacker hyperextended his right knee. Morale was not good in the UT camp.

"May the worst team win," Lemons told Jim Killingsworth before the Texas-TCU game at the Erwin Center. "I guess we both have a chance then," replied the Frog coach. The Longhorns sizzled in the first half, building a 25-point lead, and fizzled in the second half, nearly losing the game. Only by hitting eight straight free throws in the final 1:20 did UT win, 88-84. Montgomery, weakened by the flu, scored 28 points, and Carson put the clamps on TCU star Darrell Browder. Thompson, who again led the SWC in rebounding, grabbed 18.

That win, it turned out, was just a small hill in a much bigger valley. The Baylor Bears, losers of six of their last eight games, scored an 84-82 victory in Waco. Terry Teagle got 23 points and some unexpected help from three reserve teammates. Thompson, with 20 points and 18 rebounds, was UT's best. There were some tough calls, and Lemons sounded his familiar "the refs robbed us" theme.

Texas A&M came calling four days later and pulverized Texas, 108-79. Montgomery scored 26, and Thompson got 17 points and 14 rebounds despite having Vernon Smith in front of him and Claude Riley behind him all night long. Shelby Metcalf, coach of the Ags since 1964, reminded his players of the rarity of beating the Longhorns by such a wide margin in Austin. Lemons, for his part, watched the game with bare interest and preferred to speak of the future.

At 10-14, his Longhorns were almost certain to have the first losing record in six years. Lemons' witty sarcasm, once funny and endearing, was beginning to draw critics who claimed he did not care and that the game had passed him by. The Horns were just playing out the string, getting a poor season behind them, or so it seemed. Then, to their own amazement, they started winning. Thompson and Harper—whose recent contributions had been minimal—were the keys to a 65-54 defeat of Texas Tech in Austin. Except for Jeff Taylor (23), the Red Raiders' slowdown, wait-for-the-perfect-shot offense did not work.

In the close confines of Autry Court, UT took a 90-80 win over Rice to cap the regular season. Thompson and Wacker combined for 39 points, and four others reached double figures. Ricky Pierce was a one-man show for the Owls, pumping in 32 points. Lemons, miffed at impolite treatment by some Rice supporters, was happy to get out of Houston.

The same two teams met in Austin for a first-round game in the SWC tourney, attended by fewer than 4,000 fans. It was not exactly basketball at its best, but UT won, 58-44. Harper had 12 points and Wacker 11, and Wendlandt played well off the bench. Pierce was not shy about putting it up for the Owls, although he missed 19 of 25 shots.

The Longhorn juggernaut moved on to San Antonio. Lemons packed lightly, expecting a brief visit, but Texas overcame a late seven-point deficit to beat Texas Tech, 66-58. The coach had given his players some tough talk at halftime, and they responded. Thompson (21 points and 13 rebounds) took charge, aided capably by Montgomery (14) and Wacker (12). Even more surprisingly, the Horns followed that up with a 76-73 thwarting of Arkansas, the regular-season champion, ranked No. 15 in the nation. It was a heart-stopping, drama-filled game, "the most exciting game I've ever been in," Carson said. Thompson got nearly all of his 23 points in the first half, while Harper (22) was there when the action got hot and heavy in the late minutes. The team that had been reading its own obituaries two weeks earlier was in the finals, one game away from the NCAA playoffs. Lemons, who never hid his distaste for postseason conference tournaments, found himself a beneficiary and was not complaining.

Many of the 13,000-plus fans at Hemisfair Arena for the finals wore red—the Arkansas variety. They had expected to see their Razorbacks playing that Saturday night but lent considerable support to the Houston cause. Guy Lewis' Cougars needed no help in overpowering Texas, 84-59. Rob Williams (37) was magnificent, while Thompson had 27 for the losing Longhorns, who finished the year 15-15. The late run did wonders for the spirits of everyone connected to UT hoops. With Thompson and Wacker and several other quality players coming back in 1982, the future was not so dim, after all.

1982

At a press conference in the summer of 1981, DeLoss Dodds was presented as the new men's athletic director. The mantle of leadership was passed to a 44-year-old midwesterner who had given half of his life to Kansas State University. He ran track there in the late 1950s, earned a master's degree, coached the track team from 1963 to 1976 (bringing it to the Texas Relays several times), served two years as assistant commissioner of the Big 8 Conference and three years as the Wildcats' AD. Dodds had held several positions in the NCAA and was well-respected in the world of college sports. None of his eight predecessors as Texas' AD, going back to L. Theo Bellmont in 1913, had such depth and breadth of training and experience. President Peter Flawn and Athletics Council chairman Tom Morgan complimented and welcomed the new range boss. But as Dodds realized, he was stepping onto a larger stage; in terms of athletic heritage, politics and budget, the University of Texas was quite different from Kansas State, with its own set of challenges. He settled in for a long and pivotal tenure.

Football ruled the UT landscape, as it had long before Dodds' arrival. Abe Lemons' sixth basketball team, while expecting improvement over 1981, was looking at another middle-of-the-pack finish. Soph forward Mike Wacker, who appeared to have elevated his game considerably, was Texas' emotional leader. LaSalle Thompson, the other inside fixture, was dropping hints that he might depart for the NBA after one more year in Austin. Between puffs on his cigar, Lemons sang the praises of Wacker and Thompson and promised a more aggressive, higher-scoring Longhorn team. But he made no predictions: "If I knew, I'd be one of those swamis," noting that all fortune tellers and palm readers seemed to live in old, run-down houses. While no one was saying that Lemons' job was in jeopardy, the numbers over the last four seasons indicated decline—26-5 in 1978, 21-8 in 1979, 19-11 in 1980 and 15-15 in 1981.

What would prove to be an unforgettable 1982 season began with a 74-57 defeat of Hardin-Simmons. Freshman guard Jack Worthington (who had scored over 3,000 points as a Houston high school star) keyed a second-half surge, Thompson had 18 points and 16 rebounds, and another frosh, Carlton Cooper, got the first of many high-flying slam dunks in his UT career. The Cowboys were paced by center Jake Bethany with 15 points. The Colorado Buffaloes shot 68 percent and built a 12-point lead at intermission because, Lemons claimed, his team had "all the enthusiasm of a dead rat." But the Horns came back and gave their pessimistic coach and 6,506 Erwin Center fans a nice 76-64 victory. Thompson had a game-high 29 points and 16 rebounds, while swingman Denard Holmes (an Army veteran with one year of junior college experience) scored 17.

The second-half kids did it again in Des Moines. UT trailed Drake by 12 points but got serious in the last 20 minutes, beating the Bulldogs, 58-51, behind Wacker's 22 points. Worthington took a full-court pass from Howland (15) and made a three-point play to seal the win.

Back at home, Texas rolled over an outmanned Biscayne team, 91-63. The early-season schedule, as *Austin American-Statesman* and *Daily Texan* sportswriters pointed out, had been rather light—as was attendance at home games—but 4-0 was better than 0-4, and the team was learning how to play together. It became 5-0 with a 108-75 trimming of Iowa State. Holmes had 33 points, seven steals and four assists against the befuddled Cyclones.

For the fourth straight year, the Longhorns did not participate in a regular-season tournament. They traveled to New England to engage Harvard on December 18. Instead of playing at Boston Garden (as the two teams did in 1980) or the Crimson's new facility in Cambridge (it was not yet ready), they met in ancient, 1,000-seat Indoor Athletic Building, which some members of the Texas traveling party swore was the site where Dr. James Naismith hung the first peach basket in 1891. The Horns squandered a four-point lead in the last minute and had to go into overtime, but a couple of key plays by Ray Harper allowed them to escape with a 72-71 win, Lemons' 100th at UT. Joe Carrabino of Harvard led all scorers with 22 points.

Five Longhorns reached double figures in an 82-56 destruction of Drake at the Erwin Center, the second such matchup in 17 days. Frustrated by rough double-teaming in early games, Thompson had 21 points. He was right at home for the next game, against Xavier in Cincinnati. Thompson had been something of a high school legend there, and some people in the

Queen City were still hurt that he had gone to Texas. The 5,128 fans at Riverfront Coliseum must have been impressed with the performance of their guests in burnt orange. UT outrebounded the Musketeers by 34, and Thompson had 21 of them. Wacker scored 21 points in beating Xavier, 97-71. "I like this team," Lemons said. "They're playing up to their capabilities, playing good offense and good defense. They're noncomplainers. Regardless of what happens, I like this ballclub. If we don't get someone hurt, I think we can make a run at them in the Southwest Conference."

Record: 16-11
74 Hardin-Simmons 57
76 Colorado 64
58 Drake 51
91 Biscayne 63
108 Iowa State 75
72 Harvard 71 (OT)
82 Drake 56
97 Xavier 71
55 Texas Tech 50
60 SMU 51
95 Houston 83
87 Arkansas 73
105 TCU 89
88 South Carolina 71
59 Baylor 69
69 Texas A&M 71 (OT)
49 Rice 80
69 SMU 56
55 Arkansas 62 (OT)
63 Houston 77
69 TCU 81
84 North Texas 70
59 Baylor 62
70 Texas A&M 91
65 Texas Tech 67
59 Rice 60
46 Baylor 48

The Longhorns kicked off conference play with a brutal little war against Texas Tech at the Erwin Center. They blew a 13-point halftime lead and trailed by three with seven minutes left when Harper replaced Worthington at point guard and settled things down. With 14 points each from Holmes, Thompson and Wacker, Texas outlasted the Red Raiders, 55-50. If Tech's Jeff Taylor had made more than four of his 17 shots, the outcome might have been different.

Confident if not cocky before their matchup with SMU in Dallas, the Horns again took a big lead at intermission and then kept on resting. They let the Mustangs score 12 straight points (mostly by sophomore John Addison) and get back in it. For the second straight game, Lemons feared victory was slipping away. But Howland scored 24 points, and Thompson got 21 rebounds, enough to secure a 60-51 win over Dave Bliss' scrappy team, destined for another last-place finish.

Houston, 11-1 and ranked No. 10 in the nation, played host to Texas, 10-0 and No. 19, on January 12 amid considerable media attention. The Cougars, sultans of slam with 62 dunks and a kamikaze offense, had a very intriguing freshman center by the name of Hakeem Abdul Olajuwon. A native of Nigeria, his background was soccer, only lately supplanted by basketball. He had arrived at UH in utter obscurity yet made "guarantees" of 25 points and 10 blocked shots per game. Olajuwon was not quite to that point, but his raw potential was unmistakable; in time, he would become one of the greatest players in SWC—and NBA—history. A capacity crowd at Hofheinz Pavilion saw Olajuwon demonstrate his inexperience, getting in foul trouble and scoring just two points. The star of the game was Wacker, who made nine of 14 from the field for 32 points in a convincing 95-83 victory. The same team that had chewed the Horns up and spat them out three times in 1981 was humbled by Wacker, Thompson (21) and a couple of skinny frosh guards, Worthington and James Tandy. Clyde Drexler had 21 points and 13 rebounds for Houston. "A win is a win, but this was a hell of a win," Lemons said in the happy victors' locker room.

That big game was followed by another, against Eddie Sutton's No. 9 Razorbacks. There was not an empty seat in the upper reaches of the Erwin Center mezzanine when UT and Arkansas tipped off; a record 16,401 fans were there to see the Longhorns roll to an 87-73 win. When Texas went up, 10-0, in the first three minutes, the Hogs had to abandon their go-slow offense and never really came close. Tony Brown scored 24 points for the losers, and LaSalle Thompson eliminated any doubt that he was the finest big man in Longhorn history with 32 points (missing just two of 14 shots from the field), 13 rebounds, six blocks and five assists despite playing on a bad ankle. "This was a nightmare," said Sutton, the sage of the Ozarks. "Texas played a great game, and Thompson was just sensational."

The twin killing of Houston and Arkansas left the Longhorns a bit drained, and some Lemons oratory at halftime was needed before they could beat TCU, 105-89, in Austin. Virdell Howland scored 26, mostly from the outside, Wacker and Thompson (*Sports Illustrated*'s player of the week) had their way inside, and Holmes handed out 13 assists. Darrell Browder threw in 28 points for the Horned Frogs. Their coach, Jim Killingsworth, expressed surprise that UT was not yet in the top 10, but Lemons refused to be drawn into a discussion of polls. "There are 40 top 10 teams," he said. "All that stuff's irrelevant, anyway. All we worry about

the buzzer. Lemons was left to ponder a season that had gone from sublime to terrible in five weeks. The 1982 Longhorns, once 14-0, finished 16-11, tied with Rice for seventh place in the SWC. The line of demarcation, of course, had been Wacker's injury.

The season came to a thunderous conclusion on March 9 when UT athletic director DeLoss Dodds announced Lemons' firing. He declined to offer specific reasons, referring only to "a series of incidents from this and past years, along with the need for new leadership and direction." The players' response was uniformly one of disbelief because Lemons had brought Texas basketball out of the doldrums, winning 110 games in six years. He was a popular if not charismatic coach, but he was also volatile and irreverent. His acid tongue had been applied to most any and everyone—fans, players, coaches, referees, the SWC office, UT alumni, faculty and administrators. Just one player Lemons brought to Austin graduated during his tenure, and lack of academic progress was another contributing factor in the decision to cut him loose. Twenty-one seasons at a pair of little independent schools had not prepared Lemons for the University of Texas, and his refusal or inability to adjust to very different circumstances finally did him in. Lemons made some bitter comments in the days, weeks and even years after his axing, one of the most acrimonious events in UT athletic history. But that did not prevent him from being invited back for a pair of reunions in 1991 and 1998 or voted into the Longhorn Hall of Honor in 1994.

1983

So Abe Lemons was gone. But he was not quite gone, or not gone yet because he remained on the staff of the UT athletic department for a year. Before returning to Oklahoma City University to finish his coaching career, Lemons, who said he was "hibernating," made little effort to conceal his displeasure over getting busted. The players put together a petition in support of Lemons' long-time assistant, Barry Dowd, but that was a hopeless cause. Whether by perception or reality, Dowd was just too closely connected to Lemons, and AD DeLoss Dodds had determined to clean up and change the culture of the Texas basketball program.

Jack Hartman of Kansas State, Tom Davis of Boston College, Don DeVoe of Tennessee and Carl Tacy of Wake Forest were some of the coaches considered to replace Lemons, but the man chosen was 37-year-old Bob Weltlich of Mississippi. He signed a five-year contract worth $95,000 per annum on April 2, 1982. An Ohio State graduate, Weltlich did not play basketball for the Buckeyes, but his friendship with Bobby Knight (they came from the same small town in Ohio) paid off when Knight, the head coach at Army, brought him on as an assistant. When Knight went to Indiana, Weltlich followed and was part of the Hoosiers' 1976 national championship campaign. His first head coaching job was at Ole Miss, a school with a weak basketball history. Although Weltlich's record in Oxford over six seasons was slightly below .500, he got the Rebels into the NCAA tourney once and the NIT twice and developed fine players like Elston Turner, John Stroud and Carlos Clark. Knight, who won a second national title in 1981, gave Weltlich a strong recommendation, and thus he came to coach the Texas Longhorns.

A disciplinarian and teacher of fundamentals like his mentor, Weltlich preached the philosophy of strong man-to-man defense and patient offense. "The program will center around good people, good athletes and good workers," he said. "They'll be students first, players second. We're going to do it with character, not characters," evidently a comment on the fast-and-loose style employed by Lemons. Weltlich's first meetings with the players and the media were characterized by a "my way or the highway" tone. The new coach was partial to regimentation and closed practices, and he imposed an off-season training regimen, a curfew and a policy forbidding players from talking to the media without his permission. Due to Weltlich's heavy-handed manner, he absorbed a few shots even before the season began, being unkindly dubbed "Kaiser Bob." He made no attempt to court Lemons' legion of fans, who did not suffer in silence. Only winning would turn the situation around, and no one was expecting UT to win much in 1983.

Weltlich's first Longhorn team had some athletic talent, but it would not strike fear into the hearts of Southwest Conference competitors. LaSalle Thompson had begun a long if unspectacular NBA career. Mike Wacker's knee rehabilitation was a long and slow process that cost him two seasons. Denard Holmes, James Tandy and Ray Harper departed for academic and other reasons, and there were more demotions and defections to come. A late start on recruiting hindered Weltlich and Eddie Oran, the assistant he brought from Ole Miss. Some fans booed and others cheered Weltlich when he was introduced before a late-November exhibition game, an embarrassing 20-point loss to the Polish national team. The Horns began what nearly everyone conceded would be a long season at home against North Carolina Wesleyan, an NCAA Division III school. Carlton Cooper scored 12 points in a 53-42 defeat of the feisty Bishops.

The first road game was in a cozy little gym on the University of New Orleans campus close by Lake Pontchartrain. Don Smith's veteran Privateer team built a 15-point halftime lead and strode to a 74-56 win. The Horns' inexperience was manifested in many ways, starting with captain Don Ellis. A 6'5" JC transfer, he missed all four shots, turned the ball over five times and fouled out with 15 minutes left. Help was on the way, though. Bill Wendlandt, who sat out the 1982 season with an ankle injury, had missed the first two games because of an NCAA suspension for playing in an AAU summer tournament. His scoring and rebounding prowess were sorely needed on a team lacking both. Wendlandt's first game back was no Rocky Mountain high because the Colorado Buffaloes converted 15 fast breaks into layups and ran rampant over UT, 75-48, in Boulder. The Longhorns fell behind, 13-0, at the start, and only a combined 25 points from Cooper and Wendlandt made it at all respectable. Weltlich offered no excuses: "It was terribly disappointing. We just didn't do the job."

Doing the job was not easy with a 6'4" post man, even one who could jump like Cooper. And things were none too secure in the backcourt, where soph Jack Worthington and freshman Karl Willock were learning to play together. The Horns hosted the first of five straight home games on December 7 against Xavier. Anthony Hicks scored 26 for the Musketeers in a 66-64 overtime victory. The 3,729 fans could take comfort in strong offensive showings by Wendlandt (18), Ellis (17) and Cooper (13 points and 15 rebounds). Willock, who looked like a keeper, had six assists.

The Longhorns, scratching at the surface of Weltlich's master plan, used Wendlandt's 21 points and 12 rebounds to subdue Biscayne, 75-64. The crowd, 2,111, was the smallest in the six-year history of the Erwin Center, but Weltlich claimed not to care. He was quite confident of his long-range success in Austin. One of Weltlich's former Southeastern Conference foes, Georgia, came to town and put a 75-54 licking on UT. The unbeaten Bulldogs got 19 points from Vern Fleming and overwhelmed Texas inside, although Wendlandt was able to hit 11 of 14 shots. Georgia coach Hugh Durham, who heard the boos, gave Weltlich a public expression of support, saying if he could succeed at Ole Miss, he certainly could do it at Texas. Durham urged patience.

Record: 6-22

53 North Carolina Wesleyan 42
56 New Orleans 74
48 Colorado 75
64 Xavier 66 (OT)
75 Biscayne 64
54 Georgia 75
73 Harvard 58
78 Missouri Western 70
62 Santa Clara 76
60 North Carolina-Charlotte 49
54 TCU 70
43 Kansas State 51
51 Texas Tech 59
52 Houston 77
47 Rice 45
64 Arkansas 83
43 Baylor 76
52 Texas A&M 64
64 SMU 73
48 TCU 82
66 Texas Tech 78
63 Houston 106
56 Rice 71
67 Arkansas 84
57 Baylor 86
59 Texas A&M 96
67 SMU 95
48 SMU 49

Wendlandt continued his hot shooting in victories over Harvard, 73-58, and Missouri Western, 78-70. He scored a total of 47 points against those teams, neither of which were national championship contenders. The Ivy League's Crimson did not offer athletic scholarships, and the Griffons played in the NAIA, but the games were on the schedule, and the two wins counted.

Distressed at his team's poor defensive play, Weltlich held a practice session on Christmas night. Since practices—whether at Gregory Gym or the Erwin Center—were closed to everyone except players, coaches, managers and trainers, there was a certain mystery as to what went on. Weltlich vigorously instructed his men on how he thought the game should be played, and his methods caused more concern than his inattention to school traditions, such as talking while "The Eyes of Texas" was being played. Profanity and insults were the norm, and brutal charging drills, loose-ball drills and duckwalks were used to instill toughness and discipline. Weltlich, whose wife bragged that he cheerfully changed their baby daughter's diapers, cussed like a stevedore and used hard-edged motivational techniques only his friend, Bobby Knight, could get away with in the 1980s. The team's pregame meals were conducted in silence. On the other hand, some of the improvements Dodds demanded took place, such as more attention to players' academic progress, less mischief during their off time and an almost complete curtailment of contact between players and boosters. Dodds did that himself by shutting down the quasi-independent Burnt Orange Club, or at least bringing it in-house. The club's carnival atmosphere, with Lemons the star attraction, was but a fond memory for its members.

The Cable Car Classic, UT's first holiday tournament in five years, began with a 76-62 loss to host Santa Clara. The Longhorns shot 67 percent in the first half but let the Broncos score 12 straight points and seize control of the game. Harold Keeling had 20 points for Santa Clara, and Willock (14) paced Texas. The consolation game against 1-6 North Carolina-Charlotte was a 60-49 Horn victory. Willock and Cooper, recently released from Weltlich's doghouse, teamed up for 35 points in a game featuring the sticky defense and slow, careful offense the coach insisted upon.

Although their 5-5 record was a bit deceptive because they had not beaten a tough team, the Horns felt good as SWC play approached. Publicly, at least. Ellis and Wendlandt, given permission to speak, expressed optimism. And Randy Riggs of the *Austin American-Statesman* wrote, "Bob Weltlich might well turn out to be the best thing that could have happened to the program.... The young Longhorns are being molded into the kind of team Weltlich has a reputation for producing." Some fans agreed and showed displeasure at the widespread criticism of the new coach and his team, sparking something of a debate as to who the "real" fans were.

TCU, off to a 9-2 start, visited Austin on January 3 and proceeded to thump UT, 70-54. Weltlich's SWC initiation consisted of watching Joe Stephen (20) fill it up from the outside and Doug Arnold (19) from the inside. It was the Frogs' first win ever at the Erwin Center. The cold-shooting (29 percent) Longhorns then fell to Kansas State, 51-43, in a nonconference game. Needing a compass and map to find the baskets, Texas shot woefully from the field and the charity stripe, negating a strong defensive effort. Wildcat center Les Craft won scoring honors with 13 points. As they had done since the Biscayne game, UT officials included no-shows in attendance figures, giving the impression of considerably more fans in those orange seats than there really were. At the Kansas State game, for example, 4,014 fans were in the building, while 8,909 (the number of tickets sold) was the somewhat bogus figure announced.

Two losing teams with problems in the ranks, Texas and Texas Tech, met in Lubbock. Gerald Myers' team was 2-12, some players had quit and others had received the boot, but Tech used a 12-1 run in the last five minutes to grab a 59-51 victory. The Red Raiders received balanced scoring from the six players who got in the game, while Willock (16) and Wendlandt (14) were UT's best. Weltlich chatted with his team for 25 minutes before opening the locker-room door.

Seventy-eight dunks and 103 blocked shots in 14 games were some of the staggering statistics the Houston Cougars brought to Austin. Hakeem Olajuwon, Clyde Drexler, Larry Micheaux and Michael Young were the stars of one of the biggest, baddest teams in SWC history. The Horns jumped to a surprising 10-0 lead, but it could not, and did not, last. Drexler (24) led UH to a 77-52 win that caused Weltlich to wonder if the refs were not giving Guy Lewis' players the benefit of the doubt too often. Jack Worthington, who played 38 minutes, scored one point and made 13 turnovers against the Cougars, quit the team, citing pressure and purported religious reasons for his departure. To compound matters, a wrist injury to Ellis and a knee injury to Willock sidelined them for the rest of the season. Riddled by injury, defection and speculation, the Horns were in for tough times; the team already had three walk-ons, and more were coming.

Despite all their woes, the shorthanded Longhorns managed to beat Rice, 47-45, in another home game. Wendlandt scored 11 points, walk-on guard David Willett converted four clutch free throws, and Cooper tipped in a missed foul shot in the final seconds to win. The makeshift lineup held the Owls to 37 percent shooting. "I'm really proud of all those who played tonight," Weltlich said. "They've overcome a lot of adversity in the last few days."

The Abe and Eddie Show that entertained SWC audiences for six years was over since Lemons' firing.

Weltlich heard plenty about the stormy games the Horns and Hogs played during that time, and he knew it was not the same. Sutton was still coaching Arkansas, then 14-1 and ranked fourth nationally, and the Barnhill Arena fans were as ferocious as ever, but Texas' side had changed. The Horns lost, 83-64. Darrell Walker and Alvin Robertson, one of the top backcourt duos in college hoops, scored a total of 42 points, and Wendlandt distinguished himself by hitting 10 of 13 from the field. If UT had shot better than 31 percent from the free throw line, the game would have been much closer. Sutton paid Weltlich an obligatory compliment and predicted the Longhorns would be back on their feet "in a few years." Weltlich was speechless after seeing his team score just 14 first-half points in a 76-43 trouncing by Baylor in Waco. Daryl Baucham scored 22 points as the Bears snapped a four-game losing streak. In the late minutes, Weltlich inserted a couple of walk-ons, one of whom, Lance Watson, was a former Longhorn cheerleader. The media, of course, had a field day with the fact that a cheerleader made the basketball team. For the rest of the 1983 season, some fans taunted Weltlich with yells of "Put in the cheerleader!" Watson, for his part, did not understand all the fuss. He had been all-district in high school, had no illusions of stardom at UT and only wanted to help the team.

After coming to UT from Mississippi, coach Bob Weltlich won just six games his first year.

The Horns bounced back from the terrible showing against Baylor to give Texas A&M a stern test before losing, 64-52, in front of 7,119 fans at the Erwin Center. Texas led by one at the half and was close until the last five minutes when Tyren Naulls (20), Reggie Roberts (15) and Claude Riley (13) set the Aggies ahead. The UT frontcourt looked good as Wendlandt scored 15 points and Cooper got a career-high 17 rebounds. Weltlich and SMU coach Dave Bliss were friends from way back, both having served under Bobby Knight at West Point and Indiana. With big men like Jon Koncak and Larry Davis, Bliss' Mustangs were aspiring to reach the top of the SWC. Wendlandt, playing with a sore lower back, something that would require surgery after the season, scored 21 points in a 73-64 loss. The Horns handled SMU's press easily most of the time but got tired near the end. Of the 10 players Weltlich used, eight were frosh, walk-ons or both. "It may be the sorriest state a major college basketball team has been in since who knows when," wrote the *Austin American-Statesman*'s Paul Schnitt, who nevertheless believed Weltlich would eventually succeed.

Darrell Browder, TCU's first all-conference player in 11 years, got 22 points in an 82-48 defeat of Texas at Daniel-Meyer Coliseum. Although coach Jim Killingsworth mercifully chose not to press, it was UT's worst loss ever to the Horned Frogs. Weltlich did not mince words in critiquing his players, especially guards Mitch Parrish and Doug Moe. He called them "as phony as the day is long" and threatened to kick Moe off the team as the game was being played. With seven regular-season games left, morale was terrible.

Weltlich, a polar opposite of Lemons in terms of personality and offensive and defensive basketball, agreed with his predecessor on a couple of issues—poor officiating and the SWC office's halfhearted promotion of the sport. He urged commissioner Fred Jacoby to find or train better refs and to improve the league's TV package. In the meantime, the Longhorn roster continued to evolve as a player walked off and another walked on. Craig Carlton, a junior civil engineering major with solid high school and intramural experience, met his new teammates on Wednesday and was in the starting lineup against Texas Tech on Saturday before an Erwin Center crowd of 2,907. He was actually a decent player and UT's floor general the last quarter of the season. Despite 25 points and 13 rebounds from a hurting Wendlandt, the Horns lost, 78-66. Wendlandt also put the clamps on David Reynolds after the Red Raider forward scored 17 first-half points.

Huge underdogs to the fourth-ranked Houston Cougars, Weltlich's Longhorns strolled into Hofheinz Pavilion on February 15 and suffered a bruising 106-63 defeat. As was usually the case in the final games of the season, Cooper, Wendlandt and freshman David Seitz were the top scorers and rebounders. UH, en route to a first-ever SWC title and runner-up spot in the NCAA tourney, was paced by Clyde Drexler (21). Guy Lewis' biggest problem was keeping agents and NBA scouts out of his locker room. Then, it was a battle of cellar-dwellers at Autry Court as Rice and Texas squared off. The Horns were ahead by two with 15 minutes left when Wendlandt picked up four quick fouls, and the game went the Owls' way from then on. Renaldo O'Neal (21) led five Rice players in double figures, while Wendlandt made nine of 10 field goal tries before fouling out of a 71-56 loss. "We weren't tough down the stretch," said Texas' junior forward. "They just played harder than we did."

Craig Carlton and Doug Moe against Darrell Walker and Alvin Robertson. That was the guard matchup when No. 6 Arkansas visited the Erwin Center, and the result was an 84-67 defeat. The quick-handed Razorback guards caused most of UT's 33 turnovers and combined for 42 points, and soph center Joe Kleine had 11 points and 12 rebounds. Just before tipoff, UA coach Eddie Sutton surveyed 12,000 empty seats and commented, "This is the most depressing place to play I've ever seen. It looks like the YMCA gym on a Saturday morning." The final home game of the year was an 86-57 defeat administered by Baylor that had Weltlich pulling what little hair he had left. Wendlandt, playing with increasing pain in his back, hit just four of 12 shots against the Bruins.

Weltlich's lone SWC victory was 183 fewer than the number Shelby Metcalf had amassed over a 20-year career with Texas A&M. The old professor added another one in a 96-59 drilling of the Longhorns in College Station. It was never close as the Ags went up by 20 at the half and kept stretching their lead. Weltlich, who said his team resembled Clydesdales chasing quarterhorses against Arkansas, used a new analogy. "It looked like a track meet," he said. "We've got 11.0 sprinters, and they've got 9.2."

Seitz, one of those Clydesdales, those 11.0 sprinters Weltlich referred to, was proving himself a heady ballplayer. He scored a team-high 24 points in a 95-67 loss to SMU at Moody Coliseum. Dave Piehler made 13 of 14 shots from the field for the Mustangs. There was no need to return home because the Longhorns were to play SMU again two days later in the first round of the SWC tourney. Cooper was excellent, scoring 20 points and collecting 18 rebounds and almost winning the game at the buzzer. His tip-in of a missed shot was waved off by referee Lynn Shortnacy, allowing the Ponies to take a 49-48 squeaker. Twenty-five turnovers and poor free throw shooting did not help Texas' cause.

The exhausting, nightmarish season was over. Six wins and 22 losses (including the last 13 in a row) rivaled the worst UT records ever, 4-20 in 1955 and again in 1959. Cut to ribbons by the Frogs, Bears, Aggies and nearly everyone else, the 1983 Longhorns had some skilled frontcourt men in Wendlandt, Cooper and Seitz, but they sure needed help. Weltlich, who seemed willing to rebuild from the ground up, was defiant, urging his SWC colleagues to get their licks in while they had the chance. The coach with the steely blue eyes was certain he would restore a winning tradition at the Erwin Center.

1984

"Texas deserves excellence and expects it," said coach Bob Weltlich on the eve of his second year in Austin. "But I'm not going to cut corners to achieve it. We've covered some ground in recruiting and hope to have a deeper and more athletic team." Of course, it remained to be seen whether the turmoil and losing of the 1983 season would carry over into 1984. Six freshmen found out soon enough that Weltlich's practice sessions were not exactly a cruise on the Good Ship Lollipop. The returning mainstays were Bill Wendlandt (who had undergone back surgery in the summer), Carlton Cooper, Karl Willock and David

Seitz. Rehabilitation on Mike Wacker's knee continued slowly, and he remained part of the program, but he was not yet ready to play. Because Baylor had a particularly bad team, the Longhorns were not picked to finish at the bottom of the Southwest Conference.

Cooper scored 38 points in the opener against Missouri Southern on November 26, but it was Seitz' three-point play in the closing seconds that gave UT an 83-81 overtime win. Weltlich and the players were happy and yet relieved because losing to the NAIA-affiliated Lions would have been mortifying. Texas dropped a 64-58 decision to New Orleans four days later with Cooper getting 20 points and 14 rebounds. The Horns cut a 10-point lead down to one in the last minute before the Privateers took advantage of Texas' turnovers and scrambling defense to win it. Center John Harris scored 20 for UNO. Weltlich made some ominous post-game comments about older players getting "moved aside" if their performance did not improve.

One of those he had in mind was Wendlandt. The 6'7" senior's back was still tender, and he had the flu, but two-of-nine shooting against New Orleans earned him a ticket to the bench for the first road game of the year in frigid Ames, Iowa. More than 12,000 people packed Hilton Coliseum in the kind of big-time basketball environment most players dream of. Johnny Orr's Iowa State team forced 37 turnovers and took an 81-57 victory over the rattled Longhorns, who still managed a sizable rebound advantage. Barry Stevens, Ron Harris, Jeff Hornacek and the rest of the Cyclones had too much firepower for a young UT team. Wendlandt, given five minutes of mop-up duty against Iowa State, dropped a bombshell the following Monday morning by quitting. The Horns' top scorer in 1983 issued a four-paragraph statement citing unspecified personal and medical reasons for leaving the team. Wendlandt, who already had his degree from the University, decided he had just had a bellyful of Bob Weltlich, and besides, a pro team in Amsterdam sought his services, so he went.

Record: 7-21

83 Missouri Southern 81 (OT)
58 New Orleans 64
57 Iowa State 81
51 Biscayne 50
63 Long Beach State 83
77 Georgia Southwestern 60
59 Oral Roberts 74
77 San Diego State 91
62 Utah 61
67 Weber State 82
54 Kansas State 64
47 Texas Tech 74
58 Houston 69
49 Rice 63
66 Arkansas 70
67 Baylor 47
52 Texas A&M 68
81 SMU 105
53 TCU 60
65 Texas Tech 94
63 Houston 74
61 Rice 57
41 Arkansas 59
61 Baylor 54
57 Texas A&M 72
72 SMU 103
70 TCU 78
54 Texas A&M 75

With two frosh in the starting lineup, guard Mike Hess and forward Raynard Davis, the Longhorns got another win by the skin of their collective teeth—51-50 over Biscayne, an NCAA Division II team. Dane Johnson of the Bobcats scored a game-high 20 points. But on the west coast, Long Beach State shot 58 percent from the field and inflicted an 83-63 defeat on the Horns, a team clearly lacking spirit and cohesiveness. At one point, a disgusted Weltlich sent in five new players. When the game was over, he kept the squad in the locker room for a heart-to-heart talk. "I didn't yell at them," he said. "I'm tired of yelling at them. We just discussed what it means to wear that jersey with 'Texas' across the front, what responsibilities that entails."

Freshman guard Marcus Bolden scored 25 points to help dispatch Americus' team, Georgia Southwestern, 77-60. An NAIA team whose schedule contained no other remotely major school, the Hurricanes played tough all the way. UT's winning streak ended at one with a 74-59 loss to Oral Roberts in Austin. The Titans' brother duo of Mark and Jeff Acres, the sons of coach Richard Acres, combined for 42 points and 21 rebounds to wear down the smaller Horns. Cooper (24 points and 15 rebounds) was one of Texas' few bright spots.

Before the Longhorns played another game, there was more bad news: Don Ellis and Mike Hess had quit. Ellis, a senior, said he needed to apply himself academically, but Hess, a promising freshman point guard, laid it on Weltlich. The coach did not deny using Hess and Mitch Parrish as "targets" in charging drills, over and over again, a tactic that made other team members cringe. Parrish hung on until an injury ended his sophomore season, but Hess went home. Nine scholarship players had quit since Weltlich's arrival, and he expressed concern, although his faith in the long-term success of the UT basketball program seemed unshaken. Athletic director

DeLoss Dodds, who took considerable heat for firing Abe Lemons and then hiring Weltlich, was solidly behind him. "Bob's got a tough, tough job, and I don't doubt that he's going to pull it off," Dodds said. "It takes time, patience and understanding."

San Diego State's all-America forward, Michael Cage, was like a man among boys in the Aztecs' 91-77 victory over UT on December 20. He scored 37 points and grabbed 12 rebounds, just three fewer than the entire Longhorn team. Cooper (23) called Cage the finest player he had ever encountered. Of the six home games played thus far, attendance had not reached the 3,000 mark. Erwin Center crowds were late arrivers as a general rule, and sometimes the players came out on the court for pregame warmups and were dismayed to see fewer than 1,000 people awaiting them.

The 10-man Longhorn squad traveled to snow-covered Salt Lake City to play in the 16th annual Utah Classic. The Utes, hosts of the tourney, had just a 4-5 record but expected to reach the finals. Before 12,608 stunned fans, UT scored a 62-61 upset when Willock hit a layup in the waning seconds. Weltlich rushed onto the court after the buzzer and was bear-hugged by several of his players. Undoubtedly the biggest win yet in Weltlich's tenure, it snapped a streak of 21 road losses. The next night, however, the Horns had two critical dry spells in the second half and fell to Weber State, 82-67. The Wildcats got 21 points from guard John Price and 19 from 7' center Shawn Campbell.

The final pre-SWC game took place at Ahearn Fieldhouse on the Kansas State campus. Jack Hartman's Wildcats had some trouble with UT before securing a 64-54 victory highlighted by Ben Mitchell's 16 points. Cooper, who spent part of the game on the bench with a bruised leg, scored 18.

That performance, against a Big 8 team on a foreign court, gave the Horns a sense of qualified optimism, a feeling that progress was being made. But any such sanguine outlook vanished in a 74-47 blowout by Texas Tech before 5,480 fans at the Erwin Center. All 12 Red Raiders scored, and their various zone, man-to-man and pressing defenses baffled UT, which got 15 points from Cooper. In the game's late minutes, Weltlich sat with a glazed expression on his face. "Terrible, terrible, we just played terrible," he said. "Even if we'd played well, I'm not sure we could have beaten them. How's that grab you, coming from the coach?"

On television, the callow Longhorns had seen Hakeem "the Dream" Olajuwon in the Final Four the past two years (and 1984 would make three), read about him in *Sports Illustrated* and all but asked for his autograph before the Texas-Houston game at Hofheinz Pavilion. While the Cougars' great center scored just nine points in a 69-58 victory, he was in complete control of the backboards and made Cooper, Seitz, Davis and Dennis Perryman shoot poorly—just three of 25 from the field in the first half. Willock, a fine player whose offensive skills were sublimated for Weltlich's emphasis on defense, held Michael Young to 10 points. It was another of those dreaded "moral victories," but there was nothing moral about getting romped by Rice, 63-49. Tony Barnett of the Owls had 18 points and 15 rebounds, and not a single Longhorn stood out in a game Weltlich thought could be won. He again sequestered his team for half an hour, opening the visitors' locker room door just once to admit former UT star Slater Martin, who offered a few words of encouragement.

The Horns, then starting three freshmen, were going home for a pair of games. To the bittersweet amazement of 4,710 spectators, they played with intensity and confidence against Arkansas, coming back from an 18-point halftime deficit to challenge UA in the final minute but losing, 70-66. Alvin Robertson and Cooper (23) shared scoring honors in a loosely called game in which the Longhorns almost matched the Hogs' muscle. Baylor, a weak-shooting, weak-rebounding team, came to Austin on January 21 and got beaten by Texas, 67-47. A 24-2 run early in the second half effectively ended a six-game Longhorn losing streak. Seitz came off the bench to score a career-high 26 points. Bear coach Jim Haller called his team's performance "a horror show."

There was not exactly a call among other SWC teams to break up the Longhorns, but a win was a win, and Weltlich sought to build some momentum by taking Texas A&M. The Aggies, naturally, had other ideas. As freshman guard Todd Holloway keyed a second-half uprising, A&M blew by UT, 68-52, at G. Rollie White Coliseum. Despite Weltlich's pleadings from the bench, the Horns tried to run with the Ags and looked like they were hurrying from one mistake to another. Cooper (24) was the game's top scorer. And in Dallas, the SMU Mustangs scored an emphatic 105-81 victory with 22 points from center Jon Koncak, 18 from Larry Davis and 17 from Carl Wright. "We were totally dominated in every phase of the game," Weltlich said. "It was complete and total physical domination. They just manhandled us, mauled us."

With nine regular-season games left, the letters-to-the-editor sections of the *Daily Texan* and *Austin American-Statesman* were chock-full of comments regarding Weltlich and the Longhorn basketball program. Some claimed to see good effort from the players and evidence of a strong foundation being laid, but most were critical of the coach, his boring style of play and the sheer lack of success. Those readers pointed out that just 24 months earlier, Abe Lemons' last UT team was No. 5 in the nation and drawing much larger crowds.

TCU guards Dennis Nutt, Tracy Mitchell and Jamie Dixon were masters at using screens to launch long-range jumpers, which allowed the Frogs to beat Texas, 60-53, at the Erwin Center. A week later in Lubbock, Gerald Myers' Red Raiders had another easy time defeating the Longhorns (94-65), who committed 26 turnovers and were outrebounded by a two-to-one margin. Texas Tech had a deeper and better team, and that showed in every way. Cooper and Perryman combined for 45 points for UT, which dipped to a 5-15 record.

Get it out of here! Carlton Cooper displays his fabled leaping ability by rejecting a Joe Kleine hook shot in a four-point loss to Arkansas.

Fifth-ranked Houston had won 34 straight SWC games, and odds were that Texas would become the 35th victim after their meeting in Austin. The Horns lost, 74-63, but they made a game of it, entertaining a crowd of 9,548. Trailing by 21 points in the second half, they went on a 16-0 run led by the big-hearted Cooper. The Cougars got 17 points and 11 rebounds from freshman forward Rickie Winslow, and Hakeem Olajuwon blocked 11 shots. Horn fans consoled themselves that the team had not suffered a technical knockout by the UH heavyweights. "We played hard," Weltlich said. "The next step is to play smart." They looked like geniuses in a 61-57 defeat of Rice at the Erwin Center. Cooper's dunk off a half-court inbounds pass from Perryman put the finishing touches on a rare win.

Just as in 1982 and 1983, the SWC was ruled by the big two, Houston and Arkansas; only Cougars and Razorbacks would be found on the 1984 all-conference team. Arkansas, coming off a nationally televised defeat of Michael Jordan's North Carolina team, hosted UT for a Saturday afternoon game. Joe Kleine (27) gave Davis the education of his young life, and Leroy Sutton held Cooper to nine points in the Hogs' 59-41 victory. The Longhorns hit eight straight free throws in the last 27 seconds to beat Baylor, 61-54, before 2,950 fans at Heart O' Texas Coliseum. There were a total of 55 fouls and 53 turnovers in what Weltlich called "a weird game, a strange game." Willock rang up 17 points in the season's last win.

UT fell behind Texas A&M by 18 points early on but climbed back into it before a four-minute scoreless stretch ended any thoughts of an upset. The Aggies won, 72-57, as Darnell Williams, Todd Holloway and "Downtown" Kenny Brown teamed up for 60 points. The final home game of another glum season was with the SMU Mustangs, who had won 20 games for the first time since 1957. Dave Bliss' team, gunning for a berth in the NCAA Tournament, pummeled the Longhorns, 103-72. Most of the 4,352 fans did not know whether to laugh or cry at UT's ineptness. Cooper (23) and the Ponies' Jon Koncak (20) were the top scorers. It was an occasion in which the Erwin Center crowd traditionally showered appreciation on departing seniors, which—had fate not intervened—would have included Mike Wacker, Denard Holmes, Ray Harper and Bill Wendlandt. Substitute guard Craig Carlton, who played little in 1984, was the only senior.

Just seventh place in the SWC was at stake when Texas and TCU met in Fort Worth. Weltlich claimed his players were in a good frame of mind despite getting a heaping helping of humble pie. Freshman forward Carven Holcombe threw in 31 points in the Frogs' 78-70 victory, which sent UT to College Station for a first-round game in the SWC tourney. The Aggies put the Longhorns out of their misery with a 75-54 win keyed by Winston Crite's 25 points. Cooper, who had played so well in recent games, did a disappearing act, scoring just one field goal and two free throws. Even when they were way behind A&M, the Horns kept running their methodical, pass-pass-pass offense. In a postseason analysis, Weltlich was frank in saying a 7-21 mark was not good enough, but he insisted improvement was being made, both on and off the court. Gourd-green players had gained valuable experience, and the average conference loss had fallen from a margin of 21 points in 1983 to 12 in 1984. Still, those lonely souls who continued their pilgrimage to the Erwin Center wanted to see more.

1985

Plenty of people were ready to stand and deliver the opinion that two years of Bob Weltlich constituted a full-scale disaster for Texas basketball. But the worst was over, and the Longhorns were likely to field a much better team in 1985. Some 33 months had passed since Mike Wacker injured his knee in Waco. The effervescent senior forward had three operations and put himself through many hours of grueling rehabilitation for the chance to play again. While his quickness and hang time reminded no one of Julius Erving, "Wack" was back and eager to see what he could do. John Brownlee, a 6'10" junior, had warmed the North Carolina bench for two seasons before transferring to UT despite tales of cruel and unusual punishment by Weltlich. (Verbal abuse by the coach had been mitigated at the insistence of AD DeLoss Dodds.) A prolific scorer during his high school days in Fort Worth, Brownlee was the big man the Horns needed to counter behemoths like Jon Koncak of SMU and Joe Kleine of Arkansas, both members of the 1984 U.S. Olympic team and future NBA players. With Wacker and Brownlee in the middle, Weltlich moved Carlton Cooper to the perimeter. Although the experts still considered UT a second-division team in the Southwest Conference, the gloom of the past two seasons had lifted somewhat.

Karl Willock and freshman Alex Broadway joined Wacker, Brownlee and Cooper in the starting lineup for the season opener, a 77-51 defeat of Southwestern College of Kansas. Willock took advantage of the Moundbuilders' feeble zone defense to score 25 points. A lot of eyes were on Wacker, who wore a brace and was taped from foot to thigh. He looked good in another home victory, 87-52 over Northwestern Louisiana. Wacker scored 18 points against the smaller Demons, and the guards—Willock, Broadway, Marcus Bolden and George Davis—helped force 29 turnovers.

A more suitable challenge awaited the Horns in the form of LSU. More than 13,000 fans extended a lovely welcome to Baton Rouge, chanting "Tiger meat" during pregame warm-ups. Dale Brown's team, No. 16 in the nation, enjoyed a sizable lead with seven minutes to play. Cooper and Bolden narrowed it to four points, but steady free throw shooting at the end enabled LSU to win, 87-79. Brownlee (20) was the game's top scorer, followed by the Tigers' Nikita Wilson (18).

It was a disappointing loss, leading to a week of rotten practices, but the Horns answered the bell against Long Beach State with an 86-62 victory. They outrebounded the 49ers by a 41-31 margin and got 21 points from Wacker. Weltlich, who so often in the past two years heard opposing coaches make sympathetic remarks about his team, did that for Long Beach. UT fans who once sat mostly quiet, some protesting with bags over their heads, were daring to cheer for the team. There was still a semiorganized opposition to Weltlich headquartered at the Red Tomato restaurant, but those individuals found less to complain about early in the 1985 season.

In the midst of final exams, the Longhorns dropped an 82-71 decision to Oral Roberts in Tulsa. When Willock got three early fouls and went to the bench, the team seemed to come unglued. Mark Acres scored 21 for the winning Titans. Back at the Erwin Center, UT was struggling against Missouri Western when Cooper went on a brilliant three-minute stretch. He converted three jump shots, stole the ball followed by a dunk and threw in another long jumper. But Cooper was not the leading scorer in the 83-66 defeat of the Griffons because Wacker had 23 points to his 14.

A flight delay caused the team to arrive just six hours before a game with California-Riverside, and the Horns looked sluggish early, falling behind by eight points. Three late hoops by freshman Myron Lilley helped secure a 61-52 victory over the Highlanders. Two days later and a few miles down the coastal highway, Texas suffered a 71-65 loss to San Diego State. While Wacker and Brownlee combined for 34 points, 48 percent free throw shooting and poor rebounding spelled defeat. Anthony Watson (20) paced the Aztecs.

Over a span of four and a half decades at Gregory Gym and seven years at the Erwin Center, the University of Texas had never hosted a men's college basketball tournament. That surprising omission ended with the inaugural Longhorn Classic. It took a lot of time and effort; Dodds headed the steering committee, and there were six subcommittees. Thirty-one local sponsors lent their support to the tourney, attended by slightly more than 7,000 fans. Cooper scored 24 points in UT's 69-57 defeat of Army, but Brownlee, who had a bad game against the Black Knights, drew scorn from Weltlich. The Horns took the trophy with a controversial 69-68 victory over Mercer. As time ran out, Lilley blocked—or was it a foul?—Melvin Randall's shot under the basket. No whistle was blown, and that was the game. Army coach Les Wothke and Mercer's Bill Bibb both thought the officiating was inclined toward Texas. "It's sad this came down to a questionable call," Weltlich said. "But it doesn't matter now. I don't know how many Longhorn Classics there will be, but I know we won the first one."

Lubbock Municipal Coliseum, where the Horns had not won since 1978, was the site of the SWC opener. Weltlich, trying to light a fire under Brownlee, let his big man ride the pine early on. UT looked good with 10 minutes left, holding a seven-point lead. But guard Bubba Jennings (24) spearheaded a 20-4 run that allowed Texas Tech to win, 67-60. The collapse mystified Weltlich. Some of Texas' young players got jittery before the vocal Red Raider crowd, and Cooper continued to vacillate between excellent and awful.

Record: 15-13

77 Southwestern (of Kansas) 51
87 NW Louisiana 52
79 LSU 87
86 Long Beach State 62
71 Oral Roberts 82
83 Missouri Western 66
61 California-Riverside 52
65 San Diego State 71
69 Army 57
69 Mercer 68
60 Texas Tech 67
61 Houston 58
65 Rice 53
58 Arkansas 64
68 Baylor 65
61 Texas A&M 66
46 SMU 54
45 TCU 53
66 Texas Tech 61
80 Houston 94
66 Rice 65
51 Arkansas 60
75 Baylor 72
53 Texas A&M 51
60 SMU 64
52 TCU 54
71 Southern California 70
46 Arkansas 66

"The Longhorns are unlikely to win even if they do everything right," wrote Mike Blackwell of the *Austin American-Statesman* in previewing the UT-Houston game at the Erwin Center. Although the 9-2 Cougars no longer had Hakeem Olajuwon, then plying his trade for the Houston Rockets, they were rolling along and playing some strong basketball. In contrast to the events in Lubbock three days earlier, the Horns roared from 10 points down with nine minutes left to grab a 61-58 victory that had UH coach Guy Lewis mopping his face with a red-checkered towel. Davis and Willock hit key shots, Wacker collected 17 rebounds, and Brownlee asserted himself by scoring 20 points. "We finally got one to go our way," said an elated Weltlich.

Rice, too, was coming off a big upset, a three-point defeat of Notre Dame. Both the Horns and Owls had 8-4 records when they met at Autry Court on a rainy evening in January. Brownlee and Wacker combined for 48 points in a 65-53 victory. Rice stubbornly stayed with a man-to-man defense, allowing UT to exploit its height advantage. Owl star Tony Barnett scored just eight points. Up in the Ozarks, Joe Kleine (32) led Arkansas to a 64-58 win over the late-charging Longhorns. Narrowing a big halftime deficit to three points, Texas could not overcome the taller and faster Razorbacks and their noisy fans. Brownlee scored 20 for the Horns, who bounced back with a 68-65 edging of Baylor at Heart O' Texas Coliseum, scene of Wacker's injury three years earlier. That alone caused the biggest media turnout for a Bear home game all season. Wacker, who tried in vain to downplay the significance of his return to Waco, had 15 points and 14 rebounds.

Carlos Briggs scored a game-high 21 for the green and gold.

An Erwin Center crowd of 5,072 was on hand to see the Longhorns versus the Aggies, who had just two Texans on their roster. The backcourt tandem of Kenny Brown and Don Marbury scored 40 points in Texas A&M's 66-61 victory, and the Ag big men controlled the boards. UT, to Weltlich's great displeasure, seemed to lack spark throughout the game. The biggest home audience yet (11,499) in Weltlich's time as coach saw No. 2 SMU beat the poor-shooting Longhorns, 54-46. Big Jon Koncak was cooling his heels on the bench with four fouls as the Ponies led by two with six minutes left. He went back in and promptly blocked a Brownlee shot and made three of his own, putting SMU on the road to victory in a deliberately played game. It was a loss, but the Horns had held their ground against the nation's second-ranked team and threatened to win for a while. A large crowd cheered UT, and more people seemed willing to acknowledge that Weltlich knew a thing or two about basketball. Primarily a teacher of defense and the game's fundamentals, Weltlich was still not popular and never would be. But at least some demanding Longhorn fans had turned their ire away from him and toward football coach Fred Akers, whose team had recently suffered a humiliating 38-point defeat in the Freedom Bowl.

Karl Willock (right) and his teammates celebrate after winning the 1985 Longhorn Classic.

The Longhorns' offense slumped in a 53-45 loss to TCU in Fort Worth. Cooper and Willock combined to make just two of 14 shots, providing Wacker (18), whose father was the Frog football coach, with little help. Weltlich tried a number of different lineups, but nothing seemed to work.

A three-game losing streak ended when UT met the eventual SWC champions in Austin. Brownlee played 40 minutes and scored 23 points to lead the Horns to a 66-61 defeat of Texas Tech. The team's shooting drought appeared to be over as 52 percent of field goal tries went in and 16 of 19 free throws. Bubba Jennings had 22 points for the Red Raiders.

The Houston Cougars entered their Wednesday night game with Texas in a bad mood, and that meant bad news for the visiting Longhorns. UH halted a four-game losing streak with a 94-80 victory. Running and scoring almost like they did in the Phi Slama Jama glory days, the Cougars had five players in double figures, led by Greg "Cadillac" Anderson (20). Except for Wacker (22) and Broadway (13), Weltlich was not enthused about the showing of any of his players.

Their confidence a bit shaken, the Horns opened a three-game homestand by beating Rice, 66-65. Willock's two free throws in the last four seconds clinched the victory. Wacker scored 17, and Cooper, coming back from a mild shoulder separation and several poor games, had 16, including a nice dunk. The ground-bound Owls had last place to themselves. Arkansas coach Eddie Sutton did his usual fine job of working the refs in a 60-51 Hog victory before 5,330 Erwin Center fans. Despite a sagging Texas defense, Joe Kleine bulled his way to a game-high 22 points. "Kleine is the most competitive player in this league, by far," Weltlich stated. "It's not even close. He just out-competes your entire team, and he has the equipment to do it." The Longhorns held a comfortable lead over Baylor with seven minutes left when they lost their poise and nearly the game, hanging on for dear life to win, 75-72. Bear guard Carlos Briggs (28) was instrumental in the comeback, and a career-high 29 points from Brownlee was needed for the Horns to get their 13th win of the year. The BU program would soon be rocked by the resignation of coach Jim Haller when a disgruntled ex-player taped a telephone conversation with damning statements about steroids and financial improprieties.

Wacker was the hero of a dramatic 53-51 win at G. Rollie White Coliseum. Don Marbury and Todd Holloway had Texas A&M ahead by six with two minutes left, but the Horns came back and tied it up. After Brownlee blocked a potential game-winner for the Ags and secured the rebound, Texas went downcourt, where Wacker's shot was blocked by Winston Crite. He fought for his own miss and tossed the ball toward the hoop just before the buzzer sounded. It hung on the rim and fell through as a crowd of 5,897 went silent. Wacker, the game's top scorer with 22, was mobbed by his teammates. A loud group of UT fans gathered outside the locker room, eager to help celebrate the biggest road win yet for a Weltlich-coached Longhorn team.

When it became apparent that Wacker and Brownlee were not going to score enough inside points to beat No. 9 SMU, Weltlich gave his outside shooters—Cooper, Willock and Bolden—the green light of sorts. But the Longhorns fell just short of beating the muscular Mustangs in a 64-60 loss in Dallas. Jon Koncak had 18 points and 13 rebounds despite missing 10 minutes of action when an errant elbow drew blood.

Thirteen points from guard Dennis Nutt and good play from reserve center Greg Grissom were the keys to TCU's 54-52 defeat of the Horns at the Erwin Center. "We played terrible," Wacker said. "There's no other way to put it," and Weltlich concurred. Wacker, who once seemed unlikely to resume his basketball career, was UT's first all-SWC player since LaSalle Thompson in 1982. Joining Wacker were Jon Koncak of SMU, Joe Kleine of Arkansas, Bubba Jennings of Texas Tech and Dennis Nutt of TCU. The group was notable because all five players were of European-American descent; a number of all-SWC teams had been all-black since integration in the late 1960s, and the 1985 team was a quirk that would not likely be repeated.

Cooper, who had played the last two games in great pain because of a knee injury, simply could not bear it any more. A torn ligament ended his season and his career. The player who singlehandedly kept the Longhorns afloat during those two horrendous years was through. He and Wacker were the last links to the Abe Lemons era. Cooper was missed in the home finale against Southern California on March 3, although Wacker compensated with a storybook ending. The Trojans led by one point with nine seconds left when Willock fired a shot from the corner. Brownlee rebounded it and put up another shot, but it missed, too. Wacker slipped between Wayne Carlander and Rod Keller to tip the ball in, and USC was unable to score in the remaining seconds. Horns 71, Trojans 70. Brownlee and Wacker had 55 of UT's points, and Willock and Broadway combined for 12 assists.

Remarkably, there was some talk, however faint, of the Longhorns getting an NIT bid. Weltlich insisted the team was going to Dallas for one purpose—to win the SWC tourney and make it into the NCAAs. They would have to be mighty fortunate, and Wacker's knee would have to withstand three straight nights of pounding. It did not happen. Reunion Arena, a.k.a. "Barnhill South," was full of Arkansas fans calling their beloved Hogs. With Joe Kleine leading the way, Arkansas took a convincing 66-46 victory that ended UT's season. The Horns played poorly in every phase of the game, looking stale and uninspired. Yet no one, not even the most zealous Weltlich-haters, could deny that the 1985 team had been a pleasant surprise.

1986

The NBA had used a 24-second shot clock for many years, and a 30-second clock was a fixture of the women's college game, while the men debated, experimented and debated some more. Over the opposition of a few coaches who believed they would lose a measure of control, the NCAA passed a rule implementing a 45-second clock (later changed to 35) for the 1986 season. And the three-point shot was right behind, in 1987. These were two of the most fundamental and popular new rules since the elimination of the center jump after successful baskets, which was enacted five decades earlier.

As for the Texas Longhorns, not a great deal was expected after the departure of Mike Wacker. Even in a weak Southwest Conference, UT seemed unlikely to contend. Bob Weltlich's team would be smaller but quicker, extending itself on defense and pushing the ball when the opportunity arose, a welcome change after three years of mostly plodding basketball. John Brownlee was definitely the man inside, and perimeter shooting would get a higher profile because of the arrival of forward Patrick Fairs. A native of the Mississippi Delta and a junior college transfer, Fairs could really shoot from long range. Assistant coach Eddie Oran ventured a guess that the team might win 17 games, and guard Karl Willock, who got some attention for calling himself a "lifer" in Weltlich's regime, said an SWC title was possible.

Play commenced on November 25. The only patsy on the preconference schedule was Baptist College, out of Charleston, South Carolina. UT used a full-court press and some running and gunning to roll over the Buccaneers, 94-68. Fairs and Willock combined to score 35 points. The second game, also at home, was a 70-61 defeat of California-Riverside. With a 14-point scoring spree, the Highlanders led at halftime, but Brownlee (24) brought the Horns back and put them ahead.

For the third time in as many games, Texas was plagued by foul trouble, and for the first time, a loss occurred. Willock, Raynard Davis and Wayne Thomas each finished with four fouls against South Alabama in Mobile. The Longhorns were up by one with 40 seconds left when Thomas committed a turnover followed by Jeff Hodge's jumper, which won it for the Jaguars, 67-66, overshadowing a 28-point performance by Fairs. It was a frustrating defeat for Weltlich, who once had USA coach Mike Hanks as an assistant at Mississippi. Poor rebounding was the main reason for an 84-62 loss to Southern California in Los Angeles. Although they were not especially big, the Trojans got one offensive rebound after another and converted with alacrity. Freshman Tom Lewis (30) led USC in scoring. Weltlich's displeasure was evident when he held a practice session immediately after the team returned from California. "I still think we'll be competitive if we weather this period," he said.

A strangely passive Oral Roberts team lost to UT, 82-66, before 3,082 fans at the Erwin Center. In rebounding, defense and offense, the Longhorns had their way with the shorter Titans, who got 13 points from Woody Jones. Brownlee had 23 points and 12 rebounds, and Alex Broadway, who started every game in 1985, reclaimed the point guard position from Thomas.

Ahead by one and holding the ball in the last half-minute of overtime, Texas suffered a turnover, resulting in a 93-92 victory for eighth-ranked Oklahoma. Linwood Davis stripped Thomas of the ball and hit a layup that ensured the Sooners' 37th straight win at Lloyd Noble Arena. Five OU players were in double figures, while Brownlee (34 points and 16 rebounds) and Fairs (29) paced the Horns. It was Fairs' 23-foot jump shot at the buzzer that sent the game into OT.

The Longhorns had lost all three road games, but they were back at home for a while. No. 9 LSU, unbeaten in eight games, paid a visit on December 17. The Bengals were just too tall, too talented and too deep, coming from behind to grab a 72-65 victory. Nikita Wilson had 23 points for the winners, and Brownlee, who was in early foul trouble and had to play cautiously, scored just nine. As *Austin American-Statesman* writer John Maher observed, the Texas-LSU game was a good chance to see if some casual fans would join the hard-core orangebloods who regularly attended home games. Apparently not, because the Erwin Center was two-thirds empty. Nevertheless, UT had gone toe-to-toe with another strong team and almost won. Dale Brown, the Tigers' abrasive and colorful coach, claimed Weltlich was building a strong foundation and reminded people that it took him a while to attain success in Baton Rouge.

The Longhorn Classic was again won by the home team. Despite missing their first seven shots, the Horns pulled together and beat Alaska-Anchorage (coached by UT-ex Harry Larrabee), 68-57. The inside-outside tandem of Brownlee and Fairs had 47 points to help down the Seawolves. Davis scored 17 points in his first start of the year as Texas beat South Florida, 60-55, in the tournament finals. Willock and Broadway shone in the backcourt, teaming up for 16 assists.

The competition would be considerably tougher at the Cotton States Classic, held inside Atlanta's Omni. Besides 5-4 Texas, the lineup included No. 7 Georgia Tech (7-1), No. 20 DePaul (5-2) and Navy (6-2), led by 7' center David Robinson. "We've motivated ourselves for the top teams," said forward Dennis Perryman. "I think we're on the right track. We'll surprise some people." The only surprise of the first game was the huge victory margin for Bobby Cremins' Georgia Tech team, which exploded to a

90-55 win before 14,010 fans. John Salley, Duane Ferrell, Bruce Dalrymple and Mark Price were just too much; the Yellow Jackets shot 72 percent from the field and were in control throughout. DePaul won the consolation game, 63-62, largely by forcing turnovers and turning them into points. Dallas Comegys scored 16 for the Blue Demons, while Brownlee and Fairs combined for 37. Freshman forward John Sykes played well for the Horns in 22 minutes and looked like a future star.

No other Southwest Conference team had played such a difficult early-season schedule, and Weltlich and his players seemed upbeat as conference play began. Hofheinz Pavilion was the site of the first game, a 70-68 defeat of Houston. Brownlee (29) and Fairs had five fouls apiece and had to sit during the final minutes as UT clung to a slight lead. Willock had 12 assists, and Sykes and Broadway came through in the clutch. Greg Anderson scored 29 points and collected 12 rebounds for the Cougars. Two nights later and a few miles across town at Autry Court, the Horns scored another victory, beating Rice, 57-46. The Owls' zone defense collapsed around Brownlee but left Fairs (20) and Davis (17) with room to operate. Weltlich, who thought his team stood around too much against Rice, brought out the dreaded loose-ball drill in practice. "When we were losing, everybody viewed this as punishment," he said. "But when you're winning, it's great coaching. There have been a lot of defections here and a lot of complaining, but if I'm here 10 years from now, we'll still be doing the same thing."

John Brownlee, 1986 SWC player of the year.

A two-game homestand began with Arkansas. Eddie Sutton had gone on to an ill-fated stint at Kentucky and was replaced by Nolan Richardson, the SWC's first black coach. The designer of some of the worst-looking uniforms since TCU employed vertical stripes a dozen years earlier, Richardson was off to a poor start, juggling his lineup, changing the offense and losing more than Razorback fans were accustomed to. The Longhorns overcame an 11-point second-half deficit to win, 59-55, as Brownlee and Davis scored 15 points apiece, two less than the Hogs' William Mills. Almost half of the Baylor team was under NCAA suspension or had been booted entirely by coach Gene Iba. In a reminder of UT's cheerleader-turned-hoopster in the dark days of 1983, the Bears welcomed a golfer onto the team. Everyone—or at least those in orange and white—had fun in a 65-40 victory. Fairs scored 19 points and Sykes 13, while only Brandon Taylor reached double figures for BU, which was held to just nine shots in the first half and 28 in the game.

Weltlich still emphasized taking charges to draw offensive fouls. Before the UT-Texas A&M game in College Station, Aggie coach Shelby Metcalf recalled seeing the Longhorns playing for the charge a bit too obviously: "I was really impressed that when a guy dribbled into the lane, three Texas guys fell down. It looked like Bowling for Dollars." Weltlich, of course, insisted it was one aspect of solid, team defense, necessary because Brownlee was not an enforcer under the basket. Interestingly enough, one of those *faux* charges cost Texas the game against the Ags. UT led, 54-53, with just a few seconds left as Todd Holloway hurried downcourt to take a final shot. Holloway and Fairs collided, but a foul was called on the latter. Two free throws went up and in, and the game was over, to the delight of 5,882 fans. Willock (17) was the top scorer, but his two late turnovers allowed A&M to get close and then win. Trying to put that painful loss behind them, the Horns fell again. As a nearly full house at Moody Coliseum looked on, SMU outhustled Texas all the way and won, 63-56, ending a three-game losing streak. The Ponies got 19 points from Terry Williams, and Brownlee scored 16. Fairs had a poor game, committing four first-half turnovers and missing 11 of 13 shots.

The weary Longhorns, having played six of their last eight games on the road, were sinking in the SWC standings. "One thing that keeps you going when you're tired is winning," Weltlich said. "When you lose, the bubble bursts and the momentum comes crashing down." Late free throw shooting by Broadway and Willock were needed for UT to beat TCU, 56-54, in Austin. Brownlee had 21 points and 13 rebounds, and Sykes came up big again with 11 points, nine rebounds and two blocked shots. Willock, a hard-working defender, helped hold Frog stars Carl Lott and Carven Holcombe to seven of 25 from the field.

In yet another down-to-the-wire finish, UT got there first with the most, beating Texas Tech, 49-46. The Horns trailed until the final minute, when Brownlee scored and Broadway hit two free throws for the first Texas victory in Lubbock in five tries. "I give Texas credit for hanging in there when they were down," said Red Raider coach Gerald Myers. "That is the mark of an experienced team." Halfway through the conference race, UT (11-8 overall, 6-2 in the SWC and a half game out of first place) was the biggest surprise. Brownlee, Fairs, Willock and Broadway all had done more than expected. How far the Longhorns went, though, might be limited by a thin bench.

Record: 19-12

94 Baptist 68
70 California-Riverside 61
66 South Alabama 67
62 Southern California 84
82 Oral Roberts 66
92 Oklahoma 93 (OT)
65 LSU 72
68 Alaska-Anchorage 57
60 South Florida 55
55 Georgia Tech 90
62 DePaul 63
70 Houston 68
57 Rice 46
59 Arkansas 55
65 Baylor 40
54 Texas A&M 55
56 SMU 63
56 TCU 54
49 Texas Tech 46
79 Houston 63
62 Rice 56
61 Arkansas 57
55 Baylor 50
58 Texas A&M 47
58 SMU 57
54 TCU 55
62 Texas Tech 63
78 Houston 62
47 Texas A&M 55
69 New Mexico 66
65 Ohio State 71

Guy Lewis, Houston's coach for three decades—he captained the first Cougar team in 1946—announced his retirement, effective at season's end. He had tutored some of the greatest players in college basketball, such as Elvin Hayes, Otis Birdsong and Hakeem Olajuwon, and took five teams to the NCAA Final Four. The rest of the season was a long goodbye to Lewis. UH's game with the once-lowly Longhorns was not one he would care to remember. Texas jumped to a 12-1 lead and cruised to a 79-63 victory. The star of the night was Davis, who scored a career-high 28 points and helped Brownlee keep a lid on Greg Anderson. Some 9,226 fans were at the Erwin Center for the Houston contest, and about half that witnessed a 62-56 defeat of Rice. Fairs made nine of 11 shots, benefitting again from a defense fixated on Brownlee. Greg Hines scored 24 for the Owls.

At that time, rumors/news reports popped up that would have been ludicrous two years earlier. Weltlich's name was mentioned in connection with coaching vacancies at Ohio State, Minnesota and Florida State. He denied any contact with those institutions, denied any interest in leaving Austin and denied just about everything. Weltlich still had an army of detractors, but it must have been nice for him to hear that he was wanted elsewhere. When he had gone 6-22 and 7-21, speculation of a very different kind focused on who might replace him if or when he was fired.

Barnhill Arena, where the Arkansas Razorbacks had lost just eight games in 11 years under Eddie Sutton, did not seem such a fearful place in 1986. Nolan Richardson's Hogs had already lost five games there, and that number became six after a visit from UT. Broadway hit seven free throws in the last 2:19 of a 61-57 win, and Willock and Brownlee had 16 points apiece. Arkansas fans, not happy about the first losing season since 1974, reacted to a goaltending call on center Andrew Lang by bombarding the court with ice cubes and other debris.

With Arkansas and Houston down, the SWC was getting widely criticized, if not mocked. Some people called it the Southworst Conference, the Sad and Weak Conference, the So-What Conference and other derogatory names. Its members had a 1-14 record against top-20 teams. Nevertheless, Texas, TCU and Texas A&M were in a tight race for the championship. UT took a surprisingly close 55-50 victory over Baylor at dark and dank Heart O' Texas Coliseum. The Bears' Michael Williams connected on 11 of 15 shots, and Brownlee scored 21.

On the afternoon of February 15, Willock and Brownlee stood on the west side of Red River Street and took photographs of the Erwin Center marquee, which informed passersby that the Texas-Texas A&M game was sold out. Tickets to basketball games had been selling like coldcakes for much of the last four years, but the big facility was full once again. What a long, slow and painful process it had been. The 16,231 fans saw UT break open a close game to win, 58-47. Brownlee had 19 points, and Willock held Don Marbury, the SWC's top scorer, to 15. The crowd was smaller (8,884) when SMU visited three days later, but the game was even better, a 58-57 heartstopper won by the Horns, decided by Willock's free throw with 25 seconds left. The Mustangs ran the clock down to the final seconds when Glenn Puddy shot from the baseline. It missed, the ball caromed to Brownlee, and the fans unleashed a big roar.

At intermission of a more prominent game, CBS ran a two-minute, feel-good segment on Weltlich and his Cinderella team, 12-2 in the SWC. Simultaneous with that snippet of national television time, the Longhorns and Frogs met in Fort Worth. It was standing-room only at Daniel-Meyer Coliseum, although neither team was within shouting distance of the top 20. UT battled back from 13 points down to take a 54-53 lead on two Brownlee free throws with five seconds remaining. Frog guard Jamie Dixon received the inbounds pass and started weaving through a gauntlet of Longhorns trying to foul him but not get called for an intentional foul. The refs did not cooperate, however. Thomas and Willock banged Dixon, and hearing no whistle, he kept going. Just before the buzzer sounded, he threw up a 30-foot prayer and bowled over Davis in an apparent offensive foul. No call there, either. The ball went in, and Dixon's teammates and a number of purple-crazed fans hoisted him in the air to celebrate the victory. Weltlich was livid. "Totally unbelievable," he fumed. "We purposely fouled the guy three times and don't get a call. I mean, we just mugged the guy. It's a shame."

But the Horned Frogs lost their next two games, giving UT a chance to win the SWC title with a home victory over Texas Tech. Back in the driver's seat, the Horns somehow had a wreck, a 63-62 loss to the Red Raiders. The game went back and forth to the very end, when Dewayne Chism tipped in Tony Benford's missed shot to win it as the crowd fell silent. Brownlee and Fairs rang up a combined 38 points as Texas settled for a tie with TCU and Texas A&M for the conference crown. "We're still tri-champions, and our players need to be proud of that," Weltlich said. "But right now, it feels pretty hollow."

On to Dallas. The Longhorns would have to win the SWC tourney to get into the NCAAs, and in 1986, that led right back to the Final Four at Reunion Arena. Brownlee, recently named SWC player of the year, scored 33 points and secured 12 rebounds in a 78-62 defeat of Houston, the last game in Guy Lewis' coaching career. Alvin Franklin and Greg Anderson scored 16 each for the Cougars. But that preceded an inexplicable 55-47 loss to Texas A&M in the semifinals. The Aggie battle plan was to sag on Brownlee and force the other Longhorns to score. It was not original, but it worked, and to compound matters, UT played poor defense. Only Texas Tech, which beat A&M the next day, got into the 64-team NCAA tourney, not exactly a sign of high regard for the conference.

The Horns were still playing, albeit in the NIT. Mile-high Albuquerque, Willock's hometown, was the scene of a first-round game between Texas and New Mexico. Nearly 15,000 fans filled the Lobos' famous "Pit," but their team suffered a 69-66 loss to the visitors from the large state to the east. Brownlee (17), Davis and Fairs (16 each) led a balanced attack, while Johnny Brown scored 30 for New Mexico.

Road warriors, though not by choice, Weltlich's Longhorns traveled to Columbus to engage Ohio State, a team with a 7' center (Brad Sellers) and a guard (Dennis Hopson) averaging 21 points per game. There was a minor distraction when Sykes was suspended, reinstated and again suspended from the team. Academics was the first reason offered and then loafing in practice; Sykes' career with the Longhorns was over. "Everybody talks about the SWC," Fairs said. "Here's a chance to show we can play against a Big 10 team." A victory over the Buckeyes would put UT one game away from the semifinals in Madison Square Garden, a big plus for media exposure and recruiting. The Horns never made it to New York, however, because Ohio State overcame a 12-point first-half deficit to take a 71-65 victory. A big disparity in fouls and free throws favored the Buckeyes, eventual winners of the NIT. Sellers scored 25, and Fairs had 18 for Texas. Weltlich walked off the court at St. John Arena with an arm around Willock, his four-year man, the only player to endure from 1983 to 1986 and someone who helped make Longhorn basketball respectable again.

1987

Recruiting is among the most inexact of sciences. Freshmen, transfers and junior-college players may surpass or fall short of expectations, and sometimes the obscure athlete turns out much better than one with lots of newspaper clippings. Such factors as health, academics and desire also help determine who rises and who falls. Bob Weltlich and his coaching staff brought in five new players before the 1987 season. Three junior college men (David Cones, Derrick Shelton and Jerome Spinner) were almost complete washouts. George Muller, a 7'1" center with little basketball experience, was supposed to redshirt and perhaps be ready to contribute a couple of years hence, but he ended up starting 13 games for the otherwise short Longhorns. And then there was guard Travis Mays, who had put up some nice numbers (29 points and 10 rebounds per game) during his senior year in Ocala, Florida and was among the top 100 recruits in the nation. The hotshot would have to prove himself, and he did, eventually forging a mark as one of the best players Texas ever had.

Weltlich, the 1986 Southwest Conference coach of the year, had been given a contract extension. His team would not get to take any baby steps before the real competition began. At the Great Alaska Shootout in Anchorage, UT met North Carolina State in the opener. The Horns squandered an 11-point lead in the last five minutes, but a driving bank shot by Alex Broadway put them back in front. A touch-foul by Patrick Fairs at the buzzer gave the Wolfpack's Walker Lambiotte a chance to make two free throws, and Jim Valvano's team escaped with a 69-68 victory. Fairs paced Texas with 25 points (including three of five from behind the 19'9" three-point line) and nine rebounds. Alaska-Anchorage won the second-round game, 80-68, with 27 points from West German import Hansi Gnad. A game against defending national champion Louisville may have seemed hopeless, but the Cardinals, off to a poor early-season start, lost to the Longhorns, 74-70. The victory margin came on Raynard Davis' four free throws in the last 22 seconds. He and Dennis Perryman (14 points and 10 rebounds) took it upon themselves to limit the damage caused by Louisville's 6'9" all-American, Pervis Ellison.

In the home opener, UT beat Central Missouri, 88-60, as Fairs and Davis (28 and 21 points, respectively) continued their fine all-around play. The Horns went back to Albuquerque, scene of their 1986 NIT victory over New Mexico, but the Lobos would have no more of that. They took advantage of 25 turnovers and put Texas away early in an 82-72 win before 16,544 fans. Kelvin Scarborough and Hunter Greene had 24 points each for New Mexico, three more than Davis. After observing his players perform so ineptly, Weltlich had a lot to say to them after the game.

Still looking for their true colors, the Horns hosted Northwestern Louisiana and managed to win, 80-75, despite the Demons' 71 percent first-half shooting. Davis, on the way to a solid senior year, scored 31 points, the highest total of any Texas player in 1987. Broadway broke a bone in his hand and was out the next four games. Whether he would have made a difference against Oklahoma was doubtful. Billy Tubbs' Sooners were averaging 98 points per game and had some terrific players like Harvey Grant, Stacey King and Tim McCalister. UT remained within striking distance until the final minutes, but an inability to penetrate OU's tough zone defense spelled defeat, 84-65. Fairs missed nine of ten three-point shots.

But the Longhorns' senior forward bounced back to score 25 points in a 68-65 victory over Oral Roberts in Tulsa. Although the Titans led most of the way, Texas had a 36-28 rebounding edge and what it took to win. Wayne Thomas blocked a shot and hit two free throws to seal the fourth victory of the year for UT.

For the third straight season, Texas won its own tournament, one which could have used some more formidable competition. Weltlich, wearing a garish sport coat that would have made Bobby Knight pause, saw his team thump Bowling Green, 59-44. The first half was a yawner for the 2,774 fans, but Fairs (21) warmed up and brought the Horns a victory. Perryman and Thomas combined for 44 points in a 95-74 blowout of South Alabama, while the Jaguars got 22 from guard Junie Lewis. "This was a complete metamorphosis from last night," said Weltlich, who never had a Longhorn team score so many points. "Entirely different."

Perryman, MVP of the tournament, was largely responsible for Texas' fourth straight win, 75-74 over Tennessee-Chattanooga at the Erwin Center. The Longhorns needed a furious second-half comeback capped by Perryman's two free throws to tie and then beat the Moccasins. Most of the comeback was achieved with

Davis on the bench with foul trouble. The visitors' Morris Lyons (25) took scoring honors.

One of UT's sibling institutions held a holiday tournament devoid of cupcakes and attended by nearly 24,000 people. Texas-El Paso hosted the Sun Bowl Classic, welcoming the Longhorns, Iowa State and No. 5 Auburn. The hometown fans were happy to see their Miners dismantle UT, 76-51, with 21 points from Jeep Jackson and 10 from future pro star Tim Hardaway. Don Haskins' team made good use of its superior quickness. And Iowa State rode a 24-point performance by Tom Schaefer to beat the Horns, 58-57, in the consolation game. Perryman scored 19 points, which is exactly how far ahead Texas was before allowing the Cyclones to come storming back. It was the sort of loss that could shake a team's confidence. At that point, only Fairs, Davis and Perryman were offensive threats, and more was needed from the backcourt.

The Longhorns jumped into SWC competition with a 72-52 defeat of Rice in Austin. Perryman repeatedly used post-up moves inside to score a career-high 25 points against the Owls, destined for another last-place finish. Fairs had a good game, too, scoring 19 points and holding Greg Hines to six of 20 from the field.

An unforgiving schedule had Texas playing three road games in six days, and all were losses. Turning the ball over 28 times, the Longhorns got swept out of Barnhill Arena, 79-62, courtesy of Arkansas. The Hogs' victory was accomplished with 87 percent free throw shooting and a defense primed to stop Davis, Fairs and Perryman. For the first time but definitely not the last, Mays (17) was UT's top scorer. Baylor, a much-improved team with a couple of all-SWC players (Darryl Middleton and Michael Williams), stifled Texas' inside game in a 62-56 win. Middleton had 25 points, and 16 more chances at the charity stripe helped the Bears. UT had a short lineup and a short bench, and Weltlich's temper was beginning to grow short: "Ray and Dennis are busting their rear ends playing against guys three and four inches taller than them. We're not losing games because of the guys who are playing. We're losing because of guys who aren't." The Longhorns dropped another one, 68-52, to Texas A&M. A 13-point run early in the second half all but ensured the Aggies' win. Fairs paced the Horns with 22 points, and Broadway, a 5'11" guard, was the top rebounder.

Record: 14-17

68 North Carolina State 69
68 Alaska-Anchorage 80
74 Louisville 70
88 Central Missouri 60
72 New Mexico 82
80 NW Louisiana 75
65 Oklahoma 84
68 Oral Roberts 65
59 Bowling Green 44
95 South Alabama 74
75 Tennessee-Chattanooga 74
51 UT-El Paso 76
57 Iowa State 58
72 Rice 52
62 Arkansas 79
56 Baylor 62
52 Texas A&M 68
61 SMU 60
37 TCU 52
46 Texas Tech 56
59 Houston 65
70 Rice 69
78 Arkansas 73
78 Baylor 74
56 Texas A&M 58
57 SMU 55
54 TCU 70
48 Fordham 60
50 Texas Tech 62
65 Houston 64
49 Houston 59

Finally back in the Erwin Center, the Longhorns met SMU, another team off to a slow start in the SWC race. In fact, the Mustangs were winless and remained so after a 61-60 loss. Fairs (22), sometimes criticized for lacking a swoop to the hoop, proved he could do it with 15 seconds on the clock and UT clinging to a one-point lead. He knifed through the SMU defense for a layup and subsequent free throw. Carlton McKinney (21) hit a three-pointer at the other end to close the game's scoring. Weltlich saw the future in Mays (20), a superb athlete with lots of basketball savvy. The first part of his freshman season had been curtailed by minor shoulder, groin, finger, hamstring and back injuries.

Possibly the best TCU team since the early 1970s, the Frogs, preseason favorites and playing like it, scored an easy 52-37 victory over Texas at Daniel-Meyer Coliseum. And their top player, Carl Lott, was out with a broken finger. Carven Holcombe and Jamie Dixon combined for 28 points, and no Horn even reached double figures. Missing 17 straight shots during one stretch, UT finished at a miserable 25 percent. It had been 18 years since a Texas team scored so few points.

The anemic Longhorns hosted Texas Tech and came up short again, 56-46. Leading by five at intermission, UT went into another shooting funk and scored just 16 points the rest of the way. "We've just got to make the shots we're missing," Weltlich fumed. "We miss layups and follow shots. Easy shots." Red Raider guards Sean Gay (16) and Wendell Owens (15) had no such problems.

Pat Foster, the man chosen to replace Guy Lewis as Houston's coach, started a frontline of 7' Rolando Ferreira, 6'10" Greg Anderson and 6'8" Rickie Winslow, and Weltlich planned to use a variety of zone defenses to counter the big Cougars at Hofheinz Pavilion. UT might have won if not for those familiar nemeses, the turnover and the missed shot, as Houston took a 65-59 victory. Davis broke out of a prolonged shooting slump with 18 points, and Winslow had 14 for UH. The Horns returned to Harris County four days later to play Rice, whose coach, Tommy Suitts, had just been forced to resign. After an elevation of academic requirements, a downturn in athletic success was nearly inevitable, but the scholarly Owls almost beat UT. Fairs' free throw after time had expired allowed the Longhorns to take a 70-69 win before 1,200 fans. Davis had 20 points in a game with plenty of pushing, shoving and fouls (56) called.

Back home for a while, the Horns took on Arkansas and won, 78-73. Broadway made all four of his three-point attempts and engineered several rare fast breaks. Ron Huery led the Razorbacks with 15 points, and 6'11" Andrew Lang made his presence known in the paint. Coach Nolan Richardson, upset over some calls that went against his team, berated the refs at halftime and got two technicals as a result. Baylor, part of a recent bench-clearing brawl with Texas A&M, came to town for a Saturday afternoon game in which the Horns' backcourt played well. Thomas (20), Mays (16) and Broadway (15) helped muzzle the Bears, 78-74. BU made 55 percent from the field, but feeble free throw shooting lost the game, according to coach Gene Iba. UT's three-game winning streak ended in dramatic fashion against Texas A&M before a season-high crowd of 6,573 at the Erwin Center. A 12-foot bank shot by guard Darryl McDonald with four seconds left gave the Ags a 58-56 victory. "That was the biggest basket of my life," said McDonald, one of several New Yorkers Shelby Metcalf had brought to College Station. Fairs, despite the flu, scored 20 points to lead both teams.

Texas and SMU, two teams going nowhere in 1987, met in Dallas in another game decided at the end. Mays, whose traveling violation led indirectly to the Mustangs taking a one-point lead, redeemed himself by drilling a 23-foot shot over Carlton McKinney a second before the buzzer for a 57-55 win. "Not much to write home about," Weltlich said. "But the way this year is going, we'll take it."

As the season wound down, Suzanne Halliburton of the *Austin American-Statesman* penned a long article about Abe Lemons, whose Oklahoma City team was 26-0 and ranked first in the NAIA. Still launching verbal assaults against the school that fired him five years earlier, Lemons also had filed two unsuccessful lawsuits. Athletic director DeLoss Dodds told Halliburton there were no regrets about either firing Lemons or hiring Weltlich. "We don't look back," he said. "We always try to look forward." And Weltlich's job, Dodds added, was safe. John Maher, Halliburton's colleague at the local daily, backed the oft-maligned coach: "Personally, I'd like to see Weltlich succeed. He has paid more dues than any other Texas coach. While he doesn't snap off one-liners, he will, contrary to his image, joke even after tough losses. He doesn't give contrived answers. And he doesn't measure his success only on the court."

No. 16 TCU clinched the SWC championship with a 70-54 defeat of the Longhorns in Austin. The Frogs put together a 22-point halftime lead, and only a closing rush at garbage time made the final score at all close. Jamie Dixon and Carven Holcombe teamed up for 36 points, and Texas, lacking any discernible offense, was led by Mays (15).

The Horns got a break from the grind when they traveled to East Rutherford, New Jersey to play Fordham. Weltlich scheduled the game to expose UT and the Southwest Conference. Part of a doubleheader including Big East teams Villanova and Seton Hall, it reminded old-timers of how Jack Gray had taken his teams to Madison Square Garden nearly 50 years earlier. The Rams, led by center James Robinson and guard Joe Franco, beat Texas easily, 60-48, not the kind of exposure Weltlich had in mind. With 38 percent shooting and 23 turnovers, it was a weak performance. Only Fairs (19 points and nine rebounds) looked good.

A third straight defeat occurred at Lubbock Municipal Coliseum. The Longhorns could do little right in a 62-50 loss to Texas Tech. Shooting, ballhandling, defense and rebounding were all abysmal. Davis, on the bench with a groin injury, might have helped a little against the Red Raiders' Dewayne Chism (16).

Just 2,828 spectators gathered at the Erwin Center for the regular-season finale with Houston. Dodds and Weltlich did not duck the issue—poor attendance at Texas home games was a distressing reality. The Longhorn women, then shooting for a second straight national championship, drew an average of 6,639, some

2,000 more than the men. And whenever the *Dallas Morning News*, *Sports Illustrated* or *USA Today* featured a story on Jody Conradt's team, that fact was given prominent attention. In a vicious circle, the nonwinning program begat few fans, which did not thrill recruits, which made it hard to win. At any rate, not many people witnessed a 65-64 victory sealed by Mays' two free throws with 15 seconds left. Fairs, playing splendidly at the end of his college career, had 20 points, 10 rebounds and four assists. He also made some big steals down the stretch.

Six days later, the same teams met in the first round of the SWC Tournament at Reunion Arena, and the Cougars won, 59-49. Texas got run over by Greg "Cadillac" Anderson (19) and his teammates. UH forced the Longhorns to shoot from outside, and 30 percent did not get it done. While Houston joined TCU and Texas A&M in the big show, the NCAA tourney, the 14-17 Horns went home. A team Weltlich originally thought might exceed the achievements of the 1986 tri-champs had not even come close.

1988

Problems, problems. Bob Weltlich lost both of his senior guards when Alex Broadway faltered academically and Wayne Thomas injured a knee 10 days before practice started. One freshman got suspended, and two more had scarcely set foot on the Forty Acres before quitting. But those things were of little import in comparison to the real possibility of losing Travis Mays. UT's would-be sophomore had gone home to Florida in the summer of 1987 to examine his options. It was no secret Mays disliked Weltlich's slow-paced offense as well as the coach's drill-sergeant style. Although he was not pressured to return, Mays listened to assistant coach Eddie Oran and Earl Campbell—retired from the pro football wars and a new member of the Longhorn athletic department—and decided not to transfer. Weltlich, who was entering a pivotal year, named Mays captain of the team and vowed to run the ball more and ease up on the screaming and hollering in practice. Those Knightian habits were deeply ingrained, however, and little changed.

The 1988 Horns had some interesting new players, primarily 6'8" JC transfer Alvin Heggs, 6'9" Brazilian Jose Nassar and guard Courtney Jeans. High hopes were placed on these men, and while none of them ever made an all-conference team, they helped win some games over the coming seasons. The recruit who got the most attention, though, went elsewhere. LaBradford Smith, whose sisters, Annette and Audrey, had finished their eligibility with the Longhorn women's team in 1986, chose to matriculate at Louisville. Perhaps one of the best high school players in state history, Smith wanted a certifiable big-time program to springboard him to the NBA, and he heard too many unflattering words about the situation at UT to consider it.

The biggest crowd of the year was at the first game, a 100-83 loss to Iowa State, host of the 16-team Big Apple preseason NIT. More than 14,000 people saw the Cyclones employ a full-court press that unnerved Texas. Jeff Grayer led ISU with 36 points, and Mays, whose ballhandling and outside shooting skills had improved between seasons, scored 27. One loss and the Horns were out of that tournament.

Weltlich's young players had 10 days to let their bruised egos heal before the home opener against Tennessee State. The Erwin Center, known to some as the "Hum Drum" in recent years, was a bit livelier due to canned rock music, NBA-style player introductions and various ways of generating fan involvement. Nassar and Heggs combined for 43 points and 24 rebounds to help beat the Tigers, 84-72. Neither newcomer, though, was playing the kind of defense Weltlich insisted upon.

At the Apple Invitational in Palo Alto, California, the Longhorns suffered the ignominy of losing to an Ivy League team without scholarship players. Brown built a 13-point lead and held on for an 80-77 victory. The Bears' Marcus Thompson scored a game-high 23. For the consolation game with William & Mary, Weltlich shuffled his lineup, as he would do often in the first half of the season. Jeans (23) made all nine field-goal attempts, and Nassar (22) was too big and strong for the Indians in a 78-73 UT win.

In an otherwise awful game, an 86-76 defeat of Oral Roberts in Austin, Mays had a nice stretch of brilliance. He converted four free throws, a layup, a 12-foot jumper, a dunk and another free throw in just three minutes to beat the Titans, whose offensive game plan seemed to call for the first player downcourt to shoot.

Nassar was neither quick nor a great leaper. In other words, he was slow and could not jump, but he had unusual court sense and was an adept passer and shooter, as he showed in the first-round game of the Longhorn Classic. The big Brazilian had 27 points, six rebounds, five assists and four blocked shots in a 75-62 defeat of Pan American before 2,468 onlookers. Guard Lee Boddie scored 18 for the Broncs. For the first time in the four-year history of the event, the Horns failed to win their own tournament. A series of missed shots, turnovers and defensive lapses in the late minutes practically gave Utah State an 80-75 win. Jeff Anderson, a reserve guard for the Aggies, scored 29 points, one more than Mays. If UT's forwards (Heggs, Russell Green and Thomas Gipson) did not start playing better, they might get lifetime leases to Weltlich's doghouse, not a pleasant place to be.

Heggs' eight-foot jumper with three seconds left in overtime capped a wild 90-89 defeat of Southwestern Louisiana on December 16. The final play was actually designed for Jeans (20), but Heggs had the ball, stepped up and hit a game-winner. Kevin Brooks and Earl Watkins combined for 46 of the Cajuns' points.

Traveling to south Florida to engage the Miami Hurricanes, UT got ripped unmercifully, 85-56, despite the return of Broadway. "We were a step slow and a jump behind," Weltlich said. "It was a little bit of everything." Tito Horford, recently at the center of a nasty recruiting scandal involving several schools, had 21 points and eight rebounds for Miami. George Muller battled Horford as best he could but fouled out after playing just 19 minutes. Two nights later, UT wasted an 11-point first-half lead and fell to Tennessee-Chattanooga, 71-70. Mays had 20 points in a game that slipped away due to careless mistakes, some of them his.

Virginia Military Institute, 290th among 291 NCAA Division I teams, according to *USA Today*'s computer ranking, came to Austin and gave the Horns a contest. A late scoring spurt led by Mays (25) and Nassar (24) was needed to beat the lowly Keydets, 85-76. The final non-SWC game was against a 10-3 New Mexico team with more size and talent than Texas. Rob Loeffel, the Lobos' 7'1" center, had 17 points in an 86-74 win for the Western Athletic Conference club. Heggs played well (24 points and 15 rebounds) in a reserve role. Weltlich thought Heggs was better coming in off the bench, and he started just three games the rest of the season. The lineup from then on usually consisted of three guards (Mays, Jeans and Broadway), Nassar at center and Gipson at forward, replaced at the first opportunity by Heggs.

The Longhorns stayed home for the conference opener with Houston. In the final 17 seconds, three Cougars missed shots that would have tied or won the game, allowing UT to take a 65-63 victory. Mays scored 24 points, Heggs 18 and Nassar 12. The Horn center held his fellow *Brasilero*, Fernando Ferreira, to 10 points, seven below his average. "I like this three-guard offense," said Mays, SWC player of the week. "Courtney, Alex and I, we broke out and put a lot of pressure on them."

But the following game was not so gratifying. As a snowstorm raged outside Barnhill Arena, Nolan Richardson's Razorbacks administered a sound licking, 91-62. The Horns, who shot four first-half airballs, were stifled by an Arkansas defense that glided seamlessly from man-to-man to zone and back. Larry Marks scored 19 for the Hogs, and only Green (16) was at all effective for Texas.

A 29-point defeat in Fayetteville, while not exactly a welcome development, did not hurt as much as losing by two to Rice in Austin. The Owls, picked to finish last in the SWC (which they did) beat Texas, 77-75, before just 1,938 fans on a Sunday afternoon. Weltlich's teams had played poorly many times in the previous five-plus seasons, but their effort was seldom criticized until that loss to Rice. The fans, the media and even people within the UT athletic department and the basketball program realized something was wrong. "We probably need to seek professional help," Weltlich said sarcastically. "Playing like this doesn't seem to bother us. This team doesn't seem to embarrass easily."

What was more embarrassing—losing games or the attendance figures? Through nine home games, UT was averaging just 2,676, rendering the Erwin Center a white elephant of sorts. With the mezzanine closed, some people wondered aloud if it might not be better to hold some games at old Gregory Gym, and others did projections of how much potential revenue was being lost. Hundreds of thousands of dollars, depending on the numbers used. The state's high schools were producing more blue-chip players, there were NBA teams in Houston, Dallas and San Antonio, and many

Longhorn fans would not return until they got a better show. Of course, some were going to boycott as long as Weltlich stayed on as coach. Such people formed an ad hoc group known as the "Committee to Resurrect Basketball at the University of Texas." They compiled an 18-page booklet entitled *Six Years With Weltlich* packed with incendiary excerpts of articles and letters from the *Austin American-Statesman*, *Daily Texan* and other publications. It urged readers to write to UT president William Cunningham, athletic director DeLoss Dodds and members of the Athletics Council.

After a 64-55 loss to Texas Tech in Lubbock—not a particularly bad game for the Longhorns—things got worse. Television commentator Dick Vitale tabbed Weltlich as one of five coaches in trouble, and Kirk Bohls and Randy Riggs of the *Austin American-Statesman* wrote an article along the same line. "The whispers are approaching the decibel level of a roar," Bohls and Riggs stated. "And although no one in a position of authority will say Weltlich will be fired at the end of the season, all signs point in that direction."

One of UT's best ever, Travis Mays scores against Baylor.

So it seemed. The players, much too circumspect to say it publicly, were not happy for all the familiar reasons. No let's-win-for-Bob meetings were held, and yet they started winning, first with a 74-56 defeat of TCU before a decent-sized crowd, 4,931. John Lewis scored 20 for Moe Iba's Frogs, and Heggs led UT with 18, but the true hero was Mays. Advised by the team doctor not to play, he did and went 39 minutes, wearing a face mask to protect a broken nose, a corset on his back with an electronic stimulator to block pain, and tape on his knee, wrist and finger. Just a soph, he was already building a legacy as a Longhorn great.

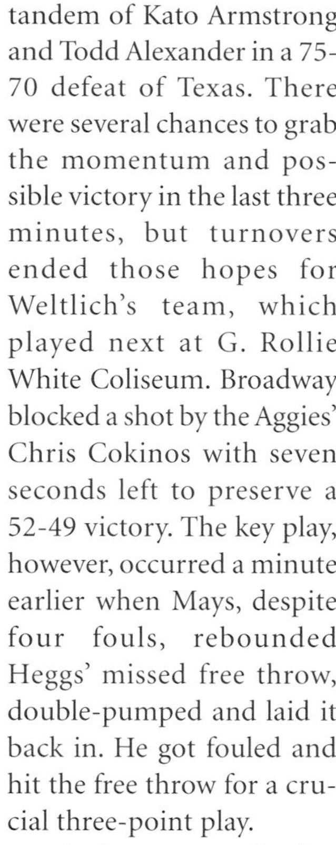

In Dallas, SMU got 31 points from its backcourt tandem of Kato Armstrong and Todd Alexander in a 75-70 defeat of Texas. There were several chances to grab the momentum and possible victory in the last three minutes, but turnovers ended those hopes for Weltlich's team, which played next at G. Rollie White Coliseum. Broadway blocked a shot by the Aggies' Chris Cokinos with seven seconds left to preserve a 52-49 victory. The key play, however, occurred a minute earlier when Mays, despite four fouls, rebounded Heggs' missed free throw, double-pumped and laid it back in. He got fouled and hit the free throw for a crucial three-point play.

A three-game Baylor winning streak ended on February 3 when the Bears missed 18 of 25 free throws in a 76-56 loss to UT at the Erwin Center. While no one could stop Michael Williams (25), Nassar and Muller did a good job on Darryl Middleton, the SWC's leading scorer and rebounder. "If you can't get motivated for the best post player in the conference, when can you?" Muller said. The Texas-Arkansas game three days later was a time for remembering as the 1978 NIT champions held a reunion and were honored at halftime. Abe Lemons, still coaching his OCU Chiefs, could not attend, but he got in the last word, as usual: "Just tell them to put my picture on a poster and parade it around the gym." If the Hogs expected an easy victory like they had up in the Ozarks, they did not get it. Before a supportive crowd of 6,095, Texas stunned league-leading Arkansas, 79-72. Mays had 25 points and a career-high 13

facility on a beautiful campus in a great city. If I can't sell this program, I should get out of the business."

In the seven months before the season began, Penders got out and talked to whoever would listen. Golf dates, luncheons with the Rotary Club, fraternities, sororities and media confabs were chances for him to discuss UT basketball. He brought one assistant, Jamie Ciampaglio, from Rhode Island and kept Eddie Oran from Weltlich's staff; the former was a fine hands-on coach, while the latter was a proven recruiter, although both were involved in every aspect of the program. By no means did Penders inherit a cold bed because only one starter exited from a 16-13 team, and two promising transfers had gained eligibility and were ready to go. Swingman Lance Blanks and guard Joey Wright had been high school stars but duds at Virginia and Drake, respectively. Blanks, Wright, Travis Mays and the rest of the players were enthusiastic about their new coach and his high-speed offense.

Following the orange and white game, a scrimmage with some Fort Hood soldiers, and an exhibition game against an Australian team, Penders' Longhorns began the season in Honolulu by playing in the Tipoff Tournament. Wright made a steal and subsequent layup in the last minute to seal an 82-79 defeat of Pepperdine. But the title game against the host team, Hawaii, was as problematic as Penders feared, and the Rainbow Warriors walked off with an 85-84 decision. "I've been coaching for 20 years, and I've seen some bad calls but nothing like that," he said. "We had our chances and should have put them away." Reggie Cross scored 26 points for Hawaii, and Alvin Heggs had a total of 40 in two games.

The starting lineup for Texas' home debut with Sam Houston State consisted of Mays, Blanks, Heggs, Courtney Jeans and Jose Nassar. Fans, a missing part of the equation during most of the Weltlich era, were eager for winning and entertaining basketball. Over 7,000 of them showed up for UT's 87-79 defeat of the Bearkats. Heggs and Tracy Pearson, all 6'8" and 300 pounds of him, led their teams with 24 points each. Despite foul trouble, Blanks showed plenty of offensive and defensive skill. A high-strung thoroughbred athlete, he was the most visible Longhorn on the court and the most quotable before and after games. Two nights later, Texas faced another lightweight, Northwestern Louisiana, and had to sweat out a 109-104 win keyed by Mays (24). It was the first time the Horns had gone over the century mark since Abe Lemons was burning stogies to celebrate victories before the crash of 1982.

Oral Roberts, a team that had beaten Alabama and LSU, hosted the Longhorns in Tulsa and got pounded, 119-91. Heggs, Mays and Wright all went over 20 points, and a school-record (soon broken again and again) 10 three-point field goals helped conquer the Titans. They were led by Greg Sutton with 22.

The Longhorn Classic, a tournament with one foot in the grave just a year earlier, looked rather healthy, although UT still did not bring in a big-name opponent. Almost 14,000 fans were at the two-day event, won by the Horns with little trouble. In a 96-73 victory over Lehigh, Blanks was the man. He hit 15 of 19 shots, including seven of nine from three-point range, handed out five assists and taunted the Lehigh players and coaches. The next night, Mays shone, throwing in 38 points as the Longhorns beat Tennessee-Chattanooga, 103-88, for the title. Texas' junior guard also had seven rebounds and played his usual tough defense. "Travis was in another world tonight," Penders said. "He was really focused."

The Horns went to California to meet Long Beach State, a team that liked to run and press, too. The 49ers got bombed, 117-86, as Heggs and Mays teamed up for 57 points. Blanks scored 20 before receiving a second technical foul and getting yanked by Penders with seven minutes left. His coaches and teammates warned the temperamental 6'4" jumping jack that he was gaining a bad reputation among officials and opponents, and he vowed to channel his energy in a more positive way, but his struggle to do so continued through the 1989 and 1990 seasons.

Blanks had no such problems when UT beat Southern Utah State, 117-78, before 8,456 Erwin Center spectators. He had 27 points in the first half, 36 in all. The Thunderbirds, who got 21 points from Jerry Naulls, never had a chance. "I was so hot, I don't think they could have stopped me if I helped them," Blanks said modestly. The team, which had exceeded 100 points five times in the past six games and was playing just the sort of basketball Penders promised, enjoyed a broad fan base of students and townspeople. Although the season was young, it looked like a new day for UT hoops.

An 8-1 record was nice, but it came against some rather weak competition. Listed among "others receiving votes" in the various national rankings, Penders insisted the team deserved to be in the top 20. That might be determined at the All-College Tournament in Oklahoma City. With 14,206 fans looking on, Richard Dumas (25) kept Oklahoma State in front most of the way, although Wright (32) brought the Horns back. The Cowboys appeared to have the game won until Blanks was fouled on a desperate shot at the buzzer. He hit a free throw to tie and another to win, 85-84. But the Horns tasted bitter defeat the next night against Oklahoma, runner-up in the 1988 NCAA tourney. Although Stacey King, their biggest star, was out with an injury, the Sooners ripped UT, 124-95. Three of OU's other frontcourt men combined for 62 points. Texas committed a staggering 39 turnovers, and only Mays (34) had a good game. "They're like a bunch of sharks," said an admiring Penders. "We saw a team with a killer instinct, which we need to acquire."

Coach Tom Penders giving instructions during a timeout.

Mays (27) went over the 1,000-point mark in his career when Texas beat Baylor, 105-85, in the Southwest Conference opener. Gene Iba's Bears, who had finished second in the conference the previous two seasons, were cellar-bound in 1989. Things were expected to be somewhat tougher when Arkansas visited the following Saturday afternoon. It would certainly be entertaining—Nolan Richardson's Razorbacks versus Penders' Horns, two up-tempo teams, the class of the SWC. A crowd of 12,647 saw UT get dunked, stuffed and snuffed by Arkansas, 99-92. Freshman Lee Mayberry (22) did a fine job of directing the Razorback offense. Blanks and Mays could not get it going, but Nassar and Heggs combined for 43 points and 23 rebounds. "I'm disappointed," Blanks said. "The fans showed some faith by coming out, and we let them down."

Mays was splendid in a 66-65 defeat of Rice in Houston. On a night when his teammates seemed hesitant to shoot, he scored 32 points, including nine three-pointers. The Owls would have won if D'Wayne Tanner's last-second shot had fallen. Three days later at Hofheinz Pavilion, another thriller went Texas' way. With five seconds on the clock and the score tied, Blanks launched an outside shot that bounced off the rim to Wright. He shot, missed, grabbed the rebound and laid it in at the buzzer to defeat Houston, 88-86, quieting a crowd of 6,698. Craig Upchurch scored 33 for the Cougars and would have had more if not for the defensive work of UT's little-used big man, George Muller.

Courting disaster as they had before, the Horns frittered away a 21-point lead and then held on for a 90-86 home victory over Texas Tech before 13,223 screaming fans. Mays and Blanks combined for 61 points, partly because their coach understood how the three-point shot had changed college basketball. Penders, in contrast to Weltlich, had a knack for getting his teams to relax and play with confidence. If the guards were open behind the line, he urged them to put it up. Jerry Mason led the Red Raiders with 22 points.

Before a big crowd in Nashville and a television audience of half the nation (or half of those tuning in to CBS), Texas played a big intersectional game with Vanderbilt. The Commodores trailed by 13 late in the first half, went on a 24-4 scoring spree, and the game was theirs, 94-79. Only Mays (30) was unaffected by Vandy's zone defense, something the Horns were usually happy to see. Frank Kornet scored 25 in the 500th career victory of coach C.M. Newton.

Moe Iba of TCU liked the same slow, ball-control style his father, Hank, had patented at Oklahoma State. The Horned Frogs were then 6-0 in the SWC. Penders was determined to force a quick pace when the teams met in Fort Worth on January 25, and the hare came in well ahead of the tortoise in a 94-84 UT win. "Texas got us out of running any kind of offense," Iba said. Center John Lewis scored 30 for TCU, and Mays had 25. He was on his way to leading the conference in scoring, the first Longhorn to do so since Larry Robinson in 1974.

An array of full-court and half-court defenses induced 27 SMU turnovers in a 96-65 Horn victory in

Austin. The Ponies, who were missing star guard Kato Armstrong (an academic casualty), attempted just 47 shots, 32 fewer than Texas. Blanks was the game's top scorer with 23 points. Texas A&M was idling along with a losing record, but the Aggies were in town and because the Longhorns were doing so well, the Erwin Center was packed when the teams met. UT shot and played poorly and yet managed an 85-80 victory, the 16th of the season. Blanks scored 23 and got unexpected offensive help from Jeans and sub forward Winn Shepard (12 each).

On a 17-degree day in Waco, the heating system at Baylor's new $12.5-million, 10,084-seat Ferrell Center refused to work, but the Horns were not exactly cold in a 110-81 blowout. Blanks and Wright had a combined 57 points, compensating for the absence of Mays, who was ejected early on for throwing a retaliatory elbow at an opponent. Julius Denton scored 21 for the Bears. That victory, coupled with an Arkansas loss, gave UT sole possession of first place—briefly. Penders' first visit to Fayetteville was one to forget, a 105-82 defeat. As they had done in Austin, the Razorbacks attacked the Texas press and got the desired results. Keith Wilson had a career-high 31 points for Arkansas, and Heggs (30 points and 14 rebounds) was the Horns' best. "Some of our guys had sub-par games, and Arkansas played with confidence and poise," Penders said. "Barnhill's a great place. The fans are super."

Back at home, UT whomped Rice, 116-74, behind 33 points each from Blanks and Mays and 15 rebounds from Nassar. "Texas is a heck of a team, especially when they're on like tonight," remarked Owl coach Scott Thompson. But that was before a perplexing 105-96 loss to Houston in front of a mere 9,623 fans at the Erwin Center. The Longhorns seemed to lack intensity, while the Cougars did not. They hit 32 of 34 free throws and were led by Richard Hollis (27) and Craig Upchurch (23).

Record: 25-9

82 Pepperdine 79
84 Hawaii 85
87 Sam Houston 79
109 NW Louisiana 104
119 Oral Roberts 91
96 Lehigh 73
103 Tennessee-Chattanooga 88
117 Long Beach State 86
117 Southern Utah 78
85 Oklahoma State 84
95 Oklahoma 124
105 Baylor 85
92 Arkansas 99
66 Rice 65
88 Houston 86
90 Texas Tech 86
79 Vanderbilt 94
94 TCU 84
96 SMU 65
85 Texas A&M 80
110 Baylor 81
82 Arkansas 105
116 Rice 74
96 Houston 105
84 Texas Tech 82
123 Miami 104
107 TCU 82
82 SMU 79
89 Texas A&M 106
93 SMU 91 (OT)
93 TCU 89 (OT)
76 Arkansas 100
76 Georgia Tech 70
89 Missouri 108

Penders took his team to the South Plains to play the much-improved Texas Tech Red Raiders, who had won five of their last six games. As a spirited sellout crowd looked on, Wright made a driving 15-foot jumper despite the best defensive efforts of Sean Gay for an 84-82 victory. A spectacular play happened late in the first half when Blanks, incensed at the remarks of some of Tech's courtside cowboys, threw down a dunk that nearly dislodged the basket.

Mays scored 40 points, and the Horns wound up with 28 offensive rebounds in a 123-104 defeat of Miami at the Erwin Center. It was a game enlivened by some comments Hurricane coach Bill Foster had made about the SWC during recruiting season. Penders, a master of us-versus-them motivation, refused to shake hands with his Florida counterpart after the buzzer. TCU came to town three days later and got beat, 107-82. While the Frogs' John Lewis (25) won scoring honors, five Longhorns reached double figures, and Muller had nine rebounds and four blocked shots in a game witnessed by 13,460 fans. That brought average home attendance to 10,009, up from 4,029 in 1988, the biggest jump in the nation. And the defeat of TCU was the tenth 100-point game of the season, easily a school record. Even Abe Lemons' 1978 NIT champs did not score so prolifically, but neither did they have the benefit of the three-point shot nor the shot clock.

The 22nd victory of the season came in Dallas as SMU fell, 82-79. But the Mustangs gave a superb effort that could have, and in their view should have, won the game. Muller blocked a shot by SMU guard Rod Hampton, and there was some contact between them, but no foul was called, drawing vociferous protests from coach John Shumate, his players and many of the 7,302 fans present. Blanks and the Ponies' John Colborne both had 26 points. The win enhanced Texas' likelihood of getting a berth in the NCAA tourney, although that was not automatic since the Horns had yet to beat a top-20 team. Defeating Texas A&M in College Station would mean a cochampionship with Arkansas, but it did not occur. The Aggies blasted UT, 106-89, before a near-capacity crowd, and they had the two leading scorers, Lynn Suber (27) and Donald Thompson (22).

Mays was chosen player of the year just before the Horns headed to Dallas for the Southwest Conference Tournament. He hit a driving layup and two free throws in the final 19 seconds of overtime to help beat SMU, 93-91, in the first round. But it was Wright (36) who took control of the game for Texas with his shooting, defense and ballhandling. In 39 minutes, Wright committed just one turnover. "This kid is one of our real keys," Penders said. "When the pressure is on, he steps forward." It was overtime again the next night as the Horns rallied past TCU, 93-89, in a game with a mind-numbing 66 fouls. Blanks had 25 points (equaling the Frogs' Craig Sibley), but five late free throws by Thomas Gipson, Wright and Mays iced the game. Both coaches, Penders and Moe Iba, barked at the refs most of the second half, and there were some questionable calls. Some 16,240 fans, most of them clad in red, watched Arkansas annihilate the Longhorns, 100-76, in the finals. Lenzie Howell, tournament MVP, had a game-high 28 points for the Hogs, who beat UT thrice in the 1989 season.

Nevertheless, the Horns were back in the NCAAs for the first time in a decade. And if the experts were right, it would not be for long because Georgia Tech had a bigger and quicker team. Yellow Jacket forwards Tom Hammonds and Dennis Scott both averaged over 20 points per game, and they had a fine coach, Bobby Cremins. But Penders was no piker, either. His last Rhode Island team had scored two tourney wins before losing to Duke by one. UT played 40 minutes of inspired basketball and stung the Yellow Jackets, 76-70. Nassar provided some crucial interior defense, and Mays scored 23 points in an upset almost as big as Texas' last NCAA win—over Houston in 1972 when Leon Black was coaching. "In the tournament, every game could be your last, and you have to play that way," Penders said. "I saw fire in their eyes tonight."

The 25-8 Longhorns played their fifth straight game at Reunion Arena on Sunday, March 19. Missouri, a tournament upset victim for Penders' Rhode Island team the year before, was the opponent. The Longhorns revved up for another giant killing but got clubbed, themselves, 108-89. The talented trio, Blanks, Mays and Wright, was responsible for 64 points, but 20 turnovers and too many Mizzou offensive rebounds made victory impossible. The Tigers' Doug Smith poured in 32 points. While the season was over, it had been one to remember for Longhorn fans, many of whom had stopped being fans until Tom Penders was hired as coach.

1990

After all their success in 1989, what could the Longhorns possibly do for an encore? Coach Tom Penders refused to make predictions and said simply, "We plan to be a better basketball team." Guards Lance Blanks, Travis Mays (captain or cocaptain for the third straight year) and Joey Wright were back. Dubbed "BMW—the ultimate driving machine" by the Texas sports information department, they were the third-best set of guards in the country, according to television commentator and hoop fanatic Dick Vitale. Penders got some muscle up front in 6'7" Locksley Collie and 6'8" Guillermo Myers. Natives of the Bahamas and Panama, respectively, they signed scholarships a few months after their junior college coach, Vic Trilli, had become a UT assistant. And sophomore swingman Benford Williams brought considerable athletic ability and a winning pedigree (three state championships) to the team. Courtney Jeans, a two-year starter, went to the bench but still played in all 33 games of another successful season for Texas.

Penders' built-for-speed Longhorns destroyed UT-Arlington in the opener, 116-66. Mays and Blanks combined for 49 points against the Mavericks, "a foil the Harlem Globetrotters would be proud of," wrote Mark Rosner of the *Austin American-Statesman*. The sixth Longhorn Classic appeared to offer two more blowout opportunities. Manhattan, a team Penders had faced often while at Columbia and Fordham, was the first victim. The Jaspers stayed within seven points at halftime, but UT made some adjustments in the locker room and came up with a 108-63 victory. The title game was much tougher as Mays (tournament MVP) scored 33 points to narrowly defeat UT-San Antonio, 89-86.

The Horns stayed at home a while longer, playing their first six games in Austin. On December 13, Long Beach State took an 89-87 win when freshman Lucious Harris hit a three-pointer at the buzzer. When it fell through, he spun around and taunted Jamie Ciampaglio, Texas' voluble assistant coach. After the 49ers gave them a rude introduction to the loss column, the Longhorns hosted No. 24 Florida. Penders urged season-ticket holders to show up, but UT fans were notorious for weak attendance at early-season games. A crowd of nearly 11,000 for the Longhorn-Gator matchup saw the unveiling of gray uniforms Penders had designed for special occasions. Despite a bruised knee, Mays scored 35, and Wright had 24 points and 17 rebounds in leading Texas to an entertaining 105-94 victory. "When a team gets hot, there's nothing you can do," said Florida's 7'2" Dwayne Schintzius, who scored 20. "Every shot seemed to be a three-pointer, and every one seemed to go in." In the midst of final exams, the Longhorns used a 60-point second half to beat Virginia Military Institute, 98-74, in the 300th victory of Penders' coaching career. The hustling Keydets had the game's top two scorers, twin brothers Ramon and Damon Williams (27 and 24 points, respectively).

It was the earliest Southwest Conference opener ever—December 23. Due to television factors, the Texas-SMU game in Dallas was moved forward, and John Colborne (27) led the Mustangs to a near upset. They slowed the pace and were ahead by six points with six minutes to play when Wright took charge from the field and the free throw line for a 73-67 UT win. The Horns really had the Wright stuff a week later in Deland, Florida. Although the game with Stetson had been arranged as a homecoming of sorts for Mays, Wright exploded for 46 points in a 102-82 defeat of the Hatters. He made 15 of 22 shots, including six of nine from behind the three-point arc, and fell just short of the school record of 49 points set by Slater Martin in 1949 and tied by Raymond Downs in 1956.

That was a nice tuneup for the big game to follow, against No. 11 LSU at the Summit in Houston. UT's post men, Collie and Myers, were still adjusting to major-college basketball, and they faced a severe challenge in the Tigers' 7'1" Shaquille O'Neal and 7' Stanley Roberts. And the guards had to contend with all-American Chris Jackson. The Longhorns lost, 124-113, but the 11,539 fans (plus several pro scouts) got their money's worth in an exciting contest. Jackson scored 51 and LSU's two big men combined for 42 points, 35 rebounds and 13 blocked shots. Blanks emerged from a five-game shooting slump with 32 points, and Mays had 30.

Conference play resumed on January 4 against Texas Tech. In what proved to be the first of 20 straight losses (extending into 1991) for Gerald Myers' Red Raiders, UT won, 109-71, before 10,721 spectators at the Erwin Center. Mays and Blanks teamed up for 51 points, and Cleveland Phelps had 22 for Tech. As part of the SWC whistle-stop tour, the officials called 44 fouls and heard from Penders and Myers on nearly every one. Regardless of fouls and free throws, there was no way the Raiders were going to win. "Texas just played a great game," Myers said. "Those guards are terrific." UT's racehorse offense was again on display in a 108-89 win over Baylor in Austin, the fourth consecutive time the Horns had gone over the century mark. Blanks, playing with familiar abandon, scored 36 points and Mays 30. The Bears got 25 each from Julius Denton and Kelvin Chalmers.

While Texas lacked a big-time rebounder and defensive intimidator, Mays, Blanks and Wright were unusually good on the boards. Collie and Myers had seven rebounds apiece when the Horns escaped Fort

Record: 24-9

116 UT-Arlington 66
108 Manhattan 63
89 UT-San Antonio 86
87 Long Beach State 89
105 Florida 94
98 Virginia Military 74
73 SMU 67
102 Stetson 82
113 LSU 124
109 Texas Tech 71
108 Baylor 89
83 TCU 80
84 Oklahoma 103
96 Texas A&M 94
107 Rhode Island 86
97 Texas Tech 77
100 Arkansas 109
96 Rice 84
93 Houston 102
96 Arkansas 103 (OT)
96 Baylor 91
85 TCU 77
79 SMU 68
79 Texas A&M 73
86 Rice 84
89 DePaul 79
79 Houston 84
92 Texas A&M 84
86 Houston 89
100 Georgia 88
73 Purdue 72
102 Xavier 89
85 Arkansas 88

Worth with an 83-80 defeat of TCU. Blanks scored 31 points, and the game would have gone into overtime if three-point shots by Michael Strickland and Tony Edmond had dropped in the final 16 seconds. One part of Penders' formula for success at Texas was exposure, and the Longhorns got plenty of it in the 1990 regular season. The first of five nationally televised games was against No. 4 Oklahoma in Norman. The relentless Sooners got their 38th straight home win, 103-84, thanks in part to UT's poor free throw shooting (16 of 31) and three-point shooting (six of 22). In a game full of jawing and attempted intimidation by both teams, OU simply had better big men—Jackie Jones, William Davis and Tony Martin. Perhaps the most encouraging sign for Texas was the play of Benford Williams, who showed some nice power moves while scoring 18 points and getting 12 rebounds in 27 minutes of play.

The season's first home sellout was a 96-94 defeat of Texas A&M. "It was a well-played game, a well-officiated game in front of a packed house," Penders said. "It was great for the Southwest Conference." The guards for both teams scored points by the barrelful—64 from Mays, Wright and Blanks and 69 from the Ags' Lynn Suber, Freddie Ricks and Tony Milton. A combined 21 rebounds by Collie and Myers indicated they were getting better. The Erwin Center was full again three days later when Penders' former team, the Rhode Island Rams, came to town. The Longhorns rolled to a 107-86 victory in which Mays (29) broke Ron Baxter's decade-old record as the top scorer in UT history. When the game was stopped briefly, Mays received the ball, hugs from teammates and warm applause from 16,231 fans aware of his role in elevating Longhorn basketball over the past four seasons. Penders, whose ex-assistant, Al Skinner, coached the Rams, saw two of his pupils, Eric Leslie and Kenny Green, score a total of 57 points in defeat.

In Lubbock, an incident late in the first half involving Blanks spurred the Horns to a 97-77 victory over Texas Tech. When Wright and Collie squared off with a couple of Red Raiders, Blanks jumped into it and either did or did not—depending on the source—spit on an opposing player. The fans were in an uproar, and Blanks gave them a universally known hand sign, for which he was assessed a technical foul. The Longhorns and Razorbacks, tied for the SWC lead, met at Barnhill Arena on a Thursday night, and Arkansas came out on top, 109-100. Nine minutes into the game, Mays fell and hyperextended a finger. His departure soon afterward helped Todd Day, a 6'8" swingman, score 34 points for the sixth-ranked Hogs. Even without Mays, the Horns hung close most of the way. Williams had 25 points and 11 rebounds, Wright (25) showed no fear driving into the lane, and Blanks—ragged constantly by most of the 9,342 fans—had a solid game.

Penders, who protested a series of calls, walked out near midcourt at one point and got himself a T. He said, "The officials in this league are going to make a maniac out of me" and issued other comments, which brought a public reprimand from SWC commissioner Fred Jacoby. Kevin Lyttle of the *Austin American-Statesman* wrote a column in defense of Penders, saying every team in the conference had athletes who could run, jump and shoot and should be allowed to play the game unfettered by so many whistles and the never-ending walk to the free throw line. Lyttle also chided the Erwin Center crowds, who were quiet and polite beyond reason. Decorum, it seemed, took precedence over decibels.

Mays was in street clothes when the Longhorns beat Rice, 96-84, in Austin. His backcourt buddies, Wright and Blanks, had a horrendous first half, missing all but four of 27 shots. But they warmed up and finished with 32 and 29 points, respectively. The Owls' frosh center, Brent Scott, had 27 points and 11 rebounds. UT hosted Houston and dropped a 102-93 decision largely because of a four-minute dry spell in the second half. Seven Cougars were in double figures, one of whom, Darrell Mickens, also grabbed 21 rebounds. Mays, playing with his injured finger heavily taped, scored 25. Penders hoped to avoid the first back-to-back losses since his arrival on the Forty Acres when No. 3 Arkansas met the Horns before a full house in Austin. It was a 103-96 overtime defeat for UT, one of the most acrimonious basketball games in years. Texas was up by three points with 14 seconds left in regulation when an unlikely chain of events occurred. After an intentional foul was called on one of his players, Razorback coach Nolan Richardson slowly and very publicly walked off the court, and yet no technical was called. It was pure theatrics. He was in the locker room when Lee Mayberry hit a three-pointer to tie the game and bring him back, amid considerable booing. The Hogs went on to win, but the game would not be forgotten.

The NCAA's chief interpreter of rules agreed that the refs erred in not slapping "Strollin' Nolan" with a technical that almost surely would have meant a Texas victory.

So the Horns had lost three of their last four games. But they were about to embark on a winning streak that restored confidence and all but guaranteed a spot in the NCAA tourney. A crowd of 9,172, the largest yet at the two-year-old Ferrell Center, saw Texas and Baylor go down to the wire before some clutch free throw shooting by Mays won it, 96-81. Blanks had 36 points for UT, and David Wesley scored 23 for the Bears.

The final two home games of the season were with TCU and SMU in mid-February. The Longhorns let a 20-point lead shrink to three in the final minute against the Frogs but hung on for an 85-77 win before 11,286 fans. Despite considerable pain in his injured finger, Mays had a game-high 27 points, two more than TCU's Craig Sibley. "I can remember when it wasn't cool to be a Longhorn," Blanks said before taking the court against SMU in a game won by UT, 79-68. Mays and Wright combined for 45 points.

Shelby Metcalf's 27-year reign at Texas A&M, during which his teams won 438 games, had ended in January when he was unceremoniously dumped and replaced by an interim coach. G. Rollie White Coliseum, the Aggies' 1950s-style arena, was the site of a 79-73 UT victory. Blanks, who struggled most of the game, was hot when it counted, but the big men helped, too; Collie scored 23, and Myers had 14 rebounds. Mays and Wright seemed tired and had subpar games, so a 10-day break was welcome. On February 28, Texas beat Rice, 86-84, at Autry Court by hitting seven free throws in the last minute. Mays had 28 points and nine rebounds, and Blanks got into altercations with the Owls' Dana Hardy and D'Wayne Tanner.

The Horns traveled to Chicago for an intersectional game with DePaul. Joey Meyer's team had lost 13 games and a promising freshman guard from Port Arthur. B.J. Tyler, who was homesick and had bumped heads with Meyer, announced his plans to transfer to UT. He was in the stands at the Rosemont Horizon when his future teammates beat his ex-teammates, 89-79. Pressure defense and long-distance shooting toppled the Blue Demons as Blanks had 30 points, four steals, four assists and no turnovers. The final regular-season game was two days later at Hofheinz Pavilion, where a record 10,660 fans saw Houston eke out its 11th straight victory, 84-79. The Cougars' Carl Herrera and Byron Smith combined for 53 points, and Mays led UT with 19. Penders, angry over one call and a noncall in the final minute, chased referee Mike Tanco off the court when it was over.

Two losses to Houston, two to Arkansas and one each to Oklahoma and LSU gave Texas a poor record against quality competition, so the Horns, despite winning 20 games, were not in the big dance yet. They probably would have to win at least one game in the SWC tourney, and the longer they played, the better chance Mays had of eclipsing the conference scoring record held by Terry Teagle of Baylor. He had already passed such luminaries as Michael Young of Houston, Sidney Moncrief of Arkansas and Rick Bullock of Texas Tech. Mays was again SWC player of the year, but Blanks (third-leading scorer in the conference) did not even make second team. His antics had alienated fans, coaches and sportswriters around the league. At any rate, Blanks scored 27 points and got an obligatory technical foul in a 92-84 first-round defeat of Texas A&M. Myers had 15 points and 16 rebounds, both career highs. The next night, Reunion Arena was again packed when UT and Houston faced off. Down by 21 points with nine minutes left, the Longhorns launched a furious comeback that fell just short in an 89-86 loss. Wright, Mays and the Cougars' Carl Herrera all had 23 points, and Blanks and Byron Smith battled verbally and physically the entire game. Penders, who was tossed after getting a third technical, ripped the officials: "I'm glad we don't have to see these guys anymore. It's a joke.... If we're going to have a circus, let's put a tent over it."

Never before had the Longhorns made the NCAAs in consecutive seasons, and their first-round opponent was Georgia at the Hoosier Dome in Indianapolis. Bulldog coach Hugh Durham knew little about Texas but after watching game films, he compared Mays, Blanks and Wright to the best guards in the Southeastern Conference. What happened on March 16 was downright a-Mays-ing. Playing with three fouls most of the game, Mays—master of the jump-stop in the lane—hit 10 of 17 field goals and 23 of 27 free throws for a career-high 44 points as the Horns beat UGa, 100-88. Forward Alec Kessler (33) had a fine game for the Bulldogs, but the 39,940 fans and media people buzzed about Mays, who had been irked to receive just honorable mention all-America honors. "If that wasn't an all-America performance, I haven't seen one," Penders said.

The second-round opponent was 22-7 Purdue, a school just 90 miles from Indianapolis. "They'll have 39,000 fans, and we'll have 200," Ciampaglio said. "It's like the Lions and the Christians." Mays sank two free throws with seven seconds left to put UT ahead, 73-72. After a timeout, the Boilermakers' Tony Jones did a full-court dash and was going for the winning layup when Myers came out of nowhere to block his shot, preserving one of the biggest wins in Longhorn basketball history. The shoe was on the other foot as Purdue coach Gene Keady went into an obscenity-laced tirade against the officials.

As Purdue's Tony Jones takes a last-second would-be winning shot, Guillermo "Panama" Myers comes in to swat it away in UT's 73-72 defeat of the Boilermakers.

Texas, so recently accused of being unable to win important games, had done it twice. Orangebloods were pinching themselves to see if the team was really in the NCAA's Sweet 16. Reunion Arena was the site of the regional, and two-thirds of the tickets were in the hands of Arkansas fans. After the Hogs beat North Carolina, coach Nolan Richardson, showing some SWC *bonhomie*, urged them to cheer for UT in the second game, against 28-4 Xavier. Mays (32), Blanks (28) and Wright (26) did most of the damage in a come-from-behind 102-89 defeat of the Musketeers. Collie collected 16 rebounds. "I think the pace got too fast for us and we wore down," said Xavier coach Pete Gillen. "We did everything we could to stop them. They drove right by us in man and zone defenses." The Musketeers got a combined 49 points and 29 rebounds from Derek Strong and Tyrone Hill.

Were the Longhorns on the road to Denver? One more win and they would be playing in the Final Four at McNichols Arena. Sure, UT had been among the last four teams in 1943 and 1947, when it was an eight-team tournament. The first was a bit deceptive because it happened during the war years. Furthermore, basketball had come a long way since the era of Slater Martin. Penders ignored media reports that he was coveted by Florida, North Carolina State and Virginia, and AD DeLoss Dodds vowed to keep him in Austin. Postseason success was bringing some serious dollars into the Texas athletic department, and Dodds, once criticized for hiring and keeping Bob Weltlich, was being called a genius for getting Penders. In the meantime, there was a big game to play, against a familiar SWC rival. It was Horns-Hogs, Part III, in the NCAA quarterfinals. Austin and UT police were prepared in case another victory celebration erupted on the Drag, as happened after the Xavier game, but there was no need. The Longhorns lost, 88-85. They came back from 16 points down with 12 minutes left and had a chance to tie it in the waning seconds when Mays' three-pointer came off the rim. Twenty-two turnovers, all seemingly at the worst possible times, hurt Texas' chances. The Razorbacks' Lenzie Howell had a game-high 21 points. The 1990 season was over, and what a run it had been. Mays' name was etched in the record book as the Southwest Conference's all-time leading scorer with 2,279 points. Penders called him the greatest player in UT history.

1991

There were many ways to measure the progress of Texas basketball entering the third year of Tom Penders' tenure, one of which was respect from the pros. Travis Mays and Lance Blanks had been first-round draft picks of the Sacramento Kings and Detroit Pistons, respectively. Penders and his assistants—Jamie Ciampaglio, Eddie Oran and Vic Trilli—were given new contracts with hefty pay raises, and why not? With a 49-18 record, hitting the century mark 21 times, two appearances in the NCAA tourney, tripled home attendance and enhanced national prestige, the Longhorn program had really evolved since Bob Weltlich's departure. The starting lineup for most of the 32 games of the 1991 season was composed of returnees: Joey Wright and Courtney Jeans in the backcourt and Locksley Collie, Guillermo Myers and Benford Williams in the frontcourt. Penders found more thunder to accompany lightning in the form of two recruits. Dexter Cambridge, the third Lon Morris JC star to follow Trilli to Texas, was advertised as another Larry Johnson, player of the year for defending national champion Nevada-Las Vegas. And 6'8" Albert Burditt, an Austin native and perhaps the top prospect in the state, signed thanks largely to Oran's long-term courting. Guard Teyon McCoy, a transfer from Maryland, was hampered in the early season by surgery to remove a benign tumor from his leg.

Arkansas, heavily favored to win the Southwest Conference for the third straight time, was doing a farewell tour. For reasons pertaining mostly to football, UA officials had decided to end an alliance with the SWC that began in 1924 and move to the Southeastern Conference. While some SWC members may have been glad to see the ferocious Razorbacks (No. 2 in the nation) depart, Penders was not. He admired the Arkansas hoop program, enjoyed the intense Hog-Horn duels and regretted the end of the rivalry. At any rate, UT was considered the only conference team capable of pushing Arkansas.

The season began nicely with a 76-74 defeat of Florida in Gainesville. The Gators, in their first game under coach Lon Kruger, had a chance to tie or win with four seconds left, but Craig Brown bricked a couple of free throws. Wright scored 26 points for the Longhorns. Three days later at the Maravich Assembly Center, Texas met an LSU team bereft of two-thirds of its renowned troika. While Chris Jackson and Stanley Roberts had gone on to the NBA, Shaquille O'Neal was back. As 14,341 fans looked on, the big fellow picked up his fourth foul early in the second half but still managed to score 26 points, collect 18 rebounds and block five shots in a 101-87 Tiger victory. After watching his team shoot poorly and commit 24 turnovers, Penders, usually so easygoing, kept the locker-room door shut for half an hour. "We're playing tough people," he said. "We want to get better for January and February, but we need a lot of work."

Brash Billy Tubbs brought his 16th-ranked Oklahoma Sooners to the Erwin Center, and their late run was enough to down the Longhorns, 96-88. Freshman Jeff Webster had 35 points and 10 rebounds, and no one seemed capable of guarding him, especially Cambridge, who fouled out in just 13 minutes. So far, at least, his shooting (eight of 27) was atrocious and his defense was even worse. Just when those comparisons to Larry Johnson were beginning to look absurd, Cambridge came through with a good game. He lit up the scoreboard for 25 points in a 112-68 defeat of Loyola-Maryland in the first round of the Longhorn Classic. Another lightweight would play Texas in the tournament finals. Wright staked the team to a big early lead, and Williams (27 points and 14 rebounds) extended it in a 116-70 blowout of UT-Pan American.

After a 10-day exam break, the Horns journeyed to the west coast to meet California-Santa Barbara. They trailed by 10 points at intermission, but time and again, Wright drove to the hoop and got fouled, converting 20 of 28 free throws in an 87-84 overtime victory. It was a tough environment in which to win a game as 6,000 demonstrative fans packed the Gauchos' little gym. The Omni in Atlanta was the scene of a doubleheader featuring Texas versus Georgia and Georgia Tech versus Loyola-Marymount. The No. 17 Bulldogs avenged their loss to UT in the 1990 NCAA Tournament with a 79-71 win keyed by Marshall Wilson (24) and Litterial Green (21). Other than Myers' 17 rebounds, it was not one of the Longhorns' better games as they shot just 57 percent from the line and had 24 turnovers.

But UT bounced back to take the opener in the Arizona State/Tribune Classic. The Horns overcame missed shots, blown free throws and errant passes to slip past Michigan, 76-74. "Going down the stretch, we feel that we are going to win no matter what," said Wright, who played 39 minutes on a sprained ankle.

"Coach Penders is real loose, so how can we feel tight?" The Wolverines, national champs two years earlier, were led by Demetrius Calip (19). Wright, Collie and Myers all fouled out in the title game, an 89-82 loss to host Arizona State. Penders, angry about Pac-10 officiating he considered biased toward the Sun Devils, refused to accept the second-place trophy, and the team headed back to Austin to prepare for SWC competition.

Joey Wright, a key figure in the Longhorns' backcourt from 1989 to 1991.

Conference officials believed there had been entirely too much woofing, profanity and violence in the 1990 season and instituted several rules to restore order on the court. Coaches, too, were told to turn down the heat or risk penalties. Penders, who had blasted league refs in the SWC tourney, was under a one-game suspension when Texas A&M visited Austin. Ciampaglio (under season-long probation for making similar strident comments), Oran and Trilli handled things while Penders listened to a radio account in the locker room. The Horns shot 60 percent in an easy 93-67 defeat of the Ags, coached for one ill-fated year by Kermit Davis. Collie, lighter and quicker than before and equipped with a drop-step move, scored 27 points as Texas beat Baylor, 94-77. Wright and McCoy had 20 points each in a game enjoyed by 13,181 fans at the Erwin Center. "Texas just came out and kicked our butt," said BU coach Gene Iba. "We didn't guard a soul in the second half."

The woeful Aggies and Bears could not simulate the "40 minutes of hell" Arkansas promised all of its opponents. The Hogs' fast-break offense and strangling, full-court pressure defense had carried them to a 13-1 record, and the Longhorns were not a good ballhandling club. Barnhill Arena was packed, as always, when the Razorbacks took a 101-89 decision, with Oliver Miller and Todd Day getting 21 points apiece. If not for some missed open shots and unforced errors, the Horns might have won. Williams had his best game yet, 32 points and 11 rebounds. Two days later in Houston, UT came back from a sluggish first half to beat Rice, 92-79. Those brainy, zany Rice students dished out plenty of abuse, and the Horns responded by winning the game and doing a taunting dance before heading to the locker room. Wright (24) and the Owls' Dana Hardy (17) led their teams in scoring.

Some 15,743 spectators were at the Erwin Center on January 17 to see the Longhorns register a 90-84 defeat of Houston. Wright and McCoy, high school rivals from Hammond, Indiana, scored 23 points each, and Byron Smith had 31 for the Cougars. With the war in the Persian Gulf intensifying, a moment of silence was observed before the game, and the Longhorns' uniforms bore yellow ribbons in commemoration. Although CBS dictated an 11:30 a.m. tipoff between UT and DePaul, the Horns seemed wide awake, gaining a 90-80 victory likely to impress the media, pollsters and NCAA Tournament selection committee. "This was a must game for us," Penders said. "It puts us in solid shape, and now we've got a chance to roll on." The Blue Demons got 28 points from guard Terry Davis, while inside men Stephen Howard and David Booth were held well below their averages. Just as they had done in Chicago a year earlier, the Horns stunned DePaul from long range, hitting 10 of 13 three-pointers. Wright (26) made all six of his.

The 10-5 Longhorns were a good team getting better. Collie and Jeans combined for 48 points in an 83-65 defeat of Texas Tech at Lubbock Municipal Coliseum. Wright, who strained a hamstring in the DePaul game, did not play. Nor did the Red Raiders' star forward, Will Flemons, out for the season with a stress fracture in his foot.

Wright was back when the Horns hosted TCU and was one of six players to reach double figures in a 90-49 drubbing of Moe Iba's Frogs before 15,775 fans. "As more and more teams go up-tempo," wrote Mark Rosner of the *Austin American-Statesman*, "the methodical style championed by folks like the Ibas is becoming a vague memory, a distant sight in the rearview mirror of college basketball." SMU, another midlevel conference team accustomed to taking it nice and slow, was trying to change, although the Ponies were still more interested in executing plays than running and scoring. They fell to Texas, 96-80, as Cambridge scored 26 points, including 13 in a row in the first half. He also hustled on defense, something the UT coaching staff had long urged him to do. Tim Mason scored 21 for the Mustangs, coached for the third season by John Shumate.

Penders' Horns had three road games in a week, and all were victories. Just 3,237 fans were on hand to witness UT's 83-74 defeat of Texas A&M. While the Aggies hit 61 percent of their shots, Texas won on rebounding, free throws and a deeper bench. Sophomore guard Brooks Thompson had a game-high 25 points for the maroon and white. Collie and Cambridge, Texas' two Bahamians, had a total of 51 points in a 100-95 victory over Baylor, a game marred by 61 fouls. Penders was again unhappy with the referees and the BU student section close behind the Longhorn bench. Several fans shot verbal arrows all through the game, and one was removed by a security guard. "It's abusive," Penders said. "I've told [Baylor athletic director] Bill Menefee about it. Sooner or later, there's going to be a full-scale riot." The Horns won their ninth straight game, 76-73 over SMU. Myers, a horrid free throw shooter, made nine of ten, including four in the last 24 seconds. He and Williams, who also played well after going scoreless against Baylor, benefitted from some pregame confidence-building talks with Penders.

Record: 23-9
76 Florida 74
87 LSU 101
88 Oklahoma 96
112 Loyola (of Maryland) 68
116 UT-Pan American 70
87 California-Santa Barbara 84 (OT)
71 Georgia 79
76 Michigan 74
82 Arizona State 89
93 Texas A&M 67
94 Baylor 77
89 Arkansas 101
92 Rice 79
90 Houston 84
90 DePaul 80
83 Texas Tech 65
90 TCU 49
96 SMU 80
83 Texas A&M 74
100 Baylor 95
76 SMU 73
65 Rice 64
73 Houston 82
96 Texas Tech 79
96 Stetson 83
70 TCU 78
99 Arkansas 86
88 Baylor 78
82 SMU 74
89 Arkansas 120
73 St. Peter's 65
76 St. John's 84

The Texas-Rice game on February 12 was too close for comfort. Brent Scott (24) brought the Owls back from an 11-point deficit with 13 minutes left, and they had a chance to win, but Sam Campbell missed an eight-foot jump shot just before the buzzer, giving the Horns a 65-64 victory. That made 10 straight wins, although the last three were by a total of nine points. Texas, ranked No. 24, saw its luck run out at Hofheinz Pavilion, where Pat Foster's Houston club won, 82-73. Byron Smith and 7'1" Alvaro Teheran combined for 51 points as the Cougars kept alive their NCAA Tournament hopes. Collie, perhaps the most improved player in the SWC, had 24 points and nine rebounds. "It's been a pretty tough run, and the kids are tired," Penders said. "We're going to take a couple of days off. We'll be back."

They were back the very next game, overpowering Texas Tech, 96-79, as 14,241 Erwin Center fans looked on. The Horns' commanding 19-point lead was sharply reduced until Wright took over, scoring 13 points in less than three minutes and finishing with a game-high 31. Three players—Steve Miles, Derex Butts and Brad Dale—accounted for all but 13 of the Red Raiders' points. The game had a poignant touch because Abe Lemons was there for the annual lettermen's reunion. Introduced before the game, the ex-coach received a 40-second standing ovation and flashed his first "hook 'em" sign in nine years. The final no-pressure game of the season was a 96-83 defeat of Stetson, although the Hatters put up a fight, getting 18 more rebounds than the taller UT team. Williams took advantage of openings in the visitors' zone defense to score 21 points.

Two nights later in Fort Worth, the Longhorns, who had beaten TCU eight times in a row, were upset, 78-70. The Horned Frogs got their final 18 points from the free throw line. Wright tallied 25, moving into third place on the Texas career scoring list, but it was a frustrating game for him. He had five turnovers and a technical foul and complained bitterly about the officiating. It was all Penders could do to refrain from unleashing similar broadsides, but he did not want to get slapped with another suspension by the SWC.

The last regular-season game was unique. Arkansas, No. 3 in the nation with a 28-2 record, came into the sold-out Erwin Center for the last time as a Southwest Conference member. The entire all-SWC team (Oliver Miller, Lee Mayberry and Todd Day for Arkansas and Wright and Collie for Texas) was on the court. And memories of Nolan Richardson's stroll in 1990 were fresh, although the Razorback coach made light of the episode. He complimented Penders (calling him "Sweet Tom"), the UT program, the fans and everything but the Austin skyline. Penders had a 0-7 record against the Boss Hog, but that changed on Sunday afternoon, March 3. Williams (22) led a 43-16 second-half run to help beat Arkansas, 99-86. It was an exciting game, and the big arena on Red River Street had not been so loud in years. "It was hard enough to beat them seven times in a row, let alone eight," said Day, the Razorbacks' top scorer with 18. "But I enjoy playing Texas. They're a good team with great fans. It's big-time basketball."

As Kevin Lyttle of the *Austin American-Statesman* put it, Penders was "Mr. March, gentle as a lamb away from the court but a master at turning his players into roaring lions at tournament time." It was getting to be that time as the SWC tourney began in Dallas with a foul-plagued 88-78 defeat of Baylor. Jeans, the quiet senior who played in a school-record 126 games, scored 26 points. BU's Kelvin Chalmers did well, getting 31 points and 15 rebounds. The Horns and Bears banged each other for 40 minutes and left the court without shaking hands. In the semifinals, Texas cruised by SMU, 82-74, with Wright getting 25 points, which led to the title game with—who else?—Arkansas. For the last time, Hog fans who had driven their Winnebagos down from the Ozarks turned Reunion Arena into Barnhill South. Whether they were getting ready for tougher competition in the SEC or leaving the SWC as unquestioned kings, the Razorbacks tattooed UT, 120-89. Seven of them, led by Oliver Miller (23) hit double figures. After the devastating loss, Penders gave Nolan Richardson's team its due.

Nevertheless, the 22-8 Longhorns were back in the NCAAs, seeded fifth in their regional in Dayton. They would face St. Peter's of the Metro Atlantic Conference, another of those bands of lightly regarded young athletes eager to score an upset and embarrass the experts who predicted a quick exit. The Peacocks strutted into the game with a 24-6 record. Texas, meanwhile, a team that had experienced heady March Madness in 1990, wanted more. As everyone knew, the Horns liked to run it and gun it, but they could adjust if necessary. When St. Peter's dictated a slow pace, UT ground out a 73-65 victory before 13,055 fans. Cambridge had 18 points, and Myers dominated inside, getting 17 rebounds and four blocked shots. Tony Walker of the Peacocks scored a game-high 21.

That led to a second-round matchup with 21-8 St. John's. Although Penders expressed fondness for Redmen coach Lou Carnesecca, he truly wanted to beat him. Little Louie had won all ten games with Penders' Columbia and Fordham teams. A victory over the Big East power would solidify Texas' reputation and help recruiting on the east coast. St. John's shot 71 percent in the first half, took a 14-point lead and held off the Horns to win, 84-76. Billy Singleton and Malik Sealy teamed up for 40 points as the Redmen advanced to the next round. Texas' tournament magic of 1990 was in short supply but not for a lack of effort. Wright, who played most of the game with a gash under one eye, ended his brilliant career by scoring 32 points. "Joey's been the guts of this team for three years," Penders said. "It's nice to see him go out with a good game. He will be sorely missed."

1992

If coach Tom Penders had his choice, Texas would have accompanied Arkansas to the Southeastern Conference, playing such worthies as Kentucky, Tennessee and LSU each year. But the Razorbacks were gone, and UT remained in the eight-member Southwest Conference—for a while longer. Changes were afoot in college athletics, and AD DeLoss Dodds, concerned about the big picture, would not let Texas become a backwater of any sort.

Penders recruited a diaper dandy in Terrence Rencher. Voted New York's "Mr. Basketball," the 6'3" guard had a polished all-around game and was counted on to help from the start. Rencher and DePaul transfer B.J. Tyler would man the Longhorn backcourt admirably in years to come. And the frontcourt was in good hands with seniors Benford Williams and Dexter Cambridge and soph Albert Burditt. Tony Watson and junior college transfer Michael Richardson were quality subs, so the Horns showed lots of potential as the season drew near.

But before a game had been played, two matters arose, destined to create turmoil. Cambridge acknowledged receiving $7,000 from a booster at his former junior college, jeopardizing his amateur status. The University was about to suspend him when his attorney convinced a judge to issue a restraining order. The case went from state to federal court, and the NCAA ruled Cambridge ineligible after four games, during which he played exceptionally well. He would be back, though. The other problem concerned assistant coach Jamie Ciampaglio, who came under investigation by the UT athletic department and then the Travis County district attorney's office for withholding players' meal money on road games, and other financial improprieties. Ciampaglio remained on the staff throughout the season but kept a much lower profile than before. He was a source of colorful, if not outrageous, quotes, and some people on campus and around the SWC enjoyed his discomfiture.

The Horns displayed their new long and baggy shorts—popularized by NBA star Michael Jordan—on November 20 against Washington at the Erwin Center. It was a first-round game in the Big Apple preseason NIT, culminating in New York. A slimmed-down Cambridge scored 29, and Tyler had a sparkling debut (28 points and 14 assists) in a 104-83 defeat of the Huskies of the Pac-10 Conference. The second-round game, also in Austin, was with Princeton. Pete Carril's Tigers, known for their patient, probing offense, were a stark contrast to the frenetic Longhorns. A crowd of 15,621 was on hand for a half-court game finally won by UT, 57-46. The free throw differential of 23-4 favoring Texas got Carril's goat, and he responded like a true Ivy Leaguer: "What does that tell you about the men in striped shirts? Are the vicissitudes of life weighing so heavily on them? I guess we were too aggressive and Texas was too passive."

Despite missing nearly half of the 1992 season due to an NCAA suspension, Dexter Cambridge averaged 22 points and nine rebounds per game and made all-Southwest Conference.

It was the Horns' first time back at Madison Square Garden since the 1978 team won the NIT championship. Penders, who coached for 10 years in New York (at Columbia and Fordham), was hailed as a returning hero by hoop aficionados and the media. And furthermore, Rencher had played for St. Raymond's High School in the Bronx the season before. Homecoming was not so sweet, however, because Georgia Tech, a team with big post men and accurate outside shooters, subdued UT, 120-107. The Yellow Jackets got a combined 53 points from Malcolm Mackey and Matt Geiger, while Cambridge had 23 points and 12 rebounds. Burditt, weak from the flu and playing poorly, was benched in the consolation game against Pittsburgh, a 91-87 loss. The Panthers could not stop Cambridge (24 points and 18 rebounds) inside, but offensive impatience on the part of Tyler and Rencher hurt the Longhorns' chances to win in the late minutes. For the next 16 games, Cambridge would be out while his case meandered through the legal system and NCAA eligibility committee. More than once during December and January, it looked like his college career was over. Although Penders strove to prevent it from overshadowing the 1992 season, *l'affaire Cambridge* got plenty of national attention.

Minus Cambridge's scoring and rebounding prowess, the team carried on. The eighth and final

Longhorn Classic began with a 124-107 defeat of North Texas. Trailing the Eagles by two at halftime, the Horns got a robust pep talk from their sidelined star and came back to win easily. Williams and Jesse Ratliff of UNT both scored 26 points. Texas dispersed San Diego State, 85-58, in the title game as Williams, tourney MVP, had 24 points, seven rebounds and three steals against the Aztecs. Tyler's ballhandling and passing were superb, but his shooting (three of 16) was not. So the Longhorn Classic gave up the ghost. UT had won 15 of 16 games in its own tournament beginning in the dog days of Bob Weltlich's coaching stint, but it simply gave little benefit to the program. Penders opted instead to take part in better-established tournaments or doubleheaders.

A more difficult challenge than North Texas or San Diego State awaited the Horns in Norman, where Billy Tubbs' undefeated Oklahoma team took a convincing 106-91 victory. Sooner fans chanted "Dexter" as Texas went cold in the early minutes of the second half. His players tired and in some foul trouble, Penders did the inconceivable for a while, holding the ball against the OU zone defense. Brent Price and Bryan Sallier combined for 49 points for the winners.

More fond memories were evoked for Penders when his alma mater, Connecticut, visited the Erwin Center. Captain and fiery point guard for the Huskies a quarter-century earlier, Penders got no mercy from Jim Calhoun's eighth-ranked team, which pounded UT, 94-77, before 14,309 spectators. Williams (31 points and 10 rebounds) had an outstanding game, and Rencher went 40 minutes, showing some shifty moves and scoring 17. Tyler had another awful night from the field, making just three of 19 shots. But Penders would not get down on Tyler, who was mercurial as a player and off the court. The coach always used a light touch, enabling him to relate well to players and keep them enthusiastic. With the ongoing news about Cambridge and Ciampaglio, that helped. A much-needed victory came at home against California-Santa Barbara, 90-77. Tyler and Williams teamed up for 50 points, and both treated the fans to some spectacular shots. Weak free throw shooting continued to plague the Horns, however.

Results were mixed at the Sun Carnival Classic in El Paso. As Clemson held a four-point halftime lead, Rencher responded to Penders' challenge, lifting the Longhorns to a 95-87 victory. Rencher had a chance to be the hero again the next night against UT-El Paso, but he missed a shot and two free throws in the last half-minute of a game won by the Miners, 92-88. As a result, a nearly miraculous comeback fell just short because the Horns had been down by 29 with 10 minutes left. Tyler scored 27 points, and Burditt had 16 rebounds and four blocked shots, while Eddie Rivera and David Van Dyke scored a total of 43 points for Don Haskins' Miners.

The biggest crowd ever to witness a Longhorn basketball game was at the Superdome in New Orleans for the UT-LSU matchup. Before 42,211 partisan fans, the Tigers nipped Texas, 84-83. Shaquille O'Neal, in his last year in college before moving on to pro stardom and attendant riches, was double- and triple-teamed but still managed 19 points, 19 rebounds and four blocked shots. Williams, who scored 23 for the Longhorns, was the intended target of Rencher's pass with 27 seconds to go but which was intercepted by LSU's Clarence Ceasar. Rencher and Tyler could not hit the side of a barn, missing all but seven of 31 shots.

The Longhorns, with an unimpressive 6-6 record, began a three-game homestand with a 93-75 defeat of Murray State. Tyler scored 28, and Burditt had 19 points and 16 rebounds and helped keep a lid on Racer star Popeye Jones. Since the departure of Arkansas, critics claimed SWC basketball was hurting, but 12,343 fans and a national TV audience might not have thought so after an entertaining 86-75 defeat of Houston. Williams had a game-high 21 points, and Watson was three of four from three-point range. With the Cougars challenging for the lead early in the second half, a call went against Texas, prompting Penders to run onto the court, walk back to the bench and fling his jacket to the ground, drawing a technical foul from referee Bryan Stout. "I got a technical," Penders said forthrightly. "I wanted one. I deserved one. I liked the crowd reaction." Rencher and Tyler took charge when UT hosted Texas Tech the following Saturday night. They combined for 55 points in leading the Horns to an 88-83 victory. "They've got great guards," said coach James Dickey, successor to Gerald Myers. "We couldn't control those guys. They really complement each other well." Will Flemons had 27 points and 13 rebounds for the Red Raiders, and freshman guard Lance Hughes, son of ex-Longhorn Brenton Hughes, scored 14.

Texas A&M, reeling under NCAA sanctions, had just eight scholarship players, and construction of a $40-million arena had been postponed—again. Fewer than 3,000 fans were at G. Rollie White Coliseum to see the thin Aggies lose, 76-73. The Horns shot just 31 percent in the first half but forced enough turnovers to fuel the fast break for a close win. It was a different story in Fort Worth, where a full house took in TCU's 80-76 upset of the Longhorns. The Frogs hit eight of nine free throws in the last two minutes to hold off a late UT rally. Rencher grabbed scoring honors with 23 points, four more than Mark Moton of TCU. "Somehow, we prevailed," said Frog coach Moe Iba. "It's great to beat Texas."

Until the Longhorns faced SMU in Austin, Tyler had made just 30 percent of his shots in conference games and 14 percent from three-point range. But in a 106-91 defeat of the Ponies, he was excellent, scoring 23 and handing out 10 assists. Rencher was hot, too, getting 28 points. In 64 minutes on the court, they committed just two turnovers. Tim Mason and Mike Wilson had a combined 59 points for SMU.

The first of three road games was a shocking 84-68 loss to Baylor. Guard David Wesley threw in 33 points, the Bears held a huge rebound advantage, and the Texas guards shot abysmally as Tyler, Rencher and Watson were a combined 12 of 49. "They took bad shots," said BU's Kelvin Chalmers. "They always do." The Horns received a break from the SWC grind and dumped Virginia Commonwealth, 105-94, behind 37 points from Rencher. But he was not the only one who played well against the Rams because Tyler scored 26 and Williams 18, going over the 1,000-point mark in his three-year career. And Burditt collected a season-high 17 rebounds. After a procession of hearings, injunctions and appeals, the NCAA restored Dexter Cambridge's eligibility. The case can be summarized thus: UT was successful in arguing that one-third of the money in question had been wages for work Cambridge performed and that missing half the season was enough punishment. If anything, the University had been overeager to report itself before all the facts were known. Regardless, the Longhorns' big forward was back and ready to go against Rhode Island in Providence. The spotlight was on him and Penders, who coached the Rams for two years before coming to Texas. Cambridge's return was spoiled by foul troubles, bad shooting and porous defense as UT absorbed a 92-79 defeat. Andre Samuels had a game-high 20 points for Rhode Island.

At 12-9, the Longhorns already had equaled the number of losses in each of Penders' first three seasons and were in danger of missing out on an NCAA Tournament berth. Whether Cambridge was in midseason shape or not, he was depended on to perform, and he did as the team embarked on an eight-game winning streak. It began with an 88-87 defeat of Rice at the Erwin Center. A free throw by Rencher (24) with seven seconds on the clock provided the margin. Brent Scott had 30 points and 12 rebounds in a lost cause for the blue and gray.

Hofheinz Pavilion, where Houston had won 87 percent of its games dating back to 1970, was the scene of an 87-72 Texas victory, one Penders called "our biggest win of the year." The quick Longhorn backcourt was responsible for forcing most of the Cougars' 24 turnovers and converting them into points. Five UT players reached double figures, one of whom, Burditt, had 12 rebounds and some newfound defensive savvy. On a Wednesday night in Lubbock, the Horns beat Texas Tech, 93-90, as Rencher (26) led the team in scoring for the fifth straight game. When Tyler fouled out, direction of the offense fell to the left-handed guard who set a school record for the most points by a freshman. The Red Raiders' Lance Hughes (22) would spend four years seeking to prove Penders had made a mistake in not recruiting him. Georgia, a talented team with a disappointing record, met UT at HemisFair Arena in San Antonio and came away with a 98-93 loss. Litterial Green had 23 points and 10 assists for the Bulldogs. Cambridge scored 21 of his game-high 30 points in the first half, Burditt blocked five shots, and Tyler, Rencher and Watson were on, too. Penders was quite pleased: "This could end up being the best team we've ever had. We've got an excellent defensive center, one of the best power forwards in the country and a great backcourt."

In sole possession of first place in the SWC, Texas played TCU in the only home sellout of the year. Ripping and running for 40 minutes, the Longhorns took a 99-77 victory over the Frogs. Cambridge, Tyler and Rencher combined for 67 points, while Reggie Smith had 26 points and 16 rebounds for TCU. As usual, the SMU Mustangs offered more resistance in Dallas than in Austin. Cambridge fought off double-team defenses for 31 points, including the winning free throws with 28 seconds left in an 88-86 win. Mike Wilson had a career-high 35 points for SMU in a game that was tightly and yet inconsistently called, just the kind that gave Penders fits. He did, however, credit Pony coach John Shumate for using a smart game plan.

The Horns returned to Austin and kept on winning. They romped Oral Roberts, 128-108, as Rencher, Tyler and Cambridge all exceeded 30 points and Williams had a couple of authoritative dunkerooskis. And Burditt broke LaSalle Thompson's season record for blocked shots. Penders' team had an angry edge when Baylor came to town. The Bears had won easily in Waco (during Cambridge's hiatus) and made some unflattering comments after the game, leading to retorts from UT players and coaches. Yet the bad blood was overshadowed by news that Penders and his agent sought to renegotiate his contract in case he was fired or reassigned—an unlikely event. His name had been mentioned as a candidate for the state's three pro teams, the Houston Rockets, San Antonio Spurs and Dallas Mavericks, not to mention Syracuse, UCLA and Nevada-Las Vegas on the collegiate level. Penders' Longhorns whipped Baylor, 97-67, for their eighth straight win. Watson, a leaper whose shooting and ballhandling continued to improve, scored 23 points and made five shots from beyond the arc. Penders and BU coach Gene Iba skipped the postgame pleasantries.

Record: 23-12

104 Washington 83
57 Princeton 46
107 Georgia Tech 120
87 Pittsburgh 91
124 North Texas 107
85 San Diego State 58
91 Oklahoma 106
77 Connecticut 94
90 California-Santa Barbara 77
95 Clemson 87
88 UT-El Paso 92
83 LSU 84
93 Murray State 75
86 Houston 75
88 Texas Tech 83
76 Texas A&M 73
76 TCU 80
106 SMU 91
68 Baylor 84
105 Virginia Commonwealth 94
79 Rhode Island 92
88 Rice 87
87 Houston 72
93 Texas Tech 90
98 Georgia 93
99 TCU 77
88 SMU 86
128 Oral Roberts 108
97 Baylor 67
97 Rice 103
86 Texas A&M 63
88 Texas A&M 69
97 Texas Tech 87
72 Houston 91
92 Iowa 98

Before the largest crowd at Autry Court since 1972, Rice defeated Texas, 103-97. In addition, the Owls attained the 20-victory level for the first time in 38 years. Marvin Moore scored 26 for Rice, and Tyler had 36 for the Horns. Five assists ran Tyler's season total to more than 200.

The unexpected loss to Rice meant UT needed a victory in the regular-season finale against Texas A&M to tie Houston for the SWC crown. The Aggies were not the team to sidetrack the determined Horns, and the result was predictable: Texas, 86-63. All of the starters were in double figures, the press unnerved the Ags, and the refs stayed out of the way. "The whole atmosphere was really intimidating—the arena, the fans, the team," said coach Tony Barone after his first visit to the Erwin Center.

The same two teams met in Dallas five days later in the first round of the SWC Tournament. Without Arkansas and its voluminous fans, Reunion Arena was just half full, prompting calls for a return to San Antonio. The game was much closer than anticipated as the overachieving Aggies held a slight lead with 13 minutes left. Michael Richardson scored all of his 18 points from then on, leading the Horns to an 88-69 win. Shedrick Anderson had 17 points and 12 rebounds for Texas A&M. In the semifinals, Cambridge played aggressively despite foul trouble, helping UT to a 97-87 defeat of Texas Tech. He and Tyler combined for 45 points in sending the Red Raiders home. But Houston, a team the Longhorns had owned in the regular season, took a 91-72 victory in the finals. The Cougars overcame an 11-point deficit, 37 percent first-half shooting and fatigue to win. Sam Mack scored 28 points and Craig Upchurch 20. Cambridge, the tourney MVP, had 29 points and 12 rebounds.

Both Houston and Texas made it into the big show, and neither team went far. The 23-11 Longhorns met 18-10 Iowa in Greensboro, North Carolina, with the winner almost certain to face defending national champion Duke. Before a crowd of 15,800, the Hawkeyes won, 98-92. The Horns made 13 of 31 three-pointers, but the press had little effect on their Big 10 opponent. Rencher scored 26 points, one more than Iowa center Acie Earl. "It was a great game," Penders said. "We just couldn't get over the hump. Iowa always answered."

The season had come to an abrupt end, and six weeks later, the same thing happened to Jamie Ciampaglio's coaching career on the Forty Acres. He was forced to resign and was convicted of a third-degree felony for tampering with governmental records. A valued assistant for Penders over the past six seasons at Rhode Island and Texas and once considered on the fast track to a head coaching job himself, Ciampaglio put a bold face on his fall from grace, quoting Abraham Lincoln and insisting he had been persecuted by the media.

1993

The buzzer had barely sounded after Texas' NCAA Tournament loss to Iowa, and Tom Penders was already booming his backcourt for 1993. B.J. Tyler and Terrence Rencher, entering their junior and sophomore seasons, respectively, might be the best guard tandem in the country, opined the Longhorn coach. For various reasons, however, 1993 would not be Tyler's or Rencher's favorite year. Expected to win the championship of the Southwest Conference (which was then discussing a football-driven merger with the Big 8), UT instead got a heaping helping of humble pie.

The season began in Tulsa, where the Horns rolled to a 136-97 defeat of Oral Roberts. It was the second-highest score in school history with 74 points coming from Rencher, center Albert Burditt and Tyler. The Titans, outrebounded by almost a two-to-one margin, were a weak team, but they played the running game Penders liked. It was a different story in the opener of the Diet Pepsi Tournament of Champions in Charlotte. Princeton's methodical pace and matchup zone defense kept the score low, but the Tigers still lost, 63-53. Mike Richardson, a quick, muscular and offensive-minded leaper, scored 17 for the Horns, three more than Chris Mooney and Rick Hielscher of Princeton. A stiffer test came the next night against North Carolina, one of the storied programs in college basketball. Dean Smith's Tar Heels, who would go on to win the 1993 national crown, drubbed Texas, 104-68. With Donald Williams (19), George Lynch (17) and Eric Montross (14) leading the way, UNC put an embarrassing defeat on the Longhorns, who shot just 29 percent. "I don't know what to say," Rencher commented. "That was the best defensive team we've played since I've been here."

After such a miserable performance, the Horns needed to play again, but they were off for two weeks due to final exams. Their next game was on the road against Utah, and television dictated a 10 p.m. tipoff. As a crowd of nearly 13,000 looked on, UT fell behind early and never got close in an 87-76 loss to the Utes. Poor shooting, a constant problem most of the season, showed up again. "Watch the Texas Longhorns," wrote Mark Rosner of the *Austin American-Statesman*. "Watch them take rapid-fire shots, unabashedly, from any angle. On the really bad days, watch one attempt after another miss. And watch the other team win."

Penders claimed to be unconcerned and determined to keep playing the up-tempo style, but he acknowledged that Rencher, Tyler and Tony Watson needed to start hitting. In the home opener against Stephen F. Austin, it was more of the same—39 percent shooting. If not for a pressing defense that forced 28 Lumberjack turnovers, Texas might not have taken an 83-70 win. Jack Little of SFA had a game-high 28 points, and Richardson, the team's only senior, came back from a groin injury to score 18 points in 19 minutes. Some of the SFA players seemed unimpressed with their opponents in orange and white. Texas assistant coach Vic Trilli put together a video of the 1990 Longhorns of Travis Mays, Lance Blanks and Joey Wright, saying, in effect: "This is how the game should be played." The ploy worked because Texas scored an 89-72 win over Illinois before 14,097 fans at the Erwin Center. Lou Henson's Illini turned the ball over 25 times, leading to many easy Texas hoops. Tyler and Deon Thomas and Andy Kaufmann of the Big 10 visitors scored 25 points each, and Burditt had another strong game—13 points, 13 rebounds and six blocked shots.

A 104-96 defeat of Weber State in the first round of the All-College Tournament was Penders' 100th victory in just over four seasons at UT. Rencher (30) ended a five-game scoring slump and was one of four Horns in double figures. The title game against Oklahoma was a hard-fought 85-76 loss. The Sooners' Bryan Sallier and Jeff Webster were too much for Burditt inside, and a lack of depth showed, with Burditt, Tyler, Richardson and Rencher scoring all but four of the team's points. Having played the ninth-ranked Sooners close, Penders and his team left Oklahoma City with a positive feeling that did not last long.

In a Sunday afternoon practice session, Tyler broke a bone in his foot, requiring an operation. The injury would sideline Tyler, a key figure on offense and defense, most of the remainder of the season. "I don't think anyone can run a fast break like B.J.," Penders said. "We may not be as good at that. We're just going to find out what we can do without him in the next few games." What happened in the next few games was none too pleasant as the Horns lost to four SWC foes. Rice won, 92-87, in Austin, a game in which Penders got two technicals and an ejection. Brent Scott, the Owls' all-time leader in points and rebounds, had 23 of the former and 12 of the latter. Richardson and Rencher launched 43 of UT's 77 shots but made just 14 of them. After the loss to Rice, Penders took the drastic step of closing practice and forbidding his players to give interviews, a policy that lasted three weeks. Behind closed doors, he sought to retool the team and focus on the substantial problems at hand. SMU, a team finally getting wise to running and three-point shooting, came into the Erwin Center and beat the Longhorns, 102-92. With 37 points from Mike Wilson and 23 from Tim Mason, the Mustangs had clutch free throw shooting in the final minutes. Richardson led UT with 26 points, and Rencher, whom Penders called "a great basketball player but not a great point guard," had 24.

At Hofheinz Pavilion, coach Pat Foster got balanced scoring from his starting five as Houston ripped Texas, 81-67. Richardson scored 19, and Burditt played every minute, accounting for 14 points, 17 rebounds and six blocked shots. Watson made four of seven three-pointers, but Rencher seemed tentative and the others were helpless. In Austin, the Horns came back from a 14-point deficit to lead Baylor by five with three minutes left. Victory went to the Bears, however, when Willie Sublett connected on a 17-foot jumper with two seconds on the clock. BU, 87-86. Richardson missed 18 of 25 shots, but Rencher (34) had one of the best games of his sophomore year, and Burditt was again a force inside, scoring 15 points, collecting 18 rebounds and blocking seven shots.

Not-so-proud owners of a five-game losing streak, the Horns got a double whammy of bad news on January 19. Burditt had become academically ineligible and was out for the year, and Rencher received a two-game suspension from Penders due to unspecified academic troubles. In a pressure cooker of a season, the coach demonstrated his commitment to the student-athlete ideal by insisting Rencher hit the books. These things happened despite UT's extensive, not to mention expensive, system of academic support for athletes on scholarship.

In Kentucky to face Murray State, the Horns' lineup included two 6'10" players, Corey Lockridge and Sheldon Quarles, whose statistics were as slim as their physiques. The fifth starter was soph guard Tommy Penders, son of the coach. Quite a star in high school and for one year at a Pennsylvania prep school, Penders, Jr. could play. In the close confines of Murray State's crackerbox gym, he found himself on the line with 19 seconds left, serenaded by chants of "Daddy's boy." But Penders hit two free throws to secure a 79-74 win over the Racers. "I've been looking forward to that situation all my life," he said. And his father added, "Tommy Penders better make those foul shots. Since he was knee-high, he's had a hoop to shoot at." Of course, it helped that Richardson had 35 points and 11 rebounds, scoring on dunks, long-range bombs and an assortment of creative shots in one of the best performances of his career.

Showing again that their obituary was premature, the Longhorns took a 92-74 victory over Texas Tech in Austin. Richardson and Watson combined for 60 points, and the Red Raiders got 19 from Will Flemons. Tech coach James Dickey had kind words for all of the UT guards, including Tommy Penders and soph Lamont Hill.

Tom Penders offers congratulations to Mike Richardson, the best player on an 11-17 team.

Penders, satisfied that Rencher had corrected his academic problems, lifted the two-game suspension on his star backcourt man. And Tyler's foot was healing fast, increasing the likelihood of his return before season's end. Maybe, Penders said, the team could heat up, win the SWC Tournament and still get into the NCAAs. That would not be easy, as Rice demonstrated with an emphatic 101-83 win in Houston. Brent Scott had 27 points and 14 rebounds for the Owls, who were bound for their best conference record since 1970. They had beaten the Horns for a third straight time, causing forward Adam Peakes to declare, "The days of Rice fearing Texas are over." Only TCU stood between UT and the SWC cellar, and that changed when the Horned Frogs took an 83-77 victory in half-full Daniel-Meyer Coliseum. If not for 58 percent free throw shooting, the Horns might have won. Rencher looked sharp, though, coming off the bench to score a game-high 31 points.

Record: 11-17

136 Oral Roberts 97
63 Princeton 53
68 North Carolina 104
76 Utah 87
83 Stephen F. Austin 70
89 Illinois 72
104 Weber State 96
76 Oklahoma 85
87 Rice 92
92 SMU 102
67 Houston 81
86 Baylor 87
79 Murray State 74
92 Texas Tech 74
83 Rice 101
77 TCU 83
81 LSU 84
82 Texas A&M 78
70 Georgia 78
60 Virginia Commonwealth 66
88 Baylor 73
57 Texas A&M 77
103 Texas Tech 105
79 Houston 86
102 TCU 84
80 SMU 96
81 Rice 76
50 Houston 58

In a Sunday afternoon game at San Antonio's HemisFair Arena, LSU scored the first 18 points, but the Longhorns, paced by Watson (21) and Rencher (19), got back in it. The Tigers' Jamie Brandon (24) hit three free throws in the last half-minute to ensure an 84-81 victory. The game was entertaining, and UT made a valiant comeback, and yet the record showed a third consecutive defeat. That trend ended—briefly—when Texas beat Texas A&M, 82-78, before 11,024 fans at the Erwin Center. Penders and Aggie coach Tony Barone had their own gripes about the officials, who made the game a free throw shooting marathon, but there were 12 lead changes in the second half and lots of hustle from both teams. The Ags' Damon Johnson took scoring honors with 27 points.

In the first of two straight nonconference games in mid-February, UT fell to a bigger and more talented Georgia team, 78-70, in Athens. Despite taking 17 more shots than the Bulldogs, Texas made just 31 percent and was cold at the line, too. Rencher and Richardson had a combined 45 points, and Cleveland Jackson scored 23 for Georgia. And back in Austin, Virginia Commonwealth won, 66-60, when the Longhorns found a lid on the basket, missing 15 straight shots over an eight-minute period. "We missed unbelievable shots," Penders said. "We were wide open and couldn't knock them down. We missed threes, followups, everything." Ram forward Tyron McCoy was the most productive player on the court, leading in points (27) and rebounds (10).

Over a span of six days, the Horns faced Baylor, Texas A&M and Texas Tech, all on the road. Richardson missed 14 of 16 field goal attempts, but Rencher (27) was on, as Texas beat the Bears, 88-73. Junior forward Gerrald Houston, who started 25 games in 1993, contributed 16 points, 14 rebounds and four steals in a much-needed win. Anthony Lewis grabbed 20 rebounds for BU. Woeful shooting doomed the Longhorns at G. Rollie White Coliseum, where they lost, 77-57. Perhaps A&M's aggressive defense deserved some credit for holding UT scoreless for a 12-minute stretch. Penders claimed he had never seen one of his teams go so frigid and had no idea why it happened. David Edwards, the Ags' gutsy little guard, scored a triple-double—12 points, 12 rebounds and 10 assists. Tyler, out the last 14 games with a foot injury, was back when the Horns and Red Raiders clashed. Penders hoped his floor leadership and passing would enhance the team's shooting. Tyler (32) hit a three-pointer to tie the game with 20 seconds left. At the other end of the court, Tech's Lance Hughes shot, missed and saw his teammate, Will Flemons, rebound the ball and put it in at the buzzer for a heart-stopping 105-103 Raider victory.

In Texas' 86-79 loss to Houston at the Erwin Center, Richardson scored 29 points. Although he put up 24 shots and did not record a single assist, he was not a selfish player. Instead, the senior swingman with boundless energy was adept at creating shots and was just a horrible passer. Charles "Bo" Outlaw, who led the Cougars with 21 points, would be voted SWC player of the year, but he was not half as fun to watch as Richardson. Texas and TCU met in Austin on March 3, and the basement belonged to the Frogs after UT scored a 102-84 victory before 10,473 fans. Richardson had 30 points in his last home game, but he was one-upped by TCU center Eric Dailey (31 points and 16 rebounds). "We're loose and playing with confidence," Penders said. "I think people are kind of keeping an eye on us."

SMU became the Southwest Conference champion with a 96-80 defeat of UT in Dallas. Pony forwards Mike Wilson and Tim Mason teamed up for 55 points, while the Horns could not counter them inside, sometimes going with a five-guard attack. After the game, the Mustangs retired to the Moody Coliseum locker room where Doc Hayes and his teams had celebrated so many titles.

The Longhorns, without an all-SWC player for the first time since 1987, were back in Dallas six days later for the conference tournament, one of the underdogs. There seemed to be agreement that five years of Tom Penders had brought significant change to the SWC. By railing against lousy officials, using a high-octane offense and competing on a national level, he had brought it forward considerably. Of course, all this occurred when the conference was beginning to unravel. Rice, a team with a three-game win streak against UT, took a fall, 81-76, in the first round at Reunion Arena. Brent Scott was a one-man gang for the Owls with 24 points and 12 rebounds. Texas, meanwhile, got 61 points from Richardson, Watson and Rencher and various contributions from Quarles, Tommy Penders, Hill and Jesse Sandstad, whom Penders dubbed the "Highland Park Flash." The 6'7" freshman walk-on played some tough defense and had six points and four rebounds in 25 minutes.

Before the semifinal game against Houston, the Longhorn camp was rocked with the news that Tyler had failed a drug test and would not play. Minus its floor general, Texas shot 32 percent and scored just 17 points in the second half of a 58-50 loss. Jessie Drain tallied 21 for UH. The 11-17 Longhorns were through for the year, and what a difficult year it had been. Penders' remarkable string of four 20-win seasons and four NCAA Tournament appearances was over.

1994

The Longhorns' free fall to seventh place in the Southwest Conference was no harbinger of things to come. Tom Penders had a potentially dynamite team as the 1994 season approached. Albert Burditt had regained academic eligibility; Terrence Rencher was coming off a "sophomore slump" in which he scored 19 points per game; B.J. Tyler, after several months at the John Lucas Center in Houston for treatment of depression and marijuana use, would rejoin the team in mid-December; a couple of transfers, Tremaine Wingfield (Louisville) and Rich McIver (Michigan) brought frontcourt muscle; and Roderick Anderson, a quick, high-scoring guard, had been recruited from the JC ranks. There was some prime-time talent, and if Penders could get them through a murderous early-season schedule, the Horns might win the SWC title and do something in the NCAAs. Penders believed Texas was a Final Four-caliber club.

After warming up in exhibitions against Fort Hood and the Red Army of Russia, it was time for the real thing. At the Maravich Assembly Center, fast-breaking and hot-shooting LSU blew out Texas, 86-66. Freshman guard Ronnie Henderson scored 21 for the Tigers, while the Longhorn offense was missing in action. "There was a lot of anxiety out there," Penders said. "I told the team to forget it. We have another game Sunday." That game was also on the road, a 78-75 defeat of Nebraska. While Rencher had a season-high 35 points, reserve guard Lamont Hill's two late steals made the difference. A three-point shot by Cornhusker forward Eric Piatkowski (35) would have sent it into overtime, but the ball bounced harmlessly off the rim. In Nacogdoches, Penders was perturbed with the sluggish play of his starters and pulled them early in the second half of a 78-66 win over the Stephen F. Austin Lumberjacks. Wingfield (18) had a good game, but Anderson, suffering from ankle and hamstring problems and still adjusting to major-college ball, did not.

The home opener came against Florida, a team bound for Charlotte, site of the 1994 Final Four. Things were a bit different at the Erwin Center; longtime announcer Wally Pryor had been replaced by Stan Kelly (who also worked the microphone for the San Antonio Spurs), and fans took note of high-tech player intros, canned music and promotional contests and giveaways at every possible break. Lon Kruger's Gators, unflustered by all that, beat UT, 76-68. Center Andrew DeClerq had 18 points for the SEC guests, while the Longhorns committed 23 turnovers and missed all but four of 27 three-point shots. Not an encouraging performance, and the best spin Penders could put on it was to say that B.J. Tyler was coming back.

Ready or not, he was in the starting lineup when the Horns met Connecticut at sold-out Gampel Pavilion. Penders' alma mater was having a hoop revival with coach Jim Calhoun, who had stars like Donyell Marshall, Doron Sheffer and Ray Allen. Ranked 16th, the new beasts of the Big East jumped to a 23-point lead, and a late UT comeback only made it respectable, 96-86. Marshall (23) led all scorers, Burditt had 20 points and 10 rebounds, and Tyler, the prodigal point guard, played well despite fatigue and unfamiliarity with his teammates.

From the wintry northeast, the Longhorns traveled to Hawaii to play in the Maui Invitational. In the first round, they encountered Big Blue, the No. 5 Kentucky Wildcats, under the baton of maestro Rick Pitino. Freshman swingman Reggie Freeman got his first start and scored a team-high 18 points, but it was not nearly enough against the mighty Cats, who took an 86-61 victory. Tony Delk led four UK players in double figures. While the loss left Texas with a 2-4 record, Penders had warned fans about the tough early schedule and the need to assimilate new players. Things began to improve immediately as the Horns bopped Tennessee Tech, 97-85, behind Rencher's 33 points. He came out of a shooting slump by driving to the basket, hitting the boards and going after loose balls. Rencher and Tyler combined for 50 points the next day in UT's 89-72 defeat of Notre Dame. Monty Williams of the Irish, who came into the game with a 27-point average, was held to 13 by the vigorous defense of Freeman and Wingfield. The Longhorns left the islands having won two of three games, Penders' goal.

In the waning days of December, the Horns scored a couple of wins at the Erwin Center. Tony Watson's three-pointer from the corner midway through the second half was the turning point in an 87-75 defeat of Oklahoma, breaking a nine-game losing streak to Billy Tubbs' Sooners. Tyler and Ryan Minor of OU both scored 24 points. And in a game that amazed and delighted 12,034 spectators, Texas grabbed a 93-91 double-overtime victory against Utah. Trailing by two with two-tenths of a second left in regulation, UT's Tommy Penders fired a full-court pass to Wingfield, who turned and hit a 17-foot shot. The score was tied at the end of the second OT when the very same thing happened—Penders to Wingfield, up and in for a win that had some Longhorns dancing on the press table. Utah coach Rick Majerus, an old friend of Penders, had doubts about either shot being launched in time, but he was gracious in defeat. Darroll Wright scored 29 for the Utes, and Burditt, who played all 50 minutes, had 17 rebounds.

Keith Van Horn's defensive effort notwithstanding, Tremaine Wingfield launches a second buzzer-beater in Texas' double-OT defeat of Utah.

No. 22 Illinois withstood the Horns' full-court pressure and 10 three-pointers to win, 83-78, before a throng of 16,129 in Champaign. Deon Thomas had 23 points for the victorious Illini, and Tyler scored 26 for the second straight game. Anderson, back from a five-game layoff, keyed a 27-4 first-half run in a 91-69 defeat of UT-San Antonio at HemisFair Arena. Knowing his team was superior to the Roadrunners, Penders experimented with a three-guard attack—Anderson at the point and Rencher and Tyler on the wings.

Favored to win the relatively weak SWC, the Longhorns had seven days to prepare for their conference opener in College Station. Things were fine and dandy with eight minutes left as Texas led the Aggies by 13. But Tony McGinnis (22) and David Edwards (18) paced a comeback that had the fans going crazy. Tommy Penders missed a pair of free throws, and Tyler's last-second shot was blocked by Joe Wilbert as Texas A&M took an 85-84 upset. Penders and assistants Eddie Oran and Vic Trilli expressed their thoughts in a locker-room session lasting more than an hour.

Playing at the Erwin Center for just the fourth time all season, Texas beat SMU, 91-79. A 20-point lead evaporated when the Horns went seven and a half minutes without a field goal and fell behind. Rather than choke, they stopped turning the ball over, started rebounding and hitting their shots to go back on top. Tyler (33) said the team lacked a killer instinct, but that should not have been necessary against what *Austin American-Statesman* writer John Maher called "a palooka of a team." Rencher, in particular, needed to get it going; the Mustangs held him to a career-low six points.

Baylor had a 10-3 record despite losing several players in an academic fraud scandal precipitated by Pam Bowers, the women's basketball coach. The Bruins could not stay with UT in a midweek game before a near-capacity crowd at the Ferrell Center, losing, 110-85. With 29 first-half points, Tyler appeared to have a chance at breaking the school record of 49, held by Slater Martin and Raymond Downs, but he cooled off and finished with 38. The senior guard also had 12 assists and just two turnovers.

Deeper and more talented than anyone else in the SWC, the Longhorns shot 63 percent and crushed Texas Tech, 108-79, in Austin. All 14 of Penders' players got in the game, and Tyler (26) was again the star. "We just got our butts kicked, plain and simple," said Red Raider coach James Dickey. "They were unbelievable. B.J. Tyler is the best point guard in America." Rather wobbly in the legs after three games in a five-day span, UT still looked good in a 107-96 defeat of Georgia at home. The taller Bulldogs got 21 points and 12 rebounds from Shandon Anderson, while the Tyler-Rencher-Anderson trio combined for 80 points. Burditt was strong inside, scoring 22 points, collecting 10 rebounds and blocking four shots.

UT jumped to a 25-point halftime lead and coasted to a 110-78 defeat of Houston. It was the Cougars' worst home loss since Hofheinz Pavilion had opened 25 years earlier. Except for Tim Moore (20) and Jessie Drain (15), UH was short on scorers. Rencher had 28, and Tyler, voted *Sports Illustrated* player of the week, was great, getting 21 points, seven rebounds and 10 steals, a Longhorn record. Late in the game, he fell and broke a bone in his hand, sidelining him for the upcoming Rice and TCU games in Austin. Neither the Owls nor the Frogs were exactly hoop juggernauts and went down without any trouble. Burditt scored 24 points on jump-hooks, dunks and spin moves down low in an 85-70 win over Rice. And Moe Iba's Frogs were rattled by UT's speed and defensive pressure from the start, losing, 95-73. Center Kurt Thomas (23 points and 12 rebounds) played well for the Cowtown visitors, but Rencher and Burditt (22 points each) and Anderson (20 points and 10 assists) were too much.

Tyler, his left hand heavily wrapped, was back when the Horns faced SMU at Moody Coliseum. Penders' group of talented and motivated young men cracked the whip on the Mustangs with a 94-66 victory. When Tyler entered the game after seven minutes, his teammates having built a big lead, he got a standing O from the burnt-orange faction of the crowd.

It was payback time when Texas A&M came to town. In the first sellout in two seasons, the Longhorns showed the Ags just who was boss with an 85-68 win. Tyler, Burditt, Rencher and

Record: 26-8

66 LSU 86
78 Nebraska 75
78 Stephen F. Austin 66
68 Florida 76
86 Connecticut 96
61 Kentucky 86
97 Tennessee Tech 85
89 Notre Dame 72
87 Oklahoma 75
93 Utah 91 (2 OT's)
78 Illinois 83
91 UT-San Antonio 69
84 Texas A&M 85
91 SMU 79
110 Baylor 85
108 Texas Tech 79
107 Georgia 96
110 Houston 78
85 Rice 70
95 TCU 73
94 SMU 66
85 Texas A&M 68
113 Baylor 91
125 Texas Tech 128 (2 OT's)
105 Lamar 75
88 Houston 70
106 Oral Roberts 69
78 Rice 70
111 TCU 78
96 TCU 75
101 Rice 89
87 Texas A&M 62
91 Western Kentucky 77
79 Michigan 84

Anderson reached double figures and appeared to have fun in beating UT's age-old rival. Joe Wilbert, the key figure in a recent brawl involving fans, coaches and players at Texas Tech (recalling similar unruly events at Gregory Gym) scored 30 points. "The crowd was absolutely phenomenal," said A&M coach Tony Barone. "No one in the league approximates this. The noise level was an intimidating factor. I told my kids after the game, this is what major-college basketball is all about." Texas, in first place in the SWC, scored another impressive victory, beating Baylor, 113-91. The Bears, led by Jerome Lambert (33 points and 12 rebounds) practically lined up after the game to give testimonials for the Longhorns. BU coach Darrel Johnson, assuming the Horns would be part of the NCAA tourney, predicted they would go far, and forward Willie Sublett said their on-court trash-talking was fully backed up.

In a wild west Texas shootout, the Horns lost to Texas Tech, 128-125, in double overtime. When Anderson's last-second three-pointer missed, many of the 6,824 fans at Lubbock Municipal Coliseum left their seats to celebrate. The Red Raiders' Jason Sasser had 34 points and Tyler 33 in the highest-scoring game in SWC history.

B.J. Tyler hoists his SWC player of the year trophy at Reunion Arena in Dallas.

The Longhorns' 10-game winning streak was over, but they continued piling up victories. McIver, who had averaged almost a foul per minute and lost his starting job in recent games, came through with 22 points and 11 rebounds in a 105-75 defeat of Lamar. Shortly after that game with the Cardinals, the long-rumored and -discussed merger with the Big 8 was announced. The UT Board of Regents and their colleagues at Texas A&M, Texas Tech and Baylor voted affirmatively to accept the deal. It meant the Southwest Conference and 80 years of athletic tradition would end two years hence. While Texas and Texas A&M were the plums (having effectively floated the smaller schools for decades), Texas Tech and Baylor got in—partly for political reasons—and the others, Rice, SMU, TCU and Houston, were out. First and foremost a matter of football, bowl games and television revenue, the change also involved basketball, baseball, track, swimming and other sports, both men's and women's.

A fair amount of anger and betrayal was felt by those schools not asked to join what would be called the Big 12, and one of them, Houston, was next on the Horns' schedule. After a defensive adjustment, Texas built a 23-point lead at intermission and went on to beat the Cougars, 88-70, before 10,502 fans at the Erwin Center. It ended with a thunderous Tyler-to-Burditt alley-oop slammer, giving the Austin senior a career-high 25 points. Seven blocked shots also equaled his school record. "Albert's been a warrior for us this year," Penders said. The final home game of the season was a nice and easy 106-69 whupping of Oral Roberts. The seniors—Tyler, Burditt, Watson and Gerrald Houston—were given special introductions with their parents. Anderson (21) and the Titans' Fred Smith (20) were the leading scorers.

During the team's participation in the Maui Invitational in December, Penders had talked about peaking in March. That month had arrived, the regular season was almost over, and the excitement of postseason was nigh. The Longhorns ground out a 78-70 win over Rice at Autry Court as defensive intensity compensated for subpar shooting. Tyler threw in 27 points, and Torrey Andrews had 26 for the Owls. In Fort Worth, where Texas had lost in 1991, 1992 and 1993, every player scored in a 111-78 conquest of TCU. The Frogs had the game's top scorer, frosh guard Jeff Jacobs (20), but they also had a share of the cellar. At the top of the standings were Penders' Longhorns, 1994 SWC champions. It was the first undisputed league title for Texas since 1974, when Leon Black was coaching and the Harry (Larrabee) and Larry (Robinson) show was playing.

Tyler led the SWC with 23 points per game and was chosen player of the year. The quicksilver guard would solidify that honor with a fine performance in the conference tournament. The No. 25 Longhorns swaggered into Reunion Arena with a 22-7 record, tipping off against TCU, a team they had beaten just five days earlier. A sparse crowd was on hand for the Thursday afternoon game. Despite 32 points and 13 rebounds by Frog forward Eric Dailey, the Horns picked up a 96-75 victory. Tyler (21) led five players in double figures. The semifinal against Rice was no more suspenseful, a 101-89 cakewalk. Burditt had 24 points and 12 rebounds, but the day belonged to Penders. As the team was leaving the court, a group of fans unfurled a banner congratulating him on his 400th career victory. He blew them a kiss and recalled winning just four games in his first year at Columbia and the unlikelihood of getting to 400. In the title game, Tyler put on a show—35 points (hitting 14 of 25 shots, including five of 10 three-pointers), eight assists and three steals in an 87-62 trouncing of Texas A&M. Burditt (17 points and 11 rebounds) was also dominant against the Aggies. The two seniors, who had ended the 1993 season with a drug suspension and academic ineligibility, savored the experience of climbing a ladder to cut down the nets. The Horns had reached the last game of the 19-year-old SWC tourney six times and finally won it.

Happy to be back in the big dance, UT faced 20-10 Western Kentucky in an NCAA first-round game in Wichita. Bill Walton, the ex-basketball star who had moved into the broadcast booth, could have had Penders in mind when he said the best tournament coaches were those who "are loose, run, press and build up players instead of tearing them down." But the Horns were unnerved in the first half by the Hilltoppers' smothering defense and long-range shooting. While Tyler was a woeful two of 13 from the field, Burditt and Anderson teamed up for 51 points to subdue Western Kentucky, 91-77. Forward Chris Robinson scored 23 for WKU.

That set up a meeting between Texas and Michigan, one of the truly high-profile programs in college hoops. Runners-up in the last two NCAA Tournaments with a group of players ballyhooed as the Fabulous Five, Steve Fisher's 1994 Wolverines had just four of them because Chris Webber had moved on to the pros. Two, Ray Jackson and Jimmy King, were Texans, and the others, Jalen Rose and Juwan Howard, would soon begin their NBA careers. Wearing black shoes, black socks and pants baggy enough to cover someone with morbid obesity, a certain strut came naturally to the Michigan team. The crowd at Kansas Coliseum was pro-Texas, but the Big 10 bullies won, 84-79, by making nine straight free throws in the final 90 seconds. Howard had 34 points and 18 rebounds. Tyler led UT with 22 points, but he missed 18 of 24 shots. "It was a very competitive basketball game between two well-coached teams," said Tyler, who would become the Philadelphia 76ers' top draft pick. "I gave my best effort, and I have to be content with that." The Wolverines won one more game and then fell to SWC-expatriate Arkansas, which went on to win the national title. And the Longhorns, as Tyler indicated, had played a great team close. They had averaged 92 points per game and compiled 26 victories, equaling the number for the 1947 Mighty Mice and the 1978 NIT champs.

1995

As it turned out, the Horns missed B.J. Tyler less than they did Albert Burditt. Guards Terrence Rencher and Roderick Anderson would be all-SWC first-teamers in 1995, but Burditt's inside scoring, defense, rebounding and outlet passes could not be duplicated, even by committee. Coach Tom Penders signed three rookies for his seventh season in Austin, forwards Sonny Alvarado and Carlton Dixon and guard Brandy Perryman. While Alvarado had scored 30 points per game in junior college—and accumulated several ejections and technical fouls along the way—and Dixon started 17 games his freshman year, Perryman, a slow-footed, long-range bomber, had the most success.

A few creampuffs graced UT's early-season schedule, but the first game would be tough: second-ranked North Carolina at the Smith Center, a.k.a. the "Dean Dome," in Chapel Hill. Dean Smith, whose Tar Heel teams had won more than 800 games in the previous 33 years, boasted a couple of talented sophomores in Jerry Stackhouse and Rasheed Wallace. Before 21,572 fans and a national TV audience, Texas and UNC put on a show not decided until the final half-minute in favor of the ACC hosts, 96-92. The stars shone brightly for both teams as Rencher and Anderson combined for 51 points and Stackhouse and Wallace 48. "It felt like an NCAA Tournament game," Penders said. "This was great basketball."

The starting lineup for the home opener against Lamar consisted of Rencher and Anderson in the backcourt and Rich McIver, Tremaine Wingfield and Reggie Freeman up front. With Freeman (24) leading the way, the Horns overcame a slow start to beat the Cardinals, 97-54. A week later, UT bloodied Southwest Texas, 105-60, in front of 12,514 fans at the Erwin Center. Except for the play of guard Tony Long (27), the Bobcats did not belong on the same floor with the Horns.

Texas got stiffer competition on December 10 against No. 6 Florida. The Gators, with most of their starters back from a Final Four team, deprived the Horns of much-wanted national recognition with a 91-73 victory in Gainesville. LeRon Williams (19) paced Florida in scoring, while UT shot bricks—38 percent from the field and 45 percent from the free throw line. After the final-exam break, the Horns dodged a bullet with a 95-94 home win over Stephen F. Austin. Ahead of the Lumberjacks by 16 points with 14 minutes left, they barely held on and avoided an embarrassing defeat. Anderson (28 points, seven rebounds and eight assists) played a fine game.

Out in the west Texas town of El Paso, the Longhorns took part in the Sierra Medical Center Sun Classic, in conjunction with the Sun Bowl, which was won by John Mackovic's UT football team. And the basketball team won the tournament after some bickering between Penders and UT-El Paso coach Don Haskins over officiating. In front of a hostile crowd, Rencher scored 20 points in an 84-73 defeat of UT-Pan American, and Tommy Penders did well in relief of Anderson, who had foul trouble and a season-low five points. Anderson bounced back to score 29 points, pass for seven assists and make five steals in the title game, 86-81 over Washington State. Anderson, whose speed, intensity and determination were evident to anyone who saw him, was named tourney MVP. Isaac Fontaine had 33 points for the Cougars.

UT had lost 13 straight games to top-25 teams, dating back to the 1991 season. That unpleasant reality ended with a 102-74 thumping of No. 19 Nebraska. Rencher and Wingfield combined for 45 points, and Perryman and forward Carl Simpson came off the bench to help beat the Cornhuskers, future Big 12 opponents. Rencher, who would average 21 points per game his senior year, continued moving up in the school and SWC scoring lists. As Nebraska was escorted out of the Erwin Center, LSU came in. Dale Brown's Bengals had defeated Texas twice in Baton Rouge and once each in New Orleans, Houston and San Antonio in the previous five seasons. The Longhorns forced 32 turnovers, hit 17 of 20 second-half free throws and grabbed an 80-71 win before a sellout crowd. Anderson and Rencher outplayed their highly touted LSU backcourt counterparts, Ronnie Henderson and Randy Livingston. "Anderson and Rencher had beautiful games," Brown commented. "And Perryman came in and hurt us."

Record: 23-7

92 North Carolina 96
97 Lamar 54
105 SW Texas 60
73 Florida 91
95 Stephen F. Austin 94
84 UT-Pan American 73
86 Washington State 81
102 Nebraska 74
80 LSU 71
98 TCU 102
115 Texas A&M 82
100 SMU 59
75 Oklahoma 100
107 Baylor 100 (OT)
99 DePaul 92 (2 OT's)
82 Texas Tech 68
96 Houston 105 (OT)
88 Rice 56
111 TCU 99
98 Texas A&M 88
91 SMU 65
70 Temple 54
87 Texas Tech 96
109 Baylor 75
96 Houston 82
108 Rice 74
78 Rice 75
107 Texas Tech 104 (OT)
90 Oregon 73
68 Maryland 82

The first of two lame-duck Southwest Conference seasons began in Fort Worth, where Texas encountered TCU, led by former Oklahoma coach Billy Tubbs. He tossed bouquets at the Horns, who had a five-game winning streak, then saw his team take a fast-paced 102-98 victory. The Frogs got 23 points and 13 rebounds from 6'10" Kurt Thomas and a surprising 26 points from guard Jeff Jacobs. Thomas, well known for his belligerence toward fans, officials, coaches, teammates and opponents, was having a great season, leading the nation in scoring and rebounding. He was not modest in proclaiming himself the best player in the SWC. McIver and Freeman, both rather short on aggressiveness, lost their starting jobs—for a while—when UT met the Aggies in Austin. Yet both contributed in the Horns' 115-82 win, seen by 14,105 fans. Six Texas players reached double figures, but Texas A&M's Tony McGinnis (24) took scoring honors.

Partly to accommodate television, UT faced five games in 11 days, the first three on the road. The minimarathon began in Dallas, where the Horns drubbed a no-name group of SMU Mustangs, 100-59. It would have been worse, but Penders called off a full-court press early in the second half. Rencher had 22 points and eight rebounds. Across the Red River, the Longhorns went from 13 points up to 24 down in one stretch and got ripped by OU, 100-75. They missed all but five of 28 three-point shots in one of the most thorough defeats of the Penders era. Ryan Minor had 30 points and 15 rebounds for the Sooners, and Rencher and Anderson failed to step up and play big games. Baylor, a team shaken by the death of forward Jerode Banks in a summer auto accident, had a new coach (Harry Miller), a promising 6'10" frosh (Brian Skinner), and a senior guard (Aundre Branch) who averaged 23 points per game. Rencher and Anderson had a combined 52 points in UT's 107-100 overtime victory at the Ferrell Center. The five-minute extra session was unusually high-scoring as Texas rang up 18 points and Baylor 11.

DePaul brought an 8-6 record into the Erwin Center and saw that fall to 8-7 when UT took a 99-92 double-overtime victory. The Blue Demons led by seven points with a minute left in regulation, but Wingfield converted a rebound, Freeman hit a three-pointer (one of a staggering 40 the team attempted) and Anderson tied it with a driving scoop shot. Anderson, playing with a strained hamstring and groin, a dislocated thumb and a touch of the flu, scored a career-high 33. Tom Kleinschmidt, who tallied 25 for DePaul, said, "I thought the game was over. I knew they were capable of coming back, but I didn't think they'd do it." When the Horns hosted preseason SWC favorite Texas Tech two days later, things were going poorly when Penders got a strategic technical foul for ripping off his jacket and throwing it high in the air. The players and the crowd of 14,127 properly enthused, Texas finished the first half with a 24-8 run and went on to eclipse the Red Raiders, 82-68. Rencher had 28 points for the Longhorns and became the sixth player in SWC history to go over 2,000. Dixon and Alvarado helped Wingfield inside, something UT would need as the season progressed.

For the third time in four games, the Horns went into overtime, but they lost, 105-96, to Houston at Hofheinz Pavilion. The Cougars got 31 points from forward Tim Moore and 25 from center Kirk Ford. While Rencher and Anderson were a combined 10 of 34 from the field, Freeman looked good, scoring 20 points before fouling out. Penders would make no excuses, saying the Cougars deserved to win. After two days of practice emphasizing defensive fundamentals, Texas got back in the winning mode with an 88-56 defeat of Rice in Austin. Willis Wilson's Owls went scoreless for almost 10 minutes of the first half. Rencher scored 21 points, and Tommy Penders made four of five three-pointers. The players and coaches were eager to take on TCU, winner of the earlier game in Fort Worth. The only empty seats at the Erwin Center were high in the mezzanine as the Horns squelched the Frogs, 111-99. TCU coach Billy Tubbs ranted and raved and protested every call that did not go his way. Kurt Thomas ("the king of preeners, scowlers and dramatic actors on a basketball court," according to Mark Rosner of the *Austin American-Statesman*) had 27 points and 16 rebounds, and Freeman and Anderson teamed up to score 55. Rencher (18), who had moved past Michael Young of Houston and Sidney Moncrief of Arkansas on the all-time SWC scoring chart, was still chasing Rick Bullock of Texas Tech, Terry Teagle of Baylor and ex-Longhorn Travis Mays.

Down at the so-called Holler House on the Brazos, Rencher scored 35 points to lead the Horns to a 98-88

From 1992 to 1995, Terrence Rencher scored a conference-record 2,306 points and played on three championship teams.

defeat of Texas A&M. The Aggie guards were no match for Rencher and Anderson (26), as coach Tony Barone conceded. "Terrence and Roderick are fantastic players," he said. "They're just too quick for us, no question about that." With refs placing a higher priority on hand-checking fouls, the UT guards were going one-on-one with great success. Rencher's velvety-smooth offensive repertoire was again on display when the Horns smoked SMU, 91-65. He made 13 of 17 shots from all over the floor. The Ponies, who went seven minutes without a field goal in the second half, were led by Matt Timme with 13 points.

Next up was a doubleheader at San Antonio's Alamodome in which Cincinnati and Maryland played, followed by Texas and Temple. During the two years he had coached at Rhode Island in the Atlantic 10 Conference, Penders was 0-5 against the Owls. John Chaney's team was hot, coming off three road wins, but the Longhorns cooled them down with a 70-54 victory before 16,716 fans. Anderson had 20 points and 10 assists, and McIver pulled down 13 rebounds and banged effectively with Temple's big men. The nationally televised game was UT's best of the year, even more impressive than the season-opening four-point loss to North Carolina.

UT and Texas Tech, easily the two strongest teams in the SWC in 1995, met in Lubbock for a high-stakes game. The joint was rocking well before tipoff, and that never changed as the Red Raiders took a frenzied 96-87 win. Jason Sasser and Lance Hughes led the red-and-black parade with 32 and 21 points, respectively. Like Sasser and Hughes, Anderson went 40 minutes, getting 25 points, one less than Freeman.

The final home games were in late February, victories over Baylor and Houston. Rencher scored 25 points and collected 10 rebounds as the Longhorns mauled the Bears, 109-75, keeping alive their hopes of sharing the SWC title with Texas Tech. BU's Brian Skinner had 22 points, 14 rebounds and five blocked shots in a game that was over by halftime. UH, which beat the Horns four weeks earlier, got its comeuppance in Austin, losing, 96-82. Penders and Cougar coach Alvin Brooks worked the referees unmercifully, but Brooks did not stay around long. He received two technicals, was ejected and left screaming as the crowd waved him goodbye. "Texas won the game legitimately," Brooks said after recovering his emotional equilibrium. "They're just hard to beat here." Tim Moore had 27 points for the Cougars, and Rencher led UT with 23. His career total was 2,201, just 78 points behind Mays. Barring some catastrophe, he seemed certain to get the record.

The regular season came to a close at the Summit, a far cry from Rice's cozy Autry Court. It was the fifth game the Owls had played there in an effort to boost their image and attendance. The 16,311-seat arena, home of the NBA-champion Houston Rockets, was less than one-third full, and most of the fans were cheering for UT. Anderson, Rencher and Freeman combined for 71 points in a 108-74 victory. Two hours later, news came that Texas Tech had lost, falling back into a tie with Texas for the league crown. In seven years as the Longhorns' range boss, Tom Penders had guided them to six 20-win seasons, in addition to his success in the NCAAs. Although he had not yet been named SWC coach of the year (a fact that rankled him somewhat), Penders was building a legacy as one of the greatest coaches in UT history. He and Jack Gray, who worked in a vastly different era, stood above the rest.

After a bye in the first round of the SWC tourney in Dallas, the Longhorns met Rice in the semifinals. The Owls took the lead midway through the first half and held it until just seven seconds remained on the clock. Anderson (22) then hit a three-pointer to secure a 78-75 win. Tommy McGhee (21) and other Rice players complained in postgame interviews about uneven officiating. In the title game the next day, there was more excitement. The Longhorns, playing in their fourth overtime contest of the year, got outrebounded by a two-to-one margin but shot 64 percent to beat Texas Tech, 107-104, before 12,852 appreciative fans. Perryman, Freeman, Anderson and Simpson sparkled down the stretch, as did Jason Sasser (28), Mark Davis, Darvin Ham and Lance Hughes of the Red Raiders. Rencher (31), MVP of the tournament, pulled within eight points of the conference career scoring mark. "I'm tired of holding my tongue," said the ordinarily quiet Rencher. "We're the best in the Southwest Conference. At the beginning of the year, everyone was talking about Texas Tech, Texas Tech. Rod and I had a hard time with that."

The Raiders' 20-9 record did not get them into the 64-team NCAA field, one that had room for a Florida International team coached by Bob Weltlich. The 22-6 Longhorns, however, were on their way to Salt Lake City to play 19-8 Oregon. The Ducks, fourth in the Pac-10, had a victory over eventual national champion UCLA to their credit. Several factors, whether real or perceived, caused the Horns to enter the tournament feeling angry and disrespected—just what Penders wanted. They minded their manners and enjoyed roast Duck in a 90-73 blowout. With a leaning jumper late in the first half, Rencher (19) became the all-time SWC scoring king. Five of his teammates were in double figures, one of whom, Wingfield, also had 13 rebounds. UT's trapping and rotating halfcourt defense had Oregon off balance most of the game. Orlando Williams paced the Ducks with 23 points.

A day between games allowed the Longhorns to rest, further acclimate to the 4,600-foot altitude and get ready for Maryland. Gary Williams' Terrapins were not completely unfamiliar to Texas because they had been part of the Alamodome doubleheader a month before. UT's frontcourt players, dubbed the Forgotten Few by assistant coach Eddie Oran, would have their hands full with 6'10" sophomore Joe Smith, soon to be an NBA lottery pick. He was magnificent that night, scoring 31 points, getting 21 rebounds and blocking seven shots in Maryland's 82-68 win. Exree Hipp put the clamps on Rencher (15), and Anderson, ice-cold at just the wrong time, missed 16 of 19 shots, reminiscent of B.J. Tyler in the 1994 season finale against Michigan.

1996

He had lost four starters, so Tom Penders was right to call it a rebuilding year. Yet he had the wood and nails, bricks and mortar to build a fine UT basketball team. Reggie Freeman, Sonny Alvarado and Brandy Perryman were back, and a couple of difference-makers had been recruited from local high schools—6'4" DeJuan "Chico" Vazquez and 6'5" Kris Clack. After sitting out a year to focus on his studies, guard Lamont Hill rejoined the Longhorns and would play a larger-than-expected role for a better-than-expected team. In the 82nd and final Southwest Conference season, Texas Tech was a strong favorite to win the title, with Texas and Houston as likely contenders.

Play began on a Saturday morning in late November when Freeman (28) paced the Longhorns to an 88-67 defeat of North Texas. Alvarado, who beat out two bigger players, Sheldon Quarles and Dennis Jordan, for the starting center job, added 19 points and 14 rebounds against the low-flying Eagles. The 26th straight home victory tied a school record set in the 1920s. Rick Majerus' Utah team came to Austin intent on avenging a controversial last-second loss to UT in 1994, and it happened in the most ironic way. The 14th-ranked Utes won, 70-69, when Ben Caton took an inbounds pass with two seconds left, hit a layup and sent 12,272 people home unhappy. The Longhorns, who squandered a 13-point lead when their shooting went cold, had trouble at the point guard spot. "It was an outstanding, unbelievable win," said the voluble Majerus. "I don't know if they blew it or we took it away."

With a shuffled lineup subject to further shuffling in the next few games, UT handed DePaul an 88-84 defeat before 11,233 fans at the Rosemont Horizon. Freeman, a supporting player to B.J. Tyler, Terrence Rencher and Roderick Anderson the past two seasons, had become the main man in the Longhorn offense. He scored 18 of his 31 points in the final 10 minutes and helped hold off the Blue Demons, who got 45 points from their backcourt duo of Jermaine Watts and Juan Gay. After a surprisingly tough 110-98 defeat of the wily Roadrunners of UT-San Antonio, Penders took his team back on the road, facing No. 23 Louisville at Freedom Hall, 40 years old but still one of the best college basketball arenas. Although two national championship banners hung from the rafters, it had been 10 years since Denny Crum's Cardinals got to the Final Four. As a crowd of 19,423 looked on, they jumped to an 18-0 lead in the first four minutes and cruised to a 101-78 victory. DeJuan Wheat had 24 points, and Samaki Walker collected 17 rebounds for Louisville. The Horns shot just 35 percent but kept playing hard, just as Penders' 1993 team had done after getting into a 17-0 hole against LSU and then nearly winning.

In the midst of final exams, UT hosted Oregon State in the first meeting of the Horns and Pac-10 Beavers since the early days of Leon Black. Held to just 19 first-half points, Texas roared back after the break to win, 83-54. "Never give up at halftime," Penders advised. "It's a 40-minute game." Freeman and Alvarado combined for 40 points. Providence came into the Erwin Center with three international players and a frosh guard by the heavenly name of God Shammgod. A young man reputed to possess rare ballhandling and offensive skills, he looked quite mortal when Hill put some tight D on him, resulting in one point and five turnovers as the Horns beat the Friars, 92-83. Freeman showed why his teammates called him "Franchise" by scoring a career-high 37 points. "He was spectacular," said Providence coach Pete Gillen. "I've been coaching a long time, and that's one of the best offensive shows I've ever seen. He was like magic."

Basketball fans in Beaumont were happy to have Penders' Longhorns there for a game with Lamar as the largest crowd in a decade gathered. Texas won it, 96-82, but not easily. Freeman, Vazquez and Hill got in foul trouble, and Perryman missed seven of eight shots, so freshman guard Titus Warmsley went in and scored 21 points. Ron Coleman had 18 for the Cardinals.

A somewhat more prominent opponent was up next—No. 11 North Carolina. Not quite a vintage Dean Smith team, the Tar Heels had a 9-1 record against a soft early-season schedule. It was the first time an ACC team had played the Longhorns in Austin, and a crowd of 16,042 and a national television audience witnessed a thrilling game. The Heels shaved a 17-point deficit down to two at the end. After Perryman missed two free throws that would have iced the victory, he redeemed himself. Three seconds showed on the clock when UNC's Vince Carter threw an inbounds pass supposed to lead to a tying or winning shot, but Perryman, not the fastest man on the team, streaked in and stole it, evoking a thunderous roar from the fans. UT 74, UNC 72. Penders called it the biggest regular-season win in his eight years in Austin. Alvarado, who played with more attitude than sheer ability, had 20 points and 14 rebounds and won praise from CBS analyst Billy Packer. Dante Calabria (15) paced Carolina.

Busting into the national rankings at No. 23, the Horns went to Lincoln to engage a future Big 12 rival, Nebraska. In a physical, foul-ridden game—93 free throws were taken—the Cornhuskers won, 85-69. UT shot just 28 percent, committed 24 turnovers and made too many poor decisions to win a game it should not have lost. Freeman (21) and Erick Strickland (17) of Nebraska were the top scorers. (The Huskers' season would include a player revolt against coach Danny Nee, followed by an NIT championship.)

Record: 21-10

88 North Texas 67
69 Utah 70
88 DePaul 84
110 UT-San Antonio 98
78 Louisville 101
83 Oregon State 54
92 Providence 83
96 Lamar 82
74 North Carolina 72
69 Nebraska 85
69 Rice 80
103 TCU 88
86 Texas A&M 70
81 SMU 63
90 Baylor 81
78 Texas Tech 79
65 Oklahoma 67 (OT)
80 Houston 63
79 Rice 64
102 TCU 81
69 Texas A&M 50
101 SMU 66
80 Baylor 72
58 Texas Tech 75
81 Rhode Island 77
76 Houston 86
86 Baylor 65
89 SMU 67
73 Texas Tech 75
80 Michigan 76
62 Wake Forest 65

That poor game was followed by another, an 80-69 loss to Rice in Austin. The Owls missed their injured 6'11" center, Shaun Igo, but Tommy McGhee made six of seven from downtown and finished with 35 points. By keeping the tempo slow, playing cohesively at both ends of the court and shutting down Freeman and Perryman, Rice led from wire to wire.

Bad weather forced the postponement of a game with Rhode Island, which allowed the Longhorns extra time to recover from the flu and take care of things in practice. Penders and assistants Eddie Oran and Vic Trilli applied their hoop acumen and got the players in a winning mode once again. Alvarado shone in a 103-88 defeat of TCU, scoring 32 points and securing 13 rebounds. Clack also had an exceptional all-around game, putting the clamps on Frog freshman star Damion Walker. On the down side, however, Perryman, a 44 percent three-point shooter the year before, had missed 21 straight. G. Rollie White Coliseum, less than half the size of the Erwin Center but sold out for the first time in seven years (again for the Horns, naturally) was the site of an 86-70 UT victory on January 16. Tony Barone's zone defense invited the Horns to break out of a perimeter shooting slump as Freeman and Perryman combined for 50 points. In a strange sequence late in the first half, Alvarado and Texas A&M's Tracy Anderson scuffled, both head coaches went on the floor, and four technicals were called.

With Freeman shaken up from a car accident the night before, Vazquez came through with 24 points in an 81-63 defeat of visiting SMU. "We had good ball movement, and I was shooting in rhythm," said Vazquez, an aggressive defender whose point guard skills were getting better. The Horns converted all 14 free throws for a new school record. Jay Poerner had 16 points and nine rebounds for the Ponies. A fourth straight win came when UT beat Baylor, 90-81, before 12,955 fans at the Erwin Center. Freeman was outstanding—29 points, seven assists and seven steals, and he got fine support from Alvarado, Clack and Warmsley. Team defense sought to keep the ball out of the hands of BU center Brian Skinner, who made nine of 11 field goals.

Texas Tech, 15-1 and still irked over getting bumped from the 1995 NCAA Tournament, was leading the SWC when the Horns went to the South Plains. Nearly 9,000 people at Lubbock Municipal Coliseum gave the usual hothouse welcome on a Sunday afternoon. Texas missed 21 of its first 25 shots but stayed close with stringent half-court defense and offensive rebounding. The Red Raiders, led by Jason Sasser (20 points and 12 rebounds) edged the Horns, 79-78. "I think Tech's a top-10 team," Penders said. "They can beat anybody in the country in this building." Back in their own building, the Longhorns lost again when Ryan Minor hit two free throws with six seconds left in overtime to give Oklahoma a 67-65 victory. Freeman (20) was one of eight Longhorns who scored but the only one in double figures. Perryman committed six turnovers and was a miserable two of 17 from behind the arc.

Austin American-Statesman columnist Kirk Bohls opined that the Horns might have played themselves right out of contention for the NCAAs by losing to the Raiders and Sooners, but there was still time to right the ship. And how better to do that than with a six-game winning streak? Houston used what looked like a five-on-one defense against Freeman, liberating his teammates in an 80-63 victory for the Horns. The lefty from New York scored 17 points, and Hill, missing in action recently, had 16. Kenya Capers led the Cougars with 19.

"Take a picture. You'll never see me here again," said Penders after his team gave Rice a sound 79-64 beating at Autry Court. If the Longhorns and Owls, conference brothers for just a few more weeks, were to meet again in Houston, it would not be in the cozy, antiquated campus gym. Tommy McGhee, who had burned UT in Austin, made but two of 16 shots, while Clack had 25 points, 10 rebounds and three blocked shots and showed why some people considered him the key to the Horns' future. In Fort Worth, Hill far exceeded his scoring average with 26 points in a 102-81 defeat of Billy Tubbs' TCU Horned Frogs. Freeman, who never saw a shot he did not like, took 29 of them and made seven, but he recorded a triple-double—22 points, 10 rebounds and 10 assists. A versatile player, he was in the conference's top 10 in scoring, steals, three-point percentage, assists, free throw percentage and rebounding.

Freeman took a back seat to a couple of youngsters in Texas' 69-50 win over the Aggies in Austin. Perryman connected on five three-pointers, and Clack controlled the boards in a game that was never close. If not for Calvin Davis (18 points and nine rebounds), Texas A&M really would have been out of it. Penders told his players they were in the part of the season in which every game was a national championship, and they responded with road wins over SMU and Baylor. The Mustangs tried to run with the Horns but, lacking the same quality and quantity of athletes, fell by a score of 101-66. In a sometimes-contentious game featuring lots of elbows thrown and three technical fouls called, Freeman had 23 points and UT outrebounded Mike Dement's team by a 48-27 margin. In Waco, the Baylor Bears used high-pressure defense and some clutch shooting by reserve guard Roddrick Miller to stay close until the end of an 80-72 Texas win. Hill and Freeman combined for 44 points, and Clack had 14 rebounds and a monster dunk.

For the first time since the North Carolina game, the Erwin Center was sold out when Texas Tech and the Longhorns met. Penders' teams had never lost to the Red Raiders in Austin, but James Dickey's men were 23-1, ranked ninth with a 16-game winning streak. It was a talented, senior-dominated team, determined to win the final SWC crown. Following an outdoor pep rally and the annual UT lettermen's game, the Raiders and Horns tipped off. Tech took a convincing 75-58 victory as Tony Battie (22), Jason Sasser (19) and their teammates looked like world-beaters. Texas' two-for-26 three-point shooting was enough to ensure defeat.

The postponed game against Penders' old school, Rhode Island, took place on February 26 before 6,020 patrons in Providence. It was a battle with NCAA tourney ramifications, and Texas came through in crunch time. Alvarado made two key defensive plays, and 10 of 11 free throws dropped for an 81-77 win. Joshua King scored 27 for the Rams and Freeman 24 for the Horns.

sparked a 17-3 Ute run early in the second half for a lead that held up despite the furious efforts of Freeman, Vazquez and Perryman. On New Year's Eve in the frigid northeast, the Horns shot 36 percent, including seven of 27 three-pointers, in a frustrating 74-66 loss to Providence. Derrick Brown (19) of the Friars and reserve guard Al Coleman (17) paced their respective teams in scoring. Penders took note of Texas' offensive problems but was heartened by a never-say-die attitude in the late going against both Utah and Providence.

He had been half of one of the wildest and most colorful acts in SWC history—the Abe and Eddie Show. While Abe Lemons was retired and living in Oklahoma City, Eddie Sutton remained in the coaching business. Best remembered for his years at Arkansas, he had a stint at Kentucky before getting the job at his alma mater, Oklahoma State. As the Cowboys took the court on January 4, Sutton quieted the boos by flashing a Hook 'em, Horns sign. In the Big 12 opener, Texas nailed 15 three-pointers and outboarded a taller OSU team by 17 en route to an easy 92-58 win. Freeman (33 points and 10 rebounds) was superb. Top-ranked and unbeaten Kansas was up next. A team blessed with size, depth and skill, the Jayhawks had two all-Americans in Jacque Vaughn and Raef LaFrentz. "I think they legitimately have a chance to go through the season undefeated," Penders said. "They're playing with a passion." A standing-room-only crowd in Lawrence roared the "Rock Chalk Jayhawk" chant as KU scored 59 second-half points to win, 86-61. Freeman (22), Clack and Jordan all fouled out for the Horns.

Coleman, a fifth-year senior long the epitome of a benchwarmer, was the man with the master plan against Kansas State. In a 104-63 victory (the only time Texas broke the century mark all season), the lithe 6'1" guard set a school record by hitting 10 three-point shots. Forward Mark Young had 17 points and 10 rebounds for the Wildcats in a game attended by fewer than 4,000 fans because of icy weather. UT hung an 86-76 overtime defeat on old foe Texas A&M in College Station. Freeman, who went the first eight minutes without a point, finished with 30, and Quarles grabbed 12 rebounds. Five players were in double figures for the Aggies, losers of seven straight. Coach Tony Barone, who had seen an industrial accident delay construction of A&M's new facility (later named Reed Arena) in the summer, kept on showing the patience of a modern-day Job.

The No. 23 Longhorns played three home games in eight days, beginning with No. 10 Louisville. Denny Crum, in his 26th year with the Cardinals, had a short, weak-shooting team but one that hustled and played good defense, good enough to reach the Elite Eight in the NCAAs. UT lost a 15-point lead, watched as swingman Eric Johnson hit from downtown at the end of regulation and let the Cards take an 85-78 OT win. Freeman and Clack, who went together like red beans and rice, combined for 53 points in a game that left Penders with a 3-21 record against top-10 teams. UT's wily coach used some histrionics when things were going poorly in the second half against Oklahoma. He walked right out onto the court to protest a noncall and got an expected technical. It had the desired effect as the Horns scored 12 straight points and went on to beat the Sooners, 76-66. Freeman (24), as usual, paced Texas, while Lou Moore (19), Nate Erdmann (17) and Corey Brewer (14) led OU, which suffered a season-high 24 turnovers. One of the radio announcers for the Texas-Missouri game was none other than ex-coach Bob Weltlich, the subject of a long retrospective entitled "Welcome back, Bob" in the *Austin American-Statesman*. The Horns blew another big lead but still managed a 78-74 victory. Quarles, the gangly 6'10" lefthander, came through with 15 points, six rebounds and four steals—one of the best performances of his UT career. The game's final minute was lively and made more so by a tussle between Clack and the Tigers' Jason Sutherland.

Only by playing a veritable "who's that?" preconference schedule had Baylor had won 12 games. So the Bears were expected to have trouble with Texas, a Big 12 heavyweight, at the Ferrell Center. But with forward Doug Brandt getting 20 points and 14 rebounds and guard Damond Mannon hitting a key three-pointer, they took a 76-72 upset victory. Upset is exactly what Penders was after the buzzer when he chased ref Jim Jenkins up the tunnel before getting stopped by a security guard. The call in question was traveling on Freeman, one of the foremost practitioners of palming the ball while dribbling, a clear competitive advantage in violation of the rules. It was an incremental trend begun a few seasons back, and since NBA officials never whistled Michael Jordan on it, why not go ahead and palm the ball? In fact, Penders later insisted the call on Freeman should not have been made because it was "an NBA move." The Longhorns had fallen the last three times they played in Norman,

Game day outside and inside the Erwin Center.

was on the bench with four fouls when his teammates put together a 19-0 run that squelched James Dickey's Red Raiders. One key play was an Anthony Goode-to-Clack alley-oop slammer that drew a foul on Tech center Tony Battie. The Horns had won a must-win game. And they also won at ancient Gallagher-Iba Arena, ripping Oklahoma State, 90-73. Freeman poured in 25 points, and Coleman and Jordan had strong games. Guard Adrian Peterson scored 25 for the Cowboys.

The loss to Baylor in Waco two weeks earlier had featured some overexuberant remarks by the public address announcer (who was quickly called on the carpet by BU coach Harry Miller and athletic director Tom Stanton) and Penders griping about small, dingy towels provided in the visitors' locker room. Both matters received plenty of media play when the Horns and Bears got together again in Austin. With seven minutes left, Baylor was up by 12, but Freeman led a comeback for UT's 70-67 win. It was not settled until an 80-foot heave by Doug Brandt glanced off the rim as time expired. The Longhorns' lack of a consistent halfcourt offense had caused trouble against the Bruins and would do so again. Freeman, Clack, Vazquez, Muoneke and Jordan had gotten sick and were full of antibiotics and penicillin when Texas engaged Nebraska in Lincoln. All five played, but none especially well; Freeman went 40 minutes and scored just nine points. Only Perryman (20) and Coleman (13) had any success in a 79-67 loss to the Cornhuskers, who were paced by fleet guard Tyronn Lue (22). "We were just hoping to hang around today, conserve energy and steal one," Penders said. "I can't give enough credit to Reggie for even playing. He had no energy."

The No. 7 Iowa State Cyclones, winners of seven of their last eight games, blew into town on a Wednesday night for a tense, low-scoring affair open to either team. The Horns trailed by one with the clock ticking down when Coleman took a jumper from the key. His shot missed, but Jordan tipped it in for a 57-56 victory after which he was mauled by delirious teammates and cheered by a "sellout" crowd that was actually about 3,000 fans short. While Dedric

and a loud, jeering crowd saw it happen again—OU 83, UT 69. Nate Erdmann (25 points and 11 rebounds) looked like all-Big 12 material, while Freeman, recently featured in flattering portrayals in *Sports Illustrated* and *The Sporting News*, made just six of 22 shots. A 38-percent shooter in 1997, Freeman was frequently double-teamed because of his ability to drive and break down defenses.

Texas was clearly struggling. Newspaper columnists and talk-show callers had begun to wonder if the Horns might not reach the NCAA tourney, an idea Penders scoffed at. The coach reminded anyone who would listen that his team was playing a tough schedule, and he anticipated more wins as the season evolved. A big-time matchup was on February 3 against No. 22 Texas Tech. A throng of nearly 16,000 filled the Erwin Center to witness an 83-67 Longhorn win. Freeman

Willoughby of ISU was the top scorer with 16, he needed 17 shots to get there. The scenario was similar three days later out on the South Plains, where Texas Tech led, 72-70, in the waning seconds. But some poor ballhandling, combined with stout Red Raider defense, meant Freeman had to shoot from 40 feet out, and it was not even close. Cory Carr scored 22 for Tech, a team that would later forfeit all of its Big 12 victories for using two ineligible players.

Ten of 52 in his last three games, Freeman was obviously not shooting well. But one of the greatest Longhorns of all time—he would finish third on the career scoring list behind Terrence Rencher and Travis Mays—got quite an ovation before his final home game, a 68-57 defeat of Texas A&M. He was upstaged by Clack, the precocious sophomore, who tallied 23 points, eight rebounds, four steals and two blocked shots. Shanne Jones had 20 points for the Ags. The regular-season finale was a desultory 83-60 loss to No. 19 Colorado in the Rockies. Freeman had a game-high 24 points, and Buff star Chauncey Billups was held to 14, but the Horns fell further and further behind in the second half. "We got whupped," said Penders, who again used the ploy of walking oncourt to get a technical. He was called for it, but his team's play changed not at all.

Champions of the Big 12's south division, Texas got a bye in the first round of the league tourney at Kemper Arena in Kansas City. Before the Horns' matchup with Missouri, however, a controversy arose regarding a pair of columns by Jason Whitlock of the *Kansas City Star*. Under the guise of humor, he intimated that the four teams from the Lone Star State were party crashers who did not really deserve to be playing in the erstwhile Big 8 Tournament and egregiously insulted the Texas fans and SWC basketball history. Kirk Bohls of the *Austin American-Statesman* and Jeff McDonald of the *Daily Texan*, among others, returned fire. What happened in KC was a quick one-and-out defeat by a Missouri team with a losing record. Norm Stewart's Tigers won a sloppy game, 80-75, with balanced scoring and coolness down the stretch. Freeman (25) pointed out a 44-to-23 free throw differential, but the problems went deeper than that. On talent alone, UT should have won the game and advanced.

Record: 18-12

83 Nebraska 81 (OT)
86 Rhode Island 79
82 Florida 64
71 North Texas 56
78 Arizona 83
98 Fresno State 86
86 Oregon State 83
68 Utah 80
66 Providence 74
92 Oklahoma State 58
61 Kansas 86
104 Kansas State 63
86 Texas A&M 76 (OT)
78 Louisville 85 (OT)
76 Oklahoma 66
78 Missouri 74
72 Baylor 76
69 Oklahoma 83
83 Texas Tech 67
90 Oklahoma State 73
70 Baylor 67
67 Nebraska 79
57 Iowa State 56
70 Texas Tech 72
68 Texas A&M 57
60 Colorado 83
75 Missouri 80
71 Wisconsin 58
82 Coppin State 81
63 Louisville 78

While skeptics abounded, the 16-11 Longhorns dusted off their boogie shoes and got ready for the big dance. They would meet Wisconsin in an NCAA first-round game in Pittsburgh on March 14. Making short work of the Badgers in a 71-58 victory, Freeman scored 31 points despite being the object of several creative defenses. Wisconsin forward Sam Okey had a nice game with 17 points and 10 rebounds. Coppin State, which had upset South Carolina, was next. The Eagles had everything it took to win again, including most of the 17,509 fans packed into the Pittsburgh Civic Arena. With Antoine Brockington (27) doing most of the damage, they went toe-to-toe with the Horns and had a shot at victory at the end. Four seconds remained when Vazquez intercepted an inbounds pass under the Coppin State hoop to preserve an exciting 82-81 UT win.

The Longhorns flew home that Sunday night and were back on a northeast-bound airplane the following Wednesday. At the Carrier Dome in Syracuse, they would get an opportunity to avenge their only home loss of the season, to Louisville. In the round of 16, Texas already had gone much further than anyone predicted just 10 days before. Beat the Cardinals, which seemed eminently doable, and Penders' team was back in the rarefied atmosphere of the Elite Eight. Texas led by six at the break, and the Cards' star guard, DeJuan Wheat, was out with an ankle injury. But Alvin Sims (25) paced Louisville to a 78-63 win before more than 30,000 spectators. The Horns missed 23 of 27 shots over the final 12 minutes and lost going away. Muoneke, looking like a star of the future, had 19 points and 12 rebounds, while Freeman could score just six points in 40 minutes.

Although the season was over, UT basketball remained in the news for several more days because, as predictable as clockwork, Penders was up for another job. His name had been mentioned for no less than 15 pro or college head coaching positions since arriving in Austin nine years earlier, but this one seemed different. Rutgers, a Big East school, allegedly had offered him a package of $700,000 per year to resuscitate a Scarlet Knight program that was as dead as a doornail. Penders, drawing $400,000 annually at Texas (with athletic director DeLoss Dodds preparing a $100,000 raise), spoke with the Rutgers AD and president and toured the campus, all in the name of "professional courtesy." His New Jersey-based agent spent several hours negotiating a deal, and sportswriters in Austin, Dallas, Houston and elsewhere read the tea leaves before weighing in on Penders' possible impending departure. The call-in shows and Internet chat rooms had no shortage of fans alarmed at the prospect of the winningest coach in Longhorn history getting away, and yet others had grown tired of his "I'm happy here, but" line and sensitivity to critical analysis of the program. Perhaps it was provincialism, but some locals wondered how he could leave warm and beautiful Austin for cold and gritty New Brunswick, New Jersey. Finally, on March 26 at a campus media conference, Penders announced that he would be staying: "Rutgers was something close to my past. I have a lot of friends and family in that area, but I'm a Texan now, and I'm proud to be the head coach at the University of Texas."

1998

Analysts of college basketball noted several disturbing trends as the century and millenium drew to a close. An increasing number of the best players were jumping to the NBA after two years or one year or sometimes without even setting foot on a college campus. And those who did matriculate were somewhat less fundamentally sound than in the past. Perhaps the generalizations are unfair, but these young athletes were more attuned to instant gratification—running constantly and throwing up indiscriminate three-pointers or striving for the spectacular dunk. All told, it led to a certain homogenization of the game. And if that were not enough, the shadow of gambling had become a major worry for the NCAA. Two point-shaving scandals would taint the 1998 basketball season, and Americans were expected to illegally wager some $3 billion on the 63-game tournament culminating with the Final Four in San Antonio's Alamodome. Despite such problems, the sport remained enormously popular.

As for the Texas Longhorns, their fans hoped they would leave hoofprints on the Big 12, although that was more likely to happen a year hence. Tom Penders and his assistants had brought in an exceptional recruiting class. Bernard Smith was the latest player hoping to take over at point guard, that crucial but hard-to-master position. Two more celebrated rookies came from Westlake High School in Austin. Bill Wendlandt, a Westlake grad and MVP of the 1983 Horn team, had coached Luke Axtell and Chris Mihm in summer basketball and helped convince them that UT was the right place. Schools all over the country wanted Axtell, a 6'9" shooting guard, and Mihm, a 7' center. If they developed quickly and merged their talents with Kris Clack, DeJuan Vazquez and the other returnees, Texas would be hard to handle.

Before the season began, however, Penders had some health problems. He lost 20 pounds from the flu and a kidney infection and then underwent preventive surgery, having a defibrillator placed in his chest. A weakened and enlarged heart was not an ideal condition for someone in the stressful business of college basketball, even a coach with the relaxed demeanor of Penders. He stayed at home while the team traveled to East Rutherford, New Jersey for a season-opening tourney, the Coaches vs. Cancer IKON Classic. Eddie Oran, a UT assistant for 15 years, was in charge. It did not go well, though. The team looked disorganized in a 62-56 loss to the methodical Princeton Tigers, who were paced by forward James Mastaglio (15). The consolation game against Georgia was just slightly better, a two-point defeat before a small gathering. Clack and Axtell combined for 44 points, while Ray Harrison had 22 for the Bulldogs. Winless in Jersey, the Longhorns slipped quietly out of the top 25 for the duration of the season.

Penders was courtside on November 22 when UT met North Texas in Denton. The opposing coach was his former assistant, Vic Trilli, who had been hired to give flight to the Eagle hoop program. Trilli's team, with no starter taller than 6'7", employed a full-court press for 40 minutes and forced 26 turnovers but lost, 116-94. Clack (26) and Mihm (25 points, 12 rebounds and seven blocked shots) were exceptional. Four nights later in the home opener against Liberty, Axtell (32) had the hot hand, making 12 of 18 shots, including six from behind the arc and a monster jam with an assist from Anthony Goode. A crowd of 8,233 witnessed the 98-70 torching of the Flames. Again, Texas and Georgia played, this time at Stegeman Coliseum in Athens. The Bulldogs used a trapping defense to jump ahead by 26 and then coasted to a 94-76 win. "They are quick and really alert," said Penders, who thought a tight schedule had something to do with the outcome. "If they had to play Wednesday and come to Austin [for a Friday night game], it might have been the other way around." The top scorers were freshman Jumaine Jones (21) of UGa and Texas forward Nnadubem Muoneke (20).

A four-game homestand commenced with a 78-62 defeat of American University. For the first time since 1984, three frosh—Mihm, Axtell and Smith—started for the Longhorns. The competition was considerably tougher later that week when defending national champ Arizona came to town. Lute Olson's Wildcats had two all-Americans, Mike Bibby and Miles Simon, in the backcourt and plenty of size, power and speed. The Erwin Center sellout crowd included Governor George W. Bush and newly hired football coach Mack Brown. The Horns were up by two at the half but fell, 88-81, as Arizona created 25 turnovers and hit several late free throws. Clack scored 21, and Ira Clark came off the bench to make all seven of his shots and grab nine rebounds. Simon and Jason Terry (20 each) paced the blue-garbed Cats. Olson, a gracious winner, said "Texas played hard and well other than, obviously, the turnover situation. That's what did them in." It was what Penders liked to call a "quality loss." Unbeaten Florida was up next. Mihm, already the best UT center since John Brownlee or perhaps LaSalle Thompson, had 16 points and 15 rebounds in an 85-82 upset of the Gators. Defensive intensity made the difference in the hotly contested game. Guard Jason Williams scored 31 for the visitors, but made just eight of 23 shots. After the exam break, the Horns hosted another Southeastern Conference team. LSU, 6-43 away from Baton Rouge in the last two seasons, took the lead in the final minutes, but some clutch play by Clack, Clark and Mihm allowed UT to win by six. Willie Anderson paced the Tigers with 22 points, while Brandy Perryman had 17 for Texas. "It was one of those games we had to get, and we got it," said the senior guard.

Junior swingman Kris Clack in action in an early-season win over American University.

A 105-80 road loss to Illinois was rather interesting. Penders got two technicals and an ejection, and a few minutes later, the same thing happened to his main assistant, Eddie Oran. The agitated coaching staff and players did not speak to the media after the game, which featured 52 free throws by the Illini. Jerry Hester of the Big 10 hosts led both teams with 24 points.

Back in Austin for two games, the Horns beat ex-SWC rival Houston, 89-71. Clack, the go-to guy since the departure of Reggie Freeman, had 22 points and nine rebounds, while Galen Robinson scored a career-high 32 for the Cougars. That marked the 200th victory for Penders in 10 years at UT. Big 12 play began on January 3 against Baylor as Harry Miller's senior-dominated team pinned an 87-81 defeat on the Longhorns. Brian Skinner, the Bears' big man in the middle, rang up 29 points, and his diminutive partner, Patrick Hunter, had 24. The Horns were a ghastly eight of 42 in the three-point department. Worse than that, Clack and Axtell suffered knee and ankle injuries, respectively, in a two-minute span of a wild second half. Penders expressed fear that Clack would be out for the season.

While Clack and Axtell did not accompany the team to Missouri, two other players were dealing with chronic injuries—Vazquez (shoulder and groin) and Mihm (thumb). The Tigers, coming off a 55-point loss to Kansas State, were not sympathetic, beating UT, 91-69. A 21-point scoring spree late in the first half put the game away for Mizzou, which got 27 points from Tyron Lee and 21 from Kelly Thames.

Austin American-Statesman writer Randy Riggs voiced a long-heard criticism of Penders' teams: "...too often recently, the offense has deteriorated into one-on-one moves and long-range shots from players who have not demonstrated they can consistently score from the perimeter." And Riggs failed to mention poor passing and free throw shooting and an absence of leadership on the court. With No. 4 Kansas visiting Austin for a Saturday morning game, things would not get any easier. One all-American (Raef LaFrentz) missed the game with an injury, but the other (Paul Pierce) was just fine, leading the mighty Jayhawks to a 102-72 victory. Pierce and Billy Thomas combined for 58 points in a basketball demonstration that impressed 13,296 fans. At least Axtell was back, scoring 18 points. Mihm had a game-high 13 rebounds but missed 10 of 13 shots and five of six free throws.

Texas sank to 0-4 in the Big 12 with a 91-75 loss to OU in Norman. In a bruising game marred by five technical fouls, Kelvin Sampson's Sooners came back from a 10-point first-half deficit by warming up from the outside. The main culprit was guard Corey Brewer, who scored 36. Oklahoma's obstreperous fans were only too glad to wave a not-so-fond goodbye to their foe from south of the Red River.

The beleaguered Longhorns finally won a conference game when they beat Texas Tech, 88-79, at the Erwin Center. Vazquez held down Big 12 scoring leader Cory Carr, Clack returned from a three-game absence, and Axtell had 17 points. "This was big," Penders said in the postgame media conference. "You don't want to get yourself in too deep of a hole. We've got 12 games left, and I honestly think we can win them all." They won the next one, shooting 55 percent in a 105-91 defeat of Nebraska. Mihm (29), Axtell (25) and Clack (22) were superb. The Cornhuskers, who saw a three-game winning streak end, got 23 points and nine assists from guard Tyronn Lue.

Penders took his club on the road, first facing Fresno State, viewed by critics as the poster boy for all that was wrong with college basketball. Jerry Tarkanian's team was in the midst of a season of scandal, including arrests, suspensions and drug abuse, featured prominently by Mike Wallace of "60 Minutes." Selland Arena was packed when the Horns and Bulldogs tipped off. Mihm had 25 points and 16 rebounds, but Fresno State's zone defense nullified him in the late going, and Tark's little angels won, 90-82. The game really came down to three-point shooting; Texas was six of 26, while Fresno State was 11 of 19. Axtell, who missed that game with a stomach virus, experienced back spasms just before UT clashed with Iowa State in Ames. The Horns had their chances, but lost a close one, 85-82. Klay Edwards of the Cyclones scored 19, and Clack (17) was one of five UT players in double figures.

Oklahoma State, 14-3 and looking like one of the best teams Eddie Sutton had developed since his Arkansas heyday, suffered an 88-73 defeat before 11,109 happy fans at the Erwin Center. The Horns blew open a close game in the first half when they hit seven three-pointers in a row. Axtell led both teams with 24 points. The tall and slender guard (whose father had played football at Texas in the mid-1970s) had fine shooting form and a quick release, drawing comparisons to former Utah star Keith Van Horn, then enjoying a strong rookie season in the NBA. "He's a tremendous young talent," said the Cowboy coach. "If he sticks with it and stays healthy, he could be a great player." Kirk Bohls of the *Austin American-Statesman* wrote that Axtell was destined to become the best shooter in school history. He added, presciently: "Let's hope he's a Longhorn for four years."

UT's final visit to raucous G. Rollie White Coliseum was an 81-80 squeaker that came down to the last shot. But Texas A&M's Steve Houston missed a mid-range jumper and victory belonged to the Horns. Aggie forward Shanne Jones, who had a career-high 32 points, got off a good quote. "To sum it up," he said, "I feel like I won the lottery but lost the ticket." A Sunday afternoon game with Oklahoma drew a big crowd, one more vocal than usual. A recent *Houston Chronicle* rating of Big 12 arenas lambasted Texas' fans, declaring that Sesame Street on Ice crowds were more intimidating. The Sooners grabbed an 81-74 win with a combined 47 points from Corey Brewer and Evan Wiley. Penders' decision to leave Mihm—who had four fouls—on the bench for most of the last 13 minutes drew critical questions from local sportswriters and commentators, and Penders, as thin-skinned as ever, ripped them in return. Mihm categorically denied rumors that he was unhappy and considering a transfer, but trouble was, in fact, brewing.

Kansas State, winning by an average of 25 points per game at home, barely held off the Horns in an 83-79 victory. The Wildcats' Manny Dies, who led both teams with 25 points, had a game-clinching dunk with 19 seconds left. Not exactly road warriors, the Longhorns traveled to the South Plains to meet Texas Tech, which, like Texas A&M, was building a new facility—the United Spirit Arena, seating 12,500 and costing $50 million, due to open in the 2000 season. Texas won, 82-80, as the usual last-second hysteria took place. The Red Raiders' Rayford Young could have sent it into overtime, but his bold drive into the heart of the Horn defense failed. Clack, Mihm, Axtell, Vazquez and Muoneke scored all but two of UT's points. And Mihm, getting better as the season progressed, had 17 rebounds.

One night after 1,000 students took part in a hoops rally just south of the Tower, the Horns hosted Texas A&M. The Ags' lame-duck coach, Tony Barone, used just six players and saw them battle valiantly only to lose by 13. Clack called it a "sloppy win," but there was nothing sloppy about Mihm's showing—25 points (12 of 14 from the field), 15 rebounds and five blocked shots.

Trying to reach the .500 mark for the first time all year, the Longhorns traveled to Waco to meet the green and gold of Baylor. While Mihm and BU center Brian Skinner played to a standoff, the Bears came back from 13 points down to win, 80-75. Clack scored 30 and Vazquez 21, but some late heroics by Baylor reserve Kish Lewis made the difference. Seven straight times, Texas had beaten Oklahoma State, dating back to 1975. That came to a crashing halt when the No. 25 Cowboys scored an 80-58 rout at Gallagher-Iba Arena. Of OSU's 29 field goals, 19 were either dunks or layups. Soph forward Desmond Morris had 27 points, and the Horns converted on a miserable four of 20 from downtown.

The regular season concluded at home against Colorado. That game also served as an occasion to honor the team that had won the NIT 20 years earlier. Abe Lemons and players like Jim Krivacs, Johnny Moore and Ron Baxter were feted and given the chance to recall their run to glory in 1978. Penders' team allowed a double-digit lead to turn into an 81-64 loss to CU, which had Longhorn fans moaning like a sinner on revival day. Except for Mihm (20) and Clack (16), no one played well. Junior guard Kenny Price scored 28 for the Buffaloes, who snapped a four-game losing streak.

With a 12-16 record and their top scorer (Clack) hurting from a shoulder injury, the Horns were seen as little more than also-rans in the Big 12 tourney. The only way to reach the NCAAs would be to win every game in Kansas City, and the KU Jayhawks were unlikely to allow that longest of long shots to happen. Things began well, albeit against another of the former SWC teams, Texas Tech. (According to Ron Flatter, who wrote a thrice-weekly Internet column, "It is hard to ignore the buzz coming out Kansas City—that Texas, Baylor, Texas A&M and Texas Tech are perceived as little more than club fighters brought in to make the rest of the Big 8 richer in both victories and in dollars.") A 20-point first half lead dwindled to almost nothing, and if Cory Carr's shot from the top of the key had connected, the Longhorns and Red Raiders would have gone into OT. Clack managed 28 points and nine rebounds, both game highs. Mihm, too, played a big role down the stretch of that 86-83 victory. The following night, Penders' team met Oklahoma State. Adrian Peterson (24) had the Cowboys up by four with 90 seconds left. Then Clack, who left the game earlier due to an ankle injury, hit a driving layup and on the ensuing play, fed Perryman in the corner. He buried the 207th three-pointer of his career, and UT had beaten OSU, 65-64. Perryman, a Kansas native with plenty of family and friends at Kemper Arena, had seen his minutes and production decline from previous seasons, so that shot was extra sweet. But reality intruded on March 7 when Kelvin

Record: 11-17

56 Princeton 62
87 Georgia 89
116 North Texas 94
98 Liberty 70
76 Georgia 94
78 American 62
81 Arizona 88
85 Florida 82
69 LSU 63
80 Illinois 105
89 Houston 71
81 Baylor 87
69 Missouri 91
72 Kansas 102
75 Oklahoma 91
88 Texas Tech 79
105 Nebraska 91
82 Fresno State 90
82 Iowa State 85
88 Oklahoma State 73
81 Texas A&M 80
74 Oklahoma 81
79 Kansas State 83
82 Texas Tech 80
87 Texas A&M 74
75 Baylor 80
58 Oklahoma State 80
64 Colorado 81
86 Texas Tech 83
65 Oklahoma State 64
55 Oklahoma 68

Sampson's Sooners lowered the boom on Texas, 68-55. Injuries and fatigue, not to mention OU's relentless pressure, spelled defeat and the end of the season for the Horns. Only Axtell (13) was in double figures. "We didn't have much gas left in the tank," Penders said. Whether 1998 had been a transition year (as the coach had called it in November) or a rebuilding year (his term of choice from January on), it had not been a good year, and those with opinions and forums to express them did so with abandon.

But the trouble ran much deeper than fans grumbling about a losing season. The day after the team returned to Austin, four players—Axtell, Mihm, Muoneke and Smith—met with AD DeLoss Dodds and in a candid discussion, expressed displeasure with Penders and mentioned the possibility of transferring. At least in the media, there were vague allegations of the coach's verbal abuse, dishonesty and failure to develop them into better basketball players; laid-back practice sessions were the norm ever since Vic Trilli took the North Texas job. Amid unpleasant private and public exchanges with Axtell, Penders, while on a Caribbean vacation, decided to suspend his star guard, although the meaning of a postseason suspension was never made clear.

The next day, Axtell's academic records were faxed to a local radio station and then read on the air. This harebrained move raised the ante because it violated a federal law guaranteeing student privacy. While assistant coach Eddie Oran took responsibility, Penders' position in the UT athletic department had grown considerably shakier. Interim president Peter Flawn assigned vice provost and general counsel Patricia Ohlendorf to investigate. For several weeks, the issue evolved and remained in the news, including an uncomplimentary article in *Sports Illustrated.* Penders hired a high-powered attorney, Roy Minton, to represent him and seemed oddly open to the idea of being reassigned within the department. The whole thing got stranger when, on March 23, Penders held a press conference in the driveway of his home to defend himself. Simultaneously, Clack and Vazquez did the same at a park in east Austin. Besides rather obvious posturing and spinning, however, little information was revealed in either instance.

As the investigation/negotiation dragged on, Penders all but guaranteed his departure when he notified the NCAA of a possible violation. Six weeks earlier, Mihm's parents had flown to an out-of-town game in the private airplane of a friend who, while not a UT alum, was a member of the Longhorn Foundation. With so much hostility circulating, the annual hoop banquet at the Erwin Center was canceled. Finally, on April 2, Penders and Dodds met the media at Bellmont Hall and announced that an agreement had been reached. Penders was resigning. The coach, who had virtually strong-armed a new contract one year earlier, had seen his base of support diminish. He denied being forced out or bought out, although he received a $657,000 golden parachute. The *Dallas Morning News*' sage sportswriter Blackie Sherrod mused, "One must wonder if we'll ever know *all* factors behind Tom Penders' 'resignation' as UofTexas hoops coach. There must be more than met the ear. Surely."

Was he the best coach in UT history? Abe Lemons enjoyed one great season (1978, when his team won the NIT title), two good seasons, two mediocre seasons and one disaster, so he cannot warrant that honor. Jack Gray, whose career took place entirely in the pre-integration era, has a stronger claim because of the Bobby Moers teams of 1939 and 1940 and the post-war teams led by Slater Martin. If not Gray, then it would have to be Penders, whose 200-plus victories and eight NCAA Tournament appearances in 10 years speak for themselves. Critics would say the program peaked in 1990 with players Bob Weltlich had brought to the Forty Acres and that not even his biggest stars (Travis Mays, Lance Blanks, B.J. Tyler and Terrence Rencher) had made more than a ripple in the pros. But after Penders quit, passions subsided considerably and people were willing to give him his due. More than 500 admirers converged on the Doubletree Hotel a week later to pay tribute to the ex-Longhorn coach. He signed autographs, reminisced a bit, made some jokes and was treated to a two-minute standing ovation.

Well before that party, attention had turned to the business of who would succeed Penders. A 10-member search committee was formed, with Dodds at its head. The media speculated about a number of candidates, primarily Rick Majerus of Utah, Bob Bender of Washington, Rick Barnes of Clemson, Kelvin Sampson of Oklahoma, Dave Odom of Wake Forest and Phil Ford, an assistant at North Carolina. Dodds was not taking direction from the media, but as it turned out, the main contenders were on that list. Majerus, whose Utes had just fallen to Kentucky in the NCAA championship game, made about $1 million per season, more than half of that deriving from a deal with Reebok, which had been UT's outfitter for several years. He had to be considered the front runner and even got an endorsement from Penders, who briefly considered a career change to sports announcing before taking the coaching job at George Washington University.

In early April, interviews were held in such disparate locales as Milwaukee, Atlanta, Dallas, Midland and Palm Springs. They involved Majerus, Sampson, Bender, Ford and Barnes, meeting with Dodds, associate AD Butch Worley and/or regents Don Evans and Tom Hicks. Was it this guy or that guy? Some sportswriters were even laying odds on who would next coach the Longhorns. Majerus gave mixed signals about his interest in the job. In the end, whether he turned down UT or vice versa, it hardly mattered. Support was growing for Barnes, an offer was made, and he agreed to a five-year contract at $700,000 per annum. He was introduced at a heavily attended media conference in the Burnt Orange Room on April 13.

Rick Barnes was a 43-year old North Carolina native, a graduate of Lenoir-Rhyne College. He served assistant coaching stints at Davidson (two seasons), George Mason (five), Alabama (one) and Ohio State (one) before taking the top job at George Mason. A 20-10 record there in 1988 brought him to Providence, where he led the Friars to five postseason appearances in six years. He returned to the South in 1995 as head coach at Clemson. That school, with little basketball tradition, was a tough place to win, but he did it, guiding the Tigers to a 74-48 record and a spot in the NIT or NCAAs each of four seasons. His 1997 team was at one point 16-1 and No. 2 in the nation. Despite Barnes' youth, he had proven himself in two of the most competitive leagues—the Big East and the Atlantic Coast Conference. He had been courted by Tennessee, Virginia and Ohio State, but the Clemson people loved and appreciated him and had given him a raise and contract extension. Barnes' Tigers got bounced in the first round of the 1998 NCAA tourney, and he may have realized the difficulty of winning big at a school in the remote reaches of western South Carolina. Fully aware of the situation at UT ("a program on the brink of self-destruction" overstated *Daily Texan* staffer Mike Finger), Barnes signed on, becoming the 23rd coach in Longhorn hoop history. He brought his entire Clemson staff with him—Ed Kohtala, Brian Cousins and Ricky Stokes. As the cameras clicked, the four smiled broadly and flashed the Hook 'em, Horns sign.

Barnes had a reputation as a flexible coach who could run or slow it down, depending on the situation. Defense, however, was always a priority with his teams at Providence and Clemson. He was a tireless recruiter

Athletic director DeLoss Dodds welcomes Rick Barnes to Austin, 37 days after the Longhorns' 1998 season ended.

and promoter who had gained unwanted notoriety three years earlier for going nose-to-nose with North Carolina's Dean Smith in an ACC game. According to Dodds, "he's a people person, the right person at the right time for the University of Texas."

He met with the returning players—minus Luke Axtell, who pondered a transfer to Kansas—and made it clear that hard work and discipline would be higher priorities than during the hang-loose Tom Penders era. Barnes laid down some rules and emphasized togetherness and family, and acknowledged what Penders had done in the past decade. Even without Axtell, he was inheriting some good players and recruits and wasted no time in getting others. The main one was Chris Owens, a 6'8" transfer from Tulane and former high school all-American. Barnes would be working at the state's flagship university, one with vast resources, alumni all over the world and a fine facility in the Erwin Center. He, his wife and two children were coming to Austin, an eminently livable city of 800,000. While he was careful not to make overblown promises, Rick Barnes knew he could win at UT.

UT Women

The Early Years: 1900-1966

Senda Berenson knew a good thing when she saw it. In 1892, she was an enthusiastic young gym instructor at Smith College in Northampton, Massachusetts, 20 miles north of Springfield, where Dr. James Naismith had invented basketball just a year earlier. Firmly imbued with Victorian ideas of proper womanliness, Berenson sought to alter the game for her students by lessening physical contact and exertion. She came up with these broad rules: (1) the court was divided into three sections with two players per team in each; (2) a player could hold the ball no more than three seconds; (3) dribbling was limited to three bounces; and (4) close guarding was prohibited. These and other rules were fluid and ever-changing, and it took more than 70 years for the special rules to be eliminated. But women's basketball was off and running, simultaneously with the development of the men's game. Protected from the elements and public scrutiny in small gyms, it spread from Smith to other colleges, schools, YWCAs and civic groups. Before 1892 was out, the first interinstitutional contest (between the University of California and Miss Head's School) was held. And Cal's female Golden Bears—surely not so called at the time—played a team from Stanford in the first intercollegiate women's basketball game in 1896.

The 1904 UT women's basketball team. Eunice Aden, who served as player, manager, coach and physical education director over a 20-year span, is on the top row, second from the left.

Clara Baer, Berenson's colleague at Sophie Newcomb College in New Orleans, brought it to the South, and the game filtered over into Texas, but the details of its arrival are sketchy. Six years before Magnus Mainland started a men's team, Eleanore Norvell instigated the first rudimentary basketball game in University of Texas history. A native of Oklahoma, she had been director of women's physical education less than a year before introducing the new sport to coed classes in the basement gym of the old Main Building. The Ideson team (including Norvell) and the Whitis team met on Saturday afternoon, January 13, 1900. The game, divided into 10-minute quarters, was won by the Whitis team, 3-2. In Austin, as elsewhere, basketball was popular because it combined pleasure with exercise. Senda Berenson, Clara Baer, Eleanore Norvell and other P.E. professionals believed it could enhance women's physical development, teach aesthetics and even moral values. Cooperation was emphasized over competition, a supposedly male trait.

UT coeds played the game in gym classes and soon formed teams to represent the freshmen, sophomores, juniors and seniors. At the end of the 1902 "season," a group of all-stars was chosen, acknowledged in the *Texan*, *Cactus* and *University*

Record as the varsity team. Norvell was the coach, and her players were captain Felton Walker, Mary Popplewell, Ada Garrison, Annie Matthews, Katie Small, Kitty Searcy, Mary Hopkins and Grace Hill. A 10-cent admission fee was charged for a 7-4 defeat of the "Town Girls." Although athletes from both teams wore modest middie blouses and serge bloomers, men were not allowed to observe, so a few stood outside and cheered through the windows.

In the next several years, the varsity played teams representing high schools in Austin, San Antonio, Belton, Cameron, Llano and Galveston, as well as other institutions. Clara Baer brought her Sophie Newcomb team to Austin in 1906 for the first intercollegiate game, but the results went unreported. The *Texan* and *Cactus* both showed exasperation over the refusal to publicize women's games, which took on an air of mystery to male students. A team representing Southwestern University played UT for the first time in 1907 and lost, 20-19. The little liberal arts college in Georgetown provided competition nearly every year, and Baylor visited a couple of times, but such instances were rare. Texas women's basketball in the early part of the 20th century was mostly an intramural, interclass affair.

Basketball practice at N Hall.

While individual recognition was frowned upon, the names of some of the better players from that era are known: Willie Thatcher, Alice Ramsdell, Viola Middlebrook, Minnie Giesecke, Helen Mobley and Eugenia Welborn. Captain of the team in 1903, manager in 1904, coach in 1905 and the new director of women's P.E. in 1911 was Eunice Aden. Recreational activities for women slowly expanded during Aden's 11-year tenure, including the building of an outdoor basketball court, surrounded by a tall fence, of course. "T" sweaters and blankets were awarded for basketball, swimming, tennis and indoor baseball, but only basketball had an intercollegiate component, slight though it was. The most significant thing a female athlete at the University of Texas could do then was to make the varsity basketball team and earn a letter. Aden and dean of women Helen Marr Kirby kept a close watch on the growing enthusiasm for basketball. They would not allow the team to play off campus, nor would they allow a full-fledged program (of which there were few in the region). Although most of their charges were obedient to such careful leadership, not all agreed. The *Daily Texan* printed occasional editorials and letters, including this excerpt from Frances McQueen in 1916: "...Each year, there has been some agitation about open athletics for women. But we have each time retreated precipitately before a cry of 'modesty and dignity!'"

Aden witnessed the construction of N Hall, a large frame building that served as the UT women's gymnasium for 15 years. When she retired in 1921 to run a girls' summer camp near San Antonio, Aden destroyed her records in order that her successor could start with a clean slate. In fact, the new era had begun even before Aden left the Forty Acres. Anna Hiss, a blue-blooded native of Baltimore, had attended Hollins College in Virginia and Sargent School of Physical Education in Boston, where she played on the basketball team against the "Seven Sisters" colleges. Tall, vivacious and a feminist long before the word had been invented, Hiss was hired as a P.E. instructor in 1918 and soon replaced Aden. For almost 40 years, she was among the most prominent women on campus. A visionary in directing physical education and intramurals, Hiss started a degree program for P.E. majors and founded the Orange Jackets and Campus League of Women Voters. Implementing idea after ambitious idea, Hiss ran her department with a strong hand and was loved by most of her colleagues and students and feared by the rest.

Be that as it may, Anna Hiss was also dead-set against intercollegiate athletics for women. She abhored the male model, governed—as she saw it—by money and skewed educational values. She was among a cohort of female P.E. professionals intent on eradicating women's intercollegiate sports, and basketball was the centerpiece of their attention. It was part of a post-World War I nationwide trend (led by Lou Henry Hoover, wife of soon-to-be President Herbert Hoover) embodied in the maternalistic mottos "a sport for every girl and a girl in every sport" and "for the good of those who play." The point system Hiss created encouraged her students to diversify their athletic interests, culminating in the big social affair known as T Night. Hiss disapproved of elite athletes receiving excessive attention, coaching and resources that could be more equitably distributed. And in the case of basketball at UT, things changed quickly and drastically. Even before Hiss succeeded Aden in 1921, games against outside schools had stopped. Texas women's basketball, although in a more structured setting, was back to intramural and interclass play.

Anna Hiss, P.E. director from 1921 to 1957. With her arrival on campus, women's intercollegiate basketball came to a sudden and seemingly permanent halt.

Through membership and leadership in state and national organizations, Hiss helped forge a concerted attack on the popular sport of basketball, which seemed unfeminine and dangerous. A progressive in many ways, Hiss held some retro ideas, believing competitive basketball (even with the modified rules) was too physically and emotionally strenuous for women. Her view got the stamp of approval in 1924 when the women's division of the National Amateur Athletic Federation issued a six-page platform stating its opposition to intercollegiate athletics for women. The platform emphasized "spirit of play for its own sake and the promotion of physical activity for the largest possible proportion of persons in any given group...under leadership and environmental conditions that foster health, physical efficiency and good citizenship." And in April of the next year, Hiss formed the Texas chapter of the Athletic Conference of American College Women. Meeting in Austin, 26 delegates from 10 institutions around the state voted unanimously to condemn intercollegiate competition for women and to endorse the intramural/interclass model. Like most unanimous votes, it was actually something less than that. Bucking the trend were members of the rival Women's Intercollegiate Association of Texas (the College of Industrial Arts [antecedent of Texas Woman's University], Baylor College in Belton, Baylor University, Southwestern University, Southwest Texas State College and SMU), who enjoyed the competition, traveling and related experiences. But before the decade was over, those schools had submitted and joined Hiss' organization.

Hiss was not interested in producing sedentary fans but players and well-rounded individuals, and she wanted each young woman under her direction to leave UT with at least one sport she could enjoy throughout life. (If nothing else, Hiss insisted her students sit, stand and walk with correct posture. She was nearly obsessed with posture.) Non-team sports like tennis, golf, archery, swimming, bowling and interpretive dance had her favor, and whenever possible, artistry was emphasized over athleticism. When Hiss revived the Women's Athletic Association (later renamed the University of Texas Sports Association) in the 1920s for those wanting to specialize in one sport, a club for basketball was not included. Several sports were added to the WAA/UTSA over the years but, again, not basketball. The University Interscholastic League had sponsored a county-level basketball program for high school girls since 1918, but Hiss and others put pressure on the UIL, forcing it to stop. They also protested, unsuccessfully, the participation of American women in the 1928, 1932 and 1936 Olympics. While it was not clear at the time, by discouraging high-level competition and the resulting popular enthusiasm and media attention, Hiss and her fellow P.E. professionals served to diminish athletic interest among female students. When things finally changed, decades hence, they had a lot of catching up to do. Through her remarkable energy and executive ability, Hiss installed a splendid spirit in generations of students who went on to become teachers, coaches and leaders of all kinds. In time, their students and daughters came to UT and overturned some of the policies Hiss had apparently chiseled in stone.

Her most lasting achievement was the construction in 1931 of the $400,000 Women's Gymnasium (renamed in Hiss' honor in 1972 after her death). During the late 1920s, Hiss toured the country at her own expense, carefully examining other facilities. She used this information in assisting architect Herbert M. Greene, who designed the building with Mediterranean-style arched windows, graceful patios and a large courtyard. No less successful for female students than Gregory Gym was for men, it featured a fine dance studio and three playing courts, all undersized, to discourage basketball competition. The pool, too, was just short of Olympic length, in keeping with Hiss' philosophy. Before the UT campus ran out of open space, the Women's Gym was surrounded by tennis courts and fields for golf, archery, field hockey and similar outdoor activities.

The classically designed Women's Gym, built in 1931 at a cost of $400,000, was renamed in honor of Anna Hiss after her death in 1972.

Women's basketball did not disappear at the University of Texas. Sororities, dormitories and other groups played intramurals (interclass games were gradually phased out), divided into orange and white brackets, with the former composed of the more advanced players. There was a tournament most years, and an all-University team was chosen to play against a group of female faculty members. That was as close as a UT coed got to serious hoop competition. While there was no rule against it, Hiss disapproved of students participating in the rambunctious games run by the city league. Teams representing the YWCA, Nixon-Clay Business College, Kash-Karry, Scarbrough's, Southwestern Bell and other entities played alongside the men at the Austin Athletic Club, located at 12th Street and Shoal Creek Boulevard. Declassé compared to the ladylike tableaux of most UT gym classes and intramurals, the teams boasted fancy satin uniforms and competed hard, before crowds of up to 500. Players got their names in the newspaper and were accorded recognition for their athletic ability. Several times in the 1920s and 1930s, the Texas Amateur Athletic Federation championship was held in Austin, and the Amateur Athletic Union national champion Tulsa Stenos (with their stars, Lillian Justice and Frances Dunlap) paid a visit in 1934. Largely as a result of the successful campaign to erase intercollegiate basketball, that was the heyday for women playing in the AAU, one of whom was a Texan, Mildred "Babe" Didriksen, who competed for a Dallas team (the Employer's Casualty Golden Cyclones) and later one in New York (the Brooklyn Yankees). The Babe, one of the greatest female athletes of all time, could never have attained such heights in track and field, golf, tennis and basketball if she had left Beaumont for Austin and played under Hiss' reign.

Some of the better female athletes at UT during this time included Helen Cline, Jane Connor, Mary Elizabeth Richter, tennis player Ruth Bailey and swimmer Jane Dillard. The most successful in her chosen sport was golfer Betsy Rawls, a 1950 graduate who later won many tournaments on the pro circuit. Men were no longer prohibited from watching intramural basketball games in the Women's Gym, so the shroud of secrecy had been torn away. With the exception of boyfriends and a few others, however, there was little interest, and anyway, the three courts had almost no room for spectators—another Hiss touch. A first of sorts took place in 1941 when two city league teams, Sammie's and Taylor's Green Devils, met in the first part of a triple-header in Gregory Gym, followed by a boys' high school game and Jack Gray's Longhorns. Sammie's won, 11-10. And a team from the National Polytechnic School of Mexico came to Austin in February 1942 to play a demonstration game in the Women's Gym. They divided into two teams, augmented by six UT students, and played before 130 spectators. "A bevy of brown bombshells did some fancy dribbling and played a brand of basketball unknown to feminine cagers here," said the *Daily Texan.*

During the long period of dormancy, things were happening. Incremental rule changes were making women's basketball less constricted and more athletic—more like the men's game, which many of them wanted to play. Why, after all, should women be limited in where they could run on the court, how many dribbles were allowed, how closely an opponent could be guarded and such things? The grumbling about that and the lack of a real team stayed mostly among a coterie of gifted athletes, but P.E. instructors and Hiss herself were aware of it. Her response for many years was unyielding; there would be no varsity teams for UT women and no outside competition. After World War II, as men returned home and to campus, Hiss permitted some corecreational sports, with male and female students playing tennis, volleyball and badminton together.

Another change came with "play days" and "sports days," in which individual women and teams from several colleges gathered for a day or weekend of competition and socializing. Most prominent in central Texas were the Baylor Olympics and Southwest Texas Sports Day; UT, following a more conservative agenda, never sponsored one. While some students enjoyed the milk and cookies, the singing of songs and assorted jollity, others—those with athletic skill and desire—savored the chance to engage in that modified version of intercollegiate sports. Some of Hiss' colleagues were more rigid than she, refusing to condone sports days and judging them an incursion of the elite, antidemocratic alternative. Peggy Vilbig, Jody Akin, Mary Ann Green, Shirley Turek, Jean Richards and Susan Janse were some of the UT students who excelled in these contests, known as extramurals (literally, "beyond the walls").

By the late 1940s and early 1950s, younger P.E. professionals were beginning to question and challenge the old assumptions. They helped revive UIL involvement in girls' high school basketball. When the statewide organization retreated under pressure in 1928, three ad hoc groups had stepped into the breach with tournaments of their own. Especially in the smaller schools in rural areas, girls wanted to play basketball, and most parents and coaches supported them. When 450 school administrators signed a petition in 1948 urging the resumption of sponsorship, the UIL found itself under pressure from a direction opposite to the 1920s. Its athletic director, Dr. Rhea Williams, a former SMU basketball star himself, was unconvinced about the supposedly evil effects of competitive basketball for female athletes and said so. Other advocates included Ruth Motley of the Houston Independent School District, Dr. Ann Dugan of Texas Woman's College and Betty Spears of the University of Texas. The issue was studied and discussed for three years before the UIL acted. Regional tournaments were held, and the first state tournament took place in Gregory Gym in March 1951, hosted in part by UT physical education majors. The winners were Comanche High School in Class A and Claude High School in Class B. The quality of play was surprisingly high, attendance was good, and it got adequate press coverage. Never considered an experiment, the girls' tourney complemented the well-entrenched boys' meet quite nicely.

Iowa is the state that kept the flame burning during those long, dark times. Girls' high school basketball there never stopped and was, if anything, more popular than the boys' game. Iowa Wesleyan pioneered—or restored—college basketball in 1943, and Wayland Baptist followed suit in 1948; the Flying Queens of Plainview, Texas, would win 10 Amateur Athletic Union titles. Temple and Ranger junior colleges also formed teams for their female students. They played AAU teams, high school teams and just about whoever else could field a competitive squad. Other schools around the country opened the door to limited intercollegiate play. There was no hurry at UT, although Hiss (who received an honorary doctorate from Boston University in 1949) had begun to accept the inevitable. She credited Roy Bedichek of the UIL with changing her mind. Bedichek wrote an article entitled "In defense of contests" that must have been very persuasive. "He taught me that you have to have competition or you can't have a game, [but] the important things are charm, energy, fearlessness and good sportsmanship," she said.

WICA, the 1946 intramural basketball champion, is on the front row. The runner-up team, Wesley Foundation, occupies the back row.

Rodney Page (back row, middle) coached the 1974 women's team, the last one not to receive full varsity status.

The team's moderate success may be attributed to having a pool of nearly 20,000 female students from which to choose. But other, smaller institutions were further advanced because they had been playing longer or they had money for equipment, travel and full-time coaches. It would be years before UT could compete with Wayland Baptist, which was fortunate to have a wealthy benefactor. And Stephen F. Austin, Baylor, Rice, and Temple and Ranger JCs were much better off. When the team, some of whose members called themselves the Lady Longhorns, played Rice in Houston, an interesting thing occurred: The father of one of the Owls, himself a UT alumnus, saw the meager circumstances they labored under and made a financial donation. Little by little, as the years passed, the situation improved.

The 1972 team, coached by Barbara Hansen—who, like Dalton, outfitted her teams in skirted uniforms—was a good one. Becky Bludau, Frances Seidensticker and the Windham sisters, Karon and Sharon, were key factors in winning the Southwest Texas Invitational and another tourney at Lamar University in Beaumont. The team qualified to go on to the regional tournament and possibly nationals, but its money had run out and so had the season. These tournaments were operated by the newly formed Association of Intercollegiate Athletics for Women, an organization paralleling the male-oriented NCAA. For its own philosophical and financial reasons, the AIAW slowly and reluctantly (under threat of a class-action suit) began to allow scholarships and recruiting by member schools.

The UTSA was serving as a de facto women's athletic department at UT, something for which it was not intended. In addition to basketball, it sponsored teams in volleyball, gymnastics, badminton, tennis, golf and swimming. Games, matches and tournaments were held on campus, and the various teams competed throughout the state, putting a growing administrative and financial burden on women's intramurals and physical education.

Another forward step came in 1973, when the Texas women began to practice and play some basketball games in the Gregory Gym annex. A referee for one of those games was Rodney Page, a recent arrival to Austin. Page, 25, had bachelor's and master's degrees from the University of Houston, where he served briefly as assistant women's basketball coach. When Hansen quit after two seasons, Page took over. His first year at the helm was the last year for the UTSA, which soon became defunct with the creation of the Texas women's athletic department. A friend of Longhorn men's coach Leon Black, he got some supplies and equipment that had previously been covered by the miniscule budget or done without entirely. Cars or vans were rented for out-of-town games, ending, mercifully, the reliance on players for transportation. Page, the coach, on-campus recruiter and public-relations man for Texas women's basketball, was responsible for the most significant change imaginable as the 1974 season approached. All home games would be played in Gregory Gym. Not in the pint-sized court at the Women's Gym and not in an obscure corner of the Gregory Gym annex, but in the venerable gym itself, where UT men's teams, good, bad and mediocre, had competed since 1931. Most of the women's games were prelims to the men's games, which did nothing to hurt awareness of Texas women's basketball. Playing in Gregory Gym, even as the Special Events Center was under construction, was a major advance and an indication of the legitimacy of the program started by Walker and carried on by Dalton, Hansen and Page.

Page was as sensitive and understanding of the physical and emotional needs of his players as any male coach could be. He took care not to use sexist language ("man-to-man" defense became "player-to-player" defense, for example) and taught and motivated carefully. But the four players who had been on Hansen's last team noticed more conditioning work and longer and harder practices. Some of the younger ones had little competitive experience or came out of the less demanding six-player game, and had to learn to deal with fatigue and play to win.

Before the season began, *Daily Texan* sports editor Herb Holland went to Dallas and spoke at the Southwest Conference winter meeting. Reminding the conference fathers of the 1972 Title IX Educational Amendments mandating equal opportunity for male and female student-athletes, Holland urged the immediate inclusion of women's sports in the SWC but got a frosty response. Students Carol Crabtree and Sue Ann Ray also played a part in the grassroots effort to draw attention to women's athletics at the University of Texas.

In the meantime, Page's first UT team put together a 7-11 record, led by Cindy Hill, Rita Egger and Treva Trice. They suffered stage fright on January 26 in their first game at Gregory Gym, a 56-36 loss to Southwest Texas prior to the UT men playing Texas Tech. Few spectators were present when the teams tipped off, but the old gym began to fill in the second half. "The players were just in a daze," Page told the *Daily Texan.* "I would tell them something and look them straight in the eye, and they wouldn't hear it."

Page and his players also had prelim games against Houston at Hofheinz Pavilion and against Texas A&M at G. Rollie White Coliseum. Although the women were not the main event, they were beginning to perform in big facilities before more than a smattering of fans. They played in tournaments hosted by Texas A&I and Texas Woman's University, and the season ended at home in a satellite tourney leading to the Texas AIAW meet in Stephenville. UT lost to St. Mary's, beat Texas Lutheran and Trinity and fell to Southwest Texas.

The team had a losing record, but 1974 was a memorable year. It was the first time a women's college team had played in Gregory Gym, the first time the Longhorn Band and cheerleaders had performed at a women's game, the first time trainers had worked with the team and the first time the roster was included in the men's game program. A month after the basketball season concluded, University president Stephen Spurr announced the creation of a separate women's athletic department, with a starting budget of $50,000, offices in Bellmont Hall and its own, presumably female, director. This development did not thrill everyone, for a variety of reasons, but it was a good move. One thing was certain—University of Texas women's athletics, with basketball the centerpiece, was moving up.

1975

What the defunct UT Sports Association had done over the past eight years, although important, was just a run-up to the establishment of a women's athletic department. Beginning in the fall semester of 1974, female students could participate on a varsity level in seven sports. If Texas had been slow to move before, that was no longer the case because the budget would increase 800 percent over the next four years. While other schools nervously awaited the Department of Health, Education and Welfare's interpretation of Title IX, UT went ahead and started building a program that would win the Texas AIAW's Babe Didriksen Award for the best overall women's athletic department every year from 1975 to 1982. Taking their cue from the administrations of Dr. Stephen Spurr and then Dr. Lorene Rogers, the leaders of the fledgling women's department (primarily June Burke, Dr. Waneen Spirduso, Dr. Dorothy Lovett, Pat Weiss and Betty Thompson) met and worked with their male counterparts (Frank Erwin, J. Neils Thompson, Darrell Royal and Al Lundstedt). It must be acknowledged that a certain amount of distrust and adversarial feeling existed between the two groups for a while. The women needed some of the men's expertise accrued from seven decades of operating a big-time program, yet they clung to the AIAW's idealistic philosophy. The men, on the other hand, had their doubts about the new enterprise and whether women's athletics would ever be self-sustaining. They sought to protect the one sport unique to their gender—football. King football had long floated other men's sports (including basketball), and it might have to do the same for women's sports. Jack Maguire, executive director of the Ex-Students' Association, wrote in the *Alcalde:* "Faced with financial, ethical and legal pressures as never before, it is not surprising that the face of intercollegiate sports may soon change forever. Perhaps, as UT Athletics Council chairman J. Neils Thompson says, 'Intercollegiate athletics, as we know them, will be gone in five to ten years.'" The sky was not really falling, but there were legitimate concerns, and the proper role of athletics in institutions of higher learning received vigorous debate.

In the meantime, Rodney Page was selecting and preparing a 14-member squad that would be the first full-fledged women's basketball team in University of Texas history. He had scholarship funds, carefully apportioned among several returning and new players. The captains were Frances Seidensticker (tallest player on the team at 5'10") and Linda Dvorak, and Cathy Self (a sophomore transfer from Temple JC) was the most promising newcomer. One of the last distinctions between men's and women's basketball was erased when the National Association for Girls and Women in Sport instituted a rule change, going from eight-minute quarters to 20-minute halves, the men's standard for many years.

Of the six home games in the 1975 season, four were stand-alone games at Gregory Gym, not prelims to the UT men. Attendance figures were not made public, but *Daily Texan* and *Austin American-Statesman* stories made clear that the crowds were sparse. There would come a time when the Texas women drew lots of fans but not in the mid-1970s. Another problem with women's college basketball then was the wide disparity in the quality of programs. Some were scarcely further along than June Walker's first team back in 1967, which meant some lopsided scores. Page had no illusions that his 1975 team was a world-beater just because it won the first four games (two against Huston-Tillotson and one each against St. Edward's and Rice) by a margin of 278-80. In one of those games, the team jumped to a 26-0 lead. But there would also

Rita Egger drives on the SWT Xochis in a 1975 game at Gregory Gym. Teammate Jere Thornhill sets a screen for her.

be instances when UT was on the other end of a blowout.

Two last-minute hoops by Self enabled UT to take a 63-62 overtime win against Houston at Hofheinz Pavilion. Page had said his team would have to play "endline to endline for 40 minutes" to beat the taller Cougars, and that is what happened.

The first loss of the season was by the demoralizing score of 116-62, courtesy of Baylor, as Lynnell Pyron and Suzie Snyder combined for 71 points. Self scored 25 for UT. The Bears had a better team and rather enjoyed whomping Texas, but the situation would soon be reversed. Thirty-seven turnovers were too much a week later when the Longhorns dropped a 77-67 overtime game to Southwest Texas (known then as the Xochis) in San Marcos, bringing their record to 5-2. On the same night in Austin, there was a fundraiser for the women's intercollegiate athletic program. A touring women's team, the All-American Redheads, defeated the UT All-Stars, with such luminaries as ex-hoopsters Mike Humphrey and Lynn Howden and football player James Street. The referee of that slightly comical game was mayor-elect Jeff Friedman.

Record: 17-10

68 Huston-Tillotson 17
62 Huston-Tillotson 19
90 St. Edward's 33
58 Rice 11
63 Houston 62 (OT)
62 Baylor 116
67 SW Texas 77 (OT)
88 SMU 53
78 St. Mary's 43
55 SW Texas 49
47 Prairie View A&M 74
58 Texas A&I 57
42 Mississippi College 95
42 West Texas 59
46 SW Texas 78
74 St. Edward's 23
84 St. Mary's 45
72 Houston 48
90 Our Lady of the Lake 24
68 Texas Lutheran 53
61 SW Texas 59
51 SW Texas 58
49 SW Texas 76
51 Baylor 75
70 Houston 67 (OT)
63 Texas A&M 62
53 Lamar 68

Page worked his team on fundamentals like ballhandling, shooting layups and passing after two straight defeats, preceding an 88-53 victory over SMU in Dallas. Self scored 26 points, mostly in the first half, and the Ponies were led by Jane Johnson (24) and Cathy Dale (19). Rita Egger had 23 points in a 78-43 home defeat of St. Mary's, a team that had beaten Texas in the 1974 TAIAW tourney. Self, who scored 12 against the Rattlers, told Andy Yemma of the *Daily Texan* that some "feminine" teams complained about bumping and other forms of rough play, but she was unconcerned. "That's the game," said the 5'8" forward who had played it since fifth grade.

The first tournament of the season was the Southwest Texas Invitational, one Page believed his team might win. They beat the host SWT "B" team on Friday afternoon but fell to Prairie View A&M, 74-47, that night. The Tamplin sisters, Creola and Ceola, combined for 32 points for the winners. In the consolation game, the Horns trailed Texas A&I by 16 points with 18 minutes left and then made a comeback to win in the final seconds. Seidensticker, Pam Smith and Self (on the bench most of the game with an injured ankle) were the key players. "The women showed a lot of character and pride," Page said. "They could have quit, but they didn't." Debbie Nelson had 24 points and 16 rebounds for the Javelinas.

Self did not play at all in the Houston Invitational, and she was missed. Mississippi College, runner-up in the AIAW national tournament the year before, inflicted a 95-42 defeat, and West Texas State won by 17 as UT shot just 26 percent from the field.

The third loss in a row came from Southwest Texas, 78-46, in Austin. Shawna Hicks and Becky Steinmeyer had 18 points each for Judy Rinker's team. The Longhorns then went on a six-game winning streak, with romps over St. Edward's (74-23), St. Mary's (84-45) and Houston (72-48). In the latter game, a prelim before the UT men played Arkansas, Self scored 25, Seidensticker grabbed 16 rebounds, and Dvorak had a lot of assists. Cougar star Cathy Bardwell was out with an injury, but Patricia Dowdell (23 points and 18 rebounds) compensated as best she could. UH coach Marilyn Krause was not happy with the game, saying, "They were fouling the hell out of us and not getting called for it."

With that run of success and Page's emphasis on conditioning and execution, Texas regained momentum in time for the TAIAW zone tourney in San Antonio. The second-seeded team (behind Southwest Texas), UT would be playing five games in three days. Seidensticker, Lorene McClellan and Labob Toles were the top scorers in a 90-24 defeat of Our Lady of the Lake. Accurate free throw shooting (27 of 32) helped beat Texas Lutheran, and one of the season's high points was a 61-59 conquest of SWT. The Xochis had had Texas' number going back several years, so it was a sign of genuine progress by the Longhorns. But that set up a rematch, a 58-51 Southwest Texas victory and then another Xochi win, 76-49, sewing up the zone title for the women from San Marcos. While Self, Seidensticker,

Toles, Egger, Dvorak and Jere Thornhill played well throughout the tournament, UT's opponents chose McClellan as the team MVP. "We have nothing to be ashamed of," said Page, who got a technical foul in the last game in San Antonio. "Our showing in this tournament is a tribute to all the girls on the team. We've beaten a lot of teams with more talent than we have."

Southwest Texas and UT advanced to the TAIAW tournament in Canyon, occasion for another first. The team flew there, a far cry from the self-provided transportation to out-of-town games just a few seasons earlier. Sixteen teams (including Stephen F. Austin and Wayland Baptist's Queen Bees, junior varsity of the Flying Queens) had qualified for the state tourney, which was played at three courts on the West Texas State campus. The Longhorns were quickly bounced, losing to Baylor, 75-51. The Bears' Lynnell Pyron scored 36, while Self led UT with 18. Playing in the consolation bracket, Texas got a 70-67 OT win over Houston when Self tied the game with seven seconds left in regulation and kept the Horns in front from then on. They had to deal with a number of pressure situations to beat Texas A&M by one point, a game Page considered the team's best of the season. But back-to-back emotionally draining games hurt UT in the consolation finals against Lamar. The teams were tied at 53 with four minutes on the clock when the Longhorns lost their shooting touch, falling by a score of 68-53. Carol Sims scored 21 for the Cardinals, and Seidensticker had 13 for UT.

With a record of 17 wins and 10 losses, the inaugural season of varsity women's basketball at the University of Texas was over. While none of the players received votes for the first-ever all-America team, a fine start was made, and they represented their school well. The 1970s were a shaking-out period for women's college basketball as some programs rose and others declined. UT was one of those in ascendance, and the process had already begun.

1976

Of the people new to Austin as the 1976 basketball season approached, two were most notable. Retha Swindell had the size (6'2") and talent to become the first great female player at UT. A dominant rebounder and defender in the two-court game still governing girls' high school basketball in the state, she nevertheless had a lot to learn about shooting and ballhandling. Texas' first black player, Swindell was a big part of the team's success over the next four years. As considerable as her impact was, it occurred only on the basketball court. Dr. Donna Lopiano, on the other hand, in a 17-year stint as athletic director, was responsible for building and shaping the entire women's athletic department. Selected from 40 applicants in the summer of 1975, Lopiano, 28, was a Connecticut native just brimming with confidence, wit and purpose. She had participated in 23 national championship tournaments in softball, basketball, volleyball and field hockey and possessed master's and doctoral degrees from Southern California. The former associate athletic director at Brooklyn College vowed to have every Longhorn women's team ranked in the top 10 and at least one national title within five years. A strong advocate and future president of the AIAW, Lopiano was on the front lines of women who made sure Title IX was enforced to the letter. She possessed enough intellect and personality to seem intimidating to some people on the Forty Acres, but Darrell Royal (who had recently told President Gerald Ford that Title IX might be the death of big-time college football) and J. Neils Thompson approved of the headstrong whiz kid during the interview process. Shortly after her arrival in Austin, Lopiano gave a Rotary Club speech entitled "Does women's athletics mean trouble for Darrell and UT?" She assured everyone that it did not, although changes were inevitable.

The new AD had high expectations, and those lacking such a commitment would not be around for long. Coach Rodney Page gave no indication of feeling pressure; with Swindell joining Cathy Self Steinle, Lorene McClellan, Rita Egger and other returnees, the 1976 basketball team was likely to be the best yet. The Longhorns were the first to wear modern uniforms, with TEXAS emblazoned on their jerseys.

Steinle scored 20 points in the season opener, a 57-47 defeat of Southwest Texas in San Marcos. Terri Anderegg had 16 for the Bobcats, who were no longer called the Xochis. Page claimed his team would have lost if not for its defensive work, and defeat is just what happened in the next three games against Baylor (92-50), Trinity (67-66) and San Jacinto JC (61-48). Sickness and injury had something to do with that little swoon, which was followed immediately by a 12-game winning streak. It began in Houston with a 78-19 slaughter of Rice and a defensive battle against UH that ended with the Longhorns up, 58-52. Cathy Bardwell, the Cougars' 6'3" ace, scored 29 points, six more than Steinle.

The first home game of the season and the only prelim to the Longhorn men (who faced Arkansas) was against Wharton Junior College on January 20. Page's team jumped to a big early lead and coasted to a 67-48 victory. Steinle and Egger combined for 43 points, and the bench responded well when Swindell got in foul trouble.

Other than what he read in the newspaper or picked up here and there, Page knew nothing about upcoming opponents. While he lacked the resources to do scouting, that was hardly necessary when the team went to Fort Worth to play TCU and Texas Wesleyan. The Horned Frogs croaked, 74-31, but TWC put up more of a fight before losing by 10. Swindell, Steinle and Egger were the top scorers, and Page complimented the play of frosh guard Marietta Hildebrandt.

Swindell blocked Texas A&M star Cissy Auclair's first shot and finished with 21 points and 10 rebounds in a 55-49 win at Gregory Gym. Auclair led the Ags with 23 points. Three days later, UT hosted the first college basketball tournament in the 46-year history of the old gym on Speedway. The Texas Classic was a Friday and Saturday affair, and the Longhorns were rude hosts, winning their own tourney and extending their winning streak to eight. In victories over Trinity (86-52) and Southwest Texas (57-43), Swindell was fabulous, scoring 53 points, getting 20 rebounds and blocking 15 shots.

She was not the only reason Texas women's basketball had come so far. There were a number of factors, Page told Dan Couture of the *Daily Texan*. "To build a class program," he said, "you have to have a good organizational structure, an organized athletic department. Then, without a doubt, there must be talent. Number three is to have a good coach, someone who has the capacity to deal with people. And fourth, it takes money and scholarships.... The fifth thing is intangible. It's character and pride. To an extent that's the nucleus of your program. It's the thing that keeps people performing when they're tired. It's a certain feeling, and it can be as important as money in building a program."

Such qualities were needed when the Horns came from behind to beat Texas A&M, 43-42, at G. Rollie White Coliseum. The place was nearly full of vocal Aggie fans for a game between the respective men's teams when Hildebrandt hit two winning free throws. After that win, UT took a couple of easy ones at home against McLennan JC (73-50) and St. Mary's (72-24). Egger and Steinle were the top scorers.

Lorene McClellan leads a fast break against Rice at Autry Court.

Page was a little upset that his team was not among those seeded—and getting a first-round bye—in the 22nd annual Houston Invitational. But when Trinity withdrew, giving Texas a forfeit victory, the point was moot. Thirty-four percent free throw shooting hurt the Longhorns, who lost for the first time in a month as Panola JC took a 49-45 decision. Texas A&M got revenge for two previous defeats by Texas, winning by four. And in UT's last game of the tourney (won by Mississippi College), Steinle scored 29 in a 62-43 defeat of Prairie View A&M. As the team departed Houston, Page said, "Win or lose, we still play with pride."

The final home game and the final game of the regular season was an 84-34 trouncing of Texas Lutheran, host of the TAIAW zone tourney in late February. As the Longhorns prepared for that and the state tourney in Nacogdoches, Lopiano made a surprise announcement: Rodney Page would not be back as coach in 1977. Explaining it primarily in financial and administrative terms, Lopiano said one full-time coach was needed for basketball and volleyball. And since Page was not versed in volleyball, he had to be replaced, although he could keep his job in the physical education department. Lopiano also intimated that he was not the hoop coach to make Texas a national contender. "Rod's had his place in our program, but it's a sign that we've gotten as much as we've got," she said. "He's done a super job and is one of the best human relations coaches I've ever met."

Record: 21-7

57 SW Texas 47
50 Baylor 92
66 Trinity 67
48 San Jacinto JC 61
78 Rice 19
58 Houston 52
67 Wharton JC 48
74 TCU 31
66 Texas Wesleyan 56
55 Texas A&M 49
86 Trinity 52
57 SW Texas 43
43 Texas A&M 42
73 McLennan JC 50
72 St. Mary's 24
Trinity, victory by forfeit
45 Panola JC 49
54 Texas A&M 58
62 Prairie View A&M 43
84 Texas Lutheran 34
63 St. Mary's 35
38 SW Texas 35
39 SW Texas 47
54 SW Texas 41
31 Abilene Christian 67
86 Tarleton 60
66 North Texas 60 (OT)
57 West Texas 53

Page, who had raised UT women's basketball considerably in three seasons with a fraction of the resources soon made available, was stunned to hear the news. His players were quite displeased if not incredulous, and seniors Lorene McClellan and Rita Egger, who had little to lose, openly defended Page. Articles and letters printed in the *Daily Texan* followed the same line. However, Lopiano was not one to hesitate in making a tough call, and it had been made. Page was a lame-duck coach when he took his team to Seguin for the zone tournament. The Longhorns made short work of St. Mary's and then won two of three with Southwest Texas to advance to the state tourney. Swindell and Steinle combined for 37 points in the last game with the Bobcats.

As the Page controversy simmered, UT headed for the Piney Woods of east Texas, where Stephen F. Austin hosted the 1976 TAIAW meet. But the Longhorns were quickly shunted to the consolation bracket. They shot 23 percent and trailed Abilene Christian by 24 at the half, losing, 67-31. Teresa Rubart had 23 points for the Wildcats. Texas came back with three victories, the first by 26 points over Tarleton State, in which Steinle scored 31. She, Egger, Hildebrandt and Swindell reached double figures in a 66-60 overtime defeat of North Texas. And in their fourth game in two days, the Horns edged West Texas, 57-53. They compiled a 21-7 record and finished fifth in the state.

Page declined an offer to serve as assistant to whomever Lopiano hired. In separate meetings with her, President Lorene Rogers, and Dr. Ronald Brown (vice president for student affairs, the office that oversaw all matters pertaining to intercollegiate athletics), Page made clear his belief that he had been treated unfairly and the whole matter handled with little discernment. Publicly, he refused to rip Lopiano, but his feelings were well articulated. In three seasons covering 73 games, Page had always emphasized effort and team play over just victories and defeats, and yet he put the program on an unmistakable upward plane, going from seven wins to 17 to 21. The University of Texas had fired a lot of basketball coaches over the years but never one with the record compiled by Rodney Page. Lopiano, the woman on the hot seat, did not flinch. To her, it was one of the "conflicts and compromises characteristic of most change processes" she had predicted when she got to Austin less than 12 months earlier.

1977

Donna Lopiano was certain about who she wanted to run the Texas women's basketball team. She began to woo Jody Conradt of UT-Arlington in December 1975 and announced her selection two days after Rodney Page coached his last game. "I've been talking to a lot of coaches from around the state, and they all keep telling me how lucky we are to get her," said Lopiano, who fended off complaints of gender and racial bias in the whole matter. Conradt, who would be UT's first full-time women's coach, was indeed highly regarded by her colleagues.

A native of Goldthwaite, Conradt scored 41 points per game in high school and played on the extramural team at Baylor, where she earned bachelor's and master's degrees. Her coaching career began at a high school in Waco, followed by four years at Sam Houston State. She handled basketball (compiling a 74-23 record), volleyball and track and moved to UT-Arlington in 1973 to build a women's athletic department from scratch. Maverick basketball (23-11 in 1976), volleyball and softball kept Conradt plenty busy, so coaching two sports, basketball and volleyball, at Texas would be comparatively easy. When she arrived, the Special Events Center was approaching completion, but the University had given no indication if or when women's basketball games would be held there. For all Conradt or Lopiano knew, Gregory Gym (with a seating capacity of 7,800, far more than women's games would need for several years) might have to suffice while the men performed at the new facility beginning in the 1978 season.

Conradt could recall playing and coaching against Longhorn teams during the extramural and UTSA days when Anna Hiss' influence remained evident. For a few seasons, the teams had performed in skirts and were as concerned with gentility as with competition. That go-slow policy at the state's flagship institution tended to hide its potential, which Page had begun to fulfill, and the boss lady, Lopiano, was surely a believer in playing to win. Conradt took the opportunity to help Lopiano build a model program. Fully aware of the controversy awaiting her in Austin, Conradt met with the players, including the seniors of Page's last team. "It doesn't bother me that the players felt loyalty to their former coach," she said after that April 1976 confab. "I just asked them to please have an open mind." Page, who had known Conradt for several years, professed no animosity and foresaw no problems. "They're big people and big players," he said. "She's spoken with all of them and feels there'll be a period of adjustment. A coach is a coach."

The coach—and her graduate assistant, Marti Fuquay—had some fine players on the 1977 team. Retha Swindell and Cathy Steinle were back, joined by Kim Basinger (who came with Conradt from UT-Arlington), Linda Andrews (an Angelo State transfer), Cathy Burns of Weatherford JC and others. Conradt's volleyball season was nearing an end when basketball got started. Of course, no one at the time knew that she would stay for 20-plus seasons, generating so many victories, championships and all-Americans. Her first UT team played a whopping 46 games, the first of which was a 72-58 defeat of McLennan JC in Waco. Burns scored 26 points before fouling out. Conradt's Austin debut was a winner, too, a 71-46 defeat of Southwest Texas in a prelim to the UT men and Oklahoma State. It was apparent early on that the team members were a compatible group who played hard (although they shot just 38 percent for the season). They liked Conradt, but some were slow to master her demanding defensive game. Jackie Swaim, a future Longhorn player, scored 19 for McLennan JC in a Gregory Gym rematch, but Swindell (22 points, 16 rebounds and some defensive intimidation) was even better in an 86-81 win. "Retha was absolutely super," Conradt said. "There's no limit to how good she can be."

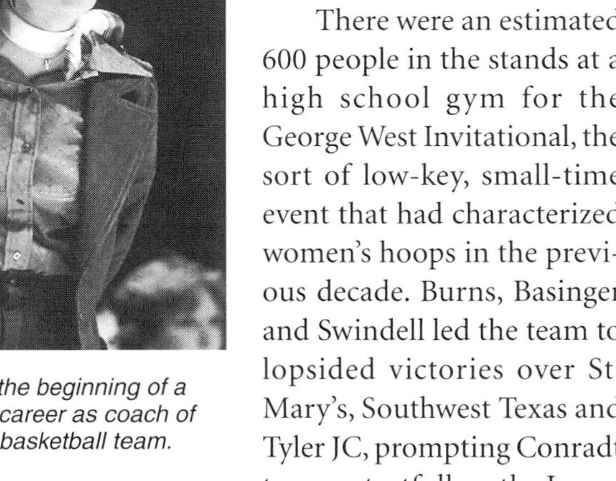

Jody Conradt at the beginning of a long and storied career as coach of the UT women's basketball team.

There were an estimated 600 people in the stands at a high school gym for the George West Invitational, the sort of low-key, small-time event that had characterized women's hoops in the previous decade. Burns, Basinger and Swindell led the team to lopsided victories over St. Mary's, Southwest Texas and Tyler JC, prompting Conradt to say—tactfully—the Longhorns needed stiffer competition. They jumped to a big lead at home against Trinity, allowing substitute Nancy Olsen (12) to be the top scorer in a 55-38 victory. Jill Harenburg had 20 for the Tigers.

Conradt had to shift gears in early December. While her Texas basketball team took a break, her volleyball team played in the AIAW national tournament, which Lopiano arranged to hold at Gregory Gym over a four-day span. Although Lopiano detested country and western music, she hired two C&W bands to entertain fans before, between and after matches. Because of poor marketing and an overall lack of experience in putting on such events, however, the tournament was a financial disaster and an embarrassment to Lopiano, who was told by her UT superiors not to let it happen again.

Two weeks after the last basketball game and two weeks before the next one, Texas took on Baylor in Austin. Olga Fallen's Bears had lost just two of 10 games (to national powers UCLA and Wayland Baptist) and were averaging 90 points per game. Their last three times against the Horns, they had won by 54, 24 and 43 points. After a high school prelim, UT scored a 66-64 upset behind 18 points from Basinger and 14 from Alisha Nelson. "If you can shoot well from the outside, you can play against the Boston Celtics," Conradt said.

In the fall, Conradt had taken the volleyball team on a trip to California and Hawaii, getting some hard-earned experience in the process. That was also the idea behind the first out-of-state trip for a Texas women's basketball team. Some of the players enjoyed or endured their first airplane flight to the northeast to take part in five games over seven days. They economized by staying at the home of Lopiano's parents in Stamford, Connecticut. The first game, against No. 15 Queens College, went poorly. Donna Geils scored 24 points as the Knights roared to a 60-37 win. Texas then traveled to central Pennsylvania to play in the Penn State Invitational. At the scene of the 1976 national tourney, Conradt's Longhorns played two fine games. They got a combined 38 points from Swindell and Burns and forced 23 turnovers in beating Penn State, 77-72. Halley Bunk had 19 points for the Lions. Texas won the tournament with a 75-64 defeat of Southern Connecticut, Lopiano's alma mater. Burns (19 points and 15 rebounds) was chosen as the meet's MVP. That surprise showing got the attention of Mel Greenberg, who covered women's basketball and conducted a weekly poll for the *Philadelphia Inquirer*. Lopiano told him, "The people at the University of Texas are making a commitment to go first class and give the women whatever it takes to be the best."

Record: 36-10

72 McLennan JC 58
71 SW Texas 46
86 McLennan JC 81
79 St. Mary's 27
64 SW Texas 44
69 Tyler JC 51
55 Trinity 38
66 Baylor 64
37 Queens 60
77 Penn State 72
75 Southern Connecticut 64
66 Montclair State 91
62 Immaculata 71
79 SMU 58
89 Texas Tech 54
110 Houston 84
100 SMU 60
96 Texas Tech 69
73 Wayland Baptist 97
83 Houston 63
72 SE Louisiana 83
63 Angelo State 40
79 Texas A&M 73
88 UT-Arlington 71
87 McLennan JC 75
64 Baylor 83
94 SW Texas 56
85 Prairie View A&M 43
84 Louisiana Tech 59
64 Baylor 70
87 Nevada-Las Vegas 81
94 Houston 58
95 Baylor 98 (OT)
80 Texas A&M 74
76 Texas Lutheran 51
72 Trinity 61
82 SW Texas 54
90 Texas Tech 72
64 Houston 63
73 Wayland Baptist 80
84 Baylor 78
86 UT-Arlington 64
67 LSU 95
80 Oklahoma State 79
109 Houston 77
94 Louisiana Tech 85

Maybe some day. The Longhorns still had games against Montclair State (in New Jersey) and Immaculata (in suburban Philadelphia), both contenders for the AIAW crown. Conradt replaced captain Cathy Steinle with Nelson to get more speed and ballhandling in the lineup, but Nelson and her teammates were helpless against the Indians' Carol Blazejowski, one of the finest players of the 1970s. She was well on her way to 49 points in an easy 91-66 win when Lopiano approached Conradt on the bench and suggested she "find somebody to cover that number 12." And the Horns led Immaculata most of the way before falling, 71-62. Basinger scored 25 against the second-ranked Mighty Macs. After getting a taste of fast and rough eastern hoops, UT flew to Dallas and beat SMU by 19 in a prelim to the men's game. When the Longhorn entourage got back to Austin, they learned of a big first in the history of the program: Greenberg's poll had Texas No. 14 in the nation.

The first-ever meeting of Texas and Texas Tech in women's basketball took place at Gregory Gym on January 15 after the men had played a Saturday afternoon TV game. Andrews made a number of steals, propelling UT to a 17-2 lead, and Burns (22) used her deadly hook shot to beat the Red Raiders, 89-54. The Horns had never broken the century mark until they took 110-84 and 100-60 wins over Houston and SMU, respectively. Conradt knew building a fan base would require good rivalries with Southwest Conference schools, although the SWC then took no note of women's athletics. The problem was, only Baylor and to a lesser extent Texas A&M or Houston could give

Texas serious competition. Rice and TCU would not get back on the Longhorns' schedule until 1983.

The team took a trip to west Texas, first beating Texas Tech, 96-69, behind Andrews' 22 points. Swindell did not play due to an ankle injury, but she was needed the next night when the Horns met No. 1 Wayland Baptist at Hutcherson Arena in Plainview. The Queens had played an important role in women's college basketball since the late 1940s with scholarships, world tours and several AAU championships. Thanks largely to the generosity of Claude Hutcherson, they had built a colorful and winning legacy while UT and other schools were still contemplating intercollegiate athletics for women. The Queens came out flying, making 60 percent of their field goals in a thorough 97-73 victory. Breena Caldwell had 26 points for Wayland Baptist, three less than Burns. "We were awful the entire night defensively," Conradt said. "Nothing worked. We went in feeling Wayland Baptist was superior. Our players grew up hearing about them." But Queen coach Dean Weese knew his team would have to contend with Texas in the future.

Eight teams, including No. 4 Stephen F. Austin, gathered at Gregory Gym for the three-day Texas Classic. The Longhorns beat Houston by 20 in front of 200 fans but lost to Southeastern Louisiana, 83-72, and missed their chance to play the SFA Ladyjacks, winners of the tournament. In a sloppy, error-filled game for third place, Texas defeated Angelo State, 63-40. Basinger made six steals, and Andrews connected on several long-distance shots.

Basinger, Swindell and Burns did most of the scoring in a 79-73 win over Texas A&M, running UT's record to 18-5. The Horns, the top seed in the Baylor Invitational, got 27 points from Andrews in an 88-71 defeat of UT-Arlington, Conradt's former team. And Swindell poured in 30 in an easy victory over McLennan JC, but the host Bears took the title game, 83-64, because Texas turned the ball over 20 times and could not stop Suzie Eppers (29).

After a 94-56 thumping of SWT in San Marcos, it was time for the Houston Invitational. In morning and afternoon games, the Horns beat Prairie View A&M by 42 and Louisiana Tech by 25. The Techsters, like UT, were not yet the great team they would later become. In the semifinal game, Texas pulled to within four of Baylor in the last minute, but the Bears held on to win. Andrews scored 32 points to lead UT to an 87-81 defeat of No. 11 Nevada-Las Vegas for third place in the tourney. Swindell also had a nice game, causing Conradt to say, "She's the best defensive player her size I've ever seen, and it's not because of my coaching."

Burns scored 21 and Basinger 17 in the last home game of the season, a 94-58 defeat of Houston. Steinle, the captain who no longer had a starting job, came off the bench to score 10 points and collect eight rebounds. No. 16 Baylor got 31 points from all-American Suzie Eppers in a 98-95 OT win at Heart O' Texas Coliseum in which Burns (25), Basinger (22) and Swindell all fouled out. That was the last time Texas lost to BU until 1994. And in College Station, the Longhorns defeated Texas A&M by just six because the subs allowed Sally Morisse, Pat Bond and the rest of the Ags to close a big lead. The game was a tuneup for the TAIAW zone tourney in Kingsville, which featured competition Conradt admitted was "pretty weak."

It was so weak that Conradt entrusted the team to her assistant, Marti Fuquay, while she stayed in Austin to watch the UIL girls' tournament and recruit. Basinger was the key offensive performer in successive wins over Texas Lutheran (76-51), Trinity (72-61) and Southwest Texas (82-54).

Sixteen teams qualified for the TAIAW state meet, hosted by Pan American and played in the hot, humid Edinburg High School gym. Realistically, however, only four teams had much chance to move into regionals—Wayland Baptist, Stephen F. Austin, Baylor and Texas. With everything to lose and nothing to gain, the Horns beat Texas Tech by 18 and Houston by one, setting up a game with Wayland Baptist. "It'll take a super effort to win," Conradt said. Led by Burns, UT was up by two points at the half, but when Swindell fouled out, hopes for a victory sank as the Queens triumphed, 80-73. Texas stormed back the next day and beat Baylor, 84-78, despite 30 points by the Bruins' Babette Metcalf. Swindell, at her best when it counted most, had 18 points and 22 rebounds.

Third place in the state tourney sent Conradt's No. 18 Longhorns to Monroe, Louisiana, scene of the regional meet. Four players were sick, but Texas had little trouble beating UT-Arlington by 22 points. Burns had 25 and Nelson, known more for her defensive work, scored 20. Mary Weems (20) paced the Mavs. Any thoughts of reaching the national tournament in Minneapolis ended with a 95-67 loss to LSU. Maree Bennie, the Tigers' Australian center, rang up 36 points, while Basinger led UT with 17. Out of the running, the

Longhorns played three consolation games, beating Oklahoma State (80-79), Houston (109-77) and Louisiana Tech (94-85). Burns scored 18, 32 and 31 points in those games.

Not so many years earlier, female basketball players had been warned not to play or practice more than twice a week, lest they suffer physical and emotional harm. And that was with the placid half-court game. Jody Conradt's first Longhorn team had played 46 full-court games, winning 36 of them, with no appreciable damage. Texas was building a powerful women's hoop program, but so were other schools.

1978

Beginning in 1978 and repeating the theme almost annually for the next decade, American media announced that women's basketball had "arrived." It was the year all colleges and universities participating in intercollegiate athletics were supposed to be in compliance with Title IX, the subject of numerous court battles. Justifying the fears of the Anna Hiss generation and later true believers in the ideals of the AIAW, money had propelled the women's game out of infancy and into a tumultuous adolescence. Female athletes were recruited, earned scholarships and played before increasingly large crowds, and the fans were seeing a more physical and sophisticated game than ever before, not a polite and pallid imitation of what the men could do. In the 1978 season, women would play stand-alone games (those not piggybacked on a men's game) in such venues as the Louisiana Superdome, Madison Square Garden and the Spectrum in Philadelphia. For the first time, the AIAW championship game would be nationally televised, albeit on a delayed basis. Big-enrollment, big-budget schools like North Carolina State, Tennessee, LSU, UCLA and Maryland were starting to take over women's college basketball from the small schools (such as Wayland Baptist, Queens, Immaculata and Delta State) that had gotten an early jump in the sport.

The pulse of change was also beating at Texas, where the $37-million Special Events Center was about to open. Damond Benningfield of the *Daily Texan* wrote a 12-part series on Longhorn women's athletics, starting with the laid-back days of the UT Sports Association and coming forward to 1978. He laid out the problems and controversies along the way but commended women's AD Donna Lopiano, who had pushed, shoved and dragged the program into national prominence. Benningfield also made clear the pressure and expectations on Jody Conradt, who coached the centerpiece sport of basketball. Volleyball (which she gave up after two seasons), tennis, swimming, track and other sports had their adherents, but basketball was the one that really needed to flourish.

Conradt's second team, ranked No. 20 in the preseason, had a fine newcomer, 6' Nell Fortner, a high school all-American from New Braunfels. But with all five starters (Retha Swindell, Cathy Burns, Linda Andrews Waggoner, Kim Basinger and Alisha Nelson) back, Fortner would have trouble getting serious playing time. "They've got a real good team, and I deserve to sit on the bench," she said. "I know I've got a lot to learn."

Frank Erwin, former chairman of the UT Board of Regents, was the person most responsible for getting the Super Drum (soon renamed in his honor) built. While the facility would fulfill many needs, foremost in Erwin's mind was that the Longhorns would finally have a fitting place to hold basketball games. The building's conception and design presumed one Texas hoop team, composed of males. Since that time, the women had gained a solid footing and deserved to play in the 16,231-seat arena, too. Although the men had played their last game in Gregory Gym, the women had occasional games there as late as 1983.

At 5:15 p.m., Tuesday, November 29, 1977 (two hours and fifteen minutes before the Texas-Oklahoma men's game), the Longhorns and Temple Junior College tipped off in the first basketball game ever held in the new building. The players had to adjust to lighting and depth perception that were quite different from old Gregory Gym. Swindell and Basinger both scored 19 points in a close 67-64 victory, and Conradt was so impressed with the Leopards' outside burners, Hattie Browning and Evwella Munn, that she decided to recruit them at the end of the season.

Defending champion of the George West Invitational, UT routed Pan American, 94-49, and Texas A&I,

75-35, before meeting Tyler JC in the finals. Bonnie Buchanan scored 29 points for the Apaches, who fell, 74-72. Burns, Basinger, Swindell and Tina Duncan all reached double figures. The tourney was enlivened by a one-on-one contest won by Swindell.

Dana Craft, one of Conradt's players while at Sam Houston, brought her Southwest Texas team to Austin for a prelim to the UT men and LSU. The SWT women, once well in advance of Texas, saw the situation had been reversed. Craft's team trailed, 28-0, after eight minutes and lost, 86-51. Basinger scored 22 for the Horns and Pat Gamble 17 for the Bobcats. The fabled Wayland Baptist Flying Queens made their first Austin visit, arriving in town in two private airplanes. The No. 1 team in the country had an 8-0 record and fine players like Jill Rankin, Marie Kocurek, Breena Caldwell and Kathy Harston, all of whom would get some kind of all-America consideration before their careers ended. The Texas women had the Super Drum to themselves for the first time, and their athletic department had to pay the rental fee otherwise covered by the men. Girls' teams from LBJ and Reagan high schools played the prelim game, and then the Queens and Longhorns came onto the court. The visitors from Plainview put on some flashy pregame drills designed to wow the crowd and their opponents. Wayland Baptist got 22 points from Rankin and won the game, 82-70, but UT played well, especially Swindell (19 points and 18 rebounds). Approximately 1,400 fans were there, so the Super Drum was not quite the giant echo chamber it might have been.

In contrast, the Longhorns' home game a week later against Houston was a prelim to the men. When the women took the floor in their burnt-orange warmups, perhaps 50 people were scattered throughout the yawning facility. The situation was not so discouraging, however, because the basketball excitement Abe Lemons' men were generating could only help the women. As for the UT-UH game, the Horns won, 97-86. Swindell scored 29 points, and Burns came out of a slump with 24, while Sharion Higgins had 23 for the Cougars. It was a physical encounter, with some rough play under the boards. But Conradt did not mind because her team was soon to return to the northeast proving grounds with eight games in five cities over 11 days. "You've got to go where the competition is when you're interested in building a top program," she said. "I'll consider the trip a success if we return with a .500 record."

Record: 29-10
67 Temple JC 64
94 Pan American 49
75 Texas A&I 35
74 Tyler JC 72
86 SW Texas 51
70 Wayland Baptist 82
97 Houston 86
89 St. Joseph's 85
79 Southern Connecticut 78
96 Penn State 67
58 Montclair State 102
100 Central Connecticut 52
91 Springfield 60
75 St. John's 41
81 Southern Connecticut 82
52 Texas A&M 59
95 Angelo State 46
81 North Texas 57
75 Stephen F. Austin 54
107 SW Texas 55
82 Houston 80
89 Temple JC 94
86 Texas A&M 60
66 Wayland Baptist 81
87 SMU 30
83 Texas Lutheran 36
94 Trinity 49
84 Texas A&M 56
106 Baylor 74
93 Stephen F. Austin 78
76 Wayland Baptist 98
85 Southern 69
78 Stephen F. Austin 80
80 Baylor 73
95 Houston 84
84 Oral Roberts 100
91 Minnesota 56
75 Kentucky 60
60 Old Dominion 70

It began in Philadelphia with an 89-85 victory over No. 8 St. Joseph's. Burns had 30 points and 14 rebounds, but the fate of the game lay in the hands of freshman Janie Denton, who made three pressure-packed free throws despite a noisy, partisan crowd. Mary Sue Garrity scored 16 for the Hawks. In the opener of the Penn State Invitational, Texas jumped to a 14-point lead and held on for a 79-78 win over No. 12 Southern Connecticut. The Horns outrebounded the Owls, 50-36, and got a combined 46 points from Swindell and Waggoner. SC's burly center, Marnie Dacko, scored 29. Although Conradt criticized her players on some technical points, she was bursting with pride over their conditioning and attitude. They proceeded to skewer the tourney host, No. 13 Penn State, by 29 points the next day, taking the trophy for the second straight year. Waggoner hit 16 of 23 from the field, totaling 35 points (and was chosen MVP), while Jen Bednarek had 20 for the Lions.

The Longhorns took a bus through drizzle and fog to reach Upper Montclair, New Jersey, hoping to extinguish "the Blaze," Carol Blazejowski, who was then averaging 39 points per game. The winner of the first Wade Trophy, symbolic of the nation's top female college basketball player, she led Montclair State to a scorching 102-58 victory on a night when nothing went right for Texas. "Thank God," she said after the game. "I'm just so glad we won. We had heard about them."

But the resilient Longhorns came back 24 hours later and put a 100-52 defeat on Central Connecticut. Because the starters got pulled early, Fortner (18) had the best game of her young career. From New Britain, the group went on to New Haven, where Southern Connecticut hosted a tourney. UT breezed by Springfield, 91-60, and St. John's, 75-41, before meeting the SC Owls for the second time on the trip. Marnie Dacko and Joan Van Ness teamed up for 46 points in an 82-81 defeat of their guests from the Lone Star State. The Horns returned home, victors in six of eight games, their bodies, emotions and national rankings having gone up and down repeatedly. It was a long and difficult trip, but for experience, recruiting and media exposure, it had been worthwhile. "They beat some eastern powers in their own ruffian-style play," wrote Lynn Flocke of the *Austin American-Statesman.* "In the east, the hack is apparently not a foul unless the refs think it impedes the ballhandler's progress."

Bad weather caused the cancelation of a game with SMU in Dallas and later, games with Texas Tech in Lubbock and Austin. Conradt's Longhorns had not played in nine days when they encountered Texas A&M in College Station. They found that the spirit of Aggieland does not discriminate on the basis of sex as a boisterous throng there mostly for the men's game cheered the maroon and white to a 59-52 victory. "The crowd made all the difference," said Ag coach Wanda Bender. Her star guard, Von Bunn (25), was the game's top scorer. Other than a disappointing loss to a big rival, no one thought too much about the Texas A&M game. It later gained significance because UT proceeded to defeat Southwest Conference teams (although women's competition was not yet a part of the SWC) 183 consecutive times, a streak that lasted until 1990. The Horns were becoming the conference bully.

Another first was recorded when the women had their own game programs during the Texas Classic in late January. Super Drum officials were surprised to see that Southeastern Louisiana, one of the teams in the tournament, had a radio broadcaster for the folks back home. Lopiano took note and began working on a similar arrangement for the Longhorns, who coasted by Angelo State and North Texas. Crowds at the early games were meager, but 2,000 people showed up for the title game between Texas and Stephen F. Austin. "They took us to the cleaners tonight," moaned Ladyjack coach Sue Gunter after her 15th-ranked team fell to the No. 12 Longhorns, 75-54. Basinger, who had matured into a fine player despite being half a step slow, scored 27 points and defended well against SFA star D.K. Thomas.

Retha Swindell, Texas' great post player of the late 1970s.

After a 52-point destruction of SWT in San Marcos, the team won an 82-80 thriller against the Houston Cougars at Hofheinz Pavilion. Waggoner scored 32 points, but the hero was Basinger, whose 15-foot jumper swished through at the buzzer, raising the Horns' record to 17-4. Ann Moon had 25 points for Dot Woodfin's team, which had closed an 11-point gap in the last three minutes only to have Basinger steal a victory. Woodfin was upset when Conradt pulled her team out of the Houston Invitational, but the Texas coach did not want to play two games within six hours, which would have been necessary in a 16-team tournament held over two days.

In something that was already becoming a rarity and would end entirely after the 1981 season, the Longhorns played a junior college team. Temple, ranked fourth in the national JC poll, got 34 points from Evwella Munn and beat Texas, 94-89.

Back in Austin, the Horns entertained Texas A&M. Von Bunn, whose sharp shooting and ballhandling had spurred the Aggies to a seven-point victory three weeks before, sprained an ankle early in the game and was not a factor. Waggoner (22) and Basinger (14) led UT to an 86-60 win, one of the team's finest performances of the 1978 season. The Longhorns needed their best when they met Wayland Baptist in Plainview. The Flying Queens were coming off a defeat of three-time national champion Delta State. Jill Rankin and Marie Kocurek combined for 37 points and 21 rebounds in beating UT, 81-66. "We played pretty well," Conradt said, "but when you play here, you need a supreme effort to win."

Three days after ripping a young SMU team, 87-30, Texas began postseason play. The TAIAW zone tournament was held at a once-familiar site, Gregory Gym. The Longhorns were prohibitive favorites to win and move on, and that is just what happened, although two starters were out with illness and injury. Fortner (22) led the scoring in an 83-36 defeat of Texas Lutheran, and Waggoner (20) did it in beating Trinity, 94-49.

Competition was expected to be much tougher at the state meet in San Angelo, but Conradt's team just kept winning. Waggoner poured in 29 points, and Burns, who had had an uneven senior season, got 19 points and 15 rebounds in an 84-56 defeat of Texas A&M. The next morning, the Horns beat Baylor by 32 points as Conradt showed her ex-coach, Olga Fallen, how it was done. Basinger scored 28 points, and Mamie Mauch had 24 for the Bears. And in the evening, UT came from behind to beat Stephen F. Austin, 93-78. But in the tourney finals against Wayland Baptist, Burns and Waggoner got in foul trouble, and the Longhorns fell behind and lost to the Queens, 98-76. "We were mismatched at every position," Conradt said. "The only thing I could think to do was call the fire department, and I don't think there's any water in west Texas."

Nevertheless, UT qualified for the regional tournament in Nacogdoches, home of the SFA Ladyjacks. The Horns committed 25 turnovers but shot 53 percent in downing Southern, 85-69. Stephen F. Austin, a loser to Texas just six days earlier in San Angelo, took an 80-78 victory as D.K. Thomas (Swindell's high school teammate) scored 34. Conradt, eager to reach the national tournament, was terribly disappointed to have her team in the consolation bracket and considered dropping out. The Horns continued playing, however, and sailed past Baylor, 80-73, and Houston, 95-84, in one day. Waggoner had 26 points against the Bears and Basinger 22 against the Cougars. Rhonda Penquite (37) and her teammates shot 67 percent as Oral Roberts pinned a 100-84 defeat on UT in the last game in Nacogdoches.

Although Conradt's 27-9 team did not make the big tournament, they received a bid to the 10th annual National Women's Invitational Tournament. An eight-team affair that originated in West Chester, Pennsylvania and later moved to Amarillo, the NWIT had been won the previous year by Wayland Baptist, but the Flying Queens had reached the AIAW nationals in 1978. Just as the NIT (which the UT men were competing in and eventually winning) hardly rivaled the NCAA tourney, nor did the NWIT claim to crown a true national champion. There were some strong teams in Amarillo, however. In the first round, Waggoner scored 23 points and Basinger had 13 assists in a 91-56 waxing of Minnesota. Someone counted 15 blocked shots or deflected passes by Swindell in a 75-60 defeat of Kentucky, setting up a March 18 title clash between Texas and Old Dominion. The Monarchs' two stars—6'5" Inge Nissen of Denmark and Nancy Lieberman, a streetball artist who had been the youngest member of the 1976 U.S. Olympic team—combined for 43 points in beating Texas, 70-60. The Longhorns finished the season ranked 15th in the nation.

1979

Lynn Flocke, the first University of Texas women's sports information director, prepared the first basketball media guide, a glossy 18-page booklet. With the program entering its fifth year, enough history had been made to merit a listing of team and individual records, a review of the preceding 29-10 season and the outlook for 1979. The cover featured Linda Waggoner, Kim Basinger and Retha Swindell in uniform outside of the Super Drum, the big marquee along Interstate 35 reading TEXAS WOMEN'S BASKETBALL.

The Longhorns would be deeper and more talented than ever before, with enough speed to play the pressing, fast-break offense coach Jody Conradt favored. She recruited two guards from Temple Junior College, Hattie Browning and Evwella Munn, and a center, Jackie Swaim, from McLennan JC. The new players fit in quickly on a team ranked No. 11 in preseason. Due in part to weak competition, Texas put up some big numbers early on, beginning with a 108-36 scrimmage win over Sam Houston in which the Gregory Gym scoreboard was turned off in the second half as a gesture of sportsmanship. And in the first four games of the year, the Horns outscored their opponents by more than a two-to-one margin.

Record: 37-4

124 UT-El Paso 48
86 UT-Arlington 30
81 North Texas 49
100 SW Texas 59
60 Tennessee 84
90 California-Fullerton 72
94 Temple JC 60
114 Minnesota 53
103 SMU 42
69 Wayland Baptist 64
83 St. Joseph's 68
89 Ohio State 59
76 Penn State 69
76 Houston 62
76 Wayland Baptist 81
91 Texas Tech 68
60 Wayland Baptist 52
75 Texas A&M 41
88 Baylor 54
89 UT-Arlington 34
84 North Texas 48
72 Stephen F. Austin 69
82 Houston 52
82 SW Texas 45
102 Temple JC 62
86 SW Louisiana 40
93 Texas Southern 58
71 Houston 47
73 Texas A&M 48
95 Baylor 67
96 Texas Tech 48
80 Texas Tech 52
102 Baylor 60
93 Houston 68
59 Stephen F. Austin 70
96 UCLA 78
69 North Texas 48
76 Oklahoma State 63
77 Oral Roberts 68
74 Louisiana Tech 77
65 Stephen F. Austin 60

There were mismatches against UT-El Paso (124-48), UT-Arlington (86-30) and North Texas (81-49) in which the subs played nearly as much as the starters. "I thought they'd give us more of a test," Conradt said. "Playing in the Super Drum is sort of an awesome feeling. When people come in for the first time, it seems to throw them off a little bit. I know playing here works in a positive way for us."

The first game away from home was no contest, either, a 100-59 defeat of Southwest Texas in which Nell Fortner had 21 points and 10 rebounds. The lack of any serious challenge showed when the Horns met No. 1 Tennessee in the Mid-America Classic in Columbia, Missouri. The two big orange schools had never met before, and Volunteer coach Pat Head boasted a couple of all-Americans—Cindy Brogdon and Holly Warlick. Tennessee held a narrow three-point edge at halftime but pulled away to an 84-60 victory before 500 fans. Brogdon scored 19, while Swindell led Texas with 14. The icy weekend in Missouri concluded with UT's 90-72 win over California-Fullerton. Basinger, held scoreless by the Vols, rang up 24 on the Titans, but Swindell (20 points and 11 rebounds) was easily Texas' best performer at the tourney. In the summer of 1978, she had been the first female Longhorn to compete on a national team, touring the Far East, and later became the first to play pro basketball. One reason for Swindell's emergence in her senior year could be traced to UT's other center, Jackie Swaim, a strong rebounder and offensive player. Much of the Longhorn half-court offense in 1979 consisted of throwing the ball in to the two big women and letting them work.

Texas further erased the memory of the loss to Tennessee, beating Temple JC by 34 points. And two days later, Conradt's team hosted Minnesota at Gregory Gym. While Title IX portended a shift in power to the large state institutions, Minnesota, one of the largest, seemed not to have caught on. The young and inept Golden Gophers took a severe beating, 114-53. Waggoner scored 31 and freshman Cheryl Hartman had 20.

The Dallas Classic was a loosely organized tournament, with games played at Bishop Dunne High School and Sprague Fieldhouse. The Longhorns got 27 points from Swaim and romped host SMU, 103-42, setting up a meeting with Wayland Baptist. Ranked seventh with a 7-1 record, the Flying Queens had a 6'3" all-American center, Jill Rankin, who was rolling along at 31 points per game. With the 1980s just around the corner, coach Dean Weese had yet to integrate his team, and strict regulation of players' off-court lives made recruiting more difficult. The loquacious Swaim, for example, showed no interest in Wayland Baptist because "They give you a demerit if you raise your window shade at night." After five losses to Wayland Baptist in the last two seasons, Texas' 69-64 win was sweet vindication. "You have to remember what Wayland has meant to basketball in this state," Conradt said. "For years, most of the kids who could not play for Wayland wanted to come back and beat them." Swaim had 26 points and helped hold down Rankin (15).

After a two-week holiday break, the No. 7 Longhorns were back in action. The team had played five games during the 1977 eastern trip and eight in 1978, which Conradt decided was just too much. They played three games in the 1979 junket and won them all, beginning with an 83-68 defeat of St. Joseph's in

Philadelphia. Basinger, who had a rather low profile on the team, took control of the offense during a surprisingly tight game and guided Texas to victory. She finished with 18 points, five fewer than Swaim. To defend their Penn State Invitational title, the Horns flew across Pennsylvania to Pittsburgh, boarded a 14-seat propeller aircraft for a white-knuckle trip through the mountains to an airport 30 miles outside of State College, and were finally bussed into town. They had no trouble beating a smaller Ohio State team by 30 as Swaim got 27 points and 10 rebounds. Kim Jordan and Frani Washington led the Buckeyes with 24 and 16 points, respectively. Penn State player Sue Martin, whose team defeated Southern Connecticut, said, "Texas will be a revenge game for us. They beat us bad last year, and we owe them one." The Lions also wanted to win before their home crowd, and they were up by one with three minutes left, but UT scored the last eight points to take a 76-69 victory and the tourney title for the third straight year. Browning came off the bench

The 1979 Longhorns, the second women's team to inhabit the Erwin Center, won 37 games and lost just four.

to score 16 points and provide steady ballhandling. Jen Bednarek led Penn State with 21. On their way back home, the Longhorns stopped in Houston and beat the Cougars, 76-62.

Wayland Baptist, long the dominant power in Texas women's basketball, was finding it no longer so lonely at the top, gradually getting squeezed by UT and Stephen F. Austin. But the Queens would not give up without a fight. As a capacity crowd in Hutcherson Arena looked on, they beat the Longhorns, 81-76. Jill Rankin poured in 34 points and Kathy Harston (back from a knee injury) was also a major factor. Swaim (23) was the top scorer for Texas, which rebounded from the loss to thrash Texas Tech, 91-68, in Lubbock.

Except for the Minnesota game at Gregory Gym, the Horns did not play a home game between December 2 and January 17. All the travel had taken a toll on her team, so Conradt did not mind that the rematch with Wayland Baptist was postponed a day to allow for Governor Bill Clements' inaugural ball at the Super Drum. Nearly as much as a victory, Conradt and AD Donna Lopiano wanted a big crowd for the season's only stand-alone game at the big new facility. "We'd eventually like to draw sufficient fan interest to play on our own and not with the men," said the Texas coach. Not only did the Longhorns win the game, 60-52, but 3,128 fans were there, the biggest home crowd yet. Swaim scored 31 points, and UT's speed and quickness forced 16 Queen turnovers.

The No. 5 Horns rode balanced scoring to a home victory over Texas A&M (75-41) and Baylor (88-54) in Waco. Both Aggie coach Wanda Bender and the Bears' Olga Fallen had high praise for Texas. "Beyond any shadow of a doubt, they're the best team we've played," Fallen said. "They've got everything. They can make it to the national tournament."

Soaring to No. 2 in the country, Texas hosted its third annual tournament at the Super Drum. Although Conradt and Sue Gunter of No. 3 Stephen F. Austin insisted upsets were possible, their teams were likely to meet in the finals. The Horns zipped by UT-Arlington and North Texas, and SFA did the same to Southwest Texas and Houston. With considerable national attention on Austin, the first UT women's basketball reunion was held, much as the men had done for decades. The ex-players reflected on humble beginnings at the Women's Gym (by then renamed in honor of Anna Hiss) and how far things had come. A record crowd of 4,800 saw a thrilling game, settled in Texas' favor, 72-69, in the last few seconds by a nice Basinger-to-Waggoner-to-Swaim play. Rosie Walker had 32 for the Ladyjacks, and Swaim (25) led the Longhorns. When it was over, Conradt, with a happy expression on her face, hoisted the big trophy.

That game, as much as any, sold a lot of people on women's hoops. But as Bill Sullivan of the *Austin American-Statesman* pointed out, such games were few and far between. Texas was averaging a 28-point winning margin, and blowouts were not conducive to gaining fans. Other big state schools like Texas A&M and Texas Tech needed to develop competitive programs because, Sullivan wrote, "Being in a class by yourself is decidedly a mixed blessing."

After the big win over SFA, the Longhorns, despite minor sickness and injuries, were on cruise control in consecutive home wins over Houston (82-52), Southwest Texas (82-45) and Temple JC (102-62). To enliven things, Conradt juggled the lineup and got good showings from Janie Denton, Fortner and Munn.

The Houston Invitational, a showcase for women's basketball long before it became fashionable, had a lackluster field apart from UT. Conradt was somewhat reluctant to go, but her team needed to play. After beating Southwestern Louisiana by 46 points in the morning and Texas Southern by 35 in the evening, the Horns got an early challenge from Houston in the finals before taking a 71-47 victory and the tourney title, the fourth of the season. Browning scored 21 for Texas, and Kip Anderson had 12 for the Cougars.

Carrying a gaudy 26-2 record, UT went to G. Rollie White Coliseum and beat the Ags, 73-48, with 17 points from Munn. Texas A&M coach Wanda Bender considered it a moral victory that Conradt did not put in her third-stringers before halftime. There were two more games to play before the state meet, both of them in Austin. Despite Baylor's sagging interior defense, Swaim (returning from a shoulder injury) scored 27 points in a 95-67 romp. Ginger Thornton and Mamie Mauch of the Bears combined for 42. Texas Tech paid a visit on February 17, and the men played first for a change. About 5,000 fans stayed around to watch the women's game, a 96-48 mauling of Gay Benson's short Red Raiders. Swaim, a rare combination of grace, quickness and power, made 15 of 20 from the field for a total of 36 points, eclipsing Waggoner's school record by one. She could have busted 40 or even 50, but Conradt pulled her with 10 minutes left.

It was time for some better competition. When sufficiently pestered by reporters, Conradt admitted her team had a chance to reach the AIAW Final Four in Greensboro, North Carolina and win the championship, yet she made no predictions. "We know this team is good, but anything can happen when you get into a one-game playoff situation," she said. "I think we're ready for it. Whatever happens now, happens."

What happened was the top-seeded Longhorns crushed Texas Tech and Baylor in the same day (the last time a Texas team would be required to play twice in one day) at SFA Coliseum in Nacogdoches to begin the state tournament. Swindell had 13 points and 16 rebounds against the Red Raiders, and Swaim scored 24 against the Bears. In the semifinals, the Horns rolled over Houston for the fourth time, 93-68, with 23 points from Denton. UT and Stephen F. Austin met in the title game, seen by an enthusiastic, if not intimidating, crowd of 7,000. Rosie Walker was nothing short of sensational, scoring 24 of the Ladyjacks' 28 first-half points, and she got enough help from her teammates in the second half to halt the Horns' 19-game win streak, 70-59. Swaim scored 25 despite getting in foul trouble, but 37 percent shooting hurt the Horns, who still qualified for the regional tourney in Tulsa.

With 10 days separating state and regionals, UT returned to Nacogdoches for a couple of doubleheaders hosted by SFA. Neither Conradt nor Ladyjack coach Sue Gunter wanted another bloodletting, so their teams avoided each other. The Longhorns met national champion UCLA first, beating the Bruins, 96-78. Swaim and Waggoner teamed up for 51 points, while Denise Curry, tabbed by *Sports Illustrated* as the super soph of 1979, was held to 16. And the North Texas Eagles fell, 69-48, the next night.

Old Dominion was ranked No. 1 in the nation, but Nos. 2 (Stephen F. Austin), 3 (Texas), 4 (Louisiana Tech) and 11 (Wayland Baptist) were in the same regional meet—of which there were 10—and only two teams would advance. The Longhorns, expecting a first-round waltz, had to come from behind to beat Oklahoma State, 76-63. Swaim, Browning, Basinger and Waggoner were in double figures, while Rhonda Kite scored 19 points for the underrated Cowgirls. Oral Roberts, the tournament's host team, had several of what Conradt called "bruisers," and the Titans did play a game that was anything but dainty, giving Texas 37 free throw attempts and losing, 77-68. Waggoner shot over the ORU zone defense for 23 points. That sent the Horns into the semifinals against Louisiana Tech, another team with more size than speed. The Techsters got second and third shots all evening and scored a 77-74 upset that knocked UT out of the national playoffs.

Elinor Griffin and Pam Kelly dominated the backboards and kept the Horns off balance, moving into the regional finals.

Conradt's team showed a lot of heart by coming back the next night and beating Stephen F. Austin (also an upset victim), 65-60, in the consolation game. Their championship hopes dashed, the players voted not to accept a spot in the National Women's Invitational Tournament the following weekend. Texas' 1979 season ended with a 37-4 record. Swindell, who first wore orange and white during the Rodney Page era, closed her career with 1,795 points and 1,759 rebounds. In the latter category, she remains—by far—the all-time leader.

1980

Athletic director Donna Lopiano and basketball coach Jody Conradt were trying to wean themselves from dependence, whether real or perceived, on the men's program. They engaged in a variety of public-relations activities and scheduled just four of 12 home games (all of them at the Super Drum) as prelims to the men. And there were other indications that Texas women's basketball had grown in popularity. Three of the Longhorns' games would be televised—a significant first—and all out-of-town games were broadcast on KUT-FM, a local radio station. A booster group, the Fast Break Club, was created for fans who wanted to show that extra measure of support. The ongoing success of the team, which featured highly conditioned female athletes playing a vigorous 94-foot game, sometimes before large crowds at the Super Drum, was also generating a young fan base. Children sought players' autographs, and high school girls in letter jackets who dreamed of joining the spectacle introduced themselves to Conradt.

Seniors Jackie Swaim, Linda Waggoner, Hattie Browning and Evwella Munn were back, but only sophomore Cheryl Hartman would start every game, and junior Nell Fortner (who had given up volleyball after two years) would be the leading scorer. Conradt's two top recruits were forward Debra Rankin and center Joy Williams. "We needed a 6'5" girl, and we just didn't get one, so we have to play around it," Conradt said. Like the 1979 Longhorns, winners of 37 games, they would be shorter than most elite teams, but a national title was not out of the question.

The No. 7 Horns got the season off to a fine start by beating Oklahoma, 66-47, in Norman, and Southwest Texas, 110-38, in San Marcos. The latter game proved that the era of unmitigated blowouts was not yet over. As a result, Conradt played mostly frosh, with Rankin (22) the top scorer.

The first game in Austin was against a team whose name carried some weight. The Delta State Lady Statesmen had won the AIAW championship thrice in the mid-1970s. With a couple of 6'3" post players, Doreen Grote and Mary Adams, and a new coach, Frances Garmon (formerly of Temple Junior College), they were trying to stay in the mix of big-time women's basketball. But a crowd of 2,000 saw UT take the wind out of their sails early with superior shooting, pressure defense and a 44-29 rebounding edge, winning by 28. Swaim and Fortner combined for 38 points. When her team was tied with Texas Tech at halftime, Conradt gave a little speech that got results as the Horns roared to a 77-47 victory, allowing the Red Raiders just 13 points in the last 20 minutes. Swaim scored 22, and Browning had 16 points and six steals. And in the fifth win of the young season, Waggoner's bombs fell hard and fast in an 88-55 defeat of Temple JC, the last home game for five weeks.

After a 31-point defeat of Conradt's old team, UT-Arlington, the Horns took a 10-day break for exams and then headed west for the Giusti Tournament of Champions in Portland. Munn came off the bench and scored 25 points, including the game-winner, in beating Oregon, 81-79. Bev Smith had 20 for the Ducks. No. 6 North Carolina State jumped in front early but could not hold the lead, even with Swaim, Munn and Browning fouling out. The Wolfpack got 24 points from 6'3" Genia Beasley but lost, 72-71. That set up a final-round meeting between UCLA and Texas. Bruin coach Billie Moore had an Olympic silver medal and an AIAW title to her credit, while Conradt was getting increased national attention for the powerhouse she had built in Austin. But no one could handle Denise

Curry, who had compiled 74 points and 30 rebounds so far in the tournament. Although UCLA's all-America forward kept it up against the Horns (28 points and 12 rebounds), she got no help from her teammates as Texas won, 74-51. The Longhorns, who left little doubt of their superiority in the minds of the 1,888 fans at Memorial Coliseum, had five players in double figures, led by Swaim (15).

The celebration was tinged with sadness, however, because Swaim injured her right knee while scrambling for a loose ball. When the team got back to Austin, doctors determined that cartilage and ligament damage had occurred, ending her participation for the year. A hopeful for all-America honors and the 1980 Olympic team, Swaim's size and savvy could hardly be replaced. "Without Jackie in the lineup, it takes us from being an awesome team to just a good one," Conradt said. "We can't overpower anybody now. Every time I think of what happened, my heart hurts." Swaim, who believed her college career was over, said: "We'll have to rely a whole lot more on our outside shooting, but we've still got a chance to win it all."

The second-highest point-producer in UT women's history, Linda Andrews Waggoner shoots against Delta State.

Several people stepped up when Swaim was injured, including Fortner, a talented forward who had drawn Conradt's ire early in the season for not working hard enough. At the UCLA-Nike Holiday Tournament, she made 10 of 15 shots for a total of 29 points in an 81-66 defeat of California. And the host Bruins, who had predicted a very different outcome at Pauley Pavilion, lost to Texas again, 74-69. Denise Curry scored 30 for UCLA, and Waggoner had 20 for UT, a team ranked fourth and still unbeaten after 11 games. Players and coaches had a little fun while out on the coast, playing beach volleyball, going to Disneyland and touring Universal Studios.

Browning (24) and Rankin (20) were about all the offense the Horns could muster in a poor showing against Pittsburgh on the second day of January. They managed to beat the unranked Panthers by three points and went east to State College to participate in the fourth annual Penn State Invitational. The first three had been won by Conradt's 1977, 1978 and 1979 teams. Hartman, who was neither fast nor shifty, made up for it with hustle and enthusiasm. She scored a total of 45 points in UT's defeats of Ohio State (87-58) and Penn State (91-51) and was named MVP of the tourney. Fortner and Browning also played splendid basketball. After four trips to central Pennsylvania and four first-place trophies, the Longhorns had worn out their welcome and were not invited back. Conradt was too kind to say it, but Texas' basketball program had surpassed the Penn State Invitational.

After spending the holidays jetting to tournaments far from home, the Horns met Houston at Hofheinz Pavilion in what Melanie Hauser of the *Austin American-Statesman* described as "a rough and tumble exhibition of street ball which, left unchecked, leaves a few bumps and bruises and a healthy share of bad feelings." In a 75-61 Texas victory, Fortner scored 27 and Sharion Higgins 14 for the Cougars.

Wayland Baptist came to Austin on January 16, but the 9-5 Queens were not flying so high. Their longtime coach, Dean Weese, had gone on to the fledgling Women's Basketball League, and their all-America center, Jill Rankin, had transferred to Tennessee. Although Conradt, perhaps to lessen the pressure of the winning streak, had begun to publicly anticipate a loss, Wayland Baptist was not the team to do it. Browning scored 23 points and held Queen star Kathy Harston to 17 in UT's 87-63 win before 3,000 fans. Browning, who led the nation in steals, Waggoner, who had more than 2,000 points in her career, and the quick-handed Munn gave the Horns a fine backcourt. They keyed a 75-49 home victory over Iowa. "You bet Texas plays like the third-ranked team in the nation," said Hawkeye coach Judy McMullen. "I'd hate to see numbers one and two."

After disposing of Baylor, 80-53, on the rubber court at Heart O' Texas Coliseum, the Horns returned to Austin and prepared for Stephen F. Austin, a recent victor of top-ranked Louisiana Tech. Even the unflappable Conradt was excited about the game with the Ladyjacks, as more than 7,000 fans gathered at the Super Drum. Hartman and Williams held all-American Rosie Walker to 21 points, while Browning (17) and Fortner (16) led the offense in beating a taller and stronger SFA team, 64-52. "I wanted this one so bad," said Fortner, one of several inside players whose game had developed in the absence of Swaim. "We proved we could play against the big boys and win."

The UT women got little competition in 30-point victories over Texas A&M, Temple JC and Houston. After seeing them destroy the Cougars in a prelim game, John Danks of the Texas men's team quipped, "They're a tough act to follow." It was a heady time for the Longhorns, who jumped into a tie with Old Dominion for No. 1. Conradt was not blowing smoke, however, when she said the Monarchs, defending national champions, were a better team, and they were soon back on top with the Longhorns at No. 2. Regardless of rankings or what happened in the AIAW playoffs, Texas and ODU were scheduled to meet in Norfolk, Virginia on February 26.

Neither fog nor sleet nor gloom of night could stay the Horns from their appointed rounds against Wayland Baptist. For the first time, Texas won (86-77) at Hutcherson Arena. Fortner scored 22, one more than the Queens' Terri Henry, in a game whose officiating displeased Conradt greatly. The Longhorns then took their 23-game win streak (which included the last game of the 1979 season) to Lubbock and beat Texas Tech, 70-58, after overcoming a 10-point deficit.

In the first part of a four-game home stretch before the state tourney, UT defeated Southern California, 85-74, with a season-high 26 points from Waggoner. The Women of Troy, who had a 15-rebound edge, played a zone defense that allowed her to set up and shoot from outside. It was ho-hum in the Drum when Texas routed Baylor, 98-49, as reserves Lee Ann Penick and Debra Rankin teamed up for 35 points. A much stiffer test was expected three days later when No. 7 Long Beach State came to town. The 49ers relied on quickness, a pressing defense and fine outside shooting, much like Texas. Their 5'10" guard, LaTaunya Pollard, who was scoring 17 points per game, was one of the best freshmen in the country. Pollard's team lost, 94-69, but she was impressive with 31 points, six rebounds and three blocked shots. The Longhorns got double-figure scoring from Browning, Munn, Hartman and Williams and dominated from the start. Long Beach coach Joan Bonvicini predicted success for Texas in the upcoming playoffs. Waggoner, Browning and Munn played their last home game against a tough, unranked Missouri team, and it was almost a defeat. Fortner, the Horns' leading scorer and rebounder, had injured a hamstring against Long Beach and did not play in the narrow 77-74 win. Browning scored 19, and Munn came through with some big plays at both ends of the court. Daina Supstiks had 22 for the Tigers.

Unbeaten so far, with state, regional and national tourneys just ahead, Conradt reflected on what the 1980 Longhorns had done: "This is a great team. I really don't think I'll have another team like this one as long as I coach."

The TAIAW meet was held in the spacious confines of the Stephen F. Austin Coliseum, and top-seeded

Record: 33-4

66 Oklahoma 47
110 SW Texas 38
84 Delta State 56
77 Texas Tech 47
88 Temple JC 55
87 UT-Arlington 56
81 Oregon 79
72 North Carolina State 71
74 UCLA 51
81 California 66
74 UCLA 69
68 Pittsburgh 65
87 Ohio State 58
91 Penn State 51
75 Houston 61
87 Wayland Baptist 63
75 Iowa 49
80 Baylor 53
64 Stephen F. Austin 52
78 Texas A&M 46
84 Temple JC 54
104 Houston 71
86 Wayland Baptist 77
70 Texas Tech 58
85 Southern California 74
98 Baylor 49
94 Long Beach State 69
77 Missouri 74
88 Lamar 55
67 Wayland Baptist 45
71 Stephen F. Austin 86
45 Old Dominion 75
97 McNeese State 65
75 Stephen F. Austin 76
96 LSU 73
81 Mercer 80
63 Maryland 68

Texas quickly dispatched Lamar, 88-55. Even without Fortner, it was no problem beating the Cardinals, who got 26 points from guard Priscilla Teal. Hartman and Waggoner combined for 29 to help the Horns defeat Wayland Baptist, 67-45, in the semifinals, easing into the title game with SFA. Both teams were certain to move on to the regionals in Baton Rouge, and their coaches, Conradt and Sue Gunter, joked about taking a bye, but there was too much hype and hoopla surrounding the Longhorn-Ladyjack rivalry to allow that. As 6,000 rowdy fans looked on, the 31-game Texas winning streak came to an end, 86-71. Stephen F. Austin's frontcourt of Rosie Walker, Barbara Brown and Vanessa Anderson had a field day against the shorter Horns, who collected just nine first-half rebounds. Waggoner did not seem especially disappointed by the defeat. "It's not state that counts, it's regionals," she said. "We want to win at regionals."

First, however, the Longhorns had a scheduled game with No. 1 Old Dominion, one that had been sold out for months. The Monarchs had taken to shouting, "We want Texas!" after every victory. The game was broadcast back to Austin, but the home folks got little to smile about. Nancy Lieberman, widely regarded as the top player in women's hoops, scored 25 points—many of them on layups after steals—and her big teammates, Inge Nissen and Anne Donovan, had their way inside, beating UT, 75-45. Only Browning (17) played well for Texas. Conradt had claimed all season that the Monarchs were the best, although not by 30 points. "They whipped us in every way," she said. "The difference tonight was intimidation, pure intimidation. I'd cry if I thought it would help."

The Longhorns had eight days to recover from that strumming, the sort they were accustomed to putting on other teams. Fortner, who played 30 minutes against ODU, was healthy again, so perhaps another winning streak was possible, one that would carry Texas to the AIAW Final Four. It started well enough in Baton Rouge, where the Horns gored McNeese State, 97-65. Fortner scored 18 points, one more than the Cowgirls' frosh star, Pat "Shoney" Jean. That set up a rubber-match semifinal between nemeses UT and Stephen F. Austin. For 40 minutes, two of the best teams in the country went toe-to-toe before it was decided in favor of the Ladyjacks, 76-75. Rosie Walker and Pam Crawford had 23 points each for SFA. Williams, the leading rebounder in nearly every Longhorn game toward the end of the season, grabbed 16. Waggoner, who missed a potential game-winner at the end, dashed into and out of the locker room, too upset to speak. All was not lost, however. UT bounced back with a 96-73 defeat of LSU to earn an at-large bid to the 24-team AIAW nationals. Fortner scored 22 and Waggoner 15, while Julie Gross led the Tigers (also known as the Ben-Gals) with 27.

To make it to the Final Four, the Horns would have to win games in three states within a week, prompting Conradt to say, "This at-large trek looks like a death march across the country." It began in Macon, Georgia, against 29-5 Mercer. Texas did not play with much enthusiasm, eking by the Teddy Bears, 81-80, on a free throw by Penick with 11 seconds left. Kathy Singletary (25) scored from the inside almost at will for Mercer, whose coach, Joan Fontaine, received postgame condolences from a swarm of fans.

The road-weary Longhorns traveled north to meet Maryland, led by 6'4" center Kris Kirchner, averaging 21 points and 12 rebounds per game. Just 400 fans were on hand at Baltimore County Coliseum to witness the Terrapins' 68-63 upset win. Texas had a chance to put them away early but failed to do so, leaving Conradt steaming. She made critical remarks about the officiating, as well as her team's inside game. Kirchner scored 19 for Maryland, and Fortner led UT with 18.

"Losing a Jackie Swaim so early in the season would crater most teams," wrote John Rooke of the *Daily Texan*. "But it never affected Texas. Linda Waggoner [who scored 2,256 points in a 161-game career], Nell Fortner, Hattie Browning, Evwella Munn, Cheryl Hartman, Joy Williams and the rest of the team all had a hand in keeping an eventual 31-game winning streak intact. They laid the foundation for several more winning seasons. Jody Conradt has taken the basketball team from the depths of anonymity to the top of the charts in only four years. It won't be too long before that light at the end of the tunnel means a national championship."

He was simply wrong by claiming UT women's basketball was in "the depths" before Conradt arrived, but Rooke was right about what she—with great support from athletic director Donna Lopiano—had achieved. Conradt was honored as AIAW coach of the year in late March in a banquet at New York's Plaza Hotel.

1981

Because of the effect of Title IX and concomitant growing success of women's basketball, the well-funded and male-dominated NCAA began making moves that led to the demise of the AIAW. Donna Lopiano, UT women's athletic director, had been elected president of the organization and was quite active in resisting the takeover. A suit against the NCAA for violation of antitrust laws eventually failed, and as a result, 1981 was the last year in which the AIAW had complete governance over the world of intercollegiate sport for women. The two antagonistic groups shared control the next year, and by 1983, the NCAA had "won." Lopiano, who observed these wrenching changes, had at first advocated merging the men's and women's athletic departments at the University of Texas, but no more. She came to believe it was better to retain some female control and identity at the institutional level.

On a related matter, UT was the subject of some gripes in the handling of Jackie Swaim's eligibility. The Longhorns' star center, who injured her knee early in the 1980 season, had gone through 10 months of rehabilitation and appeared to be completely healthy. But was she eligible? Her original request for a hardship year had been turned down on a strict interpretation of AIAW rules. Austin attorney Anthony "Curly" Ferris argued successfully that she should be allowed to play in 1981. The decision was welcomed with open arms at Bellmont Hall, headquarters for both Texas athletic departments, but not everywhere. After all, the best player on one of the best teams in the nation was back for a fifth season. "I think we're going to be criticized to an extent because of Donna's position," said UT coach Jody Conradt, "but at least Jackie stayed at the same school."

Record: 28-8

87 Temple JC 44
82 Iowa 62
74 San Jose State 54
82 Texas Tech 70
86 NE Louisiana 67
71 Delta State 67
79 Texas Southern 50
87 Portland State 51
58 Old Dominion 60
72 Oregon State 65
65 UCLA 78
106 California-Fullerton 42
89 North Carolina State 91 (2 OT's)
73 North Carolina 75
76 Wayland Baptist 68
82 Texas Tech 61
51 Old Dominion 57
67 Stephen F. Austin 84
72 Baylor 65
73 Texas A&M 42
110 Arkansas 61
83 Texas Tech 45
86 Houston 77
93 Temple JC 51
74 Wayland Baptist 65
71 Oklahoma 54
74 Baylor 66
88 SMU 56
71 Wayland Baptist 49
54 Stephen F. Austin 51
96 UT-Arlington 51
95 Nebraska 63
97 Oral Roberts 63
66 Stephen F. Austin 70
73 Southern 52
63 Illinois State 66

The 1981 Longhorns would be bigger and slower than the previous squad, but Conradt brought in some recruits destined to win a lot of games in the next four years, primarily guards Terri Mackey and Esoleta Whaley and forward Sherryl Hauglum. Ranked eighth in preseason, Conradt's fifth Texas team began by crunching Temple Junior College, 87-44, behind 14 points from Lesa Jones. And with Cheryl Hartman's 22, the Horns defeated Iowa, 82-62. Texas outrebounded the Hawkeyes by a 55-32 margin. Robin Anderson scored 21 for the home team in a prelim to the Iowa men's game.

In the 12 days preceding the first game at the newly renamed Erwin Center, UT engaged in some unofficial competition. First, the professional Dallas Diamonds came to town with Nancy Lieberman and ex-Horns Retha Swindell and Hattie Browning. The Diamonds won by 29 points. And on November 21 and 22, the University of Arkansas brought Oklahoma, South Carolina, Louisiana Tech and Texas to Barnhill Arena for a series of morning and afternoon scrimmages of 45 minutes' duration.

Swaim paced the Longhorns to a 74-54 win over San Jose State in the home opener. Despite being double-teamed by the Spartans, she scored 16 points in 21 minutes, proving her knee problem was a thing of the past. She and Nell Fortner combined for 31 points to beat Texas Tech, 82-70, as the Red Raiders unveiled a dandy freshman, Carolyn Thompson (22).

Her team was undefeated, but Conradt would not permit comparisons with the 1980 Longhorns: "We're not even in the same ballpark. This is not a good team yet. I'd like to believe we're the eighth best team in the nation, but we're not. We have too many weaknesses, no versatility, and we're not smart enough." Fans—of which there were not many—who came to the San Jose and Texas Tech games enjoyed the flash and dazzle of Mackey off the bench. She was strong and quick and a clever passer. One scouting report advised opponents to "keep the ball out of her hands and hope she's still second team."

Jackie Swaim (left) and Nell Fortner (below), seniors on the 1981 Texas team.

At Northeast Louisiana's Ewing Coliseum, Swaim had her greatest game as a Longhorn—14 of 15 from the field and 12 of 16 from the line for a school-record 40 points in an 86-67 whipping of the Indians. She got help from soph guard Nancy Walling, who handed out 12 assists. The following night in Cleveland, Mississippi, Swaim was again in charge, scoring 26 and collecting 14 rebounds in a 71-67 come-from-behind defeat of Delta State. Pressure defense by the two frosh guards, Mackey and Whaley, aided the comeback. The 1-7 Lady Statesmen got 12 points each from Andrella Gray and Mary Adams.

Texas returned home to play an exhibition game against the touring Taiwanese national team. The visitors from the Far East had just one loss so far (out of 18 games), to two-time defending champion Old Dominion, but the Horns sprang a 64-56 upset. In the first home prelim of the season, UT overcame early lethargy to beat Texas Southern, 79-50. The always-hustling Hartman (19 points and 20 rebounds) had a fine game, while the Tigers got 18 points from Nerissa Redo.

Conradt could look back 12 months and see that winning the Giusti Tournament had been a springboard to an extraordinary season. The champs were back in Oregon, and they started by overpowering the young and inexperienced Portland State Vikings, 87-51, with 14 points each from Jones and Fortner. Despite a temperature in the mid-40s inside Memorial Coliseum, things got rather hot when the tourney's two heavyweights, Old Dominion and Texas, met in the semifinals. The Longhorns forced 36 turnovers but failed to convert enough of them into baskets, falling to the Monarchs, 60-58. Anne Donovan, ODU's 6'8" center, did plenty of damage with 25 points and 17 rebounds, while Fortner scored 20 for UT. The Horns ran into another fine center the next night in Oregon State's 6'5" Carol Menken, who got 32 points. Yet Hauglum sparked the ragged Texas offense with 20 points to help beat the Ducks, 72-65. After the tournament, Fortner and Joy Williams lamented the loss to ODU and made some big predictions about what would happen when Marianne Stanley's Monarchs came to Austin on January 20.

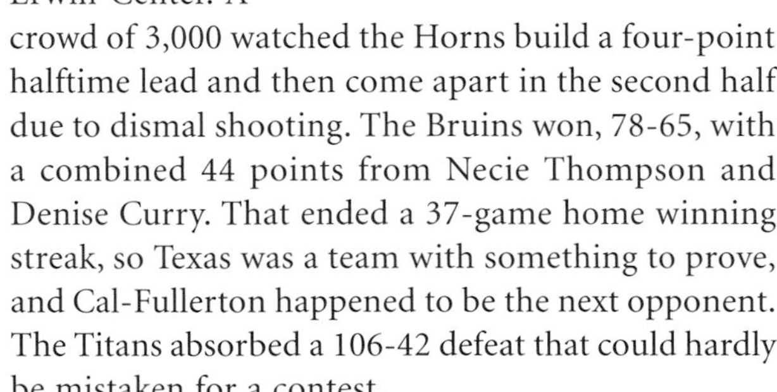

After nearly two weeks off for the holidays, UT welcomed No. 10 UCLA to the Erwin Center. A crowd of 3,000 watched the Horns build a four-point halftime lead and then come apart in the second half due to dismal shooting. The Bruins won, 78-65, with a combined 44 points from Necie Thompson and Denise Curry. That ended a 37-game home winning streak, so Texas was a team with something to prove, and Cal-Fullerton happened to be the next opponent. The Titans absorbed a 106-42 defeat that could hardly be mistaken for a contest.

"I don't have a gut feeling about where we are now," Conradt said. "I want to go on the road and be tested to see how we take the pressure." The coach got her wish because nine of the next 11 games were out of town. At the Raleigh Civic Center, No. 11 North Carolina State jumped to a 17-point lead, but UT came back, tied it and finally lost, 91-89, in double overtime. Mistakes, turnovers and fouls caught up to the Longhorns, who nevertheless got fine play from Swaim, Mackey and Jones. Trudi Lacey scored 26 for Kay Yow's victorious Wolfpack. And the next day in Chapel Hill, it was the same story as Texas lost to North Carolina by two. Conradt cited a lack of effort (except for Swaim, who had 28 points and 20 rebounds) and biased officiating because the Tar Heels ran a pressure defense and were called for just three second-half fouls. But the charge of "homer" referees was also made by coaches and players visiting Austin, so perhaps it balanced out.

"All the games are tough," Conradt said prior to leaving for west Texas. "They got an insight into the hard, cruel world last weekend. They know they're not going to win just because they show up in a burnt orange uniform." In Plainview, Fortner hit 13 of 20 shots for a game-high 28 points in a 76-68 defeat of Wayland Baptist. And in Lubbock, Debra Rankin and Nancy Walling provided a boost in UT's easy 82-61 win over Texas Tech. The No. 8 Longhorns, taller and stronger than the Red Raiders, had a lopsided rebound edge.

It was time for the rematch with Old Dominion, a team that narrowly defeated the Horns in December. The Monarchs, ranked No. 2 and carrying a 39-game winning streak, had Anne Donovan, the most dominant player in women's hoops. Before the largest Erwin Center crowd of the year (5,100), she got 26 points, 16 rebounds and nine blocked shots in a 57-51 ODU win. Texas appeared in control with 8:40 left, leading by eight points, but got outscored 17-3 from then on. The Monarchs' championship experience really showed at the end.

Subdued after that emotional defeat, UT traveled to Nacogdoches and fell to Stephen F. Austin, 84-67, the sixth loss in 10 games. More than 4,000 people were at the SFA Coliseum, some of whom showered obscenities and other verbal abuse on the visiting Longhorns. Vanessa Anderson had 23 points for the Ladyjacks, while Fortner (20) and Swaim (18) paced Texas. Conradt, whose team was sinking in the polls, cut her players no slack. But better times were ahead, in the form of a 15-game winning streak. It began with a 72-65 home defeat of Baylor. "Conradt gave me and Jackie an ultimatum, so we got our butts in there and played," said Fortner, who scored 19 points. The Horns got a breather against Texas A&M (73-42) in College Station, when Mackey moved into the starting lineup.

Texas was rested, ready and heavily favored in the first Southwest Conference Tournament, held at Hofheinz Pavilion in Houston. Women's basketball was not yet a part of the SWC, but with the NCAA takeover looming, the nine member schools chose not to wait until it became official. They needed to begin developing rivalries with each other, yet a large chasm separated the top—Texas—and the bottom, especially Rice and TCU, then part of the AIAW's Division II. The Longhorns had enjoyed robust success for several years, but some of their soon-to-be SWC sisters were scarcely beyond the club-program stage. The first-ever meeting between UT and Arkansas was a horrible mismatch (110-61) in which the Horn starters gave way to the subs early. Swaim and Fortner, the two seniors, teamed up for 36 points in an 83-45 defeat of Texas Tech. And in the title game, Vicky Finch and Sharion Higgins led the way as Houston set out to topple the mighty Longhorns. UH fell nine points short, but it was too close for Conradt, who was glad to leave Houston without suffering an upset. Fortner scored 22 and Mackey coolly guided the offense in a game witnessed by 750 souls, and that was the biggest crowd of the tournament. Nevertheless, the tourney got some media attention and gave the athletic directors and their staffs an opportunity to meet and make plans.

The Horns played three home games in a week, all of them victories. Hauglum scored 32 points in a 93-51 defeat of Temple JC, the last time UT ever played a junior college team. Wayland Baptist's scoring and rebounding leader, former Longhorn Janie Denton, collided with Swaim early in the game and injured a knee. Although the Queens missed her, they threatened to take control in the second half when Texas fluctuated between sluggish and erratic. Jones, just recovering from an ankle injury, threw in some long shots to help the Horns win, 74-65. Ranked No. 11 with a 19-6 record, Texas then played Oklahoma before 1,500 fans. The Sooners' Molly McGuire (27) was the top scorer in the game, but that was not nearly enough in a 71-54 UT victory. With the state and presumably regional and national tourneys fast approaching, Conradt felt good. "We're on the upswing," she said.

After an eight-point victory over Baylor in Waco, it was time for the AIAW state tourney in Denton. Texas proceeded to blow by SMU, 88-56. Conradt had said all the right things about Welton Brown's Mustangs, but there was hardly a chance they would win. Fortner, who led the Horns with 21 points, said, "We want to win this tournament real bad. We've been down a tough road, and it's time to take home the cake." Swaim (31) was the star the next night in a 71-49 defeat of Wayland Baptist. The Queens were miserable in the second half, committing 15 turnovers and scoring just 20 points. Of course, it came down to Texas and Stephen F. Austin in the finals, and the Ladyjacks were in charge early, leading by as much as 12. But Hauglum (16) and Fortner (15) patiently got the Longhorns back in the game, and they pulled out a 54-51 victory. The state championship, so long the property of Wayland Baptist or SFA, finally belonged to UT. "It's about time we turned the Tower orange," Swaim quipped during the raucous postgame celebration.

Because almost three weeks separated the close of the state meet in Denton and the opening of regionals in Nacogdoches, Texas hosted a couple of games in the Erwin Center. All 13 players scored in a 96-51 defeat of UT-Arlington, and Hartman got a career-high 27 points in the Horns' 95-63 steamrolling of Nebraska. Kathy Hagerstrom had 14 for the Cornhuskers. The coaches and players had some time before regionals to see what they had accomplished in a supposedly rebuilding year—26 wins and six losses, a state title, and they were peaking at just the right time.

In the first game in Nacogdoches, UT and Oral Roberts were tied at 24 with five minutes left in the first half when the Longhorns reeled off 27 straight points and never looked back in a 97-63 win. The Titans got 27 points from Sharon Tucker, while Swaim had 22 points and 12 rebounds and Mackey was credited with 12 assists. ORU coach Dixie Woodall said, "We were just outclassed. The party is over for us, but for Texas, the party has just begun." It was no party the next night against the Stephen F. Austin Ladyjacks, who were playing before a loud home crowd. Hartman injured a knee, Fortner got in early foul trouble, and SFA's Pam Crawford and Rosalind Polk combined for 46 points to beat the Longhorns, 70-66. Swaim and the freshman guards, Mackey and Whaley, kept it close all the way. They shook off Friday night's troubles with a 73-52 defeat of Southern to gain an at-large spot in the AIAW national tourney.

Try as they might, the Horns could not help looking past unranked Illinois State, their first opponent in the 24-team nationals. Playing in Austin did not seem to help, either, because the Redbirds overcame an 11-point first-half deficit, took the lead with 90 seconds left and withstood a desperate Texas rally to win, 66-63. Swaim played her last game in a Longhorn uniform, getting 22 points and 10 rebounds. "I'm at a complete loss," Conradt said. "It's really a frustrating way to end a season. You always have visions of ending things on a happy note." It would take a decade and a half of working her way up, but Fortner made Conradt happy as well as proud by becoming the coach at Purdue in 1997 and getting chosen to head the U.S. Olympic team in 2000.

1982

Nell Fortner and Jackie Swaim had graduated, and Cheryl Hartman was out for the year with a knee injury. The 1982 Texas women's basketball team would be short and green, but Jody Conradt had come up with a recruit who would have an instant impact and become one of the greatest players in school history. Annette Smith, a 5'11" center from Bay City, was a superb athlete, highly motivated and a coach's dream. The Longhorns' starting lineup seldom varied in the 39-game season—Smith in the middle, Sherryl Hauglum and Joy Williams at forward and Terri Mackey and Esoleta Whaley at guard. These players, a freshman, three sophomores and a junior, would be hard-pressed to duplicate the successes of earlier years. So Conradt and her assistants, Lynn Davis Pool and Jill Rankin, fashioned a team that compensated for lack of size with full-court defense and an explosive fast break.

It was the last year for the AIAW, most of whose key members had gone over to the NCAA. Actually, there was no discernible difference between teams under the banner of one organization or the other until postseason, when they would go their separate ways. Texas, with two staunch AIAW advocates in Conradt and athletic director Donna Lopiano, remained loyal to the female-run and female-oriented AIAW until the end. The best basketball programs still in the decade-old AIAW were Texas and Rutgers, favored to meet in the finals of a very watered-down national tournament. As far as overall athletic programs that stayed put in 1982, it was, according to Paul Schnitt of the *Austin American-Statesman*, "the giant burnt orange steer against a bunch of foundering midgets." Texas won national titles in track, swimming and volleyball in the final year of the AIAW.

After splitting exhibition games with Cuba and Taiwan, Conradt's seventh UT team began the season on the west coast. The Anheuser-Busch Classic in San Jose would be a good opportunity for the young Longhorns to gain experience. They got the best kind of experience—winning, grabbing the tourney title. Hauglum scored 18 points in an 89-78 defeat of Stanford, and Williams had 24 points and 13 rebounds in beating host San Jose State, 69-56. Williams and Smith were chosen all-tournament. In Berkeley two days later, UT squandered a 10-point lead and fell to California, 68-67. The Golden Bears, taking advantage of Smith's foul troubles, won with a combined 35 points from Chris Sellin and Cyndy Cooke.

The 2-1 Horns had their first home game against Oregon State on November 30 before 1,400 fans at the Erwin Center. After playing a tournament in Plainview, the Beavers got fogged in at the Lubbock airport, had a car accident and rode the bus into Austin, where they lost to Texas, 84-72. The Horns took a big early lead and coasted.

It was back to the coast for two tough games, beginning with Long Beach State. The No. 5 49ers boasted all-American LaTaunya Pollard, a player with strength, speed and spring. She made nine of 13 shots for a total of 22 points, and Kristen Cummings added 10 as Long Beach downed the Horns, 74-61. Smith, whose game just needed a little smoothing to match that of Pollard, scored 18, but UT turned the ball over 30 times and got 15 fewer rebounds. At the Los Angeles Forum, Southern California's McGee twins, Pam and Paula, combined for 34 points in an 83-66 thrashing of UT. The No. 4 Trojans had a narrow halftime lead and gradually stretched it out. Losing back-to-back and three of their last four may have caused the young Longhorns to doubt themselves, but with the precocious Smith leading the way, they would soon embark on a long winning streak.

The first victim was Texas Tech, a loser by 35 points. Mackey used some of her magic, including no-look passes and one full-court dash with a 360-degree spin touched off by a picture-perfect jumper to record 22 points, nine assists and four rebounds. Red Raider star Carolyn Thompson, averaging 24 points per game, was shut down by Smith. That confidence-builder was followed by another, 93-61, over Houston. Conradt was a bit embarrassed when the officials did not show, and she had to scramble for some replacements.

The SMU Classic was not exactly a tournament, just six teams at Moody Coliseum playing two games each. UT got the host team first, and Conradt was not crying wolf when she expressed concern about the Mustangs, whose star forward, Rhonda Rompola, had just transferred from Old Dominion. Conradt called Lesa Jones from the bench midway through the first half, and the senior captain made a string of baskets leading to an 84-50 victory. Hauglum hit nine of 10 in that game and 12 of 16 the next night in beating Mississippi, 69-56. It was the first loss for the much taller Rebels, who got 20 points from Eugenia Connor. "We knew that quickness beats height," Conradt said. "So the key to the game was to keep the pressure on and stop them from going inside."

The team was rusty after a two-week holiday break but managed an 80-65 defeat of McNeese State in Austin. To remedy the situation, Conradt scheduled two practices the next day, the first at 8:30 a.m. Against Missouri, the Horns were still a step slow on

Record: 35-4

89 Stanford 78
69 San Jose State 56
67 California 68
84 Oregon State 72
61 Long Beach State 74
66 Southern California 83
98 Texas Tech 63
93 Houston 61
80 SMU 54
69 Mississippi 56
80 McNeese State 65
67 Missouri 64
75 Colorado 52
66 Oregon 63
66 Kansas 47
72 Houston 67
57 Texas Tech 44
63 Wayland Baptist 57
80 Stephen F. Austin 79 (OT)
76 Baylor 69
74 SMU 55
72 Houston 50
68 Arkansas 53
88 Texas Southern 66
79 Wayland Baptist 52
93 Texas A&M 53
99 Delta State 79
81 Baylor 63
92 Mississippi College 55
78 UT-Arlington 57
87 West Texas 50
71 Wayland Baptist 57
87 Oklahoma 78
89 New Orleans 74
64 Wayland Baptist 62
67 Central Missouri 54
73 Wisconsin 61
82 Wayland Baptist 63
77 Rutgers 83

defense and out of sync on offense for most of the game. But Jones' long-range set shots and Whaley's hustle were just enough to beat the Tigers, 67-64. Annette Schwander and Lorraine Ferret had 15 points each for Mizzou.

Despite six straight wins, the Longhorns could not seem to break into the top 20, causing Conradt to speculate that her team was being blackballed because of its AIAW affiliation. What happened over the course of the next three days in frigid Wichita took care of that. In the Pizza Hut Invitational, the Longhorns bombed No. 13 Colorado, 75-52, with strong inside play from Williams and Smith. Lisa Van Goor scored 18 for the Buffs. Smith had her hands full against all-American Bev Smith of No. 9 Oregon but contained her well enough in a 66-63 upset. The championship game featured the giant-killer Longhorns versus No. 18 Kansas. The Jayhawks could not handle the frontcourt pressure of Mackey and Whaley and shot just 21 percent in the first half of UT's 66-47 victory. It was another sparkling performance by Smith—27 points and 13 rebounds. "I'm real proud of the girls," Conradt said. "They had quite a chore staring them in the face, and they came in and took care of business."

An Oregon State defender reacts to the flashy moves of Terri Mackey. She averaged 13 points per game and had 268 assists and 123 steals during her sophomore season.

The pollsters finally noticed and moved Texas to No. 12. After a rough and raucous 72-67 win over Dot Woodfin's Cougars in Houston, it was time for some west Texas hoops. Both Texas Tech and Wayland Baptist were ready and waiting for the Longhorns. A second-half comeback led by Mackey (21) was needed to drop Tech, 57-44. The Red Raiders got 24 points from Carolyn Thompson and 18 rebounds from Gwen McCray. Just a few miles up Highway 27 in Plainview, the Horns again had to come from behind to win, 63-57, offsetting a nice game by Queen center Gay Hemphill. It was a tired but happy team that flew into Mueller Airport. "We passed, but I'm not sure we made an A," was Conradt's succinct comment.

The Texas-Stephen F. Austin rivalry had produced some classic games in the past few years, and another took place at the Erwin Center before 2,238 fans. Mackey committed six turnovers, but her driving, finger-roll basket in the last 30 seconds of overtime produced an 80-79 UT victory. The Ladyjacks had several chances to score in the final frenetic half-minute and were unable to do it. Smith, who played the entire 45 minutes, had 24 points and 16 rebounds, while Tammy Mayo led SFA with 20 points.

Hauglum came out of a mild slump, making 11 of 17 shots in a 76-69 defeat of Baylor in Waco. The two backcourt bandits, Whaley and Mackey, helped the Horns take their 14th straight win. It was a prelim to the UT-BU men's game; such events still occurred, both at home and on the road, but they were becoming increasingly rare.

Formal Southwest Conference competition, sponsored by the Dallas office and reflected in its record books, did not commence until the next year. The SWC, after all, was under the aegis of the NCAA, and the nine women's athletic departments were about evenly divided between the NCAA and soon-defunct AIAW. The second and final midseason conference tournament was held at G. Rollie White Coliseum in College Station. Given that none of their SWC sisters had ever made the top 20, Texas was a marked team, but it hardly mattered. The Horns blew by SMU (74-55) and Houston (72-50). Arkansas, with Cheryl Orcholski and a couple of nice frosh, Amanda Holly and Bettye Fiscus, was the most competition the other teams could muster, and Texas beat the Hogs by 15 points, looking uninspired in the process. "I wish we played Louisiana Tech and Stephen F. [Austin] in our conference," Mackey said. "Playing against all these Southwest Conference teams is not going to get us anywhere. There's no half-stepping when you're trying to make it to the top."

While 10 of the Longhorns' past 11 games had been played away from Austin, the first half of February saw six straight home games. They were all victories, by an average margin of 24 points. First, UT beat Texas Southern, 88-66, before a paltry gathering at the Erwin Center. Because of subfreezing temperatures, the game with Wayland Baptist was delayed a day and then moved to Gregory Gym. Both the men's and women's teams regularly practiced at the old fieldhouse on Speedway, so it was a familiar setting for a 79-52 romp of the Flying Queens, highlighted by Smith's 22 points. "It was kind of fun on a cold Saturday afternoon to come in here where it's nice and warm," Conradt said. "The crowd is closer to the players, and it seems a lot more enthusiastic. It brings back memories."

The turning point in a 93-53 defeat of Texas A&M may have been the opening tipoff because Texas soon had a big lead against a weak and intimidated Aggie club. Riding a 20-game winning streak and moving up to No. 7, the Horns scored a 99-79 defeat of Delta State. Smith got 36 points, but the Lady Statesmen had an exceptional freshman, too, Ida Johnson, who finished with 27.

With just two more regular-season games left, Conradt and her 24-3 team had every right to feel upbeat. The on-court results had been most satisfying, and their chances of playing in the AIAW Final Four at the Palestra in Philadelphia seemed better all the time. Even if they won it all, though, a big asterisk would be attached since the first-ever NCAA women's championship had more money, prestige and top teams. "We're apprehensive about the playoff situation," Conradt said. "Every once in a while, a player will say something about how our playoffs are secondary. You try to guard against it, but it's there."

Mackey had 20 points and 14 assists in an 81-63 victory over Baylor witnessed by 1,700 fans. In the last regular-season game, Texas busted Mississippi College, 92-55, with Mackey again the key to the team's success. She had 23 points, 10 rebounds, seven assists and five steals. The Chocs' soph center, Deborah Mitchell, scored 22 in a losing effort.

The final Texas AIAW Tournament, held in Plainview, was no sure thing, Conradt insisted, although she agreed her team deserved the top seeding. SFA, Baylor and Houston, three teams that might have pushed the Longhorns, were not there, having moved to the NCAA. Texas took two easy victories, 78-57 against UT-Arlington and 87-50 against West Texas, advancing to the finals. Wayland Baptist, the host team, fell by a score of 71-57 as Smith connected on nine of 13 shots from the floor. The Hutcherson Arena crowd screamed for the Queens, but only Gay Hemphill (26) could do much against the Horn defense. Indicative of Texas' domination, Whaley, Smith, Hauglum and Mackey made the all-tournament team.

Every one of Conradt's teams, beginning in 1977, had reached the AIAW regionals but never won. Players like Retha Swindell, Linda Waggoner, Jackie Swaim and Hattie Browning dotted the rosters of teams that went no further than third place. The 1982 Longhorns were not necessarily better—they were quite young—but they were competing against a diluted field throughout the playoffs. Two weeks separated the end of the state tourney in Plainview and the opening of regionals in Lubbock, so fifth-ranked UT was a bit slow in the early minutes against Oklahoma. Smith scored 35, and Williams turned in a fine defensive effort in an 87-78 win. Patty McGuire had 27 points for the Sooners. Hauglum (22) led all five starters in double figures in a 89-74 defeat of New Orleans, setting up the regional title game with Wayland Baptist. The Longhorns won their 29th straight, but it was not easy. The score was 62-up in the last minute when Smith (26) forced a tie ball, won the jump, got an assist from Mackey and hit the winning shot. As usual, Gay Hemphill led the Queens with 28 points and 15 rebounds.

That victory entitled UT to host one of the four satellite tournaments whose winners would advance to Philadelphia. Hauglum was out with a foot injury, and Smith made just four of 17 shots against Central Missouri. The pressure showed as the Jennies led by five at halftime, but Mackey, Whaley and Williams came through in a 67-54 win. Only Wisconsin stood between the Horns and the AIAW Final Four, and the tall-but-slow Badgers lost, 73-61. Smith was back to her old tricks—30 points and 11 rebounds.

So the Longhorns traveled on to the Palestra, the classic gymnasium on the University of Pennsylvania campus. The AIAW title was two games away, and Conradt acknowledged, "It's there, and I want it." She joked that playing Wayland Baptist in a semifinal game was like an intrasquad scrimmage. Yes, for the fifth time that season, the Longhorns and Queens met on the basketball court, where, under other circumstances, familiarity might breed boredom more than contempt. It was close in the first half, but Texas pulled away to an 82-63 win. Mackey and Smith combined for 41 points, and frosh center Shell Bollin had 17.

Rutgers, a victor over Villanova in the other semifinal, had a 24-7 record, and UT was 35-3 entering the championship game. It was not televised—unlike the Louisiana Tech-Cheyney NCAA title game in Norfolk—and only 1,789 fans were there. It was definitely a partisan crowd for the Scarlet Knights, whose coach, Theresa Grentz, and several of her players came from the Philly area. All-American June Olkowski, playing on a bad knee, managed just four points, but teammates Patty Coyle and Terry Dorner combined for 55 in Rutgers' 83-77 victory. Smith (30), Whaley, Williams and Mackey had to play much of the second half with four fouls and thus could not apply their familiar defensive pressure. The 32-game winning streak, which began three and a half months earlier, had come to an end. Several Longhorns cried as they watched the champions cut down the nets after the game, and Conradt felt extra emotional turmoil from seeing the demise of the AIAW, an organization she and Lopiano had helped build. The AIAW, although it had its share of critics, left a legacy of making women's athletics, especially basketball, visible and highly competitive on a national scale.

1983

With the dissolution of the AIAW, a new era had arrived, symbolized by the cover of the NCAA's 436-page basketball media guide. Ralph Sampson of Virginia and Anne Donovan of Old Dominion shared cover honors, and thus was marked the beginning of full NCAA governance of women's college sport. More locally, the Southwest Conference served as the framework for women's basketball, volleyball, track, swimming, tennis and golf. The overwhelming favorite to win the first SWC hoop title was Jody Conradt's Texas team, which had nine letter-winners back and four promising recruits: forward Audrey Smith (the sister of Annette Smith), center Cara Priddy, guard Kamie Ethridge (who also had a sister, Kriss, on the team) and forward Fran Harris. Priddy, the most celebrated of the four, had averaged 37 points and 14 rebounds per game against weak competition in rural New Mexico. Of the frosh, Ethridge and Harris contributed the most in 1983 and eventually became outstanding players. The teams on which Smith, Priddy, Ethridge and Harris played would lose just nine games in four seasons.

Five of the returnees—Smith, Esoleta Whaley, Joy Williams, Cheryl Hartman and Sherryl Hauglum—played on a U.S. team in Bolivia during the summer. International competition for women was not so rare by the early 1980s; Conradt had coached such teams since 1978, although she was not fond of foreign travel. Loath to make predictions of how the Horns' season might evolve, she nevertheless called the 1983 team her deepest and most talented yet. The players, however, especially the voluble Terri Mackey, had drawn a bead on nothing less than the national title. UT had a No. 5 preseason ranking, but NCAA champ Louisiana Tech and Southern California (with fabled freshman Cheryl Miller) looked like the two best teams.

The season began with a tournament, the Nebraska Invitational. Attendance figures at Texas' two games in Lincoln were reminiscent of the glorified intramurals stage of women's basketball 10 or 15 years earlier as a total of 250 fans gathered. They saw the Longhorns eke by Indiana, 86-79, with 28 points from Smith. Rachelle Bostic got the same number for the Hoosiers. Only Mackey (20) played well in the championship game, a 78-68 loss to Colleen Matsuhara's Nebraska team. "I don't have any explanations," Conradt said after the upset. "Maybe we read the papers and thought it was going to be easy. If we don't start playing better, we'll have a real gloomy Christmas."

The Longhorns had three home games in a span of five days, beginning with No. 5 Tennessee on December 9. Texas outrebounded the taller Volunteers and got a combined 42 points from Smith and Hauglum, breaking open a close game in the late minutes to win, 74-59. It was the biggest Erwin Center crowd of the year—2,718 fans. No. 6 Kansas State brought a short and fast team to Austin, including a guard, Priscilla Gary, reputed to have a 40-inch vertical leap. But it was Smith, UT's sophomore center, who played such a dazzling game that night. She had 35 points and 12 rebounds in a crushing 93-73 defeat of the Wildcats. Conradt, after her 200th Texas win, claimed no strokes of coaching genius had been responsible for the turnaround after the poor showing in Nebraska, and yet it was another step in the inexorable march the women's basketball program had undertaken seven years earlier. "Where it ends, nobody knows," wrote Ken Murray of the *Austin American-Statesman*. "But the roadmap points to a rainbow's end and a national championship." California, a team that had beaten the Horns the season before, was next. The Golden Bears' huge frontline was as slow as molasses, and UT scored a decisive 81-63 victory. Hauglum had 20 points, but Cal coach Gooch Foster tabbed Mackey as the key to the Longhorns' success. Cynthia Cooke led the Bears with 12 points and six rebounds.

The Giusti Tournament of Champions in Portland welcomed Texas back for a third time. For some reason, UT was a sentimental favorite despite the presence of Oregon, Oregon State and Portland State. The Horns got caught looking ahead and nearly lost the opener to OSU. A 10-point Beaver lead was finally erased when Smith (31) scored with 40 seconds left and then forced a turnover in a narrow 52-50 win. That set up a clash with Louisiana Tech, the second-ranked team in the country, 1981 AIAW champion and 1982 NCAA champion. Co-head coaches Sonja Hogg and Leon Barmore had put together a dynasty in Ruston. With guard Kim Mulkey leading the way, the Techsters not only broke the UT press but scored upon it repeatedly. Janice Lawrence threw in 29 points in Tech's 86-64 victory. The game was marred by an extreme rarity in women's athletics, a fight. Mackey and Tia Sossamon tussled with nearly 10 minutes left in the game. Mackey, who had 16 points, six rebounds and six assists when the incident occurred, was perceived as the aggressor and ejected. The Horns salvaged third place by struggling to a 65-59 defeat of Oregon. Allison Lang of the Ducks had a fine game, getting 28 points and 13 rebounds and holding Smith to six of 24 from the field.

Following a nine-day layoff, UT hosted a trio of midwestern teams. The first was Drake, featuring junior center Lorri Bauman, who came in with a gaudy 28-point average and 63-percent shooting accuracy. But she was stopped cold, getting just nine points in a 94-56 Longhorn runaway. Conradt was happy with every facet of her team's play as Smith scored 29, Mackey 17 and Priddy 13 off the bench. Texas was again outstanding in a 109-71 defeat of Kansas, impressing Jayhawk coach Marian Washington. And the Horns downed a pesky Iowa State team, 79-60. Smith broke the career 1,000-point mark, and before the season was over, Williams, Hartman, Hauglum and Mackey would also go over 1,000. Of course, Smith had done it in two seasons, not three or four.

Record: 30-3

86 Indiana 79
68 Nebraska 78
74 Tennessee 59
93 Kansas State 73
81 California 63
52 Oregon State 50
64 Louisiana Tech 86
65 Oregon 59
94 Drake 56
109 Kansas 71
79 Iowa State 60
95 Stephen F. Austin 88
94 Houston 68
88 Wayland Baptist 62
75 Texas Tech 71
84 Baylor 60
88 Texas A&M 51
79 SMU 39
107 TCU 41
74 UT-San Antonio 54
77 Texas Tech 53
90 Houston 59
96 Rice 62
74 Wayland Baptist 59
89 Arkansas 67
94 Baylor 55
88 Texas A&M 57
100 Rice 49
86 Houston 62
80 Arkansas 54
84 Louisville 55
73 Kansas State 70 (OT)
58 Louisiana Tech 72

At only one court in the state had UT had never won—Stephen F. Austin Coliseum, where the Ladyjacks had taken all five matchups beginning in 1978. Conradt, who quipped that hardhats might be needed in light of SFA's boisterous fans, liked what she saw early. Smith (33) was largely responsible for building a big halftime lead, but the Ladyjacks' Tammy Mayo (25) closed it to three. Then Harris, who never really played like a freshman, made a steal, a couple of assists and totaled 19 points in a 95-88 victory. When the game was over, the Horns hardly celebrated. Recognition as the best team in Texas had once meant a lot, but it was a new day, and UT had bigger fish to fry.

While those fish were not in the Southwest Conference, Texas could not avoid obligations to the seven-decade-old league that had begun sponsoring women's competition. The nine member schools agreed to a single round-robin schedule of eight games, going to a full 16 (as per the men) the next year. History of a sort was made on January 15 before 927 spectators, but there was little suspense in UT's 94-68 demolition of Houston. Suffocating defense led by Whaley and the Mackey-to-Smith offensive combination were too much for the Cougars. Smith, 14th in the nation in scoring with 24 points per game, was the first woman to be honored as the Associated Press SWC player of the week.

Wayland Baptist, a forerunner in women's college basketball in the 1950s and 1960s, had not joined the NCAA after the AIAW folded but rather the less-competitive NAIA. As a near-blizzard raged outside Hutcherson Arena, Texas rode Smith's 36 points to an 88-62 defeat of the Queens, a game in which Conradt was slapped with two technical fouls. And while they were in the area, the No. 4 Horns stopped in Lubbock for a game with Texas Tech. Carolyn Thompson (34) led a determined upset bid, but the Red Raiders fell just short, 75-71. Marsha Sharp's team served notice that it intended to challenge the dominant Longhorns.

After that close call, UT continued drumming opponents by wide margins. The next 16 games were victories, none by less than 22 points, although Conradt and her assistants spent more time than they preferred away from the team, seeking new players. Compared to the AIAW, in which off-campus recruiting was not allowed, recruiting in the NCAA was a no-holds-barred process. The coaches had to give ever more attention to enticing prospective student-athletes to Austin. While the new development was not one Conradt liked, she had no choice but to take part. Women's college basketball was becoming less distinct from the men, yet the lack of a professional league (the WBL had gone belly-up) tended to keep the focus more clearly on education rather than making a bundle of money as a pro.

The Longhorns beat Baylor, 84-60, at Heart O' Texas Coliseum, but for the second straight game, Smith found herself bottled up by a collapsing zone defense. They rolled to an 88-51 defeat of Texas A&M in Austin, causing Aggie coach Cherri Rapp to call UT's aggressive, pressing defense the best she had seen. "If we could ever get past their guards, we might be able to play against them," she said. Whaley, in Conradt's view, was the best defensive player in the nation.

Lethargic in the first half, the Horns still romped SMU by 40 points. And TCU took a brutal 107-41 defeat in Fort Worth before 225 fans. Ken Davis, the Horned Frogs' part-time coach, tried to smile after seeing his overmatched troops sink to 3-17. Conradt offered encouraging words to TCU but wondered about the value of such a game, and she was right; TCU finished last or tied for last 12 of the 14 years of SWC women's basketball and had only one all-conference player. The UT-San Antonio Roadrunners, a team in existence for just two years, got a moral victory by losing to Texas by just 20 as Smith had 23 points and 11 rebounds.

"Women cagers deserve respect" was the title of a *Daily Texan* column by David Spangler. He described the 1983 Longhorns' exciting style of play that averaged 80 points per game, the 13-game winning streak, 23-game home streak and 51 straight wins against SWC competition. He asked why such a fine team should draw barely 1,400 fans to a typical Erwin Center game. A student body of 48,000 ought to be filling the place, Spangler noted with exasperation. Conradt, AD Donna Lopiano and sports information director Chris Plonsky were concerned, too. "We haven't found the secret to drawing fans yet," Conradt said. "Is it the day of the week? The weather? How the men's team is doing? If we had the answers, we'd do a better job of marketing the program."

A crowd of 2,113 was on hand to see Hauglum, who had given way to Harris often lately, score a season-high 21 points and lead Texas to a 77-53 decision over Texas Tech. It was not quite the closely contested game the two teams played in Lubbock three weeks earlier. Then the Longhorns took a pair of victories in Houston, beating UH, 90-59, and Rice, 96-62. Smith scored a total of 53 points, while Betty Darthard led the Cougars with 16 and Pennie Goff had 23 for the Owls.

Whaley suffered a hyperextended knee in the Houston game, which allowed Ethridge to start against Wayland Baptist in Austin. The 5'6" frosh had shown fine court sense and an ability to run the fast break about as well as Mackey or Whaley. She definitely had a future in orange and white. With Whaley dressed in street clothes and leading cheers from the bench, UT survived a series of lapses to beat the Queens, 74-59. Smith put on another show—27 points, eight rebounds and seven steals. As it turned out, that was the last time Texas and Wayland Baptist ever met, the series ending in the Longhorns' favor, 15-6.

After an 89-67 defeat of Arkansas, the SWC title belonged to UT. The Razorbacks were the only other conference team to schedule any national powers, although they lost decisively to Louisiana Tech and Kentucky. Smith had 29 points for Texas, and Bettye Fiscus scored 26 for Arkansas.

Two more games remained on the regular-season schedule, against SWC teams but not counting in the standings. On the opening tip of the Texas-Baylor game in Austin, Smith knocked the ball to Williams, who flipped it to Mackey for a layup after just three seconds had elapsed, and a 94-55 rout was on. Bear coach Pam Davis opined that UT deserved the No. 3 ranking. Smith (33 points and 15 rebounds) was a running, jumping blur in an 88-57 defeat of Texas A&M in College Station. So the Horns wrapped up their schedule with a 25-2 record and recognition as one of the best in the nation. Smith, who was born to the game but never stopped working at it, was chosen SWC player of the year.

The 1983 Horns. The youngest players on this team would taste national championship glory before they were through.

The 1983 Southwest Conference postseason tournament was the last time Gregory Gym was used for intercollegiate basketball. The Horns were hands-down favorites to win, and they had to win because the NCAA allotted just one spot for an SWC team in the playoffs. Showing no signs of rust after an 11-day hiatus, Texas rambled past Rice, 100-49. "I don't think anyone in the conference is going to touch them," said Owl coach Linda Tucker. "We were just the first victims. UT's talent is superior to everyone else." Houston gave the Horns a game for 20 minutes, but the final result was an 86-62 Texas win keyed by Smith's 24 points and nine rebounds. The championship game, held at the Erwin Center, was an 80-54 defeat of Arkansas. Smith (22) had all the right moves under the basket, and the Hogs could not stop her. Mackey, Hauglum, Ethridge and Hartman also reached double figures, and Bettye Fiscus had a strong game for Arkansas.

The Longhorns were in the 36-team NCAA Tournament, and their first game was played in Austin. Louisville, champion of the Metro Conference, could not handle UT's pressure defense and lost, 84-55. Smith struck for 21 points, and Hartman had a season-high 12 rebounds, while the Cardinals' top two scorers, Rosalind Smith and Janet McNew, got a total of seven points.

Conradt believed the NCAA was punishing Texas for staying with the AIAW in 1982 by sending it to the regional hosted by Louisiana Tech, the No. 1 team in the nation. Southern Cal, the No. 2 team, also hosted one, so why not let the Horns play in one of the other two regionals and theoretically get the best teams in the Final Four? "I've always felt we'd be paying for some time for taking a stand against the NCAA," said the UT coach. "I suppose if you're going to win the national championship, you've got to beat people and it doesn't matter where you beat them."

Texas and Kansas State met at the Thomas Assembly Center in Ruston on March 25, with the likelihood of a game against Louisiana Tech looming ahead. While the Horns had beaten the Wildcats by 20 points in December, it was not so lovely the second time around. UT needed 21 points from Smith, 16 from Mackey and some overtime heroics by Hartman and Ethridge to win, 73-70. As a result, the 30-2 Longhorns advanced to play Louisiana Tech, a team that had defeated them handily before the 25-game winning streak started. A crowd of 5,905 was on hand for a game that would send one team home and the other to the Final Four in Norfolk. The Techsters, with 76 wins in their last 77 home games, got another one at Texas' expense, 72-58. All-American Janice Lawrence scored 27 points and had help from Debra Rodman and Tia Sossamon in stifling Smith, who fouled out with 4:17 left. Conradt denied any effect from the unholy din raised by the fans, but she pointed to a gaping 32-to-2 difference in free throw opportunities. It had been a fine season, one of the best for Conradt's Longhorns. But they learned the continuing lesson that the toughest part of climbing a mountain is near the summit.

1984

In a move that shocked people outside of the UT women's basketball program but not those inside, coach Jody Conradt dismissed Terri Mackey during the summer for academic and attitude problems. The all-SWC guard, one of the Longhorns' top players for three years, was gone because Conradt insisted on the maintenance of certain standards. Mackey's backcourt replacement, soph Kamie Ethridge, was quite capable. Conradt searched high and low during recruiting season for a big (preferably in the 6'5" range) center, thought to be the final piece in the puzzle to make Texas a national champion. If she was disappointed not to get such a player, then Andrea Lloyd compensated quite well. The 6'2" forward from Idaho was a marvelous athlete who could pass, rebound and score, sometimes described as a female Magic Johnson. Two other frosh, guards Yulonda Wimbish and Paulette Moegle, and senior Sherryl Hauglum suffered knee injuries, leaving the No. 4 Longhorns short-handed before they had played a single game. Annette Smith, however, would have her greatest season yet and become the first UT player chosen as a consensus all-American.

The Horns scored an 82-56 defeat of Alabama at the Erwin Center, the first of seven victories over top-20 teams in the 1984 season. All in all, it was an impressive warm-up for another tough Southeastern Conference team, Tennessee. There in the Smoky Mountains, UT continued the quest to become queen of the hill. Volunteer coach Pat Summitt called the Longhorns "a great transition team, the best baseline-to-baseline team in women's basketball." Her team trailing by one with nine seconds left, Fran Harris spun through heavy traffic under the backboard and tossed up a prayer that fell through, and Cara Priddy blocked a potential game-winner by Mary Ostrowski at the other end to gain a thrilling 66-65 victory over No. 5 Tennessee. The remarkably composed Lloyd got 19 points, eight rebounds and six steals.

Smith, who played just 18 minutes against the Vols due to foul troubles, scored 31 points in a 90-45 rout of UT-San Antonio, one of the few nonconference "gimme" games on the schedule. She had another fine performance (34 points and 12 rebounds) when the Horns beat Cheyney, 88-78. Yolanda Laney scored 28 for the No. 20 Wolves, a team destined for the Final Four. The Longhorns had no time to catch their breath because No. 3 Georgia, with all-American Janet Harris, came to Austin for the third game in six days. The Bulldogs had a size advantage at every position, but unlike most big teams, they were quick. Texas, ahead by 12 midway through the second half, got outscored 25-7 from then on and suffered a 67-61 defeat. Smith scored 23 for UT, and Harris and Teresa Edwards combined for 35 of the Bulldogs' points. "Georgia was awesome, but we just didn't get anything from the bench tonight," Conradt said.

The Longhorns took a two-day sojourn to the midwest and got mixed results. They thrashed Kansas, 81-64, at Allen Fieldhouse but lost to Drake, 87-81, in Des Moines. All-American Lorri Bauman (the first woman to exceed 3,000 points) scored 34 as the unranked Bulldogs dictated a slow pace. Conradt, who kept the locker-room door closed for 30 minutes after the game, was worried and frustrated that her team lacked intensity, a necessary component for the pressing defense and running offense UT was known for. After a 10-day holiday break, the Horns went back to the same region to play ninth-ranked Kansas State. Lynn Hickey's Wildcats had won 31 consecutive games at home, a streak that was snapped by the orange-clad visitors, 82-78. A record crowd of 3,750 watched as the Longhorns overcame a five-point deficit in the last six minutes. Smith and K-State's Tina Dixon put up the same impressive numbers—35 points and nine rebounds. Conradt had copious kudos for Smith and nearly every other player, including sub guard Kriss Ethridge.

Her younger sister, Kamie, was a much better player, but Kriss Ethridge would get considerably more time on the court over the next two months because of a knee injury to Esoleta Whaley, heart and soul of the defense and also scoring 10 points per game. With Whaley out, UT was down to eight players, and who was up next? Defending national champion and top-ranked Southern California, with Pam and Paula McGee and basketball wunderkind Cheryl Miller. A flamboyant 6'3" forward, Miller was extending the boundaries of women's hoops. Conradt's Longhorns rose to the occasion, beating USC, 77-68, before a crowd of 3,180 at the Erwin Center. Smith and Harris both scored 20, one point less than the great Miller, and Priddy and Audrey Smith did well off the bench as

Annette Smith, two-time SWC player of the year and an all-American in 1984.

the Trojans were outrebounded, 44-38. That ended the nation's longest winning streak at 28. Just two days later, UT hosted another unbeaten California team, No. 4 Long Beach State. The Horns saw a big lead evaporate but held on for a 73-72 victory. Harris had 27 points and Kirsten Cummings 20 for the 49ers, some of whom grumbled about biased officiating.

The weakness of Southwest Conference competition was hard to deny, although Texas Tech and Arkansas (and to a lesser extent, Houston) were building respectable programs. Conference play began at home on January 7 against Marsha Sharp's 10-2 Red Raiders. Smith scored 26 points and held Carolyn Thompson to 13 in an 85-62 blasting of Texas Tech. Priddy, who was beginning to assert herself, got 16 points and 11 rebounds in just 24 minutes. Conradt gave her team, ranked No. 3, a rare day off and then began preparations for Houston and the 6'5" freshman center, Monica Lamb, who had chosen to be a Cougar instead of a Longhorn. She scored 18 points in UH's 90-69 loss at Hofheinz Pavilion, a game in which Kamie Ethridge made steal after steal and Harris had 28 points. And across town at Autry Court, Smith exploded for 46 points—an SWC record—in a 110-54 cakewalk over Rice. She really could have scored more against the flightless Owls because Conradt removed her with nearly 10 minutes left. "Annette's the most physically talented player I've ever coached in every aspect of the game," Conradt said. "She's a great offensive player, but her defense is often overlooked. You just can't ask for any more than she does. She's modest, team-oriented, everything you want. She's pretty near perfect."

One of the chief pretenders to the throne, Arkansas, came to Austin and was promptly put in its place—second place. The Longhorns pinned a 26-point defeat on the Razorbacks and followed that up by romping Baylor, 96-51. Smith had a total of 57 points in the two games. "I told Jody that she has her best team ever," said Bear coach Pam Davis. "They are strong and quick under the basket.... It's tough to recruit against the University of Texas. They have the blue-chippers. They know what they can do, and they do it well."

Rising to No. 2 in the polls, UT overcame several defensive lapses by using its offensive weapons to beat Texas A&M, 108-77, at G. Rollie White Coliseum. Ethridge had 17 assists, and Lloyd enjoyed perhaps her best game yet with 26 points and 14 rebounds. Lisa Langston scored 14 for the Aggies. Smith hit for 39 points in a 97-60 execution of SMU in Dallas, and Ethridge, known to coaches and teammates as "Brat," was relentless in running the fast break.

Before the Texas-TCU game in Austin, Horned Frog coach Frances Garmon flattered Conradt's team but said the regularity of blowouts was not helping anyone, and she was right. Nevertheless, UT scored an easy 113-62 victory with six players in double figures. *Austin American-Statesman* writer Mark Rosner described the game as "a slick sports car, racing downcourt against that old 1959 pickup that's been sitting around the yard for several years." The Ladyjacks of Stephen F. Austin, who once had Texas' number, submitted to a 91-64 beating that might have been worse. The frontline of Lloyd, Smith and Harris scored 63 points and collected 32 rebounds in a game played before 2,343 appreciative spectators. Much as it had been during the heyday of Abe Lemons' UT men's teams, the Burnt Orange Room was packed with fans before and after games.

The irresistible force known as Texas women's basketball nearly met an immovable object in Lubbock. As a big crowd screamed for the SWC heavyweight's demise, Priddy and Audrey Smith (whose big sister was triple-teamed and held to nine points) came through at the end of a 71-65 victory, ending the Red Raiders' 16-game home win streak. "We've had it too easy the last few games," Conradt said. "But I'm proud that we refused to lose."

Houston, a talented yet erratic team, committed 48 turnovers in a 103-72 loss to UT in Austin. After that win and Louisiana Tech's second defeat in a week, the 19-2 Longhorns took over the No. 1 ranking, which the 1980 team had shared briefly with Old Dominion. "It's a motivational factor for our opponents," Conradt said. "And I don't think anybody needs extra motivation to beat UT. But now that we're here, we're not planning to give it up easily."

Harris connected on 16 of 17 shots in a 113-50 defeat of Rice at the Erwin Center. Owl coach Linda Tucker said, "From what I've seen, yes, they're No. 1. Nobody likes to get romped and stomped. We can dream and think big, but we can't be at this level for quite some time. Texas has that success, and everybody wants to reach out and touch it."

A somewhat less-worshipful Arkansas coach Matilda Willis was eager to play the Longhorns in Fayetteville. Tipoff was 30 minutes after the men's game, and 3,483 fans (some wearing plastic, long-snouted pig hats) stuck around for an exciting contest. Audrey Smith's 14-foot jumper from the right side preceded a last-second shot by Amanda Holley that hung on the rim and fell out, giving Texas a 71-70 victory. Annette Smith and Harris teamed up for 47 points while Holley had 25 for Arkansas. The Longhorns' 76th straight win over SWC competition had been a 40-minute back-and-forth battle.

UT had another fast-break layup party, blitzing Texas A&M, 105-60, before the home folks. Among the big scorers was Shell Bollin (20), a 6'2" soph who customarily got the least amount of playing time. The Horns traveled to Waco to engage Baylor and took a 93-74 victory. Smith scored 31, and when Harris, Lloyd and Bollin fouled out, no reserves were left on the eight-woman team.

They had clinched a second straight SWC championship before playing in the Northern Lights Invitational in Anchorage, Alaska. There were three games in three nights, all impressive victories. Smith had 33 points and Ethridge 12 steals in beating Pepperdine, 96-68, in the first round. Florida State presented no competition, falling 32 points behind at the half and losing, 89-43. Seminole coach Janice Dykehouse admitted her team was intimidated by the tireless Longhorns, keyed by Lloyd's 19 points and 10 rebounds. Smith and Harris combined for 41 points in the title game, 82-60 over Nevada-Las Vegas. Misty Thomas scored 21 for the Rebels. Opposing coaches, fans and media raved about the tremendous showing by the nation's No. 1 team. Smith was chosen MVP, but the passing, rebounding and slashing offensive moves of Lloyd got just about as much attention.

Somewhat weary after that northern odyssey, the Longhorns did not need much rest before the final regular-season home game, a 98-63 defeat of SMU. Smith had 37 points and 11 rebounds, and Mustang center Toni Jackson scored 21. That was a typically great game for Smith, and no one knew she had performed for the last time until the 1986 season. Practicing before a Sunday afternoon game with TCU, Smith suffered a serious knee injury. Virtually the entire UT women's athletic department was in shock because Smith's dream of leading the Longhorns to the 1984

Record: 32-3

82 Alabama 56
66 Tennessee 65
90 UT-San Antonio 45
88 Cheyney 78
61 Georgia 67
81 Kansas 64
81 Drake 87
82 Kansas State 78
77 Southern California 68
73 Long Beach State 72
85 Texas Tech 62
90 Houston 69
110 Rice 54
89 Arkansas 63
96 Baylor 51
108 Texas A&M 77
97 SMU 60
113 TCU 62
91 Stephen F. Austin 64
71 Texas Tech 65
103 Houston 72
113 Rice 50
71 Arkansas 70
105 Texas A&M 60
93 Baylor 74
96 Pepperdine 68
89 Florida State 43
82 Nevada-Las Vegas 60
98 SMU 63
113 TCU 63
96 Houston 76
83 Texas Tech 73
96 Drake 60
99 NE Louisiana 91
60 Louisiana Tech 85

national championship and playing in the Los Angeles Olympics would not happen. She had been averaging 25 points per game—13th best in the country—and was just 44 points away from breaking Linda Waggoner's career scoring record. At a hastily arranged press conference at the Erwin Center during the UIL girls' tournament, Conradt expressed primary concern for Smith's health before speculating on the impact her injury would have on the already depleted team. While the SWC and NCAA playoffs suddenly looked rather perilous, UT refused to be written off.

Smith, who underwent surgery to repair ligaments and remove damaged cartilage, did not mope and feel sorry for herself but attended practices and games on crutches, wearing a smile and speaking in a positive manner. She gave ample encouragement to Priddy, her replacement in the middle, who teamed up with Harris for 41 points in Texas' 113-63 defeat of the Frogs before a handful of fans at Daniel-Meyer Coliseum.

Although Smith (again SWC player of the year) was out, Leta Whaley was back after two months of grueling rehabilitation. She played surprisingly well in the final games of her career, which began with the SWC Tournament at Hofheinz Pavilion. The Houston Cougars were licking their chops in anticipation of playing Texas without its star center, but they lost, 96-76. Harris scored 27 points and Audrey Smith 23. Conradt was beaming after the game. "Whoever has more heart can win, and this team has a lot of heart," she said. "I've got to be the luckiest person alive to have a team like this." Luck avoided Texas Tech, though. The tourney crown went to UT, which used a zone trap to force 18 second-half turnovers and break open a close game to beat the Red Raiders, 83-73. The Longhorns triumphed, but no one could handle Carolyn Thompson (30).

The first of what might prove to be an arduous five-game run to the national title was at home against Drake. The day before, the coaches and players met with Governor Mark White, who acknowledged their success and proclaimed March 15, 1984 as "women's basketball day." UT avenged the early-season loss to Drake by burying the Bulldogs, 96-60, before 4,876 fans. With 69 percent field goal accuracy and a swarming defense, Texas had the game won by halftime. Harris led a balanced attack with 21 points.

The victory advanced the Longhorns, who did not get one of four top seeds in the national tournament, to the regional meet in Ruston, home of Louisiana Tech. Decisions on where to hold regionals were made, in part, on financial considerations based on attendance figures. That inevitably meant some teams played at home, not hurting their chances a bit. UT's first game at Thomas Assembly Center was with Northeast Louisiana, led by 6'3" center Lisa Ingram and guard Eun Jung Lee, the darling of Korean-American hoop fans. Ingram was splendid, scoring 36 points, but the Indians lost a fast-paced game, 99-91. Lloyd (29) and Harris (26) offset Ingram's big offensive night.

So the 32-2 Longhorns met 29-2 Louisiana Tech to see who would go to the Final Four in Los Angeles. It was Texas' quickness, defense and fast-breaking against the Techsters' size, offense and deliberate style, and the latter prevailed resoundingly. A 20-point run in the second half won it for Tech, 85-60. Janice Lawrence scored 34 points and Pam Gant 22, while no Texas player exceeded 12. The Longhorns returned gloomily to Austin, but given the circumstances—five knee injuries including one to Annette Smith—it had been a very successful season, and that is why Conradt was chosen for the second time as national coach of the year.

1985

The 1985 season witnessed the first dunk in the history of women's hoops (by West Virginia's Georgeann Wells, albeit with the lighter and smaller ball instituted a year earlier), a crowd of more than 22,000 at a game between Iowa and Ohio State, and the NCAA Final Four in Austin. Jody Conradt's Longhorns, who spent much of the season in the limelight of a No. 1 ranking, had the talent, experience and depth to win it all on their home court the last weekend in March. "This is an exciting time in women's athletics," Conradt said. "The players are getting better, and we have more attention from the fans and media. They're not comparing us to the men anymore."

Annette Smith, sitting out the year as a medical redshirt, would be missed. But Fran Harris, Kamie Ethridge, Andrea Lloyd and the other returnees were augmented by some fine new players. Gay Hemphill, a star at Wayland Baptist, had transferred to Texas, gained eligibility and was ready to go. And Beverly Williams, a fine ballhandler and penetrator, would be one of the key figures in UT's basketball success over the next four years.

No one could accuse Conradt of arranging a creampuff schedule, certainly not at the beginning of the season. The No. 2 Horns would go on the road to play No. 3 Old Dominion and No. 1 Georgia in late November. Marianne Stanley had the finest ODU team since the AIAW champs of 1979 and 1980. The taller Monarchs outhustled and outmuscled Texas to gain a 90-80 victory in Norfolk, the first season-opening loss in Conradt's tenure. Medina Dixon led six players in double figures, while Harris (25) was UT's top scorer. Lloyd, never shy about mixing it up underneath, had 16 rebounds, nearly half her team's total. Battered by Old Dominion, the Longhorns faced an equally rugged Georgia team, although Teresa Edwards, the Bulldogs' star guard and member of the 1984 Olympic team, was out with an ankle injury. UT surged to a seven-point halftime lead and kept going, taking a sweet 83-69 win before 6,188 fans, the largest crowd yet to witness a women's game in Athens. Frosh reserves Yulonda Wimbish and C.J. Jones helped limit the points and rebounds of Georgia's inside players, Katrina McClain and Janet Harris.

The Texas Invitational, held during Conradt's first three seasons in Austin, was revived in the form of the Converse-MacGregor Texas Classic. It featured UT, UCLA (with forward Jackie Joyner, who already had won the first of several Olympic medals in track and field), No. 19 North Carolina State and Vanderbilt. Before the Longhorn-Wolfpack game, Conradt was honored when a couple of appreciative fans donated a $25,000 scholarship in her name. Texas rolled by N.C. State, 82-68, getting 21 points from Hemphill, one of the nation's leaders in shooting accuracy throughout the season. Linda "Hawkeye" Page equaled her average of 27 points for the Wolfpack, who could not handle the Texas press and committed 27 turnovers. The Horns shifted into high gear and romped Vandy, 95-71, for the tournament title. Barbara Brackman had a game-high 28 points for the Commodores, and Lloyd won MVP honors largely because of her defensive work. Prelims during the tournament were volleyball matches featuring Mick Haley's UT team. Cheerleaders and the Longhorn Band, occasional participants 10 years earlier, were by then a part of the Erwin Center scene for all women's games.

That tourney was followed by one in Las Vegas, Jones' hometown. Conradt almost pulled out of the Seven-Up Desert Classic when she realized it would not be held in the 18,500-seat Thomas and Mack Center but at an old and small gym on the Nevada-Las Vegas campus. Hemphill scored 24 and Cara Priddy 19 in an 85-53 defeat of Alabama, and Hemphill came back with 21 the next night in a 95-64 drubbing of UNLV. Conradt promised Texas would not return the next season, calling the playing conditions and officiating "bush league."

There was a major-league team coming to the Erwin Center. Tennessee had finished second in the previous NCAA Tournament, and four Longhorn players had something to prove to Pat Summitt, the Volunteer coach who headed the 1984 Olympic team; Hemphill, Lloyd and Harris were cut, while Ethridge had made it as an alternate. Summitt was surprisingly amiable after watching her team get mauled, 91-60, one of the worst defeats in Tennessee history. Ethridge, whose 15 points made her the third-leading scorer for Texas, also had nine assists and five steals. The Lubbock junior, though not so quick as the departed Esoleta Whaley, was adept at pressure defense and pushing the ball upcourt and was never afraid to admonish a lazy teammate.

After giving 2,247 fans a nicely wrapped Christmas present, a 74-48 defeat of Kansas State, the Horns dispersed and did not play again until the Trojan-Bud Light Classic in Los Angeles. It was a unique tournament, with Southern Cal hosting both a men's division and a women's division. Texas played poorly in beating Maryland, 69-40, but the intimidated Terrapins shot just 23 percent and turned the ball over 29 times. The No. 2 Longhorns and the No. 4 Trojans met in the title game. Linda Sharp's team, winner of the national championship the last two seasons, was led by Cheryl Miller, the greatest, or at least the most famous, player the sport had ever seen. She scored 36 points (14 of 17 from the field) and grabbed 20 rebounds in USC's 73-71 victory, won on Yolanda Fletcher's layup with one second left. Conradt, who searched desperately for a cohesive unit on the floor, said it was not one of her best coaching efforts.

Southwest Conference play began on January 3 in Lubbock against the No. 16 Red Raiders. Priddy, assistant coach Jill Rankin's project player, had been ineffective in recent games and was benched in favor of the versatile Wimbish at the post. Audrey Smith, who missed the early season with a knee injury, announced her presence with authority by scoring 19 points as the Horns raced to a 90-64 victory, disappointing a record crowd of 4,016.

Big Monica Lamb scored a game-high 20 points in Houston's 71-55 loss to Texas at the Erwin Center. She also blocked five shots and forced the Longhorns to alter the trajectory of several others. Hemphill had 18 points and 15 rebounds in UT's 82nd straight win against SWC competition. Conference coaches and the media began each season by saying the gap between Texas and the other teams had narrowed, but the Horns won and won, usually by substantial margins. The next seven victories were by 34, 25, 37, 22, 36, 42 and 42 points. Conradt, who sometimes acknowledged the need for stiffer competition in the SWC, still said, "I like a blowout. Anybody who doesn't must be out of their minds." Ethridge, however, had this comment: "I think it's good to be challenged. It's easier to get motivated. And it's good for the conference and women's basketball. I don't think our fans want to see 50-point blowouts every game."

Texas' fiery point guard, Kamie Ethridge.

The Longhorns packed their burnt orange uniforms for three out-of-town games, beginning with a 76-42 defeat of Rice in which Hemphill and Williams combined for 32 points. Arkansas coach John Sutherland, one of those who spoke of "parity" and "balance" in the SWC, saw UT toy with his team for a half and then pull away to an 85-60 win. Priddy made all eight of her shots, and Lloyd had 15 rebounds, while Razorback freshman Brenda Rhodes had 23 points, seven steals and four assists, earning plaudits from Conradt. And Texas beat Baylor in Waco by a score of 82-45, "a game custom-made for those who believe the world could use a dose of mercy," according to Mark Rosner of the *Austin American-Statesman.*

Solidifying their No. 2 ranking, the Horns took a pair of victories at home. Hemphill and Lloyd were the top scorers in an 80-58 defeat of Texas A&M, and it was Wimbish (19) in an 82-46 rout of SMU. The Ponies played without their court leader, Shasta Smothers-Johnson, who was ill. All 13 of Conradt's players saw action before halftime, including end-of-the-benchers Shell Bollin, Kriss Ethridge, Michele Eglinger and Lisa Lukefahr. "It was a thrill a minute," said the UT coach. "This is the most difficult part of the season, and it's real frustrating. I feel for the first time that the weakness of the conference is starting to hurt us. We're not being challenged."

TCU had nothing with which to challenge Texas, getting spanked, 95-53, in Fort Worth as Wimbish had 20 points in just 22 minutes of play. On the same night, No. 1 Old Dominion lost to Tennessee (a team the Horns had beaten by 31 points in December), resulting in a move to the top of the Associated Press poll. The Longhorns were proud to wear the tiara, although Conradt reminded them of the priority of being No. 1 at the end of the season, after the playoffs. With the countdown to the Final Four in Austin, fans and the media were in a tizzy. Photographs and stories appeared in every major newspaper in the state, and NBC, ESPN and CNN aired pieces on the Horns. Conradt's basketball dynasty was covered in *Sports Illustrated, USA Today,* the *New York Times* and most important, the *Austin American-Statesman.* Devoted fans who believed the local daily had not given the UT women adequate attention the previous season wrote voluminous letters of protest, and the situation had improved by 1985.

A 31-point scoring spree enabled the Longhorns to beat Brigham Young, 101-59, in a midseason nonconference game. Lloyd scored 21, and the Cougars' 6'7" Tresa Spaulding had 14 points, 14 rebounds and 10 blocked shots, doing most of her damage before Conradt went with a quicker lineup. Texas Tech, the winner of eight straight games since falling to Texas, came to the Erwin Center and gave the Longhorns a scare. Marsha Sharp's team successfully slowed the pace and dictated a half-court game. Because Williams was out with a knee sprain and Wimbish made just three of 11 shots, it was close, a 70-63 UT victory. Harris and the Red Raiders' Tricia Clay both scored 17 points. There were several extenuating circumstances, but the bottom line was that the women outdrew the men for the first time—3,589 fans, as compared to the 2,994 who saw Bob Weltlich's team against Texas Tech earlier in the day.

At Hofheinz Pavilion, the Longhorns took control midway through the second half and beat Houston, 79-60. Monica Lamb, in foul trouble from the start, scored just six, but teammate Sonya Watkins had 31 points and 10 rebounds. Harris and Lloyd combined for 37 points to lead UT.

Harris, who was later named SWC player of the year, twice scored 26 points in home wins over Rice (75-50) and Arkansas (89-71). "Is Fran Harris the most underrated player in the country or what?" Conradt asked rhetorically. The 6' junior from Dallas with the silky moves was known to teammates as "Automatic," so sure was her jumper. The victory over the Hogs may not have been a masterpiece, but it was one of Texas' best games since early in the season. The Longhorns clinched their third straight SWC title with an 83-53 defeat of Baylor in Austin. Conradt's thoroughbreds ran for 53 fast-break points and stole the ball 18 times. Harris, Lloyd, Priddy, Hemphill and Ethridge reached double figures, but Bear forward Terri Moore led all scorers with 23 points. "Texas has everything going for them," said BU coach Pam Davis. "This should be the year they clear the final obstacle and win the whole thing."

Davis was not the only one to say that. Since at least 1980, UT players, opponents, sportswriters and Conradt herself had spoken of bringing a national championship to Austin. After such a startling run of success, the call had grown louder and the possibility more feasible with each season. Conradt, always careful to define the national crown as a goal and not an obsession, was frank in saying what she wanted. Even with her brightest star, Annette Smith, on the sideline, it looked like 1985 might be the year.

Record: 28-3

80 Old Dominion 90
83 Georgia 69
82 North Carolina State 68
95 Vanderbilt 71
85 Alabama 53
95 Nevada-Las Vegas 64
91 Tennessee 60
74 Kansas State 48
69 Maryland 40
71 Southern California 73
90 Texas Tech 64
71 Houston 55
76 Rice 42
85 Arkansas 60
82 Baylor 45
80 Texas A&M 58
82 SMU 46
95 TCU 53
101 Brigham Young 59
70 Texas Tech 63
79 Houston 60
75 Rice 50
89 Arkansas 71
83 Baylor 53
101 Texas A&M 73
107 SMU 72
77 TCU 53
104 Arkansas 62
82 Texas Tech 62
84 Western Michigan 62
90 Western Kentucky 92

To the tune of 101-73, UT beat Texas A&M in College Station. The press was devastating, the fast break worked beautifully, and 70 percent of the shots were on target. Michell Tatum and Lisa Langston scored 50 of the Ags' points, while Hemphill led the Horns with 19 in the 400th victory of Conradt's fabulous career. She had come a long way from being a part-time teacher, coaching multiple sports and driving the team bus at Sam Houston State. With characteristic aplomb, she said, "Everybody's made a big deal out of me winning 400 games. It just means I've been at it a long time."

They were a bit mellow in the beginning, but the Horns got going at Moody Coliseum and whomped SMU, 107-72. The Mustangs were beaten by a team with a balanced offensive attack; no Texas player scored more than 26 points in a single game during the 1985 season, partly because big winning margins meant starters gave way to subs early. Another case in point was the regular-season finale, a 77-53 defeat of TCU at the Erwin Center. Williams (13) was the top scorer, and she played just 21 minutes.

As the SWC and presumably NCAA playoffs approached, Conradt wondered about her talented team, which had not shown the consistency of the 1984 Longhorns, a group of eight players who averaged 89 points per game, second in the nation. It was time to find out, starting on March 7 in Dallas. UT's opener, a 104-62 mashing of Arkansas, marked the third time in four games the Horns had broken 100. Texas made 46 of 67 shots and looked invincible, while Bettye Fiscus scored 21 in the Razorbacks' last game of the year. Texas Tech's players and coaches had talked bravely about their chances of upsetting the Longhorns in the SWC title game, but it did not happen. Slick ballhandling by

Ethridge and Harris' 23 points were the keys in a comfortable, if not easy, 82-62 victory over the Red Raiders. "I'm ready to see some new faces," Conradt said. "Our objective in the NCAA Tournament is to get back to Austin."

One of eight No. 1 seeds, 27-2 Texas would actually begin the tournament at home against 19-9 Western Michigan. Jim Hess' Broncos were young and short and making their first postseason appearance, but they battled UT in an 84-62 loss before 4,082 fans. "I knew this would be a tough game," Conradt said. "When you get down to 32 teams, everyone is tough." The WMU defense concentrated on Harris, who took just three shots, but Lloyd (21), Priddy (18) and Wimbish (16) covered for her.

That sent the Longhorns to Bowling Green, home of 26-5 Western Kentucky. A victory against the Hilltoppers, another against the winner of Tennessee-Ole Miss, and the Horns would be home and ready to triumph at the big meet. Conradt, of course, knew better than to plan so far ahead because Texas had lost to the regional host team (Louisiana Tech) the last two years. A frenzied Diddle Arena crowd of 4,900 saw UT and Western Kentucky fight it out for 40 minutes. The game ended with a bang when Hilltopper forward Lillie Mason took an inbounds pass and shot from 12 feet out, sending the ball through the net just before the buzzer for a 92-90 victory. Mason and Clemette Haskins both scored 26, while Lloyd (20 points and 18 rebounds) was valiant in defeat. Yet Mason was her defensive responsibility on the fateful last shot. And Conradt later took some heat for calling a timeout just before the play, allowing Western Kentucky to get set up. It never should have gotten to that point because the Horns hit just 16 of 31 free throws and allowed too many second- and third-shot opportunities. Topper coach Paul Sanderford said Texas would beat his team nine out of ten times, but that was small consolation.

Their dream shattered, the Longhorns came back to Austin to watch, but not participate in, the Final Four, consisting of Old Dominion, Georgia, Western Kentucky and Northeast Louisiana and won by the Monarchs of ODU. "I can't tell you how disappointed we are," Conradt said during that painful weekend. "But we only lost three games. Let's not be doomsayers yet."

1986

So serious was the knee injury she suffered in March 1984, Annette Smith's doctor advised her to give up basketball. She was back with the team as it prepared for the 1986 season, but she wore a heavy brace that limited her quickness and agility. While Jody Conradt encouraged Smith, she was careful not to place undue pressure on the fifth-year senior center, once among the top players in the game. Conradt had all five starters back, three of whom—Kamie Ethridge, Fran Harris and Andrea Lloyd—were getting preseason all-America notice. The coach, beginning her 10th season on the Forty Acres, also landed a prize recruit, Clarissa Davis, widely regarded as the finest female athlete San Antonio had ever seen. The 6'1" forward had 25 points, six rebounds, four steals and three blocked shots in the orange and white intrasquad game, giving every indication of greatness. The Associated Press, *USA Today*, *Sports Illustrated* and virtually every basketball yearbook ranked the Longhorns No. 1 before the season began, and the deep and hungry team, from Conradt on down, seemed intent on winning the national championship. "I think we are capable of going undefeated and setting marks no other women's team has ever set," Ethridge asserted. One record UT would set in 1986 was in attendance, averaging 5,289 over 16 games at the Erwin Center.

The season started, in Texas' fearless way, on the road against a couple of top-10 teams, Ohio State and Tennessee. At a snake pit called St. John Arena, 4,281 howling fans saw UT blow a 10-point halftime lead, fall behind by three and finally win, 78-76. The Buckeyes' Tracey Hall scored a game-high 22 points, and Davis had an inauspicious start, missing all seven shots but getting five rebounds. OSU coach Nancy Darsch was quite unimpressed with the supposedly ferocious Longhorns. Two days later in Knoxville, they took on Tennessee, which was eager to repay the previous season's 31-point nuking in Austin. Despite committing 32 turnovers, Texas pounded the Vols, 74-52. Harris and Smith teamed up for 29 points, and the press was effective against Pat Summitt's team. "Two-and-O and going home," Conradt chortled. "I'm having a great Thanksgiving."

The first game of the Converse-Pepsi Texas Classic was a not-so-classic 92-65 defeat of Western Michigan. The Horns played rather sloppily and made barely half of their free throws and still had no trouble with the Broncos. Davis proved that she was not long for the bench, scoring 25 points. A much tougher test came the following night against No. 3 Northeast Louisiana, a team with two players, Lisa Ingram and Chana Perry, who seemed to portend the future of women's hoops—big and bruising. They could rip down rebounds with NBA-like authority. The Indians' methodical half-court game had UT fans anxious until Beverly Williams started an 18-2 scoring spree that led to a 68-54 victory. She and Ingram shared tourney MVP honors.

Record: 34-0
78 Ohio State 76
74 Tennessee 52
92 Western Michigan 65
68 NE Louisiana 54
94 Southern California 78
81 Rutgers 63
57 Mississippi 46
70 NE Louisiana 65
92 Houston 66
70 Rice 38
75 Arkansas 44
93 Baylor 40
73 Texas A&M 59
96 SMU 58
93 Old Dominion 62
95 TCU 42
111 Brigham Young 78
64 Texas Tech 57
87 Houston 60
78 Rice 46
75 Arkansas 57
77 Baylor 45
77 Texas A&M 64
112 Miami 43
105 SMU 48
105 TCU 44
55 Texas Tech 43
81 Houston 64
77 Texas Tech 53
108 Missouri 67
85 Oklahoma 59
66 Mississippi 63
90 Western Kentucky 65
97 Southern California 81

December 10 was a rather memorable evening for Texas women's basketball as No. 5 Southern Cal, led by three-time (and soon to be four-time) all-American Cheryl Miller, came to town. "She's the best player in the world," Conradt said. "If she gets hot early, it's all over," Smith said. "Covering her last year was the toughest job I've ever had," Harris said. And while Miller scored 31 points, got nine rebounds and played in her inimitable way, the Women of Troy lost, 94-78. By far the largest crowd in UT history, 11,470, witnessed it. Smith, who went scoreless against Northeast Louisiana, had 22 points and eclipsed the school record of 2,256 set by Linda Waggoner six years earlier. It was Texas' last game for 19 days.

That was a long rest, perhaps too long, because the Horns' play showed signs of rust at the eight-team Orange Bowl-Burger King Invitational in Miami. Harris and Ethridge scored 12 apiece, offsetting a 24-point performance by Rutgers' Sue Wicks in an 81-63 UT win. By the strength of numbers, the top-ranked Longhorns rolled by No. 8 Mississippi in the second round. Jennifer Gillom (24) had the Rebels up by 12 in the first half, but Texas closed in on them in an intense, physical game, prevailing by a score of 57-46. Davis had 17 points, and Lloyd collected a like number of rebounds. "I can see why they're No. 1," said Ole Miss coach Van Chancellor. "Their second team is probably ninth or tenth." The title game, played before fewer than 800 fans, was a rematch with Northeast Louisiana, a team recently punished by the NCAA for the sort of recruiting violations Conradt had feared and predicted would happen as women's basketball evolved. Chana Perry, the key figure in those events, combined with Lisa Ingram for 46 points, but the Indians lost, 70-65. Gay Hemphill led UT with 16 points in a reserve role, and Lloyd, tournament MVP, had 12 rebounds in the last game before Southwest Conference play commenced.

No Longhorn team had fallen to SWC competition since 1978, and the 98-game streak was unlikely to end soon. Greg Williams, whose UH team upset No. 4 Louisiana Tech in December, nevertheless dreaded facing Texas, which was in the Bayou City for two games. Harris and the Cougars' Sonya Watkins both had 24 points, but Harris had a lot more help in a 92-66 victory. Many of the 1,016 fans at Autry Court were supporters of the Horns, and they saw their team blister Rice, 70-38. The Owls' Holly Jones (22) was the top scorer in the game, followed by Davis (15) and Smith (14).

John Sutherland, a mere stripling at age 26, brought his Arkansas Razorbacks to Austin and left both older and wiser after a 75-44 thumping. Baylor, too, hoped for a miracle, but the Bears just provided UT with an opportunity to work on a zone defense and half-court offense, in case the Longhorns were ever challenged. The score was 93-40.

In College Station for a Tuesday night game, the Horns won by just 14 points, which Aggie coach Lynn Hickey found encouraging. Smith went all the way, scoring 23 points and drawing praise from Conradt. Although clearly limited in what she could do, Annette

Smith still had the stuff. Sophomore guards Williams and Yulonda Wimbish teamed up for 34 points in an effortless 96-58 defeat of SMU at Moody Coliseum, leaving the Horns with a 14-0 record.

What was supposed to be a big game was actually another Texas romp. Old Dominion, the 1985 national champion, was decimated by graduation and injuries and had fallen out of the top 20 for the first time in nine years. An Erwin Center crowd of 5,517 and an ESPN television audience saw Harris connect on 13 of 16 shots in a 93-62 defeat of the Monarchs. "I think Texas is a team of destiny," said ODU coach Marianne Stanley. Two days later, the Horns met TCU in Austin. As was the custom during pregame introductions, each UT starter handed a red rose to her Frog counterpart. With the niceties out of the way, the Longhorns cruised to a 95-42 victory keyed by Davis (23) and Cara Priddy (18).

Ethridge was a tough customer, but two sore ankles forced her to miss the game with Brigham Young in Provo. And Hemphill, a top reserve, stayed at home to rest a chronic back injury. But the Horns pulled together and won, 111-78, on the strength of 26 points from Harris and 18 each from Audrey Smith and C.J. Jones. The Cougars' big center, Tresa Spaulding, scored 24 despite foul problems. Another—and much closer—road game was against Texas Tech. Hometown girl Kamie Ethridge was not supposed to play, but when UT trailed the Red Raiders by four with nine minutes left, she convinced Conradt to put her in. She got the fast break going and turned the game around with six assists and a steal as the Longhorns took a 64-57 decision. "We needed a game like this to get our adrenaline and blood flowing, but I didn't like it," Smith said.

Back in Austin, UT beat Houston, 87-60, in a physical game that caused Mark Wangrin of the *Austin American-Statesman* to describe the refs' credo as "no compound fracture, no foul." Sonya Watkins led the Cougars with 25 points, while Davis got 18 points and 13 rebounds for the Horns. Their average SWC victory margin was 32, so a 78-46 defeat of Rice was just about right. Lloyd's 20 points and 14 rebounds were the most for either team in a yawner of a game.

More than 6,000 fans stayed at Barnhill Arena after the Texas-Arkansas men's game to see the women play. Despite a number of quasi-official efforts to make the crowd as intimidating as possible, the Horns took control early and made the place rather quiet. Ethridge had a career-high 19 points in a 75-57 win. Wimbish (26) was the top scorer in a 77-45 defeat of Baylor in frigid Heart O' Texas Coliseum. Fewer than 700 fans huddled together, and Conradt wore a full-length coat. Wind-chill temperatures were not available.

The unbeaten and top-ranked Longhorns played their second straight game without Lloyd (who had an inflamed knee) when Texas A&M came to Austin. UT jumped to a 21-point lead, got complacent and saw it dwindle to seven before going on to win, 77-64. The Aggies' Lisa Langston (23) was the leading scorer. Even with Lloyd on the bench, the Horns had a 15-rebound edge.

The next three games, two at home and one on the road, were won by a combined score of 322-135 and lifted UT to a 26-0 record. The victims were Miami (112-43), SMU (105-48) and TCU (105-44), and the leading scorers were Davis (25), Harris (27) and Davis (23) again. The regular season ended at the Erwin Center on March 2 against Texas Tech. Smith converted on a couple of one-and-ones and a hook shot in the late minutes as UT gained a 55-43 victory. It was the fewest points the Horns had scored since early in the 1983 season, but Conradt did not care. After winning 16 conference games and losing none, she had to prepare her team for the SWC Tournament in Dallas. "This is the part of the season I detest," she said. "If you took a vote now, eight teams would want a conference tournament, and one would not."

That one, which Conradt coached, was heavily favored to win it and move into the NCAAs, but even if an upset happened, Texas would certainly get an at-large bid. Williams scored 18 points before fouling out, and Lloyd played well despite nursing a tender knee in an 81-64 defeat of Houston. Sonya Watkins, the leading scorer in the SWC and the only non-Longhorn chosen MVP in the first seven years of women's basketball in the conference, had 26 points in a losing effort. Whether they believed it or not, Texas Tech's coaches and players had intimated that victory was possible, an idea the Longhorns found rather irksome. It showed in a convincing 77-53 Texas win in which Williams, Davis and Harris reached double figures.

Conradt, recently honored with her third national coach of the year award, was rather blasé about winning the SWC Tournament and receiving the top seed in the 40-team NCAA Tournament. But she had to feel good about the chances of getting to Lexington, scene of the women's Final Four. After a first-round bye, the Longhorns would play a game at the Erwin Center and then—assuming that was a victory—host one of the regionals. Three wins before their adoring fans at home and they would be on their way to Rupp Arena. Of course, Conradt knew defeat was possible anywhere along the line, even against 20-11 Missouri. The Tigers had a fine player in the middle, Renee Kelly, who averaged 23 points and 12 rebounds per game. Kelly lived up to her billing, getting 28 points, but it was never close as UT jumped to a 17-1 lead with five minutes gone and won, 108-67. Harris and Davis teamed up for 45 points. "Every coach in the country is asking, 'How do you beat them?'" said Mizzou coach Joann Rutherford. "Nobody's figured it out yet."

Another Big 8 team, Oklahoma, was UT's first opponent in the regional tourney. The 24-6 Sooners had a quick, high-scoring team but not quite like Texas, which roared to an 85-59 victory before an audience of 7,474. Ethridge capped it with a fast break, 180-degree behind-the-back pass to Davis, who converted the shot for the last of her game-high 18 points. That led to a showdown with Mississippi, a team the Horns had beaten by nine in a holiday tournament. The Rebs were practically a one-woman team, relying on Jennifer Gillom for scoring, defense and rebounds. More than 10,000 fans filed into the Erwin Center for a nerve-wracking game won—barely—by UT, 66-63. Nervous and impatient on offense, the Longhorns did not get big-time performances from Ethridge, Lloyd or Harris, but Williams covered for her more famous teammates with 25 points and eight rebounds. Gillom also scored 25 for Ole Miss. "I told them early that I didn't care if we won ugly," said Conradt, who started making travel plans for the Bluegrass region of central Kentucky.

The other regional winners were quite familiar to the Longhorns: Tennessee, whom they had beaten by 22 points in the second game of the season; Southern California, who fell by 18 at the Erwin Center; and Western Kentucky, the team that dealt them a heartbreaking loss in the 1985 regional semifinals. The 32-3 Hilltoppers (including Lillie Mason, who made the climactic shot) were out to reprise that defeat of UT, while Conradt's team intended to make life miserable for Mason and her pals. All four teams in Lexington were motivated, but the Longhorns were on a mission. They destroyed Western Kentucky, 90-65, behind Davis' 32 points, 18 rebounds, four steals and four blocked shots. Harris, one of six seniors dedicated to winning the title, scored 20. Smith and Priddy held Mason to 15 points before she fouled out with seven minutes left. Although 500 Texas fans were there, most of the crowd of 9,894 were vocal supporters of Paul Sanderford's Toppers.

USC defeated Tennessee in the other semi, resulting in a Longhorn-Trojan battle for the 1986 national championship. In an indication of how far women's basketball still trailed the popularity of the men's game, many of the geographically minded fans would have preferred a Western Kentucky-Tennessee matchup, so 23,000-seat Rupp Arena was just one-quarter full when the teams took the court. The national media, which understandably loved Cheryl Miller (who had scored her 3,000th career point against the Volunteers), played up her quest for a third crown. There was considerably less attention focused on another athlete playing in her final college game—Annette Smith. Among the best before injuring a knee two years earlier, she had become merely a good player, a role player, the third-leading scorer on her team. Led by tournament MVP Clarissa Davis (24 points and 14 rebounds), UT took control of the game midway through the first half and was never really challenged in a 97-81 victory. Actually, the Women of Troy closed the gap to seven with 9:30 left when the Longhorns began celebrating prematurely. After a timeout and some straight talk from Conradt, Texas was back in charge. Miller missed 11 of 13 shots from the field, but Cynthia Cooper scored 27 for USC. Besides Davis, Texas got strong showings from Priddy (15), Harris (14), Williams (13) and Wimbish (10). Ethridge, soon to be named winner of the Wade Trophy, set a Final Four record with 10 assists. At the buzzer, Davis got a ride on her teammates' shoulders. Then the players, one by one, ascended a stepladder to perform the ceremonial cutting of the nets and accepted the championship trophy. Davis, who made believers of Miller and Trojan coach Linda Sharp, was regarded by some observers as the successor to Miller as the best female player in the game.

The 34-0 Texas Longhorns, the first team to go through a season undefeated since Louisiana Tech back in the AIAW days, flew home to Austin. They were taken in a fleet of limousines to the Erwin Center, where 3,300 people hailed the new champions. Former Congresswoman Barbara Jordan (then a UT faculty member and fan) made a brief speech. "You

Annette Smith, Clarissa Davis, Fran Harris, C.J. Jones, Cara Priddy, Kamie Ethridge and the rest of the 1986 national champs celebrate at the Erwin Center.

are the best there is," she told them in a basso profundo voice. "You've taught America a lesson. You've taught us what a team is." The following night, they spent an hour posing for photographers, professional and amateur, in front of an orange-glowing Tower, its windows lighted with the number 1. And in mid-April, the Longhorns were invited to Washington, D.C., where they (along with men's champion Louisville) met with President Ronald Reagan in the White House Rose Garden.

1987

Six seniors largely responsible for the perfect 34-0 season were gone, but Jody Conradt's coaching colleagues shed no tears of sympathy because the Longhorn roster brimmed with talent. Although her scoring and rebounding statistics had declined somewhat in 1985 and 1986, Andrea Lloyd was a preseason all-American, as was teammate Clarissa Davis. The showstopper at the Final Four in Lexington, Davis gave every indication of becoming Texas' best ever. The backcourt was in good hands with Beverly Williams and Yulonda Wimbish, and a big rookie crop included Doreatha Conwell (junior college player of the year) and high school all-American Susan Anderson, both 6'3". And why would such players not want to come to Austin, then considered the Mecca of women's college basketball? Donna Lopiano, Conradt and their many assistants had crafted a model athletic program with basketball at the pinnacle. A young woman joining the UT hoop family not only played the sport at its highest level, she also found herself in a setting that emphasized decorum, discipline and achievement. Nearly 100 percent of the student-athletes under Conradt's care left UT with diploma in hand.

"To assume that this year's team is going to take up where last year's team left off is totally unrealistic in my opinion," Conradt said. But the Southwest

Conference would again consist of the have and the have-nots as the Razorbacks, Cougars, et al. battled for second place. And nationally, Texas started in a familiar position, atop the polls. While it was not easy to make an impact in Los Angeles, fans and media there seemed genuinely pleased to have the defending champions in town to play in the USC Invitational. Against No. 7 Long Beach State, Lloyd took charge of a faltering Longhorn attack with nine minutes left to secure a 100-86 win. She credited Kamie Ethridge, then a student coach, with inspiring her to do it. "If Andrea Lloyd is not all-world, then I'm not sitting here," Conradt said. "Andy was super. I needed her everywhere." Twenty first-half points from Wimbish were helpful, too, in a fast-paced game. Southern Cal, getting used to life without Cheryl Miller, met UT in the tournament finals. Conwell, an LA native who once dreamed of wearing maroon and gold, scored 28 points in an 89-69 victory. Neither she nor Davis (24 points and 11 rebounds) had much luck in defending against Monica Lamb, a transfer from Houston. She scored 27 for the Trojans.

Andrea Lloyd, a key figure in the greatest era in UT women's basketball history. Her teams went 126-8 and won a national title.

It appeared that Conradt had a weak bench, one without the difference-makers of the year before, but there was time for young players to develop. From Los Angeles, the team traveled to Moscow, Idaho, Lloyd's hometown, to play the Idaho Vandals. The Longhorn forward was hailed as a conquering hero since most of the 16,000 residents of the quaint little town seemed to know of her role in UT's success over the past three seasons. Her 16 points were second to Davis' 21 in a lopsided game won by the Horns, 87-44. The toughest thing for Lloyd was signing autographs for 30 minutes after the game.

The Longhorns carried a 37-game winning streak into the Dr Pepper Texas Classic at the Erwin Center. Full-court defensive pressure frustrated Notre Dame's guards and was the key to an 84-59 victory. Davis scored 23 points for UT, and Heidi Bunek had 14 for the Irish. And the Horns smote No. 15 Ohio State, 99-78, in the tourney title game. Conradt was impressed with how the outmanned Buckeyes kept fighting to keep it close. Nikita Lowry (22) narrowed the gap to 12 with three minutes left, but a series of turnovers leading to Texas buckets ended the suspense. Davis (29) was chosen MVP, as she had been in Los Angeles.

It was a measure of Texas' considerable talents that the Longhorns seemed off their game in an 85-60 defeat of Northeast Louisiana in Monroe. They still outrebounded the Indians by 20, shot 57 percent and controlled things from the start. Partly because of NLU's sagging zone defense, the UT guards—Wimbish, Williams, Lyssa McBride and Paulette Moegle—accounted for 50 points.

What occurred on December 14 was the clash of the mighty orange UT's, No. 1 Texas and No. 3 Tennessee. The last two times they met had resulted in clear Longhorn victories, but Pat Summitt was getting strong play from Bridgette Gordon, Sheila Frost and frosh guard Tonya Edwards. Some 8,835 fans, the second-largest Erwin Center crowd for a women's game, saw Texas ahead by two with three minutes left, only to go scoreless the rest of the way and lose, 85-78. The Horns, harried by relentless defensive pressure, committed 27 turnovers and were worn down by a better-conditioned and deeper team. Gordon scored 26 for the Vols, and Davis had 32 for UT, but her teammates looked timid at the end. Lloyd, a big-game player so many times in the past, scored just two points and had a ghastly nine turnovers. UT was a team unaccustomed to losing, and the locker room was quiet. Conradt, while disappointed, had known defeat would come sooner or later.

Knocked off their No. 1 pedestal, the Longhorns had nearly two weeks to stew about it before the Orange Bowl-Burger King Invitational in Miami, a tournament in which Tennessee was also entered. They heard the

Austin media go on and on about the leadership and chemistry of the 1986 team that seemed, so far, to be missing from the current team. The Horns beat winless Temple, 93-57, in a loosely called game. "A couple more like that and we're going to have to call in Miami Vice to restore order," Conradt joked. The second game was not much tougher, a 97-63 defeat of Ohio State, almost a carbon copy of the earlier win over the Buckeyes. Davis made 14 of 19 shots and totaled a career-high 33 points. That led, naturally, to a rematch with Tennessee in the finals. Turnabout was fair play as the Horns toppled the Volunteers, 88-74. After Wimbish scored a basket from the foul circle in the game's early seconds, UT never trailed. Tennessee's man-to-man defense was easily solved, and Davis (29) was superb in the 448th win of Conradt's career, making her the winningest female coach in college basketball history. Texas was back in its customary place, No. 1 in all the polls. The victory in Miami announced, loud and clear, that the Longhorns were still the team to beat.

But Davis, who was averaging 23 points and eight rebounds per game, injured a foot against Tennessee. She would miss most of the next nine games, forcing the younger players to mature quickly. Six of Texas' first nine games had been against top-20 teams, and no SWC competitor reached that level in 1987, so perhaps Davis' absence could be papered over against the relatively soft conference teams. Rice had its best club since 1982 and its first all-SWC player, 6'1" Holly Jones. She scored a game-high 21 points, but the Owls fell, 85-53, at the Erwin Center. Anderson did an adequate impersonation of Davis with 19 points and eight rebounds, while Moegle made history of a sort by attempting the first three-point shot by a Longhorn. The three-point line, 19'9" from the hoop, was being tried as an experiment in 1987 and became a permanent part of the game the next year. Conradt called the three-pointer a "chip shot" for men but considered it out of range for most of her players.

The Horns hit the road for three games, the first against Arkansas, a team with an unimpressive record because of a tough preconference schedule. That was exactly what Conradt had been urging her SWC colleagues to do if they wanted to get into the big leagues. Arkansas came very close to upsetting UT and ending the 118-game streak against SWC competition. The Longhorns shot free throws at a 30 percent rate, played sorry defense and were lucky to escape the Ozarks with a 59-56 victory. Lloyd led UT with 13 points and 12 rebounds, while Lanell Dawson scored 16 for the Razorbacks.

Wimbish and Conwell combined for 40 points in an 88-58 defeat of Baylor in front of 869 fans. Four days later in College Station, the Horns romped Texas A&M, 94-60, but suffered a huge loss in the first half when Conwell went down with a knee injury, overshadowing a 25-point, 10-assist, eight-steal performance by Williams. Lloyd, too, had a fine game—19 points and 15 rebounds. But the injury to Conwell, who could rebound like a center, shoot like a forward and handle the ball like a guard, hurt, especially with Davis still on the sidelines. Conwell underwent major reconstructive surgery two days later, her season over. In fact, doctors refused to make a prognosis about her playing future.

"I feel a sense of urgency I had not felt before," Conradt said. "All of us have to be more intense, the players and the staff. We don't have the luxury of going out and testing the water." Moegle, who had come back from a knee injury herself and was something of a defensive liability, was given the starting job—briefly. Her two points and one rebound did not help much in a 91-50 thrashing of SMU in Austin. Lloyd (20 points, 16 rebounds, five assists and two blocked shots) had a terrific game. Conradt and Pony coach Welton Brown could not say enough about Lloyd's play, although she, modest to a fault, claimed it was no big deal.

C.J. Jones, a junior who sat out preseason practice and the first seven games to improve her academic status, moved into a starting role and held it the rest of the season, beginning with the TCU game in Fort Worth. The Frogs lost, 99-67, due to strong play from Lloyd, Williams and Wimbish. Teresia Hudson scored 15 points for TCU in a game seen by just 410 fans.

There were considerably more people, 9,541, at the Erwin Center to witness a nonconference game between Texas and Western Kentucky on January 21. The Hilltoppers sought to avenge the 25-point loss handed them in the Final Four ten months earlier. Jones scored all 10 of her points in the first half, and Williams and Lloyd took it the rest of way in a 63-41 victory. WKU star Clemette Haskins was ineffective because of a sprained knee.

A 74-52 defeat of Texas Tech could be attributed to Lloyd's 22 points and Williams mixing drives with outside shots. Davis played, or tried to, but struggled in 12 minutes on the court. Lisa Logsdon had 10 points for Marsha Sharp's Red Raiders.

Although the days of playing prelims to men's games had passed in Austin, it was not so elsewhere. When Texas met UH and Rice in Houston, both games were prelims. The Cougars used a slap-happy full-court press that had UT tied with 2:21 left. Then Williams (24) and reserve center Michele Eglinger came through for a 79-73 victory. If Houston had hit better than 58 percent of its free throws, the result might have been different. After missing all or most of nine games, Davis was back in the lineup against the Owls. She and Williams teamed up for 39 points in a 96-63 win.

Arkansas, emboldened by playing Texas so close before, had a 47-24 rebound deficit and seemed not to have a clue about stopping the fast break in a 91-65 Longhorn victory. Davis (29 points and 11 rebounds) looked healthy again. "To say we got outcoached is the understatement of the year," said Hog coach John Sutherland. "She [Conradt] just prepared them so much better than I did. I feel sorry for the kids because we did not have a chance." Baylor did not have much of a chance (92-41), nor did Texas A&M (96-50) in consecutive games at the Erwin Center. But more than 5,000 fans were there to watch. The UT women's athletic department had worked hard and made some good moves to boost attendance for home games. Including postseason competition, the numbers went like this: an average of 2,012 in 1984, 2,470 in 1985, 5,289 in 1986 and 6,639 to lead the nation in 1987.

Record: 31-2

100 Long Beach State 86
89 Southern California 69
87 Idaho 44
84 Notre Dame 59
99 Ohio State 78
85 NE Louisiana 60
78 Tennessee 85
93 Temple 57
97 Ohio State 63
88 Tennessee 74
85 Rice 53
59 Arkansas 56
88 Baylor 58
94 Texas A&M 60
91 SMU 50
99 TCU 67
63 Western Kentucky 41
74 Texas Tech 52
79 Houston 73
96 Rice 63
91 Arkansas 65
92 Baylor 41
96 Texas A&M 50
93 SMU 57
110 TCU 65
74 Texas Tech 52
60 Houston 55
73 Texas Tech 49
72 Arkansas 70
86 St. Joseph's 56
91 James Madison 57
85 Rutgers 77
75 Louisiana Tech 79

Davis and Anderson had a combined 29 points and 26 rebounds in a 93-57 defeat of SMU in Dallas. The Mustangs, who got 12 points from Sheila Bryant, hurt their cause by making just 27 percent of their shots. In what was really a foregone conclusion, Texas clinched its fifth straight Southwest Conference championship that Saturday afternoon.

Davis and TCU's Staci Ward both scored 25 points in a late-season game at the Erwin Center, but Davis had a much smaller percentage of her team's total, which meant the Horned Frogs got beaten soundly, 110-65. Lloyd, with 24 points and nine rebounds, became just the second Longhorn (after Retha Swindell) to go over 1,500 points and 1,000 rebounds in a career.

The Texas winning streak reached 18, the longest in the nation, with a 74-52 defeat of Texas Tech in Lubbock. Sluggish and unable to get the fast break going, the Horns relied on stout defense, rebounding and some dead-eye shooting by Wimbish and Moegle to win it. Julia Koncak had 16 points for the Red Raiders.

The last game of the regular season was against Houston, and 7,850 fans at the Erwin Center enjoyed a 30-minute concert by Johnny Dee and the Rocket 88s before tipoff. Although Cougar coach Greg Williams did not expect a five-point game, that is what happened. The Longhorns appeared distracted or perhaps just ready to get on with the playoffs as they struggled to a 60-55 victory. Williams scored 17 points, eight fewer than DeJeuna Carter of Houston.

Lloyd, the SWC's all-time rebounder, was chosen SWC player of the year and made all-conference along with Williams. In a major quirk of voting, Davis failed to make all-SWC (despite being the scoring leader), and yet she was honored with the Naismith Trophy as the top player in the nation. Texas, which finished the regular season ranked No. 1 for the fourth straight year, was far and away the class of the SWC as the tournament began at Moody Coliseum in Dallas. Conradt got fine play from her backcourt tandem, Williams and Wimbish, in a 73-49 defeat of Texas Tech. The title game with Arkansas was another matter, however. UT used a variety of zone defenses to come back from a seven-point halftime deficit and beat the Razorbacks, 72-70. Williams (27) was primarily responsible for a 22-6 scoring spree in the early minutes of the second half and earned her second straight Southwest Conference tourney MVP award. Bronwyn Wynn had 19 points for the Hogs, whose season was not over because they won the National Women's Invitational Tournament in Amarillo.

The 28-1 Longhorns again had the top seed in the 40-team NCAA Tournament, and since the Final Four was being held in Austin, a relatively smooth path had been prepared for UT to participate. "It scares me to think of not being in the Final Four at home," Lloyd said. "We're not taking it for granted." Mark Rosner of the *Austin American-Statesman* predicted that only a big-time upset would prevent the Horns from joining three other regional winners at the Erwin Center the last weekend in March.

Tournament play actually began in Austin against 23-9 St. Joseph's, a Philadelphia school with a student body 1/20th the size of UT. The Hawks, self-styled giant killers, suffered an 86-56 loss before 7,345 fans. Davis scored 24 points, the team forced 30 turnovers and started thinking about the next game.

Fayetteville, North Carolina was the site of UT's regional, and 27-3 James Madison was the first opponent. The Dukes were complete unknowns to the defending national champions, but Conradt was careful to say they were not pushovers. The Horns had no need to worry because they put it to JMU, 91-57. Davis made 11 of 16 shots, grabbed 10 rebounds and simply dominated the game. Duke coach Sheila Moorman's post-game comments were terse: "I'll spare you a bunch of questions. We were totally dominated at both ends of the court by a team that's superior to us by a wide margin. Clarissa Davis was phenomenal." And Lloyd (20) and Williams (17) were not exactly chopped liver.

If any team could derail the Longhorns, it was 30-2 Rutgers. Theresa Grentz' Scarlet Knights were led by 6'2" all-American Sue Wicks, who had a lightning-quick first step. Texas was just six minutes away from not getting a Final Four invite, but the combination of tourney MVP Lloyd (20), Williams (19) and Davis (16) rallied for an 85-77 victory. And a couple of frosh pitched in, as well. Guard Lyssa McBride made three of four medium-range jumpers, and 6'8" Ellen Bayer blocked five shots. But UT was outrebounded by a 43-28 margin. Wicks and her fellow frontcourt ace, Regina Howard, scored 24 and 23 points, respectively.

The Ultimo Quatro, the Final Four, consisted of 31-1 Texas, the host and defending champion, versus 29-2 Louisiana Tech and 26-6 Tennessee versus 33-2 Long Beach State. A lot went on in Austin during the days leading up to the two semis and then the final game. Besides heavy local, statewide and national media attention, more than 1,000 members of the Women's Basketball Coaches Association gathered at the Stouffer Hotel, the Kodak all-America team was announced (Lloyd and Davis made the 10-member team), and a large pep rally for the Longhorns was held in front of the Tower. Two of the busiest and happiest people in town were Lopiano and Conradt, who had built the UT program.

An air of electricity permeated the big circular arena between Interstate 35 and Red River Street. The presence of a five-tier media section and bands from four schools reduced capacity somewhat, but a whopping 15,303 fans were on hand for the semifinals. A bit of ticket scalping went on in the minutes before the Vols and 49ers played in the first game. Tennessee, the winner, scouted the Longhorns and Techsters in the second game. Louisiana Tech coach Leon Barmore recalled an almost-forgotten figure, Doreatha Conwell. "Texas might have been untouchable with her," he said. The blue-clad Techsters shot 58 percent and built a 10-point lead which the Horns whittled down to two in the last minute, but they never got closer in a 79-75 loss. The inside play of Nora Lewis and Tori Harrison accounted for 40 points, yet the player who won it for Tech was guard Teresa Weatherspoon (19). "We wanted to keep pressure on Weatherspoon to wear her down, but she wore us down," Conradt lamented. "She was still going strong at the end." The big crowd, overwhelmingly partisan to UT, never rattled Weatherspoon and her teammates. Davis and Williams combined for 47 points, but Lloyd, one of the players most responsible for Texas' 126-8 record over the past four years, had a poor game—seven points on two-of-nine shooting, eight rebounds, three assists, one steal, five fouls and a gash over her right eye.

The crowd, naturally, was smaller (9,283) and quieter two days hence when Tennessee beat Louisiana Tech for the national crown. Longhorn fans what-iffed the missed opportunity to win again, but just reaching the Final Four was no walk in the park because it was getting harder to excel in the world of women's basketball. If the 1987 team lacked the depth and intangibles of the 1986 champs, the Longhorns still had gone a long way on what they had, losing just twice.

1988

Depth was a question mark as the 1988 season approached, but the returning starters—Beverly Williams and Yulonda Wimbish in the backcourt and Clarissa Davis and C.J. Jones in the frontcourt—were enough to warm coach Jody Conradt's heart. And Doreatha Conwell was pushing the rehabilitation of her knee ahead of everything the doctors had predicted. If she could get in the vicinity of her former self, and if some of the youngsters came on, Texas had a chance to reach the Final Four and even win it all, as in 1986. The Associated Press pegged the Longhorns a preseason No. 2, behind defending national champion Tennessee.

And where better to begin than in the land of swaying palms, cool Pacific breezes and tropical allure? The Rainbow Wahine Classic, hosted by the University of Hawaii, was a three-day event in late November. Davis scored 20 points in an absurdly easy 93-34 defeat of Northern Arizona, 32 points to help beat Stephen F. Austin (94-71) and then had 26 points and 18 rebounds in the title game, a 91-70 win over Penn State before 884 fans. Davis, MVP of the tournament, could work the inside like no other player in women's basketball. Her quick feint-and-jab moves could keep any defense off balance, and if the Hawaii tourney was any indication, her junior season would be a scintillating one. She did have some help against the Nittany Lions as Wimbish scored 22 points and Jones held all-America guard Suzie McConnell to 14.

The home opener was against No. 13 Southern California. With 76-percent shooting in the first half, Texas crushed the Trojans, 79-62. Wimbish scored 25 points using her familiar slashing drives and soft, left-handed jumpers. Equally adept at guard or forward, the senior from Victoria used the USC game to establish herself, along with Davis and Williams, as one of UT's top three players.

A 108-50 blowout of Western Michigan hardly prepared the Longhorns for the biggest game of the young season, against No. 1 Tennessee. The Volunteers' new Thompson-Boling Arena was expected to overflow with fans if only because a fast-food chain had purchased most of the tickets and distributed them liberally. A head-on collision between the two top-ranked teams before a huge crowd with plenty of media attention was just what women's basketball needed. "You always want to play well for the sake of the sport when the world is watching," Conradt said. "On the other hand, one game isn't going to make the whole season." It was a night to remember, in more ways than one. A crowd of 24,563 jammed the arena on the banks of the Tennessee River to see their beloved Vols get ripped, 97-78. Davis came through with the greatest performance of her career—16 of 27 from the field and 13 of 14 from the free throw line for 45 points, missing Annette Smith's school record by one. Wimbish put the clamps on Tonya Edwards, Jones did the same to Bridgette Gordon, and several UT reserves played well as the huge audience seemed to put extra pressure on the home team. With seven minutes left, Vol coach Pat Summitt had her head in her hands, and many fans were on their way to the parking lot. The team returned to Austin for a nine-day exam break, and if the Horns did as well in the classroom as they had done in Knoxville, they would all be Phi Beta Kappas.

With victory well in hand, Clarissa Davis, Michele Eglinger, Susan Anderson, Lyssa McBride and Ellen Bayer cheer their teammates.

Back in the familiar No. 1 spot, Texas got good news when the team doctor cleared Dee Conwell to play. How long she could go and what she had lost would soon be evident. While Conwell was coming back, the team got a scare in practice when Davis collided with another player and hurt a knee. But Davis was in the lineup on December 18 when No. 9 Long Beach State came to town, and she had 26 points in a 99-85 victory before 8,411 fans. Penny Toler of the 49ers showed some impressive playground moves and scored 30, but Williams, often a quiet hero, also had a fine all-around game with 22 points, six rebounds, six assists and a firm hand on the Texas offensive attack. "Every time we made a run, they'd shut it down," said Long Beach coach Joan Bonvicini.

Of the eight teams entered in the Orange Bowl-Burger King Classic, only host Miami was not in the top 20. UT, seeking to win it for the third consecutive year, started with a 90-75 defeat of Illinois, a game *Austin American-Statesman* writer Randy Riggs claimed "could have been mistaken for a midnight rerun of Roller Derby." Davis shook off knee pain to score 29 points and collect 15 rebounds. "What can you say about her?" marveled Illini coach Laura Golden. "What does everyone say about her? She's a true all-American. Look up the definition of all-American, and that's what Clarissa Davis is." The Longhorns also beat Rutgers, 86-75, but it was a costly victory. With 11 minutes left in the first half, Davis streaked across court to intercept a pass and suffered a season-ending knee injury. Trainer Tina Bonci stabilized the joint and wrapped it in ice before Davis went to a nearby hospital and then to San Antonio, where surgery was performed. The team was in shock, but the games had to go on, and UT lost to Iowa in the tourney finale, 75-65. Texas dominated the Hawkeyes on the boards but committed 24 turnovers and shot just 39 percent. In pressure situations, the Horns usually looked to Davis, but she was not there in the first road loss in 43 games. Conwell, Susan Anderson and Ellen Bayer would have to step up from then on.

As Davis received get-well messages in her hospital bed, the team went from Miami to Columbus to engage No. 9 Ohio State, led by two-time Big 10 player of the year Tracey Hall. Conwell's swollen knee kept her on the bench, and Williams missed 14 of 17 shots and turned the ball over nine times in an awful 88-58 loss to the Buckeyes. Hall and Nikita Lowry combined for 51 points as a record St. John Arena crowd of 8,477 looked on. Conradt blamed herself for the defeat, saying she had not prepared the team well, but Wimbish and Williams insisted the 1988 Longhorns were far from finished.

They got back on their feet with an 89-70 defeat of Arkansas in Fayetteville. Wimbish scored a game-high 27 points, and Conwell, still limited by her knee, had 12 points and eight rebounds in just 19 minutes. Shelly Wallace and Lisa Martin scored 16 each for the Razorbacks.

Bitter icy and snowy weather caused a series of travel misadventures, and the bone-tired Horns arrived home late from a disastrous 3-2 road trip that lasted 10 days and covered nearly 4,000 miles. Waiting for them was LSU, coached by Sue Gunter. Then in her 24th year in the business, Gunter was as much of a trailblazer in women's basketball as Conradt. Wimbish came through with 26 points in a 76-61 defeat of the Tigers. The most poignant moment occurred a minute before tipoff when Davis—who made sure to wear waterproof mascara—walked to the bench on crutches and got a standing ovation from 7,528 fans. With Jones and Conwell operating inside, Texas was beginning to show some offensive efficiency.

Williams, Lyssa McBride, Bayer and Wimbish were all in double figures in an 85-60 win over Rice. "We have to open up a little bit and spread the defense out," Conradt said. "When Clo [Davis] was in there, we could just stuff it down their throat." Anderson had 17 rebounds against the Owls, who took 14 three-point shots during the game.

The No. 20 Houston Cougars sought to end the longest-running play since *The King and I* at Hofheinz Pavilion. UH coach Greg Williams, whose team had compiled an 11-1 record by playing a rather weak schedule, hoped to make history and beat Texas, ending the 136-game streak against Southwest Conference competition. Conradt believed her fellow SWC coaches made a mistake by viewing the Texas game as the World Series and Super Bowl rolled into one, but the shoe had never been on the other foot. The backcourt duo of Wimbish and Williams scored 51 points, and Bayer, all 6'9" of her, had 14 rebounds and four blocks in an 80-47 victory. UT's dominance continued, same as it ever was. The Horns also breezed by Texas Tech, 89-56, in Lubbock. Senior Paulette Moegle, starting for just the second time in her career, made 11 of 12 shots, while Reena Lynch had 17 points and 11 rebounds for the Red Raiders.

Mississippi, undefeated and ranked sixth, met No. 5 Texas at the Erwin Center, but Rebel coach Van Chancellor, always quick with a quip and a complaint, said his team was a "sacrificial lamb." Chancellor's sideline histrionics brought two technical fouls in a 74-61 loss to the Longhorns before the second-largest home crowd yet—14,413. Cynthia Autry scored 23 for Ole Miss, and Conwell had 17 points, four rebounds and two steals. It was starting to look like reports of Texas' demise were greatly exaggerated. With the Longhorns hosting an NCAA regional again, they might get to Tacoma (site of the Final Four) even without the great Clarissa.

Conradt's bench was coming on, too. Center Michele Eglinger scored 17 points, and guard Pennee Hall had 14 assists in a 102-62 crushing of TCU. A 28-2 first-half run left the Frogs demoralized in an otherwise meaningless victory, marking a full decade since UT had lost to an SWC team.

In a 17-game series dating back to 1975, 19 points was as close as the SMU Mustangs had ever come to Texas, so a 72-56 loss at Moody Coliseum did not seem so bad to the red and blue. Williams scored 25 from the outside, and Anderson had a career-high 23 from the inside in a rough game that saw Conradt working the refs constantly. An 89-61 defeat of Texas A&M was accomplished before 2,933 fans in College Station, over half of them favoring the Horns; nine chartered buses made the trek from Austin, and hundreds of people went on their own. While the Aggies reminded the visitors of their recent football supremacy, UT fans pointed to the scoreboard as indication of distaff hoop dominance.

Back in the friendly confines of the Erwin Center, the Horns jumped to a 19-2 lead and routed Pam Bowers' Baylor team, 98-52. Conwell and Williams both had 18 points, and Maggie Davis scored 23 for the Bears. In contrast with the BU game, Texas got off to a slow start against Arkansas and stormed past the Hogs in the second half of an 84-54 victory before a home crowd of 10,777. Delmonica DeHorney, much too quick for Anderson to guard, had a game-high 17 points for the Razorbacks.

After a 37-point defeat of Rice at Autry Court, the Horns came home and prepared for Houston, the second-place team in the SWC. The two W's, Wimbish and Williams, used dazzling open-court moves to chalk up 41 points in a 93-69 victory. Carla Fountain scored 21 for the Cougars. Texas Tech provided a scare on February 16, playing a patient game, committing few turnovers and using a three-post lineup to match UT in the rebound department. With the Red Raiders trailing by just five points in the late going, Wimbish took control for a 70-61 victory that guaranteed a sixth straight conference championship. "It's a game we can learn a lot from," Conradt said. "You hope you don't get tested like this, but how else do you learn?"

Texas took a break from the conference grind by meeting Western Kentucky in Bowling Green. Conradt talked about "returning to the scene of the crime," Lillie Mason's last-second shot that knocked the Horns out of a home appearance in the 1985 Final Four. There was no chance of a similar crime being perpetrated in UT's 71-52 victory. The Hilltoppers (minus star frosh Terri Mann, who was injured) played a rough game before a big and vocal crowd, but Texas had superior rebounding and a combined 35 points from Williams and Wimbish.

Having won 15 straight games, the Longhorns entered the stretch drive in good shape. There was a "relaxing"—Conradt's term—86-50 defeat of TCU in mostly empty Daniel-Meyer Coliseum. SMU tried banging the fourth-ranked Horns but still lost, 75-52. The regular-season home finale, a 79-57 win over Texas A&M, was remarkable only because Conradt had laryngitis and could not bark at the officials. The Ags'

Record: 32-3

93 Northern Arizona 34
94 Stephen F. Austin 71
91 Penn State 70
79 Southern California 62
108 Western Michigan 50
97 Tennessee 78
99 Long Beach State 85
90 Illinois 75
86 Rutgers 75
65 Iowa 75
58 Ohio State 88
89 Arkansas 70
76 LSU 61
85 Rice 60
80 Houston 47
89 Texas Tech 56
74 Mississippi 61
102 TCU 62
72 SMU 56
89 Texas A&M 61
98 Baylor 52
84 Arkansas 54
94 Rice 57
93 Houston 69
70 Texas Tech 61
71 Western Kentucky 52
86 TCU 50
75 SMU 52
79 Texas A&M 57
94 Baylor 43
72 Texas A&M 56
88 Texas Tech 61
77 South Carolina 58
79 Stanford 58
80 Louisiana Tech 83 (OT)

Donna Roper scored 23 points, two more than Wimbish. And the last women's basketball game ever played at Heart O' Texas Coliseum was a hopeless mismatch, a 94-43 defeat of Baylor. Conradt, a BU alum, bid adieu to the cavernous facility with poor lighting, often frigid temperatures, mobile home trailers masquerading as locker rooms and the lethargic effect HOT had on most visiting teams. Conwell (17 points and six rebounds against the Bears) was charging into the playoffs. She would be named MVP of the SWC postseason tourney, an honor that meshed nicely with Wimbish being chosen SWC player of the year, Conradt SWC coach of the year for the fourth time and Williams an all-American.

The *de rigueur* exercise in futility for the "other eight" known as the conference postseason tourney was again held at SMU's Moody Coliseum. The Longhorns had everything to lose and nothing to gain, but they did not lose, shooting 68 percent in the first half and cruising to a 72-56 defeat of the hard-hitting Texas A&M Aggies. That was followed by an 88-61 strumming of Texas Tech. Williams scored 19 points and Jones a career-high 18, but the day clearly belonged to Conwell, who hit nine of 13 from the field and six of seven from the free throw line for 24 points, had 10 rebounds and took care of business inside, punctuating her comeback from knee surgery 13 months earlier. "There's no way we can make a title run without Doreatha," said Conradt, who won her 500th (not including 12 victories over junior colleges) game and 383rd at Texas. "She deserves recognition. We all like a story with a happy ending."

The Longhorns, one of half a dozen teams with a legitimate chance of grabbing the brass ring, began the NCAA Tournament with a second-round game against 23-10 South Carolina at the Erwin Center. UT led by just four points three minutes into the second half when Conradt sent Hall into the fray. Lead-footed but a smart player, perhaps a poor-woman's Kamie Ethridge, she hit three quick baskets, made three steals and handed out five assists in a 77-58 victory over the Gamecocks. UT's defensive pressure, less frenetic than in past years because opposing ballhandlers had improved, forced 24 turnovers. Martha Parker had 15 points for USC.

Four teams—Texas, Stanford, Mississippi and Louisiana Tech—were in Austin for the regional tourney to decide who would move on to Tacoma. The Horns started off with the Cardinal, whose coach, Tara VanDerveer, made this comment: "The experience of being down here is an eye-opener. I don't think we've seen this caliber of basketball." Her 27-4 team was led by a couple of future all-Americans, Jennifer Azzi and Sonja Henning. The Horns advanced with a 79-58 victory keyed by Conwell's 26 points and 16 rebounds. She was wheeling and dealing inside all night long, and Williams and Jones came up big, too. Henning of Stanford scored 15 points in defeat.

One more win and the Horns were off to the Pacific northwest to seek another national championship trophy. Just Louisiana Tech, with a 20-point defeat of Ole Miss, stood in the way. Some 12,288 people were in attendance that March evening as Wally Pryor called the game and the band and cheerleaders did their part to whip up enthusiasm. Women's basketball at the Erwin Center had come to resemble a football game at Memorial Stadium. The president of the University, Dr. William Cunningham, was there, along with several members of the Board of Regents and their families, VIPs in state and city government, faculty members, prominent alumni, and business and society bigwigs. Not too many years earlier, UT coeds had tried out for teams, sewn their own uniforms, driven their own cars to away games and played in obscurity on the tiny court at Anna Hiss Gym.

None of that made any difference to Leon Barmore and his Techsters, who had dumped UT in the 1987 semifinals. It happened again as they took a gripping 83-80 overtime victory. The game was packed with momentum swings, fine individual performances and some deadly mistakes. The Longhorns trailed by one with four seconds left in OT when McBride, who was six of seven from the field, turned down an open shot and threw the ball in to Conwell. Nora Lewis intercepted it, was fouled and made two free throws to seal Tech's win. Conwell and Williams both scored 22, but Wimbish had just eight in her second consecutive subpar game. Techster guard Teresa Weatherspoon (22) was superb, gliding up and down the court throughout a 45-minute showcase for women's basketball.

"We had not been in a close game all year," said a quiet Conradt. "How do you prepare for this kind of pressure and last-second opportunities and a way to capitalize on them?...It's done. We gave our best effort and will live with the consequences." The Longhorns had gone down to the wire with the eventual NCAA champions, and the greatest player in the country—Clarissa Davis—did not even get in the game.

1989

They called it "Midnight Madness." In strict conformity with NCAA regulations, when the clock struck midnight on October 14, 1988, the Longhorn basketball teams coached by Jody Conradt and Tom Penders held a joint practice session at the Erwin Center, witnessed by 3,000 faithfuls. Later that afternoon, an ad hoc hoop workout took place at Memorial Stadium during halftime of the Texas-Arkansas football game before a considerably larger audience.

Clarissa Davis' left knee had healed enough to allow her to compete for a spot on the 1988 U.S. Olympic team, but she just missed joining Kamie Ethridge and Andrea Lloyd on that gold-medal-winning squad. Fitted with a Darth Vader-type brace, Davis seemed to have slightly less spring and quickness than before and tended to favor her right. Although her senior year would not be free of physical problems, Davis did not miss a game. There were six new faces, two of whom got the most attention. Catarina Pollini was a 22-year-old veteran of European basketball and a member of the Italian Olympic team. The 6'4" junior center was expected to make a big impact as a scorer, rebounder and defensive intimidator, but a knee injury and other circumstances limited her participation to 12 games. Real excitement followed the signing of Vicki Hall, a 6'1" guard-forward from Indianapolis. The top prospect in the nation, Hall was an intense athlete dedicated to basketball, and the demands she placed on herself—and sometimes teammates—drew comparisons to fellow Hoosier Larry Bird. While her speed and leaping ability were not exceptional, Hall could shoot and pass with élan, and most everyone believed her presence ensured UT of remaining Final Four-caliber well into the 1990s.

The starting lineup before the first game consisted of a frontline of Davis, Pollini and Susan Anderson, with soph Amy Claborn and junior Lyssa McBride as the guards. The Boilermaker Classic, 60 miles northwest of Hall's hometown, featured Purdue, Brigham Young, St. Joseph's and Texas. Davis (21) brought the Horns back from a two-point halftime deficit to beat St. Joe's, 75-69. McBride spread the Hawk defense by lighting it up from outside to lessen the double- and triple-teaming of Davis. But a first-half knee injury to Pollini (sidelining her for the next 20 games) against Purdue allowed the Boilermakers to take a 15-point lead and hold on for a 76-71 victory over the No. 3 Longhorns. MaChelle Joseph scored 22 for Purdue, and Davis had 30 points and 13 rebounds in a losing effort. "Clarissa can't play an entire team by herself," Conradt said. "We need some other people to assert themselves and show some leadership on the floor."

The last time Davis saw Rutgers was at a tournament in Florida when she was on a stretcher with ice on her injured knee. But the upset-minded Scarlet Knights found she was quite healthy, scoring 37 points in UT's 78-66 home victory. Claborn, who started every other game of the season, was out with a minor injury and was ably replaced by freshman Johnna Pointer (12). Rutgers' backcourt duo of Janet Malouf and Telicher Austin combined for 36 points. Two nights later, Hall led the Horns' 69-64 win over a flu-weakened Washington team.

Things went sour quickly, however, starting with a two-game swing through Dixie. A handful of fans at the Maravich Assembly Center in Baton Rouge saw LSU take advantage of 22 first-half turnovers and drop Texas, 94-80. Guard Dana Chatman (31) led the way as the Bengals assumed an early lead and never gave it up. Davis, who missed a week of practice because of a sciatic nerve injury, scored 32 points. Hall was out with a stress fracture in her foot as the Horns hobbled to Oxford to play Ole Miss. Davis (30) and the Rebels' Kimsey O'Neal (31) had a standoff, but O'Neal had plenty more help in an 88-67 win, the first for Mississippi in five tries against the Longhorns. McBride's 15 points made her the only other player in burnt orange to reach double figures. Reb coach Van Chancellor, who knew Davis was hurting, could not say enough about her: "You have just witnessed the best basketball player who has ever played this game. She plays with a lot of heart."

Davis was not expected to travel to California for a couple of post-Christmas games with USC and Long Beach State, but there she was. Linda Sharp's Trojans, off to a poor start themselves, had to play in the tiny Fullerton State gym because the LA Sports Arena was already booked. Anderson and Ellen Bayer provided some scoring and rebounding punch as the Horns led by four with two minutes left, but a pair of costly turnovers allowed Southern Cal to steal an 83-81 win. Karon Howell and Cherie Nelson teamed up for 42 points, giving the Longhorns a 3-4 record, the worst start in 13 years. They were sinking in the polls, and the immediate future looked dim.

No. 7 Long Beach State, which had won 95 percent of its home games in the previous five years, had a quicksilver guard combo in Traci Waites and Penny Toler. But Conradt found encouraging signs in her team's play, validated in an 87-83 defeat of the 49ers on New Year's Eve. Davis scored a game-high 37, and Anderson backed her up with 18 points and 11 rebounds. "Clarissa was awesome, but the person who really killed us was Susan Anderson," said Long Beach coach Joan Bonvicini. The guards, Claborn (10 assists), McBride and Pointer, seemingly outclassed by Waites and Toler (a combined 49 points), were more than adequate.

Record: 27-5
75 St. Joseph's 69
71 Purdue 76
78 Rutgers 66
69 Washington 64
80 LSU 94
67 Mississippi 88
81 Southern California 83
87 Long Beach State 83
80 Baylor 60
104 Arkansas 67
92 Rice 65
85 Houston 62
95 Texas Tech 49
90 Western Kentucky 67
88 TCU 68
92 SMU 70
69 Tennessee 67
88 Baylor 50
87 Arkansas 67
86 Texas A&M 61
103 Rice 61
86 Houston 72
78 Texas Tech 61
99 Old Dominion 78
100 TCU 62
105 SMU 94
78 Texas A&M 70
74 Texas A&M 59
101 Arkansas 99
83 Montana 54
88 Nevada-Las Vegas 77
71 Maryland 79

The 1989 Southwest Conference race was expected to be more of the same, with the other eight teams eating the Longhorns' dust. But they did not look so hot in an 80-60 defeat of Baylor in Austin. Bayer had 16 rebounds, and Anderson (20) shared scoring honors with Maggie Stinnett of the Bruins, whose coach, Pam Bowers, provided serious bulletin-board material. She claimed Davis (13 points and 13 rebounds) was not the Davis of old and that Texas' 150-plus game streak over SWC teams would soon end.

The main threat to the streak, Bowers believed, was Arkansas, and the Hogs were up next. There was nothing subtle about the Longhorns' 104-67 repulsion of John Sutherland's team, who left town with its porcine tail between its legs. The stat line had Davis with 33 points and 14 rebounds and McBride with 21 points on nine of 15 shooting, including three from behind the stripe. Shelly Wallace of Arkansas, who came in averaging 27 points per game, scored just 12. It was a thorough win for Conradt's Horns, who were glad to have Hall back in the lineup.

Times had changed, and UT (mostly in the form of McBride, Pointer and Hall) was shooting three-pointers with more frequency, playing some zone defense and working on a halfcourt offense. "We're definitely on an upswing," said an optimistic Conradt. "We are starting to get back." That showed in a pair of victories in Houston. Rice fell, 92-65, as Davis scored 20 and Bayer had 18 rebounds and five blocked shots. UH had no better luck, losing by a score of 85-62. Twenty-six points from Cougar center Sallie Routt kept it from being too much of a rout.

Another SWC team with an ostensible chance of upsetting UT was Texas Tech. But Davis and Hall led a 22-point first-half run that spelled defeat for the Red Raiders, 95-49, at the Erwin Center. Although Davis and Hall lobbied their coach in the late minutes, she refused to put them back in the game. "I have very few coaching friends," Conradt said. "I don't want to alienate the ones I have, so it was best that they sit next to me."

The biggest crowd yet, 11,619, gathered for the Texas-Western Kentucky matchup on January 21. Davis and Hall combined for 45 points, Claborn ran the fast break well, and McBride came off the bench with some instant offense in a 90-67 win. The same flattering comments Hilltopper coach Paul Sanderford made about the Texas program before the game were repeated afterward.

Due to early foul trouble, Davis played only five minutes in the first half against TCU in Fort Worth, and the Horned Frogs were just down by three points at intermission. In the privacy of the UT locker room, Conradt told the young women in no uncertain terms to begin playing harder. And so they did, heavily outscoring TCU in the early minutes of the second half of an 88-68 win. Hall had a fine all-around game, and center Janice Dzuik led the Frogs with 21 points. It was back home for another big crowd (8,349) and another victory, 92-70, over SMU. But Davis injured an ankle aggravated by tendinitis, and McBride sustained a bruised thigh, putting them both in doubt for the Tennessee game three days later.

McBride was indeed out, but Davis was able to practice and play against the No. 2 Volunteers, defending national champions. At least publicly, coach Pat Summitt dismissed any notion of revenge for the 19-point loss to UT before a record crowd the prior season. "That was last year," she said. "It was a long and embarrassing night for Tennessee and a tremendous display of basketball for Texas." As in Knoxville, Davis played a superlative game, getting 38 points and eight rebounds and igniting the Horns' second-half comeback to win, 69-67, before 9,614 boisterous fans. The Vols, who lost star guard Tonya Edwards to a knee injury, had a big rebounding edge but could not hit their free throws near the end. Time after time, Davis scored against a Tennessee defense that knew she would shoot. "I don't think there's any doubt who is the best player in the country," Conradt said. "If there is a better player, we'll bring them in here to play some one-on-one." Summitt, players on both teams and the media made similar assertions. Mostly because of Davis, the Longhorns had come a long way from their 3-4 start.

The first visit to Baylor's new Ferrell Center resulted in an 88-50 Texas victory as 541 fans dotted the 10,084-seat, golden-domed facility beside the Brazos River. Pam Bowers, coach of the bad-news Bears, on their way to a 3-23 record, beat a hasty exit because sportswriters wanted to know if she stood by those earlier quotes about Davis (26 points and 12 rebounds) and the Longhorns. Conradt got her 400th UT victory with an 87-67 defeat of Arkansas in Fayetteville. Davis was nothing short of stupendous, making 17 of 24 shots, and Anderson grabbed 14 rebounds. Shelly Wallace scored 22 points for the Razorbacks.

Three home games in a six-day span started with Texas A&M, a team with a couple of fine players in Donna Roper and Lisa Jordon and a fighting chance to win. The Ags did not win, missing 24 of 32 first-half shots in an 86-61 loss to Texas. The game's highlight came with 7:52 left on a McBride-to-Davis alley-oop. "I think the most difficult thing about playing here is the fear factor," said Aggie coach Lynn Hickey. "Texas has the athletes and that mystique." The subs received plenty of work in a 103-61 defeat of Rice, but the Houston game was a bit tougher. Davis got in early foul trouble, and the Cougars' Jana Crosby (22) led a nice second-half run that still fell short in an 86-72 defeat. Anderson and Hall combined for 43 points, Bayer blocked seven shots, and Claborn had 11 assists.

Pollini was back, but pain in Hall's foot kept her out of the next three games. Texas Tech fans saw their team lose, 78-61, but they got a chance to witness a typically great Davis performance—34 points, 14 rebounds and eight steals. Pollini looked rusty after 10 weeks away from competition, but Pointer (who replaced Hall in the lineup) and Anderson both scored 15.

Old Dominion brought its tradition-rich program to Austin on February 21. The Monarchs used superior frontcourt quickness to lead by three points at the half, but a 17-1 UT run erased that and more in a 99-78 victory in front of 7,698 spectators. Kim McQuarter scored 26 for ODU, and Davis had 32, leaving her two points behind ex-teammate Fran Harris as the SWC's career scoring leader. The record might have borne an asterisk, however, because Annette Smith's freshman year preceded the SWC's adoption of women's basketball; the 2,565 points scored by Smith remain at the top. At any rate, the official record was sure to fall when UT hosted TCU on Clarissa Davis Night, the first time a female hoopster had been so honored. The Austin City Council and Texas Senate drafted resolutions acknowledging her play over the past four seasons, and 11,769 fans were on hand to cheer. After the band serenaded her with *San Antonio Rose*, the lady of the hour had 16 points and 13 rebounds in Texas' 100-62 win over the Frogs, but she was outscored by both Pollini (19) and McBride (18).

A pair of road games concluded the regular season. Welton Brown's SMU team gave the sixth-ranked Horns a scare before losing, 105-94. Guard Jeannia Nix connected on 16 of 22 shots, including six of eight three-pointers for 43 points. Davis had 36 points and 12 rebounds for Texas, and Pollini, finally looking like the player she was expected to be, had another strong game inside. Davis injured a thumb in practice but seemed OK against Texas A&M. The score was tied at 68 with 2:45 left, and 2,591 Aggie fans sought to influence the outcome with every scream and whistle, but the Longhorns pulled out a 78-70 win. Southwest Conference champion and undefeated for the seventh straight time, Texas was ready for the playoffs.

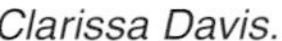

Clarissa Davis.

According to *Daily Texan* writer Ray Dise, UT's 74-59 defeat of Texas A&M in the SWC tourney semifinal was "like eating a chili dog—slow and sloppy," and Conradt did not disagree. But it sent the Horns into the finals against Arkansas at Reunion Arena. Lisa Martin (31) led the Hogs to the brink of an upset before Hall's jump shot with 17 seconds left broke a tie and gave Texas a 101-99 win. Hall, who some observers thought was unhappy and considering a transfer, denied it, and her big hoop proved she would be the Horns' go-to player in future seasons. Davis scored 36 points against Arkansas and was chosen tournament MVP, complementing her second Naismith Award, recognition as the finest player in women's college basketball.

The game's popularity and support in the South was seen in the NCAA's choice of Austin, Auburn, Ruston and Bowling Green as sites for regionals of the 48-team tournament. The 25-4 Longhorns received a bye, and the second-round game against 27-3 Montana was at home on March 18. Hall and Pointer combined for 39 points in an 83-54 defeat of the weak-shooting Grizzlies. Abstruse NCAA eligibility rules forced Pollini, after her 23rd birthday, to either stop playing or give up her senior year. She opted to play but had minimal impact in those final games.

Some 9,701 people were on hand at the Erwin Center to see Maryland beat Stephen F. Austin and Texas beat Nevada-Las Vegas as the regional tourney began. Conradt had noted the Rebels' potent inside game, so the Horns utilized an alert zone defense and the scoring talents of Davis (25) and Hall (24) for an 88-77 victory. Pauline Jordan led UNLV with 22. Hall, who hit five straight three-pointers in the second half, said, "I just want to go to Tacoma. I really want to play for the national championship and win it for Clarissa."

A tough Maryland team sought to prevent such an occurrence. The Terrapins had an all-America center, Vicky Bullett, and a quick guard in Deanna Tate, who looked and played like former Longhorn Beverly Williams. The biggest crowd of the season, 12,874 fans in full-throated roar most of the game, witnessed a 79-71 Maryland victory as Tate (32) scored from the outside, penetrated at will and bedeviled UT's much slower guards. Davis led the Horns to within three in the final minutes only to have the Terps respond. With 29 points and 10 rebounds, she enjoyed an excellent farewell game. The 1989 season had come to an abrupt end, as had the Davis era. In a 101-game career curtailed by ankle, knee, back and thumb injuries, the two-time national player of the year had scored 2,008 points, collected 882 rebounds and helped win a national title, earning a secure spot in the pantheon of the greatest players in the history of women's basketball.

1990

Was there life after Clarissa? The Texas women's basketball program had been challenging for national championships since Davis was a junior high school student in San Antonio, so there was no reason to think that would not continue. What athletic director Donna Lopiano, coach Jody Conradt and others had developed over the previous decade and a half was unlikely to falter even if Clarissa Davis' eligibility had expired. UT was on top of the Southwest Conference and near the top of the NCAA for familiar reasons: a $360,000 basketball budget, nation-leading attendance in a great facility and a mystique that aided recruiting and petrified some opponents. Annette Smith, one of the brightest names in Texas hoop lore, was added to Conradt's staff in 1990 (the first time no midseason tournament was played), along with Lynn Pool, Kathy Harston and Cherri Rapp. If further expertise were needed, Sonja Hogg, who coached Louisiana Tech to two national titles, served as an assistant AD.

Edna Campbell, a starter for two seasons at Maryland, had transferred to UT, sat out a year and was ready to jumpstart the backcourt. And in the frontcourt, Conradt welcomed center Cinietra Henderson, who had led Duncanville to a pair of state championships. Both Campbell and Henderson were impact players like sophomore Vicki Hall, so the immediate future looked bright and would have been blinding if Sheryl Swoopes had stayed. A 6' forward from the west Texas town of Brownfield, she signed a scholarship, came to Austin and was on campus just two weeks before going to a junior college closer to home. Swoopes was a promising player destined for greatness at Texas Tech.

The Longhorns started the season ranked fifth, but that did not last long. In Seattle, they suffered a 75-65 defeat by an aggressive Washington team. Karen Deden and Amy Michelson led the Huskies with 22 and 18 points, respectively, while Hall (17) paced UT. "We got outhustled on the boards, there's no doubt about that," Conradt said. "But I'm not discouraged. This loss should make us better."

They got better fast, winning the next nine games. Henderson replaced Ellen Bayer as the starting center before the Purdue game in Austin. The No. 8 Boilermakers got trounced, 89-61, as Campbell and Susan Anderson combined for 40 points. After trailing their Big 10 visitors by three at halftime, the Horns shot 62 percent in the second half and outscored Purdue by a 51-20 margin. Long Beach State, in the Final Four two of the previous three seasons, brought a quick, high-scoring, eighth-ranked team to the Erwin Center. The 49ers led by eight with 1:18 left, but Texas reeled off 11 straight points to win, 80-77, before 7,125 fans. An extra-long three-pointer by senior guard Lyssa McBride capped what Conradt called one of the most dramatic wins in recent years.

Back on the road, UT faced a fourth straight ranked opponent, No. 18 Old Dominion. The Monarchs were always tough at home, and they played Texas down to the wire. Star center Kelly Lyons (42) was fouled at the buzzer with the Horns leading, 93-92. Lyons, who had a chance to tie or win, proceeded to miss both free throws and let Texas get out of Norfolk with a victory. Campbell scored 23, and Amy Claborn, better known for distributing the ball than shooting it, had 17. The Longhorns' game with Rutgers was postponed a day because of the death of that university's president. Before a small and rather somber crowd, UT jumped to a big lead and won it, 85-63. Hall had 23 points and 11 rebounds as Texas muscled by the Scarlet Knights.

Bayer came off the bench to score 16 points, grab nine rebounds and block nine shots in an 82-52 victory over Ohio State. Beating the Buckeyes by 30 was not what Conradt expected because Harston had scouted them and considered them tougher than Washington, the only team to beat the Longhorns so far. Following a two-week holiday break, Texas hosted Big 8 champion Colorado and won, 90-67, but Conradt was not pleased with her team's play. Reserve guard Johnna Pointer (15) was the top scorer and may have caught less of Conradt's wrath in the locker room. "If she was happy with anything, she didn't let us know," McBride said.

Conference play began at home on January 2 against Texas Tech. The winning streak over SWC opponents, which had been going on for 12 years, suddenly seemed to take on greater significance. The media played it up, opponents talked about ending it, and UT players and coaches admitted taking some pride in it. Tech, one of maybe three teams with a chance to beat the fearsome Longhorns, fell, 81-46. Hall scored 23, and Bayer had a triple double—12 points,

10 rebounds and 12 blocked shots. The Red Raiders, in large part because of Texas' 6'9" center, shot miserably, just 27 percent from the field, and they were scarcely better from the free throw line. Baylor visited the Longhorns' abode three days later and got destroyed, 93-40, before a crowd of 8,396. Hall (21) and three teammates were in double figures against the cellar-dwelling Bears.

After playing before so many fans in that game, the No. 4 Horns beat TCU, 83-51, and just 775 people were at Daniel-Meyer Coliseum to see it. Hall scored 27 points in UT's ninth straight victory and one of the easiest. A team without much speed, the Horns were not using the aggressive, denying defense of the 1986 national championship team but were playing a steadier, more controlled defense, which was keeping opponents' shooting percentages and point totals low. The defense was great, but the offense was horrible when Texas lost to Western Kentucky, 61-56, in Bowling Green. Hall, the focus of the Hilltoppers' defense, made just three of 17 shots, and only Henderson and Campbell had much success. WKU enjoyed a 45-33 rebounding advantage, too. That ego-bruising loss was salved by a 95-77 win over SMU in Dallas. Hall (24) and Claborn (22) were the top scorers against the outmanned Ponies, although guard Suzanne McAnally had 25 points.

"They are a very impressive group of athletes," Conradt said about Texas A&M. "They are hard to prepare for." Perhaps, but her team thundered past the Ags, 88-67, as 9,364 fans looked on. Henderson, challenged by the coaches to hustle more, had 21 points and nine rebounds. Texas played an almost flawless game and had it won by halftime. Only Hall's sore foot caused concern because defending national champion Tennessee was next, and the game was in Knoxville.

Hall discarded her crutches and then the special boot protecting her foot. Although she was unable to run in practice, the sophomore forward was on the court as the 12-3 Vols and 11-2 Horns tipped off. Texas led by seven with six minutes left when guard Tonya Edwards took control and gave Tennessee a 76-70 win. Hall had 17 points and Bayer 15, but the latter's foul trouble sidelined her down the stretch. Anderson, who had played poorly for nine straight games, was on the bench when UT met Arkansas at Barnhill Arena. She got the message, scoring 22 points and grabbing eight rebounds in an 84-75 victory. John Sutherland's team pulled out all the stops in an effort to beat the Longhorns, and a record crowd of 6,327 was surely in favor. Delmonica DeHorney scored 17 for the Hogs, who appeared to have blown their best chance to upset the longtime SWC champions.

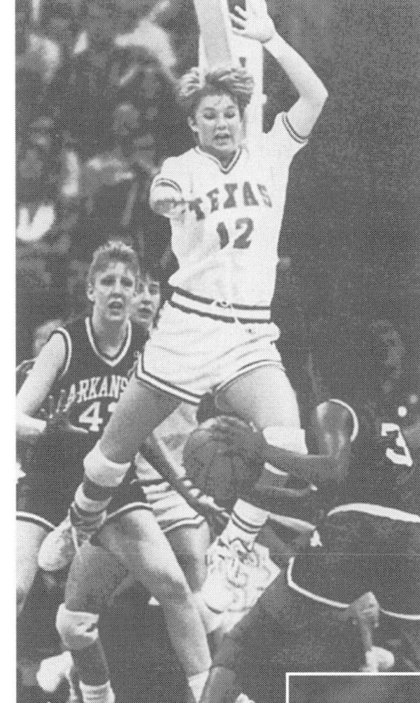

Backcourt duo Amy Claborn (left) and Edna Campbell (below).

The Erwin Center was the scene of three games over a nine-day period. All were victories, and none were too stressful. Texas reserves led the way in an 81-44 defeat of Rice, Hall scored 24 as UT ripped Houston (90-64), and Southern California got nailed, 85-44. If the Longhorns had slipped a bit since the heyday of Annette Smith, Kamie Ethridge, Andrea Lloyd, Fran Harris and Clarissa Davis, the Women of Troy had nearly fallen off a cliff compared to the Cheryl Miller era. "It's a little tough when all you have is a peashooter and they have a couple of cannons," said USC coach Marianne Stanley. Her team left Austin with a 4-13 record.

The Longhorns had tougher times in practice than offered by the SWC's weak sisters, Baylor, Rice and SMU. In Waco, the Bears were beaten, 92-62, although Texas did not play especially well. Anderson and

Campbell (15 points each) led six players in double figures. In Houston, Rice had no chance, trailing by 40 points at halftime and losing, 103-48. It was another of those games that tested Conradt's motivational powers. And in Austin, a crowd five times the combined number of the previous two games saw the Horns stroll past SMU, 105-70. Campbell, bouncing back from a thigh injury, made 10 of 12 shots, most of them coming off the fast break. Christy Scofield scored 15 points for Welton Brown's Mustangs.

More than half of the 2,043 fans at G. Rollie White Coliseum were of the hook 'em rather than the gig 'em variety, and they were treated to a 95-70 victory over Texas A&M. Hall had one of her best games yet—32 points, seven rebounds and nine assists. "This is the toughest weekend of the season," Conradt said. "I'm sure Texas Tech was sitting with their feet up tonight, waiting for us to get into Lubbock with some nice, cold weather to boot." Suzanne Halliburton of the *Austin American-Statesman* recalled that preseason prognosticators had pointed to February 18 as the day the ever-lengthening UT win streak might be halted. But an 18-point spree at the close of the first half ensured an 82-67 defeat of the Red Raiders. Campbell and Hall combined for 48 points, and Bayer collected a game-high 12 rebounds.

Record: 27-5

65 Washington 75
89 Purdue 61
80 Long Beach State 77
93 Old Dominion 92
85 Rutgers 63
82 Ohio State 52
90 Colorado 67
81 Texas Tech 46
93 Baylor 40
83 TCU 51
56 Western Kentucky 61
95 SMU 77
88 Texas A&M 67
70 Tennessee 76
84 Arkansas 75
81 Rice 44
90 Houston 64
85 Southern California 44
92 Baylor 62
103 Rice 48
105 SMU 70
95 Texas A&M 70
82 Texas Tech 67
77 Arkansas 82
91 TCU 51
91 NE Louisiana 61
77 Houston 74
101 Houston 58
63 Texas Tech 60
95 Ohio State 66
72 North Carolina State 63
57 Louisiana Tech 71

The somewhat weary Longhorns were glad to have five days before hosting Arkansas, and a big game was expected. Both teams were 20-3, and the Razorbacks' only conference loss had been to Texas. A crowd of 11,616 witnessed history as Delmonica DeHorney (26 points, eight rebounds and four blocked shots) led Arkansas to an 82-77 triumph, ending a win streak that encompassed 13 seasons. John Sutherland, his players and a handful of red-clad fans celebrated madly while their counterparts went into mourning. January 23, 1978 was the last time a UT hoop team lost to a Southwest Conference competitor (although the SWC did not sanction women's athletics until five years later), so the number came to 183. Conradt's teams had won an astounding 183 straight games against SWC foes. "It hurts," said Conradt with a grim visage. "I knew when it ended, it would be the most difficult thing for the team. Tradition has carried us through some tough times, and it will carry us again."

There was a two-hour practice session at Gregory Gym the next morning, at which time the players and coaches agreed not to discuss the streak any more. TCU was the next team to face the once-unbeatable Longhorns. Still mentally and physically down because of the Arkansas loss, UT put a 91-51 defeat on the Horned Frogs. Campbell, Hall, Anderson and Pointer all reached double figures, and Hall (who played poorly in the Arkansas game and spent a night at the Student Health Center due to exhaustion) had 13 rebounds. The final regular-season home game was a 91-61 rout of Northeast Louisiana. Henderson and Anderson teamed up for 44 points and 23 rebounds, while Derunzia Johnson scored 25 for the Indians.

Texas had some trouble beating Houston at Hofheinz Pavilion but finally managed a 77-74 victory keyed by Bayer's 20 points and 17 rebounds. The victory meant the Horns shared the 1990 SWC championship with Arkansas. Conradt worked the refs all night long and seemed to believe the Cougars were getting some extra help. "I think the conference is embarrassed by our domination," she said. "There's an undertone, a current feeling that Texas can't dominate. I'm ready to get out of conference and on the tournament road, so we can get a fair shot."

The SWC Tournament in Dallas began as it always had—with Texas getting a bye. In the second round, the Longhorns ripped Houston, 101-58, scoring on 20 of their final 25 possessions. Greg Williams of UH called it "a coach's nightmare." Campbell led all scorers with 24 points. There would be no rematch with Arkansas because Texas Tech had upset the Hogs in the other semifinal. On Saturday afternoon at Reunion Arena, the Horns and Raiders tipped off. Hall, just one for 11 in the first half, made five straight shots, including one from three-point range, in the early minutes of the second half. UT never gave up the lead from then on and won, 63-60. Stacey Siebert had 18 points and 13 rebounds for Tech, joining Campbell and Hall on the all-tourney team.

Recently expanded to 48 teams, the NCAA Tournament had room for Texas, Texas Tech and Arkansas. The Longhorns certainly had proven their ability to draw a crowd, leading the nation in attendance for the fifth straight year. They got a good deal from the NCAA, a first-round bye and a second-round game and a regional at home. Three wins at the Erwin Center and UT would head for the Final Four in Knoxville. Of course, Conradt would permit no such looking ahead. First, there was Ohio State, a team Texas had thrashed by 30 points in December. Little had changed since then as Hall (26) and Henderson (24) paced the Horns to a 95-66 victory over the Buckeyes.

The regional began on March 22 when 26-4 Texas and 25-5 North Carolina State took the court. Kay Yow's Wolfpack led by two at halftime, but Campbell (19) and Henderson (17) helped UT pull away to a 72-63 win. All-American Andrea Stinson scored 21 for the Atlantic Coast Conference team, but she made just nine of 27 shots. It was a physical game, just what the Horns needed to prepare for top-ranked Louisiana Tech, boasting a 31-0 record and an average victory margin of 35 points. All-American Venus Lacy, 6'4" of muscle and moxie, was the most prominent player on Leon Barmore's squad. The biggest crowd of the season, 12,390, saw Louisiana Tech end UT's bid for a national crown for the third time in four years. Lacy and Shantel Hardison combined for 35 points and 23 rebounds in a 71-57 Techster win. Second and third chances on missed shots were the difference for Tech, in Conradt's view. Hall (24) and others struggled to hold back tears as the Longhorn Band played "The Eyes of Texas" after the game.

1991

In the centennial year of the great game of basketball, Jody Conradt's Longhorns were accorded a reasonable chance of getting to the Final Four. Women's basketball had evolved and improved dramatically, but all the talk about parity notwithstanding, only a half-dozen or so teams could be seen as legitimate national championship contenders. While no one said Texas was at the top of the list with Virginia, Tennessee, Stanford, Auburn and Georgia, the core of guard Edna Campbell, forward Vicki Hall and center Cinietra Henderson meant the Horns had to be reckoned with. Each of them received some kind of preseason all-America recognition. Unfortunately, UT had a weak recruiting class as a junior college transfer and four frosh would make modest contributions in 1991 and the years to follow.

The season began with a trip to California, where a couple of top-25 teams awaited the Longhorns. A career-high 30 points from Campbell did not prevent Long Beach State from taking an 80-74 victory. The entire 49er starting lineup was in double figures, while Campbell was pretty much a one-woman show. Hall, playing with a broken finger, missed 11 of 13 shots. Two nights later, Tammy Story (36) and freshman sensation Lisa Leslie (30 points and 20 rebounds) sparked Southern Cal's 88-77 win. The Women of Troy built a comfortable lead with 12 minutes left and were never threatened after that, giving UT a 0-2 record with the No. 1 team in the nation, Virginia, next up.

Part of a trend toward corporate support of college athletics, the Texas-Virginia game was sponsored by a bottler of soft drinks. While the media paid scant attention, other key home games were officially connected to a bank, a newspaper, a maker of blue jeans, a haircut emporium, a fast-food company and a chain of grocery stores. The Cavaliers had Heather and Heidi Burge (at 6'5", certified by the *Guinness Book of Records* as the tallest female identical twins in the world) and a pair of fine guards in Dawn Staley and Tammi Reiss. They displayed superior shooting and passing in an 80-74 defeat of Texas before 8,844 fans. Campbell had a game-high 24 points. The Longhorns' lack of depth, quickness and intensity were quite apparent. "We can't get too hung up about our early won-loss record," Conradt said. "I could have scheduled three teams we could have had sure wins against, and we'd be 3-0. On the other hand, losing is something I cannot tolerate, and I don't think people around here can tolerate it very long, either. I'm looking for improvement or I'm going to be in a long-term bad mood." Conradt got a mood elevator when her team beat Western Michigan, 84-64. The 20th-ranked Horns struggled early but finished strong. The troika of Henderson, Hall and Campbell combined for 59 points, and senior guard Amy Claborn had 12 assists. By season's end, she would trail just Kamie Ethridge and Terri Mackey on the career list with 537.

Colorado, which recently upset national champion Stanford, was hoping for a similar result when the Longhorns visited Boulder. Conradt was concerned that her players, in the midst of final exams, might not be ready, but they trampled the Buffaloes, 93-64. Hall, with the cast removed from her broken finger, scored 21 points in the first half, and Colorado got 22 from freshman Jamillah Lang.

Cinietra Henderson, one of UT's best and most reliable players from 1990 to 1993.

Back in Austin, UT scored two more intersectional victories. The defense forced 25 turnovers and contested nearly every shot, and the bench was responsible for 34 points in an 89-63 win over DePaul. Hall (19), Campbell (16) and Fey Meeks (12) were the top scorers in a 105-48 romp of McNeese State, as the Horns went over the .500 mark seven games into the season.

After a 10-day break for the holidays, Texas participated in the Super Shootout in Hilton Head, South Carolina. Billed as the best Christmas tournament in women's basketball, its sponsors also managed to draw Tennessee, Stanford and Ohio State to a gym seating just 500 fans with a court 10 feet short of NCAA-regulation size. Stanford, with several players back from the 1990 NCAA championship team, crushed the Horns, 82-66. Campbell and Henderson had 46 of UT's points, but Hall shot poorly and no one else stepped up against Tara VanDerveer's Cardinal. Campbell sprained an ankle in that game and missed the 98-73 defeat of Ohio State the next night. Hall (25 points and 12 rebounds) and Henderson (23) carried the load in an exceptionally rough game. Monica Taylor scored 23 for the Buckeyes.

Due to injuries and subpar performances, Conradt shuffled her lineup for the Southwest Conference opener in Austin. Pointer and JC transfer Eurica Johnson got the chance to show their stuff against Texas A&M. The Horns won, 72-59, but Conradt was not thrilled, saying her team lacked cohesion and leadership, a theme she would sound over and over again as the season unfolded. Aggie guard Yvonne Hill (22) was the game's high scorer. UT was back in action two days later, overpowering Baylor, 83-49, before 6,178 fans. Henderson and Hall teamed up for 39 points, and reserves Meeks, Benita Pollard and Courtney Canavan played well down the stretch.

The University of Arkansas had announced its intention to leave the SWC at the end of the 1991 season, so the Horn-Hog game on January 8 might be Conradt's final visit to Fayetteville. And since Arkansas had ended Texas' 183-game win streak against conference teams, motivation would not be lacking. But the Longhorns limped into Barnhill Arena; Claborn and Campbell were nursing injuries and had not practiced for two days. The No. 14 Razorbacks, led by two-time SWC player of the year Delmonica DeHorney (22), beat UT, 76-61, before a vociferous crowd of 6,819. "This game was out of control from the opening tipoff to the end," Conradt said. "We totally lost our composure and got outhustled in every area. I couldn't talk to my team because of all the noise."

The next two games were rescheduled due to Governor Ann Richards' inaugural ball at the Erwin Center. Richards was one of the Horns' most prominent fans, sitting courtside along with other dignitaries like former Congresswoman Barbara Jordan and author James Michener. And the team showed its respect, not to mention gender identification, by marching up Congress Avenue in the inaugural parade. UT did beat Rice, 71-61, in Houston, but it appeared that the rest of the SWC was finally catching up. "Texas is not on top of the hill any more," crowed Rice coach Mike Dunavant. Hall played 40 minutes, scored 25 points and collected nine rebounds. The second rescheduled game was at home, a 93-79 defeat of Houston marred by the constant blowing of referees' whistles. Campbell, despite an aching ankle and Achilles tendon, scored 21 points, extending UT's all-time record against the Cougars to 42-0. Nevada-Las Vegas, undefeated and ranked fifth in the nation, came to Austin for a Wednesday night game. The Rebels had played a weak schedule, and it showed in an 89-67 Longhorn victory. Despite the looming presence of 6'6" center Merlelynn Lange, frontcourt stars Hall and Henderson combined for 51 points. For her showings against Rice, Houston and UNLV, Hall was named *Sports Illustrated*'s player of the week.

The Horns had begun an eight-game winning streak, yet critics were everywhere. A *Dallas Morning News* article was entitled "Lady Longhorns baffled by decline of dominance," the *Austin American-Statesman* ran one called "Slide from the summit," and the *Daily Texan* issued a few pearls of wisdom, too. It was not a welcome development for a program long immune from criticism. Conradt was not one to offer nor accept excuses and continued doing everything in her power to lift the team. In Lubbock, Hall had 22 points, including a driving layup with 26 seconds left to seal a 66-63 win over Texas Tech. Jennifer Buck (21) and Krista Kirkland (16) paced the Red Raiders. Three nights later at Daniel-Meyer Coliseum, the Horns jumped to an early lead and went on to defeat TCU, 84-58. Campbell, who played just 22 minutes, scored 26 points in a game that left the Frogs as so much roadkill.

Henderson had 23 points and 11 rebounds in a 93-65 home victory over SMU, coached for the last of 14 seasons by Welton Brown. Conradt, whose team won for the sixth straight time, had special praise for Henderson and defensive stopper Joanne Benton.

Record: 21-9
74 Long Beach State 80
77 Southern California 88
74 Virginia 80
84 Western Michigan 64
93 Colorado 64
89 DePaul 63
105 McNeese State 48
66 Stanford 82
98 Ohio State 73
72 Texas A&M 59
83 Baylor 49
61 Arkansas 76
71 Rice 61
93 Houston 79
89 Nevada-Las Vegas 67
66 Texas Tech 63
84 TCU 58
93 SMU 65
74 Texas A&M 65
91 Baylor 67
68 Arkansas 73
87 Rice 50
68 Houston 64
55 Tennessee 64
77 Texas Tech 53
77 TCU 40
90 SMU 52
108 Rice 61
61 Texas Tech 63
63 Lamar 77

A two-point halftime lead had Texas A&M's coaches, players and fans giddy, but it did not last as the Longhorns eliminated turnovers, shot better and played with more purpose to take a 74-65 victory at G. Rollie White Coliseum. Campbell scored 20 points on a variety of jump shots and drives, and Henderson had 19, mostly from the paint. Dena Russo (17) was one of three Aggies in double figures. It had been close, and more of the same might await UT in Waco. The Baylor Bears owned a recent victory over Arkansas and wanted nothing more than Bevo's head. BU fans were yet to fully embrace women's basketball because fewer than 800 showed up to see a 91-67 Texas win. Each of the Longhorn starters played well, but the Bears' LaNita Luckey (20) was the top scorer.

The SWC game of the year was February 9 when Arkansas and Texas collided at the Erwin Center. Tied for the league lead, they each had their reasons for wanting the game badly. A season-high 12,531 fans did their part to ensure an orange-and-white victory, but it was not to be. The Razorbacks won, 73-68, behind 21 points from Delmonica DeHorney and 16 from Blair Savage. Their passing was sure and crisp, leading to 22 assists. "It's never easy to say someone's better than you," Conradt commented. "But tonight, Arkansas was the better team. We had no offensive consistency." While it would have been inconceivable a couple of years earlier, the Horns had lost three straight games to an SWC opponent. They bounced back with an 87-50 victory over a Rice team that looked confused and scared. Hall had 21 points and was the chief contributor to UT's two-to-one rebound edge against the Owls.

Conradt said her team needed a tough game, albeit a victory, to build character and prepare for the NCAAs, and they got it at Hofheinz Pavilion. Campbell suffered another ankle injury late in the first half, and the Cougars took advantage. They were up by one with six minutes left, but Hall (20 points and 15 rebounds), Henderson (14) and Meeks (12 points and 12 rebounds) led UT to a 68-64 win. If Houston had hit better than 39 percent from the field, the result might have been different.

In accordance with CBS' contract with the NCAA, three regular-season women's games were nationally televised, including the encounter between No. 4 Tennessee and No. 15 Texas at the Erwin Center. Conradt and longtime friend and rival Pat Summitt knew their programs (and women's hoops in general) would benefit from a good showing. The glare of the cameras exposed the Horns' vulnerability to pressure defense and physical play in a 64-55 Tennessee victory before 8,225 fans. All-American Daedra Charles had 21 points and 12 rebounds for the Vols, who were headed for another national championship.

Campbell had put aside her crutches for the Tennessee game but missed the next two. On consecutive nights, Texas Tech and TCU battled the Horns in Austin. Marsha Sharp's Red Raiders, who had fallen to UT by three points twice in a row, were eager to strike a blow for their rising program. Not yet, said the Longhorns, to the tune of 77-53. Henderson was unstoppable, hitting 11 of 16 shots, and Meeks and Hall were close behind with 18 and 17 points, respectively. Hall was the star the next night, getting 27 points and 11 rebounds in UT's 77-40 defeat of TCU. Just one Frog, Liz Zeller (10), reached double figures.

As the season neared an end, the Longhorns played three straight games at Moody Coliseum. They had no trouble dispatching SMU, 90-52. Hall, Pointer and Campbell were the top scorers, and Conradt seemed pleased with every player on the roster. The SWC Tournament began in Dallas on March 6 with UT, second to Arkansas in the regular-season race, meeting Rice. The Horns had a 33-point halftime lead and finished with a 108-61 victory over the Owls. Henderson sizzled, scoring 23 points in just 21 minutes. Who could have known that would be the last victory of the year? Texas Tech showed a lot of grit and determination in beating the Longhorns, 63-61, in the semifinals before 5,211 fans. It was Texas' first loss in the nine-year history of the event and the first ever to the Red Raiders. Three Krista Kirkland free throws in the last half-minute ensured a win Tech could savor for a long time. With Claborn and Campbell hurting, Hall and Henderson did what they could, compiling 38 points and 20 rebounds.

If that loss was surprising, what happened six days later was shocking. Texas (21-8) hosted Lamar (26-3) in a first-round NCAA playoff game and got bounced, 77-63. Conradt had hoped to find redemption for a difficult season by going far in the tournament, but the Cardinals had their own plans. Slippery 5' point guard Brenda Hatchett (16) was one of five Lamar players in double figures, while UT's reliance on Campbell, Hall and Henderson was never more clear; they scored all but seven of the team's points.

Surely, 1991 was not the happiest year for Texas basketball. Home attendance, although still among the nation's leaders, declined for the second straight season. Conradt, often at wit's end, had alternately berated, praised and threatened her players to little avail. The winningest coach in the women's game, Conradt had little left to prove, but she would entertain no thoughts of retirement. Her golf clubs sat idle while she and her assistants hit the recruiting road. "The Texas mystique is dead," she told Kevin O'Keeffe of the *San Antonio Express-News*. "We're just like anybody else now."

1992

There was no doubt about it. The 1992 Longhorns would depend mostly on the showings of senior forward Vicki Hall and junior center Cinietra Henderson. But in early practices, the orange-white game and two exhibitions, the UT coaching staff saw that 5'8" freshman guard Nekeshia Henderson was a player, too. The Dallas native brought speed and enthusiasm to the team and would be a backcourt fixture for the next four years, at least when she was healthy.

Ranked twelfth in preseason, the Horns' first game was at home against Southwest Missouri. Although they represented one of those obscure "directional" schools, the Bears returned four starters from a 26-5 team that reached the second round of the 1991 NCAA Tournament. Texas won, 76-64, before a crowd of 5,185, but victory came at a steep price as Hall suffered a season-ending knee injury early in the second half. The Longhorns' leading scorer and rebounder the previous two years was fighting for a loose ball when her left knee buckled. Hall was in agony amid the fans' silence when she was wheeled off the floor. Her teammates, shocked at the development, managed to win with 21 points from Joanne Benton. Coach Jody Conradt, who always took interest in her players apart from their hoop skills, regretfully added Hall to a list of great Longhorns who had suffered serious knee injuries: Jackie Swaim, Annette Smith, Yulonda Wimbish, Doreatha Conwell and Clarissa Davis. Surgery and rehabilitation followed; the NCAA granted Hall a medical redshirt season, so she would be back in 1993.

Fey Meeks, who stepped into the starting lineup for Hall, scored 18 points as the Horns fell, 70-62, to George Washington in the first round of the Seven Up-Desert Classic in Las Vegas. Playing badly against the unranked Colonials (paced by Jennifer Shasky's 21 points), UT seemed lost without its fiery leader with the stringy blond hair. "We missed Vicki's stability more than anything," Conradt said. "She had always provided the points and rebounds when we needed them. We can't use that as an excuse, though." In the consolation game, Texas beat host UNLV, 81-65. Cinietra Henderson had 26 points and 10 rebounds in just 21 minutes.

After a 26-point home victory over Arkansas State, the Horns traveled to Charlottesville to take on the second-ranked Virginia Cavaliers. Their 5-0 record and huge average victory margin were suspect because of soft competition, but Debbie Ryan's team was for real. All-America guard Dawn Staley displayed multi-option moves and frenetic defense as the Cavs rolled over Texas, 77-47. It was the Longhorns' worst loss in four years, one featuring poor defense, rebounding, shooting and ballhandling. The Texas coaches and players returned home, red-faced.

With eight days to regroup, the Horns were ready when they tipped off with No. 13 Northwestern on December 15. Johnna Pointer (20) pointed the way as UT came from behind to win, 82-75. Michele Savage scored 19 for the Wildcats of the Big 10.

Two perennial powers, Texas and Tennessee, were chosen to play in the Naismith Hall of Fame game in Springfield, Massachusetts, where the good doctor invented the game a century earlier. Conradt and Pat Summitt, spiritual descendants of Senda Berenson—organizer of women's basketball in the 1890s—had coached their teams to over 1,000 victories. The Vols, defending national champions, still featured what one envious opponent called "corn-fed country chicks," and they used their muscle to subdue UT, 86-72. Cinietra Henderson, despite the double- and triple-teaming that would be her fate all season long, scored 21 points, and Peggy Evans (18) led five Tennessee players in double figures. The game ended with Nekeshia Henderson's hoop, launched from behind the half-court line.

After the Christmas break, the Horns scored a pair of victories at the Erwin Center. Meeks and Nekeshia Henderson (back in the starting lineup in place of Jennifer Clark) combined for 43 points in a 104-67 blowout of New Mexico State. Conradt was glad to see her team chasing loose balls and hitting the boards. "We got caught up in the smoke and spotlights," said Roadrunner coach Doug Hoselton in reference to UT's elaborate pregame introductions. In a 79-69 defeat of San Francisco, Cinietra Henderson scored 28 points to break the 1,000-point mark, barely halfway into her college career. The Dons, who wasted a big early lead, got 22 points from forward Joy Boyenga.

Seattle was the scene of a Pac 10/SWC double-header on January 4. Texas Tech did its part by beating Washington State, but No. 14 Washington played a bruising, physical game in defeating UT, 72-64. Shaunda Greene led the Huskies with 25 points.

The struggling Longhorns were not favored to win the SWC title, even with Arkansas gone to the Southeastern Conference. One of the teams with a legitimate chance to succeed the Razorbacks as champs was Houston, then 10-1 and ranked sixteenth. Before a crowd of

Record: 21-10

76 SW Missouri 64
62 George Washington 70
81 Nevada-Las Vegas 65
76 Arkansas State 50
47 Virginia 77
82 Northwestern 75
72 Tennessee 86
104 New Mexico State 67
79 San Francisco 69
64 Washington 72
65 Houston 73
65 Texas Tech 78
76 TCU 41
73 Texas A&M 74
83 SMU 81
82 Rutgers 56
76 Penn State 73 (OT)
83 Baylor 55
91 Rice 73
80 Houston 70
70 Texas Tech 63
71 Texas A&M 52
87 TCU 55
90 SMU 70
68 Tennessee 86
82 Baylor 52
84 Rice 49
84 Baylor 56
70 Houston 60
74 Texas Tech 76
81 UCLA 82

2,317 at Hofheinz Pavilion, the Cougars pulled away in the last five minutes to win, 73-65. Their inside game, led by Margo Graham (a thunderous 6'3", 240-pound player) and Darla Simpson, was too much for the Horns. It was UH's first win in a series dating back to 1975. Things got worse in Lubbock, where Texas Tech took a 78-65 victory. Compounding the Longhorns' misery was the fact that junior forward Sheryl Swoopes (32 points and 10 rebounds) had been fitted out with a Texas uniform two seasons earlier before leaving Austin rather suddenly. It would have been the merest footnote, except that Swoopes' talent improved dramatically while in junior college. She was named JC player of the year, joined the Red Raiders and continued getting better yet. Had Swoopes stayed—a source of wishful speculation by UT fans—she would have complemented Edna Campbell, Vicki Hall and Cinietra Henderson quite well. "We wouldn't be talking about rebuilding," Conradt said. "We'd be talking about knocking heads."

During the week between the loss to Texas Tech and a 76-41 defeat of lowly TCU, the Horns were treated to more newspaper articles tracing the decline of the program and the indignity of dropping out of the Associated Press' top-25 poll for the first time in 10 years. Finishing the regular season ranked first in the poll in 1984, 1985, 1986 and 1987 seemed like a distant memory. Arkansas, Texas Tech and Houston had claimed conference victories over UT, and Texas A&M did the same. Lynn Hickey's Aggies won, 74-73, before 5,602 fans in Austin. Dena Russo hit all 11 of her second-half shots, including a left-handed layup with one second on the clock. Pointer (21) and Cinietra Henderson (19) were the best of an otherwise stale Texas offense. Hickey and Russo joined a chorus proclaiming the end of UT's mastery of the Southwest Conference.

Freshman guard Nekeshia Henderson.

Athletic director Donna Lopiano penned a long piece in the *Austin American-Statesman* about "the values of educational sport." After hearing from several unhappy fans, she urged that they keep some perspective on the matter. The era of dynasties in women's basketball was over, and neither she nor Conradt had been satisfied when vintage Texas teams ran roughshod over the rest of the SWC. Furthermore, wrote the distinguished AD, the NCAA had been tightening academic requirements for the previous five years, and it was especially so on the Forty Acres. Many quality athletes who got in at other schools had no chance at Texas and were never seriously recruited. It was an interesting piece of journalism, but when Bob Weltlich made some of the same winning-is-not-everything arguments in favor of his men's program in the 1980s, he had been regarded as a whining loser.

A loss to SMU, one of the traditional doormats of the league, was not out of the question. Rhonda Rompola had taken over as coach of the Mustangs, who had a surprising 9-5 record. In a midweek game at Moody Coliseum, UT came back from an eight-point deficit to grab an 83-81 win. Cinietra Henderson was splendid, getting 27 points and 14 rebounds. Suzanne McAnally had 15 points and nine assists for the vanquished Ponies. No one knew it at the time, but the nadir of the season had passed. Conradt's Horns were on a 10-game winning streak.

Cries of glee emanated from the Texas locker room after an 82-56 taming of Rutgers in Austin. Benton limited Scarlet Knight star Tanya Hansen to six points, and Cinietra Henderson had another impressive performance—30 points and 13 rebounds, just to make sure she got the attention of Theresa Grentz, the Rutgers coach who would head the 1992 U.S. Olympic team. No. 8 Penn State came into the Erwin Center and lost an overtime thriller, 76-73. Nekeshia Henderson, quiet most of the game, scored five points in the extra session. Cinietra Henderson, who had 31 points and 13 rebounds, met her match in the Nittany Lions' Susan Robinson (29 points and 10 rebounds).

The rejuvenated Longhorns jumped back into SWC play,

hammering Baylor, 83-55, in Austin. The top scorers were Pointer (20) and the Bears' LaNita Luckey (19). Conradt was displeased. Although her star center, Cinietra Henderson, was big and strong and could handle herself, she was the object of too many knees, elbows and other rough defensive tactics by BU players. Conradt's protests drew a technical foul from referee John Lutrick. The winning continued with a 91-73 victory over Rice at Autry Court. The pesky Owls kept it close much of the game, but no one could stop Cinietra Henderson, who rang the bell for a career-high 36 points. "Cinietra has really come on for them," said Rice coach Mike Dunavant. "She is the premier center in our conference."

With five straight wins, the Horns had regained some lost respect. And they would have a chance to avenge earlier defeats by the Cougars, Red Raiders and Aggies within the space of a week. Meeks scored 16 of her 22 points at the free throw line in an 80-70 defeat of Houston. Since Pointer was slow afoot and Nekeshia Henderson lacked experience, the backcourt had trouble with UH's press in the late going. League-leading Texas Tech was beaten, 70-63, at the Erwin Center, but it was not easy. UT led by 13 at the half, fell behind and then outscored the Raiders by a 12-4 margin in the last six minutes. Pointer and Jennifer Buck paced their respective teams with 18 points. Sheryl Swoopes, dehydrated from a medical problem, had 17 points and eight rebounds for Texas Tech.

And in College Station, Texas took control from the outset and beat Texas A&M, 71-52. Meeks, known to coaches and teammates as "the energizer," scored 18 points and kept a lid on Dena Russo. "I think losing to us made them mad," Russo said. It was not 1986 revisited, but consecutive wins over UH, Tech and A&M were mighty sweet for Conradt. UT, back in the top 25 after a five-week absence, looked great in an 87-55 defeat of TCU in Fort Worth. Cinietra Henderson had 25 points and 11 rebounds, Pointer scored 23 (with four goals from beyond the arc), and the Frogs lost their 19th game. The attendance was a ghastly 196. By contrast, three days later in Austin, a season-high 7,553 fans saw the Horns drill SMU, 90-70. Texas shot 58 percent in a rough-and-tumble game with 45 fouls called. Meeks and Pointer combined for 41 points, and Vicki Walterscheid had 20 for the Mustangs.

There were several reasons for UT's 10-game win streak: the fine play of Cinietra Henderson, improved defense, adjustment to the loss of Hall, guard production and Clarissa Davis. A player whose legendary exploits were witnessed only by seniors who were frosh in 1989, she was back in Austin after another pro season abroad. Davis took part in practice and forced the 1992 Longhorns to play harder. Their streak ended at Thompson-Boling Arena, where No. 2 Tennessee took a convincing 86-68 victory. The Vols were bigger and deeper, dominating the backboards by a 46-28 margin. Peggy Evans had a game-high 20 points for the winners, and Cinietra Henderson was held to 16 in a more thorough defeat than the December game between the two UT's in Massachusetts. "This was a big disappointment and somewhat of a surprise that we didn't handle the situation better," Conradt said.

An eight-day break after the loss to Tennessee provided some much-needed rest and allowed the coaches and players, so focused on basketball since October, to get away from the game and live normal lives for a while. They were ready to go on March 4 and blasted Baylor, 82-52, in Waco. An 18-point spree in the first half decided things. Texas' regular-season finale was an 84-49 drubbing of Rice before 5,256 fans at the Erwin Center. Cinietra Henderson, recently named to the all-SWC team, had 29 points and 16 rebounds and helped limit the Owls to 33 percent shooting. As postseason play approached, Conradt spoke happily about the team's development after a 7-7 start and would not rule out a berth in the Final Four.

The SWC Tournament began when the Longhorns met Baylor on Wednesday afternoon before a small gathering at Moody Coliseum. Pam Bowers' Bears were no more able to hang with UT than before, losing, 84-56. The Horns used a balanced scoring attack and stifling defense to improve their record to 20-8. In the semifinals, Cinietra Henderson had another dominating performance—26 points and 15 rebounds in a 70-60 defeat of an aggressive Houston team paced by Margo Graham (18). Reserve guard Jennifer Clark also did well, committing just three turnovers in 31 minutes. That led to a showdown between UT and Texas Tech, the regular-season champion, at Reunion Arena. It was also a clash between the two best players in the conference, Sheryl Swoopes and Cinietra Henderson, although they played different positions and seldom covered each other. The Red Raiders swooped to a 76-74 victory. Their fine junior forward had 24 points, 14 rebounds and seven assists. "Sheryl is just a total money player," said Tech coach Marsha

Sharp. "She does everything on both ends of the court when it needs to be done." Nekeshia Henderson made 10 of 14 shots for the Longhorns, who, like the Raiders and Cougars, got NCAA tourney bids.

A tough schedule and victories in 14 of its last 16 games earned Texas a first-round bye and a home game against UCLA. The Bruins had a 1-2 scoring punch in center Natalie Williams and forward Rehema Stephens, responsible for 42 points per game in a 21-9 season. While Conradt had been around too long to assume anything, UT was expected to win and advance in the tournament. But Stephens' 17-foot jumper with 36 seconds left gave UCLA an 82-81 upset victory before a rather small crowd of 4,990. She and Williams were as good as advertised—a combined 44 points and 21 rebounds for the blue and gold. Cinietra Henderson had 28 points and 13 rebounds but was denied a shot in the game's last frantic seconds. UCLA coach Billie Moore looked up at the panoply of banners that hung from the ceiling at the Erwin Center and said, "To win in a place that has this much tradition makes the victory even sweeter."

1993

Donna Lopiano, athletic director since 1975 and the person most responsible for building the University of Texas' envied and imitated women's athletic department, was moving on. She accepted the top job at the Women's Sports Foundation in New York, where she hoped to have an even broader influence. No shrinking violet, Lopiano soon got the attention of the *New York Times* by declaring a willingness to "break the bank" of college football to achieve gender equity. Before leaving Austin, she professed to make no endorsement of any candidate to succeed her as Texas women's AD, then went ahead and endorsed Jody Conradt, whose basketball team had been the cornerstone for the success of the entire program. If she wanted it or could be talked into taking it, the job was hers. Conradt (an associate AD since 1978) briefly considered stepping up and bidding adieu to the coaching gig, but that was her passion and she was not ready to quit. Furthermore, the talented, senior-laden Longhorns were convinced 1993 would be their year. At any rate, Conradt agreed to take the AD position on an interim basis, performing double duty. After a year, she would choose one or the other or both. In addition to recruiting and teaching jump shots and half-court defenses, she would oversee a $4-million budget and such sports as track, swimming and tennis. If basketball faltered, criticism was likely to follow, although the media continued to give women's athletics the kid-glove treatment.

What some people thought might be Conradt's last team had potential greatness. Cinietra Henderson and a rehabilitated Vicki Hall were the key returnees, and guards Kim Brandl and Erica Routt were promising freshmen. The Horns had a nice blend of experience and youth, size, speed, defense and a coach who wanted to get back to the top of the Southwest Conference and even the NCAA. A preseason poll was unanimous in picking UT as the SWC winner and three Horns—Hall, Cinietra Henderson and Nekeshia Henderson—as all-SWC. Ranked 10th in the nation, Texas stumbled in the season opener, an 85-76 loss to Penn State. Katina Mack, a lightning-quick sophomore guard, abused the Horns all night, getting 29 points. "We just didn't give the effort and do the necessary things we had to do to win on the road," Conradt said.

The next four games were at the Erwin Center (equipped with a new $500,000 scoreboard), beginning with an 81-57 defeat of Arizona. The Horns built a 13-point halftime lead and never looked back. Hall made five three-pointers, and Cinietra Henderson collected 14 rebounds, while Margo Clark (15) paced the Wildcats. Conradt, who had learned the values of hard work and perseverance in a small farming and ranching town, made history on December 13 when Texas beat Creighton, 86-69. It was the 600th victory of her unparalleled career. Conradt was the first women's coach to attain that milestone, and just three active men had done it: Dean Smith of North Carolina, Don Haskins of UT-El Paso and Lefty Driesell of James Madison. In lieu of a Gatorade bath and resultant dry-cleaning bill, the players dumped a box of styrofoam pellets on Conradt when the game ended. She was swarmed by fans and players and coaches of both teams, and everyone partook of a large cake featuring the number

600. The game ball was shipped to the Naismith Hall of Fame, and Conradt was the subject of media attention as never before. She handled it all with characteristic grace.

Joanne Benton, who originally had planned to sit out her senior year, changed her mind and was back with the Longhorns when they hosted Oral Roberts. Her experience, defensive skills and unselfish play could only make the team stronger. After a 109-68 defeat of the Titans in which Hall (21) led the scoring parade, Benton was in the starting lineup the rest of the way. The first big game of the season featured the No. 11 Horns versus No. 3 Vanderbilt. The Commodores had a mobile 6'10" center, Heidi Gillingham, and an assistant coach familiar to UT hoop fans, Kamie Ethridge. The Longhorns looked hopelessly outclassed in the first half, falling behind by 25 points, but Hall spoke about pride in the locker room and Cinietra Henderson (26) led a valiant rally that fell just short in a 78-73 loss. Gillingham and Shelly Jarrard had 20 points each for Vandy.

After a week off for the holidays, Texas traveled to Piscataway, New Jersey, to headline the Bell Atlantic Tournament and got upset by Clemson, 78-75. With two minutes left, the Horns led by four points but did not score again. The game was tied when Nekeshia Henderson missed a jumper, then Tiger guard Dana Puckett canned a three-point shot at the buzzer to win. Despite having better players, UT just seemed to lack chemistry. Conradt and her staff had a day to look at films and ruminate before the consolation game against winless Maine. Jennifer Clark and Erica Routt started in the backcourt as Texas came flying out of the gate and put a 72-34 defeat on the Black Bears. Meeks scored a game-high 15 points in just 17 minutes.

The teams from the Lone Star State took both ends of another Pac-10/SWC doubleheader in Austin. First, Sheryl Swoopes scored 48 points as Texas Tech beat Washington. And Texas used a relentless defense in downing Washington State, 76-51. Benton scored 17 points, and Susie Jarosch had 13 for the Cougars. Conradt the athletic director could not have been pleased to see fewer than 4,000 fans turning out for a doubleheader. After setting an NCAA women's attendance record in 1989 (an average of 8,481), UT's fan base appeared to be shrinking for the fourth straight year. The most common explanation for the waxing and waning crowds pertained to the Longhorn men. During the lamentable six-year tenure of Bob Weltlich, some disgruntled fans shifted their allegiance to Conradt's team, then at its peak and featuring a superstar in Clarissa Davis. But when Tom Penders replaced Weltlich in 1989, the men started winning again and getting much bigger crowds. So the theory went; no one did an empirical analysis to verify it.

Record: 22-8

76 Penn State 85
81 Arizona 57
86 Creighton 69
109 Oral Roberts 68
73 Vanderbilt 78
75 Clemson 78
72 Maine 34
76 Washington State 51
64 Stanford 87
69 Santa Clara 66
82 TCU 59
93 SMU 69
82 Baylor 66
76 Texas Tech 75
72 Missouri-Kansas City 45
70 Houston 66 (OT)
74 Rice 61
58 Tennessee 72
79 Texas A&M 63
99 SMU 77
89 Baylor 75
67 Texas Tech 77
97 Houston 68
76 Rice 53
75 TCU 50
76 Texas A&M 64
87 Rice 61
95 SMU 76
71 Texas Tech 78
78 Louisiana Tech 82

The Longhorns took a quick trip to California and got routed by defending national champion Stanford, 87-64. Molly Goodenbour showed why she won MVP honors in the 1992 Final Four, recording 17 points, 12 assists and eight rebounds, overshadowing her two-time all-American teammate, Val Whiting. No Horn shot as much as 50 percent against Tara VanDerveer's Cardinal. Two nights later, Santa Clara guard Melissa King had 33 points in a losing effort as UT took a hard-earned 69-66 victory at Toso Pavilion. Brandl's four free throws in the final minute provided the difference. "Kim Brandl's very mature for a freshman," Conradt said. "I have confidence in her foul shooting, and she played well for us against Stanford. That's why she stayed in at the end of the game."

Hall and Cinietra Henderson combined for 34 points in the conference opener, an 82-59 defeat of TCU. The perpetually short-handed Frogs got 14 points each from Amy Bumstead and Rachel Hesse. The 23-point margin was close for Texas-TCU standards, and Fran Garmon, coach of the purple and white, could not resist pointing out how the current Longhorns did not resemble their sisters of yesteryear. SMU, coming off an upset of No. 8 Stephen F. Austin, was ready for more when UT rolled into Dallas. The Mustangs fell behind, 21-2, at the start of the game and were never in it as the Horns breezed to a 93-69 victory. Hall scored 22 (including four three-pointers in a two-minute span), Cinietra Henderson 20, Meeks 19, and Nekeshia Henderson broke a scoring slump with 17. Shanell Thomas, SMU's first all-SWC player, had 23. Back at the Erwin Center, the Horns compensated for miserable (36 percent) shooting by grabbing 62 rebounds in an 82-66 defeat of Baylor. Hall was the coldest, making just one of 14 shots, but Cinietra Henderson, *Sports Illustrated* player of the week, had 24 points and 16 rebounds. The Bears unveiled a nice freshman guard, Mary Lowry, who rang up 16 points. Her backcourt teammate, Kelli Donaldson, was a Texas transfer.

Lubbock Municipal Coliseum, where Texas Tech had won 24 straight games, was packed before the Red Raiders and Longhorns tipped off. "Both No. 12 Texas Tech and No. 16 Texas have their guns loaded," wrote Gene Menez of the *Daily Texan*. "And as far as they are concerned, the conference is only large enough for one true champion." It was an exciting game, won by UT, 76-75. Meeks, who scored a career-high 20 points, was fouled on a disputed call with five seconds left. Oblivious to the screams of 8,174 fans, she sank two free throws for a victory that would later grow in significance. Sheryl Swoopes scored 22 for Tech, and guard Krista Kirkland had the play of the game when she stole a pass, dribbled the length of the court, did a 360-degree turn and hit a reverse layup. The Longhorns, once cool to the point of arrogance, did not mind celebrating after the game; assistant coach Kathy Harston was seen doing an impromptu dance.

Hall surpassed Johnna Pointer as UT's three-point queen in a 72-45 scorching of Missouri-Kansas City in Austin. Her second shot from downtown brought Hall's total to 102 and counting. Ironically, the Kangaroos' Veda McNeal and Julie Jenson had gone into the game as the top three-point duo in the nation and missed 15 of 17. Brimming with confidence and optimism absent a month earlier, the 13th-ranked Longhorns met Houston on the Cougars' home court and came away with a 70-66 overtime victory. Hall, who missed a 12-foot jumper that would have won it in regulation, scored five points in the extra period. That offset a strong performance by Margo Graham (26 points and 16 rebounds) of UH. Texas won its eighth straight game, 74-61 over Rice. Yolanda Stiner lit up the Horns for 28 points, but the Owls seemed like an afterthought to most of the fans, who were keeping up with a certain Southeastern Conference game.

As the Horns beat Rice, No. 2 Tennessee upset No. 1 Vanderbilt and moved into the top spot before visiting the Erwin Center. The biggest crowd of the season (10,358) was present for a big-time game. The Longhorn Band and cheerleaders were in good form, and Volunteer coach Pat Summitt reiterated her admiration for the program Lopiano and Conradt had crafted and which Tennessee (then with three national crowns) had clearly surpassed. If the game was a measuring stick, the Longhorns still fell short, losing by a score of 72-58. With Lisa Harrison (18 points and 15 rebounds) leading the way, the Vols got repeated second- and third-shot chances. Meeks went zero for 12, and the Horns were out of it with 10 minutes left in a bruising defeat.

But Texas remained atop the SWC and stayed there with a 79-63 defeat of Texas A&M before a lively crowd at G. Rollie White Coliseum. Cinietra Henderson spent much of the game on the bench with ice on her swollen knees, but Nekeshia Henderson had 19 points and seven assists. Bouncing back from injury and academic troubles, she ran the offense with aplomb, and forward Cobi Kennedy's tenacious defense won plaudits from Conradt. The Horns got their first look at A&M's fine frosh guard, Lisa Branch, who matched Henderson's quickness and facility with the ball, scoring a game-high 22 points.

Hall and Meeks (briefly demoted from the starting lineup) combined for 40 points in a 99-77 defeat of SMU before a home crowd of just 3,636. The Ponies tried to play a fast-paced game and did well before UT took charge early in the second half. As had happened in Dallas, SMU was led by Shanell Thomas (27). "They played very hard," Conradt said of the Mustangs. "Every other team in the conference raises their level of play to match what we do. It's up to us to turn it up another notch." Texas' quest for its first outright SWC title since 1989 continued in Waco, where Hall had 21 points and 15 rebounds to send the Baylor Bears back into hibernation, 89-75. Jennifer King, Mary Lowry and Amber Seaton were responsible for all but eight of Baylor's points.

Marsha Sharp had black uniforms made and ready for a special game, and the Texas Tech coach brought them out against the Longhorns in Austin on February 17. The customary red uniforms would have sufficed as Sheryl Swoopes led the Raiders to a 77-67 victory before 9,577 fans. The gazelle-like senior forward had 37 points, eight rebounds and two steals in 40 minutes, while the Longhorns were paced by Cinietra Henderson (25). Conradt, miffed at some calls against her team, earned a technical foul but managed to refrain from ripping the officials. Sharp was happy, though: "We came here to get rid of all the ghosts, although most of the pressure was on UT. We were able to keep the crowd out of the game."

Guarded by Texas Tech's peerless Sheryl Swoopes, fifth-year senior Vicki Hall takes her best shot.

Neither the Horns nor the Raiders would lose another SWC game and ended up sharing the championship with the same conference record of 13-1. Houston, which had forced Texas into overtime a few weeks earlier, lost a laugher, 97-68, in Austin. The Longhorns shot 62 percent and got 43 points from the bench. UH coach Jessie Kenlaw, whose team looked tired in the second half, called it "an ugly game."

Cinietra Henderson, Hall and Brandl were the top scorers in the No. 14 Longhorns' 76-53 defeat of Rice at Autry Court. And a 75-50 decision over TCU in Fort Worth was nothing special except that it marked Conradt's 500th victory at Texas, setting off another round of kudos for the coach who detested being called a "pioneer." She never set foot in a covered wagon, but the 1963 Baylor grad had been a major force in building women's basketball up from glorified intramurals into something much more substantial. In consecutive wins over the Owls and Frogs, Cinietra Henderson made 20 of 25 shots, many of them on her patented spin move down near the hoop. She was no passer, however, accounting for just 17 assists despite being on the court over 800 minutes in 30 games.

The regular-season finale was a Sunday afternoon game with Texas A&M. An Erwin Center crowd of 7,382 saluted the team's seniors and witnessed a 76-64 thumping of the Ags. Cinietra Henderson had 23 points and Hall 16, while Kelly Cerny, A&M's 6'5" freshman center, helped keep it close with 15.

There was little time for self-congratulation with the SWC tourney approaching. Once just a tune-up for the NCAAs, it was getting harder for Texas to win—1990 was the last time Conradt's players held the trophy aloft at Reunion Arena. The proceedings got underway when Rice and Texas collided, and the Longhorns had the better of it, 87-61. The Hendersons, Cinietra and Nekeshia, combined for 34 points, and Tammy McCallum had 18 for the Owls. Against SMU in the semifinals, Cinietra Henderson and Hall supplied a clutch shot or rebound whenever the Ponies threatened as Texas took a 95-76 victory. The Longhorns' biggest stars combined for 43 points and 24 rebounds.

That set up a title game between the two regular-season champs, Texas and Texas Tech, far and away the best of the Southwest Conference in 1993. As 8,122 fans looked on, the Horns and Red Raiders played a fast, entertaining game. It was no time for second-stringers because both teams used just six players. Sheryl Swoopes, who led Tech to a 78-71 victory, was simply magnificent, scoring 53 points and collecting 14 rebounds. Her point total set a Reunion Arena record, surpassing by three the old mark held by Bernard King of the New York Knicks and Larry Bird of the Boston Celtics. Swoopes, whose number would soon be retired at Texas Tech, was equally adept at driving or outside shooting and could not be slowed, much less stopped. Cinietra Henderson's 21 points and Hall's 20 looked pedestrian in contrast to the electrifying Swoopes, the subject of many discussions about where she fit in the history of the game. Up there with Cheryl Miller, Clarissa Davis, Teresa Edwards and the other all-time greats, most observers agreed. A two-time all-American and 1993 national player of the year, Swoopes was not finished. She carried the Raiders all the way through the NCAA Tournament, culminating in a victory over Ohio State in the championship game.

UT's experience in the tournament was not so sweet. The Horns got their usual first-round bye and then hosted Louisiana Tech on March 20. Hoping to avoid a Tech-nical knockout, Conradt sent five seniors onto the floor—Meeks, Benton, Hall, Clark and Cinietra Henderson. Leon Barmore's Techsters compiled a 19-point second-half lead, saw it evaporate but hung on in the tense final minutes to win, 82-78. Pam Thomas, Vickie Johnson and Amy Brown reached double figures for Louisiana Tech, and Nekeshia Henderson again showed star potential with 19 points, seven rebounds and five assists. "In my mind, we weren't going down without a fight," she said. The college careers of Vicki Hall and Cinietra Henderson were over, and their expectations of Final Fours and national championships went unfulfilled. Neither received all-America honors (although they made all-SWC a total of five times), and their achievements faded a bit in the glow of what Sheryl Swoopes had done at Texas Tech. But Hall and Henderson had some great moments and finished among the top five in UT's career scoring and rebounding totals.

1994

In the months preceding the 1994 basketball season, there were developments causing concern as well as happiness. "Conradt will be pressed to reverse downhill trend" was the headline of one *Austin American-Statesman* story critical of the UT women's program, and a three-part series that ran in the summer (later rehashed by *Texas Monthly* magazine) only made matters worse. Conradt, who answered some questions cryptically and others with startling candor, dismissed all the doom and gloom and went about trying to rebuild. No longer just the interim athletic director, she was pleased to see the University settle a court case regarding enforcement of Title IX, leading to more scholarships and the addition of soccer, softball and other sports. Women, however, were bit players in the megadollar negotiations over football, television and bowl games that culminated in the impending dissolution of the Southwest Conference. Texas, Texas A&M, Texas Tech and Baylor would be joining forces with the Big 8 to form the Big 12.

The centerpiece of Conradt's recruiting class was Danielle Viglione, a 5'10" guard from California who had scored more than 3,000 points and set five national records. She, forward Amie Smith—a rare private-school recruit—and guard Angie Jo Ogletree held their own 6 a.m. practice sessions, determined to become starters and restore some luster to UT hoops. After dreaming the dreams of youth, they were indeed in the lineup when the season began in late November. The Horns were too young and too short to merit their customary SWC-favorite status, which went to defending national champion Texas Tech. By using the transition game, pressure defense and outside shooting, Conradt expected to have a competitive team. "This is going to be a throwback to the way we used to play," she said cheerfully, registering no surprise when the Associated Press' top-25 poll left the Longhorns off for the first time in 14 years. There were easier ways to begin the season than on the road against the second-ranked team, which had a 6'10" all-American (Heidi Gillingham) in the middle. She got 23 points and 11 rebounds in Vanderbilt's 93-71 victory over UT. Nekeshia Henderson scored 28, but Viglione suffered a bruised thigh and missed seven of eight shots, every one from behind the arc.

The home opener was much better, an 84-78 defeat of Oklahoma before 5,808 fans. Erica Routt awoke from a poor start to score 14 points and collect 10 rebounds in the second half as Texas' superior speed snuffed the Sooners. "Man, is she quick," said OU coach Burl Plunkett. "She blew past our players as if we were standing still."

Richmond was the site of the Central Fidelity Bank Classic, and the Horns fell to No. 24 Maryland, 75-68, in the first round. Guard Lillian Purvis (20) was one of five Terrapins in double figures. Viglione had 24 points, the first of many times she would lead the Longhorns in scoring over a four-year career. Her 23 points the next night paced UT to a 99-77 triumph over the host Richmond Spiders. Benita Pollard showed signs of coming back from knee surgery, battling effectively around the basket. Smith, just 5'10" and not much of a leaper, had led Texas in rebounding in all four games.

After a 10-day hiatus for exams, the Horns returned to action with a couple of wins in Austin. Henderson hit 10 of 12 shots in a 76-46 romp of Loyola

Marymount and helped cause 33 Lion turnovers. She had help from Ogletree, an energetic point guard with limited offensive ability but unafraid to dive after loose balls. Amy Lundquist had 18 points and 14 rebounds for the visitors. When UT and Brigham Young met, Viglione and Henderson scored 21 points apiece, and Smith secured 17 rebounds in a 95-82 defeat of the Cougars. Viglione's quick release was on display as she made three three-point shots in a one-minute span in the second half. Debbie Dimond and Behka Stafford of BYU combined for 45 points.

Arizona, a team the Horns had handled easily the season before, was improved. The Wildcats were unbeaten except for a two-point loss to No. 1 Tennessee, so it was another plus when UT took a 79-68 victory in Tucson. Viglione scored the team's first 17 points and a total of 35 with a school-record eight three-pointers. Henderson dealt 11 assists, and more production came from an unexpected source. Conradt, recalling days of yore when she coached volleyball, had recruited a player off Mick Haley's team—6'2" senior Holly Graham, who had not played competitive basketball since high school. In just 12 minutes against Arizona, she was responsible for 13 points and six rebounds. Shawn Coder and Kim Conway both scored 21 for the Cats.

Record: 22-9

71 Vanderbilt 93
84 Oklahoma 78
68 Maryland 75
99 Richmond 77
76 Loyola Marymount 46
95 Brigham Young 82
79 Arizona 68
96 California 80
90 New Mexico State 75
98 Marquette 86
78 Santa Clara 85
74 Texas A&M 75
76 SMU 71
84 Baylor 73
66 Texas Tech 65
60 Tennessee 94
100 Houston 76
77 Rice 70
85 TCU 56
81 Texas A&M 69
73 SMU 74
75 Baylor 81
61 Texas Tech 78
89 Houston 74
77 Rice 63
99 TCU 70
102 Rice 57
80 Texas A&M 75
71 Texas Tech 69
75 Oklahoma State 67
66 Seton Hall 71

The Horns were back in the Erwin Center for four games before SWC play commenced. Another Pac-10 team, California, was dispatched, 96-80. Viglione had a career-high 37 points, Smith came through with 25 points and 12 rebounds, and Ogletree ran the offense with a deft hand. Kim Robinson scored 20 for the mistake-prone Golden Bears. New Mexico State forward Anita Maxwell rang up 35 points, but it was not enough as the Roadrunners fell to UT, 90-75. The Horns' sixth straight win featured a 15-rebound edge and 23 three-point shots, 10 of which connected. Viglione again had the hot hand on January 5, scoring 40 points in a 98-86 win over Marquette. She wowed the crowd of 5,872 by hitting nine three-pointers. Warrior coach Jim Jabir was impressed with Viglione but felt the officials showed too much respect for Conradt, who declined to respond. She knew all about life on the road. Santa Clara had no such problems three nights later, employing a stiff defense to beat Texas, 85-78. Jenny Baldwin and Suzanne Ressa teamed up for 47 points for the Broncos. Viglione, recruited heavily by Santa Clara just a few months earlier, had 27. With Henderson resting a tender knee on the bench, the UT defense left something to be desired.

Texas A&M won an exciting game in College Station. The Aggies built a 15-point lead, fell behind by six, and then sophomore guard Lisa Branch (21) led a comeback in the closing minutes of a 75-74 victory. Viglione (22) failed to get off a potential game-winning shot when she committed a turnover with one second left. "We had a chance to grow up tonight," said Conradt, who got strong showings from Routt and reserve guard Tammy Jones. "It was anybody's game right down to the wire." Saddled with a two-game losing streak, the Horns met SMU at Moody Coliseum. Rhonda Rompola's Mustangs almost made it three, but they either missed shots or turned the ball over on seven of their last eight possessions to lose, 76-71. Viglione, whose name often followed the words "freshman sensation" in newspaper accounts, scored 26 points, two more than Jennifer McLaughlin of SMU. Henderson and Graham played well in UT's 31st straight win over the Ponies.

Henderson, probably the top player on the team, continued to suffer knee problems and was out for the next six games. The Horns took a sloppy 84-73 win over Baylor at the Erwin Center as the Bears' Mary Lowry (38) and Viglione (33) had a long-distance shootout. UT was a miserable 14 percent on first-half field goal attempts before warming up. Of course, Conradt's players may have had Texas Tech on their minds. The defending national champion Red Raiders, 15-1 and ranked fourth, had a dandy junior college player in Connie Robinson. On a Saturday afternoon in Austin, 12,352 fans saw Texas go scoreless the first seven minutes and yet win, 66-65. Conradt called it one of the most satisfying victories in a 25-season career. Viglione, the top scorer in the Horns' past eight games, missed 17 of 20 shots, but Routt (22 points and 12 rebounds) was superb. Robinson, on the court just 15 minutes due to foul troubles, scored 15. "It was some of the most intense basketball ever played at the Erwin Center," wrote Michael Rychlik of the *Daily Texan*. "No need to qualify that claim according to gender."

There was not much time to savor the win because the Longhorns found themselves in Thompson-Boling Arena, playing Pat Summitt's No. 2 Tennessee Volunteers. The UT-UT series, deadlocked at 7-7, tilted—rather heavily—toward the home team. Dana Johnson (20) led the Vols to a convincing 94-60 victory; their defense blocked nine shots and forced 21 turnovers. Viglione and Routt were a combined nine of 23 from the field in Texas' worst loss since 1978. "We don't see defense this physical any other place," Conradt said. "In women's basketball, you can't consider yourself a player until you've been to Knoxville and played a dominating Tennessee team."

Viglione claimed to be unconcerned over her second straight poor shooting game and kept putting it up. In a 100-76 defeat of Houston at the Erwin Center, she had the greatest night of her young career—48 points (breaking a 10-year-old UT record held by Annette Smith) and 11 three-pointers (an NCAA record). Again and again, she was well set up by the birdlike Ogletree, who had 15 assists. Following interviews with the media, Viglione got a wild reception in the Texas locker room as teammates bowed before the star, tousled her hair and hugged her. Unlike the 1993 team, which had some clashing egos, the players got along well and were eager to improve. Several times during the season, Conradt commented on how much she enjoyed coaching them.

When Cristi McKinney replaced Mike Dunavant as Rice's coach, it meant every SWC team was headed by a woman for the first time. McKinney's Owls, with a combined 38 points from Brenda Conaway and Jessica Garcia, threatened to pull an upset at Autry Court. Ogletree made four free throws in the final 14 seconds to seal a 77-70 win that had McKinney and some of her players on the verge of tears. Surprises were at a minimum when UT beat TCU (coached by ex-Longhorn Shell Bollin-Robinson), 85-56, in Fort Worth. Routt scored 25 points and got nine rebounds, and the Frogs' Donna Krueger (26) had a fine game, too.

Breaking into the top 25 for the first time in school history, leading the conference race and carrying an eight-game winning streak, Texas A&M stepped onto the Erwin Center hardwoods before a lively crowd of 11,646. In a game full of momentum swings, not to mention a timely technical foul on Conradt, the Longhorns took a sweet 81-69 victory. The three frosh, Viglione, Smith and Ogletree, made a total of 52 points, and Henderson was back, albeit for just 15 minutes. The Aggies' Lisa Branch scored 20. Three days later at the same venue, Andrea Guziec hit a layup in the closing seconds to give SMU a first-ever win over the Horns, 74-73. "We wanted this game a lot more than Texas," said the senior center. The Mustangs outhustled UT and had a 16-5 scoring edge in the last seven minutes. Smith and Routt had 20 points each, but Viglione was one of 11 from the field and sat on the bench for nearly half the game.

Losing to SMU, inconceivable just a few years earlier, hurt, but it was part of the new reality in which the worst teams of the SWC—with the exception of TCU—were getting better. As if to accentuate that fact, Baylor beat the Horns, 81-75, in Waco. Mary Lowry, a 5'8" guard en route to co-SWC player of the year honors along with Lisa Branch, scored 54 points to break Sheryl Swoopes' league record. Henderson had 23 for the Longhorns, who once again were forced to witness the we-finally-beat-Texas victory dance. The Bears actually had done it with some regularity back in the mid-1970s, but that was hardly the modern era in women's hoops. UT lost for the third straight time when Texas Tech's frontline of Connie Robinson, Michi Atkins and Tabitha Truesdale amassed 58 points and 33 rebounds in a dominating 78-61 victory. The game, played before a roaring crowd of 8,574 in Lubbock, had been sold out for weeks. Defensive breakdowns, ill-advised shots and passive play led to the Horns' defeat. Jessie Kenlaw's Houston Cougars sought to make it four in a row, but they lost to Texas, 89-74, at a mostly empty Hofheinz Pavilion. Viglione scored all of her 23 points in the first half, and Smith and Pollard continued their strong play inside. Freshman Pat Luckey led UH with 19 points and 10 rebounds.

Two games remained in the regular season, both at home. Rice lost, 77-63, although the Owls had the game's top scorer, Brenda Conaway (19). Viglione made five three-pointers, and Smith, a blue-collar player with an uncanny knack for getting her hands on the ball, had 15 points and 13 rebounds. Pollard, who spent most of her first three years watching Cinietra Henderson from the sideline, showed senior leadership the team would need in postseason play. A crowd of 7,781 saw the Horns drub TCU, 99-70. Routt and Smith had a combined 47 points, and there was a bonus. Amber Hasenmyer, a freshman with a background in Oklahoma's archaic six-player game, scored 18 points in just 17 minutes. If not for a broken foot in December, she might have made the same splash as her first-year teammates, Viglione, Smith and Ogletree. "Didn't I tell y'all Amber could shoot?" Conradt asked reporters with a smirk.

Moments after hitting a game-winner against defending national champion Texas Tech in the SWC tourney finals, Benita Pollard is pounced upon by gleeful teammates.

For the first time since the SWC began sanctioning women's athletics, there were no Longhorns on the all-conference team. They finished in third place but retained high hopes of success in Dallas and getting into the 64-team NCAA tourney. Whether they would make more than a cameo appearance—as in 1991, 1992 and 1993—remained to be seen. Leading Rice by just three points at halftime, the team got an earful from Conradt, came back out and blasted the Owls, 102-57. Viglione (23), Graham (16) and Hasenmyer (15) led the way. Everyone packed, left Moody Coliseum and headed downtown to Reunion Arena for the semis and finals. Lisa Branch was excellent in Texas A&M's 80-75 loss to the Horns, scoring 34 points, handing out eight assists and getting six rebounds. Texas got balanced scoring as Viglione (15) and four teammates reached double figures. That set up a title game between UT and Texas Tech, a game Conradt wanted. She talked about a void in the Bellmont Hall trophy case and the need to put a big, gold basketball there. Marsha Sharp's sixth-ranked Red Raiders, who had exceeded 100 points in their last three games, would not be pushovers. The 8,226 fans, roughly three-to-one for Tech, saw a contest with a breathtaking finish. The score was tied at 69 with 10 seconds left when Smith, underneath her own basket, inbounded the ball to Henderson, who broke through the defense and passed to Routt. After a brief fumble, she threw it to a screaming Cobi Kennedy in front of the UT bench. Kennedy found Pollard alone on the left side of the lane and fired a pass. Pollard caught the ball in midair and threw up a shot that hung on the rim before dropping through. She jumped in elation before falling face-down on the court and getting mobbed by delirious teammates. "I told Benita this was a once-in-a-lifetime game for her, something we all dream about," Viglione said.

But the season was not over, Conradt reminded her squad. The 21-8 Horns would be facing 20-8 Oklahoma State in the all-important NCAAs on March 16. Dick Halterman's Cowgirls, a future Big 12 opponent, rode into Austin and got thrown, 75-67. They came back from 14 points down to lead by three with five minutes left, and the Horns answered with tough defense and key hoops by Henderson and Smith. Two freshmen were the top scorers—Viglione (30) of Texas and Dawn Burnett (24) of OSU. The Cowgirls shot just one free throw all night.

The second-round game was played in South Orange, New Jersey, home of 26-4 Seton Hall. The Pirates' tiny on-campus facility made old Gregory Gym look good. If the UT mystique was dead, that was news to Seton Hall coach Phyllis Mangina: "When I saw the bracket, I said, 'Can you imagine having Jody Conradt of Texas in our gym?' I probably wouldn't be sitting here today if not for women like Jody and teams like Texas, who put women's basketball on the forefront.

It's just special to have them here." Six inches of snow lay on the ground when the Horns and Pirates tipped off. Texas rallied from a 23-point first-half deficit to tie it at 63 on a basket by Henderson with two minutes to go. But Seton Hall guard Jodi Banks (26) refused to lose and carried her team to a 71-66 victory. No one shone for the Longhorns, especially Kennedy, who had not a single point or rebound in 32 minutes. Ousted from the tournament, the team returned to Austin to host a regional in which they had expected to be playing. All things considered, it had been a fine year, the 19th straight time UT had won 20 games, with average home attendance up by nearly 2,000 and Viglione among the nation's top three-point shooters.

1995

Optimism at the beginning of a season was one trait that had helped Jody Conradt succeed for so long. She had reason to believe Danielle Viglione, Amie Smith and Angie Jo Ogletree would be better and wiser than as frosh, when they had surpassed all expectations. And senior Nekeshia Henderson and junior Erica Routt were gifted athletes who could play at the highest levels. But Texas' latest recruiting class did not feature the next Clarissa Davis, and a couple of unsettling things happened before the opening game. Viglione underwent surgery on her right ankle, and Henderson was diagnosed with a stress-reaction problem in her left leg. While Viglione was able to play, she was less than 100 percent, but Henderson would miss the first half of the season. The dress rehearsal, an 11-point loss to a Russian touring team, was not very encouraging.

The 20th-ranked Longhorns began the season with a disastrous trip to the west coast. In Berkeley, Eliza Sokolowska threw in 33 points to lead the Cal Golden Bears to a 92-82 victory. UT's defense, which had given up 73 points per game in 1994, was woeful. Except for a sterling 26-point, nine-rebound performance by Viglione, Conradt found little comfort. Two days later and a few miles to the northeast, in Viglione's hometown, the Longhorns met Sacramento State. Ogletree did not play due to a leg injury, one that lingered throughout the season. Still, an 88-85 loss to the Hornets, who had little basketball tradition, was shocking. Center Marcy Ralphs had 24 points and helped cause 37 UT turnovers. With the two best ballhandlers—Henderson and Ogletree—on the bench, the Horn offense was not a pretty sight. Conradt could only bring the team back to Austin and try to regroup.

A pair of winless teams, Texas and North Texas, met at the Erwin Center on December 3. With two freshmen, center Jaime Bailey and guard Tracie Swayden, in the starting lineup, the Horns secured a confidence-building 94-58 win. Viglione, already UT's career leader in three-point shots, made six from behind the arc for a total of 22 points, four more than the Eagles' Jaquita Deaton.

Everything was back to square zero after a 95-85 loss to future Big 12 opponent Oklahoma at Lloyd Noble Arena. Center Mandy Wade had 27 points, and the Sooners' backcourt duo of Pam Pennon and Sharee Mitchum was too much for their Texas counterparts. Viglione, who scorched the nets for a season-high 37 points, offered this frank assessment: "If we'd played our best and lost, it would have been a different story. But we didn't. We have to get this turned around right now."

The Longhorns had four straight home games up next, losing to two good teams and beating a couple of patsies. Undefeated Old Dominion stayed that way with a 73-70 victory keyed by 22 points from Clarisse Machanguana, a native of Mozambique. Texas was down by two with 15 seconds left when Ogletree (16) attempted a one-on-four drive that ended ignobly. Smith, suffering from the effects of a minor concussion, managed 13 rebounds. While the Longhorn offense sometimes appeared clueless against the Monarchs, the intensity was better. Amid media and fan speculation about UT's first-ever losing record, Conradt told Randy Riggs of the *Austin American-Statesman*, "You have to keep it all in perspective. This is my 26th year in coaching, and I guess I can handle something like this once. If I can't, it's time to move on to something else." Her Longhorns thrashed Vermont, 81-57, with 22 points from Viglione and 11 rebounds each from Smith and Ogletree, of all people. A much tougher opponent, top-ranked Tennessee, invaded Austin a week later. Before 9,419 fans, Pat Summitt's talent-laden

Volunteers won, 66-54, but it did not come easy. Defensive specialist Cobi Kennedy helped keep the Vols to their lowest score of the season. All-American Nicki McCray, coming back from a month off because of a broken finger, spent just 18 minutes on the court and was one of 10 Tennessee players to score. Viglione and Routt had 14 points each for the Horns, whose coach resisted calling it a moral victory. Routt had her best game of the season on New Year's eve, scoring 26 points and getting 10 rebounds in an 82-68 defeat of Alcorn State. A freshman, 6'4" Angela Jackson, blocked five of the Braves' shots and showed that she might be the much-needed big player in the middle.

Jackson was even better, scoring 22 points and grabbing 12 rebounds, in an 80-65 loss to Utah in Salt Lake City. Other than her, no one seemed ready to play, and Conradt promised "drastic action." Viglione, Smith and Ogletree were in an unaccustomed spot—on the bench—when the Horns met Brigham Young in Provo. Viglione, insistent that her recent poor play did not constitute a slump, scored 24 points in a 74-60 win. Debbie Dimond had 17 for the Cougars, who were taller but got outrebounded by 26.

At that point in the season, the 4-6 Longhorns had played half their games on the road, and the attendance came to two-thirds of what they drew on a typical night at the Erwin Center; the fan base remained large and loyal. A crowd just short of 7,000 was on hand when they destroyed TCU, 89-49. It was never close after the Horned Frogs committed 15 turnovers on their first 19 possessions. Jackson and Amber Hasenmyer combined for 38 points against a truly horrendous team heading for a 1-27 record.

The No. 25 Texas A&M Aggies, who had won 15 straight games at G. Rollie White Coliseum, were all too happy to put a 75-61 defeat on what they called "t.u." before 4,103 fans. Lisa Branch scored 12 of her 17 points from the free throw line, and the Horns, shooting just 34 percent, had three players with 10 points. "We probably set women's basketball way back because this was one ugly game," Conradt said. "We just have to stay positive, stay focused and get it done. We're not going to lay down and die."

Record: 12-16
82 California 92
85 Sacramento State 88
94 North Texas 58
85 Oklahoma 95
70 Old Dominion 73
81 Vermont 57
54 Tennessee 66
82 Alcorn State 68
65 Utah 80
74 Brigham Young 60
89 TCU 49
61 Texas A&M 75
74 SMU 50
69 Baylor 46
71 Florida 82 (OT)
40 Texas Tech 84
67 Houston 82
54 Rice 49
109 TCU 44
79 Texas A&M 86
75 Georgia 80
74 SMU 82
83 Baylor 78
70 Texas Tech 80
74 Houston 53
47 Rice 67
78 Texas A&M 63
65 SMU 81

Back home for three games, the Longhorns got the sobering news that Viglione was out indefinitely. The problem was not a complication from ankle surgery or her Achilles tendon, as originally thought, but a stress-reaction leg injury. In street clothes, she watched her teammates dance past SMU, 74-50. Routt had 22 points and five steals, while Kerri Delaney (16) was the only Mustang in double figures. Henderson, rusty after two months off, played 11 minutes in UT's 69-46 defeat of Baylor, witnessed by 8,647 fans. An effective pressing defense had the Bears in a 12-0 hole at the beginning of the game, and it seldom let up. BU was in an interesting position, having lost star guard Mary Lowry, who transferred to Tulane, and gained a coach with fancy credentials. Sonja Hogg, who had led Louisiana Tech to two national titles before trying her hand at some other ventures (she was an administrator at UT in the late 1980s) was back in the game. No. 13 Florida came barreling into the Erwin Center on January 25 and threatened to spank the Horns but was taken into overtime before winning, 82-71. The Gators were quicker to the ball, outrebounding Texas by 20. Merlakia Jones, twice all-Southeastern Conference, was unstoppable, scoring 44 points, more than half her team's total. Smith (24) was the top scorer for UT, which ran out of gas and made just one point in the extra session.

Marsha Sharp provided prime bulletin-board material when she said her No. 7 Texas Tech team did not have to be in peak form to beat UT. Her statement proved entirely accurate as the Red Raiders took a devastating 84-40 victory before a hostile sellout crowd in Lubbock. SWC player of the year Michi Atkins had a game-high 19 points and 13 rebounds, and only Jackson and Swayden put up any fight for the Horns. Henderson, whose minutes had been carefully monitored by trainer Tina Bonci since her return, would be in the starting lineup the rest of the way, beginning with an 82-67 loss to Houston. The best player on the court that Thursday evening was the Cougars' Stacey Johnson, who scored 37 points on a variety of acrobatic shots. UH, with a sizable rebounding advantage, won for the second time in the 52-game series.

Despite the three-game losing streak, 7,198 fans were on hand when the Horns met Rice in Austin. It was close throughout, but Texas managed a 54-49 victory sealed by Jackson's offensive rebound and short jumper near the end. She finished with 14 points and nine rebounds, while Tammy McCallum scored 14 for the Owls. The second road win of the year came against TCU, 109-44. Jackson and Smith had 19 points each against the Frogs, who were losing games by an average of 38 points.

Candi Harvey had just kicked two players off her Texas A&M team and suspended another, but the Ags were able to rally from an 11-point deficit and win, 86-79, at the Erwin Center. Before 11,247 spectators, they took full advantage when Conradt gave Henderson (32) and Smith (22) a breather with 14 minutes left. Even when those two returned, the hot-shooting Aggies kept it up. Routt, almost invisible the past five games, was thrust into the starting lineup when No. 12 Georgia came to town. She and Henderson provided 49 points in an 80-75 loss to the Bulldogs, a team destined for the Final Four. Once again squandering a big lead, the Horns played hard against a more talented foe. Georgia coach Andy Landers, who got 20 points each from La'Keshia Frett and Saudia Roundtree, had high praise for Henderson.

There was a deep reservoir of respect and affection for Conradt, built over two decades of winning, so criticism was light and fairly muted. But it existed in a season with 12 losses and counting. Some observers believed that doubling as coach and athletic director was too much (she disagreed), recruiting had slipped (she conceded some mistakes) and the program was a shadow of its former self (an overstatement, she insisted). "Ultimately, I'm my toughest critic," she told a *Daily Texan* reporter. "I've spent my lifetime trying to build this program to a consistent level, and I'm not going to coach if I don't feel that I can make a significant contribution to maintaining that standard."

The second three-game losing streak in less than a month was completed when SMU took an 82-74 victory at Moody Coliseum. Jennifer McLaughlin and ex-Longhorn Kim Brandl both scored 22 for the Ponies. Henderson, all-world in the final games of her senior year, had 27 points, 10 assists and three steals. Baylor, another team on the skids, hosted UT on February 18 and lost, 83-78. Henderson sparkled again, getting 31 points (including 15 of 18 from the line), nine rebounds, five assists and five steals. Conradt went ballistic over the first-half officiating and drew a technical foul, after which things seemed to go Texas' way. Kristin Mayberry paced the Bears with 19 points.

Eager to make amends for the 44-point shellacking they got in Lubbock a month earlier, the Longhorns were in front by three at halftime but ended up losing to Texas Tech, 80-70. A crowd of 13,378, the third largest in school history, saw Michi Atkins (31) lead the Red Raiders on a 17-0 run that ended the suspense. Tech's victory clinched a fourth straight SWC championship, formerly a birthright for the Horns. Only Henderson (24), Smith (18) and Routt (14) presented any kind of offensive threat. The final home game of a tough season was a 74-53 defeat of Houston. Henderson, Smith and Routt outscored the Cougars by themselves, and Viglione made her first appearance since mid-January, scoring five points in three minutes.

Texas, without a representative in the SWC's top-10 scoring list, needed and expected a victory over Rice to gain momentum before the tournament. For the first time in a 31-game series that began in 1983, however, the Owls won, 67-47, before a smattering of fans at Autry Court. Freshman center Angelica Smith came off the bench to tally 21 points for Rice, while Amie Smith (22) got no help from her teammates. Henderson, who had been putting up big numbers with such regularity, missed 12 of 13 shots, and Routt (two of nine) was little better.

Seeded a lowly sixth in the league tourney, the Longhorns showed they could still play the game with a 78-63 win over Texas A&M, a team that had swept them in the regular season. With stringent defense, they built an 18-point lead, suffered a typical swoon and fought back for a well-deserved victory. Henderson (27) and A&M's Lisa Branch (19), the high scorers of the game, also engaged in bumping and trash-talking once considered the sole province of male athletes. "It was really fun to see the players rewarded today," Conradt said. "We had a lot of things to prove." Two days later at Reunion Arena, UT looked physically and emotionally drained in an 81-65 loss to SMU as Jennifer McLaughlin (18) led a balanced

Mustang attack. The 12-16 Longhorns, whose hearts were more willing than their legs, got 19 points from Henderson and 16 from Viglione. For the first time since 1975, the University of Texas would not be playing in a postseason tournament. Was Conradt's program really on the other side of the mountain, as critics contended? The coach, who never had experienced anything close to a losing season going back to her days at Sam Houston State, made no excuses, but she believed 1995 had been an anomaly.

1996

In the last year of the Southwest Conference, the Texas Longhorns, humbled by their newfound familiarity with losing, drew middle-of-the-pack predictions. SMU, Texas Tech and Texas A&M were expected to engage in a three-way fight for the final league championship. Jody Conradt, a recent inductee to the Women's Sports Foundation Hall of Fame, had a couple of promising freshman guards, Vanessa Wallace and Kim Lummus, but if her team was to rebound from a miserable year, the veterans had to take responsibility.

Things got underway in late November when the Horns beat San Diego State, 69-58, at the Erwin Center. Danielle Viglione (16), who shared scoring honors with Angela Jackson, collided with a teammate toward the end and received a bloody gash over her left eye. It required 25 stitches, and she wore goggles for Texas' next game, on the road against No. 21 Florida. The Longhorns blew a six-point lead in the last three minutes of regulation and could not halt the Gators' inside attack of DeLisha Milton and Murriel Page (a combined 35 points and 22 rebounds) in a 67-64 overtime loss. "It was a hard-fought game, and you saw two teams going at it," Conradt said. "We just made some crucial errors at the end." Viglione, who took 23 of the team's 59 shots, had 28 points.

The Horns were not in great health. Jackson had a sore leg and would miss most of the next six games, to be replaced by Jaime Bailey, who herself had chronic hip problems. Amie Smith's back was hurting, and Angela Brown had a broken finger. A defensive specialist who started 21 games in the previous season, Brown would see scant action in 1996. When UT hosted and beat Lamar, 87-58, the Cardinals had the game's top two scorers—Lara Webb (23) and Lisa McMahon (21). After that lopsided win, the Horns faced a series of tough opponents, none tougher than Tennessee, a team headed for the national title. Deep in the Smoky Mountains, the Volunteers won their 68th straight home game, 83-67, over Conradt's Longhorns. Viglione and Angie Jo Ogletree were ineffective, giving way to Wallace and Lummus, who teamed up for 38 points, mostly from outside. The relentless Vols dominated the game as Michelle Marciniak ran the offense with precision and freshman star Chamique Holdsclaw got 19 points and nine rebounds.

Ten days passed between losses to Southeastern Conference powers. Vanderbilt, ranked fourth, started four players 6'1" or taller, and that size advantage, along with 80 percent free throw shooting, gave the Commodores a 61-57 win before 6,459 fans at the Erwin Center. Sheri Sam had 20 points, and Mara Cunningham pulled down 15 rebounds. Senior Erica Routt scored 18 for UT, but Viglione missed 14 of 18 shots and committed a crucial turnover in the waning seconds. "It was ugly and hard, the kind of win that turns a good season into a great one if you keep doing it," said Vandy coach Jim Foster. Returning from the Christmas break, the Longhorn players met and agreed on the importance of beating Utah. They survived a 25-point, 12-rebound performance by center Amber McEwen and hung on for a 60-56 victory. Lummus scored 16 points in just 19 minutes, and Smith added her typical frenetic hustle, but the Utes probably would have taken it if not for 1-for-14 shooting by guard Julie Krommenhoek. There was another big game two nights later when No. 4 Stanford paid a visit. The Cardinal brought an array of thoroughbred athletes, most prominently all-American Kate Starbird. It was an exciting contest featuring 13 lead changes in the second half. With less than a minute to go, the Longhorns were ahead by three when everything fell apart, and Stanford ended up winning, 72-68. Starbird, the key figure in the late run that sent UT to a heartbreaking loss, had 17 points, five rebounds, six assists and four steals, and blocked Ogletree's potential tying shot with 15 seconds left.

Seven games into the season, the Longhorns' offense was not overly impressive. They were shooting just 38 percent, their transition game was weak, and Viglione was at a career-low 14 points per game. Routt, however, had done well lately and was the closest thing Texas had to a reliable go-to player. She scored 25 points and helped dig her team out of a hole in a 75-65 defeat of Virginia Commonwealth. Guard Gabrielle Khylstedt scored 17 for the Rams, whose Franklin Street Gym contained just 511 fans during the game; it was one of four times in the 1996 season when the Horns played before crowds of fewer than 1,000. From Richmond, they traveled on to Norfolk and engaged No. 16 Old Dominion. The big and talented Monarchs laid a 98-61 defeat on UT. A 28-2 scoring spree midway through the first half ensured an embarrassing loss for Conradt's team. Shonda Deberry, Ticha Penicheiro and Clarisse Machanguana had a combined 46 points for ODU. Only Viglione (15) reached double figures for UT. "Some things you just can't explain," Conradt said. "We got whipped at both ends of the floor."

Danielle Viglione puts it up from downtown.

Despite that confidence-shaker, the Horns returned to their home state and began a six-game winning streak. Against Rice in Houston, they led by 11 and let the Owls pull back into a tie in the final minute. Jackson took what she hoped would be a game-winning shot with five seconds left, but it missed. Smith rebounded and hit a short jumper at the buzzer. Longhorns, 74-72. An unsung hero was Amber Hasenmyer, who came off the bench and bailed out the struggling Ogletree. In Fort Worth, where coach Shell Bollin-Robinson was fighting a losing battle—she would be fired at season's end—Texas drubbed TCU, 96-33. Viglione scored 25 in one of the most lopsided wins in recent years.

Back at the Erwin Center for the first time in three weeks, the Horns met Texas A&M on a Wednesday night, following the death of ex-Congresswoman Barbara Jordan, among the team's most fervent fans. Viglione, displaying the scoring magic of her freshman year, pumped in 36 points and helped UT to an 87-66 defeat of the Aggies. The Californian with the quick release made four three-pointers, played some tight defense and even handed out four assists, almost half her total in the previous season. Lisa Branch had 18 points for A&M in a rough game in which Ogletree suffered a bruised thigh. She would miss the next two games and surrender her starting job to Wallace.

There were two seconds left when former Longhorn Kim Brandl stepped to the line for three free throws. Her SMU team trailed by three. Brandl, who had made 25 straight, missed one of them, allowing UT to take a key 84-83 SWC win. The Longhorns had free throw troubles of their own, missing the front end of four one-and-ones in the final half-minute. Viglione scored 24, Routt 22, and Wallace was steady at the point. Kerri Delaney (26) paced the Mustangs. Sacramento State, which had upset the Horns out on the coast in 1995, got drilled in Austin, 90-73. The game was essentially over following a 25-point Longhorn run in the first half. The Hornets shut down Viglione, but Routt and Hasenmyer teamed up for 40 points and 22 rebounds—not bad for a couple of guards.

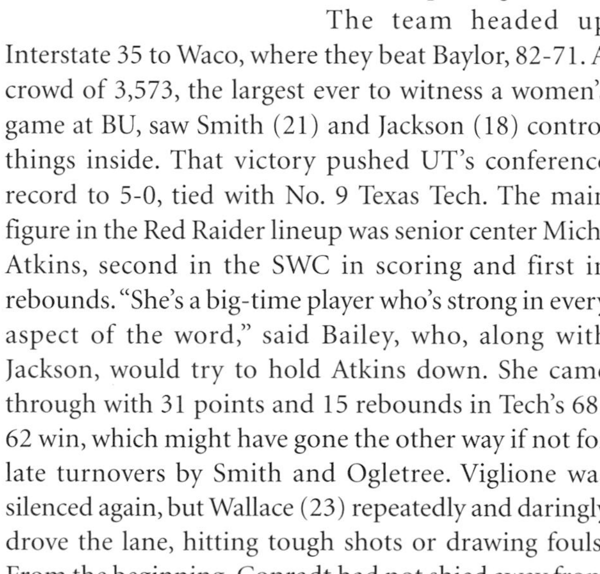

The team headed up Interstate 35 to Waco, where they beat Baylor, 82-71. A crowd of 3,573, the largest ever to witness a women's game at BU, saw Smith (21) and Jackson (18) control things inside. That victory pushed UT's conference record to 5-0, tied with No. 9 Texas Tech. The main figure in the Red Raider lineup was senior center Michi Atkins, second in the SWC in scoring and first in rebounds. "She's a big-time player who's strong in every aspect of the word," said Bailey, who, along with Jackson, would try to hold Atkins down. She came through with 31 points and 15 rebounds in Tech's 68-62 win, which might have gone the other way if not for late turnovers by Smith and Ogletree. Viglione was silenced again, but Wallace (23) repeatedly and daringly drove the lane, hitting tough shots or drawing fouls. From the beginning, Conradt had not shied away from playing the best nonconference teams, and 1996 was no different. It included a murderer's row of Florida, Tennessee, Vanderbilt, Stanford, Old Dominion and, on January 31, top-ranked Georgia. Andy Landers' Bulldogs did not lose often in Athens. La'Keisha Frett had 18 points and 14 rebounds as UGa hammered the Horns, 93-68. Conradt, who could nurture her athletes' egos when she saw fit, was upset with the play of Smith, Routt, Viglione and Ogletree. "It's time for that group to grow up," she fumed. "They've been there, done that and seen everything, and it's time for them to respond."

Things got better quickly because the Longhorns played and beat three lower-echelon teams at home in the space of a week. Against Houston, they saw a big lead get cut in half when the Cougars put on a frantic press. But with uncharacteristic free throw shooting, they regained control and won, 82-68, before 7,373 fans. Wallace, looking more like a star with every game, scored 23, while Pat Luckey had 19 for UH. Trailing Rice by eight at halftime, the Horns turned up the intensity and took an 89-75 victory. Viglione had her best game in a while with 21 points and six rebounds. Owl coach Cristi McKinney got slapped with a T and all but accused the refs of being orangebloods. The TCU Horned Frogs put up more resistance than in the earlier game but still lost, 115-82. Jennifer Hickman (26 points and 11 rebounds) acquitted herself well, and Viglione led the UT scoring parade with 20.

Over in College Station, the Longhorns and Aggies tied on a good one. With 23 points, Lisa Branch became Texas A&M's all-time scorer. Her team was ahead until Wallace took over in the final two minutes, twice penetrating the lane for a hoop, foul and free throw, giving Texas a pressure-filled 80-78 win. "We tell Vanessa to take it to the hole, and she does a great job of that," said a hoarse Conradt. "She goes in looking for bodies to lean on." With maturity and confidence sorely missing in 1995, UT next encountered SMU in Dallas. The Horns rallied from a 14-point first-half deficit to take another thriller, 79-77. Viglione, who had scored 20 points or more in the past three games, hit just three of 13 from the field, but her last one was a biggie, a three-pointer with seven seconds left that meant victory. Ogletree played a team-high 31 minutes and scored 15 points, turning the ball over just three times. Kim Brandl led the red and blue with 24 points.

According to Randy Riggs of the *Austin American-Statesman*, the UT women had made more uphill climbs than Sir Edmund Hillary. But Baylor represented something less than Mount Everest, and the Horns did not have to play well to get a 65-53 win in Austin. Kacy Moffitt and Amanda Mooney had 12 points each for the losing Bears. Their coach, Sonja Hogg, predicted UT would upset Texas Tech in the SWC game of the year three nights hence. The Red Raiders, ranked sixth, winners of 17 straight games and aiming for a bookend to their 1993 NCAA championship, were formidable. A crowd of 14,115, the largest in the nation that year, was on hand for a surprising and indubitably pleasing 76-60 Longhorn victory. Wallace (21) shared scoring honors with Tech's Michi Atkins, but several others came through with clutch performances—Jackson, Smith, Viglione, Routt and Hasenmyer. Marsha Sharp's team was outplayed from tipoff to final buzzer. "All our hard work has paid off," said Routt, UT's only senior. "We've been fighting and scratching all year to beat a top-10 team. This feels wonderful."

Virtually assured of a spot in the NCAA tourney, the Horns returned to earth the next week, playing sloppily in a 75-56 defeat of Oral Roberts. Kisa Bradley, the Golden Eagles' 6'5" center, accumulated 23 points, 13 rebounds and four blocked shots, while Viglione (17) led UT despite reverting to an old habit of shamelessly jacking up three-point shots. It was the last home game of the year for a team getting back some long-lost regional and national stature.

A loss to the Houston Cougars, always tough at Hofheinz Pavilion, would mean second place in the final SWC race, and a win meant sharing the crown with Texas Tech. Conradt and assistant coaches Kathy

Record: 21-9
69 San Diego State 58
64 Florida 67 (OT)
87 Lamar 58
67 Tennessee 83
57 Vanderbilt 61
60 Utah 56
68 Stanford 72
75 Virginia Commonwealth 65
61 Old Dominion 98
74 Rice 72
96 TCU 33
87 Texas A&M 66
84 SMU 83
90 Sacramento State 73
82 Baylor 71
62 Texas Tech 68
68 Georgia 93
82 Houston 68
89 Rice 75
115 TCU 82
80 Texas A&M 78
79 SMU 77
65 Baylor 53
76 Texas Tech 60
75 Oral Roberts 56
90 Houston 67
109 TCU 78
61 Texas A&M 75
73 SW Missouri 55
70 Kansas 77

Harston, Annette Smith-Knight and Sharon Morgan wanted that spot in the history books and conveyed the feeling to the young student-athletes on the team. Routt left nothing to chance, scoring 26 points and grabbing 11 rebounds in a thorough 90-67 victory. Savoring their cochampionship and looking forward to Dallas and beyond, the Horns had an all-SWC player (Routt) for the first time since 1993 and coach of the year in Conradt. The same columnists and talk-radio mavens who so recently had criticized her agreed that 1996 was one of her finest jobs of coaching in a career full of them.

The last Southwest Conference postseason tournament commenced with a workmanlike 109-78 defeat of TCU at Moody Coliseum. Six Longhorns were in double figures, but the best showing came from Frog guard Jackie Jenkins, who had 29 points, seven rebounds and four steals. In the semifinals at Reunion Arena, it was Texas, a recent addition to the top 25, versus Texas A&M. Candi Harvey's Ags had lost four of their last seven games and did not seem too threatening, especially after falling 18 points behind in the first half. With balanced offense and a tight man-to-man defense, A&M held on and clawed back into it. Outscoring UT by almost a two-to-one margin in the second half, the Aggies took a major 75-61 upset. Viglione (16) was the top scorer, but she and her teammates could not resist the Ags once they gained momentum.

At any rate, the 20-8 Longhorns were back in the NCAA playoffs, hoping, like 63 other teams, to win and keep on winning. Their first-round foe was 25-4 Southwest Missouri State, and the game would be played at historic Allen Fieldhouse on the campus of Kansas University. Wallace, nursing a tender foot, started but hardly played against the Bears. Viglione had 25 points (including seven of eight from behind the arc), and Smith and Jackson combined for 21 rebounds, but it was Routt who secured the 73-55 victory. Texas clung to a tenuous six-point lead early in the second half when she hit three shots, made two steals and an assist. Jessie McVay led the Missourians with 20 points. That set up a Big 12 preview between UT and 21-9 Kansas. Jayhawk coach Marian Washington used some tortured logic to give her team an underdog role, which Conradt found rather amusing. Big 8 player of the year Tamecka Dixon, blessed with dazzling quickness and ballhandling skills, scored 18 points to pace KU to a 77-70 win. The frazzled Longhorns fell behind by 15 early and never recovered. The big surprise was Lummus, who had virtually disappeared after a midseason stomach ailment; she scored 13 points in 18 minutes. Smith battled the more athletic Jayhawks for 13 rebounds. By the unforgiving nature of the single-elimination tournament, the winners moved on to the next round and the losers headed home to Austin. Conradt's Horns had time to assess their accomplishments, which were good but not great. "What happened last year should not have happened," Viglione said. "We came out this year to regain some respect, and I think we've done that."

Smiles all around after a winning effort—Angela Jackson, Amie Smith, Vanessa Wallace, Erica Routt, coach Jody Conradt, Amber Hasenmyer and Danielle Viglione face the media.

1997

They were playing in a new conference (the Big 12), they had a new floor at the Erwin Center (a $90,000 state-of-the-art model featuring load-distribution boards and rubber pads to absorb shock), and their uniforms had a new look (although the old-style quarter-sleeve jerseys remained). Jody Conradt's 21st Texas team, with seniors Amie Smith, Danielle Viglione and Angie Jo Ogletree back for a last hurrah, defeated a squad from Russia and one from Hungary in exhibitions before the season began.

The 19th-ranked Longhorns opened NCAA competition on the road as Viglione scored 18 points in a 66-54 win over Detroit Mercy. Two nights later and 80 miles to the west, UT faced Michigan State. Despite falling behind early and getting two starters in foul trouble, the Horns prevailed, 82-72, thanks mostly to a 26-5 free throw advantage. Viglione (18) and the Spartans' Jamie Wesley and Tamika Matlock (14 each) were the top scorers in a game witnessed by 1,806 fans.

On November 26, Carol Ross brought her Florida Gators to Austin. With two fine post players, Murriel Page and DeLisha Milton, combining for 44 points and 26 rebounds, the SEC visitors led most of the way but were forced into overtime. Ogletree's off-balance three-pointer with seven seconds left sent it into a second extra period, when the Horns streaked to a 97-84 win. It was the first victory over a ranked nonconference opponent since 1992. UT went to 4-0 following a 77-64 defeat of Washington, the 600th win in the history of the program. Kim Lummus scored 21 of her 23 points in the first half, but the star of the game was Husky guard Jamie Redd, who rang up 32 and made a number of dazzling plays.

After two weeks off for final exams, the Longhorns—who had moved up to No. 13—vowed not to take Virginia Commonwealth lightly, even with Tennessee coming to town shortly after the Rams. "VCU won't be easy," said reserve guard Amber Hasenmyer. "They played us tough last year. They have some Europeans and they play a different style. They have our attention." They got beat by a score of 79-58 as Angela Jackson accounted for 22 points and 16 rebounds. Meredith Sisson (16) paced the Rams. And then it was time to meet Pat Summitt's defending national champion Volunteers, led by 6'2" soph Chamique Holdsclaw. "She's the best player in the women's game right now," Conradt commented. "She's got size and quickness, and she can create her own shots." More than 9,000 fans at the Erwin Center witnessed a thriller that went to Tennessee, 68-65, in overtime. Holdsclaw (24 points and 16 rebounds) was superb in 42 minutes, but if Viglione had done just a little better than one for 10 from behind the arc, Conradt would have had a victory she thirsted for. Since Clarissa Davis' senior season, the Longhorns had lost nine straight to the Vols, who were on their way to yet another national crown.

The MCI-First American Classic in Nashville was another of those nontournament tournaments without a true winner crowned. Jackson made 11 of 15 shots, Smith collected 11 rebounds, and the UT defense shut down Seton Hall's late rally in an 83-77 victory. They beat the Pirates, so what about the host Commodores? With Lummus, Viglione and Jackson in double figures, Texas closed a 10-point deficit to two in the final minute before falling to No. 14 Vanderbilt, 67-65, before a crowd of 5,188 at Memorial Gym. While 6'7" Angela Gorsica was the best-known of Vandy's players, Lisa Ostrum (21 points and eight rebounds) had more impressive numbers that Sunday afternoon.

SMU, TCU, Rice and Houston, left out of the Big 8-Southwest Conference merger, were not to be found on the UT schedule in 1997. The Horns' first Big 12 game was with Oklahoma State in Stillwater. They jumped to a 13-point lead at intermission and watched it shrink to five with some hot shooting by the Cowgirls but finally won, 83-70. "Texas threw us out of our offense in the first half," said OSU coach Dick Halterman. "We lost our patience." Cowgirl forward Cheri Edwards (21) was the game's top scorer. On a cold night in Austin, Jackson had a career-high 24 points in UT's 87-69 defeat of Oklahoma. Carla Littleton, a powerful 6'4" freshman who started the season slowly due to a knee injury, had 11 points and four rebounds in 14 minutes against the Sooners. A fan favorite, she showed considerable promise, especially when paired with Jackson in Conradt's "twin towers" lineup.

Forecast as one of the Big 12's weaklings, Kansas State rode an effective zone defense and Missy Decker's free throw with time expired to a 68-67 win. Viglione and soph guard Vanessa Wallace combined for 29 points against the Wildcats. Back in the friendly confines of the Erwin Center, UT beat old rival Texas A&M, 100-67. Smith, recently recovered from a mild concussion that caused her to play tentatively, busted loose with 22 points and 11 rebounds. "I've always thought Amie Smith was one of the most underrated players around," said Candi Harvey, coach of the Aggies, who got 16 points each from Melinda Rollerson and Kerrie Patterson. The first big game in the Big 12 matched No. 16 Texas versus No. 11 Kansas, who had beaten the Horns in the 1996 NCAAs. UT won it, 82-72. Ogletree played one of the best games of her career, scoring 20 points, handing out four assists and playing some tough defense on Jayhawk star Tamecka Dixon (32).

The officials called a tight game when UT and OU met in Norman, somewhat negating the Longhorns' height advantage. Although Phylesha Whaley and Shonika Breedlove had a combined 43 points, the Sooners fell, 76-58. Texas freshman forward Edwina Brown contributed 11 points, three rebounds and three assists in 18 minutes. Three nights later at the Hearnes Center, the first-place Longhorns tipped off with last-place Missouri. The score was tied at halftime, but UT eked out an 84-77 win. Viglione (18) and five teammates were in double figures, and Julie Helm of the Tigers had 24. Conradt was irked to see her young athletes playing weak defense and not hustling, and they heard about it during and after the game. Nevertheless, Texas was off to a 12-3 start, the best since 1990.

In an easy 79-58 defeat of Sam Houston State (where Conradt's coaching career had begun 28 years earlier), Jackson and Wallace combined for 33 points. The third game in five days came against Sonja Hogg's Baylor team before 6,697 spectators in Austin. Lummus, Viglione and Ogletree rained in eight three-pointers to help beat the Bears, 79-61. "It's hard to keep going when they're hitting all those threes," said Nicole Palmer, who had 17 points and nine rebounds for BU.

The following Saturday, the No. 8 Horns found themselves in Boulder, playing in the opener of the Big 12/ACC Challenge; after Texas and Clemson, it was Colorado and North Carolina State. Jackson scored 21 points and Smith had 11 rebounds to help tame the Tigers, 68-53. But UT had more trouble with a familiar foe, Texas Tech. Before a crowd of 8,037 at Lubbock Municipal Coliseum, the No. 14 Red Raiders rolled to a 96-73 win. Junior forward Alicia Thompson was splendid, getting 47 points and 10 rebounds, evoking memories of Sheryl Swoopes. "I don't know what you say after something like that," lamented Conradt, whose team lacked chemistry from the start.

Still tied for the league lead, UT hosted Oklahoma State on February 8. Paced by Renee Roberts (28), the Cowgirls threatened to score an upset with three minutes left before the Longhorns increased the defensive pressure to win, 70-63. Wallace had a career-high 24 points, including 12 of 12 from the charity stripe. Due to the flu, Wallace did not play and Jackson and Viglione were weak for a Wednesday night game against Baylor in Waco. Kacy Moffitt (19) of the Bears sent it into overtime, but the Horns were in control the rest of the way for an 82-71 win. Smith scored 25 and played the entire game despite suffering from a degenerative back problem.

Kim Lummus brings the ball downcourt in the Horns' 22-8 season.

She did it again five days later at home against Nebraska, never going to the bench in an overtime win and getting 18 points, 13 rebounds and eight steals. Cornhusker star Anna DeForge (21) hit a three-pointer at the end of regulation, and the visitors were up by one in the last few frantic seconds. Jackson converted an offensive rebound into a basket for a 71-70 victory that broke the hearts of Nebraska's players and coaches. The first meeting between Texas and Iowa State since 1983 was at Hilton Coliseum, always packed for the men's games but holding fewer than 1,300 fans that evening. They liked what they saw, however. The Cyclones led most of the way, and when the Horns went scoreless for nine minutes in the second half, ISU took a 74-58 victory. Jayme Olson had a game-high 22 points, while

Hasenmyer and Smith scored 14 each for Texas. Viglione missed all but one of 11 shots.

The painful 23-point loss to Texas Tech two weeks earlier was on the Longhorns' minds before Marsha Sharp brought her red-and-black hoopsters to town. It was avenged in a 72-61 win before the largest Erwin Center crowd of the year—10,645. Alicia Thompson again played an admirable, all-America-caliber game, accounting for 39 points and 11 rebounds, but Tech was a one-woman team because the next-highest scorer had just seven. Jackson (23) and Brown (11), who had commandeered Lummus' starting job, played well for UT. "Edwina was terrific," Conradt said of her shake-and-bake frosh forward. Another big crowd was on hand for the regular-season home finale against Colorado. Erin Scholz and Raegan Scott, the Buffaloes' bruising frontcourt players, combined for 35 points and 28 rebounds to beat Texas, 60-56. The Horns whittled a 16-point second-half deficit down to as little as two in the last minute. But 32 percent shooting made victory nigh impossible.

Conradt used every player on the roster, all 15 of them, in a methodical 79-58 defeat of Texas A&M in College Station. Smith led all scorers with 17, and Viglione was part of a humorous and indicative incident in the first half. As she stood on the baseline to make an inbounds pass, the handlers of Reveille VI allowed the canine mascot to snap at Viglione's burnt orange shorts. The Ag band, Corps and spirited fans made plenty of noise, but an injury-plagued A&M team that won just three league games was not going to beat the Longhorns.

The inaugural Big 12 women's tourney was played at Kansas City's Municipal Auditorium, across town from Kemper Arena, where the men held theirs. UT, No. 12 in the nation with a 20-6 record but lacking an all-conference player, met Nebraska, a first-round winner over Missouri. Viglione and Lummus, neither of whom had been hot or even warm in recent games, made a combined nine of 16 three-point shots to help edge the Cornhuskers, 74-68. Described by *Austin American-Statesman* writer Kirk Bohls as "two hop-and-pop gunners," they accounted for more than half of UT's offensive output. Although her team won, Conradt noted several poor plays that might have spelled defeat against a stronger team like Colorado. Nothing seemed to work against the Buffaloes in the semifinals. Erin Scholz and Raegan Scott controlled things inside—as they had in Austin 10 days earlier—in a 64-50 win for CU. It was the fewest points Texas had scored in two years. Only Jackson (14 points and 11 rebounds) had any success against the Buffs, winners of the tournament.

Record: 22-8

66 Detroit Mercy 54
82 Michigan State 72
97 Florida 84 (2 OT's)
77 Washington 64
79 Virginia Commonwealth 58
65 Tennessee 68 (OT)
83 Seton Hall 77
65 Vanderbilt 67
83 Oklahoma State 70
87 Oklahoma 69
67 Kansas State 68
100 Texas A&M 67
82 Kansas 72
76 Oklahoma 58
84 Missouri 77
79 Sam Houston 58
79 Baylor 61
68 Clemson 53
73 Texas Tech 96
70 Oklahoma State 63
82 Baylor 71 (OT)
71 Nebraska 70 (OT)
58 Iowa State 74
72 Texas Tech 61
56 Colorado 60
79 Texas A&M 58
74 Nebraska 68
50 Colorado 64
66 SW Texas 38
83 Notre Dame 86

Chosen to host a subregional in the NCAA playoffs, UT faced its neighbor from San Marcos, Southwest Texas State. The Bobcats, once familiar opponents for Texas (they played 16 times in the 1975, 1976 and 1977 seasons) were coached by Linda Sharp, who had won a pair of national championships at USC before escaping the bright lights of Los Angeles eight years earlier. With average home attendance of just 621, Sharp's Cats would be playing in front of the largest crowd they had seen all year, multiplied several times over. As 8,135 fans looked on, SWT got destroyed, 66-38. Early defensive intensity set the tempo, and the frazzled Bobcats made just 25 percent of their shots. Texas got double-figure production from Jackson and Ogletree.

That set up a St. Patrick's day showdown with the Irish of Notre Dame. "We came here to win," said center Katryna Gaither. "We're not going back home without a victory." Such confidence served the Irish well in an intense game played before a partisan Texas crowd. Gaither and teammate Beth Morgan had 29 points apiece, giving Notre Dame an 86-83 lead in the final half-minute. Needing a three-pointer to go into OT, Conradt sent Lummus—on the bench except during pregame and halftime warm-ups—in to take the deciding shot, which was blocked by Gaither with three seconds left. End of game, end of season. The stat line showed Viglione with 19 points, Smith and Littleton with 14 each and Wallace with 13 assists. There were a few hugs and tears in the locker room, a phenomenon not limited to the women's tournament because some male players and coaches cried their eyes out after tough losses. Conradt saluted the Erwin Center fans: "The crowd has had the same love affair with this team that I had. It did everything possible to put us in a position to win. We build off their enthusiasm." The three overachieving seniors, although not ready to stop playing, deserved a rest. Viglione, with 1,658 points, was eighth on the UT career scoring list and first by far in the number of three-point shots made. Smith's 940 rebounds ranked fifth, and Ogletree's 403 assists were good enough for sixth. And Conradt, still serving the dual role of coach and athletic director, was just three wins short of 700. A month later, she received a contract extension worth $250,000 per year, going through the 2002 season.

1998

While those in the predicting business had Texas Tech as a heavy favorite to win the Big 12 title, Jody Conradt thought her team had a chance, too. But the 24th season of women's varsity basketball on the Forty Acres got off to an ominous start in early November, during the orange-white game. Sophomore center Carla Littleton went down with a serious knee injury. Expected to play a major role in the Longhorns' inside game (as well as throwing the shot for the track team), Littleton would spend the season in civilian clothes, watching from the end of the bench. With no new impact players, the No. 25 Horns were very thin, relying mostly on Angela Jackson, Kim Lummus, Vanessa Wallace and Edwina Brown.

Opening night at the Erwin Center was just grand, an 88-67 defeat of North Texas. Jaime Bailey had a career-high 20 points, and Taryn Brown came off the bench to grab 11 rebounds against the Eagles.

Another flock of Eagles, representing Boston College, comprised UT's next opponent. Playing in the Fleet Center, erstwhile home of the Boston Celtics, Conradt's team suffered a slump late in the first half and fell behind. Guard Cal Bouchard (32) led BC to a surprising 82-68 win. Conradt attributed the loss to shaky confidence, an issue that would dog the team throughout 1998. "We lost the game in the second part of the first half," she said. "The players got discouraged. They got down." Two nights later and many miles to the south, Texas met No. 5 Florida. With a zone defense that forced 20 turnovers and limited UT to 33 percent shooting, the Gators won, 64-51. Nobody could slow, much less stop, all-American Murriel Page, who rang the bell for 28 points and 20 rebounds. Although she played just three minutes in the first half due to foul trouble, Jackson had a team-high 14 points. Better outside shooting would have helped greatly; in three games, the Horns had made just two of 34 three-point shots.

On a day in which the big sports news was the removal of John Mackovic as UT's head football coach, Michigan State administered a heartbreaking 80-78 overtime defeat before 5,984 fans in Austin. The Spartans' Bella Engen (27) and Brown (22) were the top scorers in a game in which the Texas bench contributed but a single point. Then it was time to batten down the hatches and get ready for two-time defending national champ Tennessee at Thompson-Boling Arena. What coach Pat Summitt called "the Meeks"—Chamique Holdsclaw, Tameka Catchings and Sameka Randall—led the Volunteers to an easy 98-64 victory. Conradt opined that Tennessee might go undefeated in 1998: "Their defense and the way they run the floor will make them a team to be reckoned with." She was right; the Vols won every game and a third straight title, leading to a widespread belief that theirs was the best women's college team yet.

Her own team was slumping, but things were bound to get better with three lightweights coming to town. Texas shot 70 percent in a 103-71 strumming of Central Florida. Brown, Jackson and Wallace poured in 23, 23 and 22 points, respectively. A tense three-point defeat of the Northwestern Wildcats marked the 700th victory in the remarkable coaching career of Jody Conradt. She had been asked about the milestone at least 700 times in the days leading up to it but preferred to keep the focus on her team and its development. Just as with wins No. 500 in 1988 and No. 600 in 1993, she was praised and honored by her colleagues in the coaching profession and ex-players and was the subject of a glowing editorial in the *Austin American-Statesman.* The UT sports information department liked to point out that she joined 700-game winners Dean Smith, Adolph Rupp, Hank Iba, Ed Diddle, Phog Allen, Ray Meyer and Bobby Knight. Heady company. Austin was still buzzing when UT evened its record at 4-4 with a 77-52 defeat of Detroit Mercy. The Horns were merciless against the visiting Titans, forcing 25 turnovers. Jackson led all scorers with 19, and Dee Smith helped by getting 14 points and nine rebounds.

Washington, undefeated and ranked 13th, welcomed the Longhorns to Seattle. Much to their fans' surprise, the Huskies trailed by nine with 12:30 left in the game. Then they ran off 15 straight points in a 78-72 victory. Amber Hall and Jamie Redd combined to score 43 against UT, which lost due to fatigue, cold shooting and a 21-rebound deficit. After the game, Wallace and Brown gave their teammates what has been called a "butt-chewing." Conference play began on January 3 in Stillwater as Oklahoma State put an 82-61 loss on the Horns. With balanced scoring—all eight Cowgirls who played had at least six points—rebounding and tight defense, OSU won handily. Brown, who continued to lead UT in virtually every statistical category, needed help. That 0-5 road record brought the first of numerous media comparisons to Conradt's only losing team, in 1995.

Record: 12-15
88 North Texas 67
68 Boston College 82
51 Florida 64
78 Michigan State 80 (OT)
64 Tennessee 98
103 Central Florida 71
89 Northwestern 86
77 Detroit Mercy 52
72 Washington 78
61 Oklahoma State 82
78 Oklahoma 44
59 Texas Tech 82
71 Kansas 76
84 Oklahoma 97
53 Missouri 44
61 Georgetown 59
75 Nebraska 87
74 Iowa State 67
59 Texas Tech 79
79 Texas A&M 66
73 Kansas State 57
63 Baylor 67
63 Texas A&M 86
99 Baylor 59
66 Oklahoma State 69
75 Colorado 71
74 Texas A&M 98

After such a dreary performance, they returned to Austin and scorched Oklahoma, 78-44. Brown, playing with a sore hamstring, had another fine all-around game—19 points, six rebounds and seven assists. Sooner star Phylesha Whaley was held to just five points. "UT played like a team that wanted to win," said young OU coach Sherri Coale. "And we played like a team that expected them to win." Three days later, a season-high 8,951 fans gathered at the Erwin Center to watch the Horns battle No. 5 Texas Tech. After leading by just one at the half, the women in red and black broke it open to win big time, 82-59. All-American Alicia Thompson had a quiet night, but her teammate, JC transfer Angie Braziel, was excellent, scoring 22 points, grabbing seven rebounds and blocking two shots. Texas' backcourt veterans, Wallace and Lummus, won no kudos from Conradt: "To say our perimeter play was erratic is an understatement."

With a "crowd" of just 650 rattling around inside 16,300-seat Allen Fieldhouse, the Longhorns were up by 20 with 10 minutes left only to fall apart and let Kansas take a 76-71 victory. Fifteen second-half turnovers told part of the story, as did 19 points for the Jayhawks' Lynn Pride. And with Brown out due to a knee problem, there was no guarantee that, despite beating Oklahoma by 34 a fortnight earlier, UT would win in Norman. "The University of Texas women's basketball team continued its abysmal road show Saturday night with a 97-84 loss to Oklahoma," wrote Suzanne Halliburton of the *Austin American-Statesman.* Phylesha Whaley pumped in a school-record 38 points, ten more than Jackson. Ten three-point field goals helped the Sooner cause considerably.

Frustrated but trying to stay upbeat, the Longhorns encountered Missouri in a matchup of lower-echelon conference teams. Held to four field goals in the first half, UT was just three points down at the break and managed to win, 53-44. Lummus, with 15 points and five assists, played one of the best games of her junior season. Kesha Bonds had 18 points and 15 rebounds for the Tigers, who had lost six of their last seven. There was no Hoya paranoia as 5-11 Georgetown came into the Erwin Center.

Brown missed her third straight contest, one that nearly got away from UT. The visitors from the Big East—with two Texans in their starting lineup—were ahead by one with 12 seconds left when Wallace penetrated, hit a tough shot and followed that with a free throw to win it, 61-59. Jackson (19) was the game's top scorer.

With Brown back in the lineup, the Horns fell to a physical Nebraska team in Lincoln. The score was

87-75, but it did not seem that close to the 2,525 fans in attendance. A 17-4 run at the end of the first half effectively settled things for the Cornhuskers, who got 25 points from forward Anna DeForge. Iowa State, tied for the Big 12 lead and ranked 24th, stumbled against Conradt's Horns on February 1. Texas got ahead by 22 points and then watched the Cyclones storm back and grab the lead in the final minutes. Unlike so many other times, though, UT responded and took an exhilarating 74-67 victory. An offensive rebound and resulting three-point play by Jackson (29) might have been the key.

Lubbock Municipal Coliseum was packed when the Longhorns and Red Raiders tipped off. It was close until Texas Tech scored 16 straight points early in the second half, winning by 20. Angie Braziel and Alicia Thompson (Big 12 player of the year) combined for 59 points, while four Texas players fouled out and Conradt got a T from referee Sally Bell. Texas Tech coach Marsha Sharp said all the right things after seeing her team win its 15th game of the season.

For the second time in a week, Jackson hit a career high in scoring. Double-teamed by Texas A&M's post players, she got 30 points in a 79-66 home victory. Jackson, who had come to UT four years earlier as a passive athlete with poor footwork, had come a long way, thanks in part to the tutelage of assistant coach Annette Smith-Knight. With the Aggies thus dispatched, Kansas State was next up at the Erwin Center in a battle of 9-11 teams. The Horns built an early lead, lost it and then dominated the second half for a 73-57 win, one of their best games of the season. Brown, showing no effect from hamstring and knee problems, played 35 minutes and had these numbers: 16 points, 13 rebounds, six assists and three steals. Center Angie Finkes scored 23 for the Wildcats.

Carrying the momentum of a two-game winning streak into Waco, the Horns lost it in a 67-63 defeat by Sonja Hogg's Baylor Bears. UT gave up 25 points to Aussie guard Lara Webb and suffered from atrocious ballhandling as Wallace had seven turnovers and Brown and Smith six each. A charging call against Wallace with 12 seconds left was the Longhorns' last gasp. To make matters worse, they fell to Texas A&M, 86-68, at G. Rollie White Coliseum, in its 44th and final year as a venue for college hoops. Jackson and Brown combined for 50 points but got little support from their teammates. Prissy Sharpe (29) and Kera Alexander (17) could not help pouring salt on Bevo's wounds, making snide comments about "t.u." and "the little teasips."

Conradt, who had concluded her team lacked chemistry, communication and mental toughness even before that loss to the Aggies, turned up the heat in practice, threatening demotions and whatever else she could. But her options were severely limited by a thin bench. It was not like 1986 when the second-teamers were better than most schools' starters. "I know Coach is upset," Jackson said. "I hate being known as the worst team she's ever had."

With a bee in their collective bonnet, the Longhorns romped Baylor, 99-59, in Austin. Jackson (25) and Brown (22) led five players in double figures, while

Edwina Brown gets some serious altitude in UT's three-point loss to Oklahoma State at the Erwin Center.

the Bears helped by shooting poorly. But that preceded a Wednesday night game against Oklahoma State resulting in a 69-66 Cowgirl victory. Guard Jennifer Crow scored 21 points for OSU, but the game was decided by a staggering 26-8 second-half rebounding edge for the black-clad visitors. At the postgame media confab, coach Dick Halterman could hardly believe it, but

Conradt could: "When you're shooting 38 percent, you'd better get the rebounds."

The regular season ended in Boulder. Ceal Berry's Buffaloes were a far cry from the sweet 16 team of 1997, and their best player, guard LaShena Graham, had been injured much of the season. UT, 0-11 on the road, finally won a game outside of Austin, beating Colorado, 75-71. The second half featured seven lead changes, two technicals and an ejection of Conradt (the first of her 29-year coaching career) and some clutch free throw shooting in the final minute. Brown and Lummus combined for 46 points, and Bailey, whose playing time had declined drastically during her senior year, hit a key bucket at the end for the Horns.

A heavy favorite against Texas A&M in the first round of the Big 12 tourney in Kansas City, the Longhorns surprised everyone, including themselves, by playing miserably and losing, 98-74. Before a handful of fans at Municipal Auditorium, Candi Harvey's Ags led from wire to wire and advanced in the tournament. Kera Alexander (25) and Jackson (23) led their respective teams in scoring. And so it was over, a poor season by almost any standard, and yet one that had brought little criticism from the media or fans. As she had during the season, Conradt refused to entertain the merest suggestion of retirement. She spoke with optimism and determination of a fine recruiting class and could point to returning players like Wallace, Brown, Lummus and Littleton. Nevertheless, it would be a stiff challenge to get to the top of the Big 12, much less the NCAA, where schools like Tennessee, Old Dominion, Connecticut, Stanford, North Carolina and Texas Tech ruled. Competition had been growing more intense each year. Conradt (elected to the Basketball Hall of Fame in the summer of 1998), shuffled the coaching staff and reaffirmed her commitment to leading the Longhorns back to the elite.

INDEX

Editorial note: This index is limited to University of Texas players, head coaches and athletic directors or their antecedents. Rodney Page, women's coach from 1974 to 1976, is listed therein.

MEN

A

B

C

H

I

J

K

L

V

W

Z

WOMEN

V

W

Z